Hip Hop around the World

Hip Hop around the World

An Encyclopedia

VOLUME 2: M–Z

Melissa Ursula Dawn Goldsmith and Anthony J. Fonseca, Editors

GREENWOOD™

An Imprint of ABC-CLIO, LLC
Santa Barbara, California • Denver, Colorado

Library of Congress Cataloging-in-Publication Data

Names: Goldsmith, Melissa Ursula Dawn, editor. | Fonseca, Anthony J., editor.
Title: Hip hop around the world : an encyclopedia / Melissa Ursula Dawn Goldsmith
    and Anthony J. Fonseca, editors.
Description: Santa Barbara, California : Greenwood, [2019] | Includes
    bibliographical references and index.
Identifiers: LCCN 2018009510 (print) | LCCN 2018011517 (ebook) |
    ISBN 9780313357596 (ebook) | ISBN 9780313357589 (hardcover : set : acid-free paper) |
    ISBN 9781440849466 (hardcover : vol. 1 : acid-free paper) | ISBN 9781440849473
    (hardcover : vol. 2 : acid-free paper)
Subjects: LCSH: Rap (Music)—Encyclopedias. | Hip-hop—Encyclopedias.
Classification: LCC ML102.R27 (ebook) | LCC ML102.R27 H56 2018 (print) |
    DDC 782.42164903—dc23
LC record available at https://lccn.loc.gov/2018009510

ISBN: 978-0-313-35758-9 (set)
       978-1-4408-4946-6 (vol. 1)
       978-1-4408-4947-3 (vol. 2)
       978-0-313-35759-6 (ebook)

23 22 21 20 19   1 2 3 4 5

This book is also available as an eBook.

Greenwood
An Imprint of ABC-CLIO, LLC

ABC-CLIO, LLC
130 Cremona Drive, P.O. Box 1911
Santa Barbara, California 93116-1911
www.abc-clio.com

This book is printed on acid-free paper ∞

Manufactured in the United States of America

In memory of Duane Robinson, our wonderful neighbor and friend. We will miss your smile. The Academy of Music was lucky to have had you all those years.

Contents

List of Entries

Guide to Related Topics

ARTISTS

Above the Law
Aceyalone
Afrika Bambaataa
Akon
Allen, Harry
Ant Banks
Antipop Consortium
Anwar, Joni
Ashanthi
Ashanti
Asia One
Awadi, Didier
Babyface
Bahamadia
Banks, Azealia
Beastie Boys
Ben Sharpa
Beyoncé
Big Daddy Kane
Big Pun
Birdman
Black Eyed Peas
Blige, Mary J.
Bliss n' Eso
Blondie
The Bomb Squad

Boogie Down Productions
Brand Nubian
Briggs
Brotha Lynch Hung
Brothablack
Brown, James
Bubba Sparxxx
Bubbles
Busta Rhymes
Campbell, Don
Chance the Rapper
The Chemical Brothers
Christie Z-Pabon
Chuck D
C-Murder
Coldcut
Common
Company Flow
Compton's Most Wanted
Coolio
Crazy Legs
C-Real
Cut Chemist
Cypress Hill
Da Brat
Daara J

CONCEPTS

COUNTRIES

Afghanistan	East Timor
Albania	Ecuador
Algeria	Egypt
Angola	El Salvador
Argentina	Equatorial Guinea
Australia	Estonia
Austria	Ethiopia
The Bahamas	Fiji
Bangladesh	Finland
Barbados	France
Belarus	Gabon
Belgium	The Gambia
Benin	Germany
Bermuda	Ghana
Bolivia	Greece
Bosnia and Herzegovina	Guadeloupe
Botswana	Guatemala
Brazil	Guinea-Bissau
Brunei	Haiti
Bulgaria	Hungary
Burkina Faso	Iceland
Cambodia	India
Cameroon	Indonesia
Canada	Iran
Cape Verde	Iraq
Chile	Ireland
China	Israel
Colombia	Italy
Congo	Ivory Coast
Costa Rica	Jamaica
Croatia	Japan
Cuba	Jordan
Cyprus	Kazakhstan
Czech Republic	Kenya
Denmark	Korea
The Dominican Republic	Kuwait

Laos

Latvia

Lebanon

Lesotho

Libya

Lithuania

Macedonia

Madagascar

Malawi

Malaysia

The Maldives

Mali

Malta

Martinique

Mauritius

Mexico

Mongolia

Montenegro

Morocco

Mozambique

Myanmar

Namibia

Nepal

The Netherlands

New Zealand

Niger

Nigeria

Norway

Oman

Pakistan

Palestine

Panama

Peru

The Philippines

Poland

Portugal

Puerto Rico

Romania

Russia

Samoa

Saudi Arabia

Senegal

Serbia

Sierra Leone

Singapore

Slovakia

Slovenia

Somalia

South Africa

Spain

Sri Lanka

Sudan

Swaziland

Sweden

Switzerland

Syria

Taiwan

Tanzania

Thailand

Togo

Trinidad and Tobago

Tunisia

Turkey

Uganda

Ukraine

The United Kingdom

The United States

Venezuela

Vietnam

The Virgin Islands

Yemen

Zambia

Zimbabwe

STYLES

Bounce

Breakdancing

Brick City Club

Celtic Hip Hop

Chap Hop

Chicano Rap

Chopper

Christian Hip Hop

Clowning

Crip Walk

Crunkcore

Cumbia Rap

Dirty Rap

Dirty South

Dubstep

Gangsta Rap

G-Funk

Glitch Hop

Graffiti Art

Grime

Hardcore Hip Hop

Hip Hop Dance

Hip House

Horrorcore

Industrial Hip Hop

Jerkin'

Krumping

Kwaito

Lyrical Hip Hop

Mafioso Rap

Merenrap

Miami Bass

Motswako

Neo Soul

Nerdcore

New Jack Swing

Political Hip Hop

Popping and Locking

Reggae

Reggaetón

The Robot

Snap

Trap

Trip Hop

Uprock

M

Macedonia

Macedonia, formerly the southernmost republic of the Socialist Federal Republic of Yugoslavia, gained its independence in 1991. As of 2018, a quarter of Macedonia's population is ethnically Albanian. Despite Macedonians' having their own language, which was spoken by its majority and minority Albanian, Romanian, Serbian, and Turkish populations, under Yugoslavian rule, Macedonia's official language is Serbo-Croatian. Hip hop emerged in Macedonia during the late 1980s, with the transition from the Socialist Republic of Macedonia (1944–1991) to the current Republic of Macedonia (1991–). The earliest recorded rap by Macedonian musicians was in the antiwar song "Rapovanje" ("Rapping") by the alternative rock band Supernova (1985–1989*), released on the compilation album *Omladina '89—Subotica* (*Youth '89—Subotica*, 1989). Ethnic and political tensions were on the rise, despite the peace maintained during Macedonia's independence and the Yugoslav wars in the 1990s. Breakdancing and rapping became nonviolent ways to reinforce community building, venting frustrations over the political transition and daily life while promoting tolerance and a shared Macedonian culture.

One of the earliest hip hop artists was breakdancer and rapper Vladimir Agovski-Ago (aka Temnata strana, The Dark Side, n.d.) from Skopje, who began rapping in 1988. In 1995, Agovski-Ago's hardcore rap group the Most Wanted (1991–1996) released the first Macedonian hip hop album, *Presudniot den* (*Judgment Day*). Agovski-Ago pursued a solo career and started Macedonia's first hip hop recording label, Dolina Na Senkite (aka DNS, Valley of the Shadows, 1996–). Other pioneering acts were the rap and alternative rock group Cista Okolina (Clean Environment, 1989–) and the alternative hip hop group Mosaique (1993–1999), which fused hip hop, jazz, funk, rock, and world music. The group SAF (aka Sakam Afro Frizura, I Want an Afro Hairstyle, 1993–) incorporated turntablism and had a hit with "Miss Stone" (1996), which had an anti–drug abuse message. In 2001, SAF released its debut album *Safizam* (literally, *Sapphic*) and was the supporting act for American hip hop band Das EFX (1988–) in concert. Later 1990s acts were Da Dzaka Nakot (1991–), Nulta Pozitiv (1990–2000)*, Risto Bombata (Kristijan Gabrovski, n.d.), and producer and songwriter Darko Dimitrov (1973–).

Prominent, more politically charged Macedonian hip hop acts into the 2000s include rapper Vrcak (Rade Vrcakovski, 1980–), singer-songwriter Elena Risteska (1986–), and the groups Legijata (Legion, 2000–), Klan Istok (The East Clan, 2000–2010)*, G-Madda Funk (2006–), and Green OuT (2004–). A Macedonian diaspora due to political unrest has led to displaced Macedonian rappers, such as Skopje-born singer-songwriter and producer Jay Jay (Jovan Jovanov, 1981–), who is based in Toronto (his home) and Los Angeles.

As of 2018, a small hip hop scene can be found in the country's capital, Skopje, and its largest municipality, Kumanovo. Rapping texts are in Macedonian, but at times rappers employ urban dialects such as Kumanovski, as well as American vernacular English and Serbo-Croatian.

Melissa Ursula Dawn Goldsmith

See also: Albania

Further Reading

Balandina, Alexandra. 2017. "Rap Music as a Cultural Mediator in Postconflict Yugoslavia." In *Hip Hop at Europe's Edge: Music, Agency, and Social Change*, edited by Milosz Miszczynski and Adriana Helbig, chap. 4. Bloomington: Indiana University Press.

Ortakkov, Dragoslav. 1975. "Approaches to the Study of Macedonian Musical History." *International Review of the Aesthetics and Sociology of Music* 6, no. 2: 307–17.

Serafimovska, Velika Stojkova, Dave Wilson, and Ivona Opetceska Tatarcevska. 2016. "Safeguarding Intangible Cultural Heritage in the Republic of Macedonia." *Yearbook for Traditional Music* 48: 1–24.

Macklemore and Ryan Lewis

(2009–, Seattle, Washington)

Macklemore and Ryan Lewis is an American duo consisting of rapper and lyricist Macklemore (Benjamin Hammond Haggerty, 1983–) and DJ, artist, and producer Ryan Lewis (1988–). Macklemore is known for his narrative rapping that evokes the elements of storytelling. His tracks tend to include events that unfold over the course of a song. Though most of his lyrics are about personal experiences with addiction and with the music industry, he has also been known to invoke social justice issues.

Macklemore began rapping in high school when he was 15 years old; he eventually went on to complete a bachelor's degree at the Evergreen State College, where he continued to perform. Among his early influences were East Coast hip hop artists and groups, such as Staten Island's Wu-Tang Clan (1992–) as well as Mobb Deep (1991–2017), Nas (1973–), Talib Kweli (1975–), and Living Legends (1996–).

Under the name Professor Macklemore, he recorded an EP titled *Open Your Eyes* (2000), followed in 2005 by his first full-length album, *The Language of My World*. Following a period of intense struggle with drug addiction and alcoholism and a period spent in rehab, he began collaborating with Lewis in 2008, and the duo released *The VS. EP* (2009). Macklemore and Lewis's first studio album, *The Heist* (2012), self-released and distributed by the Warner Music Group (1958–), debuted at No. 2 on the Billboard 200 chart, sold 1.5 million copies, earned four Grammy Awards, and spawned "Can't Hold Us" and "Thrift Shop," both of which went to No. 1 on the Hot 100. "Thrift Shop" also topped the charts in France, the United Kingdom, Canada, and Australia.

Also known for activism, Macklemore has worked with the Gateways for Incarcerated Youth program at a juvenile detention facility in Chehalis, Washington, where he facilitated rap-based writing workshops. The duo's activism is apparent in "Same Love," a pro-LGBTQ+ marriage equality track that was performed at the 2014 Grammy Awards ceremony; as part of the performance, Queen Latifah (1970–) officiated the legal marriage of 33 same-sex and opposite-sex couples from the stage.

In 2016, the duo self-released *This Unruly Mess I've Made*. Prior to the album's release, the duo released the singles "Growing Up (Sloane's Song)" with English acoustic folk-pop singer-songwriter Ed Sheeran (1991–) and "Downtown," which peaked at No. 12 on the Hot 100. The track "White Privilege II" from *This Unruly Mess I've Made* is a sequel to Macklemore's solo song, "White Privilege" from *The Language of My World*. "White Privilege II" discusses the importance of the Black Lives Matter movement (2013–) and Macklemore's own experiences of grappling with white privilege. The song, which spans to about nine minutes in duration, charted on Twitter's Trending 140, which ranks songs according to how often they are mentioned on Twitter. It also features Chicago-based hip hop, R&B, and soul singer-songwriter and poet Jamila Woods (1989*–).

Lauron Jockwig Kehrer

See also: Political Hip Hop; The United States

Further Reading

Hiatt, Brian. 2013. "393 Million Macklemore (and Ryan Lewis) Fans Can't Be Wrong." *Rolling Stone* no. 1190, August 29, 41–45, 70.

Pinn, Anthony B. 2012. "What Humanism Might Learn from Hip Hop." *Free Inquiry* 32, no. 6: 31–35.

Vozick-Levinson, Simon. 2013. "Thrift Shop Hero." *Rolling Stone* no. 1180, April 11, 48–51.

Further Listening

Macklemore and Ryan Lewis. 2012. *The Heist.* Self-released.

Macklemore and Ryan Lewis. 2016. *This Unruly Mess I've Made.* Self-released.

Madagascar

Madagascar is a Southeast African island country located in the Indian Ocean about 250 nautical miles away from the continent. It gained its independence in 1960 from France. Since 1992, the country's government has been a constitutional democracy. Despite isolation, American hip hop reached Madagascar in the mid-1980s, with the Malagasies' strongest interests focusing on breakdancing and graffiti. The main hip hop center of activity is in its capital, Antananarivo. By the mid-1990s, Malagasy rap had emerged with a preference for rapping in both Malagasy and French (the country's official languages). Nicknamed *haintso haintso* (or HH Gasy), this new hip hop incorporated Malagasy traditional and popular music and instrumentation.

The group MCM Boys (1990–1995) was Madagascar's first rapping crew; it performed old-school rap. The crew was originally a four-member teenage b-boy group, but its members turned toward political and socially conscious rap. Soon the crew became Da Hopp (1995–2001, 2016–). After a 15-year hiatus, Da Hopp reunited, using old-school hip hop as a retro sound against Malagasy rap. In 2016, Da Hopp collaborated with another pioneering rap crew, Takodah sy Ngah b (1995*–), in the boombap single "Avereno ny kajy" ("Repeat the Calculation"). An early rap crew that pioneered turntablism in Malagasy hip hop was Karnaz' (1996–). Another early crew, 18,3 (1998–2005*), an MC duo formerly known as 18,2 (aka adala be, rap crazy, 1997–1998), fused Malagasy hip hop with humor, R&B, and soul.

In 1997, the Malagasy dance company Up the Rap was established, staging breakdancing and fusing it with movements from Madagascar's extraordinarily diverse traditional dance genres, such as *fampithana, joros, dihy soroka, latsitanana*, and *salegy* (the last three are circle dances), as well as Angolan *capoeira*. As Malagasy hip hop entered the country's mainstream in the 2000s, more artists have emerged. Rapper Shao Boana (aka FANJAHKKKAGNAMAKUA, Shao Masindrazana, n.d.), though recording in Paris in an effort to become international, raps in French, Malagasy, and English. He fuses Malagasy hip hop with reggae and dancehall.

Basy Gasy (Malagasy Gun, 2012–) fuses hip hop and slam poetry with reggae, ragga, and electronica, employing beatboxing, guitars, and percussion. Basy Gasy focuses on urban themes, yet actively avoids gangsta rap lyrical content. It embraces some island mentality and emphasizes rap as poetry, but its use of guitars, reggae fusion, and beatboxing create a generally softer sound than its Malagasy contemporaries.

Rapper Name Six (Narcisse Randrianarivony, 1992–) has brought Malagasy rap to worldwide exposure with his lyrical content about everyday life in the country and the social conditions of Malagasy youth since his 2007 selection as the first UNICEF (United Nations Children's Fund) Goodwill Ambassador for Eastern and Southern Africa. Female rapper (who calls herself a femcee) and singer-songwriter Farah (Andriambelona Maminiaina Faratiana, 1987–) focuses on everyday women's issues and feminist activism in Madagascar.

Melissa Ursula Dawn Goldsmith

See also: France; Reggae; South Africa

Further Reading

Boyer-Rossol, Klara. 2014. "From the Great Island to the African Continent through the Western World: Itineraries of a 'Return to the Origins' through Hip Hop Music in Madagascar (2000–11)." In *Hip Hop and Social Change in Africa: Ni Wakati*, edited by Msia Kibona Clark and Mickie Mwanzia Koster, chap. 12. Lanham, MD: Lexington Books.

Ernoff, Ron. 2002. "Phantom Nostalgia and Recollecting (from) the Colonial Past in Tamatave, Madagascar." *Ethnomusicology* 46, no. 2: 265–83.

Further Listening

Karnaz'. 2004. *Zao Zay. . . .* Kary_prod.

Mafioso Rap

Mafioso rap is a hardcore hip hop subgenre that may have been started in the 1990s by Kool G Rap (aka G Rap, Nathaniel Thomas Wilson, 1968–) and his album (as

Kool G Rap and DJ Polo) *Live and Let Die* (1992). Lyrics of Mafioso rap, like Kool G Rap's prototype, were characterized by references to the Italian American mafia, the Sicilian mafia, African American organized crime, and Latin American drug cartels. Mafioso rap became popular when East Coast rappers realized it allowed them to compete with West Coast gangsta rap and G-funk. Like gangsta rap, mafioso rap songs could take as their angle either the violence of organized crime (sometimes referred to as hustling), the mastery of crime bosses, the material benefits of an illegal underground economy, and/or the lavishness that illegal activity could bring in the way of women, cars, mansions, high fashion, jewelry, and expensive eating and drinking tastes.

Kool G Rap is an ex–Juice Crew (1983–1991) member known for his multisyllabic rhyming and hardcore lyrics. Since *Live and Let Die*, he has infused his lyrics with references to real and fictionalized mafioso bosses and criminals such as Sam Giancana (1908–1975), Al Capone (1899–1947), and Al Pacino's (1940–) fictional mobster Tony Montana from the American film *Scarface* (1983), sometimes depicting them on his albums covers.

In 1995, Kool G Rap released his solo debut *4, 5, 6* and Wu-Tang Clan (1992–) member Raekwon (Corey Todd Woods, 1970–) released his solo debut *Only Built 4 Cuban Linx. . . .* The latter contained songs such as "Incarcerated Scarfaces" and "Wu-Gambinos," and the album, which was constructed to tell a mafioso-type story, featured almost every member of the Wu-Tang Clan and used strings, piano, and samples from Kung Fu movies and mafia films. The former featured the song "It's a Shame," which references Frank Nitti (Francesco Raffaele Nitto, 1886–1943) and depicts the rapper/narrator as a drug kingpin.

In the same year, rapper AZ (Anthony Cruz, 1972–) released *Doe or Die*, which told the story of a mobster's rise and fall and featured a mob memorial on the front cover and a hand holding a cigar and a glass of champagne on the back.

LATER RECORDINGS

These three albums influenced further mafioso titles by East Coast rappers such as Scarface (Brad Terrence Jordan, 1970–), Jay-Z (1969–), the Notorious B.I.G. (1972–1997), and Nas (1973–), the latter creating a fictional drug dealer alter ego, Nas Escobar. *The Diary* (1994), by Scarface, reached No. 2 on the Billboard 200 and spawned two singles, "Hand of the Dead Body" (aka "People Don't Believe") and "I Seen a Man Die." In *Reasonable Doubt* (1996), Jay-Z creates a psychological journey through the world of organized crime set against jazz and R&B sampled beats and turntablist scratching. Like *Reasonable Doubt*, the Grammy-nominated *Life After Death* (1997), by the Notorious B.I.G.; the influential *The Untouchable* (1997), by Scarface; and *It Was Written* (1996), by Nas, were commercially successful—all made it to the top spot on the Billboard 200 albums chart. *It Was Written* is notable for its incorporation of G-funk beats and rhythms.

These albums expressed concerns with drugs, guns, materialistic excess, thievery, mob connections, and revenge, and like many mafioso rap albums, referenced the pulp novels of Al C. Clark (Donald Goines, 1936–1974), a Detroit-based crime novelist who wrote about urban organized crime. Also in 1997, Nas's hip hop supergroup the Firm (1996–1997) released the mafioso concept album *The Album*, a follow-up to *It Was Written*. It contained songs produced mainly by Dr. Dre (1965–). In 1998, Kool G Rap and AZ released further mafioso albums, *Roots of Evil* and *Pieces of a Man*, respectively.

DECLINE AND INFLUENCE OF MOBB RAP

Mafioso rap's popularity declined by 2000, although some notable albums have been released in the last two decades, such as Kool G Rap's *The Giancana Story* (2002) and *Riches, Royalty, Respect* (2011), Ghostface Killah's (Dennis Coles, 1970–) *Fishscale* (2006), Jay-Z's *American Gangster* (2007), Prodigy's (Albert Johnson, 1974–2017) *Return of the Mac* (2007), Raekwon's *Only Built 4 Cuban Linx . . . Pt. II* (2009), and Cold 187um's (Gregory Fernan Hutchison, 1967–) *The Only Solution* (2012). Women rappers have delved into the mafioso subgenre less often, the most notable example being ex–Junior M.A.F.I.A. (1992–1997, 2005–2007) member Lil' Kim (1975–), whose *La Bella Mafia* (2003) was certified Platinum.

Like G-funk, mafioso rap influenced the West Coast subgenre mobb rap, bringing gangsta rap full circle. Mobb rap is associated with the 1990s East Bay area of Oakland, California, where rappers such as Oakland's Ant Banks (1969–), Too $hort (Todd Anthony Shaw, 1966–), and Dru Down (Danyle Robinson, 1969–); San Francisco's San Quinn (Quincy Brooks IV, 1977–) and Dre Dog (Andre L. Adams, 1970–); Vallejo's E-40 (Earl Stevens, 1967–) and Celly Cel (Marcellus McCarver, 1975*–); and Hayward's Spice 1 (Robert Green Jr., 1970–) became pioneers of their own versions of mafioso rap.

Anthony J. Fonseca

See also: Gangsta Rap; G-Funk; Jay-Z; Nas; The Notorious B.I.G.; The United States

Further Reading

Harkness, Geoffrey Victor. 2014. *Chicago Hustle and Flow: Gangs, Gangsta Rap, and Social Class.* Minneapolis: University of Minnesota Press.

Lozon, Jeffrey, and Moshe Bensimon. 2017. "A Systematic Review on the Functions of Rap among Gangs." *International Journal of Offender Therapy and Comparative Criminology* 61, no. 11: 1243–61.

Quinn, Eithne. 2005. *Nuthin' but a G Thang: The Culture and Commerce of Gangsta Rap.* New York: Columbia University Press.

Further Listening

Lil' Kim. 2003. *La bella mafia (Beautiful Mafia Woman)*. Atlantic.

The Notorious B.I.G. 1997. *Life after Death.* Bad Boy Entertainment.

Raekwon. 1995. *Only Built for Cuban Lynx . . . .* Loud Records.

Malawi

Malawi, one of the smallest African countries, is located in Southeast Africa. It attained its independence from the United Kingdom in 1964 and became a one-party republic until 1994, when President Hastings Kamuzu Banda's (1898–1997) dictator-ship came to an end, resulting in the first democratically elected president, Bakili Muluzi (1943–). During the Banda administration, diaspora took place. For this rea-son, the most famous Malawian musician is singer-songwriter Lucius Banda (1970–), who moved to Johannesburg, South Africa, in the 1990s. Banda inspired Malawian reggae and hip hop artists because his songs were the first to criticize Malawian gov-ernment's corruption. By the late 1990s, privatization and expansion of radio had begun to broadcast global pop, Jamaican reggae, and American soul, R&B, and gos-pel music. By 2000, major cities had access to television channels that broadcast MTV (1981–). Radio and television are the main sources for accessing global hip hop; as of 2018, Internet access is still limited. Malawians acquired bootlegged or pirated hip hop CDs, audiocassettes, and videos from neighboring countries.

Small hip hop scenes are located in Blantyre, Malawi's business and industry capital, followed by its capital, Lilongwe. Malawian hip hop is message rap influ-enced by ragga. Lyrical content may protest corruption but concentrates on every-day life, Malawian pride and identity, and unity. Because there is no music industry in Malawi, musicians go elsewhere to record, and hip hop is usually performed live in underground clubs, in concerts, or at battling events. Since the 1990s, the pre-ferred rapping text is Chichewa, though some American vernacular is used. The rap group Bubu Lazy (formerly Boyz Lazzy, 1990–2000)* fuses hip hop with kwaito, techno, and disco music. Rapper Black Mind (aka The Gifted One, Geoff Chirwa, n.d.) and his group Black Legue (1990–2000)* fused hip hop with reggae. The most famous pioneering Malawian hip hop group was Real Elements (aka Real Elementz, 2000–) from Lilongwe. Since 2002, the group has been based in London. The rap duo Biriwiri (Greenness, 2003–) fuses hip hop with African rhumba and traditional Malawian music and rhythms, and ragga. Mid-2000s-to-2010 Malawian acts include Revolver (Kenneth Muwamba, 1989–2016), Chavura (aka Nyambaro, Mwiza Chavura, n.d.), Krazie-G (Phineus Moyo, 1992–), and Phyzix (aka Jack Trades, Noel Jack Chikoleka, 1986–).

Some more recent Malawian rappers focus on gangsta rap, using rivalry hype and braggadocio. Rapper, producer, and label owner Pop Dogg (Ibramhim Haji, n.d.) lived in the United States and Ireland after the diaspora and performed gang-sta rap in English and Chichewa. Rapper, singer, and promoter Tay Grin (Limbani Kalilani, 1984–), from Blantyre, has helped establish hip hop events in Malawi through his company Black Rhyno Entertainment (2014–).

Melissa Ursula Dawn Goldsmith

See also: Gangsta Rap; Reggae

Further Reading

Fenn, John. 2012. "Style, Message, and Meaning in Malawian Youth Rap and Ragga Per-formances." In *Hip Hop Africa: New African Music in a Globalizing World*, edited by Eric Charry, chap. 5. Bloomington: Indiana University Press.

Gilman, Lisa, and John Fenn. 2006. "Dance, Gender, and Popular Music in Malawi: The Case of Rap and Ragga." *Popular Music* 25, no. 3: 369–81.

Further Listening

Biriwiri. 2015. *The Green Album.* Ndefeyo.

Malaysia

Malaysia is a multiethnic and multicultural country, and each ethnic group has its own culture and heritage. Within this diversity, various groups of hip hop musicians and rappers perform in their native languages, including Malay, Chinese (Mandarin and Cantonese), Tamil, and English. Performers often rap about politics, life, love, and work, but rarely make references to sex or violence. Current popular rap groups, mostly from Kuala Lumpur, include Kumpulan Phlowtron (*Kumpulan* means *group*; 2000*–), Too Phat (1998–), Poetic Ammo (aka Poetic Ammunition or PMO, 1996–2004), Pop Shuvit (2001–), M.O.B. (Members of Blood, 2000s*–), and Kumpulan Teh Tarik (2000*–). Malaysia did not see its first hip hop musicians until the late 1980s, when the genre was popularized by the four-member group Krash Kozz (1989–1994), which included Najee (anonymous, n.d.), Jakeman (Jake Abdullah, n.d.), DJ Gabriel (anonymous, n.d.), and vocalist Suresh (anonymous, n.d.). The group released mixtape albums such as *Pump It Up* (1990) and *New Jack: The Street Beat* (1993).

Two of the most popular hip hop groups began as underground bands. Pop Shuvit is known for its eclectic blend of hip hop and rock, using guitars, bass, drums, and turntables. It has become a leading act at Asian music festivals with tracks in English, Japanese, Malay, Tagalog, Thai, and Spanish. Its albums include *Take It and Shuvit* (2003), *Here and Now* (2005), *Amped and Dangerous* (2006), *Tales of the Travelling Tunes* (2007), and *Cherry Blossom Love Affair* (2011). Kumpulan Phlowtron consists of Amaria Syakira (1986–), Saiful Amri (1982–), and Khalid Kamal (1979–). Its songs are sung mainly in Malay, and the music fuses hip hop with electronica. Albums include *Hip Pop* (2003) and *Warisan Senikata Malaya* (*Malay Lyrics Heritage*, 2007), and songs include "Bicara Neguran" and "Oh Cinta" ("Strike Talk" and "Oh, My Love," both 2007). Kumpulan Phlowtron has collaborated with Too Phat, a Malaysian duo consisting of Joe Flizzow (Johan bin Ishak, 1979–) and Malique Ibrahim (1977–).

A duo consisting of rappers Malique and Joe Flizzow, Too Phat poses at the 2004 MTV Asia Awards in Singapore. Hailing from Kuala Lumpur, Too Phat was the first Malaysian hip hop act to combine hip hop with both traditional Malay sounds and language. (Jun Sato/WireImage/Getty Images)

Too Phat was the first to combine hip hop with both traditional Malay sounds and language. Its single hits include "Li'l Fingaz"

(1999), "Duo Dunia" (2005), and "One Night Lover" (2012), and its albums include *Whuttadilly* (1999), *Plan B* (2001), *Phat Family* (2002), *360°* (2002), and *Rebirth into Reality* (2005). Too Phat was nominated at the MTV Asia Awards in 2001, 2002, 2004, and 2005. Poetic Ammo (1990–) consists of Yogi B (Yogeswaran Veerasingam, 1974–), Land Slyde (Chandrakumar Balakrishnan, 1971–), Point Blanc (Nicholas Ong, 1979–), and C. Loco (Sashi Kumar Balakrishnan, 1977–), and its songs are in English, Malay, Tamil, and Cantonese. Its albums include *It's a Nice Day to Be Alive* (1998), *The World Is Yours* (2000), and *Return of tha' Boombox* (2003), and the band has received numerous awards, including Best English Album in 1999 and the Best Music Video in 2000 and 2001. Too Phat's single hits include "Ipoh Mali" (in English; the song means "From Ipoh"), "KL Leng Chai" (in Cantonese; the song means "KL Handsome Guy"), and "Indian Girls" (in Tamil).

Other notable Malaysian hip hop groups include M.O.B., who were featured in operatic lyrical soprano–turned–"dance diva" Syafinaz Selamat's (n.d.) "Rindumu Rinduku" ("I Miss You," 1999) and had a subsequent hit with the highly autotuned "Don't Cha Worry, Foo'" (2002). Kumpulan Teh Tarik Crew, which fuses English with Malay in its rapping and incorporates Arabic chanting, have had hit singles that include "DooDat" and "Reminisce" (both released in 2004).

By the 2010s, Malaysian hip hop still used the same elements as it did a decade previously, and many performers have continued on in the genre. One of the most famous current acts, rapper Joe Flizzow, a former member of Too Phat, has had a solo career. His albums include *President* (2010) and *Havoc* (2013). Among other songs on his second album, "Apa Khabar" ("What's New") became a hit in 2015.

Kheng Keow Koay

See also: China

Further Reading

Bodden, Michael. 2005. "Rap in Indonesian Youth Music of the 1990s: 'Globalization,' 'Outlaw Genres,' and Social Protest." *Asian Music* 36, no. 2: 1–26.

Pillai, Shanthini. 2013. "Syncretic Cultural Multivocality and the Malaysian Popular Musical Imagination." *Kajian Malaysia: Journal of Malaysian Studies* 31, no. 1: 1–18.

Further Listening

Pop Shuvit. 2007. *Freakshow Vol. 1: Tales of the Travelling Tunes*. Shuvit Management.

The Maldives

The Maldives is a South Asian chain of 26 atolls from the Ihavandhippolhu to the Addu Atoll, southwest of India and Sri Lanka in the Indian Ocean. Its pristine beaches and beautiful marine life make it a popular tourist destination; however, a strict Sunni Islamic government prosecutes practitioners of other religions, positions women as second-class citizens, and has been accused of human rights violations. The Arab Spring (2010–2012) brought international attention to the country's political unrest, including the 2011–2012 Maldives peaceful protests and political crisis, the 2012 resignation/ousting of President Mohamed Nasheed (1967–), and his 2014 reelection. Within a tourist-oriented setting, hip hop activity has been limited to the underground and resort clubs. Maldivian hip hop is influenced by

American and Indian hip hop, including *bhangra-beat* (music that appropriates tradition Punjabi dance music and fuses it, often with hip hop, dubstep, or electronic dance music beats). Rappers opt for using the country's official language, Dhivehi.

The most notable traditional music heard in the Maldives is *boduberu* (which means big drums), an East African groove-based dance band music that involves an ensemble of 15 musicians, including a singer, backed by percussionists, who play three or four large drums made of coconut wood with goatskin membranes, a bell, and a small bamboo stick marked with horizontal grooves known as an *onugandu*. Used as part of its tourist scene, especially in the Northern Atolls, *boduberu* begins with a slow groove that speeds up to an energetic climax. Lyrical content is highly diverse. Traditional Maldivian music also favors a horizontal accordion called the *bulbul tarang*, which came from Calcutta in the early 19th century.

Since the late 1980s, hip hop has taken place mainly in the densely populated capital city of Malé. Few studios are devoted to hip hop, the most notable being Symbolic Records (2013–). Many of these studios rely on music-streaming services to disseminate Maldivian hip hop. The first band was Black Prison 8 (2005–2012), who self-released the first singles in Dhivehi in 2011 in addition to posting music videos on YouTube. Black Prison 8 fuses dubstep with hip hop. Dhebandhihaaru's (2010*–) *Magumathi* (2013), produced by Symbolic Records, was the first hip hop album produced in the Maldives. Dhebandhihaaru is a collective, with connections to Black Prison 8, that was formed by Symbolic Records. Early lyrical content focused on gangsta and party rap; however, other kinds of politically conscious rap have emerged more recently that focus on social inequality as well as concern for the country's ecological well-being. Like many Indian bhangra-beat artists, many Maldivian hip hop artists perceive themselves as black.

Human rights violations have been a concern for hip hop artists who have wanted to or are scheduled to perform in the Maldives. In 2015, internationally known R&B and hip hop artist Akon (1973–) performed a concert there to show that it is safe enough to perform in the country as well as to promote Maldivian hip hop.

Melissa Ursula Dawn Goldsmith

See also: India

Further Reading

Bano, Mukee. 2017. "Dance Trance." *Southasia*, March 31, 60–61.

Sharma, Nitasha Tamar. 2010. *Hip Hop Desis: South Asian Americans, Blackness, and a Global Race Consciousness.* Durham, NC: Duke University Press.

Mali

Mali is a West African country with a history of colonialism, political unrest, and corruption, as well as periodic droughts and famines. Despite turmoil, music is a positive aspect of Malian life and culture. Traditional music elements, such as griots and bolon players, still exist, and the oral tradition remains critical, because as of 2018, 70 percent of Mali's population was illiterate. Since the late 1980s, Malians have had some access to American, French, and Senegalese (Senrap) hip hop through pirated or bootlegged audiocassettes, CDs, and videos. Malian hip hop culture emerged in 1991 in the capital city of Bamako with the transition to a multiparty democracy and deregulation of the media. Radio expanded, but the main source for introducing Malians to hip hop was (and is as of 2018) national television because Malians have little Internet access. Rapping texts are usually in Bambara (spoken by the Mandé, Mali's largest population), though sometimes in French and American vernacular English. Lyrics protest everyday hardships such as unemployment, poverty, political corruption, censorship, and violence. Storytelling in Malian rap is especially popular if it offers moral lessons.

Rapping began underground in informal afternoon private social settings called "grins," where men conversed, drank tea, and played board games. Because of a lack of music technology, Malian hip hop began as unaccompanied rap or as rap accompanied by previously composed music played on boomboxes. Recording was done at home by privileged Malians who built makeshift private studios. In time, successful Malian rappers recorded in other countries. The pioneering Malian rap crew (for radio airplay) was the short-lived crew Sofa, which formed in 1989. It consisted of Ivory Coast–born Malian rapper, slammer, and actor Lassy King Massassy (Lassine Coulibaly, 1971*–). He is considered the father of Malian rap, as he helped drive out dictator Moussa Traoré (1936–) in 1991 through protest rapping and actual protests. The most famous Malian rap group is Tata Pound (1995–), from Bamako, which released albums such as *Rien ne va plus* (*All Bets Are Off*, 2000) and *Ni Allah sonna ma* (*If God/Allah Wills It*, 2002). It is often compared to American rap group Public Enemy (1982–) for its hardcore approach and its protesting against the government's systematic corruption.

Since Tata Pound, Malian hip hop activity has increased greatly, with hip hop concerts becoming extremely popular, but not without serious obstacles. For example, in 2012, a coup d'état leading to the occupation of North Mali by Islamicists resulted in the banning of all secular music and threats of severe punishment to Gao rappers. Rapper Amkoullel (1979–) has been critical of the situation, introducing the outside world to it through recordings and interviews, as have later acts such as rapper Iba One (Ibrahim Sissoko, 1989–) from Kayes and kora player Sidiki Diabaté (1990–) from Bamako. Notable Malian diaspora artists include rapper and Paris City Breakers (1981–) founding dancer Solo (Souleymane Dicko, 1966–) and rapper Mokobé Traore (1981–), of the French group 113 (1996–). Mokebé's music video for "Mali Forever" from his debut studio album *Mon Afrique* (2007) features shots of Bamako, the Niger River, and urban jembe drumming and dancing.

Melissa Ursula Dawn Goldsmith

See also: France; Griot; Senegal; The United States

Further Reading

Morgan, Andy. 2013. *Music, Culture, and Conflict in Mali.* Copenhagen: Freemuse.

Schulz, Dorothea E. 2012. "Mapping Cosmopolitan Identities: Rap Music and Male Youth Culture in Mali." In *Hip Hop Africa: New African Music in a Globalizing World*, edited by Eric Charry, chap. 6. Bloomington: Indiana University Press.

Further Listening

Tata Pound. 2001. *Ni Allah sonna ma* (*If God/Allah Wills It*). Mali K7.

Malta

Malta is a South European island country of three islands (Malta, Comino, and Gozo) in the middle of the Mediterranean Sea. Maltese, the national language (English is an official language), is a Latin-script, Semitic language descended from the Sicilian-based Siculo-Arabic introduced between the 9th and 12th centuries to Malta. As in other European countries, hip hop culture emerged in Malta between the early and mid-1980s. Like Italy, Malta has approached its graffiti as outsider art rather than vandalism; the little graffiti found in Malta is neverthess intended to be murals, so a more organized intent to create art, not vandalism, is expressed. American culture influenced youth to try rapping and breakdancing, although conservative preferences toward mainstream pop music and traditional Maltese music consigned hip hop music to the underground until 2000. Malta has nevertheless hosted several national rap and breakdance battle events. Malta's most populous city, Birkirkara, rather than its capital city, Valletta, is the country's center of hip hop activity.

The best-known Maltese pioneering rapper is Hooligan (Johnston Farrugia, 1980–), and the country's best-known group is No Bling Show (aka No BS, 2009*–). Inspired by Snoop Dogg (1971–), Qrendi-based Hooligan began rapping using Maltese texts at age 13. In 1999, he moved to Zurrieq to begin his rapping career. His debut album, *Originali bhali* (*Original Like Me*, 2003), became a hit in Malta and was followed by *Hooliginali* (2006) and *Triloġinali* (2012). *Triloġinali*, the first Maltese hip hop album to have songs in English, fuses hip hop with electronic dance music.

No Bling Show raps in Maltese. The group fuses traditional Maltese poetry with folk music, such as the Maltese *ghana* (peasant music for socializing and working), with newly composed rapping and beats, as well as sampling and sound effects. In 2013, No Bling Show released the album *Car kristall* (*Crystal Clear*) as a free download. The band tours internationally, spreading its consciousness-raising messages of Maltese national pride, frustration with the government, and social issues. Its lyrics also attack the conservative preferences of the general Maltese population.

Melissa Ursula Dawn Goldsmith

See also: Italy

Further Reading

Cassia, Paul Sant. 2000. "Exoticizing Discoveries and Extraordinary Experiences: 'Traditional' Music, Modernity, and Nostalgia in Malta and Other Mediterranean Societies." *Ethnomusicology* 44, no. 2: 281–301.

Griffiths, Michael. 2016. "Malta's Walls, and Its Schools, Honor Graffiti as an Art." *New York Times*, September 3, A3.

Marley Marl

(Marlon Lu'ree Williams, 1962–, Queens, New York)

Marley Marl is a pioneering American hip hop DJ, producer, house music production expert, and label owner. As a founding producer of Cold Chillin' Records

(1986–1998), Marley Marl established the Juice Crew (1983–1991), a hip hop collective consisting mostly of artists who were living in the Queensbridge Houses, a housing project in Long Island City, Queens, New York. Early members included Big Daddy Kane (Antonio Hardy, 1968–), Biz Markie (Marcel Theo Hall, 1964–), Masta Ace (Duval Clear, 1966–), Kool G Rap (Nathaniel Thomas Wilson, 1968–), MC Shan (Shawn Moltke, 1965–), and Roxanne Shanté (Lolita Shanté Gooden, 1969–). He is often credited with introducing sampling to hip hop production, as he used samples in his earliest works, and he was one of the first producers to use multilayered sampling, which was being used in electronic dance mixes as well as in electroacoustic art music, in hip hop. In addition, he was the first to create beats by making his own drum loops instead of using drum machines.

Early in his career, Marley Marl explored a drum sound each week. For example, his early albums show his experimenting with snare sounds. In the 1980s, it was practical to create a canned sound because access to technology was limited, making it practical to reuse recorded reel-to-reel tape hip hop elements. For example, the same snare drum sounds can be heard on Eric B. and Rakim's (1986–1993, 2016–) "Eric B. Is President" (1986) as on MC Shan's "The Bridge" (1985). Marley Marl's earliest work utilized an E-mu Emulator sampling keyboard, on which he could import a recorded snare drum hit and use it to create a new rhythm. This technique created his sound, which was fuller, more bass resonant (he would place more sounds to the lower left monitor or speaker field, which is used for bass), and more original than keyboard sample- and drum machine–based old-school hip hop.

FROM DJ TO PRODUCER

Marley Marl grew up in the Queensbridge Houses and took an early interest in music by watching DJs at house parties in the late 1970s and exploring turntablism with his brother's LP players. Young Marley Marl assembled the Sureshot Crew (1977–)*, a rapping crew, and worked as an intern at Unique Recording Studios (1979–2004), a five-room recording studio company in New York City, learning from DJ and record producer Arthur Baker (1955–), who had worked with hip hop and electronic music artists Afrika Bambaataa (1957–), Planet Patrol (1982–1984, 2006–), and New Order (1980–1993, 1998–2007, 2011–). Under Baker's supervision, Marley Marl's first produced album was "Sucker DJ's (I Will Survive)," a 12-inch single that was an answer to Run-D.M.C.'s (1981–2002) "Sucker M.C.s (Krush Groove 1)" (1983). Marley Marl's girlfriend, Dimples D (Crystal Smith, n.d.), recorded the track, which appeared on Partytime Records (1983–1984)* under Baker's own Streetwise Records label (1983–1986)*. At this time, Marley Marl was a DJ who battled with and shared his tools, techniques, and records with other DJs. He also worked as a radio DJ.

In 1983, Marley Marl formed the Juice Crew with Mr. Magic (John Rivas, 1956–2009), his hip hop radio DJ colleague at New York City's WHBI (now WXNY). Marley Marl's first professional production work was mixing for Tuff City Records

(1981–), an independent label that focused on New York City hip hop. His first success was Roxanne Shanté's "Roxanne's Revenge" (1984), an answer to U.T.F.O.'s (Untouchable Force Organization, 1984–1992) "Roxanne, Roxanne" (1984) that used the beats from their instrumental version. Shanté's rapping crew from Queens battled with KRS-One's (1965–) crew—to which U.T.F.O. belonged. The latter crew was from the Bronx, New York, and its members claimed that the Bronx was the real home of hip hop. Selling over 250,000 copies in New York City alone, "Roxanne's Revenge" became a hip hop classic and was the beginning of the Roxanne Wars (1984–1990*), one of the longest strings of answer records in hip hop history, many of which were produced by Marley Marl. In 1985, MC Shan (Shawn Moltke, 1965–) recorded "The Bridge," a Queensbridge pride song that sparked the Bridge Wars (1985–1990*), and more answer albums produced by Marley Marl.

COLD CHILLIN' RECORDS, LAWSUIT, AND FURTHER SUCCESS

In 1986, Marley Marl helped establish Cold Chillin' Records, which was at first run out of his sister's Queensbridge Houses apartment (nicknamed the House of Hits). Though the label was managed by Tyrone Williams (1961–) and run by its president, Kool Lenny (Len Fichtelberg, n.d.–2010), Marley Marl was responsible for most of the label's output via Juice Crew members. In 1990, he produced LL Cool J's (1968–) fourth studio album, *Mama Said Knock You Out*, for Def Jam Recordings (1983–). Certified double Platinum, the album became Marl's first huge mainstream success and created a high demand for his services as a producer and remixer.

In 1992, he produced TLC's (1990–) debut studio album *Oooooooohh . . . on the TLC Tip*, which peaked on the Billboard 200 at No. 14. In 1995, he released *House of Hits*, a compilation of his productions that marked his departure from Cold Chillin' as disputes over money and creative control reached a climax. In 1998, he won his lawsuit against Cold Chillin' Records, giving him control of his masters, which resulted in the label's closure. Marley Marl continues to produce albums in the 2000s, but at a slower pace than during the Golden Age of Hip Hop (1986–1994).

His output in the 2000s includes the compilation album *Re-entry* (2001) as well as releases and anniversary albums by rappers Nas (1973–), Busta Rhymes (1972–), KRS-One, LL Cool J, Raekwon (aka Raekwon the Chef, Corey Woods, 1970–), and M Dot (Michael Januario, 1984–).

Melissa Ursula Dawn Goldsmith

See also: Big Daddy Kane; Eric B. and Rakim; Roxanne Shanté; The United States

Further Reading

Coleman, Brian. 2007. "Marley Marle: *In Control Volume 1.*" In *Check the Technique: Liner Notes for Hip Hop Junkies*. New York: Villard.

Danois, Ericka Blount. 2010. "From Queens Come Kings: Run-D.M.C. Stomps Hard Out of a 'Soft' Borough." In *Hip Hop in America: A Regional Guide*, edited by Mickey Hess, vol. 1, chap. 3. Santa Barbara, CA: Greenwood.

Martinique

Martinique, an island in the French Antilles in the Caribbean, offers nearby musicians a place to record. For example, Guadeloupean hip hop artists need a place to record, and they sometimes record in Martinique. Although Martinique embraces French culture more than its West Indies neighbors, and French is its official language, Martinican hip hop artists, like their Guatemalan counterparts, write texts in Antillean Creole, a language natively spoken. Martinique and Guadeloupe are home to *zouk*, a fast-tempo music used for festivals, and both countries' hip hop artists adopt elements of *zouk*. In Martinque, Jamaican reggae is also influential. Some of Martinique's dance music styles, such as *chouvel bwa*, have galloping beats and, like some hip hop, contain call-and-response sections. Borders between French and French Antilles hip hop are permeable. Recently, Martinican rapper and singer Kalash (Kevin Valleray, 1988–) released his debut album *Kaos* (2016), which peaked at No. 4 on the French Syndicat National de l'Édition Phonographique (SNEP) album charts. Since 2014, Kalash has also had a string of 10 hit singles in France. *Kaos* has also peaked at No. 49 on Belgium's Ultratop album chart. Kalash raps primarily in French and Antillean Creole. In the 2000s, Kalash fused social and political hip hop with reggae, and dancehall.

French Antilles hip hop emerged in 1984, inspired by the French television show *H.I.P. H.O.P.* (1984), which was broadcast in Martinique and Guadeloupe. Breakdancing took hold, though its popularity increased later because of the 1995 arrival of David Milôme (n.d.), a b-boy and choreographer of Martinican descent from Lyon, France. In 1996, he formed his dance crew, MD Company (1996–). Due to a lack of technology, Martinican rappers, like Guadeloupean hip hop musicians, would rap over previously composed American beats. Their lyrics focused on everyday life, romance, and aspirations. One pioneer of Martinican hip hop, Nèg Lyrical (Rodolphe Richefal, 1976–), began with his group Nèg Ki Pa Ka Fè La Fèt (1989–1991*) before pursuing his solo career and helping to establish the Guadeloupean hip hop scene. Nèg Lyrical's *Kimannièoupédimwenanbagaÿkonsapéfèt?!* (the title, which is based more on sound than meaning, is a compound wordplay, 1996) was the first Antillean Creole rap album recorded in Martinique.

Rapper Lord Kossity (Thierry Moutoussamy, 1972–) was born in Paris, but his family was from Martinique, and they moved there when he was 11 years old. Since the 1990s, Lord Kossity has sold over four million copies. Lord Kossity returned to Paris after recording his debut studio album *An tèt ou sa yé* (*This Is Yourself*, 1997) in Martinique. He started recording ragga, dancehall, and reggae, but in his first recording he incorporated hip hop and zouk. His preferred rapping texts are in French and Antillean Creole, but he also uses some English.

Melissa Ursula Dawn Goldsmith

See also: France; Guadeloupe; Reggae

Further Reading

Berrian, Brenda F. 2000. *Awakening Spaces: French Caribbean Popular Songs, Music, and Culture.* Chicago Studies in Ethnomusicology. Chicago: University of Chicago Press.

Gadet, Steve. 2015. "Hip Hop Culture: Bridging Gaps between Young Caribbean Citizens." *Caribbean Quarterly* 61, no. 1: 75–97.

Further Listening
Lord Kossity. 1997. *An tèt ou sa yé (This Is Yourself)*. Killko Records.
Lord Kossity. 2005. *Booming System.* Universal Licensing Music (ULM).

Marxman

(1989–1996, London, England)

Marxman was a Dublin- and Bristol-based Irish English four-member Marxist and Celtic hip hop band that fused hardcore rap, political hip hop, and ambient electronica with traditional Irish music. It began in Dublin with graffiti artist MC Hollis Byrne (1969–) and electronic musician Oisín Lunny (aka First Born, n.d.) who became friends through their musical fathers, who performed together as part of the Irish folk pop band Emmet Spiceland (1967–1973). In 1989, Lunny reunited with Byrne in London and became the third member of Byrne's current duo with his college friend MC Phrase (aka Phrase D, Stephen Brown, n.d.). After adding DJ and turntablist Kay One (anonymous, n.d.), Marxman performed in both the London and Bristol hip hop scenes, helping to establish the Bristol sound in the 1990s, a combination of hip hop, soul, electronica, and trance that formed trip hop (downtempo), a music identified with groups such as Massive Attack (1988–) and Portishead (1991–) as well as vocalist-producer Tricky (Adrian Nicholas Matthews Thaws, 1968–).

Marxman appealed to listeners because of its combination of traditional Irish music against hardcore rap, the flexibility to perform alternative hip hop, use of turntablism, and the inclusion of political messages. Marxman's lyrical content focused on strong, militant, socialist messages, as well as protests against England's control over Ireland, economic disparity, and domestic violence. With a strong cult following, Marxman was one of the earliest bands to sign with the London-based Talkin' Loud (1990–) label.

Marxman was unusual for its combination of political hip hop and Irish folk music, but it was best known for its debut single, "Sad Affair" (1992), which was banned from British Broadcasting Corporation (BBC) radio because of its lyrics. With some borrowing from John Gibbs' (n.d.) traditional-style Irish rebel song "Irish Ways and Irish Laws" (1981), "Sad Affair" was perceived to express support of the Irish Republican Army (IRA, 1917*–). Marxman's other hit single, "All About Eve," peaked at No. 28 on the U.K. Singles Chart. Both songs were from the band's debut album, *33 Revolutions per Minute* (1993).

Ultimately, the band collaborated with acts such as Irish alternative, pop, and folk rock singer Sinéad O'Connor (1966–), American hip hop duo Gang Starr's (1986–2003) DJ Premier (aka Preem, Premo, Primo, Christopher Edward Martin, 1966–), and Celtic punk and folk band the Pogues' (1982–1996, 2001–2014) James McNally (n.d.). The last is now the composer and producer of the electronic fusion band Afro Celt Sound System (1995–). Marxman's second and last album was *Time*

Capsule (1996). As of 2018, Lunny continues as a music producer and film composer.

Melissa Ursula Dawn Goldsmith

See also: Hardcore Hip Hop; Ireland; Political Hip Hop; The United Kingdom

Further Reading

Gardner, Elysa. 1994. "New Faces: Marxman." *Rolling Stone* no. 690, September 8, 44.

Heaney, Mick. 1999. "The Son That Also Shines Underground." *Sunday Times* (London), June 13, 14.

Moriarty, Máiréad. 2015. "Hip Hop, LPP, and Globalization." In *Globalizing Language Policy and Planning: An Irish Language Perspective*, chap. 6. New York: Palgrave Macmillan.

Further Listening

Marxman. 1993. *33 Revolutions per Minute.* Talkin' Loud.

Massive Monkees

(1995*–, Seattle, Washington)

Massive Monkees is a b-boy crew that was created through the merger of Seattle's Massive Crew (n.d.) and the Universal Style Monkees (n.d.). It began competing in 1999 and is best known for winning the four-on-four category in the 2004 World B-Boy Championships in London and appearing on season four (2009) of MTV's *America's Best Dance Crew.*

While on *America's Best Dance Crew*, the crew finished third after episodes of dancing with hula hoops, incorporating *capoeira*, *bhangra* dance, and doing the Ricky Bobby dance on a trampoline. The Ricky Bobby dance is based on the eponymous character in the American film *Talladega Nights: The Ballad of Ricky Bobby* (2006), starring comedian Will Farrell (John William Ferrell, 1967–). The dance incorporates the character's moves, which include pantomiming steering a race car, posing like a celebrity, and imitating the character's sudden paralysis after a nervous breakdown, thus creating a wheelchairing motion.

In 2012, Massive Monkees won the annual international b-boy competition R-16 Korea, a dance and urban arts cultural festival, in a two-day event featuring 16 b-boy crews representing 15 countries. It became the first American crew to win in the history of the competition.

The Massive Monkees have 28 active members including rapper One Be Lo/ Nahshid Sulaiman (Ralond Scruggs, 1976–) of the former Pontiac, Michigan hip hop duo Binary Star (1998–2000, 2009–2014), who performs as the MC at their shows. The crew's style, which features humor, lots of group choreography, and acrobatics, is nonetheless traditional in its use of fundamental b-boy skills. Aside from commercial performances, the crew performs at high schools to dissuade gang violence.

In 2013, Jay Park (Park Jae-beom, 1987–) of Edmonds, Washington, who was a member of the b-boy crew Art of Movement (2002–), released a single, "Joah," which features a short dance break at the Beacon, the Massive Monkees studio in the Milwaukee Hotel building in Seattle. In 2007, the crew received the Seattle's Mayor's Arts Award.

Anthony J. Fonseca

See also: Battling; Breakdancing; Hip Hop Dance; The United States

Further Reading

Potterf, Tina. 2003. "The Art of Massive Monkees: Breakdancing Troupe Turns Moves and Ingenuity into 'Our Passion.'" *Seattle Times*, October 26, K1.

Schloss, Joseph G. 2009. *Foundation: B-Boys, B-Girls, and Hip Hop Culture in New York.* New York: Oxford University Press.

Master P

(Percy Robert Miller, 1970–, New Orleans, Louisiana)

Master P is a rap and hip hop producer, rapper, singer, and songwriter; founder/owner of No Limit Records (1990–2003); and founder/CEO of P. Miller Enterprises and Better Black Television (2008–) in New Orleans. He has also been a television executive (Better Black Television), author, philanthropist, filmmaker, and minor actor. His record company, No Limit, which became New No Limit and No Limit Forever (2010–) and is affiliated with Guttar Music (2005–2008*), is one of the major players in rap and hip hop music. Master P has released solo albums, as well as albums with the New Orleans–based groups TRU (The Real Untouchables, 1995–2002) and 504 Boyz (2000–2005), as well as project bands Louie V. Mob (2013), and Money Mafia (2015). Master P is the brother of rapper and producer C-Murder (1971–) and rapper Silkk the Shocker (Vyshonne King Miller, 1975–) and the father of rapper-actor Lil Romeo (Percy Romeo Miller Jr., 1989–), all from New Orleans.

ORIGINS AND SUCCESS OF NO LIMIT RECORDS

Originally from the Calliope Projects in New Orleans, Miller began his rap career in Richmond, California, where he had moved to attend business school and open a record store called No Limit Records. Working with In-A-Minute Records (1991–2000) in nearby Oakland, California, he transformed No Limit in February 1991 to a record label, releasing the solo album *Get Away Clean* (featuring TRU). His follow-up solos, *Mama's Bad Boy* (1992), *The Ghettos Tryin to Kill Me!* (1994, rereleased 1997), and *99 Ways to Die* (1995) saw limited success, even though the latter was distributed by Priority Records (1985–). In 1994, he started collaborating with artists on the No Limit label, with compilation albums *West Coast Bad Boyz, Vol. 1: Anotha Level of the Game* and *West Coast Bad Boyz: High fo Xmas.* Meanwhile, he had begun recording as part of the hip hop music trio TRU (originally a sextet), releasing *Understanding the Criminal Mind* (1992) and *Who's da Killer?* (1993).

In 1995, the same year that Master P moved No Limit from Richmond, California to New Orleans to create a team of Southern style rappers, TRU had its breakthrough with *True,* which peaked at No. 25 on the Top R&B/Hip-Hop Albums chart and produced the hit single "I'm Bout' It, Bout It." Armed with an in-house production team, Beats By the Pound, No Limit released Master P's *Ice Cream Man* (1995), with his second hit single, "Mr. Ice Cream Man," and TRU's *Tru 2 da Game* (1997), which stands out for its collaborations with Mia X (Mia Young, 1970–), from New Orleans, and Mo B. Dick (Raymond Poole, 1965–), from Morgan City, Louisiana.

Tru 2 da Game stands out for its diversity of sound, being influenced by Caribbean and New Orleans music, as well as sound effects and sampling. The track "I Always Feel Like" samples both Rockwell's (Kennedy William Gordy, 1964–) hit "Somebody's Watching Me" (1984) and the theme from the American anthology television program *The Twilight Zone* (1959–1964). The album was

American music producer, rapper, and singer-songwriter Master P is founder and owner of the highly successful No Limit Records, as well as P. Miller Enterprises and Better Black Television, both based in New Orleans. (Jeffrey Mayer/Wireimage/Getty Images)

also noted for its humorous interludes and popularization of the phrase "No Limit Soldier For Life," which became the label's trademark. The album starts out with Master P's talking to his son about "the game," overcoming jealousy, being supportive of other African Americans, and achieving success and independence. A daring double CD by a little-known (at the time) group, *Tru 2 da Game* is today considered a benchmark recording in gangsta rap (referred to as thug rap by No Limit) and hip hop.

SOLO CAREER AND FURTHER PRODUCTIONS

Master P's solo success came with *Ghetto D* (1997), which sold 761,000 copies in its first week and eventually was awarded triple Platinum status. Its single, "Make 'Em Say Uhh!" ranks as one of his most popular songs, and it was nominated as MTV's "Best Rap Video." His next album, *MP Da Last Don* (1998), the basis for an independent film (No Limit Films, 1997–2000) of the same name codirected and written by Master P, sold even better (turning quadruple Platinum) and debuted at No. 1 on the Billboard Top 200. In the same year, he also starred in and scored the music for *I Got the Hook Up* (distributed by Miramax). His next albums, *Only God Can Judge Me* (1999) and *Ghetto Postage* (2000), were moderate successes, but the former was released in the same year as TRU's *Da Crime Family*.

In 2000, he created a new group, 504 Boyz, and No Limit released the debut album *Goodfellas*, which peaked at No. 1 on the Top R&B/Hip-Hop Albums chart. To address the label's waning popularity, he retooled it, moved back to Los Angeles, and created the New No Limit (2001–), releasing the solo albums *Game Face* (2001) and *Good Side, Bad Side* (2004), as well as the 504 Boyz's *Ballers* (2002) and *Hurricane Katrina: We Gon Bounce Back* (2005), and TRU's *The Truth* (2005). During this time, C-Murder's murder conviction, sales, departing artists, and lawsuits forced the company into bankruptcy.

In 2005, he created the label Guttar Music, releasing the following albums and mixtapes: *Living Legend: Certified D-Boy*. Master P's albums since then have been *Ghetto Bill* (2005), *America's Most Luved Bad Guy* (2006), *TMZ* (2012), *Famous Again* (2013), *Al Capone* (2013), *The Gift* (2013), *Empire, from the Hood to Hollywood* (2015), *#CP3* (2015), *Ice Cream Man* (three mixtapes in 2016), and *Boss of All Bosses* (2016). In 2010, he created No Limit Forever, also in Los Angeles. In 2015, his most recent group, Money Mafia (2015–), released its debut album, *Rarri Boys*.

As of 2013, Miller was one of the wealthiest figures in American hip hop, worth over $300 million. Despite his wealth, he views himself as a family man and father who married his high school sweetheart; in interviews he states that he constantly fights the gangsta and thug rap image by remaining ever present in his children's lives, making sure that they are well educated, and teaching them to take over his music business.

Anthony J. Fonseca

See also: Bounce; C-Murder; Gangsta Rap; The United States

Further Reading

Chappell, Kevin. 2002. "Master P Raps about His Rapper Son, His $500 Million Empire and Why He Cleaned up His Act." *Ebony*, 57, no. 8: 57–58, 60.

Oliver, Richard, and Tim Leffel. 2006. "*Ghetto Bill*: The Man Is the Brand.'" In *Hip Hop, Inc.: Success Strategies of the Rap Moguls*, chap. 8. New York: Thunder's Mouth.

Further Listening

Master P. 1997. *Tru 2 da Game*. No Limit.

Mauritius

Mauritius is a Southeast African island nation located 700 miles east of Madagascar, in the Indian Ocean. Along with islands such as Rodrigues, Réunion, and Saint Brandon, Mauritius is part of the Mascarene Islands. In 1968, Mauritius gained its independence from the United Kingdom. Mauritians are mostly of Indian descent, with a large Creole minority, followed by small Chinese and European populations. English is the unofficial language (the Mauritian constitution deems no official language); however, French, Mauritian Creole, and Bhojpuri are national languages. Political unrest and numerous revolts took place in the 1970s and 1980s, but an increase in tourism led to an economic boost in the late 1980s, which helped Mauritius to become a republic within the Commonwealth of Nations (formerly the British Commonwealth, 1949–) in 1992. The emergence of American, French, and English hip hop coincided with the tourism boon. Interest began in 1992 with the formation of breakdance crews such as Street Brothers and Boogie Side Gang, both formed to support the Otentik Street Brothers, a *seggae* group (seggae is the fusion of reggae with traditional music of the Mascarene Islands and Mauritian *sega*, a popular dance music).

Mauritian hip hop music began in the early 1990s in capital city Port Louis and other large towns such as Beau Bassin–Rose Hill. Pioneering acts included N.A.S. Possi (1992–) and Urban Tribal Clan (2002*–). French and Mauritian Creole are the preferred languages of Mauritian hip hop, followed by American vernacular. Other popular acts included A4C (2002–), North Side Zoo (NSZ, 2004–), and Wu Team (aka Wake Up Team, 2002*–). Wu Team fuses hip hop with reggae, funk, and neo soul, and in 2006, group member Kenjee (aka KenjEe KeNnedy, 1982*–), a rapper, sound recording and film producer, and videogame sound designer, started TaffBongLab Prod (TBL, 2006–2010), a DIY home music studio label that produced several albums digitally. Its first recording was the collaborative mixtape, *Kolt'Art Mix* (2008) by the Mauritian rap collective Section Kolt'art (2008–), launched by Kenjee.

In 2010, Kenjee's Wake Up Entertainment and the Wake Up (Street) Sessions were formed, the latter a street dance battle event to promote self-esteem in Mauritian youth. TBL has also produced Mafia Swagg (2012–) and the Malagasy group Majunga (2015–). Mauritian hip hop is strongly influenced by seggae and reggae. Its lyrical content partly focuses on frustrations about the government, violence, and inequality and partly on American- and French-inspired topics, including braggadocio and partying. The best-known Mauritian hip hop diaspora acts include Paris's Mauritian All Stars (aka MAS Team, 2010–) and London-born electronica singer and percussionist Mo Kolours (Joseph Deenmamode, n.d.).

Melissa Ursula Dawn Goldsmith

See also: France; Reggae

Further Reading

Pyndiah, Gitanjali. 2016. "Decolonizing Creole on the Mauritius Islands: Creative Practices in Mauritian Creole." *Island Studies Journal* 11, no. 2: 484–504.

Thannoo, Babita. 2012. "Rap Music in Mauritius." *Wasafiri* 27, no. 4: 35–41.

Further Listening

WU Team. 2007. *T-East*. Streetbounce Productions.

MBS

(Le Micro Brise le Silence, 1988–, Algiers, Algeria)

MBS, an acronym for Le Micro Brise le Silence (The Microphone Breaks the Silence), is an Algerian rap crew of MCs that raps and sings in Algerian French and

Algerian Arabic—the latter being one of the two official languages of Algeria, the other being Tamazight, also known as Berber (a language that is a kind of Maghrebi Arabic, with a large number of loanwords from French, but also from Spanish and Ottoman Turkish). MBS combines rap with traditional Algerian music. Formed in 1988 while in the capital city of Algiers, members include their leader, Rabah Ourrad (aka Donquishoot, n.d.), along with Yacine (aka Ayad Yasine, n.d.), Red One (Cheb Redouan, n.d.), and M'Hand (aka Deymed, Touat M'hand, n.d.).

MBS focuses primarily on political rap, emerging first in response against the Algerian Government's hostile military takeover of the National Liberation Front (FLN) after the party's own dishonest cancellation of parliament elections, which would have likely led to victory for the Islamic Salvation Front (FLS) party. These events and the military government's oppression of these parties and its people led to the Algerian Civil War (1991–2002), another subject of protest found in MBS's rap. Themes include rapping and singing against government abuses, suffering under Algeria's deteriorating conditions, and youth frustrations over unemployment and failures of the Algerian education system, in addition to the horrors of witnessing massacres.

The positive reception of MBS's debut and subsequent early albums, *Ouled El bahdja* (*The Children of the Radiant*, 1998), *Hbibti Aouama* (*My Lover Is a Good Swimmer*, 1998*), and *Le Micro Brise Le Silence* (1999), the first two produced by Totem Records (1989–1998*) and the eponymous one by Universal (1996–) in Paris, as well as the band's touring and moving to Paris, helped to bring international attention and acclaim despite censorship in Algeria. After living in Paris for three years and pursuing a variety of projects as solo and duo efforts, the band released *Wellew* (*They Have Returned*, 2001, self-released) and its last album *Maquis Bla Sleh* (*Marquis Without Weapons*, 2005, Izem Prod). Both reconnect to MBS's Algerian origins and are dedicated to the people of Hussein Dey, a suburb of Algiers.

Although they are still together, as of 2018, all have worked on separate recording projects rather than producing a current album together.

Melissa Ursula Dawn Goldsmith

See also: Algeria; France; Political Hip Hop

Further Reading

Davies, Eirlys E., and Abdelali Bentahila. 2006. "Code Switching and the Globalization of Popular Music: The Case of North African Rai and Rap." *Multilingua: Journal of Cross-Cultural and Interlanguage Communication* 25, no. 4: 367–92.

El Zein, Rayya. 2016. "Call and Response, Radical Belonging, and Arabic Hip Hop in 'the West.'" In *American Studies Encounters the Middle East*, edited by Alex Lubin and Marwan M. Kraidy, pp. 106–36. Chapel Hill: University of North Carolina Press.

Further Listening

MBS. 1999. *Le micro brise le silence* (*The Microphone Breaks the Silence*). Universal.

MBS. 2005. *Maquis bla sleh* (*Marquis without Weapons*). Izem Prod

MC

MC is an honorific bestowed on rappers. A term analogous to the lead singer of a rock music band, *MC* is a shortened version of the word *emcee* and is loosely related to the idea of the master of ceremonies, the official who hosts a staged event or ceremony. By the late 1970s, in rap music jargon MC was basically synonymous with rapper, as opposed to the term DJ, an honorific bestowed upon turntablists (and sometimes producers and samplers). Early MCs were private DJs who worked parties and clubs, where their jobs were to both keep the music playing and keep the crowd engaged through call-and-response, calls to dance, and manipulation of beats and rhythms. Successful MCs were those who could master both improvised rap—what is often called freestyle—and established, prewritten rhymed verses. Usually, the MC is the liaison to the audience and as such introduces the group's DJ; however, some hip hop bands, such as Salt-N-Pepa (1985–2002, 2007–), reverse the trend and use the DJ to energize the crowd and make various announcements. The most important element of the MC's job is to engage or energize the crowd through a combination of boasts about skill and/or attacks on other rappers.

In 1979 the pioneering group Grandmaster Flash and the Furious Five released its first single, "Superappin'." The original lineup in this 1980 New York portrait featured Grandmaster Flash as DJ (center) with five MCs (clockwise from upper left): Scorpio, Kidd Creole, Keef Cowboy, Rahiem, and Melle Mel. (Anthony Barboza/Getty Images)

EARLY EXAMPLES

Perhaps the earliest American rapper to use the epithet "MC" before his name was Melle Mel (1961–), a pioneering American rapper from the Bronx, who worked as the lead rapper and songwriter for Grandmaster Flash and the Furious Five (1976–1982, 1987–1988) before embarking on a solo career. As lead rapper, he often took on the role of Master of Ceremonies during performances. His best-known hit was the classic old-school hip hop song "The Message," which appeared on Grandmaster Flash and the Furious Five's album of the same title (1982). Another rapper who acquired the epithet early was MC Hammer (1962–). He chose to do so because he acted as Master of Ceremonies at various dance clubs while on the road with the Oakland Athletics baseball team. As early as 1988, he used the term in the opening line of his guest rap on the Jon Gibson (1964–) song "This Wall," from Gibson's *Change of Heart* album (1988).

The practice itself, however, goes back further—although the term's American-ization changed practices significantly. The role of the rap-associated MC may be rooted in the *bolon player*, a male musician who plays the *bolon* (a wooden bow-shaped harp with three or four stings from West African countries such as Mali) and has the ability to criticize leadership or inequality in both serious and playfully insulting ways and some *griot* practices also found in West African countries such as Senegal, the Gambia, or Mali. It is also rooted in a combination of the Jamaican practice of toasting, which occurs when a Master of Ceremonies working also as a dance hall deejay would use rhymed introductions and announcements to engage the crowd before and after a dancer or a band performed and the African Ameri-can DJ practice of talking jive.

As Jamaican immigrants moved to New York City, they influenced hip hop, which was at that time a new music genre, by bringing to it the practice of rhythmic spoken word (rapping). The earliest American rapping MCs worked par-ties, often coming up with improvised party rhymes; such MCs are often referred to as old-school, and their styles as old-school rap or hip hop. Their rhymed impro-visations were predictably about dancing, enjoying the music, competing with others for attention from the opposite sex, and drawing attention to yourself as a superior performer; for this reason their raps were good-natured, humorous, and often included call-and-response sections so that the crowd could be involved.

THEMES AND LITERARY TECHNIQUES

Early rappers, such as Spoonie Gee (1963–) of the Sugar Hill Records (1986–1995) label's Treacherous Three (1978–1984) emphasized lyrics about love and sex. Later MCs would express lyrics that were more concerned with sociopolitical issues. Hip hop artists such as KRS-One (1965–), Public Enemy (1982–), Mos Def (1973–), Jay-Z (1969–), Nas (1973–), the Notorious B.I.G. (1972–1997), and Tupac Shakur (1971–1996) rapped about discrimination, poverty, police brutality, teen-age pregnancy, and racism; in some instances, their raps would be viewed as glamorizing crime, a criticism often leveled at Schoolly D (Jesse Bonds Weaver Jr., 1962–), KRS-One (in the early years), Ice-T (1958–), N.W.A. (1986–1991), and Public Enemy. The other major theme seen in MC raps is luxury, or the pursuit of "bling." Since the early 1990s, rappers have created boast lyrics about wealth, which usually involves a good bit of product placement in videos and name-dropping in lyrics. More recent trends in MCing have included the assimila-tion of religion into rap, as with Christian Hip Hop and the rappers who represent the Five Percent Nation (1964–), an Islamic religious and spirituality organization founded in Harlem, New York, the latter including benchmark MCs and bands such as Rakim (1968–), the Wu–Tang Clan (1992–), Brand Nubian (1989–), and Busta Rhymes (1972–).

Like other song lyricists, MCs make extensive use of simile, metaphor, word-play, rhyme, alliteration, assonance, and double entendre. For the most part, MCs use street idioms and vernacular language in their raps, and most of their imagery is derived from the urban scene. They are much more likely than lyricists in other popular music genres to use their regional dialects, since their songs are designed to tell the stories of their neighborhoods. In addition to scripted lyrics, rappers also are expected to master freestyle rap, which can be partially or entirely improvised. This further emphasizes the local, since it is easier to create on-the-spot lyrics when referencing people, places, and objects in an immediate setting. One style of free-style is the battle rap, wherein two MCs act as opponents and compete to prove their authenticity and originality through insults and boasts. As far as rap styles go, they range from breathless and frenetic to laid-back and carefully articulated, and from solo to call-and-response.

Though the majority of rappers are male, some female rappers have made their mark on the MC world, namely MC Lyte (1970–), Missy Elliott (1971–), Queen Latifah (1970–), Da Brat (1974–), Eve (Eve Jihan Jeffers–Cooper, 1978–), M.I.A. (1975–), and Nicki Minaj (1982–).

Anthony J. Fonseca

See also: Chopper; Turntablism

Further Reading

Edwards, Paul. 2009. *How to Rap: The Art and Science of the Hip Hop MC.* Chicago: Chicago Review Press.

Edwards, Paul. 2013. *How to Rap 2: Advanced Flow and Delivery Techniques.* Chicago: Chicago Review Press.

Krims, Adam. 2001. *Rap Music and the Poetics of Identity.* Cambridge, England: Cambridge University Press.

mc chris

(Christopher Brendan Ward IV, 1975–, Libertyville, Illinois)

MC Chris (stylized as mc chris) is an American hip hop musician and rapper who is often considered a nerdcore artist, even though he actively distanced himself from nerdcore until after 2010, when he became less resistant to the affiliation; he now self-identifies as a rapper who raps about nerd life. One of the most defining characteristics of his musical style is his high-pitched, androgynous voice. Other defining characteristics of his music include a lyrical alignment with subjects that are relevant to the nerdcore hip hop audience, such as obsessions with *Star Wars* ("Fett's 'Vette," 2001) and video games ("Luigi," 2014), and a preoccupation with romantic and sexual difficulties ("On*," 2008) and nerd identity ("Geek," 2003).

Unlike those of other nerdcore artists, mc chris's lyrics are often dark, explicit, and sometimes violent or aggressive. For example, "The Tussin" (2001) is an ode to robo-tripping, or intentionally overdosing on dextromethorphan, and "Tarantino" (2011) is an expletive-laden track about the American film director Quentin Tarantino (1963–). In the early part of his recording career, mc chris worked primarily with producer John Fewell (1980*–), but his music since 2008 has been produced in collaboration with Andrew Futral (1982*–).

Beginning his career as a writer and animator for several television shows on Adult Swim, the late-night animated television program block that airs on the Turner Broadcasting System's Cartoon Network, mc chris worked on programs including *Space Ghost Coast to Coast* (1994–2008), *Sealab 2021* (2000–2005), and *Aqua Teen Hunger Force* (2000–2015). His breakout role came when he voice-acted the character MC Pee Pants on *Aqua Teen Hunger Force* in the early 2000s.

In 2001, he released his first full-length studio album, *Life's a B— and I'm Her Pimp*, while he was still working at Adult Swim. He has released a total of nine full-length studio albums, as well as several EPs, compilation albums, and mixtapes. His albums frequently mix music tracks with short skits about zombies, film directors he admires, and other topics of interest.

As of 2018, his first album and all of his mixtapes are available for free download (he has noted how difficult it is to profit from sales of his other albums because many of his fans share and download the tracks online for free). In 2004, mc chris left Adult Swim permanently (approximately the time his third album, *Eating's Not Cheating*, was released) to focus on his recording career. Since then, he has written and starred in several animated pilot projects, none of which has been picked up by major networks for production or distribution.

Amanda Sewell

See also: Chap Hop; MC Frontalot; MC Lars; Nerdcore; The United States

Further Reading

Sewell, Amanda. 2015. "Nerdcore Hip Hop." In *The Cambridge Companion to Hip Hop*, edited by Justin Williams, chap. 16. Cambridge, England: Cambridge University Press.

Tanz, Jason. 2007. "White-on-White Rhyme: *8 Mile*, Nerdcore, and Mooks." In *Other People's Property: A Shadow History of Hip Hop in White America*, chap. 7. New York: Bloomsbury.

Further Viewing

Farsad, Negin, dir. 2008. *Nerdcore Rising*. Vaguely Qualified Productions.

Lamoreux, Dan. dir. 2008. *Nerdcore for Life*. Crapbot Productions.

MC Frontalot

(Damian Hess, 1973–, San Francisco, California)

MC Frontalot is an American nerdcore artist based out of Brooklyn, New York. He is credited with coining the term nerdcore hip hop in 2000 with a song of the same name and is generally regarded as the father of nerdcore by both musicians and critics. His moniker makes light of the fact that, as a nerdy white person, he is putting on a front by trying to be a rapper. Known for his humor, MC Frontalot has claimed to be the 579th greatest rapper in the world. Aside from their tongue-in-cheek lyrics, MC Frontalot's songs focus on familiar nerdcore topics, including obsessions with *Star Wars* ("Yellow Lasers," 2005), video games ("Penny Arcade Theme," 2002), and grammar ("Tongue-Clucking Grammarian," 2008); they also deal with social issues faced by nerds, such as awkwardness ("Wallflowers," 2008) and romantic rejection ("Goth Girls," 2005).

Most of his tracks are created in collaboration with Canadian producer Baddd Spellah (David T. Cheong, 1972*–) for keyboards and drum programming, as well as American Gminor7 (Gabriel Alter, n.d.) for keyboards. Although he had been releasing his music online since 1999 through the online competition Song Fight!, MC Frontalot's breakthrough came in 2002, when the web comic Penny Arcade declared him the "Official MC of Penny Arcade." In response, he recorded

"Penny Arcade Theme" the same year, and it has become one of his signature tracks.

MC Frontalot's first full-length album, *Nerdcore Rising*, was not completed until 2005, and it contained a mixture of new tracks as well as rerecorded demos and Song Fight! entries. He has released a total of six full-length studio albums, as well as dozens of demos, mixtapes, and live tracks, many of which, as of 2018, are available to download for free. He frequently collaborates with other nerdcore artists, including American rapper MC Hawking (Ken Lawrence, 1970*–) and Canadian rapper Jesse Dangerously (Jesse McDonald, 1979–). He has also worked with more mainstream hip hop artists, including South African–born American rapper Jean Grae (1976–) and Canadian DJ and Canadian turntablist Kid Koala (Eric San, 1974–).

MC Frontalot is one of the most outspoken members of the nerdcore community, having been interviewed by major news outlets such as National Public Radio and *Newsweek* magazine. He and his collaborators were the subjects of *Nerdcore Rising*, a 2008 documentary named for MC Frontalot's track and album and which also included interviews with nerdcore-affiliated artists such as mc chris (1975–) and MC Lars (1982–).

MC Frontalot has also entered 21st-century mainstream pop culture by appearing as a guest judge on the TBS reality show *King of the Nerds* (2013–2015) and performing the original track "Toilet Paper Factory" in the *Sesame Street* direct-to-DVD *Elmo's Potty Time* (2005).

Amanda Sewell

See also: Chap Hop; mc chris; MC Lars; Nerdcore; The United States

Further Reading

Braiker, Brian. 2007. "Geeksta Rap Rising." *Newsweek* 149, no. 5: 58.

Colgan, Jim. 2005. "Nerd Hip Hop, Flowing Like Han Solo." *Day to Day* (National Public Radio), November 7.

Sewell, Amanda. 2015. "Nerdcore Hip Hop." In *The Cambridge Companion to Hip Hop*, edited by Justin Williams, chap. 16. Cambridge, England: Cambridge University Press.

Tanz, Jason. 2007. "White-on-White Rhyme: *8 Mile*, Nerdcore, and Mooks." In *Other People's Property: A Shadow History of Hip Hop in White America*, chap. 7. New York: Bloomsbury.

Further Listening

MC Frontalot. 2005. *Nerdcore Rising*. Level Up Records and Tapes.

Further Viewing

Farsad, Negin, dir. 2008. *Nerdcore Rising*. Vaguely Qualified Productions.

Lamoreux, Dan, dir. 2008. *Nerdcore for Life*. Crapbot Productions.

MC Hammer

(Stanley Kirk Burrell, 1962–, Oakland, California)

MC Hammer (aka Hammer) is an American hip hop musician, old-school rapper, and dancer best known for his top-10 hits "U Can't Touch This" (1990), "Pray" (1990), and "Too Legit to Quit" (1991), as well as his catch phrase "Hammer time."

Some of his dance moves and flashy clothing, including his trademark parachute pants, helped him achieve icon status; his influence on the world of fashion was far-reaching in the 1980s and early 1990s.

His entertainment career began in 1973 as a dancer, batboy, and play-by-play analyst for the Major League Baseball team Oakland Athletics, but his music career began in 1985 after a three-year stint in the military and a brief stint with a Christian rap group (The Holy Ghost Boys, n.d.). He released the album *Feel My Power* in 1987 on his independent label, Bustin' Records, selling 60,000 copies; however, after he signed with Capitol Records (1942–) for a reported $1.75 million advance, he released of his No. 1 album *Please Hammer, Don't Hurt 'Em* (1990), which went ten-times Platinum; because of his catchy melodic lines, liberal but clever use of sampling, and extremely popular music videos featuring himself and his dance entourage, he achieved household fame.

Overall, MC Hammer has won three Grammys, and his albums have sold over 50 million copies worldwide despite a limited number of hit singles. But his influence on the hip hop genre is limited because his legacy has been that of a commercially successful entertainer and choreographed dancer, rather than a serious musician or songwriter; despite his having once signed with Suge Knight's (Marion Hugh Knight Jr., 1966–) Death Row Records (1991–), generally his songs have come to be considered commercial, having more in common with pop music than with hardcore rap, even though he attempted to become more urban in his later music.

After 2006 MC Hammer basically retired from music, becoming a Christian preacher from 1999–2006 on *Praise the Lord* (1973–) and a voice actor for the Saturday morning cartoon *Hammerman* (1991) and producer of a reality show called *Hammertime* (2009) on AandE Network. During the 1980s and 1990s, he was CEO of Bust It Records (1980*–1997), producing acts such as Oaktown's 3.5.7 (1988–1991) and Doug E. Fresh (1966–).

Anthony J. Fonseca

See also: Christian Hip Hop; Fashion; Hip Hop Dance; The United States

Further Reading

Manero, J. K. 2009. "Hammer Dance." *Bust a Move: Six Decades of Dance Crazes.* New York: ItBooks.

Small, Michael W. 1992. "Hammer." In *Break It Down: The Inside Story from the New Leaders of Rap*, pp. 91–93. New York: Carol Pub.

Further Listening

MC Hammer. 1990. *Please Hammer, Don't Hurt 'Em.* Capitol.

MC Lars

(Andrew Robert Nielsen, 1982–, Berkeley, California)

MC Lars is an American hip hop artist who calls himself the originator of post-punk laptop rap. Since he is of Scandinavian descent, he chose the family name, Lars, as his stage name because it seemed to be a humorous contrast to the African American roots of hip hop. As a producer, he often samples recordings of American and

British punk bands, including Fugazi (1987–2002), Supergrass (1993–2010), and Brand New (2000–). MC Lars is generally associated with nerdcore because his lyrics frequently refer to video games, literature and poetry, and social awkwardness. He holds a bachelor's degree from Stanford University and is the founder of Horris Records (2006–).

In 2006, MC Lars released his first full-length studio album, *The Graduate*, on which he was the lyricist, performer, and producer. The album featured "Download This Song," which has become one of his best-known tracks. Representative of his style and music technique, it features liberal sampling, in this case from American proto-punk artist Iggy Pop's (James Newell Osterberg Jr., 1947–) hit "The Passenger" (1977), which it juxtaposes against a rap that rails against record labels for not updating their sales practices to keep up with new technology. "Download this Song" also includes guest performer Jaret Reddick (1972–), the rhythm guitarist and lead singer of American rock band Bowling for Soup (1994–). Lars combines Pop's new wave sound with Reddick's post-punk and his own rap, running the song's various elements as countermelodies against one another. Other tracks on the album use an array of voices and effects and address topics such as social conformity and identity, as in "Hot Topic is Not Punk Rock," online and real-life relationships, as in "The Roommate from Hell" and "Internet Relationships (Are Not Real Relationships)," and literature, as in "Ahab."

Since 2006, MC Lars has released four full-length albums as well as several EPs and mixtapes. He is one of the few nerdcore hip hop artists who owns his own label. He frequently collaborates with other artists from a variety of genres and styles, including nerdcore hip hop artists such as mc chris (1975–) and MC Frontalot (1973–), mainstream hip hop artists such as KRS-One (1965–) and Kool Keith (1963–), rock groups such as Wheatus (1995–), and rock musicians such as Roger Lima (Rogério Lima Manganelli, 1974–).

MC Lars takes an active role in several education initiatives. He has given multiple TED Talks on the roles of poetic meter in literature, poetry, and hip hop lyrics. In 2012, he was featured at Scholastic's Art and Writing Awards, which was held at New York's Carnegie Hall. During this performance, he performed "Flow Like Poe," an analysis of poetic meter in the works of 19th-century American writer Edgar Allan Poe (1809–1849) that is rapped over a sample of the 17th-century *Canon in D*, composed by Johann Pachelbel (1653–1706). MC Lars has also served as an artist- or scholar-in-residence at several universities in the United States and the United Kingdom.

Amanda Sewell

See also: Chap Hop; mc chris; MC Frontalot; Nerdcore; The United States

Further Reading

Anon. 2009. "5 Questions for Nerdcore Rapper MC Lars." *SFGate*, March 9.

Colgan, Jim. 2005. "Nerd Hip Hop, Flowing Like Han Solo." *Day to Day* (National Public Radio), November 7.

Sewell, Amanda. 2015. "Nerdcore Hip Hop." In *The Cambridge Companion to Hip Hop*, edited by Justin Williams, chap. 16. Cambridge, England: Cambridge University Press.

Further Viewing

Farsad, Negin, dir. 2008. *Nerdcore Rising.* New York: Vaguely Qualified Productions.
Lamoreux, Dan, dir. 2008. *Nerdcore for Life.* N.p.: Crapbot Productions.

MC Lyte

(Lana Michele Moorer, 1971–, Queens, New York)

MC Lyte was one of the first women rappers to challenge sexism and misogyny in
rap music during the late 1980s. She is best known for her lyricism and distinctive
flow, which proved that female rappers could write and perform just as well as male
MCs. Although she does not shy away from the braggadocio rap battle aesthetic,
she has generally collaborated with and advocated for women rappers and other
female artists. She has also worked as an actor, appearing on TV shows such as a
1995 episode of *New York Undercover* (1994–1998), a 1998 episode of *In the House*
(1995–1999), a 2002 episode of *The District* (2000–2004), and from 2004 to 2006
as the recurring character Kai Owens on *Half and Half* (2002–2006), as well as in
the American films *Fly By Night* (1992), *Train Ride* (2000), and *Playas Ball* (2003),
among others.

MC Lyte began rapping when she was 12 years old, and at the age of 17, she
released her first album, *Lyte as a Rock* (1988) on the First Priority Music label
(FPM 1987–1997, 2001–); it was the first LP released by a solo female MC. She
followed up in 1989 with *Eyes on This*, widely considered to be her best work. It
included "Cha Cha Cha," which spent 18 weeks on the Billboard Hot Rap Singles
chart, reaching No. 1. The singles "Cappucino" and "Stop, Look, Listen" peaked
at the No. 8 and No. 9 positions on that chart, respectively.

In 1991, she released her third album, *Act Like You Know,* which was less successful but included two hit singles, "When In Love" and "Poor Georgie." For
Act Like You Know Lyte worked with producers of the new jack swing sound,
which combined musical aspects of rap, R&B, and other styles. New jack swing
songs often featured a hip hop beat combined with a pop melody and sung and/or
rapped lyrics. "Poor Georgie" is considered a classic example of new jack
swing. In 1993, MC Lyte released her fourth album, *Ain't No Other.* "Ruff-
neck," a track from this album, became the first single by a solo female rapper
to achieve Gold certification from the Recording Industry Association of
American (RIAA) and earned Lyte a Grammy nomination, the first ever for a
female rapper.

In 1996, Lyte released her first album after moving to EastWest Records (1955–
2004, 2015–), *Bad as I Wanna B.* Jermaine Dupri (Jermaine Dupri Mauldin, 1972–),
R. Kelly (Robert Sylvester Kelly, 1967–), and others produced the album. It
spawned two certified-Gold singles, "Keep On, Keepin' On" and "Cold Rock a
Party," whose single version featured Missy Elliott (1971–) and was an early success for the emerging rapper and producer.

In 1998, she released a follow-up album, *Seven and Seven* on the EastWest
label. In 2003, her seventh album, *The Undaground Heat Vol. 1*, was released

independently, and in 2015—after a 12-year hiatus—her eighth album, *Legend*, was made available only on limited release in vinyl format.

Lauron Jockwig Kehrer

See also: Political Hip Hop; The United States

Further Reading

Bradley, Adam, and Andrew Dubois, eds. 2010. "MC Lyte." Under "Part 2: 1985–92: The Golden Age" in *The Anthology of Rap*, pp. 225–32. New Haven, CT: Yale University Press.

Coleman, Brian. 2007. "MC Lyte: *Lyte as a Rock*." In *Check the Technique: Liner Notes for Hip Hop Junkies*, pp. 256–63. New York: Villard.

Young, Jennifer R. 2007. "MC Lyte." In *Icons of Hip Hop: An Encyclopedia of the Movement, Music, and Culture*, edited by Mickey Hess, vol. 1, pp. 117–40. Westport, CT: Greenwood Press.

Further Listening

MC Lyte. 1989. *Eyes on This*. First Priority Music.

MC Lyte. 1993. *Ain't No Other*. First Priority Music.

MC Opi

(Janette Oparebea Nelson, 1971–, London, England)

MC Opi is a spoken-word artist, multi-instrumentalist, and MC/DJ, who has a concurrent career as a film, radio, television, and music video director and producer. She is best known for being the first female rapper in Australia to receive national recognition, when she appeared on the 1994 Australian Recording Industry Association Music Awards (ARIA) show for the nominated hit single "The Last Train," which made her rapping sound and style famous. She has a deep, androgynous speaking voice, and her rapping style is comparable to Shaggy's (1968–) rapping and toasting.

"The Last Train," which appeared on the bonus disc of Australian pop and R&B artist Christine Anu's (1970–) electronic, hip hop, folk, and dancehall fusion album *Stylin' Up* (1995), was a dancehall/dubstep remake of Australian rock-acoustic singer-songwriter Paul Kelly's (1955–) reggae-infused "Last Train to Heaven," from his album *Gossip* (1986). Both song and video featured Anu, Kelly, and MC Opi. "Last Train" peaked at No. 93 on the ARIA Singles Chart and No. 61 on Triple J's Hottest 100 for 1993, a poll of the most popular songs of the year in Australia. *Stylin' Up* also went Platinum in Australia.

MOVE TO AUSTRALIA AND MUSIC CAREER

Born to an indigenous Australian Irish Celtic harpist (mother) and Australian of Ghanaian descent (father), MC Opi watched her parents divorce in 1979; she then moved with her mother to Sydney. Her interests in rapping, singing, turntablism, and bass guitar playing developed in the late 1980s to mid-1990s, as she began performing as MC Opi at dance parties. During her early career, she performed with the English trip hop group Massive Attack (1988–), reggae musician Lucky Dube (1964–2007), and Sydney's own electronic and dubstep duo Wicked Beat Sound System (1992–), among others. In 1990, she coproduced *Women on the Rhyme*, which was the first Australian Broadcasting Corporation (ABC) radio documentary on female Australian and New Zealand hip hop artists. She also taught scratching masterclasses to women in Sydney.

In 1993, Australian filmmaker and photographer Tracey Moffatt (1960–) asked her to be his assistant director and to appear briefly in the music video for rock group INXS's "The Messenger," from their album *Full Moon, Dirty Hearts*. At the same time, she became one of the earliest music artists to work on Australia's first dance music show, *MC Tee Vee and Alternative Arts Show*; she conducted interviews with the Beastie Boys (1981–2012), among other hip hop artists.

FURTHER ENDEAVORS

The same year that "Last Train" was released, MC Opi appeared on Sex Industrie's (1990–1994) progressive house EP *Get Lost*. From 1994 to 2000, she began working in digital entertainment, moving briefly to New York City, but then returning to Sydney, where she produced *Jezebel Complex* (2000), an industrial music project. In 2008, she completed the music and video project "The Black Hole Lovers."

In 2011, MC Opi earned a master's in digital media at the University of New South Wales, and since 2014, she has been a television producer in London for her Internet show *DotsWaves TV*, which focuses on global hip hop, among other underground arts.

Melissa Ursula Dawn Goldsmith

See also: Australia; Turntablism; The United Kingdom

Further Reading

Hardy, Marieke. 2013. "Music: She Twerks Hard for the Money." *The Monthly*, August, 52–53.

Mitchell, Tony. 2003. "Indigenizing Hip Hop: An Australian Migrant Youth Subculture." In *Ingenious: Emerging Youth Cultures in Urban Australia*, edited by Melissa Butcher and Mandy Thomas, pp. 198–214. North Melbourne, Victoria, Australia: Pluto Press.

Morgan, George, and Andrew Warren. 2011. "Aboriginal Youth, Hip Hop, and the Politics of Identification." *Ethnic and Racial Studies* 34, no. 6: 925–27.

MC Solaar

(Claude M'Barali, 1969–, Dakar, Senegal)

MC Solaar is a French hip hop and jazz rap rapper and philanthropist of Senegalese and Chadian origin. He has had six Top 10 albums, including two No. 1 albums, *Paradisiaque* (*Heavenly*, 1997) and *Géopoétique* (*Geopoetic*, 2017), on the French record chart Syndicat National de l'Édition Phonographique (SNEP, 1922–). He has also had six Top 10 SNEP singles, including two No. 1's, "Hasta la Vista" (2001) and "Inch' Allah" (2002), and he has been featured on the Missy Elliott (1971–) hit "All n My Grill" (1999). Stylistically, he is known for complex multiple rhymes that use wordplay and stream of consciousness, and his lyrical themes are informed by his experience as a minority immigrant; he usually raps in French. His solo albums have been released on the Polydor (1913–), Talkin' Loud (1990–), Sentinel Quest (1998–2011), and Play Two (2016–) labels. Talkin' Loud also released albums he was involved with while with the acid jazz hip hop crew Urban Species (1992–2000, 2008–), a London band whose music is influenced by reggae, blues, funk, dub, jazz, raga, and acoustic folk. MC Solaar is also known for his work with Boston rapper, producer, and actor Guru (aka Gifted Unlimited Rhymes Universal, Keith Edward Elam, 1961–2010) and New York–based rap duo Gang Starr (1986–2003).

His parents moved from Dakar, Senegal, to the Parisian suburb of Saint-Denis when he was a child, and he spent some of his teen years in Cairo with an uncle; there he discovered the Universal Zulu Nation (1973–) and electronica rapper Afrika Bambaataa (1957–). When he returned to France, he studied languages and philosophy at Jussieu University (aka Sorbonne University Group, 1971–), and in 1990, he released his first single, "Bouge de là" ("Get out of There"), which peaked at No. 22 on the SNEP chart. His 1991 album *Qui sème le vent récolte le tempo* (*He Who Harvests the Wind Collects the Tempo*) sold over 400,000 copies in France. His 12-nation 1992–1993 tour was very popular and set the stage for the success of his 1994 album *Prose Combat*. In 1997, he became a member of Les Enfoirés (1989–), an ensemble that raises money for charity.

Anthony J. Fonseca

See also: France; Griot; Political Hip Hop; Senegal

Further Reading

Baker, Geoffrey. 2011. "Preachers, Gangsters, Pranksters: MC Solaar and Hip Hop as Overt and Covert Revolt." *Journal of Popular Culture* 44, no. 2: 233–55.

Neal, Mark Anthony. 2016. "N—s in Paris: Hip Hop in Exile." *Social Identities* 22, no. 2: 150–59.

Further Listening

MC Solaar. 1994. *Prose Combat.* Polydor.

MC Solaar. 2017. *Géopoétique* (*Geopoetic*). Play Two.

Melle Mel

(aka Mele Mel, Grandmaster Melle Mel, Melvin Glover, 1961–, Bronx, New York)

Melle Mel is a pioneering American rapper from the Bronx, who worked as the lead rapper and songwriter for Grandmaster Flash and the Furious Five (1976–1982, 1987–1988) before embarking on a solo career. Melle Mel may have been the first rapper to use the epithet "MC" before his name. His best-known hit was the classic old-school hip hop song "The Message," which appeared on Grandmaster Flash

American rapper Melle Mel became the lead rapper and songwriter for Grandmaster Flash and the Furious Five's 1982 classic hit "The Message." Possibly the first rapper to use the epithet "MC," Melle Mel eventually led the group as Grandmaster Melle Mel before pursuing his solo career. (David Corio/Michael Ochs Archives/Getty Images)

and the Furious Five's album of the same title (1982). Unusually lengthy for a hip hop track at over seven minutes, "The Message" is often considered the first American social commentary hip hop song; it focused on inner city poverty, inequality, a lack of role models, and violence, rather than on superficial themes about parties or braggadocio. "The Message" peaked at No. 4 on Billboard's R&B chart before going Platinum. As Grandmaster Melle Mel, he released *Grandmaster Melle Mel and the Furious Five* (1984), *Stepping Off* (1985), *On the Strength* (1988), *Piano* (1989), *Right Now* (1997), *On Lock* (2001), *The Portal in the Park* (2006), *Muscles* (2007), and *Hip Hop Anniversary Europe Tour* (2009), as well as several EPs and singles. His style transcends East Coast old-school hip hop, as it also includes G-funk, hardcore hip hop, and electronica.

Melle Mel was born Melvin Glover, and was raised in the Bronx. He identifies with being Native American, since his mother was part Cherokee; rapping by the mid-1970s, MC Melle Mel was also likely the first Native American hip hop artist. In 1976, he joined DJ Grandmaster Flash (1958–) and eventually four other rappers, the Kidd Creole (Nathaniel Glover, 1960–), Rahiem (Guy Todd Williams, n.d.), Mr. Ness/Scorpio (Eddie Morris, n.d.), and Cowboy (Keith Wiggins, 1960–), to become Grandmaster Flash and the Furious Five. They quickly secured an engagement at Disco Fever and were signed with Enjoy Records (1962–1995). After the Sugarhill Gang's (1979–1985, 1994–) "Rapper's Delight" (1979), Grandmaster Flash and the Furious Five released "Superrappin'" (1979) and moved to Sugar Hill Records (1979–1985). But after a few R&B-charting hits such as "Freedom," Melle Mel became interested in writing a socially conscious rap song, resulting in "The Message," which borrowed some lines from "Superrappin'." As the last track on *The Message*, the song stood out for its sparse performance forces—Melle Mel alone, backed by an instrumental track and backing vocals by producer Duke Bootee (Ed Fletcher, n.d.). Neither Grandmaster Flash nor the Furious Five appear on the recording. The song, however, went

Platinum and peaked at No. 62 on the Billboard Hot 100 and charted internation-ally. The album peaked at No. 53 on the Billboard 200. Much later, the single was one of 50 recordings selected by the Library of Congress for the United States National Archive of Historic Recordings (2002) and the first hip hop recording inducted in the Grammy Hall of Fame (2012).

Shortly after the album's release, Grandmaster Flash departed the group, based on contract and royalty disputes with Sugar Hill Records. Melle Mel, who also argued with Grandmaster Flash, filled his shoes as leader, and the group became Grandmaster Melle Mel and the Furious Five. The Kidd Creole and Rahiem left with Grandmaster Flash as well. The new group returned to the lighter partying themes. In 1983, Melle Mel released another hip hop classic single, "White Lines (Don't Don't Do It)." The antidrug song, cowritten by Melle Mel and Sugar Hill Records owner Sylvia Robinson (1935–2011), became his second-best-known hit, peaking at No. 47 on Billboard's Hot Black Singles and No. 7 on the U.K. Singles Chart. Melle Mel gained additional notoriety for his appearance in *Beat Street* (1984). The film's title is based on "Beat Street Breakdown," cowritten by Melle Mel and Reggie Griffin (n.d.) and performed by Grandmaster Melle Mel and the Furious Five. He is also known for rapping on Chaka Khan's (Yvette Marie Stevens, 1953–) R&B hit song "I Feel for You" (1984). In 1991, he won a Grammy Award for Best Rap Performance for his appearance on the title track of Quincy Jones's (1933–) album, *Back on the Block* (1989). In 2007, Melle Mel released his debut hardcore hip hop solo album, *Muscles*, which features the track "M3—The New Message." That year, Melle Mel and the Furious Five with Grandmaster Flash became the first hip hop group inducted into the Rock and Roll Hall of Fame.

Melissa Ursula Dawn Goldsmith

See also: Grandmaster Flash; MC; Political Hip Hop; Robinson, Sylvia; The United States

Further Reading

Bradley, Adam, and Andrew Dubois, eds. 2010. "Grandmaster Flash and the Furious Five." Under "Part 1: 1978–84: The Old School" in *The Anthology of Rap*. New Haven, CT: Yale University Press.

Fricke, Jim, and Charlie Ahearn. 2002. *Yes Yes Y'All: The Experience Music Project Oral History of Hip-Hop's First Decade*. Cambridge, MA: Da Capo Press.

Stewart, James B. 2005. "Message in the Music: Political Commentary in Black Popular Music from Rhythm and Blues to Early Hip Hop." *Journal of African American History* 90, no. 3: 196–225.

Further Listening

Grandmaster Flash and the Furious Five. 1982. *The Message*. Sugar Hill Records.

Melle Mel. 2007. *Muscles*. Big Gunz Entertainment.

Merenrap

(aka Merenhouse)

Merenrap, which is short for *merengue rap*, is a style of hip hop music which blends hip hop, house music, and merengue, a Latin American and Caribbean dance music originating in the Dominican Republic, where it was promoted by Dictator Rafael Trujillo (aka El Jefe, Rafael Leónidas Trujillo Molina, 1891–1961, in power 1930–1938, 1942–1952). Merenrap emerged in the United States in the 1980s as a type of Latin house in New York City, which by 1990 had a population of nearly one million Dominicans residing mainly in barrios to create an ethnic concentration.

Early Dominican American merenhouse bands included Proyecto Uno (1989–), Ilegales (aka Los Ilegales, 1993–), Dark Latin Groove (DLG, 1995–2000, 2007–), and Fulanito (aka Little John Doe, 1996–). New York's Proyecto Uno introduced music that blended merenhouse with rap, techno, dancehall, and reggae, ultimately winning an Emmy Award. Grammy-nominated trio Ilegales charted on the Billboard Tropical. New York–based, Grammy-nominated Dark Latin Groove mixes merenhouse with salsa, reggae, and *reggaetón* (the last, also known as *reggae en Español*, originated in Panama and developed in Puerto Rico in the late 1990s and contains rapping and singing). Fulanito is a Grammy-nominated, Manhattan- and Bronx-based group that sold five million albums worldwide. Other acts that performed merenrap did so just briefly. For example, Brooklyn-born Puerto Rican rapper, singer-songwriter, and producer Vico C (Luis Armando Lozada Cruz, 1971–), who recorded merenrap in the early 1990s, continued on by focusing on reggaetón and then Christian hip hop.

Lyrical content often focuses on partying, materialism, objectifying women, and braggadocio (the last focused on authenticity and masculinity). By the late 2000s merenrap has broadened its sound by incorporating other kinds of music. For example, Fulanito's merenrap-pop album *Vacaneria!* (*Cool!* or *Great!*, 2009) has a final track titled "Culebrita," in Spanish, the feminine word for "Snake," which is also slang for "Jezebel." The song employs Arabic-sounding music and musical exoticism. Since the 2010s, merenrap has not been recorded as much. As of 2018, the most important bands, such as Proyecto Uno and Fulanito, though still active as live acts, have not released studio albums in at least four years. DLG, who broke up in 2000 and then reinvented itself in its comeback in 2007, has shifted its focus to recording and performing salsa, reggae, and dancehall.

Anthony J. Fonseca and Melissa Ursula Dawn Goldsmith

See also: The Dominican Republic; The United States

Further Reading

McGill, Lisa D. 2005. "'Diasporic Intimacy': Merengue Hip Hop, *Proyecto Uno*, and Representin' Afro-Latino Cultures." In *Constructing Black Selves: Caribbean American Narratives and the Second Generation*, chap. 5. New York: New York University Press.

Sellers, Julie A. 2004. "Merengue and Transnational Identities." In *Merengue and Dominican Identity: Music as National Unifier*, chap. 9. Jefferson, NC: McFarland.

Further Listening

Fulanito. 2007. *Vacaneria!* Cutting Records.

Various Artists. 1993. *MerenRap Tropical.* BMG International U.S. Latin/Prime Records.

Mexico

Mexico has a hip hop scene that is influenced by both Latin hip hop and gangsta rap. Its music is a result of immigration, as well as cultural cross-pollination of Mexican music and the Chicano music of the U.S. Southwest and Midwest. Such cross-influence has led to a Mexican hip hop music that is typically performed both by Mexicans and by Mexican American rappers and musicians. Mexican hip hop incorporates elements of reggae, gangsta, mobb, salsa, soca, funk, R&B, soul, and traditional dance music, and topics include urban decay and violence, social change, and social and political oppression, and more recently, feminism.

In the United States, Chicano rap artists such as Frost (aka Kid Frost, Arturo Molina Jr., 1964–), with the album *Hispanic Causing Panic* (1990) and its predominantly bass, saxophone, and vibraphone bilingual hit single "La Raza" ("The Race"), began making Mexican American hip hop viable. Frost went on to cofound the supergroup Latin Alliance, whose other members were successful rappers: Cuban-born Mellow Man Ace (Ulpiano Sergio Reyes, 1967–) and Mexican American A.L.T. (Alvin Lowell Trivette, 1970–). In California, Chicano rapper Jonny Z (John Zazueta, n.d.) and one-third Chicano group Cypress Hill (1988–) found mainstream airplay.

In Mexico, some hip hop artists, such as Control Machete (1996–2004) and, more recently, rappers C-Kan (José Luis Maldonado Ramos, 1987–) and Mare Avertencia Lirika (1986–) began to see success in the American market. Monterrey's hip hop trio Control Machete had a hit with "Sí Señor" (1999), which was used in a 2002 Levi's Super Bowl ad. Guadalajara's C-Kan, who used social networking to market his songs, incorporates elements of reggae, gangsta, and mobb, as well as chopper style rapping, and his videos feature urban decay and violence. Oaxaca's Lirika is the most prolific and multitalented female hip hop artist. Lirika raps and recites poetry about art, feminism, and social change. Songs such as "Bienvenidx," from her second album *Siempre Viva* (*Immortal*, 2016), position a hip hop beat against a distorted and sped up traditional *mariachi* brass loop (including tuba) to decry exploitation, violence, fascism, and displacement, and the album includes hip hop hybrids with funk, R&B, soul, and traditional dance music. In the last few years, both C-Kan and Lirika have toured the United States.

Other notable hip hop acts include Nogales-born but American-raised MC Magic (Marcus Cardenas, n.d.) and Monterrey's MC Davo (David Sierra Treviño, 1991–). MC Magic began as a DJ whose second and third albums, *Magic City* (2006) and *Magic City, Part II* (2008), reached the Top 10 of the Billboard's Top Heatseekers chart, the former making it to No. 1. MC Davo became popular in 2012 through social networking, getting millions of views. Monterrey's Ricky Rick (Ricardo Ruiz Pérez, 1983–) is a rapper-songwriter, beatboxer, guitarist, and percussionist who since 2006 has been active in the hip hop scene. He incorporates elements of salsa, soca, and reggae into urban beats and electronic rhythms. Others include Los Angeles-based (but from Michoacan) brother duo Akwid (2008–), which has won a Latin Grammy Award for Best Latin Rock/Alternative Album; Salt Lake City–based (but half Mexican) Bonnevilla (2007–), which has produced two mixtapes and an album full of social commentary music; Santa Catarina–based Cartel de

Santa (1996–), which has released seven critically acclaimed albums; and Mexico City's Bocafloja (Aldo Villegas, 1978–), a rapper, spoken-word artist, poet, and lecturer who has been performing hip hop that addresses racism, social and political oppression, and colonialism since 1995.

In addition to music, the most notable b-boy (breakdancer) from Mexico is RoxRite (Omar Delgado Macias, 1982–), who was born in Guadalajara. When he was 6, his family relocated to Windsor, California, and he began breakdancing at age 12. Because he first learned breakdancing in the United States, he represents the US in breakdance battles. Roxrite has won many international b-boy championships, including the Red Bull BC One title in 2011. As of 2018, Roxrite is just one of three Americans to have that title.

Anthony J. Fonseca

See also: Chicano Rap; Chopper; Gangsta Rap; The United States

Further Reading

Cru, Josep. 2017. "Bilingual Rapping in Yucatán, Mexico: Strategic Choices for Maya Language Legitimation and Revitalization." *International Journal of Bilingual Education and Bilingualism* 20, no. 5: 481–96.

Tickner, Arlene. 2008. "Aquí en el Ghetto: Hip Hop in Colombia, Cuba, and Mexico." *Latin American Politics and Society* 50, no. 3: 121–46.

Further Listening

Mare Avertencia Lirika. 2016. *Siempre viva* (*Immortal*). Thors Music.

M.I.

(Jude Abaga, 1981–, Jos, Nigeria)

M.I. is a Nigerian hip hop recording rapper-songwriter, musician, and record producer. He is also the brother of Jesse Jagz (1984–), a hip hop and reggae rapper, singer-songwriter, and record producer. M.I.'s debut studio album, *Talk about It* (2008) was critically acclaimed, and since, he has released two more studio albums, *M.I. 2* (2010*) and *The Chairman* (2014*), on the Chocolate City Music and Entertainment Company (2005–) and Loopy Records (2014) music labels. M.I.'s rapping style is laid-back, with heavy use of autotuning. He often accompanies his raps with reggae singing. His beats and music vary, although he has a predisposition for downbeat rhythms and traditional African instrumentation.

M.I. began honing his musical talents in high school, when his mother purchased some sheet music and a seven-key mini piano; this is the instrument on which he learned to write music. His early influences were Lauryn Hill (1975–), Bob Marley (1945–1981), Jay-Z (1969–), and DMX (1970–). It was the works of the last that he used as early samples when he decided to begin rapping. Even though he attended college, where he studied poetry, business, and economics, his love was music, and he performed regularly at hip hop shows and concerts. In 2003, M.I. returned to Nigeria to pursue a music career, first by recording mixtapes with a friend, and then releasing his first single, "Safe" (2009), which led to a contract for *Talk About It.*

The Chairman was a largely autobiographical, 17–track collaborative album that took two years to record and spawned various singles: "Chairman," "King James," "Bad Belle," and "Monkey." His most recent recording was the mixtape *Illegal Music 3: The Finale* (2016*), a 10-track finale to his mixtape trilogy. Along with other awards, M.I. won Best Hip Hop artist at the 2009 MTV Africa Music Awards; the next year he was nominated in the Best International Act category at the BET Awards. M.I. was appointed a UN (United Nations) Goodwill Ambassador in 2012.

Known as much for his business acumen as his music, he cofounded, along with Jesse Jagz, Ice Prince (1986–), and others, the short-lived rap group the Loop Crew in 2004, a venture which later led to his founding his short-lived Loopy Records label. The label soon folded, but fortunately, M.I. had already signed with Chocolate City, a renowned Nigerian music label. Since 2015, M.I. has been the CEO of Chocolate City Music and Entertainment Company.

Anthony J. Fonseca

See also: Ice Prince; Jesse Jagz; Nigeria; Reggae

Further Reading

Anon. 2014. "M.I. vs Ruggedman: Who's Got the Rhymes?" *The Sun* (Lagos, Nigeria), June 13, 4.

Shonekan, Stephanie. 2012. "Nigerian Hip Hop: Exploring a Black World Hybrid." In *Hip Hop Africa: New African Music in a Globalizing World*, edited by Eric Charry, chap. 7. Bloomington: Indiana University Press.

Further Listening

M.I. 2008. *Talk about It.* Chocolate City Music.

M.I.A.

(aka Maya, Mathangi Arulpragasam, 1975–, London, England)

M.I.A. is an English rapper, hip hop artist, visual artist, and activist from Hounslow, a borough in West London. Her music incorporates elements of dance, electronica, and world music, with lyrics that concentrate on political and cultural activism. As an activist, M.I.A. has spoken against the oppression and abuse of Tamils in Sri Lanka.

Her parents, both of Sri Lankan Tamil descent, relocated the family to Jaffna, Sri Lanka when M.I.A. was six months old. During a time of political upheaval there, her family lived in poverty, and her father became a Tamil activist. At 10 years old, M.I.A. and her siblings were moved back to London as refugees. The experiences she had while living in Sri Lanka provide inspiration for her music, art, and activism.

Originally a visual artist, M.I.A. got her start in the music business after designing cover art and producing videos for the London-based band Elastica (1992–2001). While video documenting a tour with Elastica, M.I.A. met Canadian alternative hip hop, electropunk, and dance-punk musician Peaches (Merrill Nisker, 1968–), who encouraged her to start making music with a Roland MC–505, which M.I.A. used to record a demo tape. Before signing a record contract, the song

"Galang" (Jamaican patois for "Go On," 2003) earned her a large following online. In 2005, M.I.A. signed to a label and released her first album, *Arular*. Featuring MC-505 beats and sequences, her album is a mix of dance and hip hop, with inspiration taken from Tamil film and Indian music.

Kala (*Black*, 2007), M.I.A.'s second album, was supposed to have been recorded in the United States, but ended up being recorded in different locations around the world after she was denied a visa. Its songs consist of an array of dance and folk styles from the places she recorded in (such as Trinidad, India, Liberia, and Jamaica) and also feature politically charged lyrics about immigration and war. "Bird Flu" (2006) was the first single released, followed by "Boyz" (2007), "Jimmy" (2007) and "Paper Planes" (2008). The song "Paper Planes" was written as a satire on the migrant stereotype, and went on to be the *Kala* track that earned her the most commercial success.

Since *Kala*, M.I.A. has released three more studio albums: *Maya* (2010), *Matangi* (2013), and *Aim* (2016). For the *Maya* single "Born Free" (2010), M.I.A. worked with director Romain Gavras (1981–) to produce a video. The explicitly violent, controversial video about the genocide of people with red hair was a metaphorical treatment of the plight of Tamil people, who were killed by the Sri Lankan army. M.I.A. and Gavras again collaborated on the video for the *Matangi* single, "Bad Girls." Filmed in Morocco, the video featured women in traditional Middle Eastern clothing performing car tricks, spinning, and skidding across the desert. The video was M.I.A's stand in solidarity with the Saudi women's right-to-drive movement.

In 2015, she released the song "Borders," which is about the struggles and stereotypes faced by migrants and refugees. M.I.A. has collaborated with Diplo (Thomas Wesley Pentz, 1978–) and Timbaland (1972–), among others.

Lindsey E. Hartman

See also: Political Hip Hop; Sri Lanka; The United Kingdom

Further Reading

Rollefson, J. Griffith. 2017. "M.I.A.'s 'Terrorist Chic': Black Atlantic Music and South Asian Postcolonial Politics in London." In *Flip the Script: European Hip Hop and the Politics of Postcoloniality*, chap. 5. Chicago: University of Chicago Press.

Saucier, P. Khalil, and Kumarini Silva. 2004. "Keeping It Real in the Global South: Hip Hop Comes to Sri Lanka." *Critical Sociology* 40, no. 2: 296–300.

Weems, Lisa. 2014. "Refuting 'Refugee Chic': Transnational Girl(hood)s and the Guerilla Pedagogy of M.I.A." *Feminist Formations* 26, no. 1: 115–42.

Further Listening

M.I.A. 2005. *Arular*. XL Recordings.

M.I.A. 2007. *Kala*. XL Recordings.

M.I.A. 2013. *Matangi*. N.E.E.T./Interscope Records.

Miami Bass

(aka Booty Bass)

Miami bass is a hip hop subgenre that emerged in the mid-1980s in Miami, Florida. Its defining characteristics are long, sustained cymbals that hiss and liberal use of snare and kick drums (usually generated by a 1984 Roland TR-808 Rhythm Composer, an early programmable transistor rhythm drum machine with a rumbling, loud low-field bass). Like other kinds of hip hop, Miami bass employs loops, samples, scratching, call-and-response vocals, shouts, and a relaxed rapping style; its lyrics are urban and emphasize sexually explicit subject matter. Its use of Latin percussion (at times electronically generated), snare and closed kick drums, and handclaps link it to electro-dance music (EDM) and house music. It also has a specific geographical appeal that sets it apart. Miami bass's fusion of hip hop, electro, and breakbeat with music from Cuba and the Dominican Republic, as well as music that has Afro-Brazilian rhythms influenced several kinds of music, including funk carioca (baile funk or favela funk), which is dance music that emerged in Rio de Janeiro, Brazil, as well as in Baltimore, Maryland. Miami bass is prevalent in freestyle and Southern hip hop, as well as in Ghettotech.

BEGINNINGS

Miami dance party DJs were the first contributors to the formation of Miami bass. In the mid-1980s, local independent record labels became interested in the sound. MC A.D.E. (Adrian Hines, n.d.) and Amos Larkins's (n.d.) "Bass Rock Express" (1985), recorded on the Fort Lauderdale-based 4-Sight (1983–) label owned by A.D.E.'s father, was likely the first popular Miami bass single. By the late 1980s, Pandisc Music Corporation (1981–) was also producing Miami bass tracks which included Maggotron Crushing Crew's (1988–1994*) "Bass Rock the Planet" (1986) and "The Bass That Ate Miami" (1988); Trinere's (Trinere Veronica Farrington, 1964–) "Can't Stop the Beat" (1989); and DJ Laz's (Lazaro Mendez, 1971–) "Journey into Bass" (1994). Maggotron's late 1980s singles show how early Miami bass was inspired not only by electro music, but also by funk, particularly Parliament-Funkadelic (1968–) and Earth Wind and Fire (1971–).

THE 2 LIVE CREW AND GLOBAL CONTEXT

Luke Skyywalker Records (1985–), which later became Skyywalker and then Luke Atlantic Records, owned by Luke (1960–) and David Chackler (1945–), took interest in Miami bass close to the same time as 4-Sight and Pandisc. At the time, Luke (as Luke Skyywalker) was also the front man for the Miami-based hip hop group 2 Live Crew (1982–1991, 1994–1998). Skyywalker produced the first Miami-certified-Platinum album, 2 Live Crew's *As Nasty as They Wanna Be* (1989), which included "Me So Horny," a song that reached No. 1 on the Billboard Hot Rap Tracks.

The band gained national attention in 1990 for having the first album ever to be deemed legally obscene by a U.S. district court. The United States Court of Appeals for the Eleventh Circuit, however, overturned the ruling, and 2 Live Crew also profited from a censored version of the album, *As Clean as They Wanna Be*. In response to the initial ruling on *As Nasty as They Wanna Be*, 2 Live Crew released the Miami bass influenced *Banned in the U.S.A.* (1990), which did better than its predecessor on the Billboard 200, but only reached Gold status. Both albums received Parental Advisory labels for their explicit content. 2 Live Crew had ear-lier been subjected to other criticism for their misogynist lyrics on "Throw the D." Anquette (1986–1993)*, an all-female Miami bass group, responded with "Throw the P" (1986).

Miami bass continued into the 2000s, but never regained its popularity. Miami bass artists active into the 2000s included Miami's own DJ Laz (Lazaro Mendez, 1971–), Pitbull (1981–), and Techmaster P.E.B. (anonymous, n.d.); as well as Fort Lauderdale band Bass 305 (1992–2011), Orlando's DJ Magic Mike (Michael Hampton, 1967*–) and DJ Baby Anne (Marianne Breslin, 1972–), and Jackson-ville bands 69 Boyz (1992–) and 95 South (1993–).

Other U.S. artists included Egyptian Lover (Greg Broussard, 1963–), Kilo Ali (Andrell D. Rogers, 1973–), Diplo (Thomas Wesley Pentz, 1978–), and Sir Mix-a-Lot (Anthony Ray, 1963–). Some Miami bass influenced artists outside of the United States include solo acts Bass Mekanik (aka Beat Dominator, Neil Case, n.d.) DJ Craze (Arist Delgado, 1977–), of Managua, Nicaragua; as well as rap crews and Black Chiney (1999–), of Kingston, Jamaica; the Wideboys (1996–), of Ports-mouth, England; and Dirtyphonics (2004–), of Paris.

Jacqueline M. DeMaio

See also: Bounce; Luke; 2 Live Crew; The United States

Further Reading

David Font-Navarrete. 2015. "Bass 101: Miami, Rio, and the Global Music South." *Journal of Popular Music Studies* 27, no. 4: 488–517.

Miller, Matt. 2010. "Tropic of Bass: Culture, Commerce, and Controversy in Miami Rap." In *Hip Hop in America: A Regional Guide*, edited by Mickey Hess, vol. 2, chap. 22. Santa Barbara, CA: Greenwood.

Further Listening

2 Live Crew. 1989. *As Nasty As They Wanna Be.* Luke Skyywalker Records.

Various Artists. 1988. *The Miami Bass Wars.* Pandisc.

Various Artists. 1991. *Miami Bass Wars II: Battle of the Boom.* Pandisc.

Various Artists. 2007. *Cut It Up: Def Miami Bass Jams.* Pandisc.

Mix Master Mike

(Michael Schwartz, 1970–, San Francisco, California)

Mix Master Mike is a Grammy Award winning American DJ (turntablist) best known for his work with the Beastie Boys (1981–2012), working on their later albums, namely *Hello Nasty* (1998), *To the 5 Boroughs* (2004), and *Hot Sauce Committee Part Two* (2011). In 2012, along with the Beastie Boys, he was inducted into the Rock and Roll Hall of Fame.

He came to prominence in 1992 when he became the first West Coast DJ to win the New Music Seminar DJ Battle in New York City, and his Rock Steady DJs (1990–) collective won the DMC World DJ Championships. He repeated the DMC championship feat in the 1993 and 1994 DMC Championships, working with DJ Qbert (1969–), with whom he later cofounded the Filipino American collective the

Invisibl Skratch Piklz (1989–2000). Mix Master Mike and DJ Qbert became judges for the 1995 DMC Championships.

His signature sound includes a heavy dose of bass and intricate, extremely quick, and precise two-turntable scratch routines, including what became known as the tweak scratch, which involves suddenly stopping the turntable's platter motor to change pitch while scratching. In his live performances, his speed and precision separate him from other turntablists, as does his showmanship—for example, he will throw in a behind-the-back scratch into the middle of a routine, or pick up and bend his vinyl record while scratching, or use a wah pedal (intended for electric guitar). He has three solo albums, *Needle Thrasher III* (1997), *Anti-Theft Device* (1998), and *Bangzilla* (2004); one of his EPs, *Eye of the Cyklops* (2000), is considered a classic of turntablism.

Mix Master Mike is the first turntablist to perform at the John F. Kennedy Center for the Performing Arts for the Kennedy Center Honors; in 2013, he did a performance of "Rockit" (2000; 2003) to honor Herbie Hancock (1940–). He has also appeared in various television venues, ranging from the sublime, with performing for the Vancouver Winter Olympics (2010) to the ridiculous, remixing the theme song "Puffy AmiYumi" for *Teen Titans Go!* (2013–) and performing in 2010 on the children's show *Yo Gabba Gabba* (2007–2015), for its "Cool Tricks" segment. As of 2018, he continues to tour and has created a virtual reality music project.

Anthony J. Fonseca

See also: Beastie Boys; DJ QBert; Invisibl Skratch Piklz; The Philippines; Turntablism; The United States

Further Reading

Katz, Mark. 2010. "The Turntable as Weapon: Understanding the Hip Hop DJ Battle." In *Capturing Sound: How Technology Has Changed Music*, rev. ed., chap. 6. Berkeley: University of California Press.

Katz, Mark. 2012. *Groove Music: The Art and Culture of the Hip Hop DJ*. New York: Oxford University Press.

Shiu, Anthony Sze-Fai. 2007. "Styl(us): Asian North America, Turntablism, Relation." *CR: The New Centennial Review* 7, no. 1: 81–106.

Tiongson, Antonio T. Jr. 2013. *Filipinos Represent: DJs, Racial Authenticity, and the Hip Hop Nation*. Minneapolis: University of Minnesota Press.

Moana and the Moahunters

(1990–1998, Auckland, New Zealand/Aotearoa)

Moana and the Moahunters was a New Zealand/Aotearoa–based popular music group which combined early hip hop and rap with pop and traditional New Zealand Māori music and instrumentation; the latter of these produced a hybrid music called *taonga pūoro*. Eventually becoming Moana and the Tribe, the group promoted Māori culture, traditions, history, and identity in its music. Moana and the Moahunters toured New Zealand, Europe, and the United States whereas Moana and the Tribe tours worldwide. Both groups are fronted by singer-songwriter Moana Maree Maniapoto (1961–), who was born and raised in Invercargill, New Zealand/Aotearoa.

MOANA AND THE MOAHUNTERS (1990–1998)

In the 1980s Maniapoto sang popular song covers in Auckland, New Zealand, nightclubs to support her law school studies. She had brief success with "Kua Makona" (either "Full" or "Sated"), an antidrinking pop song that peaked at No. 27 on the Recording Industry of New Zealand's (RIANZ) top-50 singles chart. In 1990, she formed Moana and the Moahunters with singers Teremoana Rapley (1973–), earlier a member of Upper Hutt Posse (UHP, 1985–), and Wai (Mina Ripia, n.d.). In 1991, the group released its first 12-inch single, "AEIOU (Akona Te Reo)," directed at the Māori youth who no longer regularly spoke Māori. The song lyrics loosely translate into English as "learn the language." Refrains often feature English words against background vocals in Māori. "AEIOU" urged listeners to become interested in their Māori culture and heritage, study their history and language, and preserve their traditions and identity. It peaked at No. 31 on the New Zealand Top 40 singles chart.

Moana and the Moahunters' albums *Tahi* (1993) and *Rua* (1998) reached Nos. 16 and 27 on the New Zealand Top 40 albums chart. The group's top-ranking songs included "Black Pearl" (1991) and "Tahi" ("One," 1994), which peaked at Nos. 2 and 9, respectively. Both were from *Tahi*, which was remixed and re-released in 1995. "Black Pearl," a remake of Toni Wine (1947–), Irwin Levine (1938–1997), and Phil Spector's (1939*–) 1969 hit, was recontextualized in the group's video to offer a message to female Māori to celebrate their identity, step into the foreground, and not to simply blend in to their surroundings. Adding to this message is rap from D Word (aka Te Kupu, Dean Hapeta, n.d.) of UHP. "Tahi," which featured rhythm and blues harmonies, along with chanting and Māori instruments, was released as dance mix and roots mix tracks. The song stresses Māori unity. Commercial radio in New Zealand and Australia initially resisted playing both songs. In response, the group accused the radio stations of racism against Māori musical groups.

MOANA AND THE TRIBE (2002–)

In 2002, the group reformed as Moana and the Tribe, adding Maniapoto's sister Trina Morgan (n.d.) to its singers and collaborating with the Tribe, a band of 10 musicians. The group continues combining hip hop with traditional music, more recently incorporating dubstep, ska, reggae, and electro house. The album *Toru* (*Three*, 2002) represented the group's European recording debut and entered at No. 17 on the World Music Charts: Europe (WMCE). Subsequent albums include *Live and Proud* (2007), *Wha* (*Four*, 2008), *Acoustic* (2010), the compilation *The Best of Moana and the Tribe* (2012), and *Rima* (*Five*, 2014). With Moana and the Tribe, Maniapoto has earned several awards. She was the first non-American winner of the Grand Jury Prize of the International Songwriting Competition for her song "Moko" ("Tattoo," 2004). In 2005, she was granted the New Zealand Order of Merit (NZOM), followed in 2007 when she was made an Art Laureate by the New Zealand Arts Foundation. In 2008, the Waiata Māori Music Awards recognized her work in the Māori music industry.

PERFORMANCE, USE OF MĀORI ICONOGRAPHY, AND SOUND

Both Moana and the Moahunters and Moana and the Tribe have performed concerts and festivals worldwide and are known for their performances of both hip hop and updated traditional Māori *haka*—a pre-European ritual chant and cheer most famously used as a war cry, sung in unison (heterophony) and accompanied by posture dance stomping, facial choreography, and grunts and breaths. The haka has also been used for other ritual purposes, such as praising accomplishments and welcoming guests. Although traditionally (and continued into the 20th century) men take on the main roles of singing and dancing the haka whereas women, rarely participants, dance and sing in the background, in both groups' performances, women are in the foreground. In addition, poi movements and rhythms—traditionally performed by Māori women by singing while swinging tethered weights in geometrical patterns—are incorporated in the groups' performances. Record album covers as well as videos feature Māori art, tattoos (called *tā moko*) and traditional dress. Band members wearing traditional Māori warrior attire appear in the Moana and the Tribe videos alongside images of diverse people of New Zealand/Aotearoa, who have learned to sing some phrases in Māori. Concerts also feature photographs of Māori people.

Melissa Ursula Dawn Goldsmith

See also: New Zealand; Political Hip Hop; Upper Hutt Posse

Further Reading

Mitchell, Tony. 2000. "Doin' Damage in My Native Language: The Use of 'Resistance Vernaculars' in Hip Hop in France, Italy, and Aotearoa/New Zealand." *Popular Music and Society* 24, no. 3: 41–54.

Mitchell, Tony. 2001. "Kia Kaha! (Be Strong!): Māori and Pacific Islander Hip Hop in Aotearoa/New Zealand." In *Global Noise: Rap and Hip Hop Outside the U.S.A.*, edited by Tony Mitchell, pp. 280–305. Middletown, CT: Wesleyan University Press.

Further Listening

Moana and the Moahunters. 1993. *Tahi.* Southside Records.

Moana and the Tribe. 2012. *The Best of Moana and the Tribe.* Black Pearl/Ode.

Molekane, Tumi

(aka MC Fatboy, Tumi, Stogie T, Boitumelo Molekane, 1981–, Tanzania)

Tumi Molekane is a Tanzanian-born South African rapper, singer, songwriter, poet, and record label owner, who is best known as lead singer of Tumi and the Volume (2002–2012), an experimental band that fuses hip hop with African and Latin jazz, Afropop, reggae, and rock. He has a tenor vocal range.

Molekane's parents relocated to Soweto in Johannesburg in 1992, a year after apartheid ended. Inspired by his experiences growing up, he took interest in writing poetry in English. As MC Fatboy, he joined the P.E.R.M. rap collective (2001*) and recorded *APT: An Artistic Representation of Truth* (2001). In 2002, Molekane became the frontman for Tumi and the Volume, created from band members from 340ml (2000–), who were originally from Maputo, Mozambique.

Tumi and the Volume's debut live album *Live at the Bassline* (2005) and debut studio album *Tumi and the Volume* (2006) attained critical acclaim that led it to become one of the best-known South African bands. In worldwide tours, it performed with Somali Canadian rapper, singer, songwriter, multi-instrumentalist, and poet K'naan (1978–), American hip hop groups such as the Roots (1987–) and Blackalicious (1994–), and the English trip hop Massive Attack (1988–). Molekane's debut solo effort *Music from My Good Eye* (2006), a hip hop album recorded on his label Motif Records (2006–2009, 2011–) under the name Tumi, also received critical acclaim. Tumi and the Volume's entire recorded output included *Live at the Bassline*, *Tumi and the Volume*, and *Pick a Dream* (2010).

As Tumi, he released *Music from My Good Eye* (2007), *Whole Worlds* (2009), and *Return of the King* (2015). Among other projects, he collaborated with the French electronic, trip hop, and dubstep group Chinese Man (2004–) on "Ta Bom" on their album *Remix with the Sun* (2012), pairing later on the album *The Journey* (2015).

After many music nominations, Tumi then reinvented himself as Stogie T for the album *Stogie T* (2016), whose "By Any Means" was recently a No. 1 hit in South Africa. Stogie T is a dapper version of Tumi. In comparison to Tumi's earlier work, Stogie T's current hip hop music style incorporates more pop; however his lyrics remain focused on violence, poverty, and inequality in South Africa, including the abuse of women. Even though some of his videos nevertheless objectify women, it is still generally to a far lesser extent than most of Molekane's contemporaries. Molekane is a notable exception in hip hop for supporting women's rights.

Melissa Ursula Dawn Goldsmith

See also: Political Hip Hop; South Africa; Tanzania

Further Reading

De Beer, Stephan. 2015. "Reading Psalms, and Other Urban Poems, in a Fractured City." *Verbum et Ecclesia* 36, no. 1: 1–8.

Higgins, Dalton. 2009. "What's Race Got to Do with It?" In *Hip Hop World*, chap. 3. Groundwork Guides. Berkeley: Groundwood Books.

Künzler, Daniel. 2011. "South African Rap Music, Counter Discourses, Identity, and Commodification beyond the Prophets of da City." *Journal of Southern African Studies* 37, no. 1: 27–43.

Further Listening

Tumi. 2006. *Music from My Good Eye.* Motif Records.

Tumi and the Volume. 2006. *Tumi and the Volume.* Urbnet Records.

Mongolia

Mongolia, a majority Buddhist landlocked nation in Asia, is bordered by China and Russia and has a population of around three million—half of which live in Ulaanbaatar (many in shanty towns called "ger districts"), the capital and largest city. Most citizens of this once Soviet republic are of Mongolian ethnicity. Music is important in the nation's cultural identity, and it often represents various ethnic groups: Oirats, Hotogoid, Tuvans, Darhad, Buryats, Tsaatan, Dariganga, Uzemchins, Barga, Kazakhs, and Khalha. Its modern music is influenced by the pop and rock genres of the West as seen on cable television, as well as music based on indigenous folksongs. Ulaanbaatar has a thriving pop, rock, and hip hop scene that includes soul and R&B-based boy bands such as Camerton (n.d.), Nomin Talst and Motive (n.d.), as well as R&B-based girl bands such as SweetYmotion (n.d.), Kiwi (n.d.), and 3 ohin (n.d.). Solo soul artists include Delgermörön (n.d.) and BX (n.d.). From the early 1990s, hip hop dancing crews have been formed by Mongolian youth.

The earliest Mongolian rap band was MC Boys (n.d.), who in the late 1980s rapped about social issues, philosophy, and rebellion; early rap crew Dain Ba Enkh's (War and Peace, 1997–2002). Enkhtaivan (Enxtaivan Doljingiin, 1976–2012) became Mongolia's first famous solo R&B singer-rapper. Dain Ba Enkh rapped about political and social issues against Western R&B and disco funk beats; it released two albums. Rapper Amraa (Sukhbaatar Amarmandakh, n.d.) founded the first disco and electronica dance rap band, Har Sarnai (Black Rose, 1991–), which incorporated Mongolian musical traditions (such as throat singing) into hip hop beats.

Current Mongolian hip hop artists include R&B-style rap acts Aka Odko (Odbeyer, n.d.), Lumino (1996–), and Mon-Ta-Rap (1995–); gangsta style and hardcore rap acts rapper Gee (Tugsjargal Munkherdene, 1984–) and rap band Ice Top (1996–); and G-funk style acts such as Quiza (Quiza Battsengel, 1981–). Female rappers include Gennie (1987–), who raps against the mining industry that destroys the Mongolian farmland and a government that does little for impoverished women and families. The rap group Vanquish (2000*–) opts for a big sound created by heavy synthesizer usage and 808 drums, with lots of bass kick and dramatic stingers; members rap chopper style, nonstop, and trade off verses liberally.

Experimental rap, using the skills of Mongolian throat singing and traditional instruments, can be heard with Fish Symboled Stamp (2010–), named after a traditionally used horse branding method. The duo was cofounded by bass vocalist Sanjjav Baatar (1987–) and rapper Battogtokh Odsaikhan (1985–), who imitate the sounds of nature against a continuous drone.

Anthony J. Fonseca

See also: China; Gangsta Rap; G-Funk; Hardcore Hip Hop; Russia

Further Reading

Marsh, Peter K. 2010. "'Our Generation Is Opening Its Eyes': Hip Hop and Youth Identity in Contemporary Mongolia." *Central Asian Survey* 29, no. 3: 345–58.

Whitener, John L. 2017. "Sharing Global Musics: A Multimedia View of the Music of Mongolia." *Music Educators Journal* 104, no. 1: 14–21.

Further Listening

Ice Top. 2003. *One Time.* Hi-Fi Media Group/Self-released.

Montenegro

Montenegro is a Southeastern European sovereign state on the Adriatic Sea. It is a neighbor of Albania, Kosovo, Serbia, Bosnia and Herzegovina, and Croatia. After being under communist rule within the Socialist Federative Republic of Yugoslavia

Serbo-Croatian rapper-songwriter and guitarist Rambo Amadeus incorporates absurd comedy and satire in a musical style that resembles Frank Zappa. His 1988 album *O Tugo Jesenja* (*Oh Autumn Sorrow*), which included electronica, funk, soul, rock, and hip hop, was the first Montenegrin hip hop recording. (Vyacheslav Oseledko/AFP/Getty Images)

(1945–1992) and then forming as the State Union of Serbia and Montenegro (aka Federal Republic of Yugoslavia, 1992–2006), Montenegro won its independence in 2006. The largest population is Montenegrin, followed by a large Serbian minority and smaller populations of Bosniaks, Albanians, and Croats. War and political unrest have challenged cultural development in Montenegro; however, the introduction of music education and music schools in the 20th century have produced classical musicians and composers from its capital, Podgorica, as well as the historic capital city Cetinje. Both traditional (national and folksongs played with the *gusle*, a chordophone shared with Serbia, Croatia, and Albania) and pop music, including dance music, is strongly influenced by Serbia, Croatia, Albania, and Italy. American hip hop was difficult to access in the Socialist Federative Republic of Yugoslavia, though it made its way to Serbia and Montenegro after international distribution of 1984 American hip hop films such as *Beat Street*, *Breakin'*, and *Breakin' 2: Electric Boogaloo.*

Political unrest in the late 1980s and the Yugoslav Wars (1991–2001) disrupted the development of Montenegrin hip hop, which began in the late 1980s with pioneering acts such as comedic and satirical rapper-songwriter and guitarist Rambo Amadeus (Antonije Pušić, 1963–), who has been compared to Frank Zappa (1940–1993), and Monten—s (aka Brake Boys, AE:Tell me, 1989–1999), both originating from the Mediterranean coastal city, Kotor.

Rambo Amadeus's debut studio album *O tugo jesenja* (*Oh Autumn Sorrow*, 1988), which contained electronica, funk, soul, rock, and hip hop in Serbo-Croatian, was the first Montenegrin hip hop recording. Montenegrin as a language is the Štokavian dialect of Serbo-Croatian. It became standardized in the new country by the 2000s (since 2007, it has become in Montenegro analogous to Received Pronunciation [RP] in Great Britain). Monten—s' sound included consciousness hip hop, crunkcore, and pop rap. The band's studio albums, *Tajna marenda* (*Secret Brunch*, 1996) and *Allboom* (1998), were released on the Komuna label (1985–) in Belgrade, Serbia. At the time, however, the Kosovo War (1998–1999) posed an economic drain and nearly halted all album production.

In the 2000s, Montenegrin hip hop gained popularity and included acts such as Rade Rapido (Rade Rapido Radares, 1977–) and Sivilo (Balša Krkeljić, 1988–), from Podgorica; Who See (2002–), from Kotor; Barska Stoka (2005–), from Bar; and Monten—s rapper N—or (Igor Lazić, n.d.). Montenegrin hip hop has evolved into a music that fuses a variety of musical genres, including electronica and jazz, as well as production styles such as boombap. Consciousness rap, focusing on daily life, economic disparity, and humor, remain more prominent than political rap. By the 2010s, rap collectives emerged, including TuhhtŠ (Shooting, 2010–), from the Nikšić-based rapper and producer collaboration known as naVAMga (2009–), as well as Radio Katakomba (2011–), from Budva. In addition, successful rappers such as Bacili (Illija Backovic, 1985–) and Psiho Mistik (Bojan Zeković, n.d.) emerged. As of 2018, the most successful Montenegrin battle rapper is Random (Marko Lubarda, n.d.), from Podgorica.

Melissa Ursula Dawn Goldsmith

See also: Albania; Serbia

Further Reading

Ceribasic, Naila. 2007. "Musical Faces of Croatian Multiculturality." *Yearbook for Traditional Music* 39: 1–26.

Šentevska, Irena. 2017. "*La haine et les autres crimes* [*Hate and Other Crimes*]: Ghettocentric Imagery in Serbian Hip Hop Videos." In *Hip Hop at Europe's Edge: Music, Agency, and Social Change*, edited by Milosz Miszczynski and Adriana Helbig, chap. 14. Bloomington: Indiana University Press.

Further Listening

Monten—s. 1996. *Tajna marenda* (Secret Brunch). Komuna.

TuhhtŠ. 2015. *Klasika za zvučnik* (Classics for the Speaker). Bučan Pas/Lampshade Media.

Morning of Owl

(2002–, Suwon, South Korea)

Morning of Owl is a South Korean b-boy crew that was formed in 2002 in Suwon. The original crew had four members, including its leader Sez (Lee Seung Ju, n.d.). Other original members were Issue (Kwangsuk Park, 1986–), Cho (Hyosung Joo, 1987–), and Owl'd (Park Jong Hun, n.d.). The crew gained its reputation through buskering in Suwon before winning Korean and international b-boy competitions.

Its style includes changing battle moves frequently and using impeccable footwork, multiperson freezes, and breakdance modifications. The crew is best known for their robot dance showcase.

For years South Korea had been the home of Seoul-based b-boy crews such as Gamblerz (2002–), Jinjo Crew (2001–), and T.I.P. (1996–), all of which have won international awards. This competitive atmosphere challenged Morning of Owl to become one of the world's most acclaimed crews. Morning of Owl broadened its choreography to include Korean folk dance, Brazilian *capoeira* (martial arts dance), and modern dance steps. In 2006 and 2007, Morning of Owl won the Battle of the Year–Korea, among other Korean competitions, but the crew hit its international winning stride in 2012 when it placed in the Top Four in the Battle of the Year World Finals.

In 2013, the crew won the R-16 Korea Championship, the R-16 World B-Boy Masters Championship, and the United Styles World Finals (Switzerland), among many other significant b-boy competitions. As of 2018, members include Issue, Owl'd, Pocket (Gijoo Kim, 1996–), Cho, Gon (Sanggon Han, 1991–), Mori (Seunghwan Moon, 1996–), Code (Kyumin An, 1990–), and Seung Ju Lee (1985–).

Melissa Ursula Dawn Goldsmith

See also: Battling; Breakdancing; Hip Hop Dance; Korea

Further Reading

Kim, Isaac. 2013. "Morning of Owl Tops B-Boy World." *The Korea Times*, July 28.

Tudor, Daniel. 2014. "Korea's Music Scene." In *Geek in Korea: Discovering Asia's New Kingdom of Cool*, part 8. North Clarendon, VT: Tuttle.

Morocco

Morocco is a North African populous, constitutional monarchy of over 33.8 million whose geography is characterized by mountains, desert, and a lengthy coastline. Its largest cities include Casablanca, Marrakesh, and Tangier. Moroccan music includes classical musical settings of classic poems, Chaabi and Berber folk music, Gnawa and Sufi religious music, as well as popular Westernized music such as American rock, pop, and rap, Jamaican reggae, and Algerian *raï*. Rap music was first introduced through traveling youth in the mid-1980s, and its first rap group was the band Darkheads (n.d.). The music became popular in urban centers, and a localized version of sociopolitical Moroccan rap became a fan favorite.

Contemporary hip hop acts include Dub Afrika (Mehdi Hattabi, n.d.), Casablanca-based Dizzy DROS (aka Mr. Crazy, Omar Souhaili, n.d.), Don Bigg (aka Al khasser or Rude Boy, Taoufik Hazeb, 1983–), DJ Mouss (Mouss Mounhim, n.d.), and H-Kayne (anonymous, 1996–). Dub Afrika is a rapper, songwriter, and producer. Dizzy DROS is a rapper, songwriter and producer whose 2011 song "Cazafonia" became a huge hit in Morocco and led to a successful debut album, *3azzy 3ando Stylo* (aka *33S*, 2013). Casablanca-based Don Bigg and Meknes-based H-Kayne popularized rapping in Arabic. Turntablist DJ Mouss expatriated to Paris, where he became a member of Scratch Action Hiro (2000–2001). The most popular Moroccan diaspora hip hop act is French Montana (Karim Kharbouch, 1984–), a Rabat-born rapper now based in the Bronx, New York. His album *Jungle Rules* (2017) peaked at No. 3 on the Billboard 200, with one single, "Unforgettable," peaking at No. 3 on the Billboard Hot 100.

Anthony J. Fonseca

See also: France

Further Reading

Davies, Eirlys E. 2006. "Code Switching and the Globalization of Popular Music: The Case of North African Rai and Rap." *Multilingua* 25, no. 4: 367–92.

Salois, Kendra. 2014. "The U.S. Department of State's 'Hip Hop Diplomacy' in Morocco." In *Music and Diplomacy from the Early Modern Era to the Present*, edited by Rebekah Ahrendt, Mark Ferraguto, and Damien Mahiet, chap. 11. New York: Palgrave Macmillan.

Further Listening

Dizzy Dros. 2013. *3azzy 3ando Stylo.* Funky Noise Entertainment.

Mos Def

(aka Yasiin Bey, Dante Terrell Smith, 1973–, Brooklyn, New York)

Mos Def is a rapper, singer-songwriter, keyboardist, bassist, drum programmer, record producer, actor, and activist from the Bedford–Stuyvesant neighborhood of New York City. He is primarily known as part of the duo Black Star (1997–)with Talib Kweli (1975–). His musical themes include police brutality, nationalism, and African American empowerment. His rap delivery is resonant, and his style is laid-back yet multisyllabic. Overall, he has been nominated for five Grammy Awards, including Best Rap Solo Performance (2007) and Best Rap Album (2009).

Born Dante Terrell Smith, Mos Def became a member of the Nation of Islam (NOI), following in his father's footsteps. He dropped out of high school to act, both in Hollywood and on Off-Off-Broadway. His music career began in 1994 with the short-lived family-based rap group Urban Thermo Dynamics (UTD), until 1995.

He released his first single, "The Universal Magnetic/If You Can Huh You Can Hear" (1997) on the Rawkus Records (1995–) label. While with Rawkus, he cofounded Black Star in 1997, which was mainly produced by Hi-Tek (Tony Cottrell, 1976–). The duo released the album *Mos Def and Talib Kweli Are Black Star* (1998), which reached No. 13 on Billboard's Top R&B/Hip-Hop Songs chart and No. 53 on the Billboard 200. A year later, Mos Def released his solo debut, *Black on Both Sides*, which was certified Gold and reached No. 3 on the Top R&B/Hip-Hop Albums chart and No. 25 on the Billboard 200.

Over his career, he released three other albums: *The New Danger* (2004), *True Magic* (2006), and *The Ecstatic* (2009). *The New Danger* and *The Ecstatic* both reached the Top 10 on the Billboard 200, and *The New Danger* went to No. 1 on the Top Rap Albums chart. *The New Danger*, his most commercially successful album, also produced a Grammy nominated song in "Sex, Love and Money" (2004). The same year, he released the UTD album *Manifest Destiny*, a juvenilia compilation of previously unreleased and rereleased tracks.

As an actor, he is best known for his roles in American director Spike Lee's (1957–) *Bamboozled* (2000) and season six of the American television show

Dexter (2006–2013). As a celebrity, he has hosted *Def Poetry Jam* (2002–2007). As an entrepreneur, Mos Def has designed two pairs of limited edition Converse shoes and he has created his own clothing line (both 2009). In 2011, he announced that he legally changed his name to Yasiin Bey, and in 2016, he announced his retirement from music after making various guest appearances on others' songs.

Anthony J. Fonseca

See also: Black Nationalism; Fashion; Political Hip Hop; Talib Kweli; The United States

Further Reading

Carson, Charles D. 2012. "'Melanin in the Music': Black Music History in Sound and Image." *Current Musicology* no. 93 (Spring): 95–114, 151.

Hakeem Grewal, Sara. 2013. "Intra- and Interlingual Translation in Blackamerican Muslim Hip Hop." *African American Review* 46, no. 1: 37–54.

Khabeer, Su'ad, Abdul. 2007. "Rep that Islam: The Rhyme and Reason of American Islamic Hip Hop." *The Muslim World* 97, no. 1: 125–41.

Further Listening

Mos Def. 2004. *The New Danger.* Geffen.

Motswako

Motswako is a subgenre of hip hop that emerged in the mid-1990s in Mafikeng (now Mahikeng), South Africa, a major city located near Botswana. Its emergence came just over a year after the end of Apartheid (1948–1991) and the first democratic election of a South African president (Nelson Mandela, 1918–2013, in office 1994–1999). It also came after the emergence of *kwaito*, a South African popular music genre that shares musical and cultural aspects with hip hop.

Since the late 1990s, motswako has arguably become more popular in Botswana than in South Africa. In point of fact, it was a Motswana MC originally from Francistown, Botswana, Mr T (aka Nomadic, Tebogo Mapine, n.d.), who pioneered motswako with songs such as "Malalaswii" and "Watagwan" ("What's Up?" or "What's Good?"). Within a short time after Mr T's songs aired on radio and received extremely positive reception, "motswako" was coined (the name is Setswana for "mixture," alluding to the use of both languages and the fusion of American hip hop with the gentler Mafikeng musical sound). Motswako rappers began calling themselves "Motswakolista."

Mr T was part of the P-Side Crew (1994–1999)* from Gaborone, Botswana. P-Side Crew is often credited as one of Botswana's earliest hip hop crews. Rapper Scar (Thato Matlhabaphiri, 1985–) and rapper and radio DJ Sid (Ndala Baitsile, n.d.) were also members of the P-Side Crew who had successful careers as motswako artists. Other early motswako artists included Draztik (Dave Balsher, 1973–), from Francistown; 3rd Mind (1995–2000)*, from Gaborone; Hip Hop Pantsula (1980–), from Mafikeng; and the duo Baphixile (1997*–), from Soweto in Johannesburg. Originally kwaito artists, Baphixile changed their focus to motswako. In comparison to other kinds of African hip hop, motswako rappers have been some of the earliest to collaborate with internationally renowned hip hop artists.

Early motswako used rapping texts in Setswana—a Tswana language that is Botswana's common language, which is also spoken by a large population in South Africa with American vernacular. The choice of American vernacular over South African English reflects the influence of American hip hop in both countries. Other South African languages such as Zulu and Afrikaans have also been used. One exception is South African motswako rapper, songwriter, and comedian iFani (Mzay-ifani Mzondeleli Boltina, 1985–) from Mthatha, who uses the Xhosa language. By the late 1990s, however, dominant texts are in Setswana with American vernacular.

Reggae is sometimes incorporated in motswako, which generally has a gentler sound than most American hip hop. Lyrical content includes localized sociopoliti-cal or economic protests and issues such as drug culture; however, some songs focus more on unity, localized pride, romance, objectifying women, partying, acquiring wealth, and aspirations. Musical characteristics of motswako usually include laid-back yet flowing raps, steady beat (at times four-to-the-floor, reggae-based, Afro-centric, or drum-and-bass beats), turntablism (or turntables as virtual instruments), and limited electronic music in the background to help keep rap in the foreground. Sampling is deemphasized. Unaccompanied spoken-word poetry may also be fea-tured on motswako albums or mixtapes, the two most important recording media for disseminating the subgenre in addition to streaming and posting on YouTube.

Transitioning into the 21st century, one of the most commercially successful motswako artists was Cashless Society (1999–2006), with members from Gabo-rone and Johannesburg. The band is an exception for rapping more in American vernacular than in Setswana. After 2000, some famous South African motswako acts emerged. These include Tuks Senganga (aka Tuks, Tumelo Kapadisa, 1981–) and Cassper Nyovest (Refiloe Maele Phoolo, 1990–), from Mafikeng; Spoek Mathambo (Nthato Mokgata, 1985–), from Soweto, Johannesburg; as well as Kuli Chana (Khulane Morule, 1982–) and Mo'Molemi (Motiapele Morule, 1981–), from Mma-batho, South Africa (formerly Bophuthatswana). The last was a South African farmer before pursuing a solo motswako career in Botswana.

More recent Motswana artists include Zeus (1986–) from Serowe; DJ Rade (Bob Hirschfeld, 1976–) and Dramaboi (Thuto Ramphaleng, 1993–), from Gaborone; and Apollo Diablo (Monametsi Nkhukhu, 1994–), from Francistown and Jwaneng. Stagga (aka Don Dada, Ralph Williams III, 1976–) is a London-born rapper of Tswana and Jamaican descent, who built his motswako career in Gaborone. His son Leano (2001*–) is an emerging motswako rapper. As of 2018, Stagga contin-ues his rapping career, based now in London.

Since the 2000s, there has been an increasing number of female motswako art-ists. Punah (Punah Gabasiane, n.d.), a former elementary school teacher from Serowe, began singing African jazz in cabarets before rapping. Punah fuses motswako with jazz and elements of gospel music, though motswako remains a secondary focus. Fifi Cooper (Refilwe Boingotio Mooketsi, 1991–), from Mahikeng, began as an R&B singer, but has quickly become one of the most popular female motswako rappers of her time.

Melissa Ursula Dawn Goldsmith

See also: Botswana; Namibia; Political Hip Hop; South Africa; Tuks Senganga; Zeus

Further Reading

Ditsele, Thabo. 2017. "The Promotion of Setswana through Hip Hop and *Motswakolistas*." *Journal of the Musical Arts in Africa* 14, nos. 1–2: 1–14.

Künzler, Daniel. 2011. "South African Rap Music, Counter Discourses, Identity, and Commodification beyond the Prophets of da City." *Journal of Southern African Studies* 37, no. 1: 27–43.

Masemola, Michael Kgomotso, and Pinky Makoe. 2014. "Musical Space as Site of Transculturation of Memory and Transformation of Consciousness: The Re-affirmation of Africa in the Black Atlantic Assemblage." *Muziki: Journal of Music Research in Africa* 11, no. 1: 63–70.

Molebatsi, Natalia, and Raphael d'Abdon. 2007. "From Poetry to Floetry: Music's Influence in the Spoken Word Art of Young South Africa." *Muziki: Journal of Music Research in Africa* 4, no. 2: 171–77.

Further Listening

Baphixile. 1998. *Ngoma* (*Dance*). Sony Music Entertainment.

Cassper Nyovest. 2015. *Refiloe* (*Gift*). Family Tree Records.

Cooper, Fifi. 2013. *20FIFI*. Ambitiouz Entertainment.

Zeus. 2008. *Freshly Baked*. D.I.Y. Entertainment.

Mozambique

Mozambique is a Southeast African country that borders South Africa, Swaziland, Zimbabwe, Malawi, Zambia, and Tanzania, with its coast on the Indian Ocean. Across the Mozambique Channel is Madagascar. Mozambique attained its independence from Portugal in 1975, becoming the People's Republic of Mozambique (1975–1990), under the Mozambique Liberation Front (FRELIMO), a self-proclaimed one-party communist regime. Just two years later, the Mozambican Civil War (1977–1992) began when then white-ruled Rhodesia (aka Republic of Rhodesia, 1965–1979)—an unrecognized state in South Africa—funded the right-wing nationalist, pro-Apartheid (1948–1991), and populist Mozambique National Resistance's (RENAMO) movement to oppose the government. The Mozambican Civil War (1975–1990) coincided with the emergence of hip hop in Mozambique's neighboring countries.

Whether residing abroad or in Mozambique, hip hop artists who have incorporated Mozambican music and addressed Mozambican Civil War–related issues and problems with political unrest can be found. Popular music such as Jamaican reggae, ragga, and dancehall, as well as modernized Portuguese *fado*, and Brazilian *bossa nova* and *maxixe* (aka Brazilian *tango*), are favored by hip hop artists, in addition to Mozambique's own kinds of popular music such as marrabenta (an example of Mozambican music that derives some influence from hip hop).

By the early 1990s, hip hop activity existed especially in Mozambique's capital city, Maputo, and rap there is often called Maputo rap. Although the most used native languages spoken by the black African majority are Swahili, Makhuwa, and Sena, Portuguese remains Mozambique's national language. Rapping texts also favor Portuguese, though some artists opt for English to gain further audiences. An early rap group in Maputo who recorded hip hop was Rappers Unit (1993–).

Shortly after its formation, female rapper and singer Gina Pepa (Gina Guibunda, 1976–) joined. She later pursued a successful solo career fusing hip hop with R&B. Another early Mozambican rapper was Duas Caras (Two Face, Hermío Chissano, 1978–). In 1998, *pandza*, a fast-tempo Mozambican popular music that combines *marrabenta* and *raga rock*, was created. Ziqo (aka Ziqo Maboazuda, Zico da Silva, n.d.) is often credited as its originator, and pandza has since been made popular by artists such as Mc Roger (Rogério Dinis, 1964–).

As Mozambican hip hop continues into the 2000s, more artists have produced music with accessible software. A duo from Maputo, FandG (aka Fidalgo and Gringo, 1999–), with rapper and songwriter Fidalgo (Fábio Ferreira, n.d.) and rapper, songwriter, and producer Gringo (Edson Nhamuxando, n.d.), raps in Portuguese; it fuses hip hop with funk, jazz, and neo soul. The duo's lyrical content focuses on romance, peace, and everyday street life. Using just FL Studio (formerly known as FruityLoops, 1997–), FandG released its debut studio album, *Bitologista* (*Bitologist*, 2007). The singer-songwriter, producer, entrepreneur, visual artist, and activist SIMBA (Nelson Angelo Sitoi, 1980–), also from Maputo, released Mozambique's first hip hop album in English, *Run and Tell Your Mother* (2005).

Nearly a decade afterward, with Mozambican producer and multi-instrumentalist Milton Gulli (1978–), SIMBA released *The Heroes: Tribute to a Tribe Called Quest* (2013). Azagaía (Edson da Luz, 1984–) raps in Portuguese, using some Changana. His lyrical content includes poverty, violence, and strong political criticism against the current Mozambican regime. Other notable acts are Mr. Bow (aka Bawito, Salvador Pedro Maiaze, 1982–), Laylizzy (Edson Abel Jermias Tchamo, 1988–), and Luwi Ace (Rui Mazuk, 1993–). The successful female singer-songwriter Lizha James (Elisa Lisete James Humbane, 1982–) fuses hip hop and pandza with reggae, R&B, and marrabenta.

DIASPORA ACTS

As a result of the Mozambican Civil War, a million people died, five million people were displaced, and landmines, as well as other arsenal, maimed many surviving Mozambicans. The country's first multiparty elections did not take place until 1994, resulting in its current semipresidential republic with its legislature. Mozambican diaspora acts include several hip hop artists who grew up in Lisbon, where their first contact with hip hop was Portuguese hip hop, commonly known as Hip Hop Tuga. An example of a successful expatriate Mozambican hip hop artist is Cataclysm (Mohammed Yahya, n.d.), a rapper and spoken-word artist from Maputo who was displaced by the war and raised in Lisbon. He ultimately settled in London. Cataclysm raps in English and Portuguese, focusing on political hip hop that advocates for self and societal improvement. He worked on several interfaith hip hop efforts, and with London-based rapper Anomaly MC (Daniel Silverstein, n.d.), he cofounded the first Muslim/Jewish hip hop collective in the United Kingdom.

Melissa Ursula Dawn Goldsmith

See also: Portugal; Reggae; South Africa

Further Reading

Rantala, Janne. 2016. "'*Hidrunisa Samora*': Invocations of a Dead Polital Leader in Maputo Rap." *Journal of Southern African Studies* 42, no. 6: 1161–77.

Vanspauwen, Bart P. 2013. "Cultural Struggles in the Lusofonia Arena: Portuguese-Speaking Migrant Musicians in Lisbon." *Afrika Focus* 26, no. 1: 67–88.

Further Listening

Azagaía. 2007. *Babalaze* (*Hangover*). Cotonete Records.

FandG. 2007. *Bitologista* (*Bitologist*). FandG.

Mr. B The Gentleman Rhymer

(James Burke, 1970–, London, England)

Mr. B The Gentleman Rhymer is a British rapper, producer, and multi-instrumentalist who is credited with starting the Chap Hop genre. He delivers all of his rhymes in Received Pronunciation (aka RP, or BBC English), the Standard English dialect and accent of the United Kingdom. Using the grammar and vocabulary of the Queen's English, Mr. B raps about a number of British cultural staples and stereotypes, such as playing cricket, smoking a pipe, and wearing tweed, three-piece suits, and other refined clothing.

Chap hop musician and producer Mr. B The Gentleman Rhymer raps in Received Pronunciation (aka RP or BBC English)—the Queen's English—in 2012 at Guilfest in Guildford, England. One of Mr. B's most popular songs and music videos is "Chap Hop History," from 2008, in which he raps sampled lines from important American rap songs while playing his banjolele. (Harry Herd/WireImage/Getty Images)

Many of his tracks parody familiar hip hop lyrics and concepts. For example, "Straight Out of Surrey" (2008) is a play on the American hip hop group N.W.A.'s (1986–1991) track "Straight Outta Compton," and his track "Can't Stop, Shan't Stop" (2013) is a British English adaptation of "Can't Stop, Won't Stop," the title of a 1997 track by American hip hop artist KRS-One (1965–), a 2003 hit by American hip hop duo Young Gunz (1999–), and a 2005 hip hop history book written by the Hawaiian-born American journalist and critic Jeff Chang. On most of his tracks Mr. B accompanies himself on the banjolele, a four-stringed instrument with the size and tuning system of a ukulele and the tone and construction of a banjo. He produces virtually all of his own backing beats, and he occasionally plays piano and trombone on his backing tracks, as well.

FEUD WITH PROFESSOR ELEMENTAL AND BEYOND

Mr. B first gained attention with "Chap Hop History," from his first album *Flattery Not Included* (2008), and its accompanying music video, which as of 2018 has been viewed well over one million times on YouTube. Each stanza of the track features Mr. B rapping sampled lines from important American rap songs and playing along on his banjolele. In 2010, fellow English chap hop artist Professor Elemental (Paul Alborough, 1975–) released the song and video "Fighting Trousers," a humorous critique of Mr. B. In response, Mr. B released "Like a Chap." They have appeared together both live and in recordings since.

Mr. B has released a total of five studio albums: *Flattery Not Included, I Say* (2010), *The Tweed Album* (2012), *Can't Stop Shan't Stop* (2013), and *Mr. B's Christmas Album*. His first two albums were released on the Grot Music label (2004–2010); his subsequent albums have been produced on his own label, the Chap Hop Business Concern (2012–). His label has produced two album compilations of his music: *O. G. Original Gentleman* (2011) and *Mr. B The Gentleman Rhymer: Acid Ragtime: Chapstep Volume One* (2014).

He is a popular live performer and has appeared in the Glastonbury Festival and the Edinburgh Fringe Festival, among others. In 2015, he appeared in live performances, often with his banjolele, in a series of videos called *The Bassment Sessions* that as of 2018 are available on YouTube. Mr. B also composes and produces electronica mixtapes under his pseudonym/alter ego, The Major, on his label.

Amanda Sewell

See also: Chap Hop; Nerdcore; Professor Elemental; The United Kingdom

Further Reading

Robinson, Frances. 2011. "In 'Chap Hop,' Gentleman Rappers Bust Rhymes about Tea, Cricket." *The Wall Street Journal*, April 4, A1, A14.

Walters, Simon. 2014. "Gove's Favorite Rapper Revealed: Minister Professes Love for 'Chap Hop' Star Who Calls Boris Simple, Cameron an 'Airy-Fairy Dud', and Osborne Tight-Fisted." *The Daily Mail*, March 22.

Further Listening

Mr. B The Gentleman Rhymer. 2008. *Flattery Not Included.* Grot Music.

Mr. B The Gentleman Rhymer. 2012. *The Tweed Album.* Chap-Hop Business Concern.

Mr. Len

(Leonard Smythe, 1975–, Bronx, New York)

Mr. Len is an American hip hop DJ, turntablist, and producer, best known for his role in the Brooklyn, New York hip hop band Company Flow (1993–2001) and for his collaborative production work with Grammy winner Prince Paul (1967–) from Queens, New York. His solo debut was the 2001 album *Pity the Fool (Experiments in Therapy behind the Mask of Music While Handing Out Dummysmacks)*.

Along with rapper and producer El-P (Jaime Meline, 1975–) and rapper and producer Bigg Jus (Justin Ingelton, n.d.), Mr. Len founded Company Flow. The band's their album *Funcrusher Plus* (1997) is widely regarded as one of the most important independent hip hop albums produced in the 1990s. Its success was due in equal parts to El-P's and Bigg Jus's dense, complex lyrics; the album's experimental production style, in which sampled sounds were heavily altered from their source materials and beats were often irregular; and Mr. Len's turntablism, exemplified on the songs "Lencoricism" and "Funcrush Scratch."

Company Flow disbanded in 2001, and Mr. Len went on to produce *Pity the Fool (Experiments in Therapy behind the Mask of Music While Handing Out Dummysmacks)*. The album featured rapper Jean Grae (1976–) on four tracks and other rappers including Chubb Rock (Richard Simpson, 1968–) and the members of the Juggaknots (1995–) on various other tracks. The album's key single "Taco Day," a tale of an abused girl's revenge, features lyrics by Jean Grae and originally contained samples of music from the 1985 film *Mishima: A Life in Four Chapters* by the American composer Philip Glass (1937–). Mr. Len's label, Matador, was unable to clear the samples with Glass's record label, and Mr. Len had to rework the track with entirely different samples to avoid a lawsuit.

He has released a solo compilation album, *Class X: A Tribute to Company Flow* (2003) and one digital solo album, *The Marvels of Yestermorrow* (2013), distributed via Bandcamp. He has collaborated with and appeared on tracks and albums of dozens of different artists. Along with Prince Paul, he created a fictitious doo-wop group called the Dix. The group's album *The Art of Picking up Women* (2005) scratched and looped old doo-wop recordings while parodying the culture of doo-wop in singles such as "Here Comes the Dix" and "Tears in My Eyes (Dirty Girl)." The album notes create the fictional past for the band, as having started in 1957 as the Bangkoks, with original members Orgynius, Peter O Tool, Tro John and John Handcock, reassembling as the Dix in 1965. Mr. Len was also featured prominently in the documentary film *Copyright Criminals* (2009), which detailed a number of the legal, ethical, and aesthetic issues related to sample-based hip hop.

Amanda Sewell

See also: Company Flow; Turntablism; The United States

Further Reading

Haywood, Brad. 2001. "Review: Mr. Len, *Pity the Fool: Experiments in Therapy behind the Mask of Music While Handing Out Dummy Smacks*." *Pitchfork*, November 18.

Sewell, Amanda. 2014. "How Copyright Affected the Musical Style and Critical Reception of Sample-Based Hip Hop." *Journal of Popular Music Studies* 26, nos. 2–3: 295–320.

Further Listening

Company Flow. 1997. *Funcrusher Plus*. Rawkus Records.

The Dix. 2005. *The Art of Picking Up Women*. Smacks.

Mr. Len. 2001. *Pity the Fool: Experiments in Therapy behind the Mask of Music While Handing Out Dummy Smacks.* Matador.

Further Viewing

Franzen, Benjamin, and Kembrew McLeod, dirs. 2009. *Copyright Criminals.* N.p.: Changing Images.

Myanmar

Myanmar, a Southeast Asian nation commonly called Burma, is an economically stable nation (its resources include jade, other gems and minerals, oil, and natural gas) with a huge income gap among its population of 51 million. Its largest city is its former capital, Yangon (aka Rangoon). In its early history, Burmese language, traditions, and religion (Theravada Buddhism) informed the country's culture. Hip hop emerged in the late 1990s and became the favorite musical genre of youth. Early hip hop artists included rappers Myo Kyawt Myaing (1971–), Thxa Soe (Soe Moe Aung, 1980–), Sai Sai Kham Leng (aka Sai Sai Kham Hlaing, 1979–), and Ye Lay (Ye Htun Min, 1984–), as well as rap group Acid (2000–).

Myanmar's music is greatly influenced by other musical traditions in the region, especially those in its bordering countries: India, Bangladesh, Thailand, Laos, and China. Because Theravada Buddhism eschews decadence, Myanmar's traditional music is single melody, nonharmonized, regular rhythm–oriented, with time signatures such as 4/4 (*na-yi-se*), 2/4 (*wa-let-se*), 8/16 (*wa-let-a-myan*), combined into fixed patterns and ruled by convention, although regional music styles create some diversity. Instrumentation consists of drums, pipes and flutes, bells, clappers, harps, xylophones, zithers and fiddles, and vocals. Western classical and pop music were introduced into the country during the 20th century as a by-product of its British rule period (1824–1848). Rock and roll was introduced in the 1960s and became popular in the 1980s, despite censorship by the Myanmar Music Asiayon (MMA) of lyrics dealing with political and social issues, poverty, the sex trade, democracy, or human rights.

Myaing is a singer-rapper of dance, synthpop, and remix music, as well as a producer and audio engineer; he introduced rap music to Myanmar. Thxa Soe, also an audio engineer, infused hip hop with traditional folksongs and contemporary electronic music. Sai Sai Kham is singer-songwriter, model, novelist, and actor released his debut album *Chocolate yaung yayge einmet* (*Chocolate-Colored Ice Dreams*) in 2000; his sophomore effort in 2001, *Thangegyin myar swar* (*Graduation: Friends Forever*), made hip hop more popular in the mainstream. Rapper Ye Lay is a singer-songwriter, musician, actor and model.

Acid released Myanmar's first hip hop album, *Beginning* (2000); however, its political songs against the military led to the arrest of two members. In August 2012 state censorship on music was officially abolished. Since then, rock and metal have become popular, with hip hop lagging a bit behind, although two recent rappers, Ah Boy (aka K. K. Wong, Kyaw Phyo Tun, 1985–) and Hlwan Paing (1989–), both former members of the boyband Rock$tar (n.d.), have taken the forefront in the new hip hop wave. Ah Boy is a singer-songwriter and businessman who in 2007 released his solo album *Tayoke tan* (*Chinatown*).

In 2014, rapper-singer Hlwan Paing released his electrodance-fused hip hop debut album *Gita sar so* (aka *Curse*); he was voted the country's Most Popular Male Vocalist of Year.

Anthony J. Fonseca

See also: China; India; Thailand

Further Reading

Keeler, Ward. 2009. "What's Burmese about Burmese Rap? Why Some Expressive Forms Go Global." *American Ethnologist* 36, no. 1: 2–19.

Ransley, Carol, and Toe Zaw Latt. 2007. "Burma's New Generation Political Activists." *Eureka Street* 17, no. 20: 11–14.

N

Naeto C

(Naetochukwu Chikwe, 1982–, Houston, Texas)

Naeto C is a Nigerian American Afrobeat singer-songwriter, rapper, and producer. He is the son of former Nigerian Ambassador to Ireland, Kema Chikwe (Kemafo Nonyerem Chikwe, 1947*–) and at a young age he won various poetry competitions. After finishing his secondary education in Lagos, Nigeria, the country's largest city and one of the fastest growing urban areas in the world, he moved back to the United States to attend college. He got interested in hip hop and briefly formed a trio, World Famous Akademy (2004–2008), which also featured Ikechukwu Onanaku (n.d.).

Naeto C graduated in 2004 from the George Washington University, intending to become a medical doctor (eventually he earned a master's degree in Energy Studies in Scotland). The trio returned to Nigeria in 2006 to work for Storm 360 (aka Storm Productions, 1991–), and Naeto C became an in-house producer, producing over 60 songs in his first year, including a minor hit, "I Believe" (2007), which led to the I Believe Tour (2007–2008).

His debut album *You Know My "P"* was released in 2008 and sold over a million copies. Two of its singles, "Sitting on Top" and "Kini Big Deal," made it onto various Nigerian charts, the latter becoming a club favorite. His second album, *Super C Season* (2011), spawned four singles, including "Ako Mi Ti Poju" ("My Lessons Learned" in Igbo).

As an Afrobeat artist, he uses a combination of West African musical styles (such as *fuji* music and highlife), combining those with American jazz; vocals tend to be chants, call-and-response, and polyrhythmic vocals, with harmonies and countermelodies. His instrumentation generally features bass guitar, drum kits, synthesizer, guitar, and percussion, as well as congas, brass, and saxophone. He has won two MTV Africa Music Awards, for Best New Musician (2008) and Best New Artist (2009).

Anthony J. Fonseca

See also: Nigeria; The United States

Further Reading

Adesioye, Lola. 2009. "Keep the Home Fires Burning: Nigerian Pop Musicians Have Been Ridiculed as Poor Imitators of American Hip Hop, but a Fresh Mix of U.S. Studio Polish and African Roots Is Changing All That." *The Guardian*, March 13, 7.

Künzler, Daniel. 2011. "South African Rap Music, Counter Discourses, Identity, and Commodification beyond the Prophets of da City." *Journal of Southern African Studies* 37, no. 1: 27–43.

Further Listening
Naeto C. 2011. *Super C Season.* Storm 360/Cerious Music.

Namibia

Namibia is a southern African country on the Atlantic Coast that shares borders with Angola, Zambia, Botswana, and South Africa. In 1990, Namibia attained independence from South Africa. Hip hop likely reached Namibia in the early 1980s, about the same time as it became popular in South Africa; however, the country had no music industry well into the mid-1990s, when Namibian hip hop (known as "Nam hip hop") emerged. Musicians often record in neighboring South Africa, whose hip hop and kwaito music became popular in Namibia as well. *Kwaito* developed into a mainstream music genre in Soweto, in Johannesburg, just after the end of apartheid and democratic election of President Nelson Mandela (1918–2013) in 1994. South Africa also applied apartheid to Namibia while governing the state; kwaito therefore also resonated with young Namibians. Namibian rapping texts are diverse, but mainly English, Afrikaans, and Oshiwambo are used. From kwaito, localized party and ghetto themes are part of the lyrical content of Nam hip hop; other themes have come to focus on romance (including mixed race romances), attaining wealth, and unity and tolerance.

Namibia's main hip hop scene is in Windhoek, the capital city, followed by Walvis Bay and the coastal city Skwakopmund. One of the pioneering groups of the mid-1990s was the Kalaharians (aka The Usual Suspects, 1996–2000), whose members later merged to become Dungeon Family (2000–2004*)—not to be confused with OutKast's (1991–2006, 2014–) Atlanta-based hip hop, funk, and R&B collective the Dungeon Family (1993–). Members also became the popular female R&B duo Gal Level (2004–). Unlike with other kinds of African hip hop, female Nam hip hop artists were present from the start and helped pave the way for later female Namibian acts such as rapper Snazzy (Louisa Shilongo, 1987–), who performs in English. By the late 1990s, many Nam hip hop artists also recorded kwaito and house music. One of the most critically acclaimed Namibian rappers is the Dogg (Martin Morocky, 1983–), a kwaito artist born in exile in Zambia, who also records hip hop and house music. Other famous Nam hip hop acts include rapper Gazza (Lazarus Shiimi, 1990–), rapper and crunk musician D-Jay (Diogene Ochs, 1987–), gangsta and Christian/gospel rapper D-Naff (Naftalie Shigwedha Amukwelele, 1974–), gangsta rapper Jericho (aka J-Twizzle, Jerich Jerome Gawanab, 1980–), gangsta rapper Quido (Le-Roy Quido Mohamed, 1989–), and producer WilliamMustBeControl'd (aka Willy G, William Shilamba, 1992–).

Namibia has several historically white communities, made up of mostly Afrikaners or German. As hip hop and kwaito became popular, there have been a few white Namibian artists, particularly from Windhoek. Ludik (aka Elvis se Seun, Stefan Ludik 1981–), once a cricketer, has performed hip hop, pop, and dance music since 2003, using both English and Afrikaans languages. Another Windhoek rapper of European descent is Gini Grindith (Dave Coxall, 1979–), who is part of the Johannesburg crew Abnormal Detail (2000–2010*). The most famous white Namibian rapper is EeS (Eric Sell, 1983–), who fuses hip hop with kwaito, reggae, and Afropop. He established his music career in Cape Town, where he studied sound engineering. In 2003, EeS moved to Cologne, Germany. His rap texts combine English and Afrikaans (including Camtho, which is usually used in kwaito). At times, he also uses Namlish (Namibian English) and Namibian German, also known as Namibian slang (a dialect called Südwesterdeutsch or Namsläng that combines German with Afrikaans, Ovambo, and other Bantu languages).

Though white rappers and kwaito artists exist, since the 2000s Nam hip hop and kwaito have become somewhat integrated. Eraze (Edwin Chibanga, n.d.) is a black Namibian MC, producer, and radio host from Windhoek. Active in hip hop since 1996, Eraze created the radio show *The Cypha* (2002*–), which broadcast global and local hip hop and features open mic freestyle sessions. Eraze raps in English and worked on EeS's album *Nam Flava!* (2006) and was associated with Namibian rapper Sunny Boy (Sunday Shipushu, 1983–), from Ongwediva, who records hip hop, kwaito, and *hikwa* (a combination of hip hop and kwaito that was created by Sunny Boy). Other Namibian hip hop acts that perform hikwa are OmPuff (Belmiro Hosi, 1980–) of Angolan-Namibian descent, Tre VDK (aka Tre Van Die Kasie, Tre, Tretius Kauhangengo, 1981–), and Bucharest, Romanian-born and raised Qonja (Tukonjela Haiyambo Ngodji, 1984–).

Melissa Ursula Dawn Goldsmith

See also: Botswana; Kwaito; South Africa

Further Reading

Fairweather, Ian. 2006. "Heritage, Identity, and Youth in Postcolonial Namibia." *Journal of Southern African Studies* 32, no. 4: 719–36.

van Wolputte, Steven, and Laura E. Bleckmann. 2012. "The Ironies of Pop: Local Music Production and Citizenship in a Small Namibian Town." *Africa* 82, no. 3: 413–36.

Further Listening

EeS. 2006. *Nam Flava!* EeS Records.

Nas

(aka Nasty Nas, Nasir Ben Olu Dara Jones, 1973–, Brooklyn, New York)

Nas is an American rapper, producer, film and television actor, entrepreneur, and philanthropist who is best known for his highly successful and influential albums: *Illmatic* (1994), *It Was Written* (1996), *I Am . . .* (1999), *Nastradamus* (1999), *Stillmatic* (2001), *God's Son* (2002), *Street's Disciple* (2004), *Hip Hop Is Dead* (2006), *Untitled* (2008), and *Life Is Good* (2012).

As of 2018, his first seven albums have been certified Platinum, and his last three albums were certified Gold. His albums also have an impressive charting record. All have peaked in either the No. 1 or No. 2 position on Billboard's Top R&B/Hip-Hop Albums chart. *It Was Written*, *I Am . . .* , *Hip Hop Is Dead*, *Untitled*, and *Life Is Good* peaked at No. 1 on the Billboard 200; *Illmatic*, *God's Son*, *Nastradamus*,

Street's Disciple, and *Stillmatic* peaked in or near the Top 10, as high as No. 5, on the Billboard 200.

Both his collaboration albums, *The Firm: The Album* (1997) as part of the Firm (1996–1998), a supergroup with rappers Foxy Brown (Inga DeCarlo Fung Marchand, 1978–), AZ (Anthony Cruz, 1972–), and Nature (Jermain Baxter, 1972–), and *Distant Relatives* (2010) with Bob Marley's (Robert Nesta Marley, 1945–1981) youngest son, reggae singer Damian Marley (aka Jr. Gong, 1978–), also peaked at No. 1 on the Billboard 200.

BEGINNING CAREER AND *ILLMATIC*

Nas's father is Olu Dara Jones (Charles Jones III, 1941–), a jazz cornetist, guitarist, and singer who played a variety of styles, including bebop, cool jazz, blues, funk, reggae, and jazz-rock fusion. Nas grew up in the Queensbridge Houses (1939–), the largest housing project in North America and once home to pioneering American hip hop artists such as producer Marley Marl (1962–), several Juice Crew rappers (1983–1991), and later artists such as rapper Blaq Poet (Wilbur Bass, 1969–) and the duo Mobb Deep (1991–2017). Nas showed talent in writing; however, he dropped out of school by eighth grade, about the same year his parents divorced. At this time, his best friend in the Queensbridge Houses, Ill Will (Willy Graham, 1972–1992), mentored and backed him as a DJ while he rapped. Ill Will was later murdered by a neighborhood gunman; he is referenced on Nas's debut album *Illmatic* and on Nas's independent label, ill Will Records (1999–), on which Nas released *Nastradamus*.

By the late 1980s, Nas met hip hop producer Large Professor (aka Large Pro, Extra P., William Paul Mitchell, 1973–), who produced Rakim (William Michael Griffin, 1968–). Large Professor gave Nas studio access. In 1991, Nas appeared on Canadian American hip hop group Main Source's (1989–1994) song "Live at the Barbeque." A year later, MC Serch (Michael Berrin, 1967–) of the American hip hop group 3rd Bass (1987–1992, 1998–2000) became Nas's manager and attained a record deal with Columbia Records (1887–). That year, as Nasty Nas, his solo debut was "Halftime," from MC Serch's film soundtrack to American director Oliver Stone's (William Oliver Stone, 1946–) *Zebrahead* (1992).

In 1994, Nas released *Illmatic*, which featured production by Large Professor, among others, as well as an appearance by his father. *Illmatic* earned strong critical acclaim and is considered by many critics, rappers, and scholars as a classic hip hop album. Its hardcore lyrical content contains rich use of internal rhymes, first-person storytelling that focused on Nas's inner-city experiences in the Queensbridge Houses, and alternating images of ghetto life (e.g., poverty, drug activity, and police conversations) with gangsta rap devices (e.g., braggadocio and authenticity).

SUBSEQUENT ALBUMS AND DISSING

Despite *Illmatic*'s status, Columbia Records' agenda was for Nas to work toward mainstream success. *It Was Written* featured several famous 1990s hip hop artists such as Lauryn Hill (1975–) and Dr. Dre (1965–), and it produced immediate hits and achieved chart success. *I Am . . .* followed in 1999. It was originally intended as a double album, but Nas abandoned material from the album that had been leaked onto the Internet. *Nastradamus* was released later that year to mixed critical reception. In 2000, Nas collaborated with Queensbridge hip hop legends Roxanne Shanté (1969–), MC Shan (1965–), and Marley Marl on the album *Nas and ill Will Records Presents QB's Finest*.

About this time, Nas had a well known argument with Puff Daddy (1969–) and a rivalry with Jay-Z (1969–). After collaborating on Nas's "Hate Me Now" (1999) and appearing in the music video, which featured both rappers crucified, Puff Daddy wanted to be edited out of the scene. Despite his request, the unedited version of the video aired on MTV (1981–). In 2001, Jay-Z dissed Nas on "Takeover" and Nas responded by dissing Jay-Z on "Ether." Jay-Z responded with "Supa Ugly," which contained braggadocio lines about having an affair with Nas's girlfriend.

In the meantime, Nas had a comeback with *Stillmatic*, and in 2002, Columbia Records released *The Lost Tapes*, containing Nas's unreleased earlier songs. Nas's album *God's Son* followed. At this time, Nas helped his younger brother, Jungle (aka Jabari Fret, Jabari Jones, n.d.), a member of the Queensbridge hip hop group Bravehearts (1998–), release the group's debut studio album, *Bravehearted* (2003). But a year after the 2004 release of Nas's *Street's Disciple*, the dissing continued: Nas appeared in Jay-Z's 2005 "I Declare War" concert, where they dissed each other while also performing together. The concert led to Nas's 2006 recording deal with Def Jam Recordings (1983–) while Jay-Z was president of the label. For Def Jam, Nas recorded *Hip Hop Is Dead*, *Untitled*, and *Life Is Good*.

Nas has toured worldwide and has collaborated with hip hop artists outside the United States, such as South African motswako rapper Hip Hop Pantsula (1980–). Nas has also helped create numerous scholarships, including establishing a fellowship at Harvard University in 2013 that encourages scholars and artists' creativity in connection to hip hop.

Melissa Ursula Dawn Goldsmith

See also: Gangsta Rap; Jay-Z; Puff Daddy; The United States

Further Reading

Dyson, Michael Eric, and Sohail Daulatzai, eds. 2010. *Born to Use Mics: Reading Nas's "Illmatic."* New York: Basic Civitas Books.

Pollard, Tyler J. 2014. "Conflicted State of Mind: Race, Masculinity, and Nas's Lyric Public Pedagogy." *Journal of Poetry Therapy* 27, no. 1: 1–11.

Preston, Graham Chia-Hui. 2008. "'My Pen Rides the Paper': Hip Hop, the Technology of Writing, and Nas's *Illmatic*." *Journal of Popular Music Studies* 20, no. 3: 261–75.

Further Listening

Nas. 1994. *Illmatic*. Columbia.

Nas. 2004. *Street's Disciple*. Columbia.

Nation of Islam

The Nation of Islam (NOI) was founded in 1930 in Detroit as an Islamic Black Nationalist movement. For most of the 20th century, the organization has been controversial in national discussions regarding race and racism. For most of its history, the NOI has espoused a separatist ideology that emphasizes black self-improvement and self-determination, while also protesting racial inequality. The group has also had a significant impact on the evolution of hip hop. The NOI's distinct Black Nationalist ideology inspired the lyrics, production, and aesthetics of many early rap artists. Furthermore, the group's militancy and resurgence during the final decades of the 20th century attracted many rap artists as adherents or fellow travelers, and contributed to a racially charged cultural Zeitgeist that helped shape United States–based hip hop in general.

ORIGINS AND THE U.S. CIVIL RIGHTS MOVEMENT

Wallace Fard Muhammad (Wallace D. Fard, 1877–1934*) established the Nation of Islam with the intention of using and revising the tenets of Islam to speak to the experiences of African Americans. In 1934, Muhammad disappeared, so Elijah Muhammad (Elijah Robert Poole, 1897–1975) became the group's leader until 1975. The group believed that blacks were Allah's chosen people and that white society was hostile to black interests; thus, the NOI argued that black people were entitled to a separate nation. Many members replaced their surnames with the letter "X," claiming that their original last names were those of slaveholders and not reflective of their African ancestry.

The NOI struggled to attract members during its early years, but began enjoying some success following World War II (1939–1945). The group became increasingly popular and influential during the 1960s, largely due to the charisma of Malcolm X (1925–1965). While in prison, Malcolm X converted to Islam and, following his 1952 release, became a prominent and visible minister and spokesperson. A talented public speaker, Malcolm X functioned as a more radical counterpoint to the nonviolent tradition of Civil Rights activism embodied by Martin Luther King Jr. (1929–1968). King and Malcolm X frequently disagreed publicly, but many scholars of the Civil Rights Movement in the United States (1954–1968) claim the tension between them helped propel the movement forward. Malcolm X's incendiary rhetoric often made King appear more reasonable to political leaders, while King's political successes created more space for Malcolm X's demands to be taken seriously.

Largely because of Malcolm X's visibility, the NOI became instrumental in laying the foundation for the Black Power Movement (1960–1979*); however, Malcolm X's growing celebrity also brought the organization unwanted attention from the federal government. In 1964, Malcolm X broke with the NOI over theological, political, and organizational disagreements. He converted to Sunni Islam and founded an independent Muslim organization. Tensions between Malcolm X and the NOI culminated with his assassination during a speech in 1965. To this day, the question of whether the NOI played a direct role in his death is hotly debated.

THE NATION'S ROLE IN HIP HOP

Following Malcolm X's assassination, a young Nation of Islam member named Louis Farrakhan (Louis Eugene Wolcott, 1933–) from the Bronx, New York, began climbing the ranks of the organization. Following Elijah Muhammad's death in 1975, the organization named the longtime leader's son, Warith Dean Muhammad (1933–2008), as his replacement. Muhammad began reforming the organization by trying to reconcile it with mainstream Islam. In the process, he abandoned many of his father's core teachings regarding separatism and black self-reliance. Farrakhan eventually broke with Muhammad and began reconstituting the NOI in the traditions of Wallace Fard and Elijah Muhammad. The growth of Farrakhan's revivalist organization during the final decades of the 20th century coincided with the birth of hip hop. By the end of the 1970s, many key Civil Rights leaders were dead, and once influential antiracist organizations were either gone or shells of their former selves. As the U.S. political climate moved to the right with the 1980 election of Ronald Reagan (1911–2004, in office 1981–1989) as president, poor and working-class black communities often languished due to the loss of gainful employment, the growth of street gangs, the circulation of drugs such as crack cocaine, and an intense national fixation on law and order.

Farrakhan emerged as a distinct and charismatic voice in troubling times. Whereas many prominent black figures struck a decidedly conservative tone about racial inequality, claiming that institutional racism was a thing of the past, Farrakhan bluntly claimed that the United States was still a racist nation and that black people must rely on themselves for deliverance. Under Farrakhan's leadership, the NOI engaged directly with black communities by holding antiviolence and anti-gang peace summits, visiting jails and prisons, and patrolling gang and drug-ravaged black neighborhoods. Although mainstream figures across the political and racial spectrum loathed Farrakhan, claiming he was a divisive figure who frequently engaged in anti-Semitic rhetoric, many young black people found Farrakhan's anger and message of self-reliance empowering. His status as a provocative and important black leader climaxed with the 1995 Million Man March in Washington, DC.

Many hip hop figures found Farrakhan's messages compelling. After his departure from N.W.A. (1986–1991), Ice Cube (1969–) began working with the Nation of Islam. His second solo album, *Death Certificate* (1991), contained many themes associated with the organization, and the album's record sleeve portrayed the rapper reading a copy of the organization's newspaper, *The Final Call* (1979–), which is published in Chicago. Many members of Public Enemy (1982–) also drew inspiration from the organization, which is apparent given the strong nationalist themes in their music and videos. Furthermore, the militant attire and behavior of members such as rapper, spoken-word artist, and educator Professor Griff (Richard Griffin, 1960–) mimicked the disciplined appearance of the NOI's paramilitary wing, the Fruit of Islam (FOI, 1933–1975). Crucially, many rappers' affiliations with the NOI generated significant controversy. Both Ice Cube and Griff penned lyrics or made public statements hostile toward many of the same groups the organization vocally criticized, and the NOI was attentive to hip hop. Farrakhan included prominent rappers and their young fans in NOI events. For example, following the violent deaths of Tupac Shakur (1971–1996) and the Notorious B.I.G. (1972–1997), he held a high-profile peace meeting and rap concert to bring resolution to the East Coast–West Coast feud.

In recent years, Farrakhan continues to attract controversy, but little visibility. He is less politically active due to declining health. Furthermore, individuals and organizations have stated that Farrakhan and NOI rhetoric regarding Jews, LGBTQ+s, and others is profoundly dangerous. The Southern Poverty Law Center (1971–) identifies the NOI as a hate group, despite its significant impact on racial politics for the past several decades and its central role in shaping the cultural and political context that birthed hip hop. Farrakhan has also recently expressed fascination with the controversial Church of Scientology (1954–), and has begun incorporating some of its principles into the NOI. While antiracist activism, particularly around police brutality, intensified during the second decade of the 21st century, the NOI has not figured significantly into such mobilizations at a national level. Due to the NOI's diminishing visibility in the context of contemporary U.S. racial politics, the group's influence on hip hop has significantly declined.

Bryan J. McCann

See also: Black Nationalism; Five Percent Nation; Ice Cube; Political Hip Hop; Public Enemy; The United States

Further Reading

Chang, Jeff. 2005. *Can't Stop Won't Stop: A History of the Hip Hop Generation.* New York: Picador.

Gardell, Mattias. 1996. *In the Name of Elijah Muhammad: Louis Farrakhan and the Nation of Islam.* Durham, NC: Duke University Press.

Malcolm X and Alex Haley. 1964. *The Autobiography of Malcolm X.* New York: Ballantine Books.

Further Listening

Ice Cube. 1991. *Death Certificate.* Priority Records.

Public Enemy. 1988. *It Takes a Nation of Millions to Hold Us Back.* Def Jam Recordings/ Columbia.

Native Tongues

(1988–1996, New York City, New York)

Native Tongues was a hip hop collective comprised of various artists and groups that strove to promote one another's projects and music. Part of what was considered the Golden Age of Hip Hop (1986–1994), Native Tongues strove for positive Afrocentric messages, mixed with the reality of street life. The musical techniques included sampling diversity, abstract lyricism, and a texture that was a stark contrast to the mainstream hip hop of the day; the style became known as conscious hip hop, jazz rap, or alternative hip hop. Original members included A Tribe Called Quest (ATCQ, 1985–1998, 2006–2013, 2015–), De La Soul (1987–), Jungle Brothers (1987–), Queen Latifah (1970–), Afrika Bambaataa (1957–), Lucien Revolucien (Lucien M'Baidem, aka Lucien M'B and Papalu, n.d.), Monie Love (Simone Gooden, 1970–), Black Sheep (1989–1995, 2000–), and Chi-Ali (Chi-Ali Griffith, 1976–). The members of the collective often collaborated on songs. For example, "Buddy" is a collaboration of De La Soul, Jungle Brothers, ATCQ's Q-Tip (Jonathan William Davis, 1970–), Queen Latifah, and Monie Love.

UNIVERSAL ZULU NATION AND EARLY EFFORTS

Afrika Bambaataa's extensive involvement in the Universal Zulu Nation (1973–), an international cultural group that promoted unity through dance and music in hip hop that started in the Bronx, New York, helped shape Native Tongues' music, especially in its Afrocentrism and concentration on individual identity. Zulu devotee and popular radio disc jockey Kool DJ Red Alert (Fred Crute, 1956–) managed the Jungle Brothers, and after their debut album *Straight Out the Jungle* (1988) performed poorly commercially, Red Alert promoted the song "I'll House You," which helped the band achieve notoriety. This success influenced De La Soul's groundbreaking album, *3 Feet High and Rising* (1989), which includes "D.A.I.S.Y. Age," an acronym for "Da Inner Sound, Y'all." The album focuses on peace and harmony, while incorporating skits and sampling from various mediums such as *Schoolhouse Rock!* (1973–2009) and musicians such as Johnny Cash (1932–2003), Hall and Oates (1970–), Steely Dan (1972–1981, 1993–), and the Turtles (1965–1970, 2010–). Jungle Brothers and De La Soul influenced the sound of ATCQ, whose debut album *People's Instinctive Travels and the Paths of Rhythm* (1990) failed to appeal to mainstream audiences but reached fans of alternative hip hop. The tracks "Luck of Lucien" (homage to Lucien Revolucien) and "Youthful Expression" ushered in the jazz hip hop movement. The group's second album *The Low End Theory* (1991) includes the momentous single "Scenario," a collaboration with Leaders of the New School that helped to solidify and validate alternative hip hop's presence.

In 1989, Queen Latifah released her debut album, *All Hail the Queen*, which addressed Apartheid (separateness in Afrikaans, 1948–1991) in South Africa and celebrated feminism, especially in the singles "Wrath of My Madness," "Ladies First," and "Mama Gave Birth to the Soul Children." "Ladies First" featured Monie Love, Queen Latifah's protégé, one of the first hip hop artists from the United Kingdom to be signed onto a major record label (Warner Bros., 1958–). In 1990, Monie Love released her debut album *Down to Earth*. Her singles "It's a Shame (My Sister)" and "Monie in the Middle" climbed the music charts. Black Sheep's debut album *A Wolf in Sheep's Clothing* (1991) covered topics such as sex and partying, while providing catchy beats that appealed to mainstream hip hop fans and the radio, as demonstrated in the singles "The Choice is Yours" and "Flavor of the Month." Chi-Ali was featured on the track "Pass the 40."

A SLOW BREAKUP

In the early 1990s the artists and groups affiliated with Native Tongues began to drift apart as they gradually gained momentum individually, even though the partnership's core message attracted new members: the Beatnuts (1989–), Brand Nubian (1989–), the Roots (1987–), Leaders of the New School (1989–1994), Mos Def (1973–), Da Bush Babees (1992–1997, 2005–), Common (1972–), the Pharcyde (1989–), Camp Lo (1995–), and Organized Konfusion (1987–1997, 2009–). Common's sophomore album *Resurrection* (1994) incorporated Native Tongues' positive messages. It addressed life growing up in the South Side of Chicago and personal growth in the track "Thisisme," as well as the false allure of materialism in "I Used to love H.E.R." Common's work influenced the collective called Soulquarians, a 1990s version of Native Tongues, which included successful artists Erykah Badu (1971–) and Questlove (1971–). Detroit-native producer and rapper J Dilla (1974–2006) collaborated with fellow Detroit-based rappers Baatin (Titus Glover, 1974–2009) and T3 (R. L. Altman III, n.d.) to create the group Slum Village (1996–). ATCQ's Q-Tip created the Ummah (1996–2000) with J Dilla and Brooklyn-based rapper Ali Shaheed Muhammad (1970–), with J Dilla becoming a crucial part of the sound of ATCQ's later albums. Although the founding members seem to ignore fans' pleas for a reunion—likely due to the rappers' clashing views—their messages of social awareness, unity, and adversities in urban streets echo in many hip hop artists' works of the late 1990s, early 2000s, and today.

Celeste Roberts

See also: Afrika Bambaataa; De La Soul; Jungle Brothers; Queen Latifah; A Tribe Called Quest; The United States; The Universal Zulu Nation

Further Reading

Kellerer, Katja. 2014. "Chant Down tha System 'till Babylon Falls: The Political Dimensions of Urban Grooves and Underground Hip Hop in Zimbabwe." *Journal of Hip Hop Studies* 1, no. 2: 189–207.

McGlynn, Aine. 2007. "The Native Tongues." *Icons of Hip Hop: An Encyclopedia of the Movement, Music, and Culture*, edited by Mickey Hess, vol. 1, pp. 265–92. Westport, CT: Greenwood Press.

Saucier, Paul Khalil. 2011. *Native Tongues: An African Hip Hop Reader.* Trenton, NJ: Africa World Press.

Further Listening

ATCQ. 1990. *People's Instinctive Travels and the Paths of Rhythm.* Jive.

De La Soul. 1989. *3 Feet High and Rising.* Tommy Boy/Warner Bros.

Jungle Brothers. 1988. *Straight out the Jungle.* Idlers/Warlock Records.

Neo Soul

Neo soul is an R&B subgenre that began in the 1980s as a revival movement and continued throughout the 1990s and beyond in the United States and the United Kingdom, with breakthrough artists such as D'Angelo (Michael Eugene Arthur, 1974–), Erykah Badu (1971–), Lauryn Hill (1975–), and Maxwell (Gerald Maxwell Rivera, 1973–). The phrase neo soul was not coined until the 1990s, when Motown (1959–) executive Kedar Massenburg (1963–), known for discovering Erykah Badu, used it to market the hybrid music of soul and contemporary R&B. Unlike alternative R&B, which neo soul producers and musicians considered too producer-driven and digital, neo soul goes back to traditional R&B. Typically, the instruments used in neo soul include guitar, bass, electric piano, organ, drum kits, and brass, and neo soul songs tend to be singer-songwriter- and musician-oriented, designed to showcase skill and translate well to live performance. The genre is also notable for two extramusical elements: its eschewal of commercialism and its inclusion of women.

Former Fugees singer-songwriter Lauryn Hill released *The Miseducation of Lauryn Hill*, one of the benchmark albums of neo soul, in 1998. In 2017 Hill performed at The Museum of Modern Art Film Benefit in New York City. (Nicholas Hunt/Getty Images for Museum Of Modern Art)

In a sense, neo soul, as its name implies, looks both backward and forward, as its practitioners aim to revive the elements of soul heard in songs by the likes of Marvin Gaye (1939–1984), Chaka Khan (Yvette Marie Stevens, 1953–), Al Green (Albert Leornes Greene, 1946–), and Stevie Wonder (Stevland Judkins Hardaway or Steveland Morris Hardaway, 1950–), while finding new ways to incorporate those elements into music that is relevant to fans.

MOVEMENTS FROM BEGINNING TO END

One possible source of the U.S. neo soul movement is the trio Tony! Toni! Toné! (1988–1997, 2003–) or the duo of poet and singer-rapper Gil Scott-Heron (1949–2011) and composer Brian Jackson (1952–). In the United Kingdom, artists such as Me'Shell Ndegeocello (Michelle Lynn Johnson, 1968–), Sade (Helen Folasade Adu, 1959–), and the Brand New Heavies (1985–) had success with their revitalized soul sounds. Another possible source is Me'Shell NdegéOcello's debut album *Plantation Lullabies* (1993) which was also the beginning of U.K. neo soul. Other benchmark albums in the neo soul movement included D'Angelo's *Brown Sugar* (1995), Maxwell's *Maxwell's Urban Hang Suite* (1996), Erykah Badu's *Baduizm* (1997), and Hill's *The Miseducation of Lauryn Hill* (1998), the last winning five Grammy Awards out of a record 10 nominations.

The film *Love Jones* (1997) helped propel neo soul into the popular consciousness with its soundtrack album featuring Hill, Maxwell, the Brand New Heavies, and Me'Shell Ndegeocello, among others; however, it was D'Angelo's second studio album, *Voodoo* (2000), which was produced by the hip hop collective Soulquarians (1999–2002), that marked the apex of the neo soul movement.

Neo soul's decline was a product of the conflict between its artists' rejection of commercialism and the music industry's emphasis on branding and marketing over quality; labels began to shelve their albums and cancel their contracts, and some artists responded by going on extended hiatus. Contemporary neo soul artists prefer independent labels over the major labels because of this conflict, but occasionally will realize large-scale commercial success, as did John Legend (John Roger Stephens, 1978–) and Jill Scott (1972–).

Anthony J. Fonseca

See also: Erykah Badu; Hill, Lauryn; Scott, Jill; The United Kingdom; The United States

Further Reading

Cunningham, Phillip Lamarr. 2010. "'There's Nothing Really New under the Sun': The Fallacy of the Neo Soul Genre." *Journal of Popular Music Studies* 22, no. 3: 240–58.

David, Marlo. 2007. "Afrofuturism and Post-Soul Possibility in Black Popular Music." *African American Review* 41, no. 4: 695–707.

Further Listening

D'Angelo. 2000. *Voodoo.* Virgin.

Hill, Lauryn. 1998. *The Miseducation of Lauryn Hill.* Ruffhouse Records.

Nepal

Nepal has a burgeoning hip hop scene, featuring its own style of the music, nicknamed "Nephop" by New York City–based underground rapper Aroz (Aroz Kunal, n.d.). The Nephop scene includes MCing or rapping, DJing (turntablism), b-boying (breakdancing), and the creation of graffiti art, and is centralized mainly in Kathmandu. Although in 2000 Rappaz Union (2000*–) created the first Nepalese rap album in English, Nephop evolved in 2002 when Kathmandu rapper, songwriter, and radio disc jockey Gorkhali G. (aka Girish Pranil, Girish Khatiwada, 1982–), working with an early version of the Nepali rap group the Unity (n.d.) on the album *Back Again*, went beyond the electronic mixing of classical Nepalese songs with an urban beat to releasing songs with original, commercial beats.

Considered one of the best Nephop rappers, Gorkhali G. (recording as Girish, with the Unity) released "Ma yesto chhu, Ma usto chhu" (roughly, "I'm Like This, I'm Like That"), which introduced Nepalese to a regular synth beat accompanied by chantlike, measured rapped lyrics. Following the success of this and other songs, Gorkhali G. later released a well received solo album, *Dropout* (2008). "Ma Yesto Chu Ma usto chu" gained enough popularity with Nepalese that in 2003, fellow Kathmandu rapper Nurbu Sherpa was able to gain traction with his debut album *Nurbu Sherpa Representin' K.T.M.C.*, which showed obvious Western influences: English lyrics, geographically based calls for representation, the use of autotuning, a danceable beat, rapid-fire rapping, and appearances by Aroz.

The Unity released its first full album in 2004, *Girish and The Unity Presents X with Girish Khatiwada*, which included "She's the Bomb," a song which featured turntable scratching and R&B singing, along with rap; "Malai vote deu" ("Give Me the Vote"), a satirical political song from the same album, added heavy bass, reggae beats, and sound samples of gun shots. The hero of the Nepalese underground hip hop scene is Mc Flo (Anuraag Sharma, n.d.), who since 2009 has released six mixtapes to a cult following.

Anthony J. Fonseca

See also: India

Further Reading

Greene, Paul. 2001. "Mixed Messages: Unsettled Cosmopolitanisms in Nepali Pop." *Popular Music* 20, no. 2: 169–87.

Tingey, Carol. 1994. *Auspicious Music in a Changing Society: The Damai Musicians of Nepal*. London: University of London, School of Oriental and African Studies.

Nerdcore

Nerdcore is a subgenre of American hip hop in which the artists rap about topics not typically addressed in mainstream hip hop as they are considered uncool, such as playing video games and other types of gaming, engaging in role-playing or LARPing (live-action role-playing), being a fan of the *Star Wars* franchise (1977–), enjoying fine literature, mastering computer skills, and suffering from social awkwardness or rejection. The musicians most prominently affiliated with the subgenre are Brooklyn-based MC Frontalot (Damian Hess, 1973–), mc chris (Christopher Brendan Ward IV, 1975–), and MC Lars (Andrew Robert Nielsen, 1982–). MC Frontalot coined the term nerdcore in the song "Nerdcore Hiphop" (2000). Although nerdcore rappers are superficially connected by their topical interests, several artists acknowledge that their music within the genre is actually linked by sense of isolation and marginalization. For both the musicians and the listeners, many of whom are interested in topics that are far outside the mainstream or who have difficulties with social skills, nerdcore hip hop offers a chance to belong to a community.

MUSICAL STYLES AND TOPICS

Nerdcore is one of the earliest forms of what can be called laptop hip hop, a subgenre in which all the materials of production and recording are contained in the producer's laptop. Although most nerdcore rappers, such as MC Lars, MC Hawking (Ken Lawrence, 1970*–), YTCracker (Bryce Case Jr., 1982–), and Sammus (Enongo Lumumba-Kasongo, 1986–), produce their own beats, some artists do collaborate with producers. In the early part of his career, mc chris worked with producer John Fewell (1980*–), but since 2008, his music has been produced by Andrew Futral (1982*–). Most of MC Frontalot's tracks are created in collaboration with

Canadian producer Baddd Spellah (David T. Cheong, 1972*–) and American keyboardist Gminor7 (Gabriel Alter, n.d.). MC Router (Kristin Nicole Ritchie, 1986–) and producer T-Byte (Tanner Brown, n.d.) were frequent collaborators, as are American rapper int eighty (David Martinjak, n.d.) and English producer c64 (Chris Hunger, n.d.), who form the duo Dual Core (2007–).

Nerdcore's most notable songs are those that address a variety of intellectual, obsessive, and social skills–related interests. MC Frontalot's "Yellow Lasers" (2005) and mc chris's "Fett's 'vette" (2001) are about obsession with the *Star Wars* films and franchise. Beefy's (Keith A. Moore, 1985–) "Join My Guild" (2010) addresses online role-playing games. MC Hawking's "Entropy" (2004) and Sammus's "Mae Jemison" (2014) are informed by science jargon and interests. "Level Up" (2009), by Zealous1 (Beau Fa'asamala, 1983–) is an ode to the massive multiplayer online role-playing game *World of Warcraft* (2004–), and Dual Core's "Natural 20s" (2009) is full of references to the tabletop game *Dungeons and Dragons* (1974–), as well as to other nerdcore artists. Nerdcore lyrics occasionally take on political or social issues, but usually only in the context of nerd identity and interests. For example, MC Hawking's "F— the Creationists" (2004) admonishes those who deny the existence of evolution, and MC Lars's "Download This Song" (2006) rails against record labels for not updating their sales practices to keep up with new technology.

Overall, video games play an important role in the music of many nerdcore artists. Mega Ran (aka Random, Raheem Jarbo, 1977–), whose name is a play on the 1980s Capcom video game character Mega Man, not only raps about video games but also frequently samples video game music for his beats. His album *Black Materia* (2011, released under the name Random) was based entirely on the 1997 Sony PlayStation game *Final Fantasy VII* in both its lyric content and its samples and production. YTCracker's album *NerdRap Entertainment System* (2005) features sampled and remixed music from the original 1980s-era 8-bit Nintendo Entertainment System.

Nerdcore lyrics also focus on social and romantic relationships, but tracks about relationships usually emphasize awkwardness or ineptitude. For example, MC Lars's "Internet Relationships (Are Not Real Relationships)" (2006) cautions listeners about the pitfalls of meeting friends or romantic partners online. In "On*" (2008), mc chris pleads with the navigation program OnStar to help him find a woman's clitoris. When tracks pertain to romantic relationships, nerdcore artists (the majority of whom rap in the character of the heterosexual male) often address specific groups or types of women, as in mc chris's "Nrrrd Grrrl" (2008), Beefy's "Game Store Girl" (2010), MC Lars's "Hipster Girl" (2009), and MC Frontalot's "Goth Girls" (2005). In these and other tracks, nerdcore rappers primarily lament their inability to flirt or otherwise talk to women in whom they are interested. The rare tales of romantic success often include nerd-identified women. For example, in "Dork Date" (2008), Beefy raps about inviting a girl to the comic book store, a Comic-Con convention, and an mc chris show.

KEY ARTISTS

MC Frontalot is generally regarded as the father of nerdcore hip hop by both musicians and critics. Although he had been releasing his music online since 1999 through the online competition Song Fight!, his breakthrough came in 2002, when the web comic Penny Arcade (1998–) declared him their official MC. In response, he recorded "Penny Arcade Theme" (2002), which has become one of his signature tracks. MC Frontalot's first full-length album, *Nerdcore Rising*, was not completed until 2005, and it contained a mixture of new tracks as well as rerecorded demos and Song Fight! entries.

In 2001, mc chris released his first full-length studio album, *Life's a B— and I'm Her Pimp*. Many of mc chris's tracks are aligned with nerdcore subjects, and although he is often affiliated with the nerdcore hip hop movement, mc chris himself does not claim to be associated with any specific genre or style of hip hop. For several years, he actively distanced himself from nerdcore hip hop, but in the 2010s he became less resistant to the affiliation, acknowledging himself as a person who raps about nerd life. Unlike other artists associated with nerdcore hip hop, mc chris's lyrics are often explicit and sometimes violent or aggressive.

MC Lars is generally associated with the nerdcore hip hop genre because his lyrics frequently refer to video games, literature and poetry, and a lack of social skills. MC Lars proclaims himself the originator of post-punk laptop rap because he was one of the first hip hop artists to sample post-punk recordings in his production. As a producer, he often samples recordings of American and British punk bands of various eras, including Fugazi (1987–2002), Supergrass (1993–2010), and Brand New (2000–).

MC Hawking, an animated and sometimes Photoshopped depiction of English theoretical physicist Stephen Hawking (1942–2018), is associated with lyrics that address stereotypical rap topics such as drive-by shootings, as in "All My Shootings Be Drive-bys" (2004), as well as more nerdcore-oriented topics such as science, as in "What We Need More of is Science" (2004). MC Hawking's rhymes are rendered in WillowTalk, the same computer program that Hawking has used to communicate since the 1980s when he became disabled and unable to speak as a result of amyotrophic lateral sclerosis (ALS).

RECEPTION AND DISSEMINATION

Most nerdcore hip hop is disseminated online, either through artists' websites or through file-sharing programs such as BitTorrent. No nerdcore artist is signed to a major label, although MC Lars founded his own independent record label, Horris Records (2006–), and YT Cracker created the label Nerdy South Records (2006). Most nerdcore artists acknowledge that they will not earn much money from selling their music because most of their listeners are technologically savvy enough to acquire it without paying. Instead, nerdcore artists earn revenue from tours and sales of merchandise.

Nerdcore hip hop artists frequently collaborate with each other as well as with artists from hip hop and a variety of other genres. MC Lars has collaborated with mc chris and MC Frontalot, in addition to recording with mainstream hip hop artists such as KRS-One (1965–) and Kool Keith (1963–), rock groups such as Wheatus (1995–), and rock musicians such as Roger Lima (1974–) and Jaret Reddick (1972–). MC Frontalot has recorded with other nerdcore artists, including MC

Hawking and Canadian rapper Jesse Dangerously (Jesse McDonald, 1979–), in addition to more mainstream hip hop artists such as South African–born American rapper Jean Grae (1976–) and Canadian DJ and turntablist Kid Koala (Eric San, 1974–). Further, MC Lars has opened for Nas (1973–) and Snoop Dogg (1971–).

MAINSTREAM RECOGNITION AND COLLABORATIONS

MC Frontalot is one of the most prominent and outspoken members of the nerdcore hip hop community, having been interviewed by major news outlets such as National Public Radio (United States) and *Newsweek* magazine. MC Frontalot and his collaborators were the subjects of *Nerdcore Rising*, a 2008 documentary named for MC Frontalot's track and album and which also included interviews with other nerdcore artists: MC Lars, Beefy, and YT Cracker. MC Frontalot has also made a decent showing in mainstream pop culture, appearing as a guest judge in 2013 on the TBS reality show *King of the Nerds* (2013–2015) and performing the original track "Toilet Paper Factory" in the *Sesame Street* direct-to-DVD *Elmo's Potty Time* (2005).

Beginning his career as a writer and animator for several television shows on Adult Swim, the late-night animated television program block that airs on the Turner Broadcasting System's Cartoon Network, mc chris worked on programs including *Space Ghost Coast to Coast* (1994–2008), *Sealab 2021* (2000–2005), and *Aqua Teen Hunger Force* (2000–2015). His breakout role came when he voice-acted the character MC Pee Pants (and his alter ego, Sir Loin) on *Aqua Teen Hunger Force* in the early 2000s. He left Adult Swim permanently in 2004 (approximately the time his third album, *Eating's Not Cheating*, was released) to focus on his recording career. Since then, however, he has written and starred in several animated pilot projects.

At the 2016 STARMUS Festival, which was a tribute to Stephen Hawking, MC Hawking, in collaboration with MC Lars, presented a mockumentary film about the travails of MC Hawking as well as a set of music, including the new single "Fear of a Black Hole," a play on the name of the 1990 Public Enemy (1982–) album with Def Jam Recordings (1983–) *Fear of a Black Planet*.

MC Lars is active in a variety of education initiatives. He has given multiple TED Talks on the roles of poetic meter in literature, poetry, and hip hop lyrics. In 2012, he was featured at Scholastic's Art and Writing Awards, which was held at New York's Carnegie Hall. During this performance, he performed "Flow Like Poe," an analysis of poetic meter in the works of 19th-century American poet and author Edgar Allan Poe (1809–1849) that is rapped over a sample of the 17th-century Canon in D composed by Johann Pachelbel (1653–1706).

Amanda Sewell

See also: Chap Hop; mc chris; MC Frontalot; MC Lars; The United States

Further Reading

Braiker, Brian. 2007. "Geeksta Rap Rising." *Newsweek* 149, no. 5: 58.

Colgan, Jim. 2005. "Nerd Hip Hop, Flowing Like Han Solo." *Day to Day* (National Public Radio), November 7.

Sewell, Amanda. 2015. "Nerdcore Hip Hop." In *The Cambridge Companion to Hip Hop*, edited by Justin Williams, chap. 16. Cambridge, England: Cambridge University Press.

Further Listening
mc chris. 2001. *Life's a B— and I'm Her Pimp*. Self-released.
mc chris. 2008. *mc chris is dead*. mc chris LLC.
MC Frontalot. 2005. *Nerdcore Rising*. Level Up Records and Tapes.
MC Hawking. 2004. *A Brief History of Rhyme: MC Hawking's Greatest Hits*. Brash Music.
MC Lars. 2006. *The Graduate*. Horris Records/Nettwerk America.
Mega Ran (also known as Random). 2011. *Black Materia*. Random Beats Productions.
YTCracker. 2006. *Nerd Life*. Nerdy South Records.

Further Viewing
Farsad, Negin, dir. 2008. *Nerdcore Rising*. New York: Vaguely Qualified Productions.
Lamoreux, Dan, dir. 2008. *Nerdcore for Life*. N.p.: Crapbot Productions.

The Netherlands

The Netherlands' hip hop culture has been defined by its internal struggle to characterize and cultivate authenticity in Dutch forms of hip hop. The earliest Dutch rap was performed in the 1980s by black youth of Afro-Caribbean heritage who adapted American hip hop hits by translating their lyrics into Dutch. These Dutch rappers and their audiences formed a subculture based on a set of values and attitudes shaped by their common experiences of poverty, unemployment, drugs, and inequality. By 1982, Dutch hip hop artists were creating their own beats, rhymes, and breakdance routines, but these Dutch efforts remained a small, scattered, underground phenomenon, based largely in urban areas of the Randstad (a region that houses most of the population from former Dutch colonies and migrants), throughout much of the 1980s.

At the same time as Dutch hip hop was developing underground, the commercialization of American hip hop brought an urban hip hop sound to mass audiences in the Netherlands, most notably with the Sugarhill Gang's (1979–1985, 1994–) "Rapper's Delight" (1979), which reached No. 1 on Dutch national charts. Dutch audiences were also captivated by the works of white rock artists who appropriated rap in a commercial idiom, producing hits such as Blondie's (1974–1982, 1997–) "Rapture" (1981) and the Tom Tom Club's (1981–) "Wordy Rappinghood" (1981). Dutch mass culture's interest in American hip hop was reinforced by Hollywood films such as *Breakin'* (aka *Breakdance,* 1984), *Breakin' 2: Electric Boogaloo* (1984), and *Colors* (1988). By the mid-1990s, American rappers and groups such as Wu-Tang Clan (1992–), Tupac Shakur (1971–1996) and Fugees (1992–1997) had found a ready market in the Netherlands.

NEDERHOP AND DEVELOPMENT

The developing presence of Dutch hip hop, which came to be called Nederhop, led to internal arguments regarding authenticity. A number of old-school Dutch rappers of the 1980s were from the ghetto, and most were black—from Surinam or the Antilles. They found musical role models in American hip hop and felt they shared the experiences of ghetto life, poverty and inequality that formed the background to many American hip hop songs of that era. As a result, Dutch rap music that did not have a ghetto feel was deemed inauthentic. As MCs were hired to rap over house music in the late 1980s, and rappers signed deals with commercial producers, the Dutch rappers who considered themselves authentic sought to distance themselves publicly from those who had, in their opinions, sold out.

Hardcore hip hop artists from that period who earned a degree of commercial success include the group DAMN (Don't Accept Mass Notion, 1989–1993), who with their self-titled 1989 debut offered the first full-length album of Dutch hip hop; Osdorp Posse (OP, 1989–2009), whose gangsta-style Dutch lyrics featured in its debut album, *Osdorp Stil* (*Osdorp Style*, 1992), delivered a hardcore message with direct translations of American slang; King Bee (1989–2000*), whose hits "Back by Dope Demand" and "Must Bee the Music" from the album *Royal Jelly* (1990) topped Dutch charts; and rap group 24K (1989*–), whose album *No Enemies* (1990) took on socially conscious issues such as poverty, drugs, racism, and violence.

NEDERHOP SAMPLING AND BLENDING WITH OTHER GENRES

At the same time, many commercially successful Dutch hip hop records blended rap with more popular genres. MC Miker G (Lucien Witteveen, n.d.) and DJ Sven (Sven van Veen, n.d.) released their rap-pop hit "Holiday Rap" in 1986, sampling Madonna's (1958–) "Holiday" (1983). The Urban Dance Squad (1986–2000) had gained broad popularity with their rap-rock-metal-funk hybrid sound. In 1998, the Postmen (1996–2003, 2012–) released the chart-topping hit "Cocktail," mixing reggae and rap to deliver an uplifting message about the value of life, while E-Life (Elvis de Oliveira, n.d.) in the same year released "More Days to Come," blending R&B with hip hop.

Extince (Peter Kops, 1967–) blends rock and pop with a soft, flowing rap style, delivering humorous rhymes in a soft, southern Dutch dialect. His single "Spraakwater" was a tremendous hit in 1995, with its samples from the Dutch children's television series *De fabeltjeskrant* (*The Fables Newspaper*) and its play on the word "mouthwash" as an extended metaphor for delivering rhymes. While these musical blends have expanded Nederhop's popularity, hardcore artists have decried them as sellouts; in 1996, hardcore group OP released the hip hop single "Braakwater" ("Vomit") as a parody of "Spraakwater," just one example of the many diss tracks that have come out of conflicts (often ideological) between Dutch rappers.

FEMALE ARTISTS, AUTHENTICITY, AND THE 21ST CENTURY

Questions of authenticity have also figured into the role of women in Dutch rap: hardcore Dutch rap followed the rules of masculinity to so great an extent that female rappers were not considered authentic. Some female hip hop groups such as Odie3 (a homonym of Oh, These 3, 1998*–), Nasty (Bianc Boyd, n.d.), and B—ez and Cream (n.d.) have challenged that notion while also feeling pressured to fulfill stereotypical images of femininity—from the innocent virgin to the femme fatale—in order to have their music taken seriously.

During the 21st century, Dutch hip hop has slowly gained attention from the Dutch population at large, with bands such as Relax (1998–) and Spookrijders (1996–) receiving significant airplay on Dutch radio. The group Opgezwolle (Swollen, 1997–2007) released an album entitled *Eigen Wereld* (Own World, 2006) featuring collaborations with rappers Jawat! (Raoul Geerman, 1977–) and others, reaching No. 4 on the Album Top 100, the highest chart ranking of any Dutch rap album. In the same year, MC Jawat (Raoul Geerman, n.d.) won an award at the *Grote Prijs van Nederland* (the Netherlands Grand Prize, an annual music award that recognizes the talents of new Dutch musicians, both solo artists and bands).

By the 2010s, the Dutch hip hop scene boasted over 100 hip hop acts, most associated with the Netherlands' larger cities: Alkmaar, Almere, Alphen aan den Rijn, Amersfoort, Amsterdam, Breda, Delft, Den Haag, Deventer, Eindhoven, Groningen, Nijmegen, Oosterhout, Roermond, Rotterdam, 's-Hertogenbosch, Utrecht, Vlissingen, Zwolle, and Zoetermeer. Many rappers, such as Brainpower (Gertjan Mulder, 1975–), OP, Yes-R (Yesser Roushdy, 1986–), Ali B (Ali Bouali, 1981–), Lange Frans (Frans Christiaan Frederiks, 1980–), and Extince continue to enjoy commercial success and tour internationally to establish Dutch hip hop as its own genre, with ties to Dutch cultural identity.

Jennifer L. Roth-Burnette

See also: Belgium; The United States

Further Reading

Krims, Adam. 2000. "Two Cases of Localized (and Globalized) Musical Poetics." In *Rap Music and the Poetics of Identity*, chap. 5. New York: Cambridge University Press.

Wermuth, Mir. 2001. "Rap in the Low Countries: Global Dichotomies on a National Scale." In *Global Noise: Rap and Hip Hop Outside the U.S.A.*, edited by Tony Mitchell, pp. 149–70. Middletown, CT: Wesleyan University Press.

Further Listening

Extince. 2015. *X.* TopNotch.

MC Jawat. 2005. *Ut zwarte aap (Ook Black Monkey)*. TopNotch.

Odie 3. 1998. *Odie 3.* Fonos.

New Jack Swing

(aka Swingbeat)

New jack swing is an American popular music genre that fuses hip hop elements with R&B, sometimes including funk and gospel. It was especially popular from 1987 to 1993, with unsuccessful revival efforts in 2000.

R&B and hip hop singer-songwriter, keyboardist, and producer Teddy Riley (Edward Theodore Riley, 1967–) created the sound for nightclubs in Harlem, New

York, but producers such as Babyface (1959–), Bernard Belle (1984–), Jimmy Jam (James Samuel Harris III, 1959–), Terry Lewis (1956–), and L.A. Reid (Antonio Marquis Reid, 1956–) followed suit. Some notable early example songs are Janet Jackson's (1966–) "Nasty" (1986), Club Nouveau's (1986–) "Lean on Me" (1986), Keith Sweat's (1961–) "I Want Her" (1987), and Bobby Brown's (1969–) "Don't Be Cruel" (recorded in 1987, released in 1988).

In 1987, writer Barry Michael Cooper (n.d.) named the music new jack swing in his *Village Voice* article, "Teddy Riley's New Jack Swing." American music producer, composer, musician, arranger, magazine founder, and actor Quincy Jones (1933–) read Cooper's article and asked Riley to work on the screenplay for the American crime thriller film *New Jack City* (1991). Its soundtrack included Sweat's "(There You Go) Tellin' Me No Again" (1987) and Christopher Williams's (Troy Christopher Williams, 1967–) "I'm Dreamin'" (1991). In 1989, Riley produced Wreckx-n-Effect's (1987–1996, 2014–) "New Jack Swing" to perpetuate the genre's popularity. Though it did not chart on the Billboard Hot 100, the single peaked at No. 1 on the Billboard's Hot Rap Tracks.

INSTRUMENTATION AND SWINGBEAT RHYTHM

New jack swing tends to showcase vocoder-aided vocals. It also employs typical instruments found in hip hop, such as drum machines (providing kick and snare drums and tambourines), synthesizers (ranging from electronic keyboard sounds to virtual symphonic orchestras), and scratch tones from turntablism. A funky bassline—played or sampled by either a synthesizer or bass guitar—is also added. Typical musical hardware used to create sampled beats were the E-mu SP-1200 sampler and the programmable Roland TR-808 (aka Roland TR-808 Rhythm Composer) drum machine. The usual synthesizer, if added, was either a Roland W30 or Yamaha S30. Rhythm and meter are repetitive and consistent.

Using 4/4 (quadruple meter, four beats to a measure) and a tempo typically between 100 (ballad) and 112 (dance) bpm (beats per minute), new jack swing musicians created repeated or looped core beats with kick drum beats on the first (heaviest) and third beats, combined with rapid snare drum beats that fall on the and-beats and on beats two and four. The latter results in the swing beat and syncopation. Tambourine and rapid synthesized sudden, brief orchestral sounds are used to enhance beats one and three, as well as to indicate the end of some phrases. Snare rolls also signify the end of some phrases. Sixteenth-note triplets with their first beats accented for each eighth-note value produce the swingbeat shuffle—for example, "one-and-two-and-three-and-four-and" would have snare or high hat hits three times on each word (representing an eighth-note value). The rhythmic foundation and swingbeat shuffle is found in Paula Abdul's (1962–) dance-pop hit "Straight Up" (1988).

GLOBAL PRESENCE

Into the early 1990s Billboard's Hot 100 and/or Billboard Hot R&B/Hip-Hop Singles charts were topped by new jack swing songs as well as songs that contained new jack swing elements, including Bobby Brown's "My Perogative" (1988), New Edition's (1978–1990, 1996–1997, 2002–) "If It Isn't Love" (1988), Al B. Sure's (Albert Joseph Brown III, 1968–) "Nite and Day" (1988), Babyface's "It's No Crime" (1989), Bel Biv DeVoe's (BBD, 1989–) "Poison" (1990), New Edition's Johnny Gill's "Rub You the Right Way" (1990), Boyz II Men's (1985–) "Motownphilly" (1991), and Tony! Toni! Toné's (1988–1997, 2003–) "Feels Good" (1990) and "If I Had No Loot" (1993); however, hits were not limited to the United States.

Global success stories included songs that charted in the United Kingdom, Australia, Canada, New Zealand, and Sweden. These include Bahamian singer Johnny Kemp's (Jonathan Kemp, 1959–2015) "Just Got Paid" (1988), Stockholm-born and England-raised Neneh Cherry's (1964–) "Buffalo Stance" (1988), English R&B and soul band Soul II Soul's (1988–1997, 2007–) "Keep on Movin'" and "Back to Life (However Do You Want Me)" (1989), Canadian singer Jane Child's (Jane Richman, 1967–) "Don't Wanna Fall in Love" (1990), and Australian singer Kylie Minogue's (1968–) "Word Is Out" (1991). New jack swing was also not limited to English texts. For example, the French group Tribal Jam (1994–1998), with members from Zaire, recorded several new jack swing songs using French texts. Efforts to explore new jack swing as a retro sound have taken place globally as well, as in South Korea, where BtoB's (Born to Beat, 2012–) hit "WOW" (2012) employed new jack swing.

Melissa Ursula Dawn Goldsmith

See also: Babyface; Jones, Quincy; The United States

Further Reading

Frane, Andrew V. 2017. "Swing Rhythm in Classic Drum Breaks from Hip-Hop's Breakbeat Canon." *Music Perception* 34, no. 3: 291–302.

Kojima, Rie, Teruo Nomura, and Noriyuki Kida. 2016. "Expressing Joy through Hip Hop Dance Steps: Focus on New Jack Swing." *Journal of Music and Dance* 6, no. 1: 1–11.

Lena, Jennifer C. 2006. "Social Context and Musical Content of Rap Music, 1979–95." *Social Forces* 85, no. 1: 479–83, 486–87, 489–95.

Further Listening

Keith Sweat. 1987. *Make It Last Forever.* Elektra.

Tribal Jam. 1994. *Tribal Jam.* EMI Music France.

New York City Breakers

(NYCB, aka NYC Breakers, 1981–, Bronx, New York)

New York City Breakers is a pioneering breakdancing (b-boy) crew that rivaled its Bronx, New York, contemporaries, the Rock Steady Crew (RSC, 1977–). NYCB appeared on *The Merv Griffin Show* (1962–1986), *Soul Train* (1971–2006), as well as on many other television shows and in seminal hip hop films such as *Beat Street* (1984). NYCB was the first hip hop act to perform for a current president when they danced in a 1984 *Kennedy Center Honors* show in front of then–American president Ronald Reagan (1911–2004, in office 1981–1989). At the time, NYCB's power moves included head, neck, and fist glides, in addition to head spins. The original members included Action (Chino Lopez, n.d.), Glide Master (Matthew Caban, n.d.), Lil Lep (Ray Ramos, n.d.), Kid Nice (Noel Mangual, n.d.), and Powerful Pexster (Tony Lopez, n.d.).

Originally known as Floormasters Crew, led by Action, from the Kingsbridge section of the Bronx, NYCB was created after Action becoming inspired while attending a breakdancing battle between the RSC and the Dynamic Rockers (1970–1980)* from Queens that took place in front of Lincoln Center. In 1982, the crew changed its name, as well as some of its earliest members (who remain unknown), after it defeated the RSC in battle at Negril, a club in New York City. The club's owner, Michael Holman (n.d.), a prominent hip hop impresario, music producer, filmmaker, writer, and musician, had already secured RSC as a regular act, but he wanted to host a battle instead of always hosting just one breakdancing crew. His earlier production credits included the first staged hip hop revue (1981). As a journalist, Holman is often credited as being the first writer to have the words "hip hop" published. After this battle, Holman became NYCB's manager and promoter. In 1984, Holman showcased the crew in the American film *Beat Street*, which he cowrote and coproduced, and on the first American hip hop television show *Graffiti Rock* (1984), which he created, wrote, and produced.

NYCB toured extensively worldwide and became the inspiration for other breakdancing crews. For example, the Paris City Breakers (PCB, 1984–) was a crew modeled on the NYCB after founding members attended a Gianni Ferrucci (n.d.) fashion show in Paris that featured Madonna (1958–) and the NYCB. Most of the PCB's moves, especially head spins, were styled after the NYCB; the PCB elaborated on these moves and at times refined them through cleaner and more intricate footwork than the NYCB. Years after the height of its success, and despite personnel changes, the crew has expanded. As of 2018, NYCB is an organization that still appears in breakdancing showcases and teaches hip hop dance workshops worldwide.

Melissa Ursula Dawn Goldsmith

See also: Battling; Breakdancing; Filmmaking (Feature Films Made in the United States); Hip Hop Dance; Paris City Breakers; The United States

Further Reading

Foster, Catherine. 1983. "'New' Dance Craze Blends Acrobatics, Mime, and Inventiveness." *The Christian Science Monitor*, October 14.

Fricke, Jim, and Charlie Ahearn. 2002. *The Experience Music Project Oral History of Hip Hop's First Decade: Yes Yes Y'All.* Cambridge, MA: Da Capo Press.

Schloss, Joseph G. 2009. *Foundation: B-Boys, B-Girls, and Hip Hop Culture in New York.* New York: Oxford University Press.

New Zealand

New Zealand's hip hop scene occurred as soon as the American gang culture film *The Warriors* (1979) and the Sugarhill Gang's (1979–1985, 1994–) "Rapper's Delight" (1979) reached the country. In 1980, "Rapper's Delight" peaked at No. 18 on New Zealand's hit song charts. Main centers for early hip hop activity emerged in Christchurch and Wellington, followed by Auckland. The country consists of the North Island and South Island (Te Ika-a-Maui and Te Waipounamu, meaning "The Fish of Maui" and "The Place of Greenstone" in Māori) and is located 900 nautical miles east of Australia. Mostly populated by people of European descent, New Zealand's second-largest population is the Māori people—indigenous Polynesians whose culture and language became the focus of the country's 1980s and 1990s preservation efforts. In recognition of its indigenous cultural history, another Māori word for the North Island, "Aotearoa" ("land of the long white cloud") is now used unofficially alongside "New Zealand."

EARLY HIP HOP

Old-school hip hop and reggae especially resonated with Māori and Polynesian communities. Some of the earliest successful New Zealand hip hop songs incorporated traditional Māori texts, political messages about preserving and supporting Māori culture, and the old-school sound—simple end rhymes, beat machine generated beats, funk and R&B elements, and simple lyrical refrains. In 1983, Dalvinus Prime's (Maui Dalvanius Prime, 1948–2002) "Poi E," recorded by Prince Tui Teka (aka Tui Latui, Tumanako Teka, 1937–1985) with the backing band Patea Māori Club (1983–1986)*, was the first song that fused contemporary Māori folk music with hip hop. The song's video featured traditional *poi* dancing and breakdancing (windmills and popping). Its message, to discover one's own culture, was geared toward young Māori people. "Poi E" peaked at No. 1 on New Zealand's hit singles chart. In 1988, the reggae-rap fusion group Upper Hutt Posse (UHP, 1985–) had a hit with "E tū" (aka "Stand Proud"), the first hip hop single performed by a group fully from New Zealand. Hailing from Upper Hutt, a region of Wellington, UHP was a political hip hop

Christchurch-based rapper Scribe and Auckland-based DJ P-Money collaborate during the 2005 New Zealand Music Awards ceremony held at The Aotea Centre in Auckland. A year earlier, DJ P-Money's single "Stop the Music" (featuring Scribe), from the album *Magic City*, reached No. 1 and was certified Platinum in New Zealand and certified Gold in Australia. (Phil Walter/Getty Images)

group that supported Māori sovereignty. Subsequent New Zealand groups such as Moana and the Moahunters (later Moana and the Tribe, 1990–1998, 2002–), from Auckland, eventually toured worldwide. By the mid-1990s the Urban Pasifika sound emerged.

URBAN PASIFIKA

Urban Pasifika is an Auckland-based hip hop style that combines Māori and other South Pacific Island instrumentation with English and other South Pacific Island languages, Pacific Island roots music, and African American musical genres such as hip hop, jazz, R&B, soul, Jamaican reggae, and dancehall. It may also incorporate elements of European and American punk rock and electronic dance music, including disco and dubstep. The first Urban Pasifika album was *Proud: An Urban Pacific Streetsoul Compilation* (1994), a collection recorded and cowritten by multi-instrumentalist for the Auckland-based band Otara Millionaires Club's (OMC, 1993–2010) music producer Alan Jansson (Pakeha Alan Jansson, n.d.). Auckland-born Urban Pasifika pioneer Phillip Fuemana (1964–2005) organized and promoted the *Proud* tour in New Zealand in 1994. The tour included Jansson and others featured on the album, including OMC and Sisters Underground (1990–1995). Though it failed financially, the tour led to national exposure and interest in Urban Pasifika; the Sydney label Volition (1984–2000) reissued the album and produced a 12-inch album by Sisters Underground, *In the Neighbourhood* (1995).

As one of the founding members of OMC, Fuemana was a mentor to many Auckland musicians during the 1980s and 1990s. He and his younger brother Pauly (1969–2010), also of OMC), worked with Jansson, who became one of the leading music producers of New Zealand. In 1996, OMC sold over four million copies worldwide of *How Bizarre* (1996), produced on the Huh! Records label (1995–). In 1997, it peaked at No. 40 on the Billboard 200, while the title song peaked at No. 1 on Billboard's Mainstream Top 40/Contemporary Hit Radio chart. In 1998, Fuemana released *Pioneers of a Pacifikan Frontier* on his independent Polynesian label, Urban Pacifika Records (1993*–), leading to global recognition of Urban Pasifika.

Twenty-first-century Urban Pasifika consists of many of the basic elements of its formative years, with increased emphasis on a laid-back island-inspired sound, with reggae as the main influence for bass and guitar; a concentration on Polynesian (Māori) pride and politics; and an incorporation of new-school hip hop, electronic dance music, and jazz. More current notable Urban Pasifika musicians include Auckland-based artists Che Fu (Che Kuo Eruera Ness, 1974–), Dei Hamo (aka Sani, Sanerivi Sagala, 1975–), Savage (Demetrius Savelio, 1981–), Nesian Mystik (1999–) and the duo Adeaze (2003–), as well as Wellington-based King Kapisi (Bill Urale, 1974–). Many of these artists have performed worldwide and with famous American hip hop artists such as Afrika Bambaataa (1957–), Shaggy (1968–), Missy Elliott (1971–), and the Black Eyed Peas (1995–). Since the turn of the century, many Urban Pasifika artists have recorded on internationally recognized labels such as BMG (1987–2008), Epic (1953–), and Sony (1929–).

INTO THE 21ST CENTURY

The New Zealand hip hop scene continues to expand and includes a large number of rappers and groups that have had success at least in Australia, if not worldwide. Tastes have ultimately included instrumental hip hop, hardcore, and nerdcore. Prominent New Zealand hip hop crews and rappers often turn to English texts to become internationally famous, yet they are still somewhat diverse (European, Samoan, and non–Māori Pacific Islanders). The music still focuses on discrimination and inequality, economic disparity, social action, and politics. Among others, notable artists and crews include Auckland-based Homebrew (2007–2013), Mareko (Mark Saga Polutele, 1981–), Deceptikonz (1996–), Frontline (2001–), Smashproof (2009–), and P-Money (Peter Wadams, 1978–); Christchurch-based Scribe (aka Malo Luafutu, Jeshua Ioane Luafutu, 1979–); Palmerston North City–based PNC (Sam Hansen, n.d.); and Wellington-based Tommy III (n.d.).

Melissa Ursula Dawn Goldsmith

See also: Australia; Moana and the Moahunters; Otara Millionaires Club; Reggae; Upper Hutt Posse

Further Reading

Hapeta, Dean. 2000. "Hip Hop in Aotearoa/New Zealand." In *Changing Sounds: New Directions and Configurations in Popular Music*, edited by Tony Mitchell and Peter Doyle, pp. 202–7. Sydney, Australia: University of Technology, Faculty of Humanities and Social Sciences.

Johnson, Henry. 2010. *Many Voices: Music and National Identity in Aotearoa/New Zealand.* New Castle upon Tyne, England: Cambridge Scholars.

Shute, Gareth. 2004. *Hip Hop Music in Aotearoa.* Auckland, New Zealand: Reed.

Further Listening

Jansson, Alan. 1994. *Proud: An Urban-Pacific Streetsoul Compilation.* Second Nature Records/Volition.

Nesian Mystik. 2002. *Polysaturated.* Bounce Records/Universal.

Various Artists. 1998. *Urban Pacifica Records: Pioneers of a Pacifikan Frontier.* Urban Pacifika Records.

Nicki Minaj

(Onika Tanya Maraj, 1982–, Port of Spain, Trinidad and Tobago)

Nicki Minaj is one of hip hop's most successful and critically acclaimed female acts. She combines smart, sometimes rapid wordplay with comedic and often risqué lyrics, parlaying her music career into a larger sphere with acting roles. Nicki Minaj radiates confidence in her performances, showing adeptness in both improvisational rap and in intricate prewritten rhymes. In 2009 and 2010, she was the featured guest on several songs for other artists, including Kanye West's (1977–) hit "Monster," and she produced a solo album, *Pink Friday* (2010), which was certified Platinum.

Onika Tanya Maraj, better known as Nicki Minaj, was born and partially raised in St. James, a district of Port of Spain, the capital city of Trinidad and Tobago. At a young age, however, her parents moved to New York, leaving her briefly with her grandmother. When she was five, she joined her parents in Queens, New York. An artistically gifted child, Maraj successfully auditioned for the prestigious Fiorello H. LaGuardia High School of Music and Art and the Performing Arts, where she was an acting major. After graduation, she had some success as an actor, but later turned her efforts to music.

In 2007, she signed with Dirty Money Entertainment (2006–2009)* under the stage name Nicki Minaj. Her first important success was the mixtape *Playtime is Over* (2007). She released another mixtape less than a year later, *Sucka Free* (2008), and caught the attention of the Underground Music Awards, which awarded her 2008's Female Artist of the Year prize. In 2009, another mixtape followed, *Beam Me Up Scotty*, featuring the single "I Get Crazy," which peaked at No. 20 on Billboard's Hot Rap Tracks and No. 37 on Billboard's Hot R&B/Hip-Hop Songs. She achieved greater fame after attracting the attention of rapper Lil Wayne (1982–), who in 2009 signed her to his label, Young Money Entertainment (2005–).

Nicki Minaj gained exposure by opening for Britney Spears (1981–) during Spears's Femme Fatale Tour in 2011. Nicki Minaj's second studio album *Pink Friday: Roman Reloaded* (2012) produced the singles "Starships" and "Right by My Side." Her third studio album, *The Pinkprint* (2014), featured "Anaconda," her breakthrough hit whose video reached nearly 20 million views in its first day.

Nicki Minaj has released three singles in support of her fourth studio album (yet to be released as of 2018). In 2017, she cowrote a song for rapper Jason Derulo (Jason Joel Desrouleaux, 1989–) and was featured on singles by Katy Perry (1984–) and Yo Gotti (Mario Mims, 1981–).

Nicki Minaj often slips into different personae—Harajuku Barbie and Roman Zolanski to name just two—on stage and off. She is known for elaborate outfits and makeup, and has been compared to Lady Gaga (1986–). Her rapping style, like her appearance, is eclectic. She is skilled at stereotypical hip hop boasts and posturing, and also displays a sharp cleverness in her complex wordplay and use of internal rhymes. Throughout her work, and especially in *Pinkprint*, she expresses the challenges of being a female rapper.

In 2013, she appeared as a judge on *American Idol* (2002–2016). In 2014, Nicki Minaj earned Grammy nominations for Best Rap Song for "Anaconda" and Best Pop Duo/Group Performance for "Bang Bang," with Jessie J (Jessica Ellen Cornish, 1988–) and Ariana Grande (Ariana Grande-Butera, 1993–). Recently, Nicki Minaj has built her acting resume, appearing in the films *The Other Woman* (2014) and *Barbershop: The Next Cut* (2016). In 2016, ABC Family cut the television series *Nicki* during its planning stage. The show would have been about Nicki Minaj's early years in Queens.

In 2017, Nicki Minaj surpassed Aretha Franklin for having more songs chart on the Billboard Hot 100 than any other female artist. She has also turned her attention to philanthropy. Through Twitter, Nicki Minaj offered to pay tuition, fees, or loans for 30 of her fans; she has also given donations for hurricane relief efforts after Hurricane Harvey hit Houston, and she has supported the development of small villages in India.

Christine Lee Gengaro

See also: Chopper; Dirty Rap; Fashion; Trinidad and Tobago; The United States

Further Reading

Jackson, Lauren Michele. 2017. "The Rapper Laughs, Herself: Nicki Minaj's Sonic Disturbances." *Feminist Media Studies* 17, no. 1: 126–29.

White, Theresa Renée. 2013. "Missy 'Misdemeanor' Elliott and Nicki Minaj: Fashionistin' Black Female Sexuality in Hip Hop Culture—Girl Power or Overpowered?" *Journal of Black Studies* 44, no. 6: 607–26.

Further Listening

Nicki Minaj. 2010. *Pink Friday.* Ca$h Money Records/Universal Motown.

Nicki Minaj. 2014. *The Pinkprint.* Young Money Entertainment.

Niger

Niger, the largest West African country, borders Nigeria, a country well known for its rap scene. Niger is composed mostly of the Sahara Desert, and because of severe droughts and its geography, it is one of the slowest developing African countries. Niger gained its independence in 1960 from France, but French remains the official language, though its populations speak Arabic, Buduma, Hausa, Fula, Zarma, and other languages. Most of the population is Hausa, followed by Zarma, Tuareg, and Fulani peoples. Until the late 1980s music was government-suppressed. By the 1990s, Tuareg blues, emerging from refugee camps, became Niger's best-known popular music. Rap Nigerien, the name for Nigerien hip hop, emerged in the mid-1990s, with capital city Niamey on the Niger River as the center of activity.

Rap Nigerien is mostly influenced by American, French, and Ivorian hip hop. Rapping texts often mix French, Hausa, and/or Zarma. Rap Nigerien's laidback sound often fuses hip hop with reggae, jazz, and traditional Nigerien and other West African music. Sampling is used and may include traditional musical instruments such as *tinde* (drums) or *xalam* (lutes). Topics range from sociopolitical hip hop, which protests corruption, economic equality, AIDS/HIV, and human trafficking and promotes peace and tolerance, to romance, marriage and family, adversity, and self-improvement—themes included in songs by Niger's most famous early hip hop groups, DLM (1994–2008*) and Les Black Daps (1997–).

In 1999, Lakal Kaney released the first rap Nigerien album, *La voix du ténére* (*The Voice of the Dark*). Cultural identifying lyrical content may also be added, as exemplified by the group WassWong (Hausa for Message of the Warriors, 2000–), a merger between two of the first rap Nigerien groups, Wassika Poussy (Hausa for Message and French for Posse, 1995–) and Wongari (Zarma for Warrior, 1996–); it was also important in later music by Berey Koy (Possessors of Knowledge, formerly Matassa and New Rap Connexion, NRC, 2000–). Other early groups were Lakal Kaney ("Peace of Mind" in Zarma, 1997–), Bagzam (1998–2009), Tchakey (1998–),

Metaphorecrew (2000–), Oneens (2003–), and Kaidan Gaskia ("To Act with the Truth" in Hausa, 1999–). Kaidan Gaskia's Khartoum, Sudan–born rapper, Safiat (Safiath Aminami Issoufou Oumarou, 1982–), was an early female rapper; her lyrics focus on Nigerien women's issues. ZM (Zara Moussa, 1980*–) was the first Nigerien female rapper and the first West African female hip hop recording artist.

Since the 2010s, Rap Nigerien fuses more R&B, Afropop, and trap. Some successful acts include Haské Klan (2004–), Federal Terminus Clan (aka FTC, Federal TC, 2006*–), Block S Crew (2009–), the female duo Crazy Girls (2012–), and Processus Verbal (2015*–), as well solo acts such as Alradik (aka Alradik Soldier, n.d.), Black Daps's Rass Idris (Patrice Idriss Guy, n.d.), Bagzam's Amiral JC (Mahamane Djadjé Amadou Touré, 1986–), and Metaphorecrew's Yasdi Maiwaka (aka Yas d. 1993*–). Hip hop has expanded to the city of Zinder, the origin of trap rapper Barakina (Barakina Issouf Omar, n.d.), and where hip hop acts such as rapper Kamikaz (aka Djoro G or Kadr Ali, Kaz Liman, 1980–) are being produced. From this period, a small number of diaspora acts exist. For example, Niamey-born rapper and singer Ismo One (Ismael Moussa Garba, 1985–), who records hip hop, reggae, and dancehall, has moved to further pursue his studies and hip hop career in the United States. Since 2015 Ismo One has collaborated with the Muslim rapping group MDM Crew (Méthode De la Morale, 2013*–).

Melissa Ursula Dawn Goldsmith

See also: France; Nigeria; Trap

Further Reading

Masquelier, Adeline. 2010. "God Made Me a Rapper: Young Men, Islam, and Survival in an Age of Austerity." In *Being and Becoming Hausa: Interdisciplinary Perspectives*, edited by Anne Haour and Benedetta Rossi, chap. 10. Boston: Brill.
Masquelier, Adeline. 2016. "The Mouthpiece of an Entire Generation: Hip Hop, Truth, and Islam in Niger." In *Muslim Youth and 9/11 Generation*, edited by Adeline Masquelier and Benjamin F. Soares, chap. 9. Albuquerque: University of New Mexico Press.

Nigeria

Nigeria, a populous country of 186 million, is a West African democratic republic whose capital, Abuja, has a population of about 800,000. Nigeria is made up of 36 states and some 500 ethnic groups. Reggae and hip hop emerged in the country in the late 1980s. By 2014, Nigeria had become Africa's largest economy, and it has one of the largest youth populations in the world, making it fertile ground for a proliferation of hip hop music.

Nigerian music is a combination of traditional folk and popular sounds, highly influenced by the ethnic regions in which it is produced (the largest ethnic groups are the Igbo, Hausa, and Yoruba). Traditional folksongs, like work songs, are closely tied to events and rituals, and the most common musical structures are the epic poem set to music and the call-and-response song. Instrumentation tends toward diversity, with the most common instruments being xylophones (*balafons*), marimbas, bells, scrapers (similar to *guiros*), shakers, drums, brass instruments, and woodwinds.

Popular music emerged during Nigeria's protectorate years, resulting in the emergence of *jùjú* styles (urban string-based club music) of the 1920s, the *palm-wine music* (originally known as *maringa* and from Sierra Leone and Liberia via the Kru people) of the 1950s, and the Cuban and American music as well as instruments that were imported and integrated into juju in the 1960s, leading to styles such as the short-lived Yo-pop style, *waka*, and Afrobeat. Highlife also emerged in Nigeria and neighboring Ghana in the 1950s, although it dwindled in Nigeria during the 1960s, and *apala*, a traditional style, and its offshoot, *fuji* music, became popular in the 1960s.

HIP HOP STARS

Nigerian hip hop is named Naija hip hop, after the country's nickname. American, followed by French hip hop reached Nigeria by the early 1980s with disco rap; however, the country was under a military regime and hip hop activity in the country's largest city, Lagos, remained underground. Exceptions were "The Way I Feel Rap" from Ron Ekundayo's (n.d.) album *The Way I Feel* (1981) included rap in addition to disco, boogie, and funk, and "Saturday Night Raps" from Dizzy K.'s (Kunle Falola, 1964*–) *Excuse Me, Baby (Dedicated to the DJs of the World)* (1982), which included rap, electronica, funk, and soul. Sound on Sound's (1978–1989*) *From Africa from Scratch* (1988) followed as an early Nigerian example of rap in addition to boogie, electronica, funk, and soul. The album is also an early example of Nigerian hip house, since it fuses rap with electronica. Sound on Sound's had an American connection to the creation of the first hip hop single, "Rappers Delight" (1979) through its founder Scratch (Ron McBean, n.d.), who worked as a DJ in New Jersey in the 1970s and advised Sugar Hill Records's (1979–1986) owner Sylvia Robinson (1935–2011) to base the single on American band Chic's (1976–1983, 1990–1992, 1996–) disco song "Good Times" (1979) and supervised the auditions for the Sugarhill Gang.

Other acts of this same vein, combining American sounding rap in English with disco, funk, and soul, lasted into the late 1980s. By the early 1990s, economic crisis created obstacles for obtaining music technology and software to create beats and samples. Popular music preferences included reggae, but Nigerian youth were also listening to American and French hip hop, followed by emerging African hip hop. In 1991, the trio Emphasis (1990–1999)* released *Big Deal*, often considered the earliest Naija hip hop album for its use of pidgin English (Nigerian vernacular). The rap duo Junior & Pretty (1990–1999)* followed Emphasis by also recording in pidgin English and by performing in Hausa daishikis and Igbo chieftaincy tunics.

Topics became politicized, as 1990s hip hop acts criticized military rule, a collapsing economy, high unemployment, and social issues. These 1990s acts included highlife and Afrobeat singer Fela Kuti (Fela Anikulapo Kuti, 1938–1997); Kano-based singer-rapper Eedris Abdulkareem (1974–), of the Remedies (1997–2002); Lagos-based singer-rapper and producer eLDee (1977–), of the band Trybesmen (1998–); and Nigerian American rapper Naeto C (1982–). Kuti was a multi-instrumentalist, musician, composer, activist, and Afrobeat pioneer. Eedris

Abdulkareem's 2004 solo album *Jaga Jaga* contained songs that were banned by the government.

The late 1990s also witnessed the rise of eLDee and his band Trybesmen. In 2002, eLDee moved to the United States, where he continued his solo career and gained international fame. Although he was born in Houston, Naeto C is a popular Nigerian Afrobeat and Igbo musician and record producer known for his prolific recording career. With the improved economy came the availability of computers, recording and editing software, as well as video editing software. Hip hop continued to gain popularity, and the founding of Kennis Music (1998–), and eLDee's Trybe Records (1998–), Paybacktyme Records (1999–2002*), and Dove Records (aka Dove Entertainment, 1999–) officially established the Lagos hip hop scene as well as a recording industry in capital city Abuja.

The rap duo P-Square (2000–2016), consisting of identical twin brothers Peter Okoye and Paul Okoye (1981–), began by mimicking American old-school rappers and breakdancers, but eventually moved onto the Naija hip hop use of pidgin English and focus on some localized lyrical content. The two became prolific musicians on instruments such as keyboard, drums, bass, and rhythm guitar, and eventually were certified Platinum. P-Square's third album, *Game Over* (2007), sold over eight million copies. Eedris Abdulkareem started using multilingual raps, with lyrics in English, pidgin English, and Nigerian languages such as Yoruba, Igbo, and Hausa.

Later notable acts include Nigerian American Chris Akinyemi (aka ChrisA, Olakitan Christopher Akinyemi, n.d.), M.I. (1981–), M.I.'s brother Jesse Jagz (1984–), their good friend ex–band mate Ice Prince (1986–), Ruggedman (Michael Ugochukwu Stephens, n.d.), Duncan Mighty (Duncan Wene Mighty Okechukwu, 1983–), Faze (Chibuzor Oji, n.d.), and Darey (Dare Art Alade, n.d.). Nikki Laoye (Oyenike Laoye-Oturu, n.d.) is Nigeria's most popular female rapper; she uses alternative rock, R&B, hip hop, pop, soul, funk, jazz, and Gospel in her music. Akinyemi's videos were picked up by both MTV and VH1. M.I., Jesse Jagz, and Ice Prince are all associated with the highly influential Chocolate City Music label (2005–), of which M.I. has been CEO since June 2015. M.I. has won various MTV Africa Music Awards, while Jesse Jagz popularized a reggae-infused hip hop style.

Ice Prince is known as both a rapper and actor; his song "Oleku" holds the distinction of being one of Nigeria's most remixed, and he has gone on to international fame, including winning a BET Award. Ruggedman popularized the idea of the do-it-yourself musician. A sometimes Igbo rapper, he produced his own songs and has become internationally famous as a touring act, and he later created his own record label, Rugged Records (2012–). Duncan Mighty is a musician, singer, and music producer who sings and raps in his native tongue, Ikwerre. Faze, a musician and actor, became the first Nigerian artist to have three consecutive Platinum albums; Darey, a disc jockey turned rapper and television personality, has done much to encourage rap in the 2000s, hosting various series and competitions, as well as producing anthology albums. Born into a musical family, since his father is Nigerian jazz pianist, singer, and entertainer Art Alade (n.d.), Darey became a multi-Platinum album selling hip hop recording artist. His most successful albums have been *unDAREYted* (2009) and *DoubleDare* (2011). He has also received many awards and nominations for his music videos.

IGBO RAP

Igbo rap is a Nigerian hip hop style that emerged around 2000 in Southeastern Nigeria, where the Igbo tribe is found. It infuses traditional Igbo music and hip hop beats, combined with other styles such as highlife and R&B and raps in the Igbo language. Igbo highlife emerged during the 1950s as a guitar-based music. Pioneers include Enugu-based Mr Raw (aka Dat N.—A. Raw, Okechukwu Edwards Ukeje, n.d.), whose 2005 debut launched a solo and collaborative career. Later Igbo rappers included Naeto C, and Ruggedman, and Phyno (Chibuzor Nelson Azubuike, 1986–). Phyno, a singer-songwriter, multi-instrumentalist, and producer, started out at about the same time as Mr Raw, but did not see recording success until the 2010s, although he had worked with other well known rappers such as Ruggedman. Other Igbo rappers, including Houston-born Fat Tony (Anthony Lawson Jude Ifeanyichukwu Obiawunaotu, 1988–), started out as underground acts. Female Igbo rappers include Muna (Munachi Gail Teresa Abii Nwankwo, n.d.), a graffiti artist, songwriter, model, and television personality; and London-based rapper Ninja (Nkechi Ka Egenamba, n.d.) of Brighton, England–based indie rock band the Go! Team (2000–), who raps, chants, sings, and dances.

Anthony J. Fonseca and Melissa Ursula Dawn Goldsmith

See also: Eedris Abdulkareem; eLDee; Ghana; Ice Prince; Jesse Jagz; M.I.; Naeto C; P-Square

Further Reading

Clark, Msia Kibona. 2013. "Representing Africa! Trends in Contemporary African Hip Hop." *Journal of Pan African Studies* 6, no. 3: 1–4.

Shipley, Jesse Weaver. 2017. "Parody after Identity: Digital Music and the Politics of Uncertainty in West Africa." *American Ethnologist* 44, no. 2: 249–62.

Shonekan, Stephanie. 2012. "Nigerian Hip Hop: Exploring a Black World Hybrid." In *Hip Hop Africa: New African Music in a Globalizing World*, edited by Eric Charry, chap. 7. Bloomington: Indiana University Press.

Further Listening

Phyno. 2014. *No Guts No Glory* (*NGNG*). Sputnet Records/Penthauze Music.

Ruggedman. 2007. *Ruggedy Baba.* Rugged Records.

9th Wonder

(aka 9thmatic, Patrick Denard Douthit, 1975–, Winston Salem, North Carolina)

9th Wonder is an American hip hop producer and DJ who worked with dozens of prominent hip hop artists, in addition to producing several of his own solo albums. His production style is characterized by employing samples of 1960s and 1970s soul music. The samples themselves contain vocals or vocalizations—and these source materials are layered against instrumental sounds, some of which are also sampled. 9th Wonder is also well known as a hip hop scholar who has taught courses at several American universities.

EARLY YEARS

His earliest production work was as an original member (he left in 2007) of the Durham, North Carolina, hip hop group Little Brother (2001–2010), along with rappers Phonte (Phonte Lyshod Coleman, 1978–) and Big Pooh (Thomas Louis Jones III, 1980–). The three met in the late 1990s as students at North Carolina Central University and were also members of a North Carolina–based alternative hip hop collective called the Justus League (1997–2006). Little Brother's first full-length album was *The Listening* (2003). The group's second full-length album, *The Minstrel Show* (2005), contains several scathing critiques of the hip hop industry. The album includes skits in which various aspects of African American culture are satirized and criticized. Allegedly, the Black Entertainment Television (BET) network refused to air singles from *The Minstrel Show. Source* magazine also suffered through infighting over the rating of *The Minstrel Show*, as members of the editorial staff differed (and had an irreparable falling out) over their assessment and rating of the album.

Also in 2003, 9th Wonder released his first solo effort, an online, unofficial remix of Nas's (1973–) *God's Son* (2002) called *God's Stepson*. His (9th Wonder's) production style caught the attention of Jay-Z (1969–), who enlisted 9th Wonder to produce the single "Threat" for *The Black Album* (2003). Jay-Z also introduced his then-girlfriend, now-wife Beyoncé (1981–), who was then a member of the Houston group Destiny's Child (1998–2004), to 9th Wonder's production style. 9th Wonder went on to produce Destiny's Child's "Girl," "Is She the Reason," and "Game Over" on *Destiny Fulfilled* (2004).

SOLO WORK

He released his first non-remix solo album, *Dream Merchant Vol. 1*, in 2005, followed by *The Dream Merchant Vol. 2* in 2007. Entirely produced by 9th Wonder, both albums featured many different lyricists, including Mos Def (1973–), Memphis Bleek (Malik Thuston Cox, 1978–), and Jean Grae (1976–). Phonte and Big Pooh also contributed lyrics to 9th Wonder's solo albums, both as solo artists and together as Little Brother. 9th Wonder has released five solo albums and has also produced full-length albums for various solo artists. He has produced individual tracks for dozens of hip hop soloists and groups, such as EPMD (1986–1993, 2006–), Raekwon (aka Reakwon the Chef, Corey Woods, 1970–), and Talib Kweli (1975–), as well as for both of his former Little Brother colleagues. Further, 9th Wonder produced music for multiple episodes of the Cartoon Network (1992–) television series *The Boondocks* (2005–2008, 2010, 2014), such as "Thank You for Not Snitching" (2007).

ACADEMIA

In 2007, 9th Wonder was appointed an artist-in-residence at his alma mater, North Carolina Central University. He has also taught hip hop classes at Duke University and the University of Michigan, and in 2012, he was appointed a fellow at

Harvard University, where he taught classes on beatmaking and hip hop history in the Hip Hop Research Institute, a part of the W. E. B. Du Bois Institute. His year teaching at Harvard was chronicled in a documentary film, *The Hip Hop Fellow.* In 2014, 9th Wonder helped formally launch the Hip Hop Institute at North Carolina Central University.

Amanda Sewell

See also: The United States

Further Reading

Nishikawa, Kinohi. 2014. "The Lower Frequencies: Hip Hop Satire in the New Millennium." In *Post-Soul Satire: Black Identity after Civil Rights*, edited by Derek C. Maus and James J. Donahue, pp. 38–55. Jackson: University of Mississippi Press.

Rausch, Andrew J. 2011. "9th Wonder." In *I Am Hip Hop: Conversations on the Music and Culture*, chap. 1. Lanham, MD: Scarecrow.

Further Listening

Little Brother. 2005. *The Minstrel Show.* Atlantic.

9th Wonder. 2007. *Dream Merchant: Volume 2.* 6 Hole Records.

9th Wonder. 2011. *The Wonder Years.* It's a Wonderful World Music Group.

Further Viewing

Price, Kenneth, dir. 2011. *The Wonder Year.* Wilmington, NC: Pricefilms.

Price, Kenneth, dir. 2014. *The Hip Hop Fellow.* Wilmington, NC: Pricefilms.

Norway

Norway is a Northern European Scandinavian parliamentary constitutional monarchy that shares borders with Sweden, Finland, and Russia. The vast majority of its population is Norwegian, but other native ethnic populations include Sámi, as well as Forrest Finn and Kven (both descended from the Finnish). Since the 2000s, municipalities, especially Norway's capital, Oslo, have experienced population growth as a result of immigration. The largest non-European immigrant populations are from Somalia, Iraq, Syria, the Philippines, and Pakistan. Hip hop emerged in Norway in the 1980s with the international distribution of American breakdancing films such as *Wild Style* (1983) and *Beat Street, Breakin', Breakin' 2: Electric Boogaloo*, and *Flashdance* (all 1984). As of 2018, Oslo has the largest scene, followed by a much smaller scene in Lillehammer.

Norway's folk music consists of instrumentals, such as dance music known as *Slåtter*, and vocal music, such as ballads called *Kvad*, improvised songs called *Stev*, hymns, and work songs. Traditional instruments include the *Hardingfele* (Hardanger fiddle), *Langeleik* (a box-shaped dulcimer), *Harpeleik* (a chord zither), *Tungehorn* and *Melhus* (clarinets), and *Bukkehorn* (a goat horn). Edvard Grieg (1843–1907), Norway's best-known classical composer, employed folk music and nationalistic themes. Though not as pronounced as in Sweden, popular music has had a strong market in Norway. By the 20th century, popular music included folk, rock, jazz, heavy metal (including Norwegian black metal), and hip hop.

Several early hip hop acts began in graffiti art. Musician and producer Tommy Tee (aka Father Blanco, The Crazy Minister, Tommy Flåten, 1971–), a 1980s graffiti artist and breakdancer, founded the prominent graffiti magazine *FatCap* (1989–). He later established his label, Tee Productions (1995–). The Oslo trio Warlocks (1992–), which rapped in English, became the best-selling hip hop act in Norway. Warlocks created a music video that showed the trio graffiti bombing a train car for its single "Graff Kill," from its debut album *Lyrical Marksmen* (1995).

Oslo's Gatas Parlament (Street Parliament, 1993–), also known as Kveldens-Høydepunkt (Highlight of the Evening), was the first act to record rap in Norwegian with its debut EP *Autobahn Til Union* (*Highway to the Union*, 1994). Gatas Parlament is a left-leaning political rap crew and band that protests right-wing political activity in Norway. Another early act was the hip hop–electro dance pop duo Madcon (1992–), whose members were of Ethiopian, Eritrean, and South African descent. Other 1990s acts that opted for Norwegian over English included the group Klovner I Kamp (Clowns In Camp, 1994–2006), Norwegian and Spanish rapper Diaz (Andres Rafael Diaz, 1976–), and the Christian–turned–science advocacy group Evig Poesi (Eternal Poetry, aka MHC, 1998–).

By the late 1990s into the 2000s, Oslo-based Tee Productions became Norway's largest hip hop label, producing Warlocks, Gatas Parlament, T.P. Allstars (1999–), Diaz, Son of Light (aka N-Light-N, André Martin Hadland, 1975–), and Opaque (aka Mae, Morton Aasdahl Eliassen, 1976–). Outside Tee's Productions, one of the most successful acts was the rap duo Karpe Diem (2000–). Its second-to-last studio albums, *Aldri solgt en Løgn* (*Never Sold a Lie*, 2010) was certified four-times Platinum (in Norway), and its last album, *Kors på halsen, ti kniver i hjertet, mor og far i døden* (*Cross My Throat, Ten Knives in My Heart, and My Mother and Father Die If I Lie*, 2012), reached No. 1 on Norway's VG-Lista (1967–) the country's albums chart. As multiethnic Muslims, Karpe Diem raps in Norwegian, English, Arabic, Hindi, and other languages found in prominent immigrant populations living in east Oslo. Its raps focus on discrimination, inequality, otherness, identity, stereotyping of immigrants, family, upbringing, and world politics. Contemporary acts include the collective Minoritet1 (2001–), which raps in *Kebabnorsk* (Kebab-Norwegian), a dialect spoken by multiethnic teens residing in Oslo and its eastern suburbs, as well as the pop rap duo Paperboys (2002–), who prefer rapping in English.

In contrast to the majority of Norwegian hip hop acts that consist of artists with immigrant ties, Jaa9 & OnklP (2003–), from Lillehammer, is a duo of white rappers who have been compared to the American group Beastie Boys (1981–2012) for their appearance and humor. Concurrently members of the East Coast gangsta and Dirty South–inspired group Dirty Oppland (2002–), Jaa9 (Johnny Engdal Silseth, 1982–) and OnklP (Pål Tøien, 1984–), rap in Norwegian about gangster themes, national pride, selling out, and partying. As with Karpe Diem, Jaa9 and OnklP employ wordplay. The duo's first full album-length recording, *Bondegrammatikk: The Mixtape* (*Peasants' Grammar: The Mixtape*, 2003), remains Norway's best-selling mixtape as of 2017. Of Jaa9 and OnklP's five studio albums, *Sjåre brymœ* (*Firm Breasts*, 2004), has been the duo's most successful hit, having reached No. 3 on the VG-Lista.

Meanwhile, Gatas Parlament collaborated with Swedish rapper Promoe (Mårten Edh, b. Nils Mårten Ed, 1976–) on "Antiamerikansk Dans" ("Anti-American

Dance"), from its second studio album *Fred, frihet & alt gratis!* (*Peace, Freedom, and Everything Free!*, 2004). Since 2007, Gatas Parliament and the pop and ska band Hopalong Knut (2002–) have combined to form the band Samvirkelaget (The Workers' Cooperative, 2007–), which raps in the Central Norway Trønder dialect, which tends to drop off vowel endings of words.

Contemporary acts from other cities also emerged, including Side Brok (2000–) from Ørsta and Erik og Kriss (Erik & Kriss, 2002–) from Bærum. Notable later acts include Zambia-born Norwegian alternative hip hop and reggae-rap artist Admiral P (Philip Boardman, 1982–) and Nairobi, Kenya-born STL (Stella Mwangi, 1986–), a Kenyan immigrant female rapper who focuses on discrimination. Outside Norway, multi-instrumentalist and producer Lido (Peder Losnegård, 1992–) lives in Los Angeles and records hip hop, trip hop, electronica, and wonky music, a subgenre of electronica that derives from music genres such as glitch hop, dubstep, G-funk, and crunk.

Melissa Ursula Dawn Goldsmith

See also: Gangsta Rap; Graffiti Art; Jaa9 and OnklP; Karpe Diem

Further Reading

Brunstad, Endre, Unn Røyneland, and Toril Opsahl. 2010. "Hip Hop, Ethnicity and Linguistic Practice in Rural and Urban Norway." In *The Languages of Global Hip Hop*, edited by Marina Terkourafi, chap. 9. New York: Continuum.

Uberg Naerland, Torgeir. 2014. "Hip Hop and the Public Sphere: Political Commitment and Communicative Practices on the Norwegian Hip Hop Scene." *Javnost* 21, no. 1: 37–52.

Further Listening

Admiral P. 2014. *Selvtillit & tro* (*Self-Confidence and Belief*). J.A.M. Promotions/ Knirckefritt.

Gatas Parlament. 2008. *Apocalypso.* Tee Productions.

Opaque. 2001. *Gourmet Garbage.* Tee Productions.

The Notorious B.I.G.

(aka Biggie Smalls, Christopher George Latore Wallace, 1972–1997, Brooklyn, New York)

The Notorious B.I.G. was one of the leading East Coast hip hop performers in the mid-1990s. Although he only lived long enough to release two albums, critics have praised the compelling narrative of his raps, as well as the technical virtuosity of his rhymes and easy delivery. Most rappers and scholars of rap consider him among the most talented rappers of all time, if not the very best. Just two weeks after his death, his second studio album, in the making since 1995, *Life after Death* (1997) was released to universal acclaim. The double album was a mix of glamour and grit about life in the streets, with no filler and nearly every track worthy of interest. It established the Notorious B.I.G. as a rapper whose smooth flow and effortless rhymes marked him as an MC with few peers. *Life after Death* would become one of the few rap albums to reach Diamond status, and it would also be included, deservedly so, on many lists of the greatest recordings of the past few decades. Although he left only a small recorded output, the legacy of the Notorious B.I.G. is more than sufficient to place him, along with his chief rival, Tupac Shakur (1971–1996), at the pinnacle of his art.

FROM HIGH SCHOOL DROPOUT TO SUCCESSFUL RAPPER

Christopher George Latore Wallace's parents were Jamaican-born immigrants living in Brooklyn, New York. His father abandoned him and his mother when he was two years old, and so he was raised by a single mother. He was a generally good student during his school years, but he began to engage in illegal activities, chiefly dealing drugs, around the age of 12. He also acquired the nickname Big because of his size and weight. At 17 he dropped out of high school and began to accumulate a record of arrests and jail time for charges related to drugs, guns, and probation violations.

He began rapping as a street entertainer in the Bedford-Stuyvesant neighborhood of Brooklyn while in his teens. In the early 1990s he made a tape that was heard by DJ Mister Cee (Calvin LeBrun, 1966–), who passed it along to the editors of the hip hop magazine *The Source* (1988–), who featured the then-named Biggie Smalls in its "Unsigned Hype" column. Puff Daddy (1969–) next heard the tape and signed him to a contract with Uptown Records (1986–1999) in Harlem, New York, where he began work as a backup singer and guest artist. When Puff Daddy was fired, Biggie Smalls followed him to his new label, Bad Boy Records (aka Bad Boy Entertainment, 1993–), a few months later. He had been using the name Biggie Smalls—after a gangster character in the 1975 motion picture *Let's Do It Again*—but found that another performer was using it, and so began using the Notorious B.I.G., a pseudonym he had used to record on a Mary J. Blige (1971–) track.

By August 1992, the Notorious B.I.G. had completed his first studio album, and in August his first single was released, followed a month later by his debut album, *Ready to Die*. Critics were impressed by both the honesty of the album's content and the impressive technique in his rapping. Several described him as a natural storyteller, able to convey the full range of emotions of a young black man on the streets, and not just a simplistic caricature of thug life. His ability to deliver lyrics in a deceptively effortless manner with easy, unforced rhymes was also praised. This is all the more remarkable because many of the tracks were done freestyle, either without a written text or improvised in performance. *Ready to Die* reached quadruple Platinum sales and helped to draw interest back to East Coast hip hop at a time when West Coast gangsta rap was in ascendance.

LATER CAREER, FRIENDSHIP WITH TUPAC SHAKUR, AND MURDER

Shortly after the album's release, the Notorious B.I.G. became friends with Tupac Shakur, if only for a few years. In 1995, Tupac Shakur accused the Notorious B.I.G.,

Puff Daddy, and other New York hip hop figures of involvement in a November 1994 robbery, which resulted in his suffering a gunshot wound and a significant loss of jewelry. It also escalated tensions between the two artists. In late February 1995, the Notorious B.I.G. released a B-side single, "Who Shot Ya," which was taken as a diss track aimed at Shakur, even though he claimed that the song had been written long before the robbery. Tupac Shakur responded in June of the next year with "Hit 'Em Up," an unquestionable diss that insults the Notorious B.I.G., his friends, and anyone associated with Bad Boy Records. Three months later, Tupac Shakur was gunned down in Las Vegas, Nevada, with suspicions cast on the Notorious B.I.G. and his East Coast compatriots.

In February 1997, the Notorious B.I.G. traveled to Los Angeles to attend various music industry events and to promote the impending release of his second album. In March, he attended a party, after which he and his entourage were returning to his hotel after midnight. His car was stopped at an intersection, when another vehicle pulled alongside, and a gunman in that car fired a 9 mm pistol, hitting him four times. The entourage rushed him to a hospital, where he died.

Coming so soon after the murder of Shakur, the murder of the Notorious B.I.G. attracted intense media scrutiny. Many people thought his shooting was a continuation of the feud between East Coast and West Coast rappers, while others accused the police of complicity and of covering up the facts. His relatives filed wrongful death suits against the Los Angeles Police Department and the city, but both were dismissed. The death of the Notorious B.I.G. officially remains unsolved.

Scott Warfield

See also: Gangsta Rap; Puff Daddy; Tupac Shakur; The United States

Further Reading

Coker, Cheo Hodari. 2003. *Unbelievable: The Life, Death, and Afterlife of the Notorious B.I.G.* New York: Three Rivers Press.

Lang, Holly. 2007. *The Notorious B.I.G.: A Biography.* Westport, CT: Greenwood Press.

Scott, Cathy. 2000. *The Murder of Biggie Smalls.* New York: St. Martin's Press.

Further Listening

The Notorious B.I.G. 1994. *Ready to Die.* Bad Boy Entertainment.

The Notorious B.I.G. 1997. *Life after Death.* Bad Boy Entertainment.

Further Viewing

Tilghman, George Jr., dir. 2009. *Notorious.* Beverley Hills, CA: 20th Century Fox Home Entertainment.

N.W.A.

(aka N—az wit Attitude or N—az wit Attitudes, 1986–1991, Compton, California)

N.W.A., which stands for N—az Wit Attitude or N—az Wit Attitudes, was a hip hop group that lasted just five years and issued only two studio albums, yet had a profound influence on both hip hop and broader popular culture. Although it was

In between 1988 and 1989 the American hip hop group N.W.A. went on tour with Public Enemy. Pictured backstage while in Kansas City, Missouri, in 1989, from upper left are Dr. Dre, Laylaw, and The D.O.C.; on the sofa are Ice Cube, Eazy-E, MC Ren, and DJ Yella. (Raymond Boyd/Michael Ochs Archives/Getty Images)

not the foundation of gangsta rap, N.W.A.'s debut album, *Straight Outta Compton* (1988), established the subgenre as an important commercial category of popular music and helped raise awareness about urban black neighborhood social issues. The group's forceful use of profanity and the "N-word" changed the landscape of rap. The group was associated primarily with Compton, where five of its members were born, and its music documented the decline of this city located south of Los Angeles (although Compton's problems were exaggerated by the media). Conversely, this typical 1980s and 1990s urban city contributed to the image of N.W.A.

FORMATION AND EARLY YEARS

N.W.A. began in 1986 with Eazy-E (Eric Lynn Wright, 1964–1995), a former drug dealer, who was attempting to build, along with Cleveland-based businessman Jerry Heller (Gerald Elliot Heller, 1940–2016), a record company, Ruthless Records (1986–), without much early success. This situation changed when Dr. Dre (Andre Romelle Young, 1965–), a member of the World Class Wreckin' Cru (1984–1986), and Ice Cube (O'Shea Jackson, 1969–), were brought into the company to write raps. One of Ice Cube's raps, "Boyz n the Hood" (1987), was written specifically for HBO (Home Boys Only, 1988–1990)*, but was rejected by that New York–based group as too hardcore for its image. Eazy-E then joined with Dr. Dre, Ice Cube, the Arabian Prince (Kim Nazel, 1965–), the D.O.C. (Tracy Lynn Curry, 1968–), and DJ Yella (Antoine Carraby, 1967–) from World Class Wreckin' Cru to record the track. Various members of this group also recorded three additional tracks, "Panic Zone," "8-Ball," and "Dopeman," and all were included among the 11 tracks produced by Dr. Dre on the compilation album *N.W.A. and the Posse* (1987). Just before the album's release, Ice Cube moved to Arizona, where he attended the Phoenix Institute of Technology for a year, and so Eazy-E brought MC Ren (Lorenzo Jerald Patterson, 1969–) into the Ruthless Records stable as a writer. His first project was Eazy-E's debut album, *Eazy-Duz-It* (1988), but he also contributed tracks to N.W.A. and soon became a member of the group.

STRAIGHT OUTTA COMPTON

In between 1987 and 1988, N.W.A.'s studio debut album, *Straight Outta Compton* (1988), was recorded. It was released in August 1988. Its commercial success and critical reception have distinguished this album as one of the most influential hip hop releases, an achievement notable because the extreme language made radio airplay impossible. From its opening track, "Straight Outta Compton," listeners immediately hear lyrics that required one of the first Parental Advisory "Explicit" labels, supported by beats that owe something to the aggressive sound of Public Enemy (1982–), but N.W.A. replaced the political and social issues of Public Enemy's lyrics with those that painted a grim picture of street life for black urban youths. Raps such as "Gangsta Gangsta" and "F— tha Police," positioned conspicuously as the album's second track, drew almost universal disdain, even from black critics. Police departments often refused to provide security for N.W.A. concerts, and the FBI wrote a widely circulated letter that condemned the track, but the effect was to further publicize the group and its music, especially among audiences that had not traditionally listened to hip hop. Significantly, more than 80 percent of the album's sales were in white suburban neighborhoods, whose residents had no experience with the lifestyle depicted. First charting in 1989, *Straight Outta Compton* eventually reached triple Platinum status in sales in 2015, and has been included on numerous critics' lists of best ever pop, rock, or hip hop albums.

ICE CUBE'S DEPARTURE, DISSING WITH DR. DRE, AND N.W.A.'S LEGACY

In 1989, Ice Cube left the group in a dispute over the royalties for his extensive contributions to *Straight Outta Compton*, which led to a long-lasting feud. Although Ice Cube made no mention of his former bandmates on his solo debut, *AmeriK-KKa's Most Wanted* (1990), N.W.A. immediately dissed him in its track "Real N—az" on the EP *100 Miles and Runnin'* (1990), as well as in its video. Ice Cube then responded in "Jackin' for Beats" and "I Gotta Say What Up!!!" on his own EP *Kill at Will* (1990).

N.W.A.'s second and final studio album, *Efil4za—n* (1991), the name a reversed spelling of *N—az4life*, contained multiple insults to Ice Cube, but the album is more important for the shift in sound overseen by Dr. Dre, who produced the album. The overtly aggressive beats of *Straight Outta Compton* give way to a smoother sound, characterized by slightly slower tempos, a less-accented deep bass, the use of synthesizers, and samples from earlier funk tunes, a style which would become known as *G-funk* (gangsta-funk). Though some have credited Dr. Dre with inventing this new sound, he more likely co-developed it while working with the rapper Cold 187um (Gregory Fernan Hutchinson, 1967–), who had just joined Ruthless Records in 1989.

Shortly after the release of *Efil4za—n*, Dr. Dre, who may have felt overwhelmed by his duties as head of production at Ruthless Records and who also had concerns about the label's finances, left the company to cofound Death Row Records (1991–2009). He also convinced the D.O.C. and other Ruthless artists to jump with him to the new label and thereby initiated yet another feud among former N.W.A. members. Dr. Dre struck first with insults in several early Death Row tracks, to which Eazy-E quickly responded. Even MC Ren, who technically remained with Ruthless, broke with Eazy-E and only reconciled shortly before the latter's death in 1995.

N.W.A.'s legacy has been kept alive over the past two decades with five compilation albums, most of which recycle old tracks with a few solo efforts by N.W.A. artists or guests with ties to the group. Despite several plans for a reunion, the four surviving members of N.W.A.—Ice Cube, MC Ren, Dr. Dre, and DJ Yella—did not appear together until April 2016 at the Coachella Music Festival, one week after the group was inducted into the Rock and Roll Hall of Fame.

Scott Warfield

See also: Dr. Dre; Eazy-E; Gangsta Rap; G-Funk; Ice Cube; Political Hip Hop; The United States

Further Reading

Bradley, Adam, and Andrew Dubois, eds. 2010. "N.W.A." Under "Part 2: 1985–92: The Golden Age" in *The Anthology of Rap*, pp. 232–48. New Haven, CT: Yale University Press.

Forman, Murray. 2002. *The 'Hood Comes First: Race, Space, and Place in Rap and Hip Hop.* Middletown, CT: Wesleyan University Press.

Nelson, George. 1998. "National Music." In *Hip Hop America*, chap. 10. New York: Penguin Books.

Further Listening

N.W.A. 1988. *Straight Outta Compton.* Priority Records/Ruthless Records.

N.W.A. 1991. *N—az4Life* [aka *Efil4za—n*]. Priority Records/Ruthless Records.

Oman

Oman is an Islamic absolute monarchy on the southeastern coast of the Arabian Peninsula that is considered strategically important for military and oil interests, although its economy relies heavily on tourism and agricultural trade. At its peak in the 19th century, the Sultanate of Oman had great influence in the Persian Gulf, but its power declined in the 20th century. All Omanis, regardless of age or sex, participate in music. Notable Omani musicians include *oud* (lute) player and *sawt* singer Salim Rashid Suri (1911*–1979), nicknamed the Singing Sailor, pioneer of the Sawt al-Khaleej (aka Voice of the Gulf) music genre. Traditional music is favored and pop and rock are produced sparsely. A small underground metal scene with bands such as Arabia (2000–) and Belos (1997–) exists, and there is virtually no hip hop scene as of 2018.

Some inroads have been attempted, by dancers such as Debbie Allen (1950–) and by Howard University's World Learning Program, but their effect has been minimal thus far, with acts such as Muscat- and Dubai-based DJ AA (anonymous, n.d.), known for his versatility with trip hop (downtempo), hip hop, and house. DJ Bluey (anonymous, n.d.) is an internationally known DJ who brings energy, charisma, and personality to his performances. Nonetheless, Red Bull now sponsors an annual festival called Lord of the Streets (begun in Dubai, 2006), and American old-school East Coast (U.S.) hip hop is beginning to have some influence on youth culture, with freestyle rap competitions and b-boy crews such as SNK (Serve and Knock, 2001–) and the Legends Crew (n.d.).

Anthony J. Fonseca

See also: Break dancing

Further Reading

El-Mallah, Issam, and Kai Fikentscher. 1990. "Some Observations on the Naming of Musical Instruments and on Rhythm in Oman." *Yearbook for Traditional Music* 22: 123–26.

Garratt, Rob. 2016. "How the Hip Hop Street Dance Known as B-Boying Stepped into the UAE." *The National*, July 20.

Otara Millionaires Club

(OMC, 1993–2010, Auckland, New Zealand)

Otara Millionaires Club (OMC) was a hip hop, acoustic rock, and Latin music band from Otara, one of the poorest and most troubled suburbs of South Auckland. OMC was formed when two multi-instrumentalists brothers of Niuean (Polynesian) descent, Phil (Philip Fuemana, 1964–2005) and Pauly Fuemana (Paul Lawrence Fuemana, 1969–2010), joined with producer Alan Jansson (Pakeha Alan Jansson, n.d.) to record "We R the OMC" for Jansson's *Proud: An Urban Pacific Streetsoul Compilation* (1994), the first Urban Pasifika album. OMC went on Jansson's *Proud* national tour to promote the album and sound, a combination of hip hop with R&B, reggae, and Pacific roots music (for example, log drumming and Māori ukulele and guitar strumming). OMC's lyrics focused on the irony of becoming wealthy after years of poverty and prison time, on romance, and on Auckland and Pacific pride.

All of OMC's songs were composed by Jansson and the Fuemanas in English, and its big hit was "How Bizarre" (1995), featuring Pauly's gangsta rap style. It peaked at No. 1 on hit singles charts in New Zealand, Australia, Austria, and Canada; No. 4 on Billboard's Hot 100 Airplay (now Radio Songs); No. 2 on Hot R&B/Hip-Hop Songs; and No. 1 on the Mainstream Top 40/Contemporary Hit Radio chart in the United States—making OMC the first New Zealand band to have a No. 1 hit song in the United States. This one smash hit led to Platinum and triple Platinum certification for their debut and only album *How Bizarre* (1996) in Australia and New Zealand, and Gold certification by Recording Industry Association of America (RIAA). Other songs that charted outside New Zealand from the same album were "Right On" and "On the Run" (both 1996), though in less notable positions.

In 1998, after a legal dispute over royalties, Jansson left OMC but agreed that Phil could use OMC's name as a touring solo artist. Phil founded Urban Pacifika Records (1993–2001)* and mentored subsequent Auckland hip hop acts, influencing another independent label, Dawn Raid Entertainment (1999–). In 2005, Phil died of a heart attack. Two years later, Pauly and Jansson reunited briefly to release "4 All of Us" (2007), a single featuring actress/guest vocalist Lucy Lawless (Lucille Frances Ryan, 1968–), but the single had poor sales. In 2010, Pauly died of an autoimmune disease, progressive demyelinating polyneuropathy, but his death sparked a resurgence of interest in OMC and its hit "How Bizarre" in New Zealand.

Melissa Ursula Dawn Goldsmith

See also: Gangsta Rap; New Zealand; Political Hip Hop

Further Reading

Grigg, Simon. 2015. *"How Bizarre": Pauly Fuemana and the Song That Stormed the World.* Wellington, New Zealand: Awa Press.

Shute, Gareth. 2004. *Hip Hop Music in Aoteroa.* Auckland, New Zealand: Reed.

Further Listening

OMC. 1996. *How Bizarre.* Huh Records.

OutKast

(1991–2006, 2014–, Atlanta, Georgia)

OutKast is an American Southern hip hop duo that fuses hip hop with funk, psychedelic music (from P-funk, rock, and acid jazz to trip hop), drum and bass, electronica, techno/industrial hip hop, R&B, and gospel. Consisting of American rapper,

The Southern and alternative hip hop duo OutKast consists of Atlanta-based rappers Big Boi (left) and André 3000 (right). Here OutKast performs live at a 2001 concert in Heaton Park in Manchester, England. (Jon Super/Redferns/Getty Images)

singer-songwriter, dancer, actor, and producer André 3000 (aka André, André Lauren Benjamin, 1975–) and American rapper, songwriter, actor, and producer Big Boi (Antwan André Patton, 1975), OutKast was the first hip hop act that signed to Atlanta-based LaFace Records (1989–2001). All five of its studio albums were huge successes in respect to critical acclaim and sales: *Southernplayalistica-dillacmuzik* (1994) peaked at No. 20 on the Billboard 200 and was certified Platinum; *ATLiens* (1996) and *Aquemini* (1998) peaked at No. 2 on the Billboard 200 and were certified double Platinum; *Stankonia* (2000) peaked at No. 2 on the Billboard 200 and was certified quadruple Platinum; and OutKast's double album *Speakerboxxx/The Love Below* peaked at No. 1 on the Billboard 200 and was certified Diamond.

EARLY MUSICAL INTERESTS AND FORMATION

The duo met at the Lenox Square shopping mall while rapping in public. Both attended the Tri-Cities High School for the Performing Arts, a public magnet school in the Atlanta suburb of East Point. Initially, there was some rivalry since both were rappers interested in songwriting and freestyle rhyming; however, they quickly realized they worked well together and became friends. They soon formed the duo 2 Shades Deep and continued performing in shopping malls. Eventually, a girlfriend introduced the duo to Organized Noize (1992–), an American hip hop and R&B production team based in Atlanta. Organized Noize recorded on the LaFace

(1989–2001) label and introduced then André Benjamin and Antwan Patton to the label's cofounder and producer, L.A. Reid (Antonio Marquis Reid, 1956–).

Though Reid was unimpressed with its audition, the duo continued to hone its musical skills at Organized Noize's studio and later had a successful audition that led to a recording contract with LaFace. Because both were still minors, they had to wait until mid-1993 to begin recording. That same year, 2 Shades Deep changed its name to OutKast while recording its first single, "Players Ball," for the label's compilation album, *A LaFace Family Christmas*. The single was used to promote OutKast's first studio album, *Southernplayalisticadillacmuzik*, which was produced by Organized Noize. "Players Ball" peaked quickly at No. 1 on Billboard's Hot Rap chart. Though the song alludes to a traditional gathering event of pimps in Chicago, it is mostly about living in the South and being part of its hip hop culture—an appropriate introduction of the duo to its potential fans. OutKast's debut album was released shortly afterward. Its combination of Southern hip hop and funk, as well as its energetic and colorful post-punk aesthetic, appealed to listeners and critics; it ultimately peaked at No. 20 on the Billboard 200.

The success of *Southernplayalisticadillacmuzik* was especially important at the time to the Southern hip hop scene. Although Southern hip hop had emerged in the 1990s, West Coast and East Coast rap had dominated hip hop interests and sales. The album also gave direction to OutKast's eclectic, almost throw-in-the-kitchen-sink sound, a postmodern mixture of analog and digital musical instruments, live musical instruments, old-school and new-school hip hop elements, a variety of hip hop and hip hop related music (e.g., Southern rap, trip hop, neo soul, and drum and bass), and other elements. André had a flowing rapping style that formed a chemistry with Big Boi's intense voice and rapid raps.

OutKast's second and third albums, *ATLiens* and *Aquemini*, explored its eclecticism further, adding elements of Afrofuturism, in the tradition of progressive jazz musician Sun Ra (aka Le Sony'r Ra, Herman Poole Blount, 1914–1993), disco funk musician George Clinton's (1941–) Parliament-Funkadelic (1968–), American alternative hip hop and horrorcore artist Kool Keith (Keith Matthew Thornton, 1965–), and American hip hop, neo soul, new jack swing, and R&B quartet Jodeci (1989–1996, 2001–). The albums placed Southern rap fans in the midst of unexpected and new soundscapes. *ATLiens* exhibits André's quirky lyrics and flamboyant style, which began to be a favorite at concerts as well. It also featured the singles "ATLiens" and "Elevators (Me and You)," both representing André and Big Boi's first experience as producers.

Aquemini, which was equally successful, made headlines because American civil rights activist Rosa Parks (1913–2005) sued LaFace Records in 1999 over its most successful single, which uses her name as its title. Parks objected to OutKast's use of her name and its obscenities. The initial suit reached a summary judgment in OutKast's favor, but the legal issues dragged the case into 2006 through failed appeals on Parks' and her relatives' behalf.

OutKast's fourth album *Stankonia* featured songs written and recorded just after André 3000's famous breakup with American neo soul and R&B singer Erykah Badu (1971–), which had some bearing on the change of his name from André to André 3000, which was also affected by his conscious decision to avoid being confused with American rapper and producer Dr. Dre (1965–). "Ms. Jackson," which was partly inspired by Erykah Badu's mother, combining rap with pop, became OutKast's first No. 1 pop hit. From *Stankonia*, the music videos for the angry anti-American dream rap-rock anthem "Gasoline Dreams" and the agitated drum-and-bass "B.O.B. (Bombs Over Baghdad)" give examples of OutKast's elaborate, vivid, throw-in-the-kitchen-sink visuals to match the duo's eclectic sound.

Speakerboxxx/The Love Below was a double album that became OutKast's last studio recording effort. Together, the albums were the duo's largest commercial success, attaining Diamond certification in 2004. *Speakerboxxx* is Big Boi's album, while *The Love Below* is André 3000's album, but the two appear on and produce some of each other's album. The albums also represent members' personalities with *Speakerboxxx* as boisterous, party-themed, Dirty South funk–infused rappers while *The Love Below* portrays the duo as an even, eclectic band that blends hip hop, funk, jazz, R&B, rock, and electronic music. Both Big Boi's "The Way You Move" and André 3000's "Hey Ya!" became No. 1 hits on the Billboard Hot 100. "Hey Ya!" became an instant popular standard at football games and was featured as an arrangement for plastic soprano recorders in American discount chain Target's back-to-school commercial in 2013. *Speakerboxx/The Love Below* won the 2004 Grammy Award for Album of the Year.

OTHER PROJECTS AND SOLO CAREERS

In 2006, OutKast released a soundtrack to the duo's American feature film, *Idlewild*. Written and directed by OutKast's music video director Bryan Barber (1970–) and starring André 3000 (as Percival) and Big Boi (as Rooster), *Idlewild* is a drama about a Great Depression juke joint in fictional Idlewild, Georgia, accompanied by OutKast's self-referential hip hop, funk, neo soul, acoustic blues soundtrack. The film and the album of the same title had mixed reception, though it debuted at No. 2 on the Billboard 200, peaked at No. 1 on Billboard's Top R&B/Hip-Hop Albums chart, and was certified Platinum. It fell afterward and did not measure up to OutKast's previous successes.

Between 2007 and 2013, OutKast took a hiatus. During this period, André 3000 and Big Boi focused on solo work. The two had previously finished many separate recording projects. Big Boi released *Sir Lucious Left Foot: The Son of Chico Dusty* (2010), which features appearances by André 3000 and Raekwon (Corey Woods, 1970–), among others. The album received critical acclaim and peaked at No. 3 on the Billboard 200. Big Boi's next studio album was *Vicious Lies and Dangerous Rumours* (2012), which peaked at No. 34 on the Billboard 200.

André 3000 spent this hiatus appearing as a rapper on a prolific list of hip hop and pop recordings, including those for American rapper, singer, and DJ Q-Tip (aka Kamaal Ibn John Fareed, Jonathan William Davis, 1970–), American rapper and producer Jay-Z (1969–), American hip hop group A Tribe Called Quest (1985–1998, 2006–2013, 2015–), American R&B singer-songwriter Beyoncé (1981–), and Erykah Badu. In 2007, he released the mixtape *Whole Foods*, which features many rap tracks by André 3000 in addition to appearances by R&B and neo soul singers

Macy Gray (Natalie Renée McIntyre, 1967–) and Kelis (Kelis Rogers, 1979–), as well as Big Boi. Like Big Boi, André 3000 also acted in films and television and became involved in philanthropy. In 2008, he created the "Benjamin Bixby" clothing line. André 3000 is also the creator and a voice-over actor of *Class of 3000* (2006–2008), an animated television series on the Cartoon Network (1992–).

In 2014, OutKast reunited by performing at numerous concert events worldwide. Big Boi has since recorded his solo studio album *Boomiverse* (2017), which received critical praise and peaked at No. 28 on the Billboard 200. André 3000 produced the final track on *Aretha Franklin Sings the Great Diva Classics* (2014), a cover of Prince's (Prince Rogers Nelson, 1958–2016) "Nothing Compares 2 U" (1990). Both continue to collaborate as individuals and together with other artists onstage and in recordings; however, as of 2018, OutKast has yet to release a sixth studio album, and it is unclear whether or not that album is planned. Also as of 2018, André 3000 prefers to use his birth name, André Benjamin.

Melissa Ursula Dawn Goldsmith

See also: Bounce; Dirty South; Political Hip Hop; The United States

Further Reading

Green, Tony. 2003. "OutKast: *Southernplayalisticadillacmuzik*; *ATLiens*; *Aquemint*; *Stankonia*." In *Classical Material: The Hip Hop Album Guide*, edited by Oliver Wang, pp. 131–34. Toronto: ECW Press.

Rambsy, Howard, II. 2013. "Beyond Keeping It Real: OutKast, the Funk Connection, and Afrofuturism." *American Studies* 52, no. 4: 205–16.

Further Listening

OutKast. 1994. *Southernplayalisticadillacmuzik*. LaFace Records.

OutKast. 1996. *ATLiens*. LaFace Records.

OutKast. 2000. *Stankonia*. LaFace Records.

OutKast. 2003. *Speakerboxxx/The Love Below*. LaFace Records.

P

Pakistan

Pakistan is a South Asian country of 201 million people who, through colonization and occupation, have common history with Hindus, Indo-Greeks, Muslims, Turco-Mongols, Afghans, and Sikhs. It is therefore an ethnically and linguistically diverse country with a history of ethnic civil war. In 1973, it adopted a constitution establishing an Islamic law federal government in Islamabad. Pakistani hip hop, which originated in the 1990s, was a blend of traditional Pakistani musical elements with hip hop rhythms and was heavily influenced by American hip hop, which was combined with Pakistani poetry to create a unique style.

Pakistan's popular music is diverse because of South Asian, Central Asian, Middle Eastern, and Western popular music influences, and its traditional music styles are based on the *raag* and include *dhrupad*, *ghazal*, *qawwali*, *hamd*, and *khayal*, the last being a common style with Afghanistan. Instrumentation is based on *sitar* and *tabla* interaction. Pakistani folk music, including Punjabi and Sindhi music, deals with everyday life using vernacular language, is diverse, and is based on a singer's geographical region. Pop music can be traced back to the 1960s, when Ahmed Rushdi's (Syed Ahmed Rushdi, 1934–1983) song "Ko Ko Korina" (1966) combined bubblegum, rock, and Pakistani film music to pioneer filmi-pop and opened the door for non-Muslim artists to introduce American jazz or Westernized pop. Nazia Hassan (1965–2000) released the first pop music album, *Disco Deewane* (1981), which broke national sales records and got international attention. Fuzön (2001–2004, 2007–) introduced the Western rock band concept in the 1980s.

Fakhar-e-Alam's (1972–) album *Rap Up* (1994), featured Pakistan's first rap songs. Importation of the music of Eminem (1972–) led to rappers such as Peshawar-born Party Wrecker (Mustafa Khan, n.d.) and Qzer (Qasim Naqvi, n.d.), and these performers typically came from a well-educated, socioeconomically privileged group—the people most likely to understand English. It took a decade before the first Punjabi rap emerged, but not in Pakistan; it came from San Francisco, with Pakistani American, Karachi-born rapper Bohemia (Roger David, 1979–), who rapped in Punjabi street slang. After this, rap in Punjabi, Sindhi, and Urdu—the country's refined, official language spoken by the elite—began to emerge in Pakistan.

Current Pakistani hip hop artists include Islamabad-based rapper-songwriter and producer Adil Omar (1991–), who raps in English, and also performs with producer and singer-songwriter Talal Qureshi (n.d.) in the duo SNKM (aka Sonic Nocturnal Kinetic Movement, 2015–). The duo was instrumental in getting the government to lift its YouTube ban in 2016, working with comic rapper and voice actor Ali Gul Pir (1986–). Islamabad-based teen rapper-songwriter Arbaz Khan (2001–) became popular in 2014 with his songs "Jhootha" and "12 Saal Ka Larka" ("12-Year Old Boy"), the former causing a controversy for its sexually explicit video. Also controversial is Lahore-based rapper and actor Faris Shafi (1987–), known for his explicit songs. Jhelum-based rapper Kasim Raja (n.d.), uses Punjabi and even raps about Punjabi identity, while Thatta-based rapper Meer Janweri (Shahzad Meer, n.d.) uses Sindhi and celebrates its culture in his raps—including Sufi poetry.

Diaspora rappers include Bohemia; Tingbjerg, Denmark–based rapper Ataf Khawaja (n.d.), Amsterdam-based urban singer-songwriter Imran Khan (1984–), Detroit-based American rapper-songwriter and physician Lazarus (Kamran Rashid Khan, n.d.), Orlando, Florida–based American rapper, singer-songwriter, and physician Osama Com Laude (Syed Osama Karamat Ali Shah, 1987–), and Danish rap group Outlandish (1997–2017), which contains members who are immigrants from Morocco, Pakistan, and Honduras.

Anthony J. Fonseca

See also: India; Political Hip Hop

Further Reading

Goldsmith, Melissa, and Anthony J. Fonseca. 2013. "Bhangra-Beat and Hip Hop: Hyphenated Musical Cultures, Hybridized Music." In *Crossing Traditions: American Popular Music in Local and Global Contexts*, edited by Babacar M'Baye and Alexander Charles Oliver Hall, chap. 9. Lanham, MD: Scarecrow.

Maira, Sunaina. 2000. "Henna and Hip Hop: The Politics of Cultural Production and the Work of Cultural Studies." *Journal of Asian Studies* 3, no. 3: 329–69.

Further Listening

Bohemia. 2017. *Skull and Bones: The Final Chapter.* T-Series.

Palestine

Palestine is a Middle Eastern region along the Jordan River, made up of most of the religiously important territory claimed by Israel, known as the Holy Land, the birthplace of Judaism and Christianity. As of 2018, the State of Palestine is recognized as a *de jure* sovereign state by about 136 of 193 member states of the United Nations (UN). In 2012, the State of Palestine became a nonmember observer state in the UN. Since 1967, Israel has occupied the State of Palestine. Palestinian music is a subgenre of Arabic music, and it is influenced by the many ethnic groups that reside in the region, including Arab Muslims, Arab Christians, Sephardic Jews, Mizrahi Jews, Ashkenazi Jews, Samaritans, Circassians, and Armenians. Palestinian hip hop began in the late 1990s by blending Arab and Hebrew melodies, lyrics, and instrumentation with Western beats. Rap trio DAM (aka Da Arabian MCs, 1998–), based in Lod, Israel, popularized rap in 1999 with Arabic, Hebrew, and English songs about the Israeli Palestinian conflict and living in poverty.

Traditional music began as a combination of the music of trade groups, such as agrarian farmers who sang work songs such as those in the popular four-verse

Refugees of Rap is a Palestinian-Syrian hip hop band formed in 2007 by brothers Yaser and Mohamed Jamous, who were born at Yarmouk, a refugee camp in Damascus. Relocating to Paris, the band openly criticizes violence in Syria, the actions of Syrian President Bashar al-Assad, as well as the world's perceptions and treatment of Palestinians. (PHILIPPE LOPEZ/AFP/Getty Images)

ataaba (a traditional Arabic musical form sung at weddings, festivals, and work) or *dal'ona* style (meaning love and longing), to accompany fishing, shepherding, harvesting, and making olive oil; the epic songs of professional storytellers and musicians; and event songs (usually accompanied by an event dance). Popular music, which featured legends such as Sayed Darwish (1892–1923) and Umm Kulthum (Umm Kulthum Ibrahim, 1898–1975), drew from these categories.

With the creation of Israel in 1948, the geographic centers for Palestinian music, Nazareth and Haifa, became part of Israel, and Arab Palestinian musicians found themselves in exile or refugee camps. Palestine's current most popular singers are therefore diaspora musicians such as Manchester, England–based Reem Kelani (1963–), Cairo-based Jaffa Phonix (2003–), and New Orleans–based DJ Khaled (Khaled Mohamed Khaled, 1975–), who created songs about living under Israeli occupation and longing for peace and a return to Palestine.

Hip hop collective Ramallah Underground (2005–), based in Ramallah, creates hip hop and trip hop (downtempo) nationalistic music in Arabic that Arabic youth find relatable. Some Palestinian musicians fear governmental censorship and reprisal from Islamic fundamentalists since the 2005 elections, which gave the militant Sunni Islamic Palestinian Hamas party (1987–) more political power. The most popular Palestinian rapper is Saz (Sameh Zakout, 1983*–), from Ramle, Israel. Saz's lyrical content focuses on Palestinian and Arab identity as well advocates for Arab-Israeli peace.

Anthony J. Fonseca

See also: Israel; Political Hip Hop

Further Reading

Maira, Sunaina. 2012. "Hip Hop from '48 Palestine." *Social Text* 30, no. 112: 1–26.

McDonald, David A. 2008–2009. "Carrying Words Like Weapons: Hip Hop and the Poetics of Palestinian Identities in Israel." *Min-Ad: Israel Studies in Musicology Online* 7, no. 2: 116–30.

Further Listening

DAM. 2012. *Dabke on the Moon.* 48 Records.

Panama

Panama is a Central American country whose largest city is Panama City, home to nearly half of Panama's four million people. With the backing of the United States, Panama became an independent republic in 1903, and the United States gave the Panama Canal over to the country in 1999, which resulted in a revenue boon. The music of Panama is a combination of influences: indigenous peoples, Americans, Africans, and peoples of Jamaica and other Caribbean islands—with musical influences such as *bolero, cumbia,* calypso, jazz, *mejorana,* reggae, rock, and salsa. Pop and rock reached Panama by the 1960s with doo-wop music; Spanish reggae, dancehall, and eventually reggaetón (aka reggae en Español in Panama) became popular in the mid-1970s with pioneering act El General (Edgardo Armando Franco, 1969–), who made Spanish-language rap famous with two 1990 dancehall hits, "Te ves buena" ("You Look Good") and "Tu pun pun" ("You Play with Words"). El General paved the way for Nando Boom (Fernando Orlando Brown Mosley, 1977–), Renato (Leonardo Renato Aulder, 1961–), Aldo Ranks (Aldo Vargas, 1973–), Kafu Banton (Zico Alberto Garibaldi Roberts, 1979–), Eddy Lover (Eduardo Mosquera, 1985–), El Roockie (Iván Vladimir Banista, 1977*–), Joey Montana (Edgardo Antonio Miranda Beiro, 1982–), and Makano (Hernán Enrique Jiménez, 1983–). Women were also involved in the reggaetón scene, with artists such as La Factoría (1999–2013) and Lorna (Lorna Zarina Aponte, 1983–).

Like El General, Nando Boom added rap to reggae and salsa in the 1980s. Renato became internationally famous for "La Chica de los Ojos Café" ("The Brown-Eyed Girl," 1990), which combines reggaetón with *mariachi* music. El Roockie is well known for his lyrical prowess and has been nicknamed "Maquina de Lirica," which loosely translates to "Lyric Machine." Makano began his music career at the age of 12, and has had several No. 1 hits in Panama. La Factoría was led by female rapper-singer Demphra (Marlen Romero, 1977–) and had an international hit (with guest musician Eddy Lover) with the R&B-influenced "Perdóname" ("Forgive Me," 2006). Rapper Lorna's electronic funk and disco-influenced "Papi Chulo . . . Te Traigo El MMMM . . ." ("Papi Chulo . . . I Bring the MMMM . . . ," 2003) went to

No. 1 in France, No. 2 in Italy, Belgium, and No. 3 in the Netherlands. Among expatriate hip hop acts, the Grammy nominated Oakland duo Los Rakas (2006–) offers G-funk style beats and electronic dance music that is politically conscious, with English and Spanish rapping. Its song "Sueño Americano" ("American Dream"), from the album *El negrito Dun Dun and Ricardo* (*The Bold Dun Dun and Ricardo*, 2014), describes how immigrants are left out of the American Dream, working for low wages under the table, or earning their money on the streets.

Anthony J. Fonseca

See also: Puerto Rico; Reggae; Reggaetón

Further Reading

Rivera, Raquel Z., Wayne Marshall, and Deborah Pacini Hernandez. 2009. *Reggaetón.* Durham, NC: Duke University Press.

Rivera-Rideau, Petra. 2016. "From Panama to the Bay: Los Rakas' Expressions of Afrolatinidad." In *La Verdad: An International Dialogue on Hip Hop Latinidades*, edited by Melissa Castillo-Garsow and Jason Nicholls, chap. 4. Columbus: Ohio State University Press.

Further Listening

El General. 1994. *Es mundial* (*Is Worldwide*). BMG/U.S. Latin/RCA.

Panjabi Hit Squad

(PHS, 2001–, London, England)

Panjabi Hit Squad (PHS) is an English collective of DJ/Producers that formed in 2001 in Southall, West London. Its music has been called urban South Asian fusion, a style that employs hip hop with *bhangra-beat*, BollyHood, and *Desi* (a term that refers to South Asian–related people, culture, art, and products) *beats*. The group's members are all self-identified British Asians who worked separately as DJs in the West London club scene in the 1990s. PHS includes core members Rav (anonymous, n.d.) and Dee (anonymous, n.d.), which are the collective's main production duo, as well as others such as Markie Mark (Mark Ian Strippel, 1974–) and Amo (anonymous, n.d.).

They joined together to release their first and second albums, *Panjabi Hit Squad: The Album* (2001) and *The Streets* (2002), on London's India Sound label (2000–2003), a short-lived recording label that released Bollywood, classical Indian music, and urban Desi compilations, and Tiger Entertainment (2000*–2004), which specialized in world music. PHS's Youtube hit "Hai Hai" first appeared as a garage track toward the end of the band's second album.

In 2002, PHS collaborated on the single "Stolen (Dil)," which featured Jay-Z (1969–). But PHS's biggest success took place in 2003, when it rerecorded "Hai Hai" as a 12-inch promotional single for Def Jam U.K. "Hai Hai" was the first Asian song to reach No. 1 on the MTV Base chart. It featured Ms Scandalous (Savita Vaid, 1985–), a Southall-based bhangra-beat singer and rap artist. "Hai Hai" also featured Punjabi singer Satwinder Bitti (1975*–), who appears on the remix of the song on the EP *Desi Beats Vol 1* (2003).

"Hai Hai" is a bilingual song that fuses bhangra-beat and hip hop, English rap, Punjabi and Hindi singing, and Desi beats. PHS later produced Ms Scandalous's "Aaja Soniyah" ("Come, Darling" or "Spread Love"), the second track of her album *Ladies First* (2005). Ms Scandalous's song reached No. 4 on the MTV Base chart. Also for Def Jam, PHS remixed Ashanti's (1980–) "Baby" (2002) in 2003, Mariah Carey's (1970–) "Boy (I Need You)" in 2002, and Jay Sean's (Kamaljit Singh Jhooti, 1979–) "Maybe" and "Ride It" in 2008.

In 2006, Amo and Markie Mark left PHS. Markie Mark became the Head of Music at the BBC Asian Network, a British radio station with an English-speaking South Asian target audience. A duo since 2006, PHS produced Ms Scandalous's second album *Aag* (*Fire*, 2008), on which the title song was also a hit. This album also began PHS's collaboration with the pop and Bollywood playback singer Alyssia (Alyssia Sharma, 1985–). From 2004 until 2009 PHS has hosted the radio show *Desi Beats Show* on BBC 1Xtra. Rav and Dee have remained regulars on radio, hosting the Saturday night show *Panjabi Hit Squad, Hit Squad House Party* on BBC's Asian Network.

In 2012, Panjabi Hit Squad released *World Famous*, which reached No. 1 in the United Kingdom as well as on the Apple iTunes World album chart. As of 2018, the current PHS is still touring, working on studio albums, collaborating with artists, and hosting radio shows.

Melissa Ursula Dawn Goldsmith

See also: India; The United Kingdom

Further Reading

Baddhan, Raj. 2005. "Music: It Is Ladies First for Ms Scandalous." *Evening Mail* (Birmingham, England), May 13, 66.

Goldsmith, Melissa, and Anthony J. Fonseca. 2013. "Bhangra-Beat and Hip Hop: Hyphenated Musical Cultures, Hybridized Music." In *Crossing Traditions: American Popular Music in Local and Global Contexts*, edited by Babacar M'Baye and Alexander Charles Oliver Hall, chap. 9. Lanham, MD: Scarecrow.

Um, Hae-Kyung. 2012. "The Politics of Performance and the Creation of South Asian Music in Britain: Identities, Transnational Cosmopolitanism, and the Public Sphere." *Performing Islam* 1, no. 1: 57–72.

Further Listening

PHS. 2002. *The Streets*. Tiger Entertainment.

Panjabi MC

(Rajinder Singh Rai, 1973–, Coventry, England)

Panjabi MC is a British Indian musician (DJ) and producer best known for the *bhangra-beat* hits "Mundian To Bach Ke" ("Beware of the Boys," 1998) and "Jogi" ("Yogi," 2003). The former, from his fifth album *Legalised,* was a YouTube hit, which led to Panjabi MC's being signed by Superstar Recordings (1994–). A remix version featuring Jay-Z (1969–) was released in 2003 as "Beware of the Boys" and debuted at No. 5 on the U.K. charts while selling 100,000 copies in two days in England and Germany, and eventually one million copies worldwide. Panjabi MC popularized the combining of Western and traditional instruments in bhangra-beat music, using the traditional *tumbi, dhol, dholki,* and *tabla,* along with the standup bass, electric bass, and drum kit. He also uses both male and female singers and vocal samples in much of his music.

Panjabi MC's studio albums include *Souled Out* (1993), *Another Sell Out* (1994), *100% Proof* (1995), *Grass Roots* (1996), *Magic Desi* (1996), *Legalised* (1998), *Dhol Jageroo Da* (2001), *Desi* (2002), *Indian Breaks* (2003), *Mundian To Bach Ke* (aka, *Beware of the Boys,* compilation, 2003), *Steel Bangle* (2005), *Indian Timing* (2008), and *The Raj* (2010). He has won awards at the MTV Europe Music Awards, the U.K. Asian Music Awards, the World Music Awards, and the Panjabi Music Awards.

As of 2018, he is performing internationally and has partnered with Apple Inc. to market its iTumbi, which allows musicians access to tumbi sounds via the iPhone.

Anthony J. Fonseca

See also: India; Jay-Z; The United Kingdom

Further Reading

Goldsmith, Melissa, and Anthony J. Fonseca. 2013. "Bhangra-Beat and Hip Hop: Hyphenated Musical Cultures, Hybridized Music." In *Crossing Traditions: American Popular Music in Local and Global Contexts,* edited by Babacar M'Baye and Alexander Charles Oliver Hall, chap. 9. Lanham, MD: Scarecrow.

Hankins, Sarah. 2011. "So Contagious: Hybridity and Subcultural Exchange in Hip Hop's Use of Indian Samples." *Black Music Research Journal* 31, no. 2: 193–208.

Um, Hae-Kyung. 2012. "The Politics of Performance and the Creation of South Asian Music in Britain: Identities, Transnational Cosmopolitanism, and the Public Sphere." *Performing Islam* 1, no. 1: 57–72.

Wartofsky, Alona. 2003. "Rap's Fresh Heir: Panjabi MC, Making Some Noise on the Hip Hop Scene with a South Asian Sound." *The Washington Post,* July 13, N01.

Further Listening

Panjabi MC. 1998. *Legalised.* Nachural Records.

Paris City Breakers

(PCB, 1984–, Paris, France)

The Paris City Breakers (PCB) was the first breakdance and b-boy crew in France. Cofounded by choreographer, breakdancer, and DJ Frank le Breaker Fou (Franck II Louise, n.d.) and breakdancer Scalp (Pascal Grégoire, n.d.), the PCB was modeled on the New York City Breakers (NYCB, aka NYC Breakers, 1981–), a breakdance crew and a rival hip hop dance crew to the Rock Steady Crew (RSC, 1977–) of the Bronx, New York. Another member, the rapper Solo (Souleymane Dicko, 1966–), whose parents were from Mali, made the original PCB a trio. More members were added later.

The inspiration for the Paris City Breakers first came during a Gianni Ferrucci (n.d.) fashion show in Paris that featured Madonna (1958–) and the NYCB. The PCB became regular performing guests on the nationally broadcast television show *H.I.P. H.O.P.* (1984), France's first television show on the country's hip hop scene that also introduced American hip hop artists. Most of the PCB's moves were styled after the NYCB, especially head spins; the PCB elaborated on these moves and at times had cleaner and more intricate footwork than the NYCB.

From European tours and television shows in mid-1980s to touring Africa, the Paris City Breakers have often been credited as early inspiration to breakdancing crews from outside the United States. Crediting the PCB for their inspiration, French breaking crews emerged in Paris: Aktuel Force (1984–) formed the same year as the PCB, and the Vagabond Crew (2000*–) emerged later in Paris. Other French crews also emerged, first in the northeast Alsace and Burgundy regions and then in east-central Auvergne-Rhône-Alpes. Breaking crews from Brussels, Belgium followed. Soon after PCB's African tour, breakdancing crews based on PCB, such as the Bamako City Breakers (from Mali) and the Abidjan City Breakers (from Ivory Coast), developed in urban cities in West and South Africa.

Melissa Ursula Dawn Goldsmith

See also: Breakdancing; France; Hip Hop Dance; New York City Breakers

Further Reading

Eric Charry. 2012. "A Capsule History of African Rap." In *Hip Hop Africa: New African Music in a Globalizing World*, edited by Eric Charry, chap. 1. Bloomington: Indiana University Press.

Schloss, Joseph G. 2009. *Foundation: B-Boys, B-Girls, and Hip Hop Culture in New York*. New York: Oxford University Press.

Peru

Peru's hip hop scene is mainly located in its capital and largest city, Lima, and since more than 70 percent of Peru's 31 million citizens—with 76 percent living in urban areas—speak Spanish, Peruvian rappers rap mainly in that language. Peruvian rap has a strong sociopolitical focus. Comité Pokofló's (2012–) 2015 boombap album, *El fin de los tiempos* (*The End of Time*), exemplifies contemporary Peruvian hip hop's style with its political stance, its elaborate use of orchestral instrumentation and quirky effects (for example, using chimes), and its quick-paced, almost frenetic rapping. However, the country's population is multiethnic, including Amerindians, Europeans, Africans, and Asians, and this cultural mix causes diversity in instrumentation and styles for music, which has Andean, Spanish, and African roots. This musical diversity has resulted in a slow buildup of hip hop popularity, as it has to compete with traditional and popular music styles.

Despite the population concentration and odds against its popularity, hip hop is growing in other areas of Peru, such as coastal northwestern Trujillo and Huancayo, in the central highlands. The first Peruvian rap group was Golpeando la Calle, formed in 1991 by musicians who were leaders of the country's hip hop movement. The duo M Sony M and DJ Pedro (1998–) were the fathers of Movimiento Hip Hop Peruano, an attempt to unite the country's rap community. In 1998, Droopy G (Isaac Shamar, n.d.), one of the pioneers of Peru's Christian rap scene, released Peru's first hip hop record, *Cadenas Invisibles* (*Invisible Chains*). Peruvian rappers to follow included Clan Urbano (2002–), whose big break came in 2010 when it won Festival Claro with the song "Esta es mi casa" ("This Is My House") and Rapper School

(2001–), whose single hit "Psicosis" (2010) created a national following, while "Pase lo que pase" ("Whatever Happens," 2012) received over 20 million YouTube views.

Women have also carved out a niche in Peruvian hip hop, with bands such as the duo Las Damas (n.d.), Las Hermanas del Underground (H.D.U., n.d.), and Sipas Crew (2012–). The nation is slowly embracing hip hop culture: on the last Friday of every month, 150 b-boys, graffiti artists, and rappers gather in Parque Kennedy de Miraflores (downtown Lima) to show off their skills.

Anthony J. Fonseca

See also: Bolivia; Christian Hip Hop

Further Reading

Jones, Kyle E. 2014. "'Searching and Searching We Have Come to Find': Histories and Circulations of Hip Hop in Peru." *Alter/Nativas: Latin American Cultural Studies Journal*, no. 2: 1–32.

Lewis, Eshe. 2012. "'Más Peruano que el Macchu Picchu' ["More Peruvian than Macchu Picchu"]: Creating Afro-Peruvian Rap." *Latin Americanist* 56, no. 1: 85–106.

Further Listening

Comité Pokofló. 2015. *El fin de los tiempos* (*The End of Time*). No label.

Pharrell

(Pharrell Lanscilo Williams, 1973–, Virginia Beach, Virginia)

Pharrell is an American music and motion picture producer, recording executive, singer-songwriter, drummer, keyboardist, and rapper, who often fuses hip hop with R&B, funk, neo soul, and/or electronic music. He primarily sings lyrical melodies that are either featured or support rappers. Pharrell is a tenor, whose signature falsetto is heard as soloist in his hit "Happy" (2013) and in contrasting passages to American rapper Jay-Z (1969–) in the hit "Frontin'" (2002) and to American rapper Snoop Dogg (1971–) in the hit "Beautiful" (2002). Pharrell also composed and performed songs for the American animated comedy films *Despicable Me* (2010) and *Despicable Me 2* (2013). Since the 2000s, Pharrell and his music have appeared often in American films and television series. In music camp and junior high school marching band in Virginia Beach, Virginia, percussionist Pharrell befriended saxophonist Chad Hugo (Charles Edward Hugo, 1974–). In high school they formed the production-songwriting duo the Neptunes (1992–). Teddy Riley (Edward Theodore Riley, 1967–), the American record producer and singer-songwriter credited for creating new jack swing and hits for artists such as Michael Jackson (1958–2009) and Bobby Brown (1969–), discovered the two during a local talent competition.

American rapper N.O.R.E.'s (aka Noreaga, Victor Santiago Jr., 1976–) "Superthug" (1998), which peaked at No. 36 on the Billboard Hot 100, was the Neptunes' first hit. Employing a prominent bass line, drum machine beats, samples, world music virtual instruments and Pharrell's falsetto, the Neptunes have had a prolific number of hits such as Jay-Z's "I Just Wanna Love U (Give It 2 Me)" (2000), Britney Spears's (1981–) "I'm a Slave 4 U" (2001), and Nelly's (Cornell Iral Haynes Jr., 1974–) "Hot in Herre" (2002).

The Neptunes released *The Neptunes Present . . . Clones* (2003), which was certified Gold and peaked at No. 1 on the Billboard Hot 100. In 2001, the Neptunes, as fans of the *Star Trek* original series (1966–1969), created the recording label Star Trak Entertainment (2001–), under the parent company Universal Music Group (1996–). Star Trak coreleased Snoop Dogg's *RandG (Rhythm and Gangsta): The Masterpiece* (2004), which peaked at No. 6 on the Billboard 200 and was certified Platinum. Since 1999, the Neptunes have doubled as a funk-rock band, N*E*R*D (No-one Ever Really Dies, 1999–). N*E*R*D's albums *In Search of . . .* (2002) and *Fly or Die* (2004) peaked at Nos. 56 and 6, respectively, on the Billboard 200 and went Gold. Subsequent albums *Seeing Sounds* (2008) and *Nothing* (2010) peaked at Nos. 7 and 20 on the Billboard 200.

In 2003, Pharrell began his solo career. As of 2018, he continues producing, recording, performing, and collaborating with internationally known hip hop artists. His solo studio albums *In My Mind* (2006) and *G. I. R. L.* (2014) peaked at Nos. 3 and 2, respectively, on the Billboard 200. *In My Mind* was certified Silver. As of 2018, Pharrell has won 10 Grammy Awards.

Melissa Ursula Dawn Goldsmith

See also: New Jack Swing; Snoop Dogg; The United States

Further Reading

Lester, Paul. 2015. *In Search of Pharrell Williams*. London: Omnibus Press.

Williams, Pharrell, Buzz Aldrin, Ian Luna, and Lauren A. Gould. 2012. *Pharrell: Places and Spaces I've Been*. New York: Rizzoli.

Further Listening

Williams, Pharrell. 2014. *G. I. R. L.* I Am Other/Columbia Records.

The Philippines

The Philippines is an archipelago located in Southeast Asia and was a colony of the United States from 1898 until 1946; therefore, America has had a profound impact on the country's culture, including its hip hop scene, known as Filipino hip hop, Pinoy hip hop, or Pinoy rap. After the Philippines gained independence, the United States maintained military bases in the country. American service members stationed there helped introduce hip hop to Filipinos, and the exchange of music between Filipino immigrants in the United States and their friends and family in the Philippines helped spread it faster than in other Southeast Asian countries. The origins of Pinoy rap can be traced back to the emergence of the Sugarhill Gang's (1979–1985, 1994–) "Rapper's Delight" (1979), which became so popular in Manila that Filipino singer and comedian Dyords Javier (George Javier, n.d.) recorded a parody called "Na onseng delight" ("Led to Believe," 1980). Along with Vincent Dafalong's (1953*–2017) "Nunal" ("Magical Mole," 1980), it was one of the first rap tracks recorded in the Philippines.

The two most influential Pinoy hip hop artists are Francis M. (Francis Magalona, 1964–2009), of Mandaluyong, and Andrew E. (Andrew Ford Valentino

Espiritu, 1967–), of Parañaque. The popularity of Magalona's nationalistic themed track, "Mga Kababayan" ("My Countrymen," 1990) exposed Pinoy hip hop to a wider audience. Andrew E.'s first hit track, "Humanap Ka ng Panget" ("Look for Someone Ugly," 1990), led to a starring role in a movie with the same name. A promising career in both music and cinema helped Andrew E. bring Pinoy hip hop into the mainstream.

Pinoy hip hop is rapped and sung in Tagalog, English, Cebuano, Ilokano, Biko-lano, and other languages; however, there have been disputes between artists who use Filipino languages and those who use English only, especially in the main-stream. Many rap artists believe that the Philippines' music industry suffers from a colonial mentality, favoring those who rap in English only. Although language is an ongoing issue affecting Pinoy hip hop identity, it is uniquely Filipino because it represents Filipino roots, experiences, and national pride.

CURRENT PINOY ARTISTS

Current notable Pinoy hip hop artists include Michael V. (Beethoven del Valle Bunagan, 1969–), from Manila; Denmark (Denmark Repuyan, n.d.); Bass Rhyme Posse (1990*–), from Las Piñas; and Rapasia (1990*–) and Gloc-9 (Aristotle Pol-lisco, 1977–), both from Binangonan. Significant female rappers, who choose to remain anonymous or give obvious pseudonyms as their birth names, include Lady Diane (anonymous, n.d.), MC Lara (aka Glenda Resureccion, anonymous, n.d.), and Chill (aka Audra Bio, anonymous, n.d.). In the early 1990s, turntablism gained exposure, especially with the debut of the group Mastaplann (1992*–).

Inspired by American hip hop group N.W.A. (1986–1991), Death Threat (1993–2003, 2010–) emerged with its hardcore and gangsta style of Pinoy rap. The band's lyrics expressed frustration and anger with the social problems facing Metro Manila and other areas in the Philippines, such as crime, drugs, and violence, with "Gusto Kong Bumaet" ("I Want to Be Good") becoming an instant radio hit around the country.

Antonette Adiova

See also: DJ Babu; Gangsta Rap; Invisibl Skratch Piklz; Mix Master Mike; The United States

Further Reading

Devitt, Rachel. 2008. "Lost in Translation: Filipino Diaspora(s), Postcolonial Hip Hop, and the Problems of Keeping It Real for the 'Contentless' Black Eyed Peas." *Asian Music* 39, no. 1: 108–34; 147.

Perillo, J. Lorenzo. 2012. "An Empire State of Mind: Hip Hop Dance in the Philippines." In *Hip Hop(e): The Cultural Practice and Critical Pedagogy*, edited by Brad J. Por-filio and Michael J. Viola, chap. 2. New York: Peter Lang.

Further Listening

Death Threat. 2005. *Da Best of Death Threat.* Real Deal Entertainment.

Francis M. 1992. *Rap Is FrancisM.* PolyEast Records.

Mastaplann. 1993. *Mastaplann.* Universal Records.

Pitbull

(Armando Christian Pérez, 1981–, Miami, Florida)

Pitbull is a Grammy Award winning American hip hop and reggaetón rapper and record producer. He has released 10 albums since 2004, when his debut *M.I.A.M.I.*, which included production by Lil Jon (Jonathan Smith, 1971–) and Jim Jonsin (James Scheffer, 1970–), was released by under TVT Records (1985–2008). He had previously self-released three mixtapes. *M.I.A.M.I.* went to No. 2 on the Top Rap Albums chart and reached No. 14 on the Billboard 200. Born to Cuban expatriates, Pitbull could recite, at the age of three, the poems of José Martí (José Julián Martí Pérez, 1853–1895) in Spanish. He also began to appreciate music, especially the Miami bass sound, as well as the salsa and merengue of Celia Cruz (Úrsula Hilaria Celia de la Caridad Cruz Alfonso, 1925–2003) and Willy Chirino (1947–).

He was raised by his mother and in a foster home; he decided to become a rapper in high school. He released three mixtapes in 2002 and 2003 and first appeared on Lil Jon's (Jonathan Smith, 1971–) album *Kings of Crunk* (2002). His song "Oye" was featured on the soundtrack to *2 Fast 2 Furious* (2003).

Pitbull Starring in Rebelution became Pitbull's first No. 1 rap album in 2009, and also reached the Top 10 of the Billboard 200. It was the first to be released on his Mr. 305 Inc. (2008–) label. His rap album *Global Warming* (2012) also reached No. 1, and one other, *Planet Pit* (2011), reached the Top 10. Pitbull has released seven solo Top 10 hits on the Hot 100, including two No. 1 songs, "Give Me Everything" (2011) and "Timber" (2013). He is also known for his part in the song "We Are One (Ole Ola)," the official theme of the 2014 FIFA World Cup, which he sang with Jennifer Lopez (aka J.Lo, 1969–) and Claudia Leitte (Cláudia Cristina Leite Inácio Pedreira, 1980–). In 2005, Pitbull and Puff Daddy (1969–)

Active since 2001, rapper and producer Pitbull had his first hit in 2009 with the Eurodance single "I Know You Want Me (Calle Ocho)," which reached No. 2 on the Billboard Hot 100. Here, he is pictured performing in 2010 in New York City, just a year before he had a No. 1 hit single with his hip house song "Give Me Everything." (Michael Loccisano/FilmMagic for Vh1/Getty Images)

cofounded Bad Boy Latino, a subsidiary of Bad Boy Entertainment (aka Bad Boy Records, 1993–) label. Pitbull heads the A&R division of the label (talent searching and development), and he hosted a variety show, Pitbull's La Esquina (2007–2009).

The city of Miami granted Pitbull a Key to the City in 2009, and in 2010, he released a full-length Spanish-language album, *Armando*. In 2014, it was announced that Pitbull would be receiving a star on the Hollywood Walk of Fame. He has been used for various product endorsements, including Kodak, Dr Pepper, Voli Vodka, Budweiser, and Miami Subs Pizza and Grill. In 2015, Pitbull launched a new Sirius XM Satellite Radio (1990–) channel, Pitbull's Globalization Radio. He has appeared in film, on television, and in video games.

Anthony J. Fonseca

See also: Cuba; Miami Bass; Puff Daddy; Reggaetón; The United States

Further Reading

Ginger, Andrew. 2018. "International Love? 'Latino' Music Videos, the Latin Brand of Universality, and Pitbull." In *Branding Latin America: Strategies, Aims, Resistance*, edited by Djunja Fehimović and Rebecca Ogden, chap. 7. Lanhan, MD: Lexington Books.

Hoard, Christian. 2004. "Pitbull Unleashed." *Rolling Stone* no. 957, September 16, 28.

West-Durán, Alan. 2004. "Rap's Diasporic Dialogues: Cuba's Redefinition of Blackness." *Journal of Popular Music Studies* 16, no. 1: 4–39.

Further Listening

Pitbull. 2012. *Global Warming*. Polo Grounds Music.

Poland

Poland has a hip hop scene that began in the early 1990s. Polish hip hop is a combination of the influences of American rap and 1980s Polish punk rock, alternative rock, disco, funk, and traditional Slavic music. Polish rap's earliest appearance was the cassette *East On Da Mic* (1995) by Liroy (as PM Cool Lee, Piotr Krzysztof Liroy-Marzec, 1971–). Like many urban areas, Warsaw, the capital and largest city of Poland, with a population of about three million residents, became the Polish center for hip hop after radio station KOLOR broadcast songs by hip hop artists in 1995, the year that Liroy released *Albóóm* (a wordplay on *Album* and *All Boom*).

Polish rappers are known for their expression of pride in Polish culture (a sentiment that has made its way into the English hip hop scene as well, with Polish immigrants in the United Kingdom). Polish immigrant rappers in the United Kingdom, such as Popek (Paweł Ryszard Mikołajuw, 1978–), often rap in English, to a fan base that is mostly Polish. Many of them have become grime rappers, practicing the cheaper, DIY London-based music genre that emerged in the early 2000s from U.K. garage, jungle, dancehall, hip hop, and raga. As such, they use rapid, syncopated breakbeats (130 to 140 bpm), an aggressive or jagged electronic sound, and lyrics that depict gritty depictions of urban life.

Some of the other best-selling hip hop artists in Poland are the street rap and hip hop group Slums Attack (1993–) and related rapper Peja (Ryszard Andrzejewski,

1976–); rapper, musician, audio engineer, and record producer O.S.T.R. (Adam Ostrowski, 1980–); musician, music producer, and sound engineer Donatan (Witold Czamara, 1984–); early Warsaw street rap group Molesta (aka Mistic Molesta, 1994–) and related group Hemp Gru (1998–); rapper Trzyha (Warszafski Deszcz, 1994–); and rap group WWO (W Witrynach Odbicia, Sites of Reflection, 1999–). O.S.T.R., from Łódź, is a classically trained violinist from the Academy of Music in Łódź and is famous for his freestyle rap skills and unique beats. WWO is one of the most famous polish hip hop band; it spawned the solo rapper Sokół (Wojciech Sosnowski, 1977–), who has released two Platinum albums and founded the Prosto (1999–) record label and clothing company.

Donatan, from Kraków, is known for extremely controversial rap topics and for criticizing the government, which has not affected his success. Recently, he has teamed with singer Cleo (Joanna Klepko, 1983–), who represented Poland in the Eurovision Song Contest 2014—and as a duo they are becoming internationally famous by creating a niche with songs that depict rural Polish life in hypersexualized, stereotypical hip hop video vixen fashion. The video to the song "Brać" ("Take" or "Assume") from the album *Hiper Chimera* (2014), depicts farm girls in Daisy Dukes and tight shirts washing tractors against a music that features elements of Slavic folk music and *klezmer*, including punk accordion. From the same album, "Slavica" ("Slavik") uses elements of Western hip hop, and its video, which has had nearly 16 million views in just weeks (as of 2018), features twerking Slavic women wearing skin-tight leather shorts, juxtaposed against images of farm roosters, honey harvesting, and powdered amber (believed to have medicinal properties in Polish folk medicine).

Anthony J. Fonseca

See also: The United States

Further Reading

Miszczynski, Milosz, and Przemyslaw Tomaszewski. 2014. "'Spitting Lines-Spitting Brands': A Critical Analysis of Brand Usage in Polish Rap." *European Journal of Cultural Studies* 17, no. 6: 736–52.

Miszczynski, Milosz, and Przemyslaw Tomaszewski. 2017. "Wearing Nikes for a Reason: A Critical Analysis of Brand Usage in Polish Rap." In *Hip Hop at Europe's Edge: Music, Agency, and Social Change*, edited by Milosz Miszczynski and Adriana Helbig, chap. 8. Bloomington: Indiana University Press.

Further Listening

Donatan. 2012. *Równonoc. Słowiańska Dusza (Equinox: Slavic Soul)*. Urban Rec.

Donatan and Cleo. 2014. *Hiper Chimera*. Urban Rec.

Political Hip Hop

Political hip hop exists worldwide, as hip hop is often used to express political stances and to advance political agenda. While specific political issues that make their way into hip hop songs vary widely from culture to culture, common themes that can be seen internationally include cultural-political identity, indigeneity (the attribute of being born or produced naturally in a given region), race, gender, human rights, and the need to often take an antigovernment stance (resistance).

NORTH AMERICA

Though hip hop began in the 1970s in the United States as party music, the continued oppression of African Americans in post–Civil Rights United States (after 1968) led to hip hop's use as an expressive vehicle for the African American community to speak out boldly on social, political and economic matters. By the early 1980s, politically conscious hip hop had emerged. Brother D (Daryl Aamaa Nubyahn, n.d.) in "How We Gonna Make the Black Nation Rise?"(1980), raps about poverty, poor housing, and violence against African Americans, over an uptempo funk beat sampling Cheryl Lynn's (Lynda Cheryl Smith, 1957–) "Got to Be Real" (1978). Grandmaster Flash and the Furious Five's (1976–1982, 1987–1988) "The Message" (1982) was the first widely known politically conscious rap: its gritty narrative about poverty, violence and the prison system is delivered emphatically over a bare-bones, tense synth beat. The chorus warns that African Americans are close to the edge, a warning about the precarious state of urban African American community at large.

These and similar early hip hop recordings would pave the way for Public Enemy (1982–) and N.W.A. (1986–1991) to deliver increasingly strident political messages. Public Enemy's third album, *Fear of a Black Planet* (1990) sought to capture Dr. Frances Cress Welsing's (Frances Luella Cress, 1935–2016) theories of color confrontation; Public Enemy's creative vision was well established as one that confronted head-on sociopolitical issues.

As gangsta rap emerged, it overlapped significantly with political rap: Groups such as N.W.A. and rappers such as Ice-T (1958–) stridently and explosively delivered political statements over hard-driving, swirling, forceful beats. N.W.A.'s debut album *Straight Outta Compton* (1988) dealt uninhibitedly with issues such as racism, drugs, and violence, while Ice-T and Body Count's (1990–2006, 2009–) "Cop Killer" (1992) protested rampant police brutality against blacks. Gangsta rap criticized the inner city blight of Los Angeles, whose poverty and unemployment rates affected a whole generation of black youth; the power in its message hinges on the idea that social realism, drawing attention to a striking lack of opportunity for and active criminalization and oppression of the black community, is itself a political statement. At the same time, gangsta rap's frequently misogynistic culture and lyrics fly in the face of politically forward feminism. This misogyny, rooted in economic oppression and lack of access to other signs of heterosexual masculine power, grapples with the issue of limited personal and political power by displacing expressed aggression onto women instead of directing it toward perceived oppressors. Ice Cube's *AmeriKKKa's Most Wanted* (1990) reflected the commonly held sense in the African American youth community that they were stereotyped, targeted, and criminalized by the criminal justice system and by a mass media that chose to dwell on expressions of sexism and misogyny instead of on positive aspects such as personal empowerment, antidrug rhetoric, and black community building.

Since the beginning of his career with C.I.A., then N.W.A., to his successful solo career and group Westside Connection, American rapper Ice Cube has written rap songs that serve as sociopolitical commentary. In 2012 Ice Cube released the music video for his non-album single "Everythang's Corrupt," just a day before the U.S. presidential election. (Starstock/Dreamstime.com)

In the late 1990s New Orleans emerged as a burgeoning hip hop center with labels No Limit Records (1990–2003) and Ca$h Money Records (1991–) generating large revenues while drawing attention to urban life in the city's wards. In the aftermath of Hurricane Katrina's (2005) devastation of New Orleans and particularly its ninth ward, rap artists drew attention to community impacts in the predominantly African American city while criticizing government response. Mos Def (1973–) included in his album *True Magic* (2006) the track "Katrina Klap," which is based on the rhythm and hook of "Nolia Clap"—a pro–New Orleans rap by MC Juvenile (Terius Gray, 1977–) on *The Beginning of the End* (2004)— and expresses disgust with the U.S. government's mismanagement of the disaster, cleanup, and community revitalization.

The campaign and election of President Barack Obama (1961–) in 2008 brought on a new wave of political activism in hip hop, and a resurgence of conscious rap, reinvented around new media associated with digital, online communities. During the election year, mixtapes were used as a vehicle for hip hop political discourse. Obama-themed digital mixtapes were circulated online, encouraging young voters to be politically active, and capturing the hope and personality of the campaign, many tracks quoting directly from Obama's speeches. Will.i.am (1975–) released the single "Yes We Can" on YouTube, featuring Obama's words echoed by celebrities in a call-and-response manner. Nas (1973–) centered "Black President" (2008) around Obama's spoken words, set alongside the hook from the posthumous release of Tupac Shakur's (1971–1996) "Changes" (1998). In this track, he expresses both hope and questions about Obama's future accountability to the African American community. Since the 2016 election, American rappers have produced songs challenging President Donald Trump's (1946–) policies on immigration and race.

In Canada, the Toronto-based Dope Poet Society (1992–) is known for their rapid-fire deliveries of politically charged messages, confronting throughout their career issues such as sexism, the neo-Nazi movement, political oppression, U.S. responses to terrorism, and global inequalities. Their album *Third World Warriors No. 1* (2008) deals with global politics as well as a response to the question of why Dope Poet Society chooses to enact political activism in their music. Palestinian-Canadian Belly (Ahmad Balshe, 1984–) released the mixtape *Mumble Rap* in 2017 both as a nod to the activism of 1990s politically conscious rap, and to offer his version of a 21st-century rap style, with fast-flowing lyrics that have to be followed consciously, even worked out over multiple hearings, to be understood by the listener. In *Mumble Rap* Belly takes the media and conservative politicians to task for their attacks on rap music, and deals with issues such as immigration and human rights. In addition, Native American hip hop artist Shibastik (meaning Underground Flow in Cree, Chris G. Sutherland, n.d.), awarded for his work with at-risk youth, used hip hop music and art to promote environmental responsibility and the political perspectives of First Nation culture. Recordings such as "Landslide" (2015) drew attention to the white appropriation of Native American lands, tying those events to current-day pollution and ecological disasters. His albums include *Wild Game* (2003), *Moose River* (2007), *Wild Life* (2012), and *Underground Flow* (2016).

EUROPE

French hip hop, popular among the large African and Caribbean community since the 1970s, offers urban poor a way to express discontent with French political structures, racism, ghetto life, and immigrant status. The group Suprême NTM (1989–2001) was known for its confrontational material and conflicts with French authorities. In "Qu'est-ce qu'on attend" ("What Are We Waiting For," 1995), a beat based on the Meters' (1965–1977, 1989–) easygoing, funk instrumental "Oh, Calcutta!" (1969) is played against hard-hitting lyrics that denounce the suffering of ghetto youth, an anger that has risen to an exploding point, the discomfort of the juxtaposition of lighthearted beats against strident lyrics highlights an intense frustration. IAM's (1989–), in *De la planète Mars* (1991), takes on French colonialism and predicts the end of colonization at the expense of original inhabitants.

Much British-produced hip hop has focused on rave-jam remixes of U.S. styles; however, British Asians have used hip hop to address cultural legitimacy and egalitarianism. Fun-Da-Mental (1991–), founded by Aki Nawaz (Haq Nawaz Qureshi, n.d.), incorporates Indian and Afro-Caribbean sounds into its beats, while rapping about the discrimination faced by British Asians and Afro-Caribbeans. The band's third single, "Wrath of the Blackman" (1993), exemplifies its outspokenness in favor of African American Islamic radicalism and the separatist policies of the Black Panther Party (1966–1982).

Before the fall of the Soviet Union in 1991, hip hop's potential political power was sensed by East German authorities, who after the release of the American film *Beat Street* (1984), mounted a public campaign to recharacterize it as a warning about the dangers of capitalist competition. By the end of the 20th century, hip hop groups such as Freundeskreis (Circle of Friends, 1996–2007) had emerged as a politically active underground, with overtly political texts connected deeply to their upbringings in a Black Panther household and a Marxist collective. Freundeskreis's *Quadratur des Kreises* (*Squaring the Circle*, 1997) called on listeners to be keenly aware of their place in political history. The group Advanced Chemistry (1987–), whose members are German citizens with immigrant backgrounds, tackle controversial political issues such as immigrant status and racism.

Dutch hip hop (Nederhop) groups such as DAMN (1989–1993) and Osdorp Posse (1989–2009) used hip hop to explore sociopolitical inequality and the postcolonial migrant experience. Basque Country underground group Negu Gorriak (1990–1996) spoke out in favor of Basque nationalism and indigenous language revival. The Galician hip hop collective Dios Ke Te Crew (2003–) code-switch between majority language (Spanish) and indigenous or migrant dialects—resistance vernaculars—to protest a Spanish-centric language standard. In the Italian rap track "Fight da faida" ("Fight the Blood Feuds," 1993), Frankie Hi-NRG MC (Francesco De Gesù, 1969–) calls for a cessation of a blood feud between the Camorra and Mafia families, which he considers a major cause of social and political ill. In 1994, the Italian group 99 Posse (1991–2005, 2009–), known for its left-wing views, staged a national Incredible Opposizione Tour to share messages about exploitation, antifascism, and political incompetence.

Afro-Ukrainian hip hop artists such as Tanok na Maidani Kongo (TNMK, Dance in Congo Square, 1989–), which formed in a teen educational summer camp, have used hip hop to fight cultural and political oppression, and to influence public opinion regarding black identity in Ukraine. Latvian hip hop artist Gustavo (Gustavs Butelis, 1978–) raps about the years under Soviet control, and how those years continue to affect the Latvian people. In an example of government manipulation of hip hop, in the mid-1990s Russia's NDR (Our Home) party, led by Prime Minister Viktor Chernomyrdin (1938–2010, in office 1993–1998), invited rapper MC Hammer (1962–) to perform three concerts without informing him that the concerts were part of a political campaign intended to motivate voters.

THE MIDDLE EAST AND AFRICA

Hip hop was heard in much of the Arab world by the 1990s, but came onto the world stage as a political agent in 21st-century Arab revolutionary movements that have protested and overthrown dictatorships in the Middle East and North Africa. "Rayes Lebled," Tunisian rapper El Général's (Hamada Ben Amor, 1989*–) direct criticism of President Ben Ali (Zine El Abidine Ben Ali, 1936–, in office 1987–2011), became a battle cry for protesters in Tunisia, and was used similarly in Egypt, Libya, Syria, and beyond. Hip hop recording artist Bahram Nouraei (1988–) likewise rapped against President Mahmoud Ahmadinejad (Mahmoud Sabbaghian or Saborjhian, 1956–, in office 2005–2013) in Teheran.

Though U.S. and U.K. cultural diplomacy efforts have attempted to take credit for hip hop's emergence in Lebanon, Yemen, Libya, and elsewhere, each Middle Eastern and North African nation has its own distinct hip hop culture, typically featuring indigenous instruments and language, and frequently speaking against oppressive government regimes and against western involvement. Many Arab rappers, such as Iranian hip hop recording artists Shahin Najafi (1980–) and Salome MC (1985–), have fled their countries of origin and continue to deliver strident political messages from abroad; meanwhile, diaspora rappers such as Syrian American Omar Offendum (1981–) and Libyan American Khaled M (Khaled Ahmed, 1985*–) form a transnational hip hop community, drawing worldwide attention to Middle Eastern political situations from outside. Middle Eastern female rappers such as Amani Yahya, (1993*–) from Yemen, Ramona Khabiri (1995*–), from Afghanistan, and Nazila (1987–2012), from Iran, challenge traditional gender roles and limitations on women's political freedom.

By the 1990s, African hip hop groups had begun to speak to their specific political situations. Positive Black Soul (PBS, 1989–) was one of the first hip hop collectives in Senegal, and urged people to become active in government, to fight political corruption, and to combat a negative global media perspective on Africa. The Senegalese grassroots hip hop coalition Y'en a Marre (Fed Up, 2011–2012) protests ineffective government and encourage the youth to register to vote. It stood against incumbent President Abdoulaye Wade (1926–, in office 2000–2012) in his 2012 run for a third presidential term, leading to some members' arrests.

In Kenya, hip hop's revolutionary energy focuses on the problems of poverty and violence and expresses an anticolonial view. The group Ukoo Flani Mau Mau (1994–), whose members hail from the slums of Nairobi and Mombasa, rallies around the memory of the revolutionary Mau Mau Uprising (1952–1960), fighting against British hegemony and government oppression. In Zimbabwe, hip hop underground groups such as A Peace of Ebony (POE, 1992–) actively defied state policies that encouraged young artists to record only progovernment or apolitical music. In their album *From the Native Tongue* (1992), POE fused hip hop beats with indigenous instruments such as the *mbira*, and blended Shona language with French and English, to confront sexual exploitation and protest unchecked violence. In South Africa, groups such as Prophets of da City (1988–2001) and Brasse Vannie Kaap (BVK, 1996–2006) criticize apartheid and its associated political ideologies. The all-female group Godessa (2000–) protests gender violence and promote AIDS awareness.

ASIA

Asian hip hop began largely as a commercial enterprise, though several political examples have emerged. On one hand, in "911," Japanese group King Giddra (1993–1996), part of a right-wing nationalist hip hop movement, reflects on the aftermath of the atomic bombings of Japan in 1945 and the terrorist attacks on the United States in 2001. On the other hand, Japanese group Rhymester (1989–), part of a hip hop underground, addresses social and political issues not openly discussed in Japanese society, such as the Japanese government's support of the invasion of Iraq.

A 21st-century Chinese hip hop youth underground has elevated local-dialect rapping as a way of reinforcing cultural and political identities. In Mongolia, hip hop artists have resisted the control of the Mongolian People's Party (1920–) over their music's political messages, particularly after the economic downturn that followed the end of Soviet subsidies. For example, the group Dain Ba Enkh (War and Peace, 1997–2010) names the government as the main obstacle preventing the Mongolian people from realizing its potential.

AUSTRALIA

In the early 1980s hip hop came to Australia, becoming a voice for the under-privileged. The underground group Sound Unlimited (1990–1994), with members who grew up in Australian immigrant communities, rap about poverty and racism in their album *Postcard from the Edge of the Underside* (1992). Hip hop music and art has become a way of life for Aboriginal youth in areas such as the poor hous-ing of inner-city Redfern-Waterloo (in Sydney), who felt marginalized by sociopo-litical and economic forces. Through hip hop, these youth crystallized their cultural identity, setting Aboriginality as a primary identification. The group Local Knowl-edge (2002–2006), and its descendants the Last Kinection (2006–) and Street Warriors (2007*–), form part of a grassroots underground movement focusing on the poverty, unemployment, and discrimination faced by indigenous people.

CENTRAL AND SOUTH AMERICA AND THE CARIBBEAN

Hip hop in Central and South America has taken on pointed political topics such as poverty and lack of government services. Mare Advertencia Lirika (1986–) raps confrontationally about women's rights, women's education, and the government's failure to protect women against endemic violence in Mexico. The Guatemalan group B'alam Ajpu (2010–) asserts a cultural and political identity as primarily Mayan, rapping in the Mayan language and challenging hegemonic assumptions about ethnic identity in Guatemala. In Brazil, the group Racíonaís MC's (1988–) released *Sobrevivendo no Inferno* (*Surviving in Hell*, 1997), which describes the struggle to end slavery and military dictatorship, and blames the massacre of 111 prisoners. The Argentinian group Actitud María Marta (1995–) raps about the need to be informed about political leaders. Cuban diaspora group Krudas Cubensi (aka the "raw native ones from Cuba and the Caribbean representing the world," 1999–) began in Havana, later moving to Austin; it raps about gender politics, black femi-nism, and freedom of speech.

Jennifer L. Roth-Burnette

See also: Black Nationalism; Bolon and Bolon Player; Five Percent Nation; Hip Hop Diplo-macy; Nation of Islam

Further Reading

Barrett, Rusty. 2016. "Mayan Language Revitalization, Hip Hop and Ethnic Identity in Guatemala." *Language and Communication* 46 (March): 144–53.

Beighey, Catherine, and N Prabha Unnithan. 2012. "Political Rap: The Music of Opposi-tional Resistance." *Sociological Focus* 133, no. 2: 133–43.

Gueye, Marame. 2013. "Urban Guerilla Poetry: The Movement Y'en a Marre and the Socio-Political Influences of Hip Hop in Senegal." *Journal of Pan African Studies* 6, no. 3: 22–42.

Hammett, Daniel. 2012. "Reworking and Resisting Globalizing Influences: Cape Town Hip Hop." *Geojournal* 77, no. 3: 417.

Helbig, Adriana N. 2014. *Hip Hop Ukraine: Music, Race, and African Migration.* Bloomington: Indiana University Press.

Kellerer, Katja. 2013. "'Chant Down the System 'Till Babylon Falls': The Political Dimensions of Underground Hip Hop and Urban Groovers in Zimbabwe." *Journal of Pan African Studies* 6, no. 3: 43–64.

Koster, Mwanzia. 2013. "The Hip Hop Revolution in Kenya: Ukoo Flani Mau Mau, Youth Politics and Memory, 1990–2012." *Journal of Pan African Studies* 6, no. 3: 82–105.

Loureiro-Rodríguez, Verónica. 2013. "'If We Only Speak Our Language by the Fireside, It Won't Survive': The Cultural and Linguistic Indigenization of Hip Hop in Galicia." *Popular Music and Society* 36, no. 5: 659–76.

Marsh, Peter K. 2010. "Our Generation Is Opening Its Eyes: Hip Hop and Youth Identity in Contemporary Mongolia." *Central Asian Survey* 29, no. 3: 345–58.

Martinez, George, and Christopher Malone. 2014. *The Organic Globalizer: Hip Hop, Political Development, and Movement Culture.* New York: Bloomsbury Academic.

Mitchell, Tony. 2001. *Global Noise: Rap and Hip Hop Outside the U.S.A.* Middletown, CT: Wesleyan University Press.

Morgan, George, and Andrew Warren. 2011. "Aboriginal Youth, Hip Hop and the Politics of Identification." *Ethnic and Racial Studies* 34, no. 6: 925–47.

Rose, Tricia. 1994. *Black Noise.* Middletown, CT: Wesleyan University Press.

Poor Righteous Teachers

(PRT, 1989–1996, Trenton, New Jersey)

Poor Righteous Teachers is an American hip hop trio known for classic Golden Age of Hip Hop (1986–1994) singles such as "Rock Dis Funky Joint" (1990), "Shakiyla (JRH)" (1991), "Easy Star" (1992), and "Word Iz Life" (1996). Despite a lack of commercial success, PRT's musical output received critical acclaim. Its lyrical content emphasized black unity, avoiding materialistic greed, eschewing street violence, and improving oneself through knowledge.

In 1989, lead MC and vocalist Wise Intelligent (Timothy Grimes, 1971*–), producer and backing vocalist Culture Freedom (aka Kerry Williams, n.d.), and DJ and producer Father Shaheed (aka Devine, Scott Phillips, 1969–2014) founded PRT in Trenton, New Jersey. That year, the trio released its first singles, "Time to Say Peace" and "Butt Naked Booty Bless." Both appeared on PRT's debut studio album, *Holy Intellect* (1990). Its second album, *Pure Poverty* (1991), marks the beginning of PRT's use of internal rhymes, triplets and quadruplets based on multisyllabic words, double-time rap, and diverse musical fusion; however, it was less commercially successful and critically acclaimed than *Holy Intellect*. PRT nevertheless continued recording studio albums into the 1990s with *Black Business* (1993) and *The New World Order* (1996). All were produced by Profile Records (1981–), a New York City label, and charted on Billboard's Top R&B/Hip-Hop Albums. PRT's first three albums peaked at Nos. 142, 155, and 167, respectively, on the Billboard 200.

PRT's lyrical content focused on Five Percenter rap messages—pro–Black Consciousness teachings of the Nation of Gods and Earths (aka the Five Percent Nation, Five Percenters, 1964–), a movement founded by Clarence 13X (Clarence Edward Smith, 1928–1969), a former member of the Nation of Islam (NOI, 1930–). PRT based its name on the Five Percenter role of being those who both know the truth and seek to educate the rest of the population through teaching.

PRT fused hip hop with elements of funk, as heard with its sampling the 1970s funk band War's (1969–) "Slippin' into Darkness" (1971) in the background of its "Rock Dis Funky Joint." PRT also used reggae, as heard with the toasting in "Easy Star." It sampled not only other music, but also speeches that resonated within the Five Percent Nation and the NOI, such as Malcolm X's (1925–1965) "Words from the Wise." Instrumental hip hop tracks often appeared on PRT's albums—exhibiting the work of DJ and producer Tony D (Anthony Depula, 1966–2009), who produced PRT's first three albums.

In 2001, the trio reunited to release the underground album *Declaration of Independence*, the single "I Swear ta God," and the 12-inch album "Dangerous"/"Save Me." In 2006, *Rare and Unreleased*, a compilation and remix album, was released. Since 1995, while still with the group, Wise Intellect pursued a solo career. He recorded seven studio albums, including *The Talented Timothy Taylor* (2007) and *The Blue Klux Klan* (2017). In 2014, Father Shaheed died in a motorcycle accident.

Melissa Ursula Dawn Goldsmith

See also: Five Percent Nation; Nation of Islam; Political Hip Hop; Reggae; The United States

Further Reading

Coleman, Brian. 2007. "Poor Righteous Teachers: *Holy Intellect*." In *Check the Technique: Liner Notes for Hip Hop Junkies*, pp. 333–47. New York: Villard.

Miyakawa, Felicia. 2005. "Sampling, Borrowing, and Meaning." In *Five Percenter Rap: God Hop's Music, Message, and Black Muslim Mission*, chap. 5. Bloomington: Indiana University Press.

Further Listening

PRT. 1991. *Pure Poverty.* Profile Records.

Pop'in Pete

(Timothy Earl Solomon, 1961–, Fresno, California)

Pop'in Pete is an American dancer, choreographer, and one of the original poppers, dancers who developed popping moves—quickly contracting and relaxing muscles to create individual jerking movements known as pops or hits. He began as a first-generation member of the Electric Boogaloos (1977–). Since he began popping, Pop'in Pete has wanted to define the hip hop dance subgenre as an art form, and as a specialist in popping, he stood out among his peers with unique battle pauses, moves, and beatbox sounds he makes in lieu of counting beats. He has been called on to judge dancing competitions worldwide. In addition to popping, he originated moves such as the ET, spider man, and crazy legs.

EARLY DANCE YEARS WITH THE ELECTRIC BOOGALOOS

Born Timothy Solomon, Pop'in Pete and his brother Sam (later Boogaloo Sam, 1959–) grew up in Fresno, California, where they absorbed funk-inspired street dance moves from television, as well as from dancers at clubs and house parties in their neighborhood. Sam, the older of the two, started mastering popping moves first, wanting to create his own kind of dance. In 1975, after watching late 1960s television dancers who were using the locking technique in their moves, Sam took the stage name Boogaloo Sam and began thinking about forming the Electric Boogaloo Lockers. His moves combined locking and roboting with smooth, relaxed, and flowing steps. Pop'in Pete found the Electric Boogaloo too difficult to learn, so Boogaloo Sam encouraged him to specialize in popping. In 1977, Boogaloo Sam dropped the word "Lockers" from his crew's name, and began recruiting other dancers.

In 1978, Pop'in Pete joined the Electric Boogaloos, whose original crew members included the two brothers, Robot Dane (Dane Parker, n.d.), Puppet Boozer (Marvin Boozer, n.d.), Creep'n Sid (Cedric Williams, 1959–), and Scarecrow Scalley (Gary Allen, n.d.). The brothers' cousin, Stephen Nichols (n.d.), was already a locker (a dancer who uses the locking technique) and wanted to join the crew, so he trained in popping, joined the crew, and took the stage name Skeeter Rabbit. With just a boombox to supply their music, the Electric Boogaloos buskered in Hollywood and Los Angeles, until an agent discovered them and got them an audition for dancer and choreographer Jeff Kutash (1945–) and his traveling Vegas-type show. Kutash hired them. Appearances on many television shows followed.

After the crew's 1980 *Soul Train* (1971–2006) appearance, it was approached by Michael Jackson (1958–2009) to choreograph his music videos for "Thriller" and "Beat It" (both 1983). The crew developed a partnership with Jackson, choreographing many of his subsequent music videos and live performances, even giving Jackson dance lessons.

Pop'in Pet himself has worked with a long list of popular music acts, including Janet Jackson (1966–) and the Black Eyed Peas (1995–). The 2010 music video for hip hop rapper, singer-songwriter, and dancer Chris Brown's (1989–) electro-pop and house track "Yeah 3x" was a tribute to Pop'in Pete, featuring his choreography and the two dancing together. As of 2018, Pop'in Pete is still dancing and teaching numerous celebrities his signature moves.

Melissa Ursula Dawn Goldsmith

See also: The Electric Boogaloos; Hip Hop Dance; Popping and Locking; The United States

Further Reading

Anon. 1995. "So. L.A. a Hoofer's Place in History before Popping, Posing, Breaking, Hip Hop, and Even Disco, There Was Locking, and Don Campbell Invented It." *Los Angeles Times*, July 23, 16.

Guzman-Sanchez, Thomas. 2012. *Underground Dance Masters: Final History of a Forgotten Era*. Santa Barbara, CA: Praeger.

Reeves, Marcus. 2009. "Generation Remixed: Past-Nationalism and the Black Culture Shuffle." In *Somebody Scream: Rap Music's Rise to Prominence in the Aftershock of Black Power*, chap. 1. New York: Farrar, Straus, and Giroux.

Popmaster Fabel

(Jorge Pabon, 1965*–, Harlem, New York)

Popmaster Fabel is an old-school pop and lock style hip hop dancer most associated with the Rock Steady Crew (RSC, 1977–); he is known for his distinctive style and for bringing West Coast dance styles to the New York scene. Unlike the more robotic pop and lock dancers, he used his tall, thin frame to give the impression of long, loose, fluid movements, often keeping his legs straight to accentuate his height. His slower steps prefigure dubstep, although they are usually executed more quickly (a more rapid transitions between locks than in dubstep), something which he terms "electric boogaloo" dancing. His trademark is an emphasis on minute movements using his arms, hands, and fingers, with lots of sudden locking between smooth movements.

Fabel was born and raised in Spanish Harlem, where he developed a dance and choreography career that has been showcased internationally since 1982. His connections with various dance crews amounts to a who's who crew list: he was the president of the Hierophysics Crew (1970–1979)* of the Bronx, New York; senior vice president of the RSC in the Bronx; member of Magnificent Force (1970–1989)* of the Bronx; and an honorary member of the Electric Boogaloos (1997–) of Fresno, California. Fabel also broke into documentary film in *The Freshest Kids: A History of the B-Boy* (2002) and the film short *Musically Inclined* (2008) as a featured dancer. A hip hop activist, he engages in graffiti art and is cofounder with his wife Christie Z-Pabon (1969*–) of the Tools of War Park Jam series (2003–), a New York City grass roots hip hop promotion organization and battling event that brings hip hop artists and culture back to New York City parks—hip hop's initial venue. He has also taught hip hop courses at New York University and Cornell University.

Anthony J. Fonseca

See also: Battling; Dubstep; Hip Hop Dance; Rock Steady Crew; The United States

Further Reading

Guzman-Sanchez, Thomas. 2012. *Underground Dance Masters: Final History of a Forgotten Era.* Santa Barbara, CA: Praeger.

Khabeer, Su'ad Abdul. 2016. *Muslim Cool: Race, Religion, and Hip Hop in the United States.* New York: New York University Press.

Schloss, Joseph G. 2009. *Foundation: B-Boys, B-Girls, and Hip Hop Culture in New York.* New York: Oxford University Press.

Popping and Locking

Popping and locking are American hip hop dance moves sometimes associated with a third move, called dropping. Combined, the dance moves create the illusion of the body's motion being slowed or even reversed, as in dub step dancing. Popping consists of various techniques that cause it to differ greatly from most break-dancing techniques, as there is very little floor work, or dance moves performed while lying down, positioning oneself upside down, or sitting down, in popping. Popping best creates its illusions when the dancer is standing. Locking, today used extensively in hip hop, was originally a funk dance technique. Like popping, it is a dance technique designed to create a robotic illusion, achieved by starting with a fast, usually large-scale movement, and then immediately freezing and locking into a statuesque position. This freeze is typically held for a while, which makes locking different from popping, which is more consistently fluid. Locking is also more upper body specific, while popping generally uses the whole body. Mastery of both techniques relies heavily on how tightly a dancer can synchronize movements with music.

ROOTS OF POPPING: THE ROBOT

Popping is related to robotic dance, made famous by the Robot, a 1960s and 1970s dance that traces its origins back to 1920s miming. The Robot, which was made internationally famous in a scene from the British film *Chitty Chitty Bang Bang* (1968) wherein English actress and dancer Sally Ann Howes (1930–) dances on a pedestal, pretending to be a life-sized music box dancer, while American actor and dancer Dick Van Dyke (1925–), for contrast, dances as loosely as possible, imitating a rag doll. In her dance Howes keeps her muscles contracted or flexed the entire time, while constantly stopping and then starting her arm motions, to create the effect of having motorized limbs that have been pieced together with hinges instead of elbows and wrists. The Robot, however, was already a minor dance craze by then, as West Coast dancers were already using continuous robotic moves choreographed to the rhythm of funk and R&B music.

Popping differs from the Robot in that it uses not just the flexing of the muscles, but the relaxing of them as well (alternating between flexing and relaxing, a movement called a hit or a pop) to create not so much the illusion of robotics as the illusion of moving in either slow motion or under a strobe light. The time differential in the pops corresponds to the beat in the music, although pops can be done double-time or faster. Nonetheless, it is a smoother dance than the Robot, much less prone to the Robot's jerking movements. As well, popping makes the movements more minute, sometimes concentrating on moving small digits (fingers) or on moving larger body parts, such as arms, just an inch or so at a time, with moves being separated by a dime stop (an immediate stop, named from the phrase "stopping on a dime").

THE POPPING ILLUSION

Popping fits into the category of illusory dance techniques, such as roboting, waving, worming, strobing, and tutting (moving the arms, hands, and fingers in an angular fashion to suggest Egyptian hieroglyphics). Popping also differs from funks's electric boogaloo (aka boogaloo or boog), which uses a lot of hip sway and drops to create the illusion of bonelessness, and dubstep's floating, which uses heel to toe lifts, combined with foot twists and glides to create the effect of frictionless floor sliding. However, popping often incorporates those two techniques because they create concurrent leg moves that compliment popped arm moves. Because of their visual appeal, popping techniques are used in breakdancing battles, where b-boys and b-girls, usually as parts of crews, dance competitively against one another. In battles, improvisation and freestyle during solo dances in essential, so mastering techniques such as popping are absolutely necessary.

Early popping dancers used 1970s funk music as their background, but in the 1980s synthesized music and electronica became favorites, as did some hip hop beats. Generally, the best music for popping uses a quadruple (4/4) time signature, has few starts and stops, and has at least 90 beats per minute with a pronounced backbeat.

ROOTS OF LOCKING: CAMPBELLOCKING AND THE LOCKERS

Like popping, locking has roots in funk music. Unlike popping or dubstep, where dancers dress in urban styles and tend to use drab, serious colors, lockers generally prefer very colorful costumes when performing. Clothing must be appropriate to dance moves that include acrobatics and gymnastics, such as jumps, landings, and splits. Unlike popping, locking can be traced to one dancer, and is actually named after him. Don Campbell (1951–) created a dance called the Campbellock in the late 1960s when he started adding dime stops to his performances. By the early 1970s, he was a regular dancer on the dance variety show *Soul Train* (1971–2006). He then joined forces with his then girlfriend, choreographer Toni Basil (Antonia Christina Basilotta, 1943–), to form the Lockers (1971–1976), which included actor and dancer Fred Berry (1951–2003), who danced under the stage name Mr. Penguin and later became iconic as the character Rerun in the American television series *What's Happening!!* (1976–1979), which resulted in locking's being given a prime time television outlet, as Berry often danced on the series. The Lockers appeared on the show to dance with Berry in some episodes.

The Lockers became a huge influence on future locking dancers, both for dance moves and clothing, at one point even performing on *Saturday Night Live* in 1975. The Lockers were known for their distinctive costumes, which included striped knee socks, suspenders, oversized hats, and oversized short pants. During some performances, dancers would wear costumes that were covered with lighted bulbs. The basic moves of the Lockers included arm locks, slapping hands with a dance partner (based on the "give me five" handshake), back to front claps, points, splits, dives, and knee drops.

THE LOCKING ILLUSION

Since a highly respected film choreographer managed the group, the Lockers influenced actual dances, working either solo, sometimes using the *Soul Train* (1971–2006) Line technique, or as dance partners, interacting with handshakes and hand offs (where the dancers create the illusion that a move is passed from dancer to dancer). Usually, the essence of locking is humor or lightheartedness. The basic locking moves are bending knees and elbows, rotating forearms, hopping, and pointing the fingers. Moves range from the uplock, which is basically pretending there is a metal bar in one's hands and then bringing the arms up to lock them in a muscleman flex; to the point, which is moving one arm across the chest in an exaggerated motion to then move it back to its side and point upward, while shifting the head to look at the spot pointed at; to walking, punching, or kicking in place; to flourishing the end of a move by reaching up and rotating a worn oversized cap or hat. The aforementioned exaggerated handclaps, handshakes, and handoffs are also commonly incorporated.

Like popping, locking relies on improvisation, but just about every dancer has a set of signature moves or a favored freeze position. For example, later in the development of locking, one of the Lockers, Leo Williamson (n.d.), who danced under the stage name Flukey Luke, introduced a unique lock. He placed the outer ridge of both of his hands on his waist and locked his elbows forward. This improvisation became his signature move and was named the Leo Lock.

Anthony J. Fonseca

See also: Campbell, Don; The Electric Boogaloos; Hip Hop Dance; Pop'in Pete; The Robot

Further Reading

Rajakumar, Mohanalakshmi. 2012. *Hip Hop Dance.* Santa Barbara, CA: Greenwood.

Schloss, Joseph G. 2009. *Foundation: B-Boys, B-Girls, and Hip Hop Culture in New York.* New York: Oxford University Press.

Walter, Carla Stalling. 2007. *Hip Hop Dance: Meanings and Messages.* Jefferson, NC: McFarland.

Portugal

Portugal boasts a vibrant hip hop scene that is influenced by African music from countries such as Mozambique, Angola, Guinea-Bissau, Equatorial Guinea, Cape Verde, and São Tomé and Príncipe, where combined, over 56 million Portuguese-speaking people live. The sound owes a lot to reggae, *zouk* (a rapid carnival beat originating from Guadeloupe and Martinique), and traditional Portuguese *fado* music. Commonly called Hip Hop Tuga, Portuguese hip hop differs from mainstream hip hop because of these musical influences. Compared to American hip hop, it is more political, and it favors the laid-back West Coast and Dirty South sound, usually with only one rapper (with no harmony rapping). Instrumentation shows heavy funk brass, African percussion, and reggae influences, combined with a pronounced electronica aesthetic.

ORIGINS OF HIP HOP TUGA

Hip Hop Tuga came into being when immigrant rapper General D. (Sergio Matsinhe, 1971*–) came to Lisbon from Mozambique and became the first rapper to garner a major recording contract (with Valentim De Carvalho, Música Lda., part of EMI Records, 1931–) for two albums, *Pé na tchôn, karapinha na céu* (*Foot in the Sky* or *Karapincha in the Sky*, 1994) and *Kanimambo* (*Thank You*, 1997).

Early Portuguese hip hop acts included rapper Chullage (Nuno Santos, 1977–); hip hop brother band Da Weasel (1993–2010), an Almada-based group that fuses elements from hard rock, pop, rap, acid jazz, and ska; and Allen Halloween (Allen Pires Sanhá, 1980–), an alternative and horrorcore immigrant rapper, singer, and producer from Guinea.

Other early hip hop artists included Dealema (1996–), an amalgamated band from Porto and Vila Nova de Gaia; Mind Da Gap (aka Da Wreckas, 1993–), a group from Porto; and Sir Scratch (Benigno António, n.d.), a rapper and producer from Angola. California native artist and poet Ithaka (Ithaka Darin Pappas, 1966–), vocalist of "So Get Up" (*Underground Sound of Lisbon*, 1994), lived and recorded in Lisbon and is often considered an early Hip Hop Tuga success. "So Get Up" has been in constant reissue and remix since its 1994 release.

Current Hip Hop Tuga stars include Valete (Keidje Torres Lima, 1981–) and Sam the Kid (Samuel Martins Torres Santiago Mira, 1979–), both from Lisbon. Valete, the cofounder of the hip hop duo Canal 115 (1997–1999), and later soloist, recorded the influential Portuguese political hip hop album *Serviço Público* (*Public Service*, 2007). Sam the Kid is famous for creative sampling; his instrumental album, *Beats Vol. 1: Amor* (2002), was a fan favorite, and as of 2009, he has been a member of the rap band Orelha Negra.

Anthony J. Fonseca

See also: Angola; Brazil

Further Reading

Pardue, Derek. 2015. "Kriolu Interruptions: Local Lisbon Rappers Provoke a Rethinking of 'Luso' and 'Creole.'" *Luso-Brazilian Review* 52, no. 2: 153–73.

Simões, José Alberto, and Ricardo Campos. 2017. "Digital Media, Subcultural Activity, and Youth Participation: The Cases of Protest Rap and Graffiti in Portugal." *Journal of Youth Studies* 20, no. 1: 16–31.

Further Listening

Valete. 2007. *Serviço Público* (*Public Service*). Horizontal Records.

Positive Black Soul

(1989–, Dakar, Senegal)

Positive Black Soul (aka PBS) was one of the first hip hop collectives in Senegal. Founding members Didier Awadi (aka DJ Awadi, Didier Sourou Awadi, 1969–) and Doug E-Tee (aka Duggy Tee, Amadou Barry, 1971–), after performing together at a party in Dakar, created PBS as a vehicle for their political activism and philosophy. The acronym PBS is a play on PDS, which stands for Parti Démocratique Sénégalais, the Senegalese Democratic Party. Throughout its career, PBS has used hip hop as a platform to urge Senegalese people to participate in government and vote in elections and to project a positive image of Africanness. The duo considered rap an accessible forum for issues such as corruption, politics, and the AIDS epidemic.

Senegalese rappers have been referred to as "modern griot," linking rap to West African verbal traditions and spoken-word art such as *taasu*. Awadi's technique is to go beyond the griot as journalistic reporting of social and political realities, to the griot as praise for kings or chronicle of history. The PBS single "Return of Djelly" ("Return of the Griot"), features Doug E-Tee's impersonation of a griot, using the Mande language term *djelly*, a more universal term than the Wolof term *géwël*. The song is completely in English, sung-rapped in a ragga style, while retaining the rapid-fire delivery, lyrical complexity and pervasive rhymes typical of rap. The track opens with a native Senegalese flute, followed by a synthesized melodic figure that evokes the sound of the *kora* (a 21-string harp played by Mande griots). In the djelly persona, Doug E-Tee exhorts all black people to look to their ancestry for a cultural identity that will lift them out of pessimism, promoting a positive pan-African future.

PBS achieved fame during the 1990s, rapping in English, French, and Wolof. After a 1992 music festival performance at the Dakar French Cultural Center, PBS was invited to open for internationally known French Senegalese–Chandian rapper MC Solaar (1969–) and continued performing with him in France. PBS was then featured in the album *Firin' in Fouta* (1994) by Baaba Maal (1953–), and soon after signed with Mango Records (whose parent company is Island Records, 1959–) for their debut album, *Salaam* (1995).

PBS's first international release, *New York/Paris/Dakar* (2002), initially sold in Senegal as a cassette, and was remastered in 2002 for distribution outside the country, with collaboration from American rapper KRS-One (1965–), who shared PBS's pan-African philosophy, which seeks to strengthen solidarity among people of African descent, believing that the unity of common history can be channeled to forge a common, positive destiny. In 2002, PBS appeared in the Red Hot Organization compilation album *Red Hot + Riot*, paying tribute to Nigerian musician Fela Kuti (Olufela Olusegun Oludotun Ransome-Kuti, 1938–1997), who died of AIDS. During the 21st century, PBS members began solo projects, though in 2009 the collective performed in Dakar to celebrate its twentieth anniversary.

Jennifer L. Roth-Burnette

See also: Awadi, Didier; Griot; Political Hip Hop; Senegal

Further Reading

Tang, Patricia. 2012. "The Rapper as Modern Griot: Reclaiming Ancient Traditions." In *Hip Hop Africa: New African Music in a Globalizing World*, edited by Eric Charry, chap. 5. Bloomington: Indiana University Press.

Winders, James A. 2006. "Paris, Dakar, and Bamako: New Directions in Music and Migration." In *Paris African: Rhythms of the African Diaspora*, chap. 6. New York: Palgrave Macmillan.

Further Listening

PBS. 2002. *New York/Paris/Dakar.* Africa Fête Diffusion.

Professor Elemental

(Paul Alborough, 1975–, Norwich, England)

Professor Elemental is an English hip hop artist associated with chap hop. He is best known for his affiliation with the steampunk movement and for his 2010 feud with fellow chap hop artist Mr. B The Gentleman Rhymer (1970–). His persona evokes the French science fiction of Jules Verne (1828–1905), as he frequently sports a pith helmet while in cargo shorts (caravan wear) and refers to himself as a mad scientist. He is accompanied by an orangutan butler named Geoffrey, with whom he conducts scientific experiments. Because of its close affiliation with and evocation of elements of the Victorian era (1837–1901), Professor Elemental and his music are closely associated with the steampunk movement. He regularly appears at steampunk events and has been the headlining act at the Steeampunk World's Fair, a convention held in the United States annually since 2010, and Waltz on the Wye, a steampunk festival held since 2011 in Chepstow, a town on the border of England and Wales. Visual aspects of steampunk humor appear throughout his videos.

Professor Elemental first came to prominence with the track "Cup of Brown Joy" (2010), from his debut album *Rebel without Applause* (2009). The song is an ode to tea (more precisely, to black tea, not to herbal ones) and was remixed on his subsequent album, *The Indifference Engine* (2010). The album combines hip hop, swing jazz, elements of musical exoticism, and animal sound effects. Most of his music is produced by Sussex- and Yorkshire-based Tea Sea Records, a label that specializes primarily in hip hop and hip hop remixes.

The Indifference Engine was followed up with *More Tea?* (2011), an album that consists entirely of remixes of previous tracks. This time, "Cup of Brown Joy" samples Edgar Sampson's (1907–1973) jazz standard "Stompin' at the Savoy" (1934) in the background and places chords from a slightly out-of-tune spinet piano more in the foreground.

Professor Elemental became irritated when people frequently mistook him for Mr. B The Gentleman Rhymer. Like Mr. B, Professor Elemental raps in Received Pronunciation (RP), the Standard English, also known as BBC English, used in the United Kingdom. In 2010, Professor Elemental released the song and video "Fighting Trousers," in which he started a comic feud. In response to Professor Elemental's track, Mr. B released "Like a Chap" (2012). After the tongue-in-cheek feud, the two have performed together both live and in recordings. During a 2011 performance, they engaged in a "chap-off" in which they had a rhyme battle over whose "chap" was superior. In 2012, Mr. B was a guest artist on "The Duel," a track on Professor Elemental's album *Father of Invention*.

Professor Elemental's entire album *Apequest* (2016) was devoted to a galaxy-wide search for his orangutan companion, Geoffrey. The same year *Apequest* was released, he released *Professor Elemental and His Amazing Friends*. Though none of his albums or singles have charted or entered the mainstream, Professor Elemental's cult following has grown since his famous feud with Mr. B and his 2013 appearance on the "Steampunx" episode of American television show *Phineas and Ferb* (2007–2015).

Amanda Sewell

See also: Chap Hop; Mr. B The Gentleman Rhymer; Nerdcore; The United Kingdom

Further Reading

Anon. 2010. "Chap Hop Turns Slightly Nasty." *The Chap*, December 16.

Robinson, Frances. 2011. "In 'Chap Hop,' Gentleman Rappers Bust Rhymes about Tea, Cricket." *The Wall Street Journal*, April 4, A1, A14.

Further Listening

Professor Elemental. 2010. *The Indifference Engine.* Tea Sea Records.

Professor Elemental. 2016. *Apequest.* Tea Sea Records.

Professor Elemental and Various Artists. 2011. *Professor Elemental: More Tea?* Tea Sea Records.

Professor Jay

(formerly N—a J, Joseph Haule, 1975–, Songea, Tanzania)

Professor Jay is a Tanzanian rapper who raps in Swahili and English. In 1994, he began rapping and became the MC of Tanzania's first rap crew, Hard Blasters (1989–). With Hard Blasters, Professor Jay (then known as N—a J), pioneered Tanzanian hip hop, known as Bongo Flava, from the capital city of Dar Es Salaam. His version of hip hop fused hip hop beats with reggae, dancehall, Afrobeat, and R&B, as well as Tanzanian traditional and popular music such as *taarab* or *dansi* (aka *musiki wa dansi*, dance music in Swahili), Swahili jazz, and/or Tanzanian rhumba (deriving from the Congolese soukous).

When Professor Jay joined Hard Blasters in 1994, the crew released its debut album *Mambo ya mjini* (*City Affairs*). In 2000, Hard Blasters released *Funga kazi* (roughly, *Finish the Job*, 2000) and had a hit song with "Chemsha Bongo" ("Quiz" or "Crossword"), which contrasts the life of child prostitutes to happier and wealthier people in the city. Professor Jay's solo career began in 2001 and consists of six solo studio albums: *Machozi jasho na damu* (*Tears of Sweat and Blood*, 2001); *Mapinduzi halisi* (*Real Revolution*, 2003); *J.O.S.E.P.H.* (2006), *Aluta continua* (*The Struggle Continues*, 2007); *Izack Mangesho* (2014); and *Kazi kazi* (*Work, Work*, 2016). Since his first solo studio album, Professor Jay has won critical acclaim and awards in Tanzania. Hit songs, among others, include "Ndio mzee" ("Yes, Sir," 2001), and "Nikusaidiaje?" ("How Can I Help You?" 2007). He also released "Zali lamentali" (2004), a Swahili phrase meaning when something from out of the blue changes one's whole life for the better.

Professor Jay's politically driven lyrical content focuses on politicians' questionable behavior, socioeconomic disparity, HIV/AIDS in Africa, and unity, among other topics. Sometimes he creates personae and uses humor in his message rap and storytelling. For example, in "Ndio Mzee," he plays the role of a politician who promises anything, no matter how absurd, to get elected. Ironically, in 2015, Professor Jay became an elected member of parliament (MP), representing the county of Mikumi, running on the Chadema party ticket. The Chadema party (1992–), a shortened name for Chama cha Demokrasia na Maendeleo (Party for Democracy and Progress), is a right-of-center political party that campaigns on an anticorruption platform.

He started his own recording studio and label Mwanalizombe (2014–) in Dar Es Salaam, but as of 2018, he is based in Mikumi county, where he has promised to rebuild his studio to help educate youth via hip hop.

Melissa Ursula Dawn Goldsmith

See also: Political Hip Hop; Tanzania

Further Reading

Casco, José Arturo Saavedra. 2006. "The Language of the Young People: Rap, Urban Culture, and Protest in Tanzania." *Journal of Asian and African Studies* 41, no. 3: 229–48.

Mbuya, Mejah. 2014. "Tanzanian MCs vs. Social Discourse." In *Hip Hop and Social Change in Africa: Ni Wakati*, edited by Msia Kibona Clark and Mickie Mwanzia Koster, chap. 11. Lanham, MD: Lexington Books.

Ntarangwi, Mwenda. 2009. "Economic Change and Political Deception." In *East African Hip Hop: Youth Culture and Globalization*, chap. 5. Urbana: University of Illinois Press.

Perullo, Alex. 2005. "Hooligans and Heroes: Youth Identity in Dar es Salaam, Tanzania." *Africa Today* 51, no. 4: 74–101, 117.

Further Listening

Professor Jay. 2001. *Machozi jasho na damu* (*Tears of Sweat and Blood*). FKW.

Prophets of da City

(aka POC, 1988–2001, Cape Town, South Africa)

Prophets of da City (aka POC) was one of the earliest pioneering South African hip hop crews to become internationally famous. The crew from Cape Town was originally inspired by old-school American hip hop such as the Sugarhill Gang's (1979–1985, 1994–) "Rapper's Delight" (1979) and the American hip hop music and production styles of the Bomb Squad (1986–) with Public Enemy (1986–) and Ice Cube (1969–). POC fuses politically conscious hip hop (at times incorporating Black Nationalism) with reggae, electronica, and traditional West African rhythms and South African vocal music and raps in Cape slang (a local Afrikaans dialect) and English vernacular. Its discography includes *Our World* (1990), *Boom Style* (1992), *Age of Truth* (1993), *Phunk Phlow* (1994), *Universal Souljaz* (1995), and *Ghetto Code* (1997). POC's early development and success had been inspiring to many musicians in Africa and worldwide because the crew produced politically conscious hip hop in the final years of Apartheid (meaning "separateness" in Afrikaans, 1948–1991), years before South Africa's first democratic election of President Nelson Mandela (1918–2013, in office, 1994–1999).

POC began in 1988 as a studio effort led by rapper Shaheen Ariefdien (n.d.) and DJ Ready D (Deon Daniels, 1968–), who used Arefdien's father's studio equipment since he came from a musical family—his father is jazz musician Issy Ariefdien (n.d.). The resulting demo became *Our World* (1990) and was South Africa's first hip hop release. From the album, the song "Dallah Flét" ("Do It Thoroughly") was the first recorded hip hop song in Cape slang. The album is a seminal recording of POC's style, since it included a fusion of hip hop with South African musical instruments such as the *goema* (a hand drum that is used in Cape Jazz as well as in Cape Minstrel Carnivals) and South African music such as *mbaqanga* (black urban music with Zulu roots) on the tracks "Our World" and "Stop the Violence," as well as dub versions of "Our World" and "Stop the Violence." Scratching (turntablism) is also present on this early album. After several attempts with other South African production companies that were generally more drawn to lighter hip hop themes such as partying or sex, Ku Shu Shu Records (1990–1991) was set up as POC's production company, which found international distribution with Teal-Trutone Music (1940s–1995)*. A year after the album's success, Ku Shu Shu became the Johannesburg label, Ghetto Ruff (1991–) and continued producing POC's albums. To reinforce album sales, POC toured extensively and was involved in an antidrug campaign that also introduced their music to thousands of youth. Other members have since joined POC, but personnel shifts often took place. The crew had between five to eight members on tour.

Its second album, *Boom Style* (*Tree Style*, 1991), included the use of TR-808 drum machine kick drum sounds as a way of play on the idea of kicking—American vernacular for cool, as well as the motion of kicking in playing a kick drum, dancing, playing, and fighting back. The track "Ons Stem" ("Our Voice") was an ahead-of-its-time, daring attack against apartheid. The title was a response to "Die Stem" ("The Voice"), the racist apartheid national anthem. Though the video for "Kicking Non Stop" was censored because it features POC placing a portrait of then–South African president P. W. Botha (1916–2006) in the refrigerator "to chill," legendary American composer, musician, and producer Quincy Jones (1933–) and successful Los Angeles–based South African composer and singer Caiphus Semenya (1939–) invited POC to perform at the Montreux Jazz Festival in Switzerland in 1992. At the transition between the end of apartheid and Mandela's election, POC continued traveling extensively, but always spent some of its time educating youth through antidrug campaigns or hip hop workshops.

In 1994, POC performed "Excellent, the First Black President" at Mandela's inauguration. The performance is often understood as rap's entrance into the mainstream of South African popular music. *Boom Style*, as well as *Age of Truth* and *Phunk Phlow*, marked POC's height in popularity. *Universal Souljaz* was stylistically different from previous albums for its inclusion of more hip house and contained gangsta rap. POC's last album, *Ghetto Code*, was a return to its previous sound.

Melissa Ursula Dawn Goldsmith

See also: Jones, Quincy; Political Hip Hop; South Africa

Further Reading

Ariefdien, Shaheen. 2011. "Daalah Cape Fléts: Hip Hop, Resistance, and Hope." In *Searching for South Africa*, edited by Shereen Essof and Daniel Moshenberg, chap. 7. Pretoria: Unisa Press.

Haupt, Adam. 2001. "Black Thing: Hip Hop Nationalism, 'Race,' and Gender in Prophets of da City and Brasse Vannie Kaap." In *Colored by History, Shaped by Place: New Perspectives on Colored Identities in Cape Town*, edited by Zimitri Erasmus, chap. 10. Cape Town, South Africa: Kwela Books.

Further Listening

POC. 1991. *Boomstyle.* Trutone Music.

POC. 1993. *Age of Truth.* Tusk Music.

P-Square

(aka Peter and Paul, 2003–, Jos, Nigeria)

P-Square is a Nigerian hip hop duo made up of identical twin brothers Peter Okoye and Paul Okoye (1981–). The duo, both of whom are rappers and dancers, has specialized since 2003 in R&B-based, African- and reggae-influenced, highly autotuned danceable hip hop. P-Square is associated with its own United Kingdom–based record label Square Records (2001–), with Akon's (1973–) Konvict Muzik label (2004–), and with Universal Music Group (1996–), although the duo has produced and released most of its albums since 2008 through Square Records.

FROM J-TOWN, NIGERIA TO SETTLING IN THE UNITED STATES

P-Square began in a small Catholic school in Jos (aka J-Town), an urban city of one million in the Middle Belt of Nigeria and the administrative capital of Plateau State. The brothers joined the music and drama clubs, which gave them a chance to sing, rap, dance, and learn American hip hop music by imitating artists such as MC Hammer (1962–), Bobby Brown (1966–), and Michael Jackson (1958–2009).

They formed an a cappella quartet, MMMPP (aka MMPP, 1996–99), and began to practice the dance moves of Jackson, including breakdancing; in 1997, the brothers formed a group named after Jackson's song "Smooth Criminal" (1988). The brothers kept both the Smooth Criminals (1997–1999) and MMMPP going simultaneously, working on choreographed dance routines—these routines soon got the duo and its groups small gigs. The brothers then decided to return to school to develop their musical skills, studying keyboard, drums, bass, and rhythm guitar, and to study business administration. They then formed a duo, eventually named P-Square.

In 2011, the duo signed with Konvict Muzik, and in 2012, P-Square signed a record distribution deal with Universal Music South Africa. P-Square has released six albums: *Get Squared* (2005), *Game Over* (2007), *Get Squared: Reloaded* (2008), *Danger* (2009), *The Invasion* (2011), and *Double Trouble* (2014). The duo has released one EP, *Bizzy Body II* (2006). *Get Squared* was the first of three albums released under Square Records, and it has sold over eight million copies in Nigeria, as have *Game Over* and *Danger*. In 2010, P-Square was named the Artist of the Year at the Kora Awards, given annually for musical achievement in sub-Saharan Africa, winning one million dollars.

P-Square differs from many hip hop bands in that the Okoye brothers handle most of their production and beatmaking in house by reconstructing drum patterns, chord progressions, and sampled lyrics to create an electronic dance and hip hop sound that focuses on typical party themes: beauty, romance, materialism, dancing, and enjoying the moment. In 2014, the brothers moved to the United States and bought mansions next door to one another in Atlanta.

Anthony J. Fonseca

See also: Nigeria; Reggae; The United States

Further Reading

Inyabri, Idom T. 2016. "Youth and Linguistic Stylization in Naija Afro-Hip Hop." *Socio-linguistic Studies* 10, nos. 1–2: 89–108.

Shipley, Jesse Weaver. 2017. "Parody after Identity: Digital Music and the Politics of Uncertainty in West Africa." *American Ethnologist* 44, no. 2: 249–62.

Shonekan, Stephanie. 2012. "Nigerian Hip Hop: Exploring a Black World Hybrid." In *Hip Hop Africa: New African Music in a Globalizing World*, edited by Eric Charry, chap. 7. Bloomington: Indiana University Press.

Further Listening

P-Square. 2009. *Danger.* Square Records.

PSY

(Park Jae-sang, 1977–, Seoul, Korea)

PSY is a K-pop (Korean pop) singer, rapper, songwriter, musical comedian, and producer known for "Gangnam Style" (from *Psy6, Six Rules, Part 1*, 2012), an international hit. The song's video was the first ever to reach one billion YouTube views, won best video at the 2012 MTV Europe Music Awards and a Billboard Music Award, and its refrain ("oppan Gangnam style") was listed by *The Yale Book of Quotations* for 2012.

Born in an affluent family in the Gangnam District, Park Jae-sang started out studying business in the United States but switched majors and studied instead at the Berklee College of Music in Boston, then dropped out and returned home to become a musician. He made his first television appearance in 2000 on Korean national television, but by 2012 he was performing "Gangnam Style" on *The Today Show* (NBC) in New York City.

His first album, *PSY from the Psycho World!*, was released in 2001 and led to his being fined by the South Korean government for inappropriate content. His second and third albums, *Ssa 2* and *3 Mai* (both 2002), brought the singer notoriety and more censorship, but led to his receiving a Seoul Music Award, and his fourth and fifth albums, *Ssajib* (2006) and *PsyFive* (2010), were recognized at the SBS Music Awards, the Mnet Asian Music Awards, and the Melon Music Awards.

Overall, his music is techno-based, high-energy dance–infused hip hop which contains chantlike, catchy refrains in both Korean and English. PSY has also been at the center of controversy for lyrics that criticize the U.S. detention camp at Naval Station Guantanamo Bay, Cuba, and adult-themed lyrics in his songs. His seventh album, *Chiljip Psy-da* (aka *This Is Psy's Seventh Album*), was released in 2015.

Anthony J. Fonseca

See also: Korea; Nerdcore

Further Reading

Tan, Marcus. 2015. "K-Contagion: Sound, Speed, and Space in 'Gangnam Style.'" *TDR: The Drama Review* 59, no. 1: 83–96.

Tudor, Daniel. 2014. "Korea's Music Scene." In *Geek in Korea: Discovering Asia's New Kingdom of Cool*, Part 8. North Clarendon, VT: Tuttle.

Public Enemy

(1982–, Long Island, New York)

Public Enemy is an American hip hop group regarded as one of the progenitors of socially conscious or political hip hop, and scholars often rank Public Enemy as one of the most important hip hop groups of all time. Current members include Chuck D (Carlton Douglas Ridenhour, 1960–), Flavor Flav (William Jonathan Drayton Jr., 1959–), Professor Griff (Richard Griffin, 1960–), DJ Lord (Lord Aswood/Aswod, 1975–), Davy D (aka Davy DMX, David Franklin Reeves Jr., 1960–), and Khari Wynn (1981–). Former members of the group include Terminator X (Norman Rogers, 1966–) and Sister Souljah (Lisa Williamson, 1964–). Since 1986, Public Enemy's music has been produced by the Bomb Squad (1986–). Chuck D's explosive delivery and socially conscious lyrics are among the most defining features of Public Enemy's style. His lyrics often feature complex poetic meters that vary in style widely both within individual tracks and across entire albums. "Fight the Power," a single from the 1990 album *Fear of a Black Planet*, is one of Public Enemy's most influential tracks.

ORIGINS

In the early 1980s, Chuck D was a student at Adelphi College in New York, where he met Flavor Flav; Brooklyn, New York–born journalist and critic Harry Allen (1964–); and other people who would become key figures in Public Enemy's formative years. Chuck D recorded an early demo track called "Public Enemy Number One" (1985) in response to what he perceived as persecution in the local music scene. The track featured Flavor Flav but no other members of what would later become Public Enemy; on the basis of the demo, however, Rick Rubin (Frederick Jay Rubin, 1963–) signed Chuck D and his group to the new Def Jam Recordings New York–based label (1983–).

INITIAL ALBUMS AND STYLE

Public Enemy's first studio album, *Yo! Bum Rush the Show* (1987), was followed by critical and commercial successes *It Takes a Nation of Millions to Hold Us Back* (1988) and *Fear of a Black Planet*. All three of these albums were produced by the Bomb Squad and exemplify Public Enemy's sound. In these and all subsequent albums, Public Enemy promotes a pro-black stance, encouraging black listeners to be aware and to educate themselves. In "Fight the Power," Chuck D alludes to various funk and soul artists and songs, such as Bobby Byrd's (1934–2007) "I Know You Got Soul" (1971) and James Brown's (1933–2006) "Funky Drummer" (1970). The song also accuses individuals and institutions—most notably Elvis Presley (1935–1977)—of being racist, and encourages black listeners to find their own heroes, even if those heroes are not necessarily recognized by the white American mainstream.

Rapper Flavor Flav serves as the hype man and as the counterbalance to Chuck D's more serious lyrics. His interjections between Chuck D's verses and phrases, particularly his catch phrase "yeah, boy!" (with the diphthong extended), are as much a marker of Public Enemy's style as are Chuck D's lyrics. Flavor Flav did provide lead vocals on a few tracks, such as "911 Is a Joke" (1990), an admonishment of emergency crews and their slow response time when summoned to black neighborhoods.

The Bomb Squad's production style is characterized by a dense sonic texture and frenetic energy. Its music from this period contained sampled sounds from dozens of different source tracks; some of the albums that the Bomb Squad produced for Public Enemy in the late 1980s and early 1990s contain hundreds, possibly more than a thousand, sampled sounds. The members of the Bomb Squad drew samples from their enormous personal record collections that consisted of many different kinds of African American popular music, such as soul, funk, and R&B. They also drew sounds from spoken-word sources, such as Richard Pryor's (1940–2005) and Robin Harris's (1953–1990) comedy albums, and political speeches by civil rights figures such as Jesse Jackson (1941–) and Dick Gregory (1932–). The Bomb Squad also frequently sampled snippets of Chuck D's and Flavor Flav's voices for new tracks. For instance, samples of Chuck D's voice from the 1987 single "Bring the Noise" have appeared in several other Public Enemy tracks, such as "Black Steel in the Hour of Chaos" (1988) and "Night of the Living Baseheads" (1988). Moreover, The Bomb Squad sampled sounds that were sometimes abrasive, such as the shrill saxophone sound (which has come to be called the teakettle sample) in the introduction to "The Grunt" (1970), a track by the J.B.'s (1970–1985), Brown's backup band.

Other key members of Public Enemy at the time included Terminator X, the group's DJ, and Professor Griff, sideman and the leader of the Security of the First World, or S1W, which performed live stage routines during Public Enemy's concerts that were a combination of military drills and the African American percussive dance style known as stepping. Professor Griff also served as the group's Minister of Information, giving interviews on behalf of the other group members. Allen's primary role is the go-between for Public Enemy and the mainstream media. In 1989, shortly after the release of Public Enemy's *It Takes a Nation of Millions to Hold Us Back*, Professor Griff gave an interview to the *Washington Post* in which he expressed both homophobic and anti-Semitic ideas. Allen's responsibility was to defuse the tension created by Griff's comments and to keep Public Enemy in good standing with the media.

INTO THE 1990s

Public Enemy's popularity peaked in the early 1990s, following the release of its initial three albums, as well as the commissioning of its single "Fight the Power" by American director Spike Lee (Shelton Jackson Lee, 1957–) for his film *Do the Right Thing* (1989). The group saw several changes in its personnel, reception, and style during this decade.

Public Enemy released four albums in the 1990s (not including *Fear of a Black Planet*, which was slated to be released in 1989 but had to be held over until early 1990). Although none received particularly poor reviews, Public Enemy's albums from this period also did not capture the same praise from critics that its music from the late 1980s had. By the early 1990s, due to legal issues and copyright restrictions, the Bomb Squad began sampling fewer source tracks, resulting in a notable change in its musical sound and style. Terminator X left the group in 1999 and was replaced by DJ Lord. Following Professor Griff's anti-Semitic remarks to the media, Sister Souljah temporarily replaced him as Public Enemy's Minister of Information. Sister Souljah made controversial comments, published in the *Washington Post*, about the 1992 Los Angeles riots, calling them "payback" and suggesting that black young people were "at war." Her comments drew national attention and were criticized by Bill Clinton (1946–), then a candidate for president of the United States.

PUBLIC ENEMY IN THE 21st CENTURY

Public Enemy has continued to record albums into the 21st century, although none have come close to the commercial or critical acclaim its first three albums achieved. For example, *How Do You Sell Soul to a Soulless People Who Sold Their Soul???* (2007) was reviewed favorably by critics, most of whom agreed that Public Enemy's message had not changed in 20 years, for better or for worse. Hype man Flavor Flav experienced a surge in popularity in the mid-2000s, appearing on several reality television shows on the VH-1 network (1985–). He released a solo album, *Hollywood* (2006), during this period, his only solo effort to date and a project that had taken nearly seven years to complete. Two tracks from his solo album were incorporated into *How Do You Sell Soul to a Soulless People Who Sold Their Soul???*

Public Enemy still works closely with the Bomb Squad, but the group has also increased its use of live and acoustic instruments. Bass player Davy D has toured with Public Enemy since 2010. In the early 2000s guitar player Khari Wynn regularly appeared as a guest with the group. He formally became Public Enemy's music director in 2011. The group's use of live guitar and bass also indicate its reduced reliance on sampled sounds.

In 2016, Chuck D announced that he and other members of Public Enemy would be teaming up with members of the Los Angeles–based alternative rock band Rage Against the Machine (1991–2011) and the South Gate, California hip hop group Cypress Hill (1988–) to form a hip hop supergroup called Prophets of Rage. The group's name is based on a single from Public Enemy's *It Takes a National of Millions to Hold Us Back*.

Amanda Sewell

See also: Allen, Harry; The Bomb Squad; Chuck D; Five Percent Nation; Flavor Flav; Political Hip Hop; The United States

Further Reading

Danielsen, Anne. 2008. "The Musicalization of 'Reality': Reality Rap and Rap Reality on Public Enemy's *Fear of a Black Planet*." *European Journal of Cultural Studies* 11, no. 4: 405–21.

Katz, Mark. 2010. "Music in 1s and 0s: The Art and Politics of Digital Sampling." In *Capturing Sound: How Technology Has Changed Music*, rev. ed., chap. 7. Berkeley: University of California Press.

Mills, David. 1992. "Sister Souljah's Call to Arms; The Rapper Says the Riots Were Payback." *The Washington Post*, May 13, B1.

Sewell, Amanda. 2014. "How Copyright Affected the Musical Style and Critical Reception of Sample-Based Hip Hop." *Journal of Popular Music Studies* 26, nos. 2–3: 295–320.

Further Listening

Public Enemy. 1988. *It Takes a Nation of Millions to Hold Us Back.* Def Jam.

Public Enemy. 1990. *Fear of a Black Planet.* Def Jam Recordings.

Public Enemy. 2007. *How Do You Sell Soul to a Soulless People Who Sold Their Soul???* SlamJamz.

Puerto Rico

Puerto Rico, a United States commonwealth, is a small Spanish-speaking island in the Caribbean. The political status of the island grants U.S. citizenship to Puerto Ricans, which has historically enabled migration between the two, and has led to a large Puerto Rican community in New York City. Because of the steady movement of Puerto Ricans between the island and New York City, hip hop in Puerto Rico is almost as old as hip hop in the Bronx, the borough in which the majority of Puerto Ricans settled between the 1970s and 1990s, the formative years in the birth and growth of hip hop. Puerto Ricans traveling back and forth then carried hip hop to Puerto Rico via vinyl records and audiocassettes, hip hop dance, and conversation about hip hop culture. As a result, the music formed deep roots in Puerto Rico, particularly in its impoverished urban neighborhoods.

Puerto Rican hip hop is diverse in sound and content. Musically it reflects the stylistic priorities of early 1990s New York City–based hip hop: jazz bass and piano riffs, multilayered and diverse percussions, and synthesized instrumentals. Puerto Rican hip hop also mirrors the 2000s evolution of the music, with deep and highly danceable bass beats, hi-hat percussions, heavily synthesized sounds, and vocal manipulation techniques such as autotuning.

The parallel trends of New York and Puerto Rican hip hop reflects the continued movement of people between both locales, which helps to form shared aesthetic tastes and forms of musical production. Puerto Ricans on the island were drawn to the familiarity of music video and other media images and stories; these mirrored their lives in Puerto Rico's urban communities. By the late 1980s, Puerto Rican MCs, called *raperos*, were on the rise, and breakdancing (or b-boying/b-girling) was becoming a specialized skill of many youth. Graffiti murals could also be seen adorning the walls of *caseríos*, or low-income housing communities.

Stylistically, contemporary Puerto Rican hip hop maintains the integrity of old-school, late 1980s and early 1990s, lyrical content. Songs boast of the skill of an MC while defaming another, share stories about the living conditions of poverty and violence, or make political observations about the world. Tego Calderón (Tegui Calderón Rosario, 1972–), for example, is an MC that is revered for exposing racial discrimination and injustice against Afro–Puerto Ricans in his songs. Other themes that exemplify developing trends in the music as it becomes more commodified are the acquisition of wealth, extravagant spending, and the dealings and conflict of the underground drug economy.

Notable Puerto Rican MCs include San Juan–based Vico C (Luis Armando Lozada Cruz, 1971–), originally born in Brooklyn, New York; Ñengo Flow (Edwin Laureano Rosa Vazquez Ortiz, 1981–); and Arecibo-based MC Ceja (Alberto Mendoza Nieves, 1978–). Artists such as Ivy Queen (1972–) and Calderón bridge hip hop and reggaetón. The Bronx-born rapper Big Pun (1971–2000), who is widely considered one of the most lyrically skilled rappers of all time, was of Puerto Rican descent.

Sabia McCoy-Torres

See also: Big Pun; Ivy Queen; Reggae; Reggaetón; The United States

Further Reading

Arroyo, Jossianna. 2010. "'Roots' or the Virtualities of Racial Imaginaries in Puerto Rico and the Diaspora." *Latino Studies* 8, no. 2: 195–219.

Flores, Juan. 2000. *From Bomba to Hip Hop: Puerto Rican Culture and Latino Identity.* New York: Columbia University Press.

Rivera, Raquel Z., Wayne Marshall, and Deborah Pacini Hernandez. 2009. *Reggaetón.* Durham, NC: Duke University Press.

Further Listening

Ivy Queen. 2010. *Drama Queen.* Machete Music.

Tego Calderón. 2015. *El que sabe sabe* (*He Who Knows, Knows*). Siente Music.

Vico C. 1991. *Hispanic Soul.* Prime Records.

Puff Daddy

(aka P. Diddy, Love, Brother Love, Sean John Combs, 1969–, New York)

Puff Daddy, also known professionally at various times as P. Diddy, Diddy, Puffy, Sean Combs, and most recently as Love or Brother Love, is a leading producer, performer, entrepreneur, and celebrity. Although his successes as both a producer and performer cover multiple styles, with his work leaning toward a more popular, dance-oriented sound, he epitomizes the East Coast hip hop style. His business ventures, including a successful line of men's fashions, restaurants, a digital media channel, and other products, have made him one of the wealthiest executives in the entertainment industry. Unlike many hip hop producers, he has embraced the role of industry mogul, and he is more likely to be seen in a smartly tailored suit than in the hoodies and backward ball caps of most rappers.

CHILDHOOD AND EARLY WORK IN THE RECORDING INDUSTRY

Puff Daddy was born Sean John Combs in public housing in Harlem, New York City, where his father, Melvin Earl Combs (1938–1972), was an associate of Frank Lucas (1930–), one of the city's most notorious drug dealers. When he was three, his father was killed in a botched drug deal, and his mother, Janice Combs

(1940–), raised him alone. He graduated from Mount Saint Michael Academy in the Bronx, and he then attended Howard University for two years before dropping out. Starting as an unpaid intern at Uptown Records (1986–1999) in Harlem, he was quickly promoted to the position of talent director. He worked with new acts, notably Jodeci (1988–1996, 2014–), Father MC (Timothy Brown, 1967*–), and Mary J. Blige (1971–). Generally, he was quite successful in helping these R&B-oriented performers to develop grittier urban images and to achieve strong showings on their debut albums. Despite his many accomplishments for the label, tension developed between him and Andre Harrell (1960–), Uptown's founder and chief executive, and in 1993, Puff Daddy was dismissed without notice.

BAD BOY RECORDS

Within a few weeks, he had founded his own company, Bad Boy Records (1992–), and in July 1994, the label released its

Most recently renaming himself Brother Love, Puff Daddy has been a prominent and award-winning American rapper, hip hop producer, and fashion designer. His label Bad Boy Records produced his own Platinum-certified albums, as well as for the Notorious B.I.G., Mase, and Faith Evans, among others. (Feature Flash/Dreamstime.com)

first recording, a hit single by Craig Mack (1971–), "Flava in Ya Ear," which was followed in September by Mack's debut album, *Project: Funk da World* (1994), which reached Gold status. Those recordings were quickly surpassed; however, by the debut album of the Notorious B.I.G. (1972–1997), *Ready to Die* (1994), which had been released just a week before Mack's album. The Notorious B.I.G. had signed initially with Uptown Records and was singing as a guest on recordings by other Uptown artists when he began working under Puff Daddy's guidance to record his own debut album. But that project stalled when Puff Daddy left Uptown. After a brief hiatus, the Notorious B.I.G. moved to Bad Boy Records, where he finished the album, which would reach quadruple Platinum in sales.

Ready to Die established the Bad Boy label as a major player in the music industry and also reasserted the importance of East Coast hip hop, which had been eclipsed by the rise of West Coast gangsta rap. Puff Daddy would also produce and promote two additional albums by the Notorious B.I.G.—after his murder in 1997. They achieved Diamond and double-Platinum status.

Puff Daddy was known for a strong eye for talent, and he has been able to attract and develop a number of new performers at Bad Boy Records. For example, he served as Executive Producer for the debut album *Faith* (1995), by R&B singer Faith Evans (1973–), as well as for the R&B trio Total's (1994–2000, 2010–) eponymous album (1996). He also produced the Harlem-based rapper Ma$e's (Mason Durrell Betha, 1977–) album *Harlem World* (1997) and the pop teen girl group Dream's (1998–2003) *It Was All a Dream* (2001), all of which reached Platinum certification. This lineup testified to the variety of styles he produced, most of which were aimed toward middle-of-the-road pop audiences, as well as his association with hip hop soul, a mixture of traditional R&B with hip hop elements, a sound that he helped to pioneer.

DEBUT ALBUM, BUSINESS VENTURES, AND FASHION DESIGN

In 1997, Puff Daddy released his own debut album, *No Way Out* (under Puff Daddy and The Family), which included a number of guest appearances by Bad Boy artists. The album earned a Grammy Award the next year and went on to sell over seven million copies. Combs's subsequent albums, *Forever* (1999), *The Saga Continues* (2001), *Press Play* (2006), and *Last Train to Paris* (2010), have all sold reasonably well, but none have come close to the sales of his first album.

Criticism of his work has usually been mixed to positive, with complaints centering on his frequent use of guest performers, the repeated sampling of his earlier hits, and a general tendency to water down hip hop into a more saleable sound. His music, whether his own or tracks that he produces for other performers, almost always has a more mainstream sound, with richly orchestrated accompaniments (adding an elegant, luxurious sound, called *luxe*) and backing vocals that are much closer to traditional R&B than to the raw beats of West Coast gangsta rap. His lyrics are also less violent and obviously vulgar than their West Coast counterparts, although there are occasional exceptions.

His sense for the market is reflected in his other business ventures, notably his Sean John fashion line, which he founded in 1998 with a men's sportswear collection. The company, which earned an industry award in 2004, subsequently expanded to include numerous related lifestyle products and since 2010 has been sold exclusively at Macy's department stores. His personal celebrity is also aimed at the broadest audiences and is widely covered by the mainstream media. His occasional run-ins with the law, a high-profile relationship with singer and actress Jennifer Lopez (aka J.Lo, 1969–), a leading role in a 2004 Broadway revival of the play *A Raisin in the Sun* (1959) and its subsequent television adaptation, and a series of superficial name changes over the years have all helped to keep the name Sean Combs in the news. Puff Daddy nevertheless has also been notable for his frequent charity work with inner city youth, his honorary degree from Howard University, and his public pride in his children's accomplishments.

Scott Warfield

See also: Fashion; Gangsta Rap; The Notorious B.I.G.; The United States

Further Reading

Jones, Jen. 2014. *Sean "Diddy" Combs: A Biography of a Music Mogul.* Berkeley Heights, NJ: Enslow Publishers.

Ro, Ronin. 2001. *Bad Boy: The Influence of Sean "Puffy" Combs on the Music Industry.* New York: Pocket Books.

Further Listening

Puff Daddy and The Family. 1997. *No Way Out.* Bad Boy Entertainment.

Quarashi

(1996–2005, 2016–, Reykjavík, Iceland)

Quarashi is an Icelandic hip hop group that fuses old- and new-school hip hop, funk, electronica, nu-metal, hard garage rock, and techno. In 1996, rapper, singer, and producer Hössi Ólafsson (Höskuldur Ólafsson, 1977–) and rapper Ómar Öm Hauksson (aka Ómar Swarez, 1975–) met at a protest against a U.S. military base in Reykjavík. DJ, keyboardist, percussionist, rapper, and songwriter Sölvi Blöndal (1975–) soon joined and invited rapper Steini (aka Stoney, Steinar Orri Fjeldsted, 1976–) to establish Quarashi. The Arabic name means supernatural, but it was also Steini's nickname as a champion ice skater, as well as a commonly seen Reykjavík graffiti tag. Originally, Steini was the lead MC, but by 2002 he had left the group and was replaced by Ólafsson. Guitarist Tarfur (Smári Jósepsson, n.d.), bassist Gaukur Úlfarsson (n.d.), and DJ Dice (anonymous, n.d.) joined Quarashi during their concerts.

Early Quarashi had a boyish, high-pitched rapping sound set against rock guitars; the band sounded like a combination of the Beastie Boys (1981–2012) and Limp Bizkit (1994–2006, 2009–); however, the band showed rapping flexibility, strong presence of turntablism and synthesized sounds, and lush instrumentals on its studio albums. Its lyrics were often about partying and gangster life (drugs, attaining wealth, committing crimes). Quarashi's videos ranged from garage band, such as "Surreal Rhyme" (from *Xeneizes*), to black-and-white minidramas, such as "Baseline" (2002), which featured Quarashi rapping and playing on a naval ship. The more recent "Chicago" (2016) is also a black and white music video that shows a more mature, metrosexual Quarashi, with contrasting rapping styles and vocal ranges.

ALBUMS AND SUCCESS

Rapping completely in English, Quarashi experienced early national success with its EP *Switchstance* (1996), as all 500 copies sold in one week. Between 1996 and 1998, Quarashi toured Iceland to promote the album, opening for internationally known American hip hop groups such as the Fugees (1992–1997) and released its eponymous debut studio album (aka *The Egg Album*, 1997). Quarashi's second album, *Xeneizes* (1999) topped the Icelandic album chart and was certified Gold in Iceland. Its third studio album, *Kristnihald undir Jökli* (*Christianity under the Glacier*, 2001), was an instrumental soundtrack album to 20th-century Icelandic novelist, poet journalist, and playwright Halldór Laxness's (Halldór Guðjónsson,

1902–1998) play of the same title and—with just 500 copies made—is now a rare find.

Quarashi's fourth album, *Jinx* (2002), was the group's only album released internationally and recorded on a major American label, Columbia Records (1887–), in New York City. Ironically titled, *Jinx* attained mixed reception, peaking at No. 104 on the Billboard 200. But just a week later, the album fell to No. 144, and Quarashi began having issues with Columbia. *Jinx* sold just 100,000 copies in the United States, and in 2004, the label dropped Quarashi. Returning to Reykjavík, Hössi left the band to attend the University of Iceland and was replaced by rapper Tiny (Egill Olafur Thorarensen, 1984–).

Quarashi's fifth studio album, *Guerilla Disco* (2005), was well received, though with Tiny's influence it represented a change in Quarashi's sound from pop-infused rap to gangsta rap. After a worldwide tour in 2005, Quarashi broke up. In 2016, Quarashi, including Hössi, reunited. "Chicago" (2016) is the new lineup's first new single.

Melissa Ursula Dawn Goldsmith

See also: Beastie Boys; Gangsta Rap; Iceland; Turntablism

Further Reading

Marino, Nick. 2002. "Q&A Rappers from Iceland—How Warped Is That?" Interview with Quarashi. *Florida Times Union* (Jacksonville), August 2, WE13.

Mitchell, Tony. 2015. "Icelandic Hip Hop from 'Selling American Fish to Icelanders' to Reykjavíkdætur (Reykjavík Daughters)." *Journal of World Popular Music* 2, no. 2: 240–60.

Further Listening

Quarashi. 1997. *Quarashi.* Japis.

Quarashi. 2004. *Guerilla Disco.* Dennis.

Queen Latifah

(Dana Elaine Owens, 1970–, Newark, New Jersey)

Queen Latifah is known as the First Lady of Hip Hop. She has had a rich and varied career, from being an Afrocentric and feminist rapper to a sitcom actor, film actor, talk show host, jazz vocalist, *Cover Girl* model and spokesperson, and Curvation lingerie model. Her raps explore themes of African American female empowerment and stands in stark contrast to her contemporary male rappers. The name Latifah is Arabic and means sensitive, kind, and beautiful. It is her stage name, but Owens says she adopted it when she was eight years old. In 1989, she added the moniker "Queen" when she released her first album, *All Hail the Queen*. Unlike some female rappers, such as Lil' Kim (1975–) and Roxanne Shanté (1969–), Queen Latifah is famous for her refusal to package her body as a sexual object, preferring instead athletic wear, comfortable clothes, or sophisticated, dignified styles of dress. She has also insisted on maintaining artistic and financial control of her music. In 1995, with Shakim Compere (1967–), she founded her own label and management company, Flavor Unit Entertainment (1995–), which she took over from Flavor Unit, a collective of MCs and DJs that was founded around 1990. Queen Latifah's voice is in the contralto or first alto range. It is clear and strong, and her diction and intonation are impeccable, both in singing and rapping. Her lyrics are thus easy to hear and take the foreground in all of her music, whether in rap, jazz, or R&B. The R&B influence is heard clearly in her rap songs, whose beats often use horns and saxophone.

A CAREER IN RAP

Queen Latifah launched her rapping career at the age of 18 with her single "Wrath of My Madness" (1988), released by Tommy Boy Records (now Tommy Boy Entertainment, 1981–). A year later, she released the album *All Hail the Queen* (1989). Her hit single from this album, "Ladies First," a duet with British rapper and Native Tongues Posse (1988–1996) member Monie Love (Simone Gooden, 1970–), established her reputation as a serious rapper with a strong female message. Over beats with horns and wailing saxophone riffs, Queen Latifah ends one memorable phrase by pointing out her music will place "ladies first."

During the early 1990s, she was connected with two important Afrocentric rap collectives, Afrika Bambaataa's (1957–) Universal Zulu Nation (1973–) and the Native Tongues Posse. Her second album was *Nature of a Sista'* (1991, also with Tommy Boy), and after lukewarm reviews, she moved to Motown Records (1959–), where she produced *Black Reign* (1993). Her hit song "U.N.I.T.Y." from *Black Reign*, like "Ladies First," is a hymn to black female empowerment, and won the 1995 Grammy for Best Rap Solo Performance. The song was a call for unity in the African American community to stop putting down black women by calling them names such as *b—* or *ho*. As a testament to this hit's far-reaching influence, Queen Latifah performed it at the 2014 Nobel Peace Prize Concert. Her subsequent albums, *Order in the Court* (rap, Flavor Unit/Motown, 1998), *The Dana Owens Album* (jazz standards, Interscope, 2004), and *Trav'lin' Light* (pop standards, Verve, 2007), did not achieve the hit status of *All Hail the Queen* or *Black Reign*. "Ladies First" and "U.N.I.T.Y." remain her two most famous rap hits.

FROM RAPPING TO ACTING

In the early 1990s, concurrent with her rising success as a rapper, Queen Latifah established herself as a television and film actor. By the 2000s, her career shifted away from rap and toward acting. She played the lead role of Khadijah James in the syndicated television series *Living Single* (1993–1998) and appeared in single episodes of various television shows including *The Fresh Prince of Bel Air* (1991), *Spin City* (2001), *Eve* (2004), and *30 Rock* (2010), among others. She also plays the voice of Ellie in the American animated *Ice Age* films from Blue Sky Studios, a division of 20th Century Fox. Notable film appearances include Matron Mama Morton in *Chicago* (2002), for which she was nominated for an Oscar as Best Actress in a Supporting Role and won a BET award for Best Actress, Motormouth Maybelle in *Hairspray* (2007), and Angela in *Miracles from Heaven* (2016).

In 2015, she played the Wiz in an innovative new genre, the live television production of a musical, *The Wiz Live!* The move away from rap in the 2000s toward an acting career enabled Queen Latifah to extend her influence into mainstream American popular culture. In 2006, she became the first hip hop artist to be awarded a star on the Hollywood Walk of Fame. As of 2018, she remains a role model for the next generation of female rap artists.

Terry Klefstad

See also: Fashion; Missy Elliott; Native Tongues; The United States; The Universal Zulu Nation

Further Reading

Hirji, Faiza. 2007. "Queen Latifah." *Icons of Hip Hop: An Encyclopedia of the Movement, Music, and Culture*, edited by Mickey Hess, vol. 1, pp. 217–42. Westport, CT: Greenwood Press.

Roberts, Robin. 1994. "'Ladies First': Queen Latifah's Afrocentric Feminist Music Video." *African American Review* 28, no. 2: 245–57.

Further Listening

Queen Latifah. 1989. *All Hail the Queen.* Tommy Boy.

Queen Latifah. 1993. *Black Reign.* Motown.

Queen Latifah. 2009. *Persona.* Flavor Unit Records.

Queen Pen

(Lynise Walters, 1972–, Brooklyn, New York)

Queen Pen is an American rapper and author, best known for her collaborations with BLACKstreet (1991–), from New York, and Me'Shell Ndegeocello (Michelle Lynn Johnson, 1968–), born in Berlin, as well as for recording one of the first hip hop tracks that openly portrayed the LGBT experience, "Girlfriend" (1997). Following the release of her second album, *Conversations with Queen* (2001), Queen Pen has shifted her career toward writing, having self-published *Situations* (2002), a book of short stories, and *Blossoms* (2006), a novel. She also works closely with the New York nonprofit Children of Promise, an organization devoted to breaking the cycle of intergenerational involvement in the criminal justice system.

Queen Pen first gained widespread recognition when she performed as a featured rapper on BLACKstreet's 1996 multimillion-selling single "No Diggity." She was a protégé of producer and band member Teddy Riley (1967–), who included her on a verse of "No Diggity" and also produced all of the tracks on her first full-length album, *My Melody* (1997), which included "Girlfriend." The song featured neo soul artist (and out lesbian) Me'Shell Ndegeocello's playing bass and singing. The chorus of "Girlfriend" borrows the chorus of her single "If That's Your Boyfriend (He Wasn't Last Night)" (1993) by substituting the word "girlfriend" for "boyfriend" and thereby suggesting a same-sex encounter. Critical of the lack of music available for lesbians of color, Queen Pen wanted to convey the experiences of an underrepresented group in the track. In interviews (for example, in the *New York Times*), she has been cagey about disclosing her own sexual orientation, claiming that she would not discuss the topic (1998), that she was straight (2001), and that she was bisexual (2008).

Although "Girlfriend" garnered praise and was widely regarded by critics as a milestone for its subject, not everyone was a fan of the track or its message. In 1998, rapper Foxy Brown (Inga DeCarlo Fung Marchand, 1978–) recorded two different diss tracks, "10% Diss" and "Talk to Me," both of which contained a number of homophobic slurs directed at both Queen Pen and Queen Latifah (1970–). Critics suggested that Queen Pen's single "I Got Cha" (2001) was a response to Foxy Brown, but Queen Pen denied those claims.

Amanda Sewell

See also: Political Hip Hop; The United States

Further Reading

Jamison, Laura. 1998. "A Feisty Female Rapper Breaks a Hip Hop Taboo." *The New York Times*, January 18, B34.

Keyes, Cheryl. 2000. "Empowering Self, Making Choices, Creating Spaces: Black Female Identity via Rap Music Performance." *Journal of American Folklore* 113: 255–69.

Further Listening

Queen Pen. 1997. *My Melody.* Interscope.

Queen Pen. 2001. *Conversations with Queen.* Motown.

R

Reggae

Reggae is a musical genre that originated in 1960s Jamaica, becoming popular when Kingston bands such as Bob Marley and the Wailers (1963–1981) and Toots and the Maytals (1962–1981, 1997–) invented a new sound that combined beats from mento, ska, rock steady, R&B, and gospel. The term *reggae* itself was possibly introduced in 1968 in a single by the Maytals titled "Do the Reggay," based on the name of a dance made popular by the new music that was replacing rocksteady music (and rocksteady dance) in Jamaica. The single was part of a package deal, the B side being "Motoring," by Beverley's Records (1961–1971) combination band, Beverley's All Stars. The single was also picked up in 1968 by Pyramid Records (1961–1971) in the United Kingdom.

EARLY CLASSICS

Despite the Maytals' benchmark recordings in the development of reggae, it was Bob Marley (Robert Nesta Marley, 1945–1981) who internationalized the music through his key collaborations with London producer Chris Blackwell (Christopher Percy Gordon Blackwell, 1937–). Ska and rocksteady musician and producer Prince Buster (Cecil Bustamente Campbell, 1938–) from Kingston, Jamaica, provided the financial investment needed to internationalize reggae, bringing the sound to Great Britain in the 1960s. By 1962, Blackwell had collected five thousand dollars from financial backers to recreate Island Records, Ltd. (1959–) into a distribution outlet for leading Jamaican records.

Blackwell put his trust in Marley and his Jamaican cohorts, Bunny Livingston (aka Jah B, Neville O'Riley Livingston, 1947–) and Peter Tosh (Winston Hubert McIntosh, 1944–1987), two members of the original Wailers, and helped them release solo albums. During Blackwell's sustained collaboration with Marley, Island Records released the Wailers' *Catch a Fire* (1973) and *Burnin'* (1973), as well as Bob Marley and the Wailer's *Natty Dread* (1975), *Rastaman Vibration* (1976), *Exodus* (1977), *Kaya* (1978), *Babylon by Bus* (1978), *Survival* (1979), and *Uprising* (1980).

The wide success of Bob Marley and the Wailers was also made possible by those of the three female backing vocalists, known as the I-Threes (n.d.), who played in the band. These three black women were Marcia Llyneth Griffiths (1949–), Rita (Alpharita Constantia Marley, 1946–), and Judy (Judith Veronica Mowatt, 1952–). These women provided not only morale and emotional support for the group, but also singing skills, appeal, class, and deportment that helped propel the band to success and popularize the classic image of the "Rastawoman" that has now influenced hairstyle, fashion, and other popular cultures worldwide.

The phenomenal success of Bob Marley and the Wailers inspired the contiguous rise and prominence of other reggae stars, including Burning Spear (Winston Rodney, 1945–) and Dennis Brown (Dennis Emmanuel Brown, 1957–1999). Known as "The Crown Prince of Reggae," Brown was one of the first musicians who, like Marley, left indelible imprints on development of reggae. Unfortunately, Brown, like Marley, died young, collapsing in 1999 from illnesses ascribed to asthma and drug use. Between 1978 and 1998, Brown performed at nearly every Reggae Sunsplash, the largest gathering of reggae artists held in Jamaica annually, influencing all genres of Jamaican music, from roots reggae to dancehall and ragga.

Brown's music has had a cultural/historical as well as musical impact on reggae, due in large part to his infusion of rock-and-roll rhythms and R&B vocal syncopations into reggae. His impact can be seen with contemporary reggae musicians such as Jamaica's Freddy McGregor (1956–) and Junior Reid (Delroy Reid, 1963–), and London's Maxi Priest (Max Alfred Elliott, 1961–) and the band Aswad (1975–), as well as other bands that popularized the original forms of dancehall.

OFFSHOOTS: DANCEHALL AND RAGGA MUFFIN

Since the early 1990s, the term "dancehall" has been used to describe reggae that deemphasized slower tempos and spiritual concerns to create a more danceable music so that people could enjoy a more vibrant and energetic reggae experience, one that catered to physical movement more than meditation. Rather than from traditionalists roots music, dancehall came about as a version of ragga (aka Ragga Muffin), a music associated with Kingston acts such as Shabba Ranks (Rexton Rawlston Fernando Gordon, 1966–), Buju Banton (Mark Anthony Myrie, 1973–), Sizzla (aka Sizzla Kalonji, Miguel Orlando Collins, 1976–), and Patra (Dorothy Smith, 1972–), as well as Islington, Jamaica's Capelton (Clifton George Bailey III, 1967–) and Trelawny, Jamaica's Anthony B (Keith Blair, 1976–).

Roots and dancehall versions of reggae share a common celebration of Rastafarianism (1930s–) and rebelliousness against oppression. Some traditionalist roots artists and bands include these Kingston acts: U-Roy (Ewart Beckford, 1942–), Yabby You (Vivian Jackson, 1946–2010), Big Youth (Manley Augustus Buchanan, 1949–), Horace Andy (1951–), Mutabaruka (Allan Hope, 1952–), Don Carlos (1952–), Gregory Isaacs (1951–2010), Jacob Miller (1952–1980), Johnny Clarke (1955–), Sugar (Lincoln Barrington Minott, 1956–2010), Michael Prophet (Michael George Haynes, 1957–2017), Eek-A-Mouse (Ripton Joseph Hylton, 1957–), Michael Rose (1957–), Earl Sixteen (Earl John Daley, 1958), Hugh Mundell (1962–1983), Junior Reid (Delroy Reid, 1962–), Frankie Paul (Paul Blake, 1965–2017), Tenor Saw (Clive Bright, 1966–1988), and Mark Wonder (Mark Andrew Thompson, n.d.), among many others.

In addition to these legends are a number of acts from outside Kingston: Saint James Parish, Jamaica's Jimmy Cliff (James Chambers, 1948–); Clarendon, Jamaica's Freddie McGregor (1956–); Birmingham, England's Steel Pulse (1975–); and

Falmouth, Jamaica's Twinkle Brothers (1962–). Others include Christiana, Jamaica's Ijahman Levi (Trevor Sutherland, 1946–); Ann Parish, Jamaica's Max Romeo (1947–); Annotto Bay, Jamaica's Beres Hammond (1955–); Port Antonio, Jamaica's Mikey Dread (Michael George Campbell, 1954–2008); and Clarendon Parish, Jamaica's Everton Blender (Everton Blender Everton Dennis Williams, 1954–), Cocoa Tea (Calvin George Scott, 1959–), and Barrington Ainsworth Levy (1964–); as well as Manchester Parish, Jamaica's Garnet Silk (Garnett Daymon Smith, 1966–94), Luciano (Jepther McClymont, 1974–), and many other icons.

These other idols include bands such as the Paragons (1960s–), the Melodians (1963–), the Gladiators (1968–), Inner Circle (1968–), the Wailing Souls (1968–), the Abyssinians (1969–), the Mighty Diamonds (1969–), the Mystic Revealers (1970–), Israel Vibrations (1970s–), Black Uhuru (1972–), Third World (1973–), the Meditations (1974–), Misty in Roots (1975–), the Congos (1975–), the Revolutionaries (1975–), the Itals (1976–), Culture (1976–), Morgan Heritage (1994–), and many other groups.

DUB REGGAE

Dub reggae is a mostly instrumental subgenre of reggae that emerged in the 1960s. It was named after producers' activity of dubbing previously recorded reggae and modifying that material—usually in ways that emphasized the drum and bass, often removing the vocal parts. "Dub" may also refer to the resultant recording, the modified yet recognizable double of the original. Just a couple of pioneers of dub reggae include Lee Scratch Perry (1936–) and King Tubby (1941–1989). Transforming reggae by electronically stretching the possibilities of voice, pitch, sound, rhythms, tonality, and other musical patterns with the dexterity of highly talented live musicians, dub reggae artists and technicians have defined a genre that appeals to selected fans from around the world.

Big names of dub reggae artists include Sir Coxsone (Clement Seymour Dodd, 1932–2004), Mad Professor (Neil Joseph Stephen Fraser, 1955–), the Scientist (Hopeton Overton Brown, 1960–), the Heptones (1965–), the Upsetters (1968–), Dub Syndicate (1982–), the Aggrovators (1970s–), Black Uhuru (1972–), Sly and Robbie (1976–), Roots Radics (1978–), Zion Train (1990–), John Brown's Body (1995–), Basque Dub Foundation (1990s–), and the Black Seeds (1998–). Dub reggae would become highly influential to other genres of music, most notably electronica, hip hop, and trip hop.

NEW JAMAICAN ROOTS REGGAE

Drawing from the legacy of early conscious reggae music, a new generation of roots artists has evolved out of Jamaica since the 1990s. These icons include Bob Marley's children, such as Cedella Marley (1967–), Ziggy Marley (David Nesta Marley, 1968–), Jr. Gong Marley (Damian Robert Nesta Marley, 1978–), Raggamuffin Marley (Stephen Robert Nesta Marley, 1972–), Julian Ricardo Marley (1975–), and Ky-Many Marley (1976–). Besides the Marley family, Peter

Tosh's son and Bunny Wailer's (aka Jah B, Neville O'Riley Livingston, 1947–) nephew, Andrew Tosh (Carlos Andrew McIntosh, 1967–); Joseph Hill's (1949–2006) son Kenyatta Hill (1979–); and legendary dub musician Augustus Pablo's (Horace Swaby, 1954–1999) son Addis Pablo (1989–) have, among other offspring of legends, kept their parents' legacies alive.

Other male reggae icons include St. Croix's legend, Vaughn Benjamin, former member of the Midnite band and now member of Akae Beka and Jamaica's Jahmali (Ryan Thomas, 1972–), Jah Cure (Siccature Alcock, 1978–), Tarrus Riley (Omar Riley, 1979–), I Wayne (Cliffroy Taylor, 1980–), Duane Stephenson (1976–), Jesse Royal (Jesse David Grey, 1989–), Chronixx (Jamar McNaughton, 1992–), and Raging Fyah (2011–).

Although men have generally dominated Jamaican reggae, women have played a role in the music as well. Several women stars preceded or followed the footsteps of their male pioneers and contemporaries, expanding reggae's reach to the United States, Europe, and the rest of the world. These stars include Hortense Ellis (1941–), Phyllis Dillon (1944–), Millie Dolly May Small (1946–), Dawn Penn (1952–), Sister Nancy (Ophlin Russell, 1952–), Diana King (1970–), and Tanya Stephens (1973–). Treading on their elders' paths, another generation of Jamaican women artists have reinvigorated reggae. These stars include the Jamaicans, Queen Ifrica (Ventrice Morgan, 1975–), Etana (Shauna McKenzie, 1984–), Alaine Laughton (1978–), and the mystic voice of St. Croix, U.S. Virgin Islands, Dezarie (n.d.). These women are as talented as their male peers who have also strengthened reggae's stature over the past 15 years.

INTERNATIONALIZATION

Since the early 1980s, reggae's internationalization has created a complex system of musical borrowing whereby the Jamaican music first had to be introduced to the rest of the world and then had to make its way back to its homeland, in new versions, from many parts of the world; thus, many artists from Africa, Europe, the Americas, the Caribbean, Asia, Australia, and Oceania have contributed to reggae's global development. For instance, in the 1980s, Dimbokro, the Ivory Coast's Alpha Blondy (Seydou Koné, 1953–) created a new form of reggae that draws on the musical roots and spirituality of Jamaican reggae, and mixes them with elements of Afrobeat, R&B, and rock 'n' roll. Combining reggae with rhythms from his Dioula, Muslim, and Christian backgrounds, Alpha Blondy invented a music that appealed to international audiences, earning him the title of "Africa's Bob Marley."

Jamaican reggae musicians have influenced other major African musicians, including Dakar, Senegal's Xalam (1969–), Ndiaga Diop (n.d.), Super Diamono de Dakar (1975–), and Youssou N'dour (1959–); Ziguinchor, Senegal's Touré Kunda (1978–); Podor, Senegal's Baba Maal (1953–); Sierra Leone's Sebanoh 75 (1975–1979); Enugu, Nigeria's Sonny Okosun (1947–2008); Ermelo, Mpumalanga (Transvaal), South Africa's Lucky Dube (1964–2007); Morocco's Momo Cat (Mohammed Quiat, 1990s–); and Ethiopia's Teddy Ab (2010s–), to name just a few.

Outside Africa and Jamaica, equally strong reggae musicians have emerged. Beside the bands Aswad and Steel Pulse, England has produced internationally famous reggae bands such as UB40 (1978–), from Birmingham; Black Roots (1979–), from Bristol; and Alien Dread (1986*–). From the United States, major reggae bands such as Big Mountain (1988–), from San Diego, California; SOJA (Soldiers of Jah Army, 1997–), from Arlington, Virginia; and Rebelution (2004–), from Isla Vista (Goleta), California have carried reggae's burning torch.

Germany, Italy, France, and other parts of Europe have produced captivating roots reggae that has evolved over the past decades. Headliner acts such as Osnabrück, Germany's Gentleman (Tilmann Otto, 1975–) and Lage, Germany's Uwe Banton (Uwe Schäfer, 1966–); Sicily, Italy's Alborosie (Alberto D'Ascola, 1977–); and Kingston, Jamaica's T.O.K. (1996–2015) have shown that reggae knows no race, color, nationality, or creed, that it belongs to anyone who has the strong will to spread justice, love, and equality throughout the world and carry the message of Jah Rastafari, a title based on the birth name of Ethiopian emperor Haile Selassie I (Ras Tafari Makonnen Woldemikael, 1892–1975; reign, 1930–1974), whom many Rastafarians believe is a messenger of God and his incarnation on earth.

WORLDWIDE POPULARITY AND GENRE CROSSING

Reggae's worldwide popularity has led to both the creation of related musical styles as well as fusion. For example, reggaetón, a music born in Puerto Rico after the popularity of Shabba Ranks' song "Dem Bow" (1990), uses reggae conventions as its basis. Ska and rocksteady, precursors to reggae, have always been associated with reggae. Sounding like reggae but played at a faster tempo, ska has enjoyed an international popularity, surging in the 1980s into the 1990s; its worldwide popularity has enhanced reggae's own popularity. Dub music, a subgenre of reggae that began in the 1960s, is a precursor of dubstep, which has become popular worldwide in the electronic dance music scene (beginning in the late 1990s in the United Kingdom). Since the late 1970s, reggae has also had a major influence on punk music, with bands such as the Clash (1976–1986), and by the 1980s it had been incorporated in new wave and hip hop.

Countless hip hop artists and bands worldwide embrace reggae in their music, some placing more emphasis on reggae than others. Just a few artists and bands who not only fuse reggae with hip hop, but have also made reggae a major part of their sound are Positive Black Soul (PBS, 1989–), Shaggy (1968–), Fugees (1992–1997), Michael Franti and Spearhead (1994–), Moana and the Moahunters (aka Moana and the Tribe, 1991–1998, 2002–), Akon (1973–), Daara J (1997–), Intik (1988–2001), Ivy Queen (1972–), Don Omar (William Omar Landrón, 1978–), Vico C (Luis Armando Lozada Cruz, 1971–), Super Cat (William Anthony Maragh, 1963–), and Snow (Darrin Kenneth O'Brien, 1969–).

Babacar M'Baye

See also: Daara J; Franti, Michael; Fugees; Intik; Ivy Queen; Jamaica; Moana and the Moahunters; Reggaetón; Shaggy

Further Reading

Chang, Kevin O'Brien, and Wayne Chen. 1998. *Reggae Routes: The Story of Jamaican Music.* Philadelphia: Temple University Press.

Thompson, Dave. 2002. *Reggae and Caribbean Music.* San Francisco: Backbeat Books.

White, Timothy. 2000. *Catch a Fire: The Life of Bob Marley.* New York: Henry Holt.

Further Listening

Alpha Blondy. 2007. *Jah Victory.* Mediacom.

Bob Marley and the Wailers. 1984. *Legend: The Best of Bob Marley and the Wailers.* Island Records.

Marley, Bob. 2007. *Remixed & Unmixed.* Music Brokers.

Marley, Ziggy. 2016. *Ziggy Marley.* Tuff Gong Worldwide.

Shabba Ranks. 1990. *Rappin' with the Ladies.* Greensleeves Records.

Super Cat. 1995. *The Struggle Continues.* Columbia.

Touré Kunda. 1980. *É'mma Africa (Ms. Africa).* Celluloid.

UB40. 1983. *Labour of Love.* Virgin.

Yellowman & Fathead, Purpleman, and Sister Nancy. 1983. *The Yellow, The Purple, and The Nancy.* Greensleeves Records/Shanachie Records.

Reggaetón

Reggaetón is a music genre that combines vibrant percussive beats, synthesized sounds, and the instrumental components of various genres of music. Some of the musical aspects that reggaetón incorporates are the percussive and vocal styles of dancehall, R&B singing, *salsa*, *merengue*, rapping or MCing, and the guitar and horn riffs of *bachata* (dance music from the Dominican Republic that derives from Cuban *bolero* and *son*, and sometimes Dominican *merengue*). In terms of its rhythmic structure, the most notable characteristic of reggaetón is the *dem bow* (pronounced "dem-boh," which when translated from Jamaican patois means "them bow," the rhythm that is at the core of most songs). It is a rhythm derived from legendary reggae and dancehall musician Shabba Ranks' (Rexton Rawlston Fernando Gordon, 1966–) classic Jamaican dancehall hit "Dem Bow" (1991), which was notable for its "boom-chick-boom-chick" beat. Just as notable as the dem bow percussive rhythm is in reggaetón, so too is the hip hop lyrical delivery of reggaetón artists. When they are not singing in the R&B style, most are rapping in Spanish.

EARLY HISTORY

The early history of reggaetón traces to Panama, but its evolution into the music genre that is known today occurred in Puerto Rico. In the mid-1800s, Afro-Caribbean people from the English-speaking Caribbean islands (also referred to as the West Indies) began immigrating to Panama to work on the construction of the Panama Canal. Most remained in the country after its construction was complete, and others continued to immigrate to work on banana plantations. Afro-Caribbean people maintained cultural and musical traditions that originated in the West Indies. Reggae developed in Jamaica in the late 1960s.

In the 1980s dancehall, a faster paced, urban themed subgenre, developed, Afro-Caribbean people imported both kinds of music to Panama by exchanging records and audiocassettes with family members. In order to reflect their Panamanian culture and use of Spanish, Afro-Caribbean people made *reggae en español* (reggae in Spanish) and the roots of reggaetón were planted. Early reggae en español had a sound more similar to the dancehall music of Jamaican artists such as Shabba Ranks and Buju Banton (Mark Anthony Myrie, 1973–) than the "roots reggae" music of Bob Marley (1945–1981). Panamanians El General (Edgardo Franco, 1959–) and 1980s musician Nando Boom (Fernando Orlando Brown Mosley) are widely acknowledged as reggaetón's pioneers.

As early reggae en español was transported throughout the Caribbean via travelers, migrant laborers, families relocating, and friends sharing music, it took root in Puerto Rico, a small island in the Caribbean. Puerto Rico is an unincorporated territory of the United States in which people have U.S. citizenship. Because of their citizenship status, Puerto Ricans have historically traveled frequently between the island and the U.S., particularly New York City. At a crossroads between countries, Puerto Rico's location in the Caribbean made it a place where people immigrate to and from other islands (especially the Dominican Republic) to work, and its connection to the United States made it a prime location for different genres of music to meet and be hybridized into a new genre. Hip hop, R&B, salsa, merengue, and bachata were infused into reggae en español, transforming it into reggaetón.

TEXTS AND NOTABLE ACTS

The lyrics of reggaetón span a range of topics. Some songs focus on elements of nightlife leisure, such as being with friends, dancing, courting, and seeking sexual conquests with romantic partners. There are also reggaetón songs that thematically are concerned with love, national identity and pride, and social critique. Tego Calderón (Tegui Calderón Rosario, 1971–), from Santurce, has protested racial inequality in Puerto Rico in various songs, and has been a pioneer of consciousness raising reggaetón. Some other prominent reggaetón artists from Puerto Rico include Wisin y Yandel (1998–), Don Omar (William Omar Landrón, 1978–), Calle 13 (2004–), Zion Y Lennox (2004–n.d.), and Ivy Queen (1972–). Calderón, Calle 13, Don Omar, Ivy Queen, and Wisin y Yandel are also hip hop artists.

Reggaetón's reach extends to the United States and throughout the Spanish speaking Caribbean where reggaetón artists are building fame in the Dominican Republic and Cuba. It is also popular throughout Mexico, as well as Central and South America, where it remains among the most celebrated and enjoyed popular music. Reggaetón's broad Latin American appeal has converted it for many into a symbol of pan-Latino identity and pride.

Sabia McCoy-Torres

See also: Ivy Queen; Panama; Puerto Rico; Reggae

Further Reading
Baker, Geoffrey. 2011. *Buena Vista in the Club: Rap, Reggaetón, and Revolution in Havana.* Durham, NC: Duke University Press.

Rivera, Raquel Z., Wayne Marshall, and Deborah Pacini Hernandez. 2009. *Reggaetón.* Durham, NC: Duke University Press.

Rivera-Rideau, Petra. 2016. "From Panama to the Bay: Los Rakas' Expressions of Afrola-tinidad." In *La Verdad: An International Dialogue on Hip Hop Latinidades*, edited by Melissa Castillo-Garsow and Jason Nicholls, chap. 4. Columbus: Ohio State University Press.

Further Listening

Don Omar. 2003. *The Last Don.* VI Music.

Nando Boom. 1991. *Reggae Español.* Shelly's Records.

Shabba Ranks. 1990. *Just Reality.* VP Records.

Rihanna

(Robyn Rihanna Fenty, 1988–, Saint Michael, Barbados)

Rihanna is an internationally known Barbadian singer-songwriter, model, actress, and fashion designer who performs primarily R&B, pop, reggae, and electronic dance music; her music often employs hip hop elements such as rapping, beats, and loops. Her studio albums that contain hip hop include *Good Girl Gone Bad* (2007), *Rated R* (2009), and *Talk That Talk* (2011), and many of her Billboard Hot 100 hit singles contain hip hop elements: "We Ride" (2006); "Umbrella" and "Don't Stop the Music" (both 2007); "Hard," "Wait Your Turn," and "Rockstar 101" (all 2009); "Te Amo" and "What's My Name?" (both 2010); "Talk that Talk" (2011); "Where Have You Been" (2012); and "Work" and "Nothing Is Promised" (both 2016).

After moving to New York City at 16, Rihanna signed with Def Jam Recordings (1983–). She has collaborated with hip hop producers and artists, including Jay-Z (1969–), Kanye West (1977–), Drake (1986–), Eminem (1972–), Ne-Yo (Shaffer Chimere Smith, 1979–), Nicki Minaj (1982–), and Chris Brown (1989–). In 2009, Rihanna's relationship with Brown made media headlines when he physically assaulted her in a domestic violence incident.

A mezzo-soprano, Rihanna participates in hip hop by singing contrasting lyrical passages to featured rappers, but since *Good Girl Gone Bad*, Rihanna sometimes raps. Her rapping, usually autotuned, can be heard in "Wait Your Turn," "Hard," and 2012's "Cockiness (Love It)." Her rap lyrics focus on love, money, and fashion.

As of 2018, Rihanna is the youngest solo artist to have as many as 12 No. 1 singles on Billboard's Hot 100. She has also won eight Grammy Awards, and all eight of her studio albums have been certified Platinum or multi-Platinum.

Melissa Ursula Dawn Goldsmith

See also: Barbados; Reggae; The United States

Further Reading

Fleetwood, Nicole R. 2012. "The Case of Rihanna: Erotic Violence and Black Female Desire." *African American Review* 45, no. 3: 419–35.

Jones, Esther. 2013. "On the Real: Agency, Abuse, and Sexualized Violence in Rihanna's 'Russian Roulette.'" *African American Review* 46, no. 1: 71–86.

Rodier, Kristin, and Michelle Meagher. 2014. "In Her Own Time: Rihanna, Post-Feminism, and Domestic Violence." *Women* 25, no. 2: 176–93.

Further Listening
Rihanna. 2009. *Rated R.* Def Jam Recordings/SRP Records.
Rihanna. 2011. *Talk That Talk.* Def Jam/SRP.

Rob Base and DJ E-Z Rock

(1985–2014, Harlem, New York)

Rob Base (Robert Ginyard, 1967–) and DJ E-Z Rock (aka Skip, Rodney Bryce, 1967–2014) were a New York–based hip hop duo known for the old-school braggadocio and party rap and dance song "It Takes Two" (1988), which reached Nos. 36 and 17 on the Billboard Hot 100 and Hot R&B/Hip-Hop Songs chart, respectively. Along with the Sugarhill Gang (1979–1985, 1994–), Run–D.M.C. (1981–2002), DJ Jazzy Jeff and the Fresh Prince (1985–1994), MC Hammer (1962–), and Young MC (Marvin Young, 1967–), Rob Base and DJ E-Z Rock is considered one of the pioneers of mainstream rap music.

"It Takes Two", from the Platinum album *It Takes Two* (1988), also reached No. 3 on the Hot Dance Club Songs chart and was certified multi-Platinum. The song uses multiple samples, from "Think (About It)," a 1972 funk song by Lyn Collins (Gloria Lavern Collins, 1948–2005), and from various songs by James Brown (1933–2006).

The album spawned two more hits, the synthesizer- and bass-heavy "Get on the Dance Floor" and the drum- and bass-heavy "Joy and Pain." The former went to the top spot on the Hot Dance Club Songs chart and reached No. 6 on Billboard's Hot Rap Songs chart; the latter was the duo's third Top 10 hit on the Hot Dance Club Songs chart, peaking at No. 9, and its second Hot 100 hit—it also reached No. 5 on the rap songs chart and No. 11 on the Hot R&B/Hip-Hop Songs chart.

Unfortunately, DJ E-Z Rock soon had to leave the duo because of personal issues. Rob Base recorded one studio solo album in 1989, *The Incredible Base*, but it was not a commercial success, nor was the duo's 1994 reunion album, *Break of Dawn.*

Anthony J. Fonseca

See also: The United States

Further Reading
Kelly, Dennis. 1991. "Base and E-Z Rock Rap Way from Flop to Million-Sellers." Interview with Rob Base and DJ E-Z Rock. *Morning Call* (Allentown, Pennsylvania), April 5, 1991, D01.
Webber, Stephen. 2008. *DJ Skills: The Essential Guide to Mixing and Scratching.* Burlington, MA: Focal Press.

Further Listening
Rob Base and DJ E-Z Rock. 1988. *It Takes Two.* Profile Records.

Rob Swift

(Robert Aguilar, 1972–, Queens, New York)

Rob Swift was an American DJ, turntablist, producer, and member of the DJ collective the X-Ecutioners (aka X-Men, 1989–), with whom he released three studio albums: *X-Pressions* (1997), *Built from Scratch* (2002), and *Revolutions* (2004). Rob Swift employs regular style scratching (as opposed to hamster style— reverse scratching that developed after his early years). His strengths include improvisation and musical swing. Though some techniques demonstrated athletic showmanship such as some ambidexterity (he favors scratching on the left deck while using his right hand to control the fader, but easily shifts hands when using the right deck) and choreography, Rob Swift's turntablism is focused more on sound than on show or speed.

Born Robert Aguilar to immigrant parents from Colombia, he grew up in Queens, New York. His father was a salsa and meringue DJ with a large record collection. By age 12, he learned turntablism, including selecting albums, by watching his older brother practice DJ and by studying videos of DJs at park jams. Through his father's collection, he was introduced to jazz and funk. He also learned of the work of DJs such as Grandmaster Flash (1958–) and GrandWizard Theodore (1963–). In 1990, Rob Swift worked as a DJ while attending Baruch College, where he majored in psychology. Around this time, Rob Swift's second mentor was Dr. Butcher (Andrew Venable, n.d.). A year later, both joined the X-Men (later the X-Ecutioners), a turntablist crew known for their skills at beat juggling.

Built from Scratch and *Revolutions* charted on the Billboard 200 at Nos. 15 and 118, respectively. The crew toured worldwide and appeared on national television shows. Rob Swift joined the X-Ecutioners in 1991, the same year he won the DMC East Coast DJ Championship and just five years before his X-Ecutioners colleague and friend Roc Raida (aka Grandmaster Roc Raida, Anthony Williams, 1972– 2009) won the DMC World Championship title.

In 2004, he left the X-Ecutioners to pursue a solo career in which he applied turntablism to jazz, soul, funk, electronica, and classical music. His studio albums include *Soulful Fruit* (1997), *The Ablist* (1999), *Sound Event* (2002), *Under the Influence* and *Who Sampled This?* (both 2003), *OuMuPo 2* (2004), *War Games* (2005), and *The Architect* (2010), and he had one compilation album, *Airwave Invasion* (2001).

Although he left the collective, Rob Swift continued to collaborate with the X-Ecutioners on the albums *General Patton vs. The X-Ecutioners* (2005), *Ill Insanity* (2008–), and *Ground Xero* (2008). Three years after Roc Raida's untimely death from cardiac arrest due to surgery following a martial arts accident, Rob Swift released a collection of songs, both previously released and unreleased, interviews, and battle style routines on the album *Roc for Raida* (2012). Proceeds benefited Roc Raida's family. Rob Swift's solo albums demonstrate his eclectic musical tastes, sometimes fusing hip hop with funk, soul, as well as Caribbean and Cuban music. In *Wargames* he paired turntablism with political hip hop. Rob Swift also teaches turntablism, from making videos for turntablists to study and appearing in documentaries, to workshops and classes. Since 2014, he has held the position of professor at the New School for Liberal Arts in New York City, teaching the course DJ Skills and Styles.

Melissa Ursula Dawn Goldsmith

See also: Battling; Roc Raida; Turntablism; The United States; The X-Ecutioners

Further Reading

Katz, Mark. 2012. *Groove Music: The Art and Culture of the Hip Hop DJ.* New York: Oxford University Press.

Webber, Stephen. 2008. *DJ Skills: The Essential Guide to Mixing and Scratching.* Burlington, MA: Focal Press.

Further Listening

Rob Swift. 1997. *Soulful Fruit.* Stones Throw.

Rob Swift. 2005. *War Games.* Coup De Grace.

Robinson, Sylvia

(Sylvia Vanderpool 1936–2011, New York City, New York)

Sylvia Robinson, often called the "Mother of Hip Hop," was an American singer, songwriter, guitarist, and record producer. While still in her early teens, she recorded under the name Little Sylvia and later learned guitar to become half of the R&B duo Mickey and Sylvia (1956–1961). She is best known as co-owner and CEO of Sugar Hill Records (1979–1985), which was the first recording label to specialize in hip hop. The year it was founded, Sugar Hill Records released "Rapper's Delight" (1979) by the American hip hop and disco group the Sugarhill Gang (1979–1985, 1994–). This became the single that made hip hop popular in the United States and worldwide. Many other notable old-school hip hop artists, groups, and pioneers signed to the label soon afterward. These included Crash Crew (1977–), Funky 4 + 1 (1977–1983), Grandmaster Flash and the Furious Five (1976–1982, 1987–1988), the Sequence (1979–1985), Treacherous Three (1978–1984), and the West Street Mob (1981–1984).

FROM LITTLE SYLVIA TO MICKEY AND SYLVIA

As a child, Sylvia Vanderpool enjoyed singing blues and began taking an interest in R&B. When she was 14, a Columbia Records staff member discovered her. Robinson was a soprano with a breathy quality that could sound sultry. After singing for Columbia, she moved onto Jubilee Records (1946–1970), a label specializing in R&B, doo-wop, and novelty songs. Her 45-RPM singles were "Drive Daddy Drive"/"I Found Somebody to Love" (1952), "A Million Tears"/"Don't Blame My Heart" (1952), and "Blue Heaven"/"The Ring" (1953). In 1953, Jubilee became the first independent record label to have a popular song by a black vocal group, the Orioles' (1946–1956) "Crying in the Chapel," reach a white audience.

Meanwhile, Robinson began recording for Atlantic Records' (1947–) Cat label (1954–1957*) and studied guitar with Mickey Baker (MacHouston Baker, 1925–2012), a jazz and R&B guitarist from Louisville, Kentucky, who was inspired by the husband-wife duo Les Paul and Mary Ford (1950–1964). In 1954, he and Robinson formed their duo, and in 1956, they had a hit with the classic "Love Is Strange," an R&B song written by blues guitarists and singers Bo Diddley (Ellis Otha Bates, 1928–2008) and Jody Williams (Joseph Leon Williams, 1935–). The duo bought their own nightclub and formed a publishing company and record label. Mickey and Sylvia had lesser known hits with "There Oughta Be a Law" (1957), "What Would I Do" (1960), and "Baby, You're So Fine" (1961). In 1959, they briefly broke up when she married real estate agent Joseph Robinson (n.d.), who became her manager and soon took interest in the music business. From 1960 to 1961, Mickey and Sylvia reunited and became backup singers for the R&B, soul, and rock and roll duo Ike and Tina Turner (1960–1976). After Mickey and Sylvia split up in 1961, Robinson began her solo career.

FROM "PILLOW TALK" TO SUGAR HILL RECORDS AND HIP HOP PIONEER

In the late 1960s, the Robinsons moved to Englewood, New Jersey and began their own record label, All Platinum (1967–1979), which specialized in soul and R&B. In 1973, Sylvia Robinson had a huge hit (as Sylvia) with "Pillow Talk," from her funk and disco album of the same title, which was certified Gold. But the hits and high sales ended, and her subsequent albums *Sweet Stuff* (1976), *Sylvia* (1976), and *Lay It on Me* (1977) on Vibration (1969–1978), a division of All Platinum, were modest successes with mixed reception.

After the company purchased the last remaining songs of the Chess Records (1950–1975) catalog, All Platinum fell into bankruptcy in 1979. That year the Robinsons founded Sugar Hill Records in partnership with Milton Malden (n.d.) and with funding by Morris Levy (Moishe Levy, 1927–1990), who owned Roulette Records (1956–2013), the New York mob-connected label that bought Jubilee's catalogue. From the very beginning, Sugar Hill specialized in hip hop. This decision was Sylvia Robinson's idea, after hearing Harlem World nightclub MC Lovebug Starski (Kevin Smith, 1960–) rapping during the instrumental breaks. Searching for talent, Robinson heard pizzaria manager Big Bank Hank (Henry Jackson, 1958–2014) rapping over a PA system while working; she asked him to record and then teamed him up with a high school student known as Master Gee (Guy O'Brien, 1963–) and a flower salesman known as Wonder Mike (Michael Anthony Wright, 1956–) to form the Sugarhill Gang, named after an wealthy section of Harlem.

The Sugerhill Gang's "Rapper's Delight" was a 12-inch single that had a duration of 15 minutes. Robinson played bass and joined in on the instrumental backing track, a sample (technically) of "Good Times" by Chic. The single sold over eight million copies and peaked at No. 36 on the Billboard Hot 100 and No. 4 on Billboard's R&B chart. Globally, it topped charts in Canada and the Netherlands, and it held Top 10 status in Austria, France, Germany, Norway, Sweden, Switzerland, and the United Kingdom—all of which later developed lucrative hip hop markets. In 1980, the Sequence's "Funk You Up" success followed "Rapper's Delight" as did a string of other early hip hop hits for Sugar Hill Records, such as by Grandmaster Flash and the Furious Five's "The Message" (1982) and Melle Mel's (1961–) "White Lines (Don't Don't Do It)" (1983).

Sylvia Robinson's work at Sugar Hill Records required her to wear many hats as she was involved in A&R (talent searching and developing), promotion, sound engineering and production, backing music and vocals, marketing, and finances. All were balanced by her being a supportive and involved wife, mother, and grandmother. Financial and legal issues led to the end of Sugar Hill Records in 1985, and subsequently Sylvia divorced Joe Robinson while they were dealing with litigation against Wonder Mike and Master Gee (who lost their case against Sugar Hill Records and had to relinquish their band name). In addition, the Robinson's dealt with litigation against MCA Records (1934–2003) over a distribution deal. In 1994, Rhino Records purchased Sugar Hill Records' masters. The couple retained the studios in Englewood until a fire destroyed them.

In 2011, Sylvia Robinson died at age 76 of congestive heart failure. In 2015, her autobiography and the most driven side of her personality became the basis of the television character Cookie Lyon on Fox's *Empire*, a show about the rise of a New York hip hop and entertainment company. In 2018, a biographical miniseries on Robinson, *The First Family of Hip Hop*, aired on Bravo in the United States.

Melissa Ursula Dawn Goldsmith

See also: Grandmaster Flash; Melle Mel; The Sequence; Spoonie Gee; The Sugarhill Gang; The United States

Further Reading

Charnas, Dan. 2010. "Album One: Number Runners." In *The Big Payback: The History of the Business of Hip Hop*, chap. 1. New York: New American Library.

George, Nelson. 1999. "Hip Hop Wasn't Just Another Date." In *Hip Hop America*, chap. 2. London: Penguin Books.

Further Listening

Sylvia Robinson. 1973. *Pillow Talk*. Vibration.

The Robot

(aka Roboting, Botting, or The Mannequin)

The Robot is an illusionary dance style which has been incorporated into the moves of hip hop dancing since the 1970s, when funk and soul legend James Brown (1933–2006) performed robotlike moves on stage while singing. The moves can be traced back into the 1960s, when it was used as part of the funk dance repertoire, as West Coast dancers were already using robotic continuous robotic moves choreographed to the rhythm of funk and R&B music. Robotting can also be a performance rather than a dance, if the performer is a mime or statue imitator, imitating a robot without any music.

EARLY DEVELOPMENT

The techniques it uses (roboting or botting) go back much farther, at least to the mimes of the 1920s. The technique is basically one of moving the arms, legs, neck, and head with stiff, quick, jerking motions that constantly start and stop, to mimic the movements of a robot or an automaton. The illusion created is one of the dancer's being motorized and having stiff hinges rather than flexible joints. Though it should not be confused with popping and locking, which alternate between flexed (stiff) and relaxed movements, roboting is related and has been incorporated into popping and locking dances. In hip hop, the robotic stops do not turn into freezes. Rather they are dimestops, which are abrupt and last only a fraction of a second.

The Robot was made internationally famous in a scene from the movie *Chitty Chitty Bang Bang* (1968) when English actress and dancer Sally Ann Howes (1930–) danced on a pedestal, pretending to be a life-size music box dancer. Meanwhile, American actor and dancer Dick Van Dyke (1925–) dances as loosely as possible (marionetting), imitating a rag doll, for contrast. In her Robot, Howes keeps her muscles contracted or flexed the entire time, while constantly stopping and then starting her arm and head/neck motions, to create the illusion of a music box dancer with motorized limbs.

POPULARITY

The Robot gained further popularity when Michael Jackson (1958–2009) and then two of his brothers used the dance's techniques when the Jackson 5 performed their billboard Hot 100 No. 2 hit "Dancing Machine" (1974, from the album *Dancing Machine*) live on the music variety show *Soul Train* (1971–2006). Unlike most dances, the Robot lends itself to the dancer's using vocalizations rather than music. For example, a dancer could vocalize a series of beeping sounds or the sounds of a belt moving a mechanical limb; this is often done in solo performances in full costume; however, the visual impact of roboting is most effective when moves (and dimestops) are timed out to coincide with the beat (or backbeat) of a song.

Considered one of the best *Soul Train* dancers ever, Damita Jo Freeman (1953–) specialized in doing the Robot, at one point performing a solo on stage during a James Brown performance on the show, further popularizing roboting as a funk, soul, and hip hop technique that could be incorporated into various dance styles. As of 2018, hip hop dancers still use roboting in combination with other dance styles such as popping and locking or with fluid steps such as moonwalking in competitive performances.

Anthony J. Fonseca

See also: The Electric Boogaloos; Hip Hop Dance; Popping and Locking

Further Reading

Gaunt, Kyra Danielle. 2006. "Mary Mack Dressed in Black: The Earliest Formation of a Popular Music." In *The Games Black Girls Play: Learning the Ropes from Double-Dutch to Hip Hop*, chap. 3. New York: New York University Press.

Guzman-Sanchez, Thomas. 2012. "The Next Evolution in Oakland." In *Underground Dance Masters: Final History of a Forgotten Era*, chap. 4. Santa Barbara, CA: Praeger.

Roc Raida

(aka Grandmaster Roc Raida, Anthony Williams, 1972–2009,
New York City, New York)

Roc Raida is an American DJ, turntablist, producer, and member of the DJ collective the X-Ecutioners (aka X-Men, 1989–). In 1995, he won the DMC World DJ

Championship—his routine involved constant, quick switches of records, unexpected tempo changes, posing/dancing during minutely timed silences, and efforts of showmanship such as turning his back to the turntable and reaching over himself to play records with the opposite hand. In 1999, he was inducted into the DMC Hall of Fame.

With the X-Ecutioners, Roc Raida released three studio albums: *X-Pressions* (1997); *Built from Scratch* (2002); and *Revolutions* (2004). Roc Raida also DJed as part of a duo with underground MC MF Grimm (Percy Carey, 1970–). He released several solo albums, usually through his label AdiarCor Records (2000–2009); these used beats, including his Beats for Jugglers series, that could be used in DJ competitions. His early self-released, solo mixtapes include *The Adventures of Roc Raida . . . One Too Many!* (1997) and *The Adventures of Roc Raida: "Stuck in the Past"* (1997). Once Roc Raida established himself, he released *Crossfaderz: Roc Raida of the X-Ecutioners, a Turntablists Throwdown* (2000), on the Moonshine Music (1992–) label and *Champion Sounds* (2003), as Grandmaster Roc Raida, on the DMC (Disco Mix Club, 1983–) label. He also coreleased with DJ Vlad (aka Vlad the Butcher, Vladimir Lyubovny, 1973–) and Mike Shinoda (1977–) of Linkin Park (1996–) the album *Rock Phenomenon: Hip Hop vs. Rock Mashups* (2005), which blended rock songs with hip hop beats and songs. *Rock Phenomenon* won the Mash-Up Mixtape of the Year at the Justo Mixtape Awards. One of his last releases, *Beats, Cuts and Skits* (2007), was on AdiarCor.

As a producer, he has worked with the duos Ill Al Skratch (1993–1997, 2012–), Showbiz and A.G. (aka Show and A.G., 1990–), and Smif-N-Wessun (aka Cocoa Brovaz, 1993–), as well as bands and solo rappers such as Linkin Park (1996–), Jungle Brothers (1987–), Ghostface Killah (Dennis Coles, 1970–), and Big L (Lamont Coleman, 1974–1999). The biggest name with whom Roc Raida worked as a turntablist was Busta Rhymes (1972–).

Roc Raida continued DJing until his death in 2009 from an unexpected cardiac arrest due to surgery after a martial arts accident. Three years afterward, fellow X-Ecutioner Rob Swift (Robert Aguilar, 1972–) released a collection of songs, both previously released and unreleased, interviews, and battle style routines, on the album *Roc for Raida* (2012). Proceeds benefitted Roc Raida's family.

Anthony J. Fonseca

See also: Battling; Rob Swift; Turntablism; The United States; The X-Ecutioners

Further Reading

Katz, Mark. 2012. *Groove Music: The Art and Culture of the Hip Hop DJ.* New York: Oxford University Press.

Webber, Stephen. 2008. *DJ Skills: The Essential Guide to Mixing and Scratching.* Burlington, MA: Focal Press.

Williams, Damon C. 2003. "Roc at the Top: DJ Raida Hones the Art of Turntablism." Interview with Rock Raida. *Philadelphia Daily News*, October 30, 29.

Further Listening

Roc Raida. 1997. *The Adventures of Roc Raida . . . One Too Many!* Self-released.

Roc Raida. 2000. *Crossfaderz: Roc Raida of the X-Ecutioners, a Turntablists Throwdown.* Moonshine Music.

Rock Steady Crew

(RSC, 1977–, Bronx, New York)

The Rock Steady Crew (RSC), formed in 1977, by Jojo (Santiago Torres, n.d.) and Jimmy D (Jamie White, n.d.), is one of the first and most enduring b-boy crews in the Bronx, New York. With many film appearances, ranging from feature films such as *Flashdance* and *Wild Style* to documentaries such as *Style Wars* (all three released in 1983), the RSC was, for many outside New York, responsible for introducing the public to hip hop dance. Their work has reached further into the mainstream than any other crew of its kind.

The RSC gained wider attention in 1981 when Henry Chalfant (1940–), who also produced *Style Wars,* invited them to perform at the Lincoln Center Outdoors Program. This event became a battle with Dynamic Rockers (1979–) from Queens, New York and garnered much media coverage in New York as well internationally, in *National Geographic*. Through television and film appearances and tours throughout the United States and Europe, including a prominent role in the Roxy Tour (1982), the first international hip hop tour that also included the Bronx native Afrika Bambaataa (1957–), as well as Fab Five Freddy (1959–), and other artists and DJs, the crew continued to broaden their audiences. That same year, the RSC became part of the hip hop awareness group Universal Zulu Nation (1973–), underscoring a commitment to education, community, and preservation of hip hop culture. A 1983 invitation to perform for Queen Elizabeth II (1926–, reign 1952–) confirmed their mainstream success.

The RSC grew out of the Untouchable Four B-Boys (1977), which included JoJo and Jimmy D, who decided that expansion was in their best interest and formed the Rock Steady Crew. At this time, potential members had to battle existing members to join. According to Jojo, the name was both literal and metaphorical. It took into account the hardness of the floors on which dancers often performed (Rock), the desire to preserve the art of b-boying (Steady), and the teamwork needed to support one another (Crew). The crew now has chapters throughout the world and has included such famed dancers from the Bronx as Crazy Legs (Richard Colón, 1966–), Frosty Freeze (Wayne Frost, 1963–), Popmaster Fabel (Jorge Pabon, 1965*–), and Ken Swift (Kenneth James Gabbert, 1966–).

In the late 1980s creative difficulties among the members led to a brief hiatus. Responding to pressure to regroup from several quarters, Crazy Legs reunited the group in 1989. Several members contributed to a critically acclaimed Off-Broadway musical, *So! What Happens Now?* (1991), considered the first piece of hip hop theatre. The crew still hosts annual anniversary parties, which serve as large-scale community events, and is active in providing dance instruction.

Susannah Cleveland

See also: Crazy Legs; Filmmaking (Feature Films Made in the United States); Frosty Freeze; Ken Swift; Popmaster Fabel; The United States; The Universal Zulu Nation

Further Reading

Chang, Jeff. 2005. *Can't Stop, Won't Stop: A History of the Hip Hop Generation.* New York: Picador.

Mills, David. 1993. "A Leg Up for Hip Hop: Dance Masters Pass on the Art, and the History." *The Washington Post*, May 25, B01.

Schloss, Joseph G. 2009. *Foundation: B-Boys, B-Girls, and Hip Hop Culture in New York.* New York: Oxford University Press.

Further Viewing

Israel, dir. 2002. *The Freshest Kids: A History of the B-Boy.* Chatsworth, CA: QD3 Entertainment.

Lathan, Stan, dir. 1984. *Beat Street.* Santa Monica, CA: MGM Home Entertainment.

Lee, Benson, dir. 2007. *Planet B-Boy.* New York: Mental Pictures.

Silver, Tony, dir. 1983. *Style Wars.* Los Angeles: Public Art Films.

Rokafella

(Ana García, 1971–, New York City, New York)

Rokafella is a pioneering American b-girl and choreographer from Spanish Harlem in New York City. She is also a writer on hip hop dance. When she was 11 years old, she began breakdancing despite the fact that it went counter to her Puerto Rican family's and community's expectations for acceptable female behavior. Her earliest inspirations were Puerto Rican dancers such as Rita Moreno (Rosa Dolores Alverío, 1931–) and Iris Chacón (Iris Chacón Tapia, 1950–), as well as other American dancers and hip hop artists. She also idolized poet La Bruja (Caridad de la Luz, 1977–) and Afro-Antillian/Puerto Rican rapper, hip hop artist, and activist Lah Tere (1979*–). Rokafella is known for exceptional, elaborate footwork; this specialization may also have reflected her interests in the tap, jazz, and modern dance of Gregory Hines (1946–2003) and Alvin Ailey (1931–1981). She is best known for dancing and choreography, as well as serving as a judge at

Rokafella was a pioneering female breakdancer (b-girl) and choreographer from Spanish Harlem, New York, who danced with veteran breakdancer (and later husband) Kwikstep and his crew, Full Circle, as well as with GhettOriginal and other prominent New York City dance crews. Starting in the late 1990s, she also has been the lead singer of her band, RPM. (Johnny Nunez/WireImage/Getty Images)

b-boy competitions; however, she also participates in hip hop through singing (fronting the band RPM, 1996*–), acting, filmmaking, teaching, and writing. She has been active in hip hop preservation through making radio appearances and conducting interviews of hip hop artists. In 1991, veteran breakdancer Kwikstep (Gabriel Joseph Torres Dionisio, 1968–) began mentoring Rokafella. Kwikstep, whose own career began in 1981 in New York City, toured worldwide at age 19 with the New York Express (n.d.) dance crew when it appeared that hip hop music had already ended its commercial peak in the United States. Mentored by Kwikstep, Rokafella joined several notable dance crews, including the Breeze Team (n.d.), the Transformers (n.d.), New York City Float Committee (n.d.), and Kwikstep's own New York City–based crew Full Circle (1992–), as well as the dance company GhettOriginal (1994–). Eventually, Rokafella and Kwikstep married, and they founded Full Circle Productions (1996–), a nonprofit hip hop dance collective that educates young people in the Bronx, New York.

As of 2018, she continues teaching hip hop dance masterclasses that also cover hip hop's historical and cultural aspects.

Melissa Ursula Dawn Goldsmith

See also: Battling; Breakdancing; Hip Hop Dance; Puerto Rico; The United States

Further Reading

Burbach, Elizabeth A. 2013. "Hittin' the Streets with the NYC Tranzformerz." *Voices* 39, nos. 1–2: 32–35.

Kramer, Nika and Martha Cooper. 2005. *We B*Girlz*. Introduction by Ana "Rokafella" García. New York: powerHouse Books.

Schloss, Joseph G. 2009. *Foundation: B-Boys, B-Girls, and Hip Hop Culture in New York*. New York: Oxford University Press.

Romania

Romania, whose name goes back to 1866, is a sovereign state located in Southeastern Europe. Its population of 20 million includes two million citizens of Bucharest, its largest city; Romanian citizens are mainly Eastern Orthodox Christians (consisting also of Greek Orthodox Christians) who speak Romanian. The country's music is varied and multicultural and includes classical, religious, and secular folk as well as pop, metal, rock, and hip hop. Traditional instrumentation is region-specific and includes violins, *tárogatós* (woodwinds that resemble shawms or clarinets but sound like saxophones), *ţilincă* (flutes), *cobza* (lutes), and more recently double basses, accordions, *hidede* (a trumpet played by bowing a violin fret board), *tambal* (open piano–type string instruments played with mallets), and drums. Romania was introduced to jazz and easy listening (called romanţe) after World War I, and after World War II, orchestral dance music and pop (called *manele*). The 1960s introduced nouveau traditional (called *etno*), contemporary acoustic folk, and underground rock (which became mainstream after 1989 and divided into rock, metal, and punk styles), and the 1980s saw the emergence of synthesized dance music, house music, and hip hop.

Romanian hip hop and break dancing were introduced in Bucharest in 1982 but stayed underground until the Romanian Revolution. The first Romanian hip hop group was Vorbire Directă (Direct Speech, 1992–), and the first hip hop album was *Rap-sodia efectului defectului* (*Defect Effect Rap-sody*, 1995), by Bucharest-based hardcore sociopolitical rap crew R.A.C.L.A. (aka Rime Alese Care Lovesc Adânc, Handpicked Rhymes with a Deeper Meaning, 1993–2007, 2014–). R.A.C.L.A. was involved in a three-way Romanian diss track war, with rival groups B.U.G. Mafia (aka Black Underground, Bucharest Underground Mafia, 1993–) and La Familia (1996–), two rap crews that popularized gangsta rap in Romania. B.U.G. Mafia started by rapping about governmental corruption, poverty, and crime in English, but in 1995 transitioned to writing in Romanian. Also from Bucharest, La Familia became popular in the late 1990s and early 2000s, and despite legal problems, continue to tour as of 2018. Another rap pioneer, rap trio Parazitii (The Parasites, 1994–), introduced atmospheric hip hop beats and dark political humor, as well as created the 20CM Records label in 2003. The current most popular Romanian hip hop acts include rapper Guess Who (Laurențiu Mocanu, 1986–) and rap group Șatra B.E.N.Z. (2015–). Bucharest-born Guess Who has released four albums since 2005, and Șatra B.E.N.Z. introduced trap music in 2015 with its album *θ.$.θ.D.*

Anthony J. Fonseca

See also: Breakdancing; Gangsta Rap; Political Hip Hop; Mafioso Rap; Russia

Further Reading

Merila, Isabela, and Michaela Praisler. 2009. "Textually Constructing Identity and Otherness: Mediating the Romanian Hip Hop Message." In *Subcultures and New Religious Movements in Russia and East-Central Europe*, edited by George McKay, Christopher Williams, Michael Goddard, Neil Foxlee, and Egidija Ramanauskaitė, chap. 5. Oxford, England: P. Lang.

Șorcaru, Daniel, and Floriana Popescu. 2009. "On Linguistic Politics: The Stylistic Testimonies of Romanian Hip Hop." In *Subcultures and New Religious Movements in Russia and East-Central Europe*, edited by George McKay, Michael Goddard, Neil Foxlee, and Egidija Ramanauskaitė, chap. 6. Oxford, England: P. Lang.

Further Listening

B.U.G. Mafia. 2011. *Inapoi in viitor* (*Back to the Future*). Casa Productions.

Șatra B.E.N.Z. 2015. *θ.$.θ.D.* Seek Music.

The Roots

(aka The Square Roots, 1987–, Philadelphia, Pennsylvania)

The Roots is an American alternative and activist hip hop and rap band that incorporates elements of neo soul and contemporary jazz into its music. The band was formed as the Square Roots by MC Black Thought (Tariq Luqmaan Trotter, 1971–) and drummer Questlove (aka ?uestlove, Ahmir Khalib Thompson, 1971–) as a jazz-influenced hip hop act that would feature traditional musical instruments. Soon afterward, the duo added electric bassist Rubberband (Josh Abrams, n.d.) for a brief time. The first stable lineup of the band consisted of Black Thought and Questlove, along with second MC Malik B. (Malik Abdul Basit, 1972–), keyboardist Scott Storch (n.d.), and bassist Hub (Leonard Nelson Hubbard, n.d.). The band's name was changed to the Roots in 1992 to avoid confusion with a different local band called the Square Roots.

FORMATION, ALBUMS, AND TRACK COUNTING

The band originated as a street busker act in Philadelphia, where Questlove played bucket drums while Black Thought rapped. Both were schoolmates from the Philadelphia High School for the Creative and Performing Arts. The Roots released its first album, *Organix* (1993) on an independent label; the album lead to offers from major music labels, including Geffen Records (1980–), with whom the Roots signed. The band's follow up album, *Do You Want More?!!!??!* (1994), and appearances at Lollapalooza and the Montreux Jazz Festival, bolstered its popularity, and the album reached No. 28 on the Billboard 200.

Beginning with *Do You Want More?!!!??!*, the Roots began an idiosyncratic continuous track listing of all its songs, calling attention to its music as a continuous endeavor. The third album, *Illadelph Halflife* (1996) reached No. 21, but it was the fourth album and the band's first on MCA Records (1934–2003), *Things Fall Apart* (1999), which finally broke the Top Ten, peaking at No. 4; it became the band's first certified-Platinum record and was nominated for a Grammy. The single "What They Do," a parody of the rap scene, became the first of only two Top Forty hits for the band, peaking at No. 34 on the Hot 100.

Over time, band members have departed to pursue other careers, with only Black Thought and Questlove remaining constant members. A membership change occurred before each of the next two albums, *Phrenology* (2002), which earned a Grammy nomination, and *The Tipping Point* (2004), which earned two more Grammy nominations, as did the next album, *Game Theory* (2006), which marked the Roots' moving to Def Jam Recordings (1983–). *Game Theory* honored the dying hip hop producer J Dilla (James Dewitt Yancey, 1974–2006). The band released four more studio albums, *Rising Down* (2008), *How I Got Over* (2010), *Undun* (2011), and *. . . And Then You Shoot Your Cousin* (2014). A new album, *End Game*, was released in 2018. The band continues to tour extensively, including an annual pre-Grammy jam session and an annual summer Roots Picnic.

As of 2018, the Roots has released 11 studio albums, two mixtapes, and one live album, as well as a handful of collaborative albums with musicians such as John Legend (John Roger Stephens, 1978–) and Elvis Costello (Declan Patrick Mac-Manus, 1954–). It was the house band on *Late Night with Jimmy Fallon* (2009–2014) and is the current house band on *The Tonight Show Starring Jimmy Fallon* (2014–). The band has had six albums reach the Billboard 200 Top Ten, had 10 albums reach the Top Ten of the Top R&B/Hip-Hop Albums chart, and has been nominated for 11 Grammy Awards, winning three. It has won two NAACP Image Awards and was the first hip hop band to perform at the Lincoln Center in 2002. Band members have been featured in four films, and the band has been involved with the Red Hot Organization's (1990–) musical projects to raise money and awareness for AIDS victims.

Anthony J. Fonseca

See also: Black Nationalism; Neo Soul; The United States

Further Reading

Marshall, Lewis Miles. 2015. "Root Theory." *Ebony* 70, no. 12: 86–93.

Questlove and Ben Greenman. 2013. *Mo' Meta Blues: The World According to Questlove.* New York: Grand Central.

Further Listening

The Roots. 1999. *Things Fall Apart.* MCA Records.

The Roots. 2006. *Game Theory.* Def Jam Recordings.

The Roots and Elvis Costello. 2013. *Wise Up: Ghost.* Blue Note.

Roxanne Shanté

(Lolita Shanté Gooden, 1969–, Long Island, New York)

Roxanne Shanté is an American rapper who grew up in the Queensbridge housing projects of New York and was active primarily from 1984 to 1992. She is best known for her debut song, a diss track called "Roxanne's Revenge." Roxanne Shanté got her start as a rapper in 1984, when at 14 she recorded a response to "Roxanne, Roxanne," a song by the Brooklyn, New York hip hop group U.T.F.O. (UnTouchable Force Organization, 1984–1992). The original track features U.T.F.O. members describing a woman named Roxanne who dismisses their advances. Her response, "Roxanne's Revenge," was the first of many subsequent answer records that made up what is now referred to as the Roxanne Wars. Marley Marl (1962–) produced the song, which originally featured an instrumental taken from U.T.F.O.'s original, but after a lawsuit, it was rereleased in 1985 with a new beat track.

"Roxanne's Revenge" is a boast rap, with Roxanne Shanté claiming to be the woman about whom U.T.F.O. raps. Her lyrics proclaim that other MCs will take note of her rhymes. Like "Roxanne's Revenge," many of her other tracks were also boast records, where she promoted herself as a skilled MC above all others. "Queen of Rox (Shanté Rox On)" (1985) and "Def Fresh Crew" (1986), which features beatboxer Biz Markie (Marcel Theo Hall, 1964–), are two well known examples. Many of these tracks reportedly originated as freestyles, and showcase her direct, battle-rap style, intricate lyrics and raps, and girlish voice.

She was a member of Juice Crew (1983–1991), which Marley Marl cofounded with radio DJ Mr. Magic (John Rivas, 1956–2009). They recorded on the New York City–based label Cold Chillin' Records (1986–1998) and were involved in a number of hip hop rivalries and arguments, in addition to the Roxanne Wars, including a long-running rivalry with South Bronx, New York–based Boogie Down Productions (1985–1992). She appears on the track "Wack Itt," from the album *In Control, Vol. 1* (1988), which features various members of Juice Crew, including Biz Markie, Heavy D (Dwight Errington Myers, 1967–2011), and Big Daddy Kane (1968–). She was the crew's only female member.

Throughout the mid- to late-1980s, She released numerous singles. Her collaboration with Rick James (James Ambrose Johnson Jr., 1948–2004), "Loosey's Rap" (1986), was a No. 1 hit on the Billboard R&B chart. In 1989, She released her first full-length album, *Bad Sister*, on Cold Chillin' Records. The album was primarily produced by Marley Marl and included the tracks "Knockin' Hiney" and "Feelin' Kinda Horny." In 1992, her second album, *The B— Is Back*, was released. Her songs have also appeared on the soundtracks for the American films *Colors* (1988), *Lean on Me* (1989), and *Girls Town* (1996).

Roxanne Shanté largely stopped performing after 1992 but has used her expertise to mentor other female rappers. In 2008, she appeared in this capacity on the VH1 network's reality show, *Ego Trip's Miss Rap Supreme* (2008), to help contestants prepare for rap battles.

Lauron Jockwig Kehrer

See also: Juice Crew; Marley Marl; The United States

Further Reading

Bradley, Adam, and Andrew Dubois, eds. 2010. "Roxanne Shanté." Under "Part 2: 1985–92: The Golden Age" in *The Anthology of Rap*, pp. 283–89. New Haven, CT: Yale University Press.

Mshaka, Thembisa S. 2007. "Roxanne Shanté." In *Icons of Hip Hop: An Encyclopedia of the Movement, Music, and Culture*, edited by Mickey Hess, vol. 1, pp. 51–68. Westport, CT: Greenwood Press.

Further Listening

Roxanne Shanté. 2002. *The Best of Cold Chillin': Roxanne Shanté.* Landspeed Records.

Run-D.M.C.

(1981–2002, Queens, New York)

Run-D.M.C. was an extremely successful early American hip hop trio from the Hollis neighborhood of Queens, New York. Its members included vocalists D.M.C. (Darryl Mc Daniel, 1964–) and Run (born Joseph Simmons, 1964–), and turntablist Jam Master Jay (Jason Mizell, 1965–2002). The band is generally regarded as one of the most influential hip hop acts of all time, having achieved many hip hop and rap firsts: the first Gold record, the first Platinum record, the first multi-Platinum record, and the first Grammy nomination. The trio was also the first hip hop group to have its music videos played on MTV and to have its image appear on the cover of *Rolling Stone* magazine. Run-D.M.C. is the second hip hop group to be inducted into the Rock and Roll Hall of Fame, after Grandmaster Flash and the Furious Five (1976–1982, 1987–1988).

ORIGINS AND EARLY EFFORTS

Run and D.M.C. grew up near each other, and Run's older brother Russell Simmons (1957–) was at the time an aspiring hip hop promoter—he later cofounded Def Jam Recordings (1983–) in New York City. Russell Simmons encouraged the two to pursue hip hop and recruited Jam Master Jay to be the group's DJ. He also coined the group's name. Run-D.M.C.'s first single, "It's Like That (Sucker MCs)," was released in 1983 and reached No. 15 on the R&B/hip hop songs chart. The group released its self-titled debut album in 1984 and achieved modest success, with singles including "Rock Box" and "Jam Master Jay." "Rock Box" was typical of the group's style, with a hard rock edge and socially conscious lyrics.

KINGS OF ROCK

Following the success of *Run-D.M.C.*, the group released two albums back to back: *King of Rock* (1985) and *Raising Hell* (1986). Singles such as "King of Rock" and "Can You Rock It Like This" helped propel *King of Rock* to Platinum status, and *Raising Hell* reached No. 3 on the Billboard 200. Jam Master Jay's production style included sampled and manipulated guitar riffs, and in 2012, *Spin* magazine named Jay one of the greatest guitarists of all time because of his ability to transform sampled guitar sounds.

The group joined forces with producer Rick Rubin (Frederick Jay Rubin, 1963–) for *Raising Hell*, which would become one of the best-selling hip hop albums of all time. The album included iconic singles such as "It's Tricky," "My Adidas" (which would land the group an endorsement deal with the athletic apparel brand), and "Peter Piper." Run-D.M.C.'s cover version of Aerosmith's (1970–) single "Walk This Way," which featured new performances by Aerosmith's Steven Tyler (1948–) and Joe Perry (1950–), reached No. 4 on the Billboard Hot 100, and "You Be Illin" achieved Top 40 status. Run-D.M.C. also appeared in films, including *Krush Groove* (1985), a fictionalized version of Simmons's efforts to start Def Jam.

FINAL ALBUMS

Run-D.M.C.'s fourth album, *Tougher Than Leather* (1988), was a departure from the group's earlier rock-based sound. Jam Master Jay incorporated a greater variety of sample sources, including funk and soul, and both Run and D.M.C. included more internal and polysyllabic rhymes in their lyrics. The pseudo crime caper film *Tougher Than Leather* (1988) was released as a tie-in to the album. Directed by Rubin and featuring guest appearances by the Beastie Boys (1980–2014) and Slick Rick (1965–), *Tougher Than Leather* was nearly universally panned by critics.

During the 1990s, Run-D.M.C. struggled to remain relevant and to avoid sounding dated. Critics trashed its 1990 album *Back from Hell* for its preachy lyrics and attempts to incorporate the sounds of new jack swing. Each of the three group members battled personal, criminal, and substance abuse problems during this time, and both Run and D.M.C. became religious in response. Run became an ordained minister in 1993 and has gone by Rev. Run ever since. Run-D.M.C.'s next album, *Down with the King* (1993), returned to the earlier sounds of *Tougher Than Leather*, and some of the album's lyrics subtly reflected the religious values that both Run and D.M.C. had adopted.

DEATH OF JAM MASTER JAY AND DISSOLUTION

Run-D.M.C. recorded one final studio album, *Crown Royal* (2001), the recording and release of which were delayed by conflicts within the group. Run and D.M.C. had completely different visions for the group's songs. These disputes, coupled with D.M.C.'s struggles with depression and substance abuse, meant that he appeared on only three of the album's tracks. Although Run-D.M.C. embarked on a very successful tour with Aerosmith following the release of *Crown Royal*, the three band members seemed to agree that they would not record any more albums. Their decision was tragically cemented in 2002, when Jam Master Jay was murdered at his recording studio in Queens. As of 2018, the murder remains unsolved. Following his death, Run and D.M.C. formally disbanded the group and retired its name.

LEGACY

Run-D.M.C.'s legacy cannot be overstated. Nearly every hip hop artist or group since the early 1980s has cited Run-D.M.C. as having a major influence on their music. Run-D.M.C. nearly singlehandedly helped hip hop achieve mainstream recognition in many areas that had previously been off-limits. Its fusion of rap and rock influenced artists ranging from the Red Hot Chili Peppers (1983–) to Rage against the Machine (1991–2000, 2007–2011) and Sublime (1988–1996).

Its live onstage configuration, in which the two rappers were backed by the DJ and two turntables, that is, the "two turntables and a microphone" setup—a phrase made mainstream in "Where It's At," a 1996 song by Beck (Bek David Campbell, 1970–)—became the template for other hip hop groups to follow. Further, Run D.M.C.'s street-based fashion, with fedoras, gold chains, Adidas tracksuits, and laceless sneakers, set the standard for hip hop fashion for the next three decades.

Amanda Sewell

See also: Jam Master Jay; Turntablism; The United States

Further Reading

Adler, Bill. 2002. *Tougher Than Leather: The Rise of Run-D.M.C.* Los Angeles: Consafos Press.

Ronin Ro. 2005. *Raising Hell: The Reign, Ruin, and Redemption of Run-D.M.C. and Jam Master Jay.* New York: HarperCollins.

Further Listening

Run-D.M.C. 1985. *King of Rock.* Profile Records.

Run-D.M.C. 1986. *Raising Hell.* Profile Records.

Further Viewing

Logan, Guy, dir. 2008. *2 Turntables and a Microphone: The Life and Death of Jam Master Jay.* N.p.: Image.

Rubin, Rick, dir. 1988. *Tougher Than Leather.* Burbank, CA: New Line Cinema.

Russia

Russia saw its hip hop culture emerge in the mid-1980s, the waning years of the Soviet Union. Breakdancing became popular through performances by crews such as Mercury (1985*–) and Magic Circle (1985*–), as well as through shows by Arsenal (1980–1990)*, a jazz-rock fusion ensemble whose leader Alexei Kozlov (n.d.) would b-boy during concerts. After the fall of the Soviet Union in 1991, rap artists began to gain attention. The first Russian rap album was *Rap* (1984*), by the group Chas Pik (n.d.). Popular Russian rappers in the 1990s included Bogdan Titomir (1967–), from Sumy, Ukraine, known as half of the Moscow-based techno-pop duo Car-Man (1990–), and Lika Star (Lika Pavlova, 1972–), from Vilnius, Lithuania, as well as rap groups Raketa (Rocker, n.d.) and Malchishnik (1991–1994, 2000–). These rappers were influenced by both pop rock styles and American rappers such as MC Hammer (1962–).

The 1990s saw a rise of hip hop that coincided with the rise of a social oligarchy that benefitted from lucrative government contracts (and accumulated vast amounts of wealth). Concurrently, the Communist Party retained a great deal of control over media. As a response, commercially successful Russian hip hop artists such as Moscow's Timati (Timur Ildarovich Yunusov, 1983–) and

Moscow rapper, singer-songwriter, and record producer Timati performs in concert in 2015 at the Space Moscow Nightclub. Timati's style embraces 1990s American gangsta rap themes like acquiring wealth, partying, and womanizing, and he was one of Russia's early commercially-successful hip hop artists. (Hurricanehank/ Dreamstime.com)

Krovostock (2002–) imitated American bands, promoting an urban lifestyle and a socially defiant posture, but with no political implications. Timati has collaborated with Detsl (aka Le Truk, Kirill Aleksandrovich Tolmatski, 1983–), also from Moscow, and Georgian rapper L'One (Levan Gorozia, 1985–), from Yakutsk, garnering some international renown. Groups such as Moscow's Centr (2004–), who were apolitical but promoted illegal drug use, gained popularity through the Internet and with live concert tours.

The Russian chanson, whose most famous poet was Moscow's Vladimir Vysotsky (1938–1980), has had a strong influence on some Russian rap. It confronted issues of repression, social injustice, and political corruption, all veiled in highly poetic lyrics and a folk song–like musical style. Russian hip hop artists such as Kasta (1995–), from Rostov-on-Don, Krestnaya Semya (2002–2005), from Stavropol, and Yu.G. (2001*), took their inspiration from this style and wrote about poverty and crime. The rise of the Internet allowed some Russian musicians to build their careers independent of official Russian media, leading to the emergence of social justice rappers such as Dino MC47 (1982–), from Moscow and Noize MC (Ivan Aleksandrovich Alekseev, 1985–), from Yartsevo, whose "Mercedes S666" from the album *Latest Album* (2010) protests the death of two young Russian women as a result of reckless driving by a Russian oil executive.

Popular Russian rappers of the 2000s include St. Petersburg's Kasta, Timati, Detsl, and Bad Balance (1989–). Moscow's R&B-influenced hip hop artists include Band'Eros (2005–). As of 2018, Russian hip hop bands exemplify a variety of styles, rooted in everything from the 1960s Russian chanson, to American rock music and gangsta rap. An early center of rap was the southwestern port city Rostov-on-Don, but by the mid-2000s an underground hip hop scene had emerged in Moscow. In 2009, Russian prime minister Vladimir Putin (1952–), who is known for his conservative if not closed-minded musical tastes, voiced approval of breakdancing, rap, and graffiti during a guest appearance on the Muz-TV rap competition show *Fight for Respect* (2008–), remarking that rap and breakdancing, when separated from alcohol and drugs, promote a healthy lifestyle.

Terry Klefstad

See also: Breakdancing

Further Reading

Ivanov, Sergey. 2013. "Hip Hop in Russia: How the Cultural Form Emerged in Russia and Established a New Philosophy." In *Hip Hop in Europe: Cultural Identities and Transnational Flows*, edited by Sina A. Nitzsche and Walter Grünzweig, chap. 4. Zürich, Switzerland: LIT Verlag.

Wickström, David-Emil. 2014. *Rocking St. Petersburg: Transcultural Flows and Identity Politics in the St. Petersburg Popular Music Scene*. Stuttgart, Germany: Ibidem-Verlag.

Further Listening

Bad Balance. 2012. *World Wide.* Soyuz.

Detsl. 2014. *MXXXIII.* Rasta Mafia.

Noize MC. 2010. *Greatest Album.* Studio Monolit.

Ruthless Rap Assassins

(1987–1992, Manchester, England)

Ruthless Rap Assassins was an English hip hop group formed by MC and DJ Kermit (aka Kermit La Freak, Paul Leveridge, 1966*–), Dangerous Hinds (Anderson McConley Hinds, n.d.), and Dangerous C (Carson Hinds, n.d.). Drummer Ged Lynch (Gerard Lynch, 1968–) joined the group soon after its creation. The band was much a product of Manchester's (which was nicknamed Madchester) music scene, which included rappers such as MC Tunes (Nicholas William Dennis Hodgson, 1970–), techno and drum-and-bass musicians such as A Guy Called Gerald (Gerald Simpson, 1967–), and techno bands such as 808 State (1987–). Ruthless Rap Assassins quickly earned a cult following because the band rapped using British English (rather than aping American rappers), imbued its songs with a wry sense of humor and incorporated diverse musical influences and styles, including rock and electronica dance. The band used samples from indie rock, reggae, pop, jazz, and classic rock, as well as funk and hip hop. Its lyrics showed a wide range of interests, from parody and metatextuality to social commentary on issues such as urbanism, the black experience, the country's failing economy, and the racism that accompanied immigration. Like the Roots (1987–) in the United States, Ruthless Rap Assassins was known for its live performances because it used traditional instrumentation (drum kits, guitars, bass, and keyboards).

ALBUMS AND SOUND

A violin player, one-time DJ, and ex-member of the breakdance crew Broken Glass, Kermit recorded "Style of the Street" (1984) with the group Broken Glass (made up of the breakdance crew) for the compilation album *Street Sounds Electro U.K.* (1984) album on the Street Sounds label (1982–), and was then asked to record six more tracks for the album under various names. Kermit then met the Hinds brothers, who were performing as the Dangerous 2. With much sought after producer Greg Wilson (1960–) as its manager, the trio founded the Ruthless Rap Assassins.

The band's first release was the single "We Don't Kare" (1987). The band's 14-track debut album, *Killer Album* (1990), released on EMI (1931–), contained both serious political songs and tongue-in-cheek tracks, as well as old-school, singsong rapping and more urban, angry, frenetic rapping (both accompanied by scratching, hip hop diva singing, and pitch-adjusted samples). The album spawned two singles, "Just Mellow" and "And It Wasn't a Dream," and was well received by the hip hop community; however, U.K. radio stations thought the band too incendiary to give its songs airplay—sales were not very good.

The band's second album *Th!nk, It Ain't Illegal Yet* (1991), like its predecessor, did well with critics, but its sales were not robust. The band split up in 1992, and Kermit and Lynch joined with Shaun Ryder (1962–) of Happy Mondays (1980–1993, 2004–) to form Black Grape (1993–1998, 2015–), which did have successful sales. Kermit later left Black Grape to form the short-lived band Big Dog (2000–2001).

Dangerous Hinds left the music industry altogether. As of 2018, rumors persist that the Ruthless Rap Assassins's members may reunite for an album.

Anthony J. Fonseca

See also: Industrial Hip Hop; Political Hip Hop; The United Kingdom

Further Reading

Ott, Brian, and Cameron Walter. 2000. "Intertextuality: Interpretive Practice and Textual Strategy." *Critical Studies in Media Communication* 17, no. 4: 429–46.

Simpson, Dave. 2001. "The Home Boys: Who Needs Eminem and P-Diddy When We've Got Perfectly Good British Rappers?" Interview with Roots Manuva and the U.K. Posse. *The Guardian*, September 13, 2.16.

Wood, Andy. 2002. "Hip Hop." In *Companion to Contemporary Black British Culture*, edited by Alison Donnell, pp. 141–42. London: Routledge.

Further Listening

Ruthless Rap Assassins. 1990. *Killer Album.* EMI.

S

Salt-N-Pepa

(1985–2002, 2007–, Queens, New York)

Salt-N-Pepa is an American hip hop trio notable for being one of the first all-female hip hop groups to achieve both commercial and critical success. The group's permanent members are Brooklyn, New York native Salt (Cheryl James, 1964–), Pepa (Sandra Denton, 1964–) from Kingston, Jamaica, and Spinderella (Deidra Muriel Roper, 1971–), also a Brooklyn native. Latoya Hanson (1965*–), the group's original Spinderella, was permanently replaced by Roper in 1987. The group's breakthrough came with a remix of the single "Push It" in 1987; it became its first Billboard Hot 100 hit.

Salt-N-Pepa began in the mid-1980s as a duo called Super Nature and released the single "The Showstopper" (1985), a response record to "The Show" (1985) by Doug E. Fresh (1966–). The single achieved modest success, and the duo was signed to Next Plateau Records, an independent label. With the addition of DJ Spinderella, the duo became a trio. Its next album, *Hot, Cool and Vicious,* was produced by Hurby Azor (Herby Azor, 1965–), who served as the group's manager at the time. A few singles from the album charted modestly in the United States and the United Kingdom, but a remix of "Push It," created by San Francisco radio DJ and Mixx It service creator Cameron Paul (1957*–), made Salt-N-Pepa famous nationally. The song was not originally released as part of its debut album *Hot, Cool and Vicious* (1986), but rather as a B side to "Tramp," but the remix's success led to its being added to subsequent pressings of the album. As such, the song's success helped *Hot, Cool and Vicious* sell over one million copies—making it the first album by a female hip hop artist (solo or group) to achieve both Gold and Platinum status. The remix reached No. 19 on the Hot 100.

FOLLOW-UP ALBUMS

The group released four more albums in the 1980s and 1990s. *A Salt with a Deadly Pepa* (1988) was also produced by Azor. It included several modest hits, such as a cover of "Twist and Shout" as well as "Shake Your Thang." *Blacks' Magic* (1990) and *Very Necessary* (1993) relied less heavily on Azor than the previous two albums, and the members of the group began writing and producing their own songs. "Shoop" (1993), from *Very Necessary*, was coproduced by Pepa; it reached No. 4 on the Hot 100, becoming Salt-N-Pepa's second biggest hit next to "Whatta Man," which reached No. 3.

Salt-N-Pepa took on sex, gender, and sexuality head-on in its music. The single "None of Your Business," an indictment of slut-shaming and sexual double standards, won a Grammy award for Best Rap Performance by a Duo or Group in 1995, making Salt-N-Pepa the first female hip hop artists ever to win a Grammy. The trio's single "Let's Talk about Sex" (1991) describes both the positive and negative aspects of sexuality and encourages listeners to discuss and practice safe sex. An alternate version was later rerecorded as "Let's Talk about AIDS," with the lyrics tailored more directly toward AIDS-related topics.

In 1997, Salt-N-Pepa released its fifth and final album, *Brand New.* By this time, the trio had legally severed all ties with Azor, and he was not involved in the writing or the production of the album. *Brand New* had been released on Salt-N-Pepa's own label, Red Ant, but Red Ant filed for bankruptcy at the same time the album was released. Without promotion from a label, *Brand New* saw far lower sales than its predecessors.

Salt-N-Pepa formally disbanded in 2002, but the trio has continued to perform together since 2007, at live events such as the 2008 BET Hip Hop Awards, and in 2012, the trio opened for Public Enemy (1986–) during the Martin Luther King Jr. Concert Series. In 2016, Salt-N-Pepa was a headline act in the I Love the '90s Tour. Members also starred in one season of their own reality television show, *The Salt-N-Pepa Show,* which aired on VH-1 from 2007 to 2008.

Amanda Sewell

See also: Black Nationalism; DJ Spinderella; Political Hip Hop; Turntablism; The United States

Further Reading

Elafros, Athena. 2007. "Salt-N-Pepa." In *Icons of Hip Hop: An Encyclopedia of the Movement, Music, and Culture,* edited by Mickey Hess, vol. 1. Westport, CT: Greenwood.

Phillips, Layli, Kerri Reddick-Morgan, and Dionne Patricia Stephens. 2005. "Oppositional Consciousness within an Oppositional Realm: The Case of Feminism and Womanism in Rap and Hip Hop, 1976–2004." *Journal of African American History* 90, no. 3: 257–77.

Further Listening

Salt-N-Pepa. 1986. *Hot, Cool, and Vicious.* Next Plateau.

Salt-N-Pepa. 1993. *Very Necessary.* Next Plateau/London Records.

Samoa

Samoa, comprised of six islands in the South Pacific, consists of two areas, American Samoa and Western Samoa. American Samoa, located in Southeast Samoa, has been an unincorporated United States territory since 1889, whereas Western Samoa (the rest of Samoa) attained independence from New Zealand in 1962. The International Dateline serves as a boundary for Western and American Samoa, and Western Samoa has the largest islands and settlements, Savai'I and 'Upolu. Since the early 1980s, Samoa has had a hip hop scene since its residents, including stationed military, traveled from the United States with hip hop cassettes, and albums, followed by videocassettes and CDs. Breakdancing found fertile ground and became popular because dance was already an essential aspect of Samoan culture.

Samoan hip hop favors rapping texts in English, rarely using the Samoan language; however, hip hop music is not produced there, and there are no prominent native hip hop artists. Popular acts come from mainland United States or New Zealand, most having been recorded there, or in Australia; hence, lyrical content hardly ever focuses on Samoan life, but on West Coast gangsta rap concerns. There is little native influence on the music itself, although Samoan hip hop may fuse it with Pacific roots music, reggae, or jazz. Samoan-based Boo Yaa T.R.I.B.E. (aka Too Rough International Boo-Yaa Empire or the Blue City Crew, 1988–), which originated from Carson, California, fused West Coast gangsta rap, G-funk, rock, and heavy metal, as well as music from 1980s Samoan hip hop artist Kosmo (aka K.O.S.-163, Kosmo Faalogo, n.d.), who learned breakdancing while visiting Los Angeles in the mid-1980s and helped bring hip hop dance to Wellington, New Zealand. Boo Yaa T.R.I.B.E. identifies both with its members' Samoan roots and their Los Angeles upbringing, as heard in their albums *New Funky Nation* (1990) and *Angry Samoan* (1998).

Other Samoan-associated acts include Drew Deezy (anonymous, n.d.), a Samoan rapper from San Jose, California who favors West Coast hip hop and hyphy music, and Savage (Demetrius Savelio, 1981–), a South Auckland, New Zealand rapper and member of the hip hop group Deceptikonz (1996–) until 2005. Savage's debut solo album, *Moonshine* (2005), reached No. 2 on New Zealand's album chart. The title track, featuring American rapper Akon (1973–), was certified Platinum in New Zealand and Gold in Australia, peaking at Nos. 1 and 9, respectively. After American rappers and producers Soulja Boy (aka Soulja Boy Tell 'Em, DeAndre Cortez Way, 1990) and Pitbull (1981–) remixed Savage's "Swing"—a party track calling on women to dance provocatively—the single peaked at No. 45 on the Billboard Hot 100 and became certified Platinum in the United States.

Scribe (aka Jeshua Ioane Luafutu, Malo Luafutu, 1979–) is a Samoan rapper from Christchurch, New Zealand whose debut album *The Crusader* (2003) was certified five-times Platinum there and in Australia, peaking at Nos. 1 and 12, respectively. His album *Rhyme Book* (2007) was certified Gold in New Zealand, peaking at No. 4 there and No. 9 in Australia. Scribe's cousin, Ladi6 (Karoline Tamati, 1982–) is a critically acclaimed singer who combines hip hop with neo soul, funk, R&B, and reggae. Her albums *Time Is Not Much* (2008), *The Liberation of . . .* (2010), and *Automatic* (2013), focus mostly on romance. They peaked at Nos. 4, 6, and 3, respectively, on the New Zealand album chart.

Melissa Ursula Dawn Goldsmith

See also: Breakdancing; Gangsta Rap; New Zealand; The United States

Further Reading

Henderson, April. 2006. "Dancing between Islands: Hip Hop and the Samoan Diaspora." In *The Vinyl Ain't Final: Hip Hop and the Global of Black Popular Culture*, edited by Dipannita Basu and Sidney J. Lemelle, chap. 12. Ann Arbor, MI: Pluto Press.

Henderson, April. 2010. "Gifted Flows: Making Space for a Brand New Beat." *The Contemporary Pacific* 22, no. 2: 293–315.

Further Listening
Boo Yaa T.R.I.B.E. 1997. *Angry Samoans.* Bullet Proof Records.

Sarkodie

(Michael Owusu Addo, 1985–, Tema, Ghana)

Sarkodie is one of the most critically acclaimed Ghanaian rappers of the 2000s. His music incorporates hip hop, hiplife, and *azonto*, the latter a Ghanaian musical genre that employs fast-paced dance beats to accompany a dance that is characterized by hand movements that pantomime everyday activities to amuse and relay coded messages to an audience. Sarkodie's rap texts are primarily in Twi, but he also raps in English. He has a tenor vocal range, and his singing voice is often auto-tuned. His lyrics focus primarily on love in the form of admiring or fixing a gaze on women, as well as breaking up, praising God, seeking friendship, hustling, and living the street life.

EARLY RAPPING INTEREST AND RECORDING CAREER

Since he was a boy, Sarkodie rapped as a response to living with an abusive aunt. Fortunately, he was able to move back with his mother in Tema, Ghana, but his shyness led him away from public performance. Inspired by Michael Jackson (1958–2009), he became a talented dancer, and he eventually studied for a degree in graphic design at the University of Ghana, Accra. While in college, he built confidence and skill by winning rap battles and appearing on radio.

He met Ghanaian hip hop and hiplife producer Hammer of the Last Two (aka Hammer, Tony Starks, Edward Nana Poku Osei, 1976–) and impressed him with his flowing rap style in Twi, freestyle rhyming, and knowledge of many rapping styles. He signed a five-year contract on Hammer's label, the Last Two Music Group (1999*–). After appearing on Edem's (Denning Edem Hotor, 1986–) debut album *Volta Regime* (2009), he quickly developed a fan base, and he took the stage name Sarkodie, an Ashanti surname that he believed attracted wealth and success, as well as sounded like the Twi word for eagle.

Sarkodie returned to Duncwills Entertainment (n.d.), a label on which he previously signed, to release his debut album *Makye* (2009), which included "Baby," a huge national hit. He followed this success in 2011 with another hit, "You Go Kill Me," which employed azonto beats and was produced by Ghanaian rapper EL (1986–) for his second and most successful album, *Rapperholic* (2011). This album was also released in the United States and garnered multiple awards in Ghana and abroad. A 2013 remix featured Sarkodie, EL, Nigerian hip hop, Afrobeat, reggae, and dancehall singer-songwriter Wizkid (Ayodeji Ibrahim Balogun, 1990–), Nigerian rapper and singer-songwriter Ice Prince (1986–), and Ugandan rapper and producer Navio (Daniel Lubwama Kigozi, 1983–). It brought further global attention to his music. *Sarkology* (2014) and *Mary* (2015) followed this album; *Mary* was produced on Sarkodie's SarkCess Music label (2013–).

Having his own stylish appeal, Sarkodie began his own fashion line and shop, Sark Collections by YAS, in 2012. Success from this business, his albums, and product endorsements have helped rank Sarkodie at No. 8 of the 2013 *Forbes* magazine List of Top Ten Richest/Bankable African Artists. In 2013, he began the Sarkodie Foundation, a philanthropic organization that provides aid and food to underprivileged children in Ghana.

Melissa Ursula Dawn Goldsmith

See also: Christian Hip Hop; Ghana

Further Reading

Clark, Msia Kibona. 2012. "Hip Hop as Social Commentary in Accra and Dar es Salaam." *African Studies Quarterly* 13, no. 3: 23–46.

Collins, John. 2012. "Contemporary Ghanaian Popular Music Since the 1980s." In *Hip Hop Africa: New African Music in a Globalizing World*, edited by Eric Charry, chap. 10. Bloomington: Indiana University Press.

Osumare, Halifu. 2012. *The Hiplife in Ghana: West African Indigenization of Hip Hop.* New York: Palgrave Macmillan.

Shipley, Jesse Weaver. 2013. "Transnational Circulation and Digital Fatigue in Ghana's Azonto Dance Craze." *American Ethnologist* 40, no. 2: 362–81.

Further Listening

Sarkodie. 2009. *Makye.* Duncwills Entertainment.

Saudi Arabia

Saudi Arabia's hip hop scene began to emerge in underground culture around the turn of the 21st century—this underground scene flourishes today because Western images of gangsta rappers suggested cultural stereotypes that were antithetical to the conservative values of the region. The eschewal of gangsta rap also led to the emphasis by performers and hip hop advocates on some of the same core values of early American hip hop, including a focus on spirituality and self-improvement. These themes, combined with the lyricism of the genre, have helped it to gain wider traction. Some artists, however, still feel the need to keep their activities secret from friends and family, as any kind of singing and dancing can be problematic, since many perceive rappers as being less Arab or less Muslim because of their interest in hip hop. This is despite the pervasiveness of Muslim themes in much of the work. Where clubs and concerts are nonexistent, making a place for a live music form is difficult, but performers and media are working to change this dynamic.

MTV ARABIA AND NOTABLE ARTISTS

The 2007 launch of MTV Arabia (2007–2015) provided a platform for exposing Arabs to a combination of programming from the United States and locally produced youth-culture programming. The talent show, *Hip Hop Na* (*Our Hip Hop*, 2006–), hosted by Saudi rapper Qusai (aka Don Legend, Qusai Kheder, 1978–) and

Palestinian American producer Fredwreck (Farid Karam Nassar, 1972–), sought to find new rappers in the Middle East, in an attempt to create a much bigger representation in Saudi popular music for the hip hop scene. Qusai was one of the first professional Saudi rappers whose solid commercial reputation and album sales led to his appointment as the host of *Hip Hop Na*.

As an early competitor on that program, the rap group Dark2Men (n.d.) became one of the more prominent Saudi hip hop groups. Its members rap in both English and Arabic and include Muslim themes in their lyrics. Another rap group, Blak-R (2003*–) starred in the first hip hop concert in Saudi Arabia. Its lyrics focused on issues of youth empowerment. Jeddah FAM (aka J-FAM, 2008*–) was a bilingual Arabic and English rapping group whose members are mainly from Saudi Arabia, although the lineup includes musicians from outside the country. Its lyrics focused on positive messages grounded in Islam.

In 2011, *Laisch hip hop* (*Why Hip Hop*) became Saudi Arabia's first hip hop radio program, exposing Arab audiences to hip hop and to non-Western artists not heard on mainstream radio. The show marked the first time that many Arab artists received airplay. Arab hip hop culture began to be documented in the magazine *Re-Volt* (2013–).

Despite these forays into hip hop culture, the scene has not been completely embraced by society because of fear of censorship. This fear pervades much of Saudi hip hop and controls its themes and styles. While artists largely avoid lyrics related to off-limits topics, such as sexuality, other ideas are explored, such as social problems and the frustrations of the country's youth. Nonetheless, artists are still left open to critique for issues of racism or for implied insults to the royal family. Still, the music is readily available to all, as most Saudi hip hop is available as online downloads.

Susannah Cleveland

See also: Political Hip Hop; The United States

Further Reading

Kahf, Usama. 2007. "Arabic Hip Hop: Claims of Authenticity and Identity of a New Genre." *Journal of Popular Music Studies* 19, no. 4: 359–85.

Urkevich, Lisa. 2015. *Music and Traditions of the Arabian Peninsula: Saudi Arabia, Kuwait, Bahrain, and Qatar.* New York: Routledge.

Further Listening

Qusai. 2012. *The Inevitable Change.* Platinum Records.

Scott, Jill

(1972–, Philadelphia, Pennsylvania)

Jill Scott is an American neo soul singer-songwriter, poet, actress, model, and philanthropist who is known for her eclectic style. Her music can best be described as alternative hip hop fused with neo soul, R&B, jazz, and spoken word. Scott's flexible soprano voice has a wide range. She has the ability to hit the whistle register, producing full sound. Her thematic concerns, established as early as her debut album, focus on uplifting messages, romance, and metatextuality (on writing poems or musical inspiration), among other topics. Scott is an outspoken critic on hip hop's treatment of women of color in both songs and music videos.

MUSIC CAREER AND SOUND

An only child raised in Philadelphia by her mother and grandmother, Jill Scott took interest in poetry and music by the time she was 13 years old. She attended Temple University, where she studied secondary education to become a high school English teacher; however, after her third year and brief teaching experience, she dropped out.

Eventually, Scott started performing live poetry readings at open-mic events, where in the late 1990s percussionist Questlove (aka ?uestlove, Ahmir Khalib Thompson, 1971–) of the American alternative hip hop and neo soul group the Roots (1987–) discovered her and asked Scott to collaborate with the band. Scott cowrote "You Got Me" (1998) and recorded proto-vocals for the refrain and bridge that were rerecorded by Erykah Badu (1971–). In 2000, Erykah Badu and the Roots won a Grammy Award for Best Rap Performance by a Duo or Group. Other collaborations followed for Scott, as well as a singing role in a Canadian production of the Broadway musical *Rent* (1996). But in 1999, after one year on tour, Scott decided that she was better suited for working in the recording studio.

Scott's prolific recording career began with her debut studio album, *Who Is Jill Scott? Words and Sounds Vol. 1* (2000), which peaked at No. 17 on the Billboard 200 and No. 2 on Billboard's Top R&B/Hip-Hop Albums chart, also charted internationally, and was certified double Platinum.

Scott's neo soul follow-up albums *Beautifully Human: Words and Sounds Vol. 2* (2004), which peaked at No. 3 on the Billboard 200 and No. 1 on Billboard's Top R&B/Hip-Hop Albums chart, and *The Real Thing: Words and Sounds Vol. 3* (2007), which peaked at Nos. 4 and 2 on these two charts, were both certified Gold.

She has toured worldwide and has acted in American films and television. In 2005, she published a volume of poems, *The Moments, the Minutes, the Hours* (St. Martin's Press). Her later neo soul and R&B albums, *The Light of the Sun* (2011) and *Woman* (2015), received critical acclaim and debuted at No. 1 on the Billboard 200.

Melissa Ursula Dawn Goldsmith

See also: Neo Soul; The Roots; The United States

Further Reading

Lee, Shayne. 2010. "Sultry Divas of Pop and Soul: Janet, Beyoncé, and Jill." In *Erotic Revolutionaries: Black Women, Sexuality, and Popular Culture*, chap. 2. Lanham, MD: Hamilton Books.

David, Marlo. 2007. "Afrofuturism and Post-Soul Possibility in Black Popular Music." *African American Review* 41, no. 4: 695–707.

Whaley, Deborah Elizabeth. 2002. "The Neo-Soul Vibe and the Post-Modern Aesthetic: Black Popular Music and Culture for the Soul Babies of History." *American Studies* 43, no. 3: 75–82.

Further Listening

Scott, Jill. 2000. *Who Is Jill Scott? Words and Sounds, Vol. 1.* Hidden Beach Recordings/ Epic.

Scott-Heron, Gil

(Gilbert Scott-Heron, 1949–2011, Chicago, Illinois)

Gil Scott-Heron, who has been nicknamed the "godfather of rap" and the "Black Bob Dylan," was an influential jazz-poet, proto-rapper, singer-songwriter, musician, writer, and spoken-word recording artist. He is best known for his spoken-word recordings from the 1970s and 1980s, which serve as precursors of jazz rap and alternative hip hop and fused political and social lyrical content with percussive beats, jazz, soul, and blues. Lyrical content included autobiography, racism in America, anticonsumerism, and frustrations over white Americans' obsession with television and its lack of understanding African Americans' conditions in inner cities. He also included positive messages geared toward black listeners on education, creativity, community, and love.

EARLY YEARS, WRITING TALENT, AND MUSICAL INTERESTS

Gil Scott-Heron grew up in a musical family. His mother, Bobbie Scott-Heron (n.d.), was an opera singer who once performed with the New York Oratorio Society. His father, Gil Heron (n.d.), was a Jamaican soccer player who became the first black man to play for the Celtic Football Club in Glasgow, Scotland. They raised him in the Bronx, New York, but because of his parents' separation and professional careers, Scott-Heron's maternal grandmother Lillie Scott (n.d.) raised him in Jackson, Tennessee when he was a teenager. As a teenager, Scott-Heron already demonstrated exceptional talent as writer and student, and he earned a scholarship to a prestigious preparatory school. At the Fieldston School, despite academic success, he became alienated: Scott-Heron was one of only five black students there and he was a "scholarship kid."

Scott-Heron attended Lincoln University in Pennsylvania, the college of his first choice since Langston Hughes (James Mercer Langston Hughes, 1902–1967) was previously a student there. As an undergraduate, Scott-Heron met Brian Jackson (1952–), who was a flutist and keyboardist. This began their lifelong musical collaboration. Scott-Heron and Jackson were inspired to form their own band, Black and Blues (1969–1970)*, after attending a performance of the Last Poets (1968–). The band, however, was short-lived, since Scott-Heron intended to take a year off from his undergraduate studies to write two novels, *The Vulture* (1970), which earned critical acclaim, and *The N— Factory* (1972). Scott-Heron would never complete his bachelor's degree at Lincoln; however, in 1972, he earned a creative writing master's degree from Johns Hopkins University with his thesis *Circle of Stone*.

RECORDING SPOKEN WORD AND SONGS

While writing his novels, Scott-Heron began his first sound recording projects with the album *Small Talk at 125th and Lenox* (1970), in collaboration with Jackson and produced on the Flying Dutchman Records label (1969–1984*). The album featured 14 tracks with Scott-Heron's speaking in the foreground and sparse accompaniment on conga, percussion, and vocals. Scott-Heron followed *Small Talk* with *Pieces of Man* (1971), *Free Will* (1972), and *The Revolution Will Not Be Televised* (1974). Autobiographical and politically charged themes used in *Small Talk*, as well as Scott-Heron's reading of his poem, "The Revolution Will Not Be Televised," were employed again on Scott-Heron's best-known album, *The Revolution Will Not Be Televised.* He followed with *Winter in America* (1974), another collaboration with Jackson, but this time on the jazz label Strata-East Records (1971–).

Scott-Heron's recordings featured proto-rap, funk, and jazz, and these albums won critical acclaim, establishing Scott-Heron's notoriety and legacy as a jazz poet, songwriter, and musician. Scott-Heron's albums, particularly *The Revolution Will Not Be Televised* and *Winter in America*, inspired rappers such as Public Enemy's (1986–) Chuck D (1960–), KRS-One (1965–), Wu-Tang Clan's (1992–) Ghostface Killah (Dennis Coles, 1970–), Snoop Dogg (1971–), Talib Kweli (1975–), and Kanye West (1977–), among other hip hop, rock, and indie music artists.

Scott-Heron's studio album *The First Minute of a New Day* (1975) marked his move to Arista Records (1974–2011). For Arista, he recorded *From South Africa to South Carolina* (1976), *It's Your World* (1976), *Bridges* (1977), *Secrets* (1978), *1980* (1980), *Real Eyes* (1980), *Reflections* (1981), and *Moving Target* (1982), in addition to the live album *It's Your World* (1976). Scott-Heron released several recordings that addressed apartheid in South Africa, criticizing how the United States was lacking in its handling of racial issues. Examples of this kind of lyrical content are found in *From South Africa to South Carolina* and the single "Johannesburg" (1979). In 1985, Arista dropped Scott-Heron, who stopped recording for nearly 10 years; however, he continued live performances, touring, collaborating, and writing songs, such as "Let Me See Your I.D.," on *Artists United Against Apartheid*

In 1993, Scott-Heron recorded *Spirits* on TVT Records (1985–2008). On "Message to the Messengers," he mentors rappers to become knowledgeable if they were going to teach using rap, including knowing the work and history of previous generations, in order to build communities. In the song, he also criticizes the braggadocio of gangsta rap—how rappers brag about having guns. His comeback to recording was interrupted by drug addiction and legal problems. In 2001, Scott-Heron was sentenced to two years imprisonment for possession of cocaine. In 2002, he appeared on West Coast alternative hip hop group Blackalicious's (1994–) album *Blazing Arrow* while he was briefly out of prison.

Scott-Heron's release and parole followed in 2003, but he faced another arrest for possession of a crack pipe and received a six-month prison sentence. In 2006, Scott-Heron was arrested for drug possession again. This time, he was sentenced to four years imprisonment after violating a plea deal and leaving a drug rehabilitation center because the center failed to provide him HIV medication. Though he was to serve prison time until 2009, he was released and paroled in 2007.

From his release until his death, Scott-Heron performed concerts and recorded. He also enjoyed notoriety for his earlier recordings and was the subject of several radio and television documentaries and interviews. Returning to working with Jackson, Scott-Heron recorded *I'm New Here* (2010) for the independent label XL

Recordings (1989–). The title track features Heron's deeper, weathered voice, reciting and singing autobiographical words about having a second chance and turning one's life around and starting anew. As of 2018, Scott-Heron's spoken-word recordings and songs have been sampled over 300 times.

Melissa Ursula Dawn Goldsmith

See also: Chuck D; Filmmaking (Documentaries); The Last Poets; Political Hip Hop; South Africa; The United States

Further Reading

Baram, Marcus. 2014. *Gil Scott-Heron: "Pieces of Man."* New York: St. Martin's Press.

Gosa, Travis L., and Erik Nielson, eds. 2015. *Hip Hop and Obama Reader.* Oxford, England: Oxford University Press.

Scott-Heron, Gil. 2012. *The Last Holiday: A Memoir.* New York: Grove Press.

Stewart, James B. 2005. "Message in the Music: Political Commentary in Black Popular Music from Rhythm and Blues to Early Hip Hop." *Journal of African American History* 90, no. 3: 196–225.

Further Listening

Scott-Heron, Gil. 1974. *The Revolution Will Not Be Televised.* Flying Dutchman.

Scott-Heron, Gil. 1974. *Winter in America.* Strata-East Records.

Scott-Heron, Gil. 2010. *I'm New Here.* XL Recordings.

Senegal

Senegal can trace its rap scene to the years 1988 and 1989, when the music of Positive Black Soul (PBS, 1989–) introduced hip hop. Since then, the genre has developed to become more diverse and more egalitarian, as both female and male artists from many parts of the country have contributed—even though the music remains dominated by urban male youth, especially those from Dakar. Still, female artists and artists from other regions have increasingly participated in what is called *Rap Galsen* or *Hip Hop Galsen*, terms that describe the blending of bold and revolutionary messages calling for social, cultural, and political consciousness and equality.

RAP AGAINST POLITICAL CORRUPTION

The radical quality of Rap Galsen is apparent in the song "Niap Sa" ("F— Your . . . , 2007), in which Canabasse (aka Abdou Basse Dia, n.d.), a rapper from Dakar who is influenced by Eminem (1972–), raps about ending corruption through musical preaching, ironically performed by rappers, who were at one time referred to as male whores. Despite their sexist lyrics, Canabasse's songs are important since they depict corrupt politicians as the real prostitutes—since they are the leaders who pretend to teach moral truth but rob the people. Another rapper who criticizes governmental corruption is Fou Malade (Malal Almamy Tall, 1974–). In 2011, along with other Senegalese rappers and journalists, he founded the Y'en a Marre Movement (Enough Is Enough or Fed Up) to protest corruption and ineffective government officials, as well as to encourage young people to vote.

In addition to subtle criticisms of corruption, Rap Galsen celebrates the virtues of notable leaders of the past. One example is the song "Yaay mbër" ("What a Fighter You Are," 2013), in which hip hop legend Pacotille (1975*–2015) praises ordinary Senegalese people, who have dignity and are resourceful and resilient, as were many Sufi Senegalese Islamic figures such as Mame Cheikh Ibra Fall (aka Sheikh Ibrahima Fall, 1855–1930), Serigne Touba (aka Cheikh Ahmadou Bamba Mbacké or Khadimu 'r-Rassul, Ahmad Ibn Muhammad Ibn Habiballah Ibn Al Khair, 1852*–1927), Serigne Limamoulaye (aka Seydina Mouhammadou Limamou Laye, 1843–1909), and Foutiyou Tall (aka Umar al-Omar Futi or Seydou Tall, 1797–1864). These historical heroes were touted as models of survival and resistance.

OTHER THEMES

Equally meaningful themes are discernible in the songs of ALIF, or Liberation Attack of the Feminist Infantry (Attaque Libératoire de l'Infanterie Féministe, 1997–), inspired by Positive Black Soul, Daara J (1997–), and Xuman (Pee Froiss, 1993–). ALIF became the first well known Senegalese female rap group to raise social consciousness. While decrying the rampant pickpocketing and other forms of crime in Dakar, ALIF's "Addu Kalpin" (2004) notes that such criminal activities would decrease if the youth had a future—but a lack of employment opportunities and food had robbed the youth of a law-abiding and humane means of survival. A similar emphasis on societal ills is noticeable in "Mane" ("I Say," 2016), a rap song by Toussa (aka Astou Guèye, 1991*–) in which the narrator declares her resilience in a male dominated world, one in which she has to be a *jambar deugeu* (real warrior) whose survival is due to the fact that she refuses to give up and steadfastly holds to her work ethic when it comes to bringing messages to the youth via rap. The image of the hip hop artist as wrestler is pervasive in Senegalese music; it serves as a national symbol of resistance against atrocity.

Babacar M'Baye

See also: Awadi, Didier; Daara J; France; The Gambia; Griot; MC Solaar; Positive Black Soul

Further Reading

Appert, Catherine. 2016. "On Hybridity in African Popular Music: The Case of Senegalese Hip Hop." *Ethnomusicology* 60, no. 2: 279–99.

Fredericks, Rosalind. 2014. "'The Old Man Is Dead': Hip Hop and the Arts of Citizenship of Senegalese Youth." *Antipode* 46, no. 1: 130–48.

Gueye, Marame. 2013. "Urban Guerilla Poetry: The Movement *Y'en a marre* and the Sociopolitical Influences of Hip Hop in Senegal." *Journal of Pan-African Studies* 6, no. 3: 22–42.

Neff, Ali Colleen. 2015. "Roots, Routes, and Rhizomes: Sounding Women's Hip Hop on the Margins of Dakar, Senegal." *Journal of Popular Music Studies* 27, no. 4: 448–77.

Further Listening

ALIF. 2006. "Addu Kalpin." *Dakamerap.* Out Here Records.

Fou Malade. 2008. *"On va tout dire: Fou malade et le bat'haillons blin-d."* Lalu Production Music single.

Pacotille. 2013. *Yaay mbër*. Prince Arts.

Retour vers le futur, Part 1. 2010. Ghetto fab soldats. Vol 2. Pr4productions and Malik Bledoss.

Toussa. 2016. *Toussa: EP Fam Musik*. Senetunes.

The Sequence

(1979–1985, Columbia, South Carolina)

The Sequence was a hip hop, funk, and disco trio that was formed by three high school cheerleaders: Angie Brown Stone (aka Angie B., Angela Laverne Brown, 1961–), Cheryl the Pearl (Cheryl Cook, n.d.), and Blondie (Gwndolyn Chisolm, n.d.). They were discovered by Sugar Hill Records (1986–1995) co-owner Sylvia Robinson (1936–2011) when they ran up to the stage at a Sugarhill Gang performance and started to sing backing vocals for the group with Robinson. The Sequence became the first female trio and the first female group to release a rap single, "Funk You Up" (1979). Its two eponymous albums (1980 and 1982) and third noncharting album, *The Sequence Party* (1983), were recorded on the Sugar Hill Records label (1986–1995).

SOUND AND SUCCESS

Similar to the Sugarhill Gang, the Sequence performed funk-infused old-school hip hop at the height of disco. Its sound, however, had a broader range, since the trio also sang R&B and 1970s style soul ballads. In addition, Angie Brown Stone not only sang; she also rapped.

In 1979, the Sugarhill Gang released "Rapper's Delight," the first rap single to become a Top 40 Billboard hit, reaching No. 36. Soon afterward that year, the Sequence had a hit with "Funk You Up," which peaked at No. 15 on Billboard's R&B Singles chart. The Sequence continued on the Sugar Hill label in 1980 by backing Sugar Hill artist Spoonie Gee (1963–) on his early rap single, "Monster Jam" (*Spoonie Gee Meets the Sequence*). That year, the Sequence also released the single "And You Know That."

Both the Sequence's first and second singles, as well as its third single release "Funky Sound (Tear the Roof Off)" appeared on the trio's debut album, *Sugar Hill Presents the Sequence* (1980). "Funky Sound (Tear the Roof Off)" was another hit, peaking at No. 39 on Billboard's Black Singles in 1981. The song was a remake of the psychedelic funk and soul group Parliament's (1968–1970, 1974–1980) 1976 hit "Funk You Up (Tear the Roof off the Sucker)."

In 1982, the trio released its second album, *The Sequence* (1982), which reached No. 51 on Billboard's R&B Albums chart and featured another hit, the ballad "I Don't Need Your Love (Part One)," which reached No. 40 on Billboard's R&B Singles chart. In 1983, the trio released its final album together, *The Sequence Party*. Although there were a few single releases from the album between 1983 and 1984, such as "Here Comes the Bride" and "I Just Want to Know," none of these singles charted. The group's final releases were the remix "Funk You Up '85" (1984) and "Control" (1985).

BREAKUP AND LEGACY

When Sugar Hill folded in 1985, the Sequence broke up. Nevertheless, "Funk You Up" became frequently sampled. The hip hop group Boogie Down Productions (1985–1992) used it in "Jimmy" (1988). The song has lived on in sample culture in tracks such as De La Soul's (1987–) "This Is a Recording 4 Living in a Fulltime Era (L.I.F.E.)," Dr. Dre's (1965–) "Keep Their Heads Ringin'" (1995), and Erykah Badu's (1971–) "Love of My Life Worldwide" (2003).

Angie Brown Stone joined Vertical Hold (1988–1996), an R&B and soul trio based in New York City. In 1993, she sang lead on Vertical Hold's Billboard Top 20 R&B hit "Seems You're Much Too Busy." She continued on with a successful solo career, having a 1999 hit, "There's No More Rain in This Cloud," from her certified-Gold album *Black Diamond*.

Comparisons can be drawn between the sound and legacy of the Sequence and its more mainstream pop-oriented contemporaries Sister Sledge (1971–). The Sequence employed rap and often allowed for more loosely organized unison vocals; however, the recorded sound was lively and seemed appropriate for the Sequence's lighthearted romantic and partying lyrical themes. The Sequence clearly influenced subsequent female hip hop trios such as TLC (1990–) and Salt-N-Pepa (1985–2002, 2007–) in the United States, but also female hip hop groups worldwide, for example, Auckland, New Zealand's Sisters Underground (1990–1995) and Moana and the Moahunters (1990–1998).

Melissa Ursula Dawn Goldsmith

See also: Moana and the Moahunters; Robinson, Sylvia; Salt-N-Pepa; Sisters Underground; TLC; The United States

Further Reading
Bradley, Adam, and Andrew Dubois, eds. 2010. "Sequence." Under "Part 1: 1978–84: The Old School" in *The Anthology of Rap*, pp. 85–89. New Haven, CT: Yale University Press.
George, Nelson. 1999. *Hip Hop America*. London: Penguin Books.

Further Listening
The Sequence. 1980. *Sugar Hill Presents the Sequence*. Sugar Hill Records.
The Sequence. 1982. *The Sequence*. Sugar Hill Records.

Serbia

Serbia is an Eastern European nation that was once part of the Socialist Federative Republic of Yugoslavia (1945–1992), until it attained its independence and became the Republic of Serbia (1992–). As of 2018, most Serbs live in Serbia, though Serbian minority communities exist in countries that formerly belonged to the Socialist Federative Republic of Yugoslavia, such as Bosnia-Herzogovina and

Slovenia. Although during the early 1980s there was limited access to American hip hop music, Serbs took an interest in breakdancing shortly after the international distribution of 1984 American hip hop films such as *Beat Street*, *Breakin'*, and *Breakin' 2: Electric Boogaloo*.

The center for early Serbian hip hop activity was in Serbia's capital city, Belgrade. Meanwhile, Bosnian Serbs interested in breakdancing sparked the beginnings of Serbian hip hop in Bosnia-Herzogovina's capital, Sarajevo. Hip hop in Serbia was less disrupted than in neighboring countries that gained independence in the early 1990s and during the Yugoslav Wars (1991–2001). Serbia nevertheless experienced political criticism and economic crisis. Between 1998 and 2001 the Kosovo War (1998–1999) posed an economic drain and nearly halted all album production.

FOUR WAVES OF HIP HOP

Serbian hip hop is often thought of as occurring in four waves, in conjunction with Serbian conflicts and war. The earliest Serbian hip hop release was the Master Scratch Band's (early 1980s–1996*) *Dégout* EP (1984), which introduced rap in Serbian and English; it was released on the Jugoton label (1947–), based in Zagreb, Croatia (then part of the Socialist Federal Republic of Yugoslavia). The tracks "Break War" and "Jailbreak" became national hits. Despite having no financial means of acquiring samplers at the time, the Master Scratch Band, an electro breakbeat group, produced samples by using limited recorders, mixers, vocoders, synthesizers, and drum machines. In 1986, the band moved to London, but other Serbian hip hop acts emerged, including groups such as Badvajzer (Budweiser, 1987*–1991), Who Is the Best? (1988*–), Sanšajn (Sunshine, aka Green Kool Posse, 1993–), CYA (1994–2003)*, rappers Gru (Dalibor Andonov, 1973–), Ajs Nigrutin (Vladan Aksentijević, 1977–), Juice (Ivan Ivanović, 1981–), and St. Petersburg, Russia, natives Straight Jackin' (aka Strejt džekin, 1994–).

Emerging at the end of the first (late 1980s–2000) and beginning of the second waves (2001–2005), Beogradski Sindikat (1999–) became the most internationally famous Serbian hip hop act with its album *BSSST . . . tišinčina* (*Pssst . . . Silence*, 2001) and the EP *Govedina* (*Beef*, 2002), which used imagery of coffee, cloves, and sausage, alongside the double meaning of the word "beef" in its tracks to harshly criticize the Milošević government. *Govedina* also focused on Serbia's poor economic conditions and Belgrade's antiquated attitude toward marijuana and homosexuals. Group member Škabo (Boško Ćirković, 1976–) had a successful concurrent solo career. The comedic rap group Bad Copy (1996–2008, 2012–) and one of its rappers, Struka (Ognjen Kostić, 1983–), were contemporaries of Beogradski Sindikat. By the turn of the 21st century, localized gangsta style rap as well as political (including antiwar) protest rap became accepted more in the mainstream.

In 2005, Serbian hip hop producer Oneya (Vanja Ulepić, 1979–) established the Belgrade label Bassivity Music and, through its record stores, improved the distribution of Serbian, Croatian, and Bosnian hip hop. Bassivity produced second wave acts such as VIP (2002–), Marčelo (Marko Šelić, 1983–), Rasta (Stefan Đurić, 1989–), and Don TRIALeon (aka Trial, Don Trialeon, n.d.). Contemporaries included Skaj Vikler (aka Wikluh Sky, Đorđe Miljenović, 1980–), Prti BeeGee (2001–), and Bvana (aka Bvana Herbalizer, Nikola Ćosić, 1983–). VIP's Ikac (Ivan Jović, n.d.) and Demian (aka Rexxxona, Relja Milanković, 1982–) have also had successful solo careers. The end of Bassivity's dominance and the incorporation of R&B marked the third wave (2006–2011), in which acts such as Elitni Odredi (Elite Units, 2005–2015) emerged. This duo fused turbo-folk and electro house with hip hop. Turbo-folk, also known as Serbwave, is a fusion genre consisting of Balkan folk music and dance pop—it began in Serbia in the 1980s, and its popularity has grown in Croatia, Bosnia and Herzegovina, Macedonia, Montenegro, Slovenia, and Bulgaria. Third wave artists included Cvija (Stefan Cvijović, 1989–), Marlon Brutal (Vukašin Jasnić, 1989–), and Mikri Maus (Nikola Jelić, 1981–). In 2008, the Belgrade label Ltdfm Music (Live to Die for My Music) was established and produced artists such as Juice, Prti BeeGee, and Bvana.

The use of trap music marks the beginning of the fourth wave (2012–), which demonstrates further diversity of lyrical content. For example, Sajsi MC (Ivana Rasic, 1981–), who comes from Vracar, a wealthy neighborhood in Belgrade, raps in affected Serbian about Belgrade's nouveau-riche snobbery. Her alter ego, Tiffany, is named after the jewelry store. Other artists include Mimi Mercedez (1992*–) and the alternative hip hop band Mr. Rabbit (2013–). By the late 1990s, several Serbian diaspora acts such as Canada's Illuminati X (aka Street Team, Balkan Beasts, 2005–), Australia's X-PynSyv™ (Sylvia Peric 1983–), Germany's Toni der Assi (1978–), and two Austrian rappers, Svaba Ortak (Pavle Komatina, 1993–) and Manijak (Denis Abramović, 1991–), emerged. As of 2018, there are no significantly successful Serbian hip hop artists in the United States.

Melissa Ursula Dawn Goldsmith

See also: Bosnia and Herzegovina; Croatia; Macedonia; Montenegro; Slovenia

Further Reading

Baker, Catherine. 2009. "War Memory and Musical Tradition: Commemorating Croatia's Homeland War through Popular Music and Rap in Eastern Slavonia." *Journal of Contemporary European Studies*, 17, no. 1: 35–45.

Šentevska, Irena. 2017. "*La haine et les autres crimes* [*Hate and Other Crimes*]: Ghetto-centric Imagery in Serbian Hip Hop Videos." In *Hip Hop at Europe's Edge: Music, Agency, and Social Change*, edited by Milosz Miszczynski and Adriana Helbig, chap. 14. Bloomington: Indiana University Press.

Further Listening

Beogradski Sindikat. 2001. *BSSST . . . Tišinčina (Pssst . . . Silence)*. Tilt.

Mr. Rabbit. 2016. *Postmoderna Komedija (Poatmodern Comedy)*. Lampshade Media.

Shaggy

(Orville Richard Burrell, 1968–, Kingston, Jamaica)

Shaggy is a Jamaican American rapper, singer, and DJ who had hit albums and singles in the 1990s and 2000s that fused reggae with alternative rock, pop, R&B, dancehall, dubstep, and hip hop. Shaggy also uses toasting in his music. His biggest international hit singles include a dancehall cover of John Folkes's (n.d.) 1958

Singer-songwriter Shaggy fuses his signature reggae toasting sound with rap and hip hop beats. The prolific Jamaican-American's combination of musical style and uplifting messages have contributed to his huge international following. (Neil Mockford/Alex Huckle/GC Images/Getty Images)

ska song "Oh Carolina" (1993), "Boombastic" (1995), "It Wasn't Me" (1999), and a reggae fusion song titled "Angel" (2000) that uses the refrain melody from Chip Taylor's (James Wesley Voight, 1940–) country pop hit "Angel of the Morning" (1968) and the bass line from Steve Miller's (1943–) rock hit "The Joker" (1973). His collaboration album with Sting (Gordon Matthew Thomas Sumner, 1951–), *44/876*, was released in 2018.

EARLY CAREER AND SUCCESS

Nicknamed Shaggy because of his wild hair, Burrell began songwriting in high school. By age 19, he took singing lessons and buskered, singing reggae songs. Although he soon recorded several reggae songs with Spiderman (Lloyd Campbell, 1948–), he was poor and wanted to escape the tough Brooklyn street life; he therefore enlisted in the United States Marine Corps during the First Gulf War (1990–1991). In the meantime, he developed his melodic and strongly accentuated rapping, as well as his raspy baritone.

In 1992, he resumed his music career, appearing on Dope's (aka K-Dope, Kenny Gonzalez, 1970–) hip hop album *The Kenny Dope Unreleased Project* (1992) and releasing his own debut album, *Pure Pleasure* (1993). A prerelease single, "Oh Carolina," peaked at No. 59 on the Billboard Hot 100. He followed with *Original Doberman* (1994), without any singles released before it. His most critically acclaimed album, *Boombastic* (1995), spawned a title song that peaked at No. 3 on the Billboard Hot 100 and No. 1 on the Billboard R&B chart. Most significantly, *Boombastic* was No. 1 on Billboard's Reggae Album chart for a record 30 consecutive weeks. In 1996, the album won a Grammy Award for Best Reggae Album. *Boombastic* peaked at No. 34 on the Billboard 200 and was certified Platinum.

Shaggy's following album, *Midnite Lover* (1997), paled in comparison to *Boombastic*, but he followed it with his most successful album, *Hot Shot* (2000), which was RIAA certified six-times Platinum and peaked at No. 1 on the Billboard 200. In 2002, a remix of this album was released, while his following album, *Lucky Day*, attained Gold certification.

AFTER *HOT SHOT*

Although many of Shaggy's later albums, including *Clothes Drop* (2005), *Intoxication* (2007), *Shaggy and Friends* (2011), *Summer in Kingston* (2011), *Rise* (2012), and *Out of Many, One Music* (2013), have attained critical acclaim, they have not reached the same status as *Boombastic* and *Hot Shot*. Shaggy's themes include romance and breaking up, admiring or objectifying women, thanking those who love and support him (despite difficulties), protesting economic unfairness, and the need for philanthropy. "Rise Again" (2010) supported the victims of the Haiti earthquake.

Throughout his career, Shaggy has created reggae fusion renditions as well as employed elements of many popular hits. As of 2018, Shaggy continues recording and has maintained collaborations with prominent American and global hip hop artists in both the studio and while touring worldwide.

Melissa Ursula Dawn Goldsmith

See also: Jamaica; Reggae; The United States

Further Reading

Daniel, Jeff. 1995. "A True Reggae Toastmaster Shaggy Takes the Music Back to Its Melodic Roots." *St. Louis Post-Dispatch*, October 26, 15.

Locilento, Micah. 2002. *Shaggy: Dogamuffin Style.* Toronto: ECW Press.

Further Listening

Shaggy. 1995. *Boombastic.* Virgin.

Shaggy. 2000. *Hot Shot.* MCA.

Shebang!

(1999–, Toronto, Canada)

Shebang! Is a b-girl crew formed in 1999 by Ms. Mighty (Sara Fenton, n.d.) and Blazin' (Peggy Lau, n.d.), who became the crew's cochoreographers. What was originally intended as a support group for women of hip hop became the first Canadian b-girl crew whose efforts included advocacy for women, girls, and youth. In 2003, Shebang! competed in the World B-Boy Championship in London, finishing in seventh place. That year it also battled in the Rocksteady Anniversary in New York City and the Battle of the Year–North America in Montreal.

The crew became internationally famous for performing with the hip hop group Beastie Boys (1981–2012), Canadian pop and hip hop singer/songwriter Nelly Furtado (1978–), and DJ Kool Herc (1955–). In the early 2000s, Shebang! hosted Break and Enter, a b-boy and b-girl battle in Toronto. In 2003, the Canadian Floor Masters presented the Absolut Canadian B-Boy/B-Girl Award to Shebang, recognizing its efforts to encourage women to pursue breakdancing, educating youth about hip hop through classes and workshops, and preserving breakdancing in Canada. Ms. Mighty eventually moved to Los Angeles, where she teaches choreography coaching to actors and dancers. As of 2018, Shebang! continues to compete.

Melissa Ursula Dawn Goldsmith

See also: Battling; Breakdancing; Canada; Hip Hop Dance

Further Reading

Caldwell, Rebecca. 2003. "The Throwdown of B-Girling and Movers Shebang!" *The Globe and Mail* (Toronto), January 25, R4.

García, Ana "Rokafella." 2005. Introduction to *We B*Girlz* by Nika Kramer and Martha Cooper. New York: powerHouse Books.

Gupta-Carlson, Himanee. 2010. "Planet B-Girl: Community Building and Feminism in Hip Hop." *New Political Science* 32, no. 4: 515–29.

Sierra Leone

Sierra Leone is a West African country on the Atlantic coast that borders Liberia and Guinea. Many factors interfered with the development of hip hop in 1990s Sierra Leone. The Sierra Leone Civil War (1991–2002) destroyed the country's infrastructure, displaced over two million people, and set up problems with handling the 2014 Ebola outbreak. Before the Sierra Leone Civil War, popular music tastes were extremely diverse. For example, one of the most famous funk bands, Muyei Power (aka Orchestre Muyei, 1970*–1979), combined Sierra Leonean beats with Congolese and Nigerian music, American soul, and Jamaican reggae. But the Sierra Leone Civil War destroyed the country's music industry.

As of 2018, nearly all Sierra Leonean acts are from the capital city of Freetown. Singer-songwriter, rapper, actor, radio host, sound recording producer, film producer, and director Jimmy B (Jimmy Yeani Bangura, n.d.) is a pioneering rapper who fused hip hop and R&B. Jimmy B began his successful music career in Johannesburg, South Africa, but moved to Freetown to establish Paradise Records (2000–) to promote Sierra Leonean music and rebuild the country's music and film industry. In 2002, Jimmy B signed Freetown rapper YOK D Sniper (aka YOK Seven, anonymous, n.d.), who was a refugee in Guinea during the Sierra Leone Civil War. YOK Seven's track "A-Bo," from *Paradise Records Compilation, Vol. 1* (2002), calling for officials to stop the war, was the first hit rap song in Krio (an English-based Creole language) released in Sierra Leone.

Rapper and singer-songwriter Daddy Saj (Joseph Gerald Adolphus Cole, 1978–), also a Freetown refugee in Guinea, had global commercial success with his Krio and English album *Corruption: "E de so"* ("It Is So," 2003), focusing on political corruption in his home country. At times, Daddy Saj's music fuses hip hop with traditional Bahamian goombay music. Other Freetown rappers are K-Man (Mahomad Saccoh, 1984–), who fuses hip hop with reggae, ragga, and Kao Denero (aka Kao D, King Denero, Amara Denise Turay, n.d.), who fuses pop and rap. English is the official language of the country, but Krio is spoken by nearly all of Sierra Leone's highly diverse population. Sierra Leonean hip hop employs both languages.

Many Sierra Leonean acts still reside outside the country. Groups include G Force (2005–), based in Gävle, Sweden and Bajah + the Dry Eye Crew (2000–), who reside in New York City. Both fuse hip hop with dancehall and reggae. Chosan (Sheku kef-Kamara, n.d.), who was born in Sierra Leone, lived in Canada, began his rapping career in the United Kingdom, and is based in the United States. Chosan has supported hip hop acts in concert such as Busta Rhymes (1972–), dead prez

(1996–), and Jadakiss (Jason Phillips, 1975–), and performed the introduction for Kanye West's (1977–) music video for "Diamonds from Sierra Leone" (2005). Rapper Black Intellect (Jerry Kai Lewis, n.d.), born in Freetown, grew up in Baltimore, relocated to Johannesburg, and became a member of the hip hop band Cashless Society (1999–2006). Chief Boima (Boima Tucker, n.d.) is a Milwaukee, Wisconsin-born Sierra Leonean-American DJ, sound recording producer, and songwriter of hip hop, hyphy, Trinbagonian *soca*, Ivory Coastan *zouglou*, jazz, minimalist music, techno, and ambient electronica. Chief Boima toured with the San Francisco eclectic art music band Beaten by Them (2005–), produced remixes for the Brooklyn, New York–based recording label Dutty Artz (2008–), and is currently half of the Brooklyn-based house duo the Kondi Band (2007–), playing turntables with Sierra Leonean *mbira* (thumb piano) player Sorie Kondi (Sorie Koroma, 1968*–). In 2013, Chief Boima formed the production group Africa Latina (2013–), and in 2017, he relocated to Rio de Janeiro, Brazil.

Melissa Ursula Dawn Goldsmith

See also: Reggae

Further Reading

Lahai, John Idriss. 2014. "The Musicscapes of a Country in Transition: Cultural Identity, Youth Agency, the Emergent Hip Hop Culture, and the Quest for Socio-Political Change in Sierra Leone." In *Hip Hop and Social Change in Africa: Ni Wakati*, edited by Msia Kibona Clark and Mickie Mwanzia Koster, chap. 13. Lanham, MD: Lexington Books.

Shepler, Susan. 2010. "Youth Music and Politics in Post-War Sierra Leone." *Journal of Modern African Studies* 48, no. 4: 627–42.

Tucker, Boima. 2013. *Musical Violence: Gangsta Rap and Politics in Sierra Leone.* Uppsala, Sweden: Nordiska Afrikainstitutet.

Further Listening

Daddy Saj. 2003. *Corruption: "E De So."* Super Sound.

Singapore

Singapore's hip hop scene goes beyond just music to include graffiti arts, breakdancing, and beatboxing—a variety of artistic expressions matched by the diversity of its creators, who are Chinese, Malay, Indian, and Eurasian. Hip hop was first brought to the country in the mid-1980s by stationed military and international business traders. Singaporean rap is primarily in English (or its variant, Singlish), though Mandarin Chinese, Bahasa Melayu, and Tamil are also used.

The first commercially successful rap artist was the duo Construction Sight (1990–2000)*, which mainstreamed rap music. Ex–Construction Sight member Sheikh Haikel (Sheikh Haikel Bin Sheikh Salim Bajrai, 1975–) became a solo rapper and now runs a music school in Kuala Lumpur, where hip hop is taught. The new, young hip hop talent includes the popular ShiGGa Shay (Pek Jin Shen, 1992–), rapper-songwriter, video director, and music producer, and ex-member of the hip hop collective Grizzle Grind Crew (2013–); he is the youngest hip hop artist to have charted in Singapore, with "LimPeh" ("Your Dad," 2013), a song rapped in

Hokkien. Bandmate Lineath (Lineath Rajendran, 1994–), a rapper and producer, raps in Tamil, a practice he began in 2014 on the song "Grizzle Grind Anthem." Achieving international success, rapper and activist Kevin Lester (aka Lion City Boy, Kevin Lester Sarjit, 1984–) has signed to Black Eyed Peas (1992–) member apl.de.ap's (Allan Pineda Lindo, 1974–) BMBX (2014–) record label.

Underground hip hop success stories include Q-Dot (Ern Quek, n.d.), a rapper and producer known for his wordplay and lyricism and who came into the scene with his 2013 free-for-download mixtape *The Qoncrete Jungle*, while diaspora hip hop acts include Masia One (Maysian Lim, 1980*–) of Toronto, a rapper and record label owner (The Merdecka Group, aka the M1 Group, 2003–) and Akeem Jahat (1989–), who is part of the underground Malaysian hip hop scene and raps in Malay. Top Singaporean hip hop producers include Azrael (Muhammad Izaril Ismail, 1983–), a rapper and hip hop activist, and Don M (Syed Muhammad Fayk Alaydrus, 1985–), who has more than 250 songwriting credits to his name and is working toward an evolving and unique Singaporean hip hop sound. Though not involved in the music scene per se, beatboxer Dharni (Dharni Ng, 1987*–) has become famous in Singapore. He was the first person to win the Grand Beatbox Battle Championship consecutively, in 2013 and 2014, and has placed fourth in the World BeatBox championships. Among hip hop dancers, Radikal Forze (1998–), a pioneering b-boy crew, is perhaps the best known, especially for its spawning the acting career of ex–crew member Tosh Zhang (Tosh Zhang Zhi Yang, 1989–), a dancer and hip hop singer.

Anthony J. Fonseca

See also: Beatboxing; Breakdancing; Graffiti Art

Further Reading

Mattar, Yasser. 2003. "Virtual Communities and Hip Hop Music Consumers in Singapore: Interplaying Global, Local, and Subcultural Identities." *Leisure Studies* 22, no. 4: 283–300.

Tan, Shzr Ee. 2009. "Singapore Takes the 'Bad' Rap: A State-Produced Music Video Goes 'Viral.'" *Ethnomusicology Forum* 18, no. 1: 107–30.

Sisters Underground

(1990–1995, Auckland, New Zealand/Aotearoa)

Sisters Underground is a duo best known for its hit song "In the Neighbourhood" (1994), a groundbreaking single for New Zealand/Aotearoa hip hop. Part of the subgenre Urban Pasifika, the single combines Māori and other Pacific Island roots music with African American music genres. The song's success gave international attention to the Auckland hip hop scene and paved the path for other Urban Pasifika hits, which incorporated music styles such as hip hop, jazz, R&B, and soul.

"IN THE NEIGHBOURHOOD" AND AFTERWARD

Before becoming Sisters Underground, Brenda Makammeoafi (1976*–) and Hassanah Iroegbu (1976*–) met at Hillary College in Otara, South Auckland.

Afterward, they performed at Auckland dance parties as an a cappella R&B and soul singing, scat, and old-school rap act in the Voodoo Rhyme Syndicate (n.d.). That year, they were introduced to Alan Jansson (Pakeha Alan Jansson, n.d.), who was recording *Proud: An Urban Pacific Streetsoul Compilation* (1994). Sisters Underground's two tracks on the album, "In the Neighbourhood" and "Ain't It True," were the result of their edgy street-themed songwriting about living in Otara, combined with Jansson's reworking of lyrics and adding hip hop beats and acoustic guitar accompaniment.

The songs interweave rap with a lyrical R&B style refrain and close harmonies. Topics include racism, street violence, youth unemployment, city nightlife, dancing, and aiming to live a peaceful life. Greg Semu (1971–) directed the music video of "In the Neighbourhood" in the duo's home and in South Auckland's streets; it became the most frequently played music video on New Zealand television in 1994. The single peaked at No. 6 on the New Zealand singles chart and at No. 62 on Australia's ARIA Singles Chart.

In 1995, Sisters Underground won the award for Most Promising Group at the New Zealand Music Awards. After they toured Australia, Sony Music Australia offered an album deal, but Iroegbu had moved to Hawaii. The album was never recorded.

"In the Neighbourhood" enjoyed renewed popularity in the 2000s. In 2001, it was ranked No. 58 in the APRA (Australian Performing Rights Association) Top 100 New Zealand songs, and in 2002, New Zealand's TV2 commissioned producer, songwriter, and multi-instrumentalist Jansson, to remix the song as the station's promotions theme. Jansson reunited the duo for the recording, and airplay of the remix inspired a resurgence of interest in the original video. In 2003, "In the Neighbourhood" was included in the six-part New Zealand rock 'n' roll television miniseries *Give It a Whirl*, as well as on its 2005 soundtrack album.

Iroegbu studied jazz and pursued a solo career in the United States, working as a guest vocalist with De La Soul (1987–) in New York (2003), as a guest vocalist on Soane's (anonymous, n.d.) "Runaway" track on *Tonganchic* (2005), and as a featured vocalist on Atlanta rapper Young Jeezy's (anonymous, 1977–) "What You Talkin' Bout" (2006) on *The Inspiration*. Since 2013, Sisters Underground has reunited to perform "In the Neighbourhood" several times. As of 2018, Iroegbu is active in the Miami hip hop scene, and Makammeoafi (now Brenda Pua) is pursuing a solo career in Australia.

Melissa Ursula Dawn Goldsmith

See also: New Zealand

Further Reading

Hapeta, Dean. 2000. "Hip Hop in Aotearoa/New Zealand." In *Changing Sounds: New Directions and Configurations in Popular Music*, edited by Tony Mitchell and Peter Doyle, pp. 202–7. Sydney, Australia: University of Technology, Faculty of Humanities and Social Sciences.

Johnson, Henry. 2010. *Many Voices: Music and National Identity in Aotearoa/New Zealand.* New Castle upon Tyne, England: Cambridge Scholars.

Shute, Gareth. 2004. *Hip Hop Music in Aotearoa.* Auckland, New Zealand: Reed.

Further Listening
Jansson, Alan. 1994. *Proud: An Urban-Pacific Streetsoul Compilation.* Second Nature
    Records/Volition.

Slick Rick

(aka Rick the Ruler, MC Ricky D, Richard Martin Lloyd Walters, 1965–,
London, England)

Slick Rick is an English American rapper known for his storytelling raps, as well
as for his use of multiple character voices, narrative structures, and quick-wit
humor. His smooth, melodic sounding rap, use of British English (from Received
Pronunciation to vernacular), and storytelling of adventures loosely make him an
early precursor to chap hop, an English style of rapping that emerged in the 2000s
that contains elements of British chap culture and sometimes steampunk. Slick
Rick's initial success was as MC Ricky D, in Barbadian American beatboxer, rapper, and producer Doug E. Fresh's (Douglas E. Davis, 1966–) Get Fresh Crew
(1985–2003).

EARLY CAREER

Richard Martin Lloyd Walters was born in London to parents of English Jamaican descent. When he was 18 months old, Walters was blinded in the right eye by
a flying piece of glass from a broken window. Walters began wearing his trademark eye patch at an early age. Both the accident and the eye patch contributed to
Walters's shyness, so he opted to write stories by himself rather than play with
others. He also developed talent as a visual artist. In 1976, Walters's family moved
to the United States and settled in the Bronx, New York.

He majored in visual art at the prestigious Fiorello H. Laguardia High School of
Music and Art and Performing Arts, where he befriended American rapper Dana
Dane (Dana McLeese, 1965). The duo became the Kangol Crew (1980*–1984),
which became part of the New York City hip hop scene by performing at parks,
clubs, and local school rapping battles. The two parted ways after he was hired by
Doug E. Fresh.

He became part of the the Get Fresh Crew, and the group's first single, "The
Show" (1985) achieved Gold certification. The B side, "La Di Da Di," featuring
Slick Rick rapping over Doug E. Fresh's beatboxing, gained cult popularity and
marked the beginning of Slick Rick as being one of the most sampled rappers in
hip hop history.

SOLO ALBUMS, INCARCERATION, AND
IMMIGRATION ISSUES

In 1988, Slick Rick released his solo debut studio album *The Great Adventures
of Slick Rick* on Russell Simmons' (1957–) Def Jam Recordings label (1983–). Produced by Slick Rick, Jam Master Jay (Jason William Mizell, 1965–2002), and the

Bomb Squad (1986–), *The Great Adventures* peaked at No. 31 on the Billboard 200 and No. 1 on Billboard's Top R&B/Hip-Hop Albums chart.

His studio solo albums had varying success. *The Great Adventures*, *The Ruler's Back* (1991), *Behind Bars* (1994), and *The Art of Storytelling* (1999) coincided with difficult times in his life. Simmons had met Slick Rick in a New York mental ward after the rapper had smoked too much PCP (phencyclidine, aka angel dust). Slick Rick had a worse problem with his bodyguard and cousin Mark Plummer (n.d.). After Plummer made numerous extortion attempts and threats to Slick Rick's life, the rapper purchased guns to protect himself and his family. In 1990, Slick Rick, feeling threatened, fired shots that hit Plummer— and an innocent bystander. No one suffered life-threatening injuries, but attempted murder, firearms, and immigration charges resulted in a five-year prison sentence.

Slick Rick recorded his second album, *The Ruler's Back*, after Simmons posted his bail. The album peaked at No. 29 on the Billboard 200 but received mixed reception. Recorded while in jail, *Behind Bars* peaked at No. 51 on the Billboard 200 and No. 11 on the Billboard Top R&B/Hip-Hop Albums chart; however, sales were mediocre. But *The Art of Storytelling* was Slick Rick's comeback album, featuring several hip hop artists who had been inspired by him, such as Nas (1973–) and Snoop Dogg (1971–). *The Art of Storytelling* became Slick Rick's most successful album, peaking at No. 8 on the Billboard 200 and No. 1 of Billboard's Top R&B/ Hip-Hop Albums chart.

Further issues with immigration took place in 2001 when Slick Rick finished performing on a Caribbean cruise and reentered the United States. Because of his previous felonies, he endured threats of deportation and spent over one year in prison. In 2008, New York Governor David Paterson (1954–, in office 2008– 2010) granted him a full and unconditional pardon on his attempted murder charges.

Slick Rick has been active in many humanitarian efforts, from teaching children to avoid violence to donating artifacts to the Smithsonian National Museum of African American History and Culture. In 2016, he was granted U.S. citizenship.

Melissa Ursula Dawn Goldsmith

See also: Doug E. Fresh; Nas; Snoop Dogg; The United Kingdom; The United States

Further Reading

Bradley, Adam, and Andrew Dubois, eds. 2010. "Slick Rick." Under "Part 2: 1985–92: The Golden Age" in *The Anthology of Rap*, pp. 289–96. New Haven, CT: Yale University Press.

Coleman, Brian. 2007. "Slick Rick: *The Great Adventures of Slick Rick*." In *Check the Technique: Liner Notes for Hip Hop Junkies*. New York: Villard.

Inoue, Todd. 2003. "Slick Rick: *The Great Adventures of Slick Rick*." In *Classical Material: The Hip Hop Album Guide*, edited by Oliver Wang, pp. 147–48. Toronto: ECW Press.

Further Listening

Slick Rick. 1988. *The Great Adventures of Slick Rick*. Def Jam.

Slick Rick. 1999. *The Art of Storytelling*. Def Jam Recordings.

Slovakia

Slovakia is a Central European country that borders the Czech Republic, Austria, Poland, Hungary, and the Ukraine. Slovak hip hop began in the late 1980s, just before the end of communist rule in 1989, with leading scenes in the capital city, Bratislava, and in its largest eastern city, Kosice. Rapping texts are in Slovak, the country's official language, and lyrics focus on political upheavals; protesting communism, socialism, and capitalism; economic inequality; and corruption. The studio album *Rezimy* (*Regimes*, 2011), with lyrics composed mostly by Michal Kovac (n.d.) of the Slovak rock group O.B.D. (Orchester Bronislava Dobrotu, 1993–), is an alternative hip hop album that features various artists recording storytelling raps about 30 years of Slovak regimes against a jazz background; however, most famous Slovak hip hop takes after West Coast gangsta rap.

Until the 1990s Slovak hip hop was considered an alternative to the ubiquitous airplay of American rock, R&B, and jazz. One early rapping crew was the Rap Steady Crew (1993*) from Kosice, who in 1993 released the first Slovak hip hop album, the gangsta rap influenced *Pozor! Vsade je plno rapu!* (*Beware! Everywhere Is Full of Rap!*) with mostly Slovak language texts, mixed with some urban American vernacular English. Other early crews were Jednotka slovenskej starostlivosti's (Slovak Care Unit, JSS, 1997–), from Prievidza; Názov Stavby (1996*–), from Bratislava; and Trosky (formerly Crabb and Sickle Syndicate, 1992–2003), from Zlaté Moravce. After Trosky disbanded, DJ and rapper Vec (Branislav Kovac, 1976–) pursued a solo career combining rap and pop. By the 2000s, Slovak hip hop had grown in popularity.

The most famous Slovak hip hop artist of this time is the group Kontrafakt (2003–), from Piest'any. Kontrafakt's rapping texts emulate gangsta rap, including its vulgarity. Kontrafakt released four studio albums and collaborated with American rapper, singer, and actor Nate Dogg (Nathaniel Dwayne Hale, 1969–2011), American DJ Premier (aka Preem, Premo, Primo, Christopher Edward Martin, 1966–) of Gang Starr (1986–2003), and Czech producer DJ Wich (Tomas Pechlák, 1978–). In 2006, Kontrafakt's founding member, Rytmus (Patrik Vrbovsky, 1977–), of Slovak and Romani descent and born in Kromeriz, Czechoslovakia, began his successful solo career with his first studio album *Bengoro*, followed by *Král* (*The King*, 2009) and *Fenomén* (*Phenomenon*, 2011). Rytmus's single "Technotronic Flow" peaked at No. 1 on the Slovak singles chart.

Melissa Ursula Dawn Goldsmith

See also: Czech Republic

Further Reading

Barrer, Peter. 2009. "'My White, Blue, and Red Heart': Constructing a Slovak Identity in Rap Music." *Popular Music and Society* 32, no. 1: 59–75.

Barrer, Peter. 2017. "'The Underground Is for Beggars': Slovak Rap at the Center of National Popular Culture." In *Hip Hop at Europe's Edge: Music, Agency, and Social Change*, edited by Milosz Miszczynski and Adriana Helbig, chap. 6. Bloomington: Indiana University Press.

Further Listening

Kontrafakt. 2004. *E.R.A.* Epic.

Slovenia

Slovenia is a Southeastern European country that shares borders with Austria, Croatia, Hungary, and Italy. In 1991, as the result of protests and mass support of a parliamentary democracy, Slovenia was one of the first countries to gain its independence from the Socialist Federative Republic of Yugoslavia. Slovenia's earliest hip hop scenes can be traced as far back as the late 1970s and early 1980s, but it was not until the 1990s that the music became popular. Olympic champion skier Jure Kosir (1972–) popularized hip hop music with his short-lived rap crew Pasji Kartel (1996–2000*), but its 1996 debut album release was preceded by two years by pioneer Ali En (aka Dalaj Eegol, Ali Dzafic, n.d.), who released the popular, energetic *Leva Scena* (*Left Scene*, 1994) on the Macji Disk (1993–2001) label.

Ali En's early songs were rap against hip hop beats, infused with traditional music, American funk, rock, and metal elements, with heavy use of turntables and guitars. Rap duo Dandrough (n.d.), which released *Ko pride bog . . .* (*Who Comes to God*) in 1996 on the Conan label (1995–2001), introduced G-funk beats created by heavy bass and snare- and tom-based drum sounds, combined with synthesizer, looped samples, various character voices, and offbeat vocalized sound effects. Solvenia's first career rapper emerged in 2000, when Ljubljana (the capital and largest city of Slovenia) gruff-voiced rapper KlemenKlemen (aka Klemen de Klemen, Klemen Dvornik*, 1977–), who has been rapping since age 13, released *Trnow stajl* (*Trnow Style*), which featured the hit "Kes Picke" ("What's Up?"), on the Nika label (1990–), the most prolific early record label for Slovenian hip hop. He followed his successful debut with *Hipnoza* (2003) and continues to tour and record as of 2018.

Hip hop did not have an easy start in Slovenia. Breakdancing and hip hop dancing were referred to derogatorily in Slovenia in the 1980s and early 1990s, but by 2001, the first Slovenian freestyle rap championships were being organized. Freestyle competitions launched the career of 6pack Čukur (Bostjan Cukur, 1978–), from Velenje, who released three albums, *Ne se čudit* (*Do Not Be Surprised*, 2001), *Keramicarska lirika* (*Ceramic Lyrics*, 2003), and *GangstaDillaPlayaGorilla* (2009).

Recent hip hop acts originate in either Ljubljana or Maribor (the second-largest city in Slovenia). These include the duo Murat and Jose (2002–), who quickly developed a reputation as clean rappers, with songs that are not about gangs, drugs, or sex; Emkej (Marko Kocjan, n.d.), a solo rapper and member of Tekochee Kru (2007–); Ledeni (aka Denile, Damijan Kovacic, n.d.), a rapper and producer who introduced trap music; N'toko (Miha Blazic, 1980–), a prolific underground rapper and singer known for socially critical lyrics and freestyle abilities in both Slovenian and English, with a music that combines rap with dark electronic, video game, and metal; AMO (2003–), a rap, reggae, and dancehall trio; and Trkaj (Rok Terkaj, 1983–), a theology student turned rapper known for his freestyle. Emkej cofounded Wudisban Records (2012–), which is becoming the label of choice for Slovenian rappers.

Anthony J. Fonseca

See also: G-Funk

Further Reading

Kline, Barbara Majcenovič. 2013. "2pac or 6pack: Slovene Gangsta Rap from a Sociological Perspective." In *Words and Music*, edited by Victor Kennedy and Michelle Gadpaille, chap. 10. Newcastle upon Tyne, England: Cambridge Scholars.

Šabec, Nada. 2013. "The Influence of English on Slovene Rap Lyrics." In *Words and Music*, edited by Victor Kennedy and Michelle Gadpaille, chap. 9. Newcastle upon Tyne, England: Cambridge Scholars.

Further Listening

Ali En. 1994. *Leva Scena* (*Left Scene*). Mačji Disk.

N'toko. 2010. *Parada Ljubezni* (*The Parade of Love*). Beton Records.

Smif-N-Wessun

(aka Cocoa Brovaz, 1993–, Brooklyn, New York)

Smif-N-Wessun is a hip hop duo consisting of rappers Tek (Tekomin B. Williams, 1973–) and Steele (Darrell A. Yates Jr., n.d.), who were both from Brooklyn, New York. Tek and Steele are two of the eight members in the Brooklyn-based hip hop supergroup Boot Camp Clik (1993–). Their music is unique for its use of smooth jazz rhythm (horns, bass, high hats) backgrounds against which the duo rap, often with some type of foregrounded instrument more indicative of rap music, such as turntables. Both Tek and Steele match their rapping against the rhythm track, so that the rap becomes part of the music's rhythm, and in many cases is the driving force behind an individual song's rhythm (in other words, songs are differentiated more by the rap rhythms than by the rhythm section). Other qualities of their sound include a tendency to prioritize an atmospheric sound, soft dynamics, and low pitches; a combining of drug culture and gangsta rap motifs, and the occasional use of Jamaican patois.

As Smif-N-Wessun, Tek and Steele debuted on the Brooklyn-based hip hop group Black Moon's (1992–2006, 2011–) 1993 album *Enta da Stage*, appearing on two tracks. They released a single, "Bucktown," in early 1994, and it peaked at No. 93 on the Billboard Hot 100, also reaching No. 14 on the rap chart. This helped the Smif-N-Wessun market its debut album, *Dah Shinin'* (1995), which peaked in the top 5 in the Top R&B/Hip-Hop Albums chart and became an influential album in the hardcore New York hip hop scene. In 1996, the duo changed its name to Cocoa Brovaz when the Smith and Wesson firearms manufacturer threatened to sue them. Also, as part of the Boot Camp Clik, Tek and Steele were going to collaborate on an album with Death Row Records' (1991–2008) Tupac Shakur (1971–1996), but the project fell through.

In 1998, as Cocoa Brovaz, the duo released *The Rude Awakening*, but its sales were moderate. The duo appeared on a number of compilation albums over the next few years, and finally, in 2005, Tek and Steele returned as Smif-N-Wessun with *Smif 'n' Wessun: Reloaded*. The duo's fourth album, *Smif-N-Wessun: The Album*, was released in 2007. Its fifth album, *Monumental*, was a collaboration with producer/rapper Pete Rock, released in 2011 on Duck Down Music (1995–). In 2013, the duo returned to its earlier Jamaican sound and released a reggae-inspired EP, *Born and Raised*, also on the Duck Down label. As a solo artist, Steele has released two mixtapes, *Amerikkka's Nightmare* (2004) and *Hotstyle Takeover* (2007), and two albums, *Welcome to Bucktown* (2009) and *Amerikkka's Nightmare, Pt. 2* (2010); Tek has released no solo albums but has produced three mixtapes, *It Is What It Is: The Street Album* (2003), *I Got This* (2006), and *Underground Prince* (2009).

Anthony J. Fonseca

See also: Jamaica; Reggae; The United States

Further Reading

Cramer, Jennifer, and Jill Hallett. 2010. "From Chi-Town to the Dirty-Dirty: Regional Identity Markers in U.S. Hip Hop." Chap. 10 in *The Languages of Global Hip Hop*, edited by Marina Terkourafi. New York: Continuum.

French, Kenneth. 2017. "Geography of American Rap: Rap Diffusion and Rap Centers." *GeoJournal* 82, no. 2: 259–72.

Marshall, Wayne. 2005. "Hearing Hip Hop's Jamaican Accent." *Newsletter—Institute for Studies in American Music* 34, no. 2: 8–9, 14–15.

Smith, Christopher Holmes. 1997. "Method in the Madness: Exploring the Boundaries of Identity in Hip Hop Performativity." *Social Identities: Journal for the Study of Race, Nation, and Culture* 3, no. 3: 345–74.

Further Listening

Smif-N-Wessun. 1995. *Dah Shinin'.* Wreck Records.

Smith, Will

(Willard Carroll Smith Jr., 1968–, Philadelphia, Pennsylvania)

Will Smith is best known as one of Hollywood's most bankable actors and producers, but he began his career as a rapper and songwriter known as the Fresh Prince. His early style, which featured lighthearted storytelling of everyday life and inoffensive lyrics, found popularity with mainstream audiences, and this led to a successful television show, *The Fresh Prince of Bel-Air* (1990–1996), whose rap theme song he performed and co-composed, and later a Hollywood career. Since the mid-1990s, Smith has been one of the world's most successful actors, having starred in some of the highest grossing films of all time. As of 2018, he continues to produce occasional hip hop recordings.

SUCCESS IN HIP HOP, TELEVISION, AND FILM

Smith was born into a middle-class family in West Philadelphia's Wynnefield neighborhood, where in 1985 he met DJ Jazzy Jeff (Jeffrey Allen Townes, 1965–), who was performing alone at a house party. Smith originally served as his hype man, and based on their strong connection, the pair soon joined with Smith's friend, beatboxer Ready Rock C (Clarence Holmes, 1968–), to form DJ Jazzy Jeff and the Fresh Prince (1985–1994). The trio's first single, "Girls Ain't Nothing but Trouble," was issued by the local Word Up label (1986–1987), and the success of that recording led to a contract with Jive Records (1981–2011) and the release of their first album, *Rock the House* (1987).

Their follow-up album, *He's the DJ, I'm the Rapper* (1988), was the first double-disc hip hop release on vinyl, and with triple-Platinum sales, is the group's most popular work. The second single from that album, "Parents Just Don't Understand" (1988), won the first ever Grammy Award for Best Rap Performance (1989). The group's growing success, especially with mainstream audiences, led to the perception, beginning with *And in This Corner . . .* (1989), that they had sold out artistically, but the album reached Gold status.

Smith neglected his finances and owed the IRS $2.8 million in back taxes, so he accepted an offer from NBC to star in a situation comedy based on his Fresh Prince persona. *The Fresh Prince of Bel Air* introduced hip hop to audiences in middle America, which also grew to like the show's theme song and Smith's Fresh Prince character. By 1993, with his first major role in the American drama film *Six Degrees of Separation*, Smith had begun turning toward a film acting career. Smith broke through as a motion picture star in the blockbusters *Independence Day* (1996) and *Men in Black* (1997).

Meanwhile, Ready Rock C left the group, so Smith recorded two additional albums with DJ Jazzy Jeff alone, before releasing his own debut solo album on the Columbia label, *Big Willie Style* (1997), which would be his most successful commercial effort. The album's release was preceded by a single tied to the motion picture *Men in Black*, a marketing strategy used on the subsequent album, *Willenium* (1999), and the title track from the motion picture *Wild Wild West* (1999).

His subsequent solo albums were *Born to Reign* (2002) and *Lost and Found* (2005). Though both of these albums charted on the Billboard 200, they were met with mixed critical reception. Some have criticized Smith's later albums for their pop-friendly approach to hip hop, but strong album sales suggest that Smith is a performer beyond the reach of critics.

At the same time, Smith's acting career reached critical acclaim: He was nominated for Academy Awards for his starring roles in *Ali* (2001) and *The Pursuit of Happyness* (2006). He has also been nominated for five Golden Globe awards.

Both of Smith's children have emerging careers in entertainment. His son, Jaden Smith (1998–), has appeared with his father in *The Pursuit of Happyness* and *After Earth* (2013). In 2010, Smith's daughter, Willow Smith (2000–), signed on Jay-Z's (1969–) label Roc Nation (2008–), and her hip hop and pop hit "Whip My Hair" peaked at No. 11 on the Billboard Hot 100.

Scott Warfield

See also: DJ Jazzy Jeff; Filmmaking (Feature Films Made in the United States); The United States

Further Reading

Corrigan, Jim. 2007. *Will Smith.* Philadelphia: Mason Crest Publishers.

Palmer, Lorrie. 2011. "Black Man/White Machine: Will Smith Crosses Over." *Velvet Light Trap: A Critical Journal of Film and Television* 67 (Spring): 28–40.

Further Listening

DJ Jazzy Jeff and the Fresh Prince. 1988. *He's the DJ, I'm the Rapper.* Jive.

Smith, Will. 1997. *Big Willie Style.* Columbia.

Snap

Snap is a hip hop musical style derived from crunk and popularized in the early-to mid-2000s Atlanta hip hop musical style derived from crunk. Snap became mainstream and popular for a short time between 2005 and 2007 but declined shortly thereafter. Popular snap artists included D4L (2003–2006), whose single "Laffy Taffy" topped the Billboard Hot 100 chart in 2006. The song appeared on D4L's debut album *Down for Life* (2005), which reached No. 22 on the Billboard 200 and No. 4 on the Top R&B/Hip-Hop Albums chart.

"Laffy Taffy" is a sex song that has a textbook snap beat created by a melodic loop displaced by an octave—a series of three notes/beats on a synthesizer—with a muted bass kick accompaniment and a finger snap on the third synthesizer note/beat that reverbs to become part of the fourth beat, which is bass kick with the snap decay, while the synthesizer rests; this is repeated over and over with slight variation where the synthesizer disappears and the bass kick and snap carry the beat. The simplicity of the song, like the snap genre itself, was its appeal, and "Laffy Taffy" became a multi-Platinum hit.

POPULARITY

The banner year for snap music was 2006, with hits such as "Lean wit It, Rock wit It" by Dem Franchize Boys (2002–2012); "Do It To It," by Cherish (2003–); and "Snap Yo Fingers," by Lil Jon (Jonathan Smith, 1971–); all Atlanta-based acts. Earlier in 2004, Dem Franchize Boyz signed to Universal Music Group (1996–) and released a self-titled debut album with hit single "White Tee," but the group's biggest hit was "Lean wit It, Rock wit It" from the album *On Top of Our Game*, which reached No. 5 on the Billboard 200 and No. 2 on Billboard's Top R&B/Hip-Hop Albums chart. The song was the band's only Top 10 hit, reaching No. 7 on the Billboard Hot 100 and No. 2 on Billboard's R&B/Hip-Hop Songs chart. It features the ubiquitous snap Roland TR-808 bass drum kick, snapping on the third beat (followed by a bass kick on the fourth beat), a synthesizer produced clicking percussion sound, and synthesized strings that produce the song's dramatic atmosphere and main groove. As with "Laffy Taffy," vocals take the form of repetitive group chants alternated with solo raps.

Female snap rap group Cherish had a hit single with "Do It to It," from the album *Unappreciated*, which reached No. 4 on the Billboard 200. The song was the band's biggest hit, reaching No. 12 on the Billboard Hot 100 and the Top 10 on Billboard's Hot R&B/Hip-Hop Songs chart. Unlike many snap songs, it features handclaps more prominently than snaps; these are set against a bass kick and synthesizer groove that is mainly soft strings.

Lil Jon's "Snap Yo Fingers" features a catchy, uptempo rhythm. It peaked at No. 7 on the Billboard Hot 100 and topped the Hot R&B/Hip-Hop Songs chart. The song is slightly more complex than most snap music, as its main groove is created by a quick, rhythmic, synthesizer progression of notes displaced by an octave that pan from left to right as they are getting higher, and against this groove the typical kick bass and finger snap beat is juxtaposed, but an ostinato played on the triangle is added. The effect is the impression that the music constantly builds in intensity, which works well against Lil Jon's gruff vocals and grunts. Lyrics, however, are chantlike and simple, as with most snap hits.

BEYOND 2006 AND SNAP'S DECLINE

Other Atlanta-based snap hits included the Grammy nominated "It's Goin' Down" by Yung Joc (Jasiel Amon Robinson, 1983–) and the multi-Platinum Grammy nominated "Crank That (Soulja Boy)" by Soulja Boy Tell 'Em (DeAndre Cortez Way, 1990–), which spent seven weeks at No. 1 on the Billboard Hot 100 in 2007. "It's Goin' Down" is a character song that features a gangsta style synthesized loop and heavier bass, with both 808 drums and snaps; "Crank That (Soulja Boy)" is a dance song known for its steel drum loop, which is played against 808 drums, snaps, a heavy bass kick, and synthesized orchestral stingers (for dramatic effect).

In 2008, V.I.C. (Victor Grimmy Owusu, 1987–) released a hit snap single called "Get Silly." Both snap song and snap parody, it peaked at No. 29 on the Billboard Hot 100 and was certified Gold. The song's groove is a series of orchestral stingers and heavy bass kick, with snaps being distorted to sound like nutshells cracking, and a melodic loop based on a minor scale, reminiscent of the opening of the *Inspector Gadget* theme played on a toy piano.

Snap artists not from Atlanta include two hip hop groups from Texas, Arlington's GS Boyz (2005–2012) and Dallas's Trap Starz Clik (2007–), and two from Georgia, College Park's Mr. Collipark (Michael Crooms, 1970–) and Decatur's Nitti (Chadron S. Moore, n.d.). After 2008, snap music lost its commercial viability.

Anthony J. Fonseca

See also: Crunkcore; Dirty South; The United States

Further Reading

Grem, Darren E. 2006. "'The South Got Something to Say': Atlanta's Dirty South and the Southernization of Hip Hop America." *Southern Cultures* 12, no. 4: 55–73.

Miller, Matt. 2004. "Rap's Dirty South: From Subculture to Pop Culture." *Journal of Popular Music Studies* 16, no. 2: 175–212.

Sanneh, Kelefa. 2006. "'Laffy Taffy': So Light, So Sugary, So Downloadable." *The New York Times*, January 12, E1.

Snoop Dogg

(aka Snoop Lion, Snoop Doggy Dogg, Calvin Cordozar Broadus Jr., 1971–, Long Beach, California)

Snoop Dogg is highly influential and prolific pioneering American rapper and singer-songwriter who later became a record producer, actor, and television personality. Snoop Dogg's musical sound recording output includes 15 studio albums that have all charted on the Billboard 200, including the Top 10 *No Limit Top Dogg* (1999), *Paid tha Cost to Be da Boss* (2002), *R&G (Rhythm & Gangsta): The Masterpiece*

(2004), *Tha Blue Carpet Treatment* (2006), *Ego Trippin'* (2008), *Doggumentary* (2011) and three No. 1's, *Doggystyle* (1993), *Tha Doggfather* (1996), and *Da Game Is to Be Sold* (1998). Seven of his albums reached Platinum or multi-Platinum status, and two Gold. Snoop Dogg's singles have crossed over into mainstream popularity, with Billboard Hot 100 charting hits that included "What's My Name?" and "Gin and Juice" (both 1993), "Still a G Thang" (1998), "Beautiful" (2003), "Drop It Like It's Hot" (2004), and "Sexual Eruption" (2007). Snoop Dogg's prolific recording output also includes 17 compilation albums, 20 mixtapes, one EP, 14 promotional singles, and many appearances and collaborations with internationally renown hip hop artists. His success has also enabled him to record music in other genres. In 2012, he became Snoop Lion, converted to Rastafari, and recorded the reggae album *Reincarnated* (2013). Since 2015, he has returned to using the name Snoop Dogg.

MUSICAL SUCCESS AND MURDER TRIAL

Born Calvin Broadus, he took an interest in singing and playing piano while attending church. He started songwriting and rapping by sixth grade, but he also started got involved in the from Long Beach's Eastside Rollin' 20 Crips gang. After graduating high school, he was arrested for cocaine possession and served some prison time in the early 1990s. When he was at home, he recorded and formed the trio 213 (1990–2011), named after the Los Angeles, California telephone area code with his cousin, rapper Nate Dogg (Nathaniel Dwayne Hale, 1969–2011), and best friend, rapper and producer Warren G (Warren Griffin III, 1970–). His freestyle rapping caught the attention of Dr. Dre (Andre Romelle Young, 1965–), a founding member of N.W.A. (1986–1991) and co-owner and coproducer of Death Row Records (1991–). In 1992, after an invitation to audition from Dr. Dre, he signed on with Death Row and took the stage name Snoop Doggy Dogg (based on Snoopy, his childhood nickname).

The two began working together, and Snoop Doggy Dogg showed great potential in rhyming, lyrics, and delivery (a smooth, laid-back style), in addition to having a low tenor voice. Dr. Dre had N.W.A. collaborator and Death Row cofounder the D.O.C. (aka Doc T, Tracy Lynn Curry, 1968–) work with Snoop Doggy Dogg on lyrical and musical structure, forming hooks and choruses, and creating theme-based verses. Snoop Doggy Dogg quickly became a central pioneer of West Coast G-funk hip hop, first working on a theme song for the feature crime film drama *Deep Cover*, as well as on Dr. Dre's debut solo album, *The Chronic* (both 1992). At this time, Dr. Dre created Tha Dogg Pound (1992–2002, 2005–), a rapping duo with Kurupt (Ricardo Emmanuel Brown, 1972–) and Daz N—ga Daz (aka Daz Dillinger, Delmar Drew Arnaud, 1973–), who appeared on *The Chronic* as well as on Snoop Doggy Dogg's debut studio album *Doggystyle* (1993). The latter also featured 213, who had a minor hit with "Ain't No Fun (If the Homies Can't Have None)." *Doggystyle* topped Billboard's Top R&B/Hip-Hop Albums chart and a year later was certified quadruple Platinum. Its strongest hit singles were "Gin and Juice," which peaked at Nos. 52 and 73, respectively, on Billboard's Hot 100 and

R&B/Hip-Hop Songs charts, and "What's My Name," which peaked at Nos. 62 and 75, respectively, on the same charts. The album was not only a G-funk classic; Snoop Doggy Dogg's soft spoken, smooth sound, as well as contrasting lyrical content about his mother, added depth and dimension to G-funk, which was still being criticized for its foul language, misogyny, and violence.

Toward the end of recording *Doggystyle*, however, Snoop Doggy Dogg—who underwent his first name change to Snoop Dogg—was arrested in 1993 for his connection to the murder of rival gang member Philip Woldemariam (n.d.), who was shot to death by Snoop Dogg's bodyguard McKinley Lee (n.d.). Defended by Johnnie Cochran (1937–2005), who became famous for his work on the defense and acquittal of O.J. Simpson (1947–), both Snoop Dogg and Lee were acquitted, though had legal battles into 1996—the same year Snoop Dogg recorded *Tha Doggfather* and Death Row's dominance of the rap charts would come to an end with the death of Tupac Shakur (1971–1996). Dr. Dre and Snoop Dogg eventually left the label because of Death Row cofounder Suge Knight's (Marion Hugh Knight Jr., 1965–) public feuding with hip hop artists such as Luke (1960–) and Puff Daddy (1969–).

In 1998, Snoop Dogg signed with Master P's (1970–) No Limit Records (1990–2003), which ultimately enabled him to focus on launching his own label, Doggystyle Records (aka Dogghouse Records, 1995–), a business that Snoop Dogg established just before his own legal issues. Meanwhile, Death Row continued to release some of Snoop Dogg's final work there, including the successful compilation album with *Death Row: Snoop Doggy Dogg at His Best* (2001), as well as an 18-minute short film *Murder Was the Case* (based on his murder trial, 1994) starring Snoop Dogg, with a soundtrack supervised by Dr. Dre. This practice, including releasing recordings by Tha Dogg Pound, was continued into the 2000s, long after Death Row went bankrupt in 2006 (the lawsuit led to a two-million-dollar loss for Snoop Dogg). Death Row became part of the Global Music Group (aka Global Music Entertainment, 2008–), and in 2009 it released *Death Row: The Lost Sessions, Vol. 1* with Snoop Dogg's recordings from 1993 to 1997. With No Limit, Snoop Dogg continued his success with three albums: *Da Game Is to Be Sold, Not to Be Told* (1998), *No Limit Top Dogg* (1999), and *Tha Last Meal* (2000). Doggystyle Records released *Snoop Dogg Presents Tha Eastsidaz* (2000), with his trio Eastsidaz (1997–2004, 2014–), as well as Eastsidaz *Duces 'n Trayz: The Old Fashioned Way* (2001), and the promo single *Loosen Control* (2001). Though his recording career remained prolific, Snoop Dogg's venture with his label and his intent to use it to support other rappers came to fruition for just a brief time. One issue was that Eastsidaz—consisting of Snoop Dogg, Big Tray Deee (Tracy Lamar Davis, 1966–), and Goldie Loc (Keiwan Deshawn Spillman, 1980–)—was under contract with Virgin Records (1972–).

In 2012, Snoop Dogg announced a name change to Snoop Lion and a new career as a reggae artist after a trip to Jamaica. Previously, he had been a member of the Nation of Islam (NOI). In 2013, he released *Reincarnated*. That same year, a documentary film with the same title was released, which focused on Snoop Dogg's conversion to Rastafarianism. The name and career change was short-lived, and three years later with *Bush* (2015), he announced changing his name back to Snoop Dogg; he began recording West Coast style hip hop again.

SUPPORT OF OTHER ARTISTS, PERFORMANCE PRACTICE, AND ENDEAVORS BEYOND MUSIC

Despite a prolific recording career, Snoop Dogg often tours and supports other hip hop artists beyond just lending his name and escalating sales. Snoop Dogg appeared on *The Art of Storytelling*, Slick Rick's (1965–) comeback studio album, which became Slick Rick's most successful album, peaking at No. 8 on the Billboard 200 and No. 1 of the Billboard's Top R&B/Hip-Hop Albums chart. He has supported and collaborated with Pharrell (1973–) numerous times, including having Pharrell's label Star Trak Entertainment (2001–) corelease Snoop Dogg's *R & G*. He also appeared dancing the Crip Walk in Pharrell's "Drop It Like It's Hot" (2004) music video. Thai American hip hop group Thaitanium's (2000–) 2014 remix of his "Wake Up (Bangkok City)" from *Tha Doggfather* features Snoop Dogg in the recording and video, and he appeared on Thaitanium's 2014 U.S. tour.

His concert appearances and recordings are a combination of previously written and memorized rap and freestyle lyrics. The latter is Snoop Dogg's strength—impressive for line length, internal rhymes, alliteration, and an unshakable laidback delivery. Though he is from Long Beach, Snoop Dogg's rapping voice has a drawl; all these attributes, in addition to content, made Snoop Dogg influential to Southern rap. Known for making impromptu appearances in intimate venues, Snoop Dogg also tends to work to form a rapport with his audience through simply talking with them, improvising by incorporating their involvement in a rap performance, or through call-and-response.

In 2009, Priority Records appointed Snoop Dogg as creative chairman. He appeared on film and television with main roles in the American motion pictures *The Wrecking Crew* (1999), *Bones* (2001), *The Wash* (2001), *The Tenants* (2005), *Mac & Devin Go to High School* (2012), and *Dispensary* (2015). A large part of Snoop Dogg's image involves cannabis smoking. In 2007, he was certified for medical marijuana to treat migraines. He has used this image and his advocacy to become an investor in the California-based medical marijuana delivery business, Eaze, in 2015. That same year, he established a digital media business, Merry Jane, which presents news about marijuana in addition to another business, Leafs by Snoop, which sells cannabis products. In 2016, Snoop Dogg bought the soul food chain Roscoe's House of Chicken and Waffles out of bankruptcy.

Melissa Ursula Dawn Goldsmith

See also: Crip Walk; Dirty South; Dr. Dre; Gangs (United States); Gangsta Rap; Slick Rick; The United States

Further Reading

Gosa, Travis L. 2015. "The Fifth Element: Knowledge." In *The Cambridge Companion to Hip Hop*, edited by Justin Williams, chap. 5. Cambridge, England: Cambridge University Press.

Oliver Wang. 2003. "Dr. Dre: *The Chronic*; Snoop Doggy Dogg: *Doggystyle*." In *Classical Material: The Hip Hop Album Guide*, edited by Oliver Wang, pp. 57–59. Toronto: ECW Press.

Quinn, Eithne. 2005. *Nuthin' but a G Thang: The Culture and Commerce of Gangsta Rap*. New York: Columbia University Press.

Westhoff, Ben. 2016. *Original Gangstas: The Untold Story of Dr. Dre, Eazy-E, Ice Cube, Tupac Shakur, and the Birth of West Coast Rap.* New York: Hachette Books.

Further Listening
Snoop Dogg. 1993. *Doggystyle.* Death Row.
Snoop Dogg. 2004. *R & G (Rhythm & Gangsta): The Masterpiece.* Geffen.

Somalia

Somalia is a Northeastern African country that gained its independence from the United Kingdom in 1960 originally as the Somali Republic (1960–1969), unifying people living in former British and Italian Somalilands. But hostilities flared, leading to Somali nationalism, ethnic tensions, and violent power struggles. In 1969, a coup d'état led to the dictatorship of general Mohamed Siad Barre (1910–1995, in office 1969–1991), who began suppressing music, so hip hop had no presence in the early to mid-1980s, and as of 2018, more research on 1990s Somali hip hop needs to be conducted; however, Somali culture has historically placed emphasis on music and poetry. In point of fact, Somalia is nicknamed the "Nation of Bards" or the "Nation of Poets."

Traditional music includes Somali folklore (folksongs) and *dhaanto* (urban dance songs), with Arabic influences. Popular music includes protest songs, *balwo* (passionate love songs combined with poetry), and Somali blues, with influences from American and pan-African jazz, Afrobeat, Jamaican reggae, and American funk. Radio and television disseminated popular music in Somali, Arabic, and English with stations from Hargeisa and Somalia's capital city, Mogadishu. By the 1970s, Somali popular music included a fusion known as Somali funk. Though hip hop was not part of the mainstream, protest songs against the Siad Barre regime were recorded, and many musicians therefore departed to escape punishment.

Growing resistance to the Siad-Barre regime led to the Somali Civil War (1986–), which continues (as of 2018) despite the 1990 defeat of the Siad-Barre regime; regional forces and clan militias compete for power still. The Somali Civil War has led to diaspora, and virtually all Somali hip hop is a diasporic musical activity. The most famous Somali rapper is K'naan (1978–), a singer-songwriter and poet from Mogadishu, who is based in Toronto. K'naan raps in English and Somali, and some of his lyrical content focuses on Somalia, the war, and refugees. K'naan's aunt was the singer Magool (Halima Khaliif Omar, 1948–2004), a traditional Somali singer known for patriotic songs during the Ethio-Somali War (aka the Ogaden War, 1977–1778), love songs, and Islamic protest songs against the late 1970s Somali government. She left Somalia in self-imposed exile.

The duo Malitia Malimob (Militia of Griots, 2011*–) formed in Seattle and raps about the Somali immigrant experience in the United States, including stereotyping. The hip hop collective Waayaha Cusub (New Era, 2002–) was formed by Somali expatriates in Nairobi, Kenya. Female singer-rapper Falis Abdi (1989–) leads the collective. As of 2018, Waayaha Cusub is based in London and belongs to the music initiative "I'm with the Banned," which protests the travel bans proposed in 2017 by United States president Donald Trump (1946–, in office 2017–).

Ethiopian-born Somali English singer-songwriter, multi-instrumentalist, producer, and actor Aar Maanta (Hassan-Nour Sayid, n.d.) performs and records a fusion of R&B, pop, and hip hop, with traditional Somali music. Further examples of hip hop artists of Somali descent are message rapper and singer-songwriter OMVR (aka Omar, Omar Mohamed Ahmed, 1988*–), from Norway, and pop, hip hop, electronica, and jazz singer-songwriter, multi-instrumentalist and producer Mocky (Dominic Salole, 1974–), from Canada.

Melissa Ursula Dawn Goldsmith

See also: K'Naan

Further Reading

K'naan. 2011. "A Son Returns to the Agony of Somalia." *The New York Times*, September 25, SR5.

Sobral, Ana. 2013. "The Survivor's Odyssey: K'naan's 'The Dusty Foot Philosopher' as Modern Epic." *African American Review* 46, no. 1: 21–36.

Further Listening

K'naan. 2006. *The Dusty Foot Philosopher.* Sony BMG Music Entertainment Canada.

South Africa

South Africa is located at the southern tip of the continent Africa. It borders both the Atlantic and Indian Oceans, as well as Botswana, Mozambique, Namibia, Swaziland, and Zimbabwe. South Africa also surrounds Lesotho, which won its own independence from the United Kingdom in 1966. Though its largest city is Johannesburg (nicknamed Jozi), South Africa has three capital cities: Pretoria (executive); Cape Town (legislative); and Bloemfontein (judicial). Its population of 55 million consists of a vast majority of black Africans and minorities of whites (who are either descendants of Afrikaners, Anglophones, or other Europeans), Indians and racially mixed populations still self-identify as "coloureds." By the early 1980s, American hip hop arrived in these large cities; however, for political, economic, and cultural reasons, it was unable to gain immediate popularity there. For the same reasons, South African hip hop has also had challenges with its emergence and development. Artists faced the challenge of either using English to reach large audiences or a South African language (sometimes mixed with some American vernacular). But unlike other countries that could resolve the issue by opting for a native common language or a regional vernacular, South Africa has so many spoken languages from which to choose. For artists opting to use a South African language, the question became which language(s) to use.

Languages in South African hip hop mirror the country's language diversity: The most spoken languages are Zulu, Xhosa, and Afrikaans, followed by English. Other recognized spoken languages include Khoe, Lobedu, Nama, Northern Ndebele, Northern Sotho, Phuthi, San, Tswana, Sesotho, Southern Ndebele, Swati, Tsonga, and Venda. Fanagalo (based on Zulu and some Afrikaans) is just one example of several kinds of pidgin English languages spoken. Not only do South Africans often speak an English influenced by Afrikaans; spoken English there often sounds much closer to British English than American English. For those from elsewhere, it is easy to mistake South African pidgin English for British English.

Another backdrop to South African hip hop is the country's lengthy history as a victim of European colonialism that reached its height in between the late 19th to early 20th centuries. Though first explored by the Portuguese in the 1400s, Dutch and English colonization did not begin until the early 1600s. Anglo-Dutch rivalries for power led to conflicts in South Africa that included the Anglo-Zulu War (1879), which led to the end of an independent Zulu nation, and the First and Second Anglo-Boer Wars (1880–1881 and 1899–1902); both were mainly between England and Boers (descendants of Dutch-speaking Cape settlers). In addition, German rule and colonialism took place in western South Africa (including Namibia) much later, starting in 1884 until South Africa, backed by the United Kingdom, defeated German forces at the end of World War I (1914–1918). South Africa contributed to fighting on the Allied Forces' side during World War II (1939–1945), despite internal pressure from nationalists who were Nazi sympathizers.

By the late 20th century, South African government's institutionalization and brutal enforcement of Apartheid (meaning separateness in Afrikaans, 1948–1991), a white nationalist system of laws and policies that violated human rights with its severe racial segregation and imposed violence against blacks and its disenfranchisement of black voters, received worldwide criticism and economic sanctions. During this time, many black South Africans lived in exile in other countries while others faced poor living standards, crime, and police brutality in segregated township ghettos (e.g., Soweto in Johannesburg) or within the homeland system of separate states (each one was called a *Bantustan* or black state). Botswana and Swaziland were also vulnerable to South Africa's economic and political pressures, though Lesotho opposed apartheid and became home to black South African refugees. In 1990, Namibia declared independence from South Africa, which applied apartheid there as well. Global economic and political pressure brought the end of apartheid and the Bantustans by 1994, less than a year after the country's first democratic election of a South African president (Nelson Mandela, 1918–2013).

Colonialism, white nationalism, and European immigration contributed to a European influence on traditional and popular South African music. Since the 19th century, some American influence on music took place through cultural exchanges with South Africa and the West Indies. Black South Africans responding against European colonialism embraced black-identified American music such as jazz, soul, funk, rock, and ultimately hip hop. Reggae from Jamaica has also been a favorite kind of South African popular music and remains influential on the comparatively gentle sound of South American hip hop.

Though American hip hop arrived by the early 1980s, South Africa's late-20th-century political history affected how the music was received and how its own hip hop developed. During President P. W. Botha's (1916–2006) last years in office, South Africa was on one hand facing alienation for apartheid and related human rights violations that ultimately included harsh globally imposed economic sanctions, while on the other hand philanthropic efforts responded to the plight of apartheid's victims and South Africa's extreme poverty. American artists also found ways to relate to victims of apartheid. For example, Chicago-born Gil Scott-Heron (Gilbert Scott-Heron, 1949–2011) released several recordings that addressed apartheid in South Africa, criticizing how the United States was lacking in its handling of racial issues. Examples of this kind of lyrical content are found in *From South Africa to South Carolina* and the single "Johannesburg" (1979). Other artists who responded include alternative hip hop group A Tribe Called Quest (ATCQ, 1985–1998, 2006–2013, 2015–), who recorded "Steve Biko (Stir It Up)" (1993), titled after the slain anti-apartheid and South African human rights activist (1946–1977).

South Africa nevertheless had more music studios than all other African countries. Despite its own political turmoil, South Africa was a destination for other African recording artists. In addition, the establishment of RiSA (Recording Industry of South Africa, formerly Association of the South African Music Industry) in the 1970s helped create South Africa's own promising popular music industry. But, because of economic sanctions, South Africans interested in creating music had extremely limited access to the kind music technology that was being used in American hip hop.

EARLY HIP HOP

Pioneering hip hop was an underground activity centered in Cape Flats, the poor outskirts of Cape Town. Breakdancing and graffiti occurred first, followed by music. By the mid 1980s Soweto, in Johannesburg, became the other prominent scene, followed in the 1990s by Durban, Grahamstown, Port Elizabeth, and the diamond mining town, Kimberley.

Two of South Africa's earliest Cape Town acts were Black Noise (formerly Chill Convention, 1986*–) and Prophets of da City (aka POC, 1988–2001). Both were inspired by old-school American hip hop and focused on guarded political conscious hip hop—creating message rap through metaphor, coding, and addressing serious subject matter through using lighthearted humor. In 1990, POC released its debut studio album, *Our World*, which became the country's first hip hop release. POC rapped in English and Cape slang (an Afrikaans dialect) on the album. The band also employed South African music such as *mbaqanga* (black urban music with Zulu roots). In 1992, Black Noise, fronted and cofounded by pioneering b-boy and rapper Emile YX? (Emile Lester Jansen, 1968–), released its debut studio album, *Pumpin' Loose da Juice*.

Despite South Africa's alienation and political suppression of lyrical content, these early hip hop acts managed to attain international exchange and attention. POC toured extensively, was involved in an antidrug campaign geared toward South Africa's youth, and, after its 1991 release "Ons Stem" ("Our Voice")—an ahead-of-its-time attack on the racist apartheid national anthem "Die stem" ("The Voice") and government censorship for its music video "Kicking Non Stop" (1991), POC played for the 1992 Montreaux Jazz Festival in Switzerland as invited guests of Quincy Jones (1933–). In 1993, Emile YX? participated in Universal Zulu Nation's (1973–) Twentieth Anniversary event in New York City in an effort to share South African hip hop with Americans. In 1994, Emile YX?, also a schoolteacher, and members of Black Noise supported South Africa's democratization and participated in voters' education.

EMERGENCE OF KWAITO AND MOTSWAKO

Mandela's election sparked the acceptance of hip hop into the mainstream. In 1994, POC performed "Excellent, the First Black President" at Mandela's inauguration. Just a couple years prior to this performance, Ku Shu Shu Records (1990–1991), which was formed and became the Johannesburg label, Ghetto Ruff (1991–), emerged as the nation's largest independent South African label that focuses on hip hop.

Post-Mandela hip hop was diverse yet splintered because of multiple languages and competing music cultures. Famous Cape Town act 5th Floor (1996–) raps in English, while rap crews Kallitz (pronounced "Coloureds," 1998–) and Brasse Vannie Kaap (BVK, 1996–2006) rap in Afrikaans. Another Cape Town crew, Maniac Squad (1998*–), featured rapper Rattex (Thabo Twetwa, 1981–), who performed in Xhosa, English, and Cape Flats slang. Skwatta Kamp (1996–2009)* from Soweto rapped in English and American vernacular. Skwatta Kamp, the first South African hip hop group to secure a major recording contract, would later have a Platinum-certified album with *Mkhukhu Funkshen* (*Mkhukhu Function*, 2003, *Mkhukhu* is a Zulu name). Skwatta Kamp's Slikour (Siyabonga Metane, 1981–) also had a solo career.

As access to music and music technology began to improve in the mid to late 1990s South African hip hop music exhibited an increasing diversity. For example, Krushed & Sorted (1997–) is a DJ and production duo from Cape Town that performs hip hop, breakbeat, drum-and-bass, electronica, and dubstep. Also from Cape Town was Moodphase5ive (1999–2002), a hip hop, trip hop (downtempo), dubstep, drum-and-bass, and jazz-funk band with members from South Africa and Namibia.

Though rival popular music genres informed each other, they also divided attention and sales. Another urban music, *kwaito*, developed when Soweto-born Arthur Mafokate (Sello Arthur Mafokate, 1962–) had the first kwaito hit in South Africa, "*Kaffir*" (1995). With lyrical content that was far less political than hip hop, kwaito used South African languages that may be known in Botswana, such as Afrikaans, Zulu, and American vernacular English. Kwaito, a subgenre of house music, consisted of some of the same elements as hip hop, but used slowed-down house music beats, drum loops, African music samples, and heavy bass. As South African hip hop began to more explicitly address inequality, poverty, street violence, police brutality, HIV and AIDS, cultural identification, and the ravages of colonialism, kwaito focused on localized gangster topics, partying, and other lighthearted subject matter as a means for escape. Some youth opted for kwaito over hip hop because kwaito was perceived as a truly South African. Others opted for kwaito because some South African youth were critical of the United States' role and responsibility in poor economic conditions that exist in the world.

Ghetto Ruff Records quickly expanded to become the largest kwaito label. The most famous kwaito artists are from Soweto, Cape Town, and Durban. These artists include Boom Shaka (1993–2000), Thebe (Thebe Mogane, 1973–), Mdu Masilela (1970–), Brenda Fassie (aka MaBrrr, 1964–2004), Mandoza (Mduduzi Edmund Tshabalala, 1978–2016), Trompies (1995–), TKZee (TaKe It Eezy, 1996–), Bongo Maffin (1996–), Baphixile (1997*–), and Big Nuz (2002–), Pitch Black Afro (Thulani Ngcobo, n.d.), Zola (Bonginkosi Dlamini, 1981–), and TKZee's Bouga Luv (Kabelo Mabalane, 1976–). Skwatta Kamp's Flabba (Nkululek Habedi, 1977–2015) had a concurrent hip hop and kwaito solo career from 2007 until his death. Kwaito rapper Pitch Black Afro (Thulani Ngcobo, 1976*–) had a certified-Platinum hit album with *Styling Gel* (2004). Kwaito also found popularity in Namibia, Lesotho, and Zimbabwe. In the 2000s, *sghubu*, a hardcore subgenre of kwaito, emerged and was performed by South African artists such as the duo Major League Djz (2008–).

Another kind of music that was a rival to South African hip hop was *motswako*, which emerged in South Africa. *Motswako* is a subgenre of hip hop that emerged in the mid-1990s in Mafikeng (now Mahikeng), a South African major city located near Botswana. Since the late 1990s, motswako has arguably become more popular in Botswana than in South Africa. In point of fact, it was a Motswana MC originally from Francistown, Botswana, Mr T (aka Nomadic, Tebogo Mapine, n.d.), who pioneered motswako (the name is Setswana for mixture, alluding to the use of two languages and the fusion of American hip hop with the gentler Mafikeng musical sound). Since early motswako, rapping texts were mainly in Setswana—a Tswana language that is Botswana's common language, but also spoken by a large population in South Africa. It also employed American vernacular, as well as South African languages such as Zulu, Afrikaans, and Xhosa. Lyrical content includes localized sociopolitical or economic protests and issues such as drug culture; however, some songs focus more on unity, localized pride, romance, objectifying women, partying, acquiring wealth, and self-actualization. Musical characteristics of motswako usually include laid-back yet flowing raps, steady beat (at times four-to-the-floor, reggae-based, Afrocentric, or drum-and-bass beats), turntablism (or turntables as virtual instruments), and limited electronic music in the background to help keep rap in the foreground. Sampling is deemphasized. An early South African motswako artist was rapper and singer-songwriter Hip Hop Pantsula (aka HHP, Jabba, Jabulani Tsambo, 1980–). Other early motswako acts included rapper Khuli Chana (Kulane Morule, 1982–) and Baphixile. The latter started as a kwaito duo, but shifted to motswako. One of the most commercially successful motswako artists was Cashless Society (1999–2006), with members from Johannesburg and Gaborone, Botswana. Post 2000s South African acts are Tuks Senganga (aka Tuks, Tumelo Kapadisa, 1981–), Cassper Nyovest (Refiloe Maele Phoolo, 1990–), Spoek Mathambo (Nthato Mokgata, 1985–), Kuli Chana (Khulane Morule, 1982–), Mo'Molemi (Motiapele Morule, 1981–), iFani (Mzayifani Mzondeleli Boltina, 1985–), JR (Tabure Thabo Bogopa Junior, 1987–), Fifi Cooper (Refilwe Boingotio Mooketsi, 1991–), and Blaklez (Cliff Lesego, n.d.).

Other kinds of South African hip hop is *spaza* (a Cape Town hip hop subgenre that blends Xhosa and township slang) and Kasi Rap (a combination of kwaito and hip hop). Spaza acts include Middle Finga (aka Rhamncwa, Mangaliso Sauka, 1980–) and Manqoba (The Winner, E. Mendu, n.d.).

INTO THE 21st CENTURY

In 2002, *Hype*, a bimonthly magazine devoted to hip hop, was founded to inform and stimulate interest in South African hip hop. Recent acts continue to use many languages. They fuse hip hop with reggae, Afrobeat, R&B, pop, indie rock, jazz, electronica, and other kinds of music. Multiracial crews such as Etc. (2000–) from Cape Town have emerged and so have crunkcore groups such as Jozi (2006–) from Johannesburg, which until 2009 included DJ and producer Bongz (Bongani Fassie, 1985–), the son of singer Brenda Fassie.

Twenty-first-century acts include Snazz D (Julian Du Plessis, 1977–), Raiko (Grant Spreadbury, 1980–), Jack Parow (Zander Tyler, 1982–), Bliksemstraal (Lightning Bolt, Charl van der Westhuizen, 1986–), Anatii (Anathi Mnyango, 1993–), Godessa (2000–), the Constructus Corporation (2002–2003), Tykoon Suit (2002–), and Writers Block (2005–), all from Cape Town; Driemanskap (2001–), Terror MC (Nazeer Abdol, 1985–), and DOOKDOOM (2013–), all from Cape Flats; Black M.O.S.S. (Black Master of Spontaneous Sentences, Phakamisa Blessing Majola, 1986–), DJ C-Live (Clive Tshabalala, 1991–), and Nasty C (David Junior Ngcobo, 1997–), all from Durban; Simphiwe Dana (1980–), QBA (Cuba, Nondumiso "Sharon" Nkosi, 1981–), J-Bux (Jason Fraser, 1982–), and King Daniel (n.d.–2010), all from the Eastern Cape; Imbube (Zulu for Lion, 2000–), Spoek Mathambo (aka MC Einaar, Nthato James Monde Mokgata, 1985–), Kwesta (Senzo Mfundo Vilakazi, 1988–), DJ Speedsta (Lesego Nkaiseng, 1992–), Tweezy (Tumelo Thandokuhle Mathebula, 1992–), the Surreallist'z (2002–), Sake Of Skill (aka SOS, 2003–), WitchcrAft (2007–), Gigi Lamayne (Genesis Gabriella Tina Manney, 1994–), and Shane Eagle (Shane Patrick Hughes, 1996–), of Irish descent, all from Johannesburg; Proverb (Tebogo Thapelo Sidney Thekisho, 1981–), from Kimberley; the Anvils (2006*) from Pretoria; and Kwabulawayo Kraal (formerly OAU, Omnipotent Army Underground, 2000–), Spaceman (Diau Madisha, 1982–), Emtee (Mthembeni Ndevu, 1992–), Saudi Western (2005–2011*), and Robo (aka Robo the Technician, n.d.–2013), all from Soweto.

Johannesburg labels such as Reck Shoppe Tunez (2007–) and CashTime Life (2010–) were formed. CashTime Life with its collective CashTime Fam (2010–) produces and records both hip hop and *skhanda* (a combination of kwaito and HHP-inspired rap). Later skhanda acts include Teargas (2004–2012)* and K.O. (Ntokozo Mdluli, n.d.), both from Soweto. K.O. went solo after being a member of Teargas. Another skhanda act is rapper and producer A.K.A. (Kiernana Jordan Forbes, 1988–) from Cape Town whose albums *Altar Ego* (2011) and *Levels* (2014) were certified as Gold and Platinum, respectively, in South Africa.

As of 2018, the most internationally renown South African hip hop act is the rap-rave group Die Antwoord ("The Answer" in Afrikaans, 2008–) from Cape Town. Formerly MaxNormal.TV (aka Max Normal, 2001–2002, 2005–2008), Die Antwoord raps in Afrikaans and English, as well as a local slang associated with *zef* (a South African counterculture). After signing with the American recording label Interscope Records (1989), the band released the studio albums *O* (2009), *Ten$ion* (2012), *Donker Mag* (2014), and *Mount Ninji and da Nice Time Kid* (2016). The band's visual image is intentionally shocking and edgy with odd contact lenses (e.g., blacked-out eyes or yellow ones with dollar signs for pupils), grills, multiple tattoos and piercings, and odd costumes, and Die Antwoord's music uses foulmouthed lyrics rapped over catchy musical motifs and infectious beats, fusing hip hop with rave elements. Lyrical content ranges from chaotic absurd parodies of South African *zef* stereotypes to honed harsh criticism of major players in the American-dominated music industry, such as Lady Gaga (Stefani Joanne Angelina Germanotta, 1986–).

INFLUENCE AND DIASPORA ACTS

South Africa has contributed to the nation's influence on music not only in neighboring countries, but also farther-away countries that underwent political strife and suppression of music. For example, the country offered safety and a starting point for Angolan hip hop during the Angolan Civil War (1975–2002). These acts include Mutu Moxy (now Intelektu, aka Genio Lyricista, n.d.), Tribo Sul (Tribe of Soldiers, 1995*–), and Jamayka Poston (1976–). From Sierra Leone, singer-songwriter, rapper, actor, radio host, sound recording producer, and film producer and director Jimmy B (Jimmy Yeani Bangura, n.d.) began his successful music career in Johannesburg before returning to Freetown, where he established Paradise Records (2000–). In addition, the Zimbabwean-Zambian act the Innovators (2000–), was formed in Grahamstown, on the Eastern Cape. Neighboring Namibian hip hop and kwaito artists have also recorded in South Africa to introduce themselves to a much larger music industry. These acts include Gini Grindith (Dave Coxall, 1979–) and EeS (Eric Sell, 1983–).

Because of apartheid, some South African acts would first experience hip hop elsewhere before returning home. Rapper and producer Ben Sharpa (Kgotso Semela, 1979–), from Soweto, grew up and learned to rap in Chicago. But in 1994, his family returned to Johannesburg, where he created the rap crew Audio Visual (1996–), which eventually folded into the collective GroundWorks (2001–). He then started a solo career in 2002, eventually releasing his debut album, *B. Sharpa* (2008). Ben Sharpa's lyrics are in English and focus on social issues, such as police brutality, government corruption, and the problems of teenage pregnancy. He also records songs about spirituality.

Another famous example is Tanzanian-born South African rapper, singer, songwriter, poet, and record label owner Tumi Molekane (aka MC Fatboy, Tumi, Stogie T, Boitumelo Molekane, 1981–), who is best known as lead singer of Tumi and the Volume (2002–2012), an experimental band that fuses hip hop with African and Latin jazz, afropop, reggae, and rock. Molekane's parents relocated a year after the end of apartheid. By the 2000s he had a solo career, including reinventing himself as the debonair Stogie T. In 2012, he formed the short-lived duo T-Z Deluxe with Zubz (Ndabaningi Mabuye, 1976–), a Zambian-born, Zimbabwean-raised, South African rapper. Other examples are Young Nations (formerly K.A.S.H., Kept in Africa's Subliminal Hold, Zosukuma Kunene, 1976–), an English and Zulu rapper now based in Durban, who was born in exile in London and raised in Los Angeles; Jozi's Da L.E.S. (Leslie Jonathan Mapmpe Jr., 1985–), who was born in Washington, D.C., raised in Houston, and currently resides in Johannesburg; Yung

Swiss (Steve Dang, 1994–), a Cameroon-born South African rapper and singer-songwriter, who also lives in Johannesburg; producer, composer, and DJ Nyambz (Inyambo Imenda, 1985–), who is a Lusaka, Zambia-born South African whose family relocated to Pretoria in 1989; rapper Kilani Rich (n.d.–2013) from Soweto, who grew up in Detroit, Los Angeles, and Oakland, California before returning to South Africa; and Trusenz (Lungelo Nzama, 1980–), an MC from Durban, who lived in Boston's Jamaica Plain before relocating to East London, South Africa.

Some diaspora acts include Cape Town–born and Brooklyn, New York–raised singer-songwriter, rapper, and comedian Jean Grae (1976–); the LOX's (1994–) founder, Styles P (David Styles, 1974–); and rappers Earl Sweatshirt (aka Sly Tendencies, Thebe Neruda Kgositsile, 1994–) and Reason (Sizwe Moeketsi, 1987*–).

Melissa Ursula Dawn Goldsmith

See also: Botswana; Die Antwoord; Kwaito; Lesotho; Molekane, Tumi; Motswako; Mozambique; Namibia; Political Hip Hop; Prophets of da City

Further Reading

Battersby, Jane. 2003. "'Sometimes It Feels Like I'm Not Black Enough': Recast(e)ing Colored through South African Hip Hop as a Postcolonial Text." In *Shifting Selves: Post-Apartheid Essays on Mass Media, Culture, and Identity*, edited by Herman Wasserman and Sean Jacobs, chap. 6. Cape Town, South Africa: Kwela Books.

Hammett, Daniel. 2012. "Reworking and Resisting Globalizing Influences: Cape Town Hip Hop." *GeoJournal* 77, no. 3: 417–28.

Kunzler, Daniel. 2011. "South African Rap Music, Counter Discourses, Identity, and Commodification beyond the Prophets of da City." *Journal of Southern African Studies* 37, no. 1: 27–43.

Molebatsi, Natalia, and Raphael d'Abdon. 2007. "From Poetry to Floetry: Music's Influence in the Spoken Word Art of Young South Africa." *Muziki: Journal of Music Research in Africa* 4, no. 2: 171–77.

Schoon, Alette. 2014. "Digital Hustling: ICT Practices of Hip Hop Artists in Grahamstown." *Technoetic Arts* 12, nos. 2–3: 207–17.

Watkins, Lee. 2012. "A Genre Coming of Age: Transformation, Difference, and Authenticity in the Rap Music and Hip Hop Culture of South Africa." In *Hip Hop Africa: New African Music in a Globalizing World*, edited by Eric Charry, chap. 2. Bloomington: Indiana University Press.

Further Listening

Brasse Vannie Kaap. 2000. *Yskoud* (*Frosty* or *Freezing*). Ghetto Ruff.

Moodphase5ive. 2000. *Steady On.* African Dope Records.

Pitch Black Afro. 2004. *Styling Gel.* Ghetto Ruff.

Skwatta Kamp. 2003. *Mkhukhu Funkshen* (*Mkhukhu Function*). Gallo Record Company.

Spain

Spain's hip hop scene took American and U.K. hip hop and flavored it with traditional music styles such as *flamenco* and *rumba*, and then cross-pollenated the sound with Latin American hip hop, incorporating genres such as *reggaetón*. Torrejón de Ardoz's American military base and its radio station may have been the

Rapper Mala Rodríguez, one of Spain's best known hip hop artists, performs in 2014 in Santander, Spain. Rodríguez employs a smooth rapping delivery along with an articulated, slow vocal style. (Juan Manuel Serrano Arce/Redferns via Getty Images)

gateway to hip hop in Spain, as soldiers would bring in American hip hop music. One of the early acts introduced in this way was the Mean Machine (1981–), a Puerto Rican rap group on the Sugar Hill Records (1979–1986) label; it rapped and sang in English and Spanish. During the 1980s, hip hop music and culture spread through Spain as skate culture, graffiti, breakdance, and hip hop radio in Madrid and Barcelona, and at the turn of the decade, the Madrid-based group El Club de los Poetas Violentos (aka CPV, The Violent Poets Club, 1991–) made hip hop more fashionable with atmospheric melodies, backgrounded samples, throaty vocals, and well-placed scratching.

Since then, the Spanish hip hop music industry has grown into a multinational one, with international tours and collaborations; however, like all rap cultures, it is locally focused and socially conscious, having a strong presence in working-class neighborhoods in larger, urban areas with large populations such as Madrid, Barcelona, Zaragoza, Seville, and Málaga. Early hip hop began with loops and samples, with Spanish as the main language for lyrics, although English, Spanglish, and American urban slang made their way into songs. Spanish public radio currently features two hip hop radio shows, *La cuarta parte* (*The Fourth Part*) and *El rimadero* (*The Rim-Pot*, but a wordplay on *rima*, which means rhyme).

The first Spanish hip hop record was released in 1989 on the short-lived Troya DSCS and RCRS (1889–1990) label. Its *Madrid Hip Hop* was a compilation of four bands from Madrid. Hip hop slowly caught hold in the underground music scene, but during the 1990s it began to be mainstreamed. Spain's long-standing hip hop stars include El Club de los Poetas Violentos: 7 Notas 7 Colores (The Club of the Violent Poets: 7 Notes 7 Colors, 1993–2000, 2007–), who collaborated with the American hip hop band Company Flow (1993–2001) and at one time recorded in the United States; and prolific Siempre Fuertes De Konciencia (aka SFDK, Forever Strong In Conscience, 1993–), which has expanded American Southern Rap and reggae-influenced hip hop with simple rhymes, dry humor, and social criticism through its 16 albums, EPs, and mixtapes.

Some of the newer rap stars in Spain include C. Tangana (aka Crema, Antón Álvarez Alfaro, 1990–), a soft-spoken rapper who raps about sadness and romance and emphasizes middle-class values in his lyrics and videos; Yung Beef (Fernando Gálvez, 1990*–), a trap artist who since 2013 has released hundreds of tracks as albums and mixtapes, both as a soloist and with various project bands; Kaydy Cain (Daniel Gómez, n.d.), who uses old-school hip hop beats and raps about materialism and sex; and Khaled (Jalid Rodríguez, 1990*–), a Spanish Moroccan rapper with a throaty and aggressive style who sports the American hip hop gold chain look, uses autotuning, and showcases popping moves in his hand gestures. The most popular female rapper is Mala Rodríguez (aka La Mala, María Rodríguez Garrido, 1979–), whose smooth delivery and articulated, slow vocal style enjoys a huge following in Latin America.

Anthony J. Fonseca

See also: Reggaetón; The United Kingdom

Further Reading

Corona, Victor, and Sophie Kelsall. 2016. "Latino Rap in Barcelona: Diaspora, Languages, and Identities." *Linguistics and Education* 36: 5–15.

Morgade, Marta, Alberto Verdesoto, and David Poveda. 2016. "Hip Hop Echoes in South Madrid Teenagers' Soundscapes." *Linguistics and Education* 36: 27–34.

Further Listening

El Club de los Poetas Violentos. 2012. *Siempre* (*Always*). BOA.

Rodríguez, Mala. 2013. *Bruja* (*Witch*, *Sorceress*, or *Hex*). Universal Music Group.

Spoonie Gee

(aka The Love Rapper, Gabriel Jackson, 1963–, Harlem, New York)

Spoonie Gee is an American hip hop and funk musician and rapper best known for his association with the Treacherous Three (aka Spoonie Gee and the Treacherous Three, 1978–1984), an early old-school rap group he cofounded. As part of the Treacherous Three, which featured Grammy Award winner Kool Moe Dee (1963–), and as a solo act, he was one of the few rap artists to release records in the 1970s. Some credit him with coining the term hip hop, a claim which cannot be proven or disproven. Nonetheless, he was one of the first rappers to introduce themes into music that dealt with issues such as gang violence. Spoonie Gee was also one of the first rappers to use Jamaican-influenced echo and reverb in his vocals. Marley Marl (1962–) produced Spoonie Gee's debut album, *The Godfather of Rap* (1987). His output, however, ended there due to various arrests and imprisonments.

EARLY UPBRINGING AND SOUND RECORDING CAREER

Nicknamed "spoonie" because he would eat only with that utensil as a child, he was born in Harlem, New York, but when Spoonie Gee was 12, his mother died, and he moved to New York City with his uncle, Bobby Robinson (1917–2011), an independent record producer and songwriter who had produced the Shirelles (1957–1982) and Gladys Knight and the Pips (1952–1989), and was soon to produce Grandmaster Flash and the Furious Five (1976–1982, 1987–1988). Robinson was associated with various labels, including Red Robin Records (1951–1956), Fury Records (1957–1976), Fire Records (1959–1962), and Enjoy Records (1962–1987).

American rapper Spoonie Gee (pictured ca. 1970) is one of the earliest pioneering hip hop musicians. Originally from Harlem, he was active as a member of Treacherous Three and recorded on the Enjoy! and Sugar Hill Records labels before pursuing his own solo career. (Michael Ochs Archives/Getty Images)

Spoonie Gee would practice his rapping in his uncle's apartment, and a connection of his uncle's, Peter Brown (n.d.), a producer and multiple-label owner based in New York City, gave him his first opportunity to record a rap, "Spoonin' Rap" (1979), on the Sound of New York, U.S.A. (1979–1983) imprint, a disco and early hip hop label. "Spoonin' Rap" referenced legal problems and arrests, themes that would become prominent in gangsta rap. Spoonie Gee then joined his uncle's Enjoy Records label, and released two singles, "The New Rap Language" (as part of the Treacherous Three) and "Love Rap" (as a solo, 1980). "Love Rap" was an experimental low-key rap accompanied by only a drum kit and congas. In 1981, Spoonie Gee moved over to Sugar Hill Records (1978–2015) to record the minor hit "Spoonie's Back." Finally, he settled at the Tuff City label (1981–) for most of his releases, including the diss track "That's My Style" (1986), which attacked Schoolly D (Jesse Bonds Weaver Jr., 1962–).

The Godfather of Rap turned out to be Spoonie Gee's one and only album. His only other non-single recording was the 2008 EP, *The Boss Is Back*.

Anthony J. Fonseca

See also: Chopper; Kool Moe Dee; Marley Marl; The United States

Further Reading

Bradley, Adam, and Andrew Dubois, eds. 2010. "Spoonie Gee." Under "Part 1: 1978–84: The Old School" in *The Anthology of Rap*, pp. 89–96. New Haven, CT: Yale University Press.

Cramer, Jennifer, and Jill Hallett. 2010. "From Chi-Town to the Dirty-Dirty: Regional Identity Markers in U.S. Hip Hop." In *The Languages of Global Hip Hop*, edited by Marina Terkourafi, chap. 10. New York: Continuum.

French, Kenneth. 2017. "Geography of American Rap: Rap Diffusion and Rap Centers." *GeoJournal* 82, no. 2: 259–72.

Gosa, Travis L., and Erik Nielson, eds. 2015. *Hip Hop and Obama Reader*. Oxford: Oxford University Press.

Further Listening

Spoonie Gee. 1987. *The Godfather of Rap*. Tuff City.

Sri Lanka

Sri Lanka, located almost 900 miles southeast of India, has a hip hop scene that is strongest in its capital city, Colombo. Though no one knows when hip hop first emerged there, underground culture was not new to 1980s Sri Lankans. Following the Sri Lankan Civil War (1983–2009), closed-down schools and widespread unemployment gave teens the time to express their discontent through graffiti and songs. Meanwhile, foreign pop music, notably the overplayed hits of Swedish rock band ABBA (1972–1983), dominated Sri Lanka's musical preferences. In the mid-1990s, Brown Boogie Nation (1995–2002*), likely Sri Lanka's first hip hop musical group, became the first group there to have a music video broadcast on national television. Their antiwar single "Lions and Tigers" (1997) was about Sri Lanka's strife. One of the teens who founded the band was rapper and Colombo-based R&B singer-songwriter Randhir (Randhir Yasendra Witana, n.d.), who left the band to work with Bathiya and Santhush (BnS, 1998–).

Several American rappers inspired Randhir. These include Jay-Z (1969–), Kanye West (1977–), and Tupac Shakur (1971–1996). In 2000, Randhir joined BnS, which was becoming the most commercially successful hip hop duo in Sri Lanka. BnS's debut album *Vasanthaye: A New Beginning* (1998) was the first to combine Western musical styles such as hip hop and R&B with traditional Sri Lankan music. Also from Colombo, BnS consists of Bathiya Jayakody (1976–) and Santhush Weeraman (1977–), two music school students who studied Western classical music, jazz, and musical theatre. Randhir's main work was with BnS's fusion of folk music and hip hop; these were called folk-hop remixes, and they used English, Sinhala, and Tamil texts, as well as some Hindi verses. In 2002, BnS became the first Sri Lankan artists to sign a major record label with Sony BMG (2004–2008). By 2008, Randhir had begun his own solo career, rapping in Sinhala.

Working with BnS led to other hip hop artists' success. For example, hip hop rapper and R&B singer Ashanthi (1981*–), a crewmember in 2000, eventually became the first female Sri Lankan hip hop artist to have an international record contract when she signed with Universal Music Group (1996–) in 2006. Previously, she was part of the successful yet short-lived pop and R&B duo Ashanthi 'n' Ranidu

(2001–2002) with songwriter Ranidu (Ranidu Lankage, 1982–), who has also had a successful solo career. Sri Lankan hip hop has yet to spread globally, but in 2005, DeLon (Dilan Jayasingha, 1990–), who was born and raised in Los Angeles, became the first artist of Sri Lankan descent to have hits in the United States, charting at No. 15 on the Billboard's Hot Singles Sales with "Calor de la Salsa" ("Heat of the Salsa").

As of 2018, several Sri Lankan hip hop artists continue to aspire to becoming internationally known. These include Ashanthi, whose *Rock the World* (2013) was her first album in English. The best-known artist, however, is London-born M.I.A. (1975–), of Tamil descent, who started her music career in 2002. Her politically charged work has received critical acclaim while her singles and albums have charted internationally. The political nature of M.I.A.'s raps serves as contrast to Ashanthi and other Sri Lankan artists who perform in the country; most Sri Lankan lyrical content is about romance, partying, antiwar sentiments (more currently in a global rather than local sense), and lighthearted topics.

Melissa Ursula Dawn Goldsmith

See also: Ashanthi; India; M.I.A.; The United Kingdom

Further Reading

Rollefson, J. Griffith. 2017. "M.I.A.'s 'Terrorist Chic': Black Atlantic Music and South Asian Postcolonial Politics in London." In *Flip the Script: European Hip Hop and the Politics of Postcoloniality*, chap. 5. Chicago: University of Chicago Press.

Saucier, Paul Khalil, and Kumarini Silva. 2014. "Keeping It Real in the Global South: Hip Hop Comes to Sri Lanka." *Critical Sociology* 40, no. 2: 295–300.

Further Listening

BnS. 2002. *Tharunyaye: The 3rd Album*. Sony Music.

Stetsasonic

(1981–1992, Brooklyn, New York)

Stetsasonic was one of the earliest rapping crews that used a live hip hop band. The band's style, which combined old-school hip hop with jazz, funk, R&B, rock, dancehall, and reggae, was a precursor to that of numerous alternative hip hop bands and groups worldwide. Stetsasonic's lyrical content was among the earliest that focused on positive black consciousness, humor, and metatextuality.

FORMATION AND EARLY USE OF HIP HOP WITH JAZZ

In 1981, Stetsasonic formed in Brooklyn, New York, originally as the Stetson Brothers with three MCs who donned Stetson hats. The original rapping crew consisted of Daddy O and MC Delite (Marvin Shahid Wright, n.d.). In 1983, rapper, beatboxer, and producer Wise (aka the Stetsa-Human Mix Machine, Leonardo Roman, 1965–) joined the band, and the crew changed its name to Stetsasonic the Hip Hop Band, shortened soon afterward to Stetsasonic. In 1984, after watching him at a DJ battle in Brooklyn, Daddy-O recruited DJ and turntablist Prince Paul.

It was at this time that rapper Frukwan (aka Sun Star, Fu Kwan, Arnold Hamilton, n.d.), DJ, keyboardist, and drummer DBC (aka The Devastating Beat Creator, Da Bad Creator, Marvin Nemley, n.d.), and drummer Stetsa-drum (Bobby Simmons, n.d.) also joined.

Stetsasonic's first big break was a recording deal with Tommy Boy Records (aka Tommy Boy Entertainment, 1981–) after the DBC played a live audition of the bassline from the funk-infused "If You Can't Say It All, Just Say STET" (1985). The band's debut album, *On Fire* (1986), peaked at No. 32 on Billboard's Top R&B Albums chart, but had a mixed reception because of the new sound, at times simple rhymes, and combination of light party themes with more serious Afrocentric ones.

In contrast, its second album, the ambitious double LP *In Full Gear* (1988), won critical acclaim. The album exemplifies Stetsasonic's mature sound, which included incorporating more R&B, sophisticated beatboxing techniques, sampling from jazz and funk, and spoken word. This album featured one of Stesasonic's most memorable tracks, "Talkin' All that Jazz," which sampled American cool jazz, jazz fusion, soul, and funk keyboardist Lonnie Liston Smith's (1940–) "Expansions" (1974). "Talkin' All that Jazz," defends hip hop by defining it as an art form, a new kind of jazz.

After *Blood, Sweat, and No Tears*, Stetsasonic went on hiatus so that members could pursue solo careers. Prince Paul and Frukwan founded the East Coast hardcore hip hop group Gravediggaz (1990–2002, 2010–2016). Prince Paul (Paul Edward Huston, 1967–), Daddy-O (Glenn Bolton, 1961–), and DBC became successful record producers.

While recording, Stetsasonic continued performing live, ultimately touring worldwide. The group's sound influenced future artists and groups, such as Gang Starr (1986–2003) and the Roots (1987–), from the United States; Dream Warriors (1988–2002) and BBNG (BADBADNOTGOOD, 2010–), from Canada; Urban Species (1992–2000, 2008–) and the Herbaliser (1995–), from England; Tumi and the Volume (2002–2012), from South Africa; and 1200 Techniques (1997–2005), from Australia. In 1991, Stetsasonic disbanded, but as of 2018, the band still reunites for concerts.

Melissa Ursula Dawn Goldsmith

See also: Reggae; The United States

Further Reading

Blatt, Wendy. 1987. "Rap Voice of Social Responsibility." *Los Angeles Times*, July 19, 92.

Shusterman, Richard. 1995. "Rap Remix: Pragmatism, Postmodernism, and Other Issues in the House." *Critical Inquiry* 22, no. 1: 150–58.

Further Listening

Stetsasonic. 1988. *In Full Gear.* Tommy Boy.

Sudan

Sudan is composed of North Sudan and South Sudan, two North African countries that border Egypt, Ethiopia, Eritrea, Central African Republic, Chad, Libya,

Kenya, Uganda, and the Democratic Republic of Congo. In 1956, Sudan won its independence from the United Kingdom and Egypt. The First Sudanese Civil War (1955–1972) and the Second Sudanese Civil War (1983–2005), between the northern and southern regions, led to nearly three million dead, and displaced nearly five million people from the southern region. In 2011, South Sudan won its independence. Because of the civil wars and other factors such as Islamic extremism and fundamentalism, little research about hip hop's emergence has been done, and early hip hop musicians have been persecuted. For example, Muslim Nubian singer-songwriter Mohammed Wardi (1932–2012) was arrested and self-exiled to Egypt from 1989 until 2003. After the Nairobi Comprehensive Peace Agreement in 2005, signifying the end of the Second Sudanese Civil War, limited hip hop activity and radio airplay took place in Khartoum, North Sudan's capital city, and Juba, South Sudan's capital city; however, most Sudanese hip hop is created by artists living elsewhere as a result of diaspora.

The United States–based hardcore hip hop collective and Sudanese Arabic label NasJota (aka Jota, 2003*–) from Khartoum, raps against Sudanese government corruption, including election rigging. NasJota, consisting of Sudanese and Arab rappers who perform in Arabic and English, released "B Sotak" ("With Your Vote"), which was included on *Sudan Votes: Music Hopes* (2010), a sampler of R&B, Afropop, and hip hop. Compiled by German hip hop, R&B, and pop singer-songwriter and producer Max Herre (Maximilian Herre, 1973–), it was Sudan's first national recording. Washington, DC–born rapper Oddisee (Amir Mohamed el Khalifa, 1985–), of Sudanese descent, appears on this recording. NasJota also released the antidictatorship song "LA Dictatorship" (2012). Hip hop and R&B singer-songwriter and music producer Nile (Moawia Ahmed Khalid, 1983–), based in the United Arab Emerates, also criticizes the Sudanese government in English.

Hip hop in South Sudan evolved from favoring Nuer texts and using sticks as percussive accompaniment to using diverse texts that reflect its population. Rapper Emmanuel Kembe (1969–) was an early hip hop singer; however, in 1994, he escaped imprisonment and took voluntary exile for his political protest song "Shen Shen" ("A Cry for Sudan"). In 2007, Kembe returned to Khartoum, his hometown, Wau, and settled in Juba. His return reflects the postwar return of many South Sudanese. Rapper and former child soldier Emmanuel Jal (Jal Jok, 1980*–), from Tonj, raps about peace, unity, and everyday life in war-torn South Sudan in Nuer, English, Juba Arabic, Swahili, and Dinka. After living in Kenya, where he first took interest in hip hop, Jal has lived in Canada and England. Rapper and singer-songwriter Bangs (aka Ur Boy Bangs, Ajak Chol, 1990–), from Juba, has also chosen a career outside South Sudan, in Australia, whereas rapper L.U.A.L. (Lyrically Untouchable African Legend, Lual D'Awol, 1985–), who was born in New York City and grew up in Baltimore, returned to Juba.

Melissa Ursula Dawn Goldsmith

See also: Political Hip Hop

Further Reading

Serpick, Evan. 2008. "Rapper Mines Life as Child Soldier in Sudan." *Rolling Stone* no. 1052, May 15, 2008, 24.

Wilson, Michael. 2012. "'Making Space, Pushing Time': A Sudanese Hip Hop Group and Their Wardrobe-Recording Studio." *International Journal of Cultural Studies* 15, no. 1: 47–64.

Further Listening
Jal, Emmanuel. 2011. *See Me Mama.* Gatwitch Records.

The Sugarhill Gang

(aka The Original Sugarhill Gang, 1975–1989, 1994–, Englewood, New Jersey)

The Sugarhill Gang, also known as the Original Sugarhill Gang, is an American hip hop band consisting of Master Gee (Guy O'Brien, 1963–), Wonder Mike (Michael Anthony Wright, 1956–), and Big Bank Hank (Henry Lee Jackson, 1958–2014). The band is best known for its hit song "Rapper's Delight," released in 1979 on the Sugar Hill Records label (1986–1995) and produced by Sylvia Robinson (1936–2011); the record eventually sold eight million copies.

Robinson had earlier achieved success in the music industry as part of the duo Mickey and Sylvia (1955–1965*), which had a No. 1 single with "Love Is Strange" (1956). Sugar Hill Records had been founded in 1979 by Robinson and her husband, Joe (n.d.), funded by Morris Levy (Moishe Levy, 1927–90) of Roulette Records (1957–1989) in New York, even though the Robinson's prior label, All Platinum Records (1967–1978*), went into bankruptcy. "Rapper's Delight" became the first rap single to become a Top 40 Billboard hit, reaching No. 36. The song also reached No. 4 on the R&B chart and topped the charts in Canada and the Netherlands, also reaching Top 10 status in Austria, France, Germany, Norway, Sweden, Switzerland, and the United Kingdom.

Overall, the Sugarhill Gang recorded five studio albums between 1979 and 1999. Its sound can best be described as a funk-infused hip hop, featuring a heavy beat accentuated by claps and a heavy bass, with constant rapping alternated by the three MCs; singing occurs sparingly and tends to be singsong when it does, coming across as a conscious parody of itself.

"RAPPER'S DELIGHT" AND THE FORMATION OF THE SUGARHILL GANG

"Rapper's Delight" is also important for its early use of sampling, as it uses the bass track from the Chic (1976–) hit "Good Times," a 1979 No. 1 hit on both the Billboard Hot 100 and R&B charts, as well as "Here Comes That Sound Again" by British disco group Love De-Luxe (1979–1980*). The song caused some controversy as Chic's Nile Rodgers (1952–) and Bernard Edwards (1952–1996) threatened legal action over copyright and received a settlement and songwriter credits. It also raised eyebrows in New York, where rap music first emerged, as early rappers accused the Sugarhill Gang of appropriating their music.

To the surprise of many, the song, coming in at 14:36 (a seven-minute radio-friendly version was also released) and recorded in a single take, became a hit at a time when rap songs did not find their way to commercial radio. The song was in fact ignored by radio stations until WESL in St. Louis, Missouri, picked it up, leading the way for other stations.

It broke through the barriers of race, ethnicity, and genre; prior to its release, rap was generally relegated to nightclubs, parties, and competitions, the former being the venue where Sylvia Robinson first heard rap music in 1979 and realized its potential after witnessing the genre's call-and-response appeal. "Rapper's Delight" made the genre into a viable studio production and a marketable commodity by introducing it to a wider audience.

The song is a breathless 14-minute rap by all three MCs, and Robinson added some calls and responses to the song in studio, including a high pitched "say what?" during Big Bank's Hank's verses, one of the song's signature moments, which marks the introduction of audience response.

Generally, its lyrics are a boast about the trio's ability to rap, its financial success (an early version of the concern with bling), and its ability to move people to dance. Generally speaking the song is clean, although it references sexuality and "super sperm."

Sylvia Robinson assembled the trio in 1979, naming them after the Sugarhill neighborhood in Harlem. "Rapper's Delight" was released as a single to introduce the band's debut album *Sugarhill Gang* (1980), which reached No. 4 on the R&B chart despite not charting in the Billboard 200. The band's second album, *8th Wonder* (1981), was its sole album to break into the Billboard 200, reaching No. 50 (as well as No. 15 on the R&B chart). The song "8th Wonder" became a minor hit and introduced a more conscious and pronounced call-and-response as well as Latin rhythms.

AFTER "RAPPER'S DELIGHT"

The next two albums, *Rappin' Down Town* (1983) and *Livin' in the Fast Lane* (1984), did not chart. In the 1990s, the trio reunited for various concerts, and in 1999, a Sugarhill Gang reunion produced a hip hop children's album, *Jump on It!* On the Kid Rhino label. The band's history was also marred by a lawsuit brought by Wonder Mike and Master Gee against Sugar Hill Records, where the duo lost its case and had to relinquish the band name; however, they were allowed to tour as Wonder Mike and Master Gee of the Original Sugarhill Gang.

Big Bank Hank died of cancer in 2014, the same year that the band was inducted into the Grammy Hall of Fame for "Rapper's Delight." The song has achieved the status of music icon—considered a benchmark in the history of popular music. It was named to the National Recording Registry of the Library of Congress in 2011. It is the first song referenced by Mr. B the Gentleman Rhymer (Jim Burke, 1970–) in his song "Chap Hop History," from his album *Flattery Not Included* (2008). The song has, as of 2018, had more than 1.2 million views on YouTube.

Anthony J. Fonseca

See also: Robinson, Sylvia; The United States

Further Reading

George, Nelson. 1999. "Hip Hop Wasn't Just Another Date." In *Hip Hop America*, chap. 2. London: Penguin Books.

Kajikawa, Loren. 2015. "'Rapper's Delight': From Genre-less to New Genre." In *Sounding Race in Rap Songs*, chap. 1. Oakland: University of California Press.

Newman, Maria. 2002. "Fire Razes a Pioneering Rap Music Recording Studio." *The New York Times*, October 12, B4.

Further Listening

The Sugarhill Gang. 1980. *Sugarhill Gang.* Sugar Hill Records.

Suge Knight

(Marion Hugh Knight Jr., 1965–, Compton, California)

Suge Knight is the cofounder and main force behind Los Angeles–based Death Row Records (1991–2008), the main competitor to Ruthless Records (1987–2010*), which famously produced the West Coast gangsta rap band N.W.A. (1986–1991). Suge Knight's cofounders included N.W.A. members Dr. Dre (Andre Romelle Young, 1965–) and the D.O.C. (aka Doc T, Tracy Lynn Curry, 1968–). Dre, the D.O.C., and Michel'le (Michel'le Toussaint, 1970–) left Ruthless Records to join Death Row, which then dominated the rap charts with Dre, Tupac Shakur (Lesane Parish Crooks, 1971–96), and Snoop Dogg (Calvin Cordozar Broadus Jr., 1971–). Death Row fell apart after Shakur was killed and Suge Knight was incarcerated in September 1996, going bankrupt by 2006 (after a lawsuit) and being sold in 2008 to Global Music Group (2008–), now Global Music Entertainment.

EARLY SUCCESS AS A MUSIC PUBLISHER AND PRODUCER

Around 1989, Suge Knight became a music publisher, making a considerable amount of money from Vanilla Ice's (Robert Matthew Van Winkle, 1967–) "Ice, Ice, Baby" (1990). Around this time, he also began collaborating with the D.O.C., who was already interested in leaving N.W.A. They formed Death Row, and Knight managed a distribution deal with Interscope (1989–). The result was that Dr. Dre's *The Chronic* (1992) went triple Platinum, and Snoop Dogg's *Doggystyle* (1993) went quadruple Platinum.

Suge Knight also literally purchased Shakur by offering to pay his bail if he signed with the label. In 1994, Death Row released, under the moniker 2Pac, the promotional EP *Pain*, followed by the singles "California Love" and "Dear Mama" (1995). Two more singles followed in 1996, and the 2Pac album *All Eyez on Me* (his fourth and final studio album) was released in 1996.

SUBSEQUENT PRODUCTIONS AND KNIGHT'S FALL

Suge Knight, however, began feuding with East Coast rappers 2 Live Crew (1982–1991) and Puff Daddy (Sean John Combs, 1969–). Dr. Dre and Snoop Dogg eventually left the label because of Suge Knight's feuding (Snoop Dogg went to No Limit), but before doing so, Dr. Dre had supervised the soundtracks for *Above the Rim* (1994) and *Murder Was the Case* (1994), the last an 18-minute short film starring Snoop Dogg.

In 2009, Death Row released *The Chronic: Re-lit* as a reissue with seven bonus tracks and a DVD. This was the same year the label released *Death Row: The Lost Sessions, Vol. 1* with Snoop Dogg's recordings from 1993 to 1997. Snoop Dogg had a string of success with *Tha Dogg Pound–Dogg Food* (1995), *Tha Doggfather* (1996), and a compilation album *Death Row: Snoop Doggy Dogg at His Best* (2001).

Other artists who recorded on the Death Row label since Dr. Dre's and Snoop Dogg's departures include Kurupt (Ricardo Emmanuel Brown, 1972–) and member of the rap group Tha Dogg Pound (1992–2002, 2005–), R&B and neo soul singer Danny Boy Steard (1977–), the Los Angeles gangsta rap group O.F.T.B. (Operation from the Bottom, 1990–2013), and R&B singer Jewell (aka Ju-L, Jewell Caples, 1968–). None came close to the success experienced in the years Dr. Dre, Shakur, and Snoop Dogg recorded for Death Row.

Ultimately, in 2013, Entertainment One (aka eOne, 1970–) purchased the rights to the entire Death Row catalog. In 2015, Suge Knight, who was in and out of prison on various charges for a decade, was arrested after a fatal hit-and-run in Compton, California.

As of 2018, Tupac Shakur's *All Eyez on Me* has been certified Diamond. As 2Pac, Tupac Shakur produced hundreds of tracks during his time at Death Row, most of which would be released posthumously.

Anthony J. Fonseca

See also: Dr. Dre; Gangsta Rap; N.W.A.; Snoop Dogg; Tupac Shakur; The United States

Further Reading
Diehl, Matt. 2015. "The Endless Fall of Suge Knight." *Rolling Stone* no. 1239–1240, July 6, 46, 48–51, 72.
Thompson, Robert. 2010. "A Dirge for Death Row." *Canadian Business* 83, no. 3: 38–41.

Sway

(Derek Andrew Safo, 1982–, London, England)

Sway is an English grime and hip hop rapper, songwriter, and producer of Ghanian descent. His studio albums, *This Is My Demo* (2006), *The Signature LP* (2008), and *Deliverance* (2015) have peaked at Nos. 45, 51, and 150, respectively, on the U.K. Albums Chart. Born and raised in Hornsey, a district of North London, he learned music production at his high school, followed later by studying music engineering at City and Islington College. He began writing rap, honing on storytelling techniques, humor, and speed when he was 14 years old. At the same time, he was a member of several rap groups. His influences included American hip hop groups such as Bone Thugs-N-Harmony (1991–) and Wu-Tang Clan (1992–), as well as English drum and bass artist MC Skibadee (Alfonso Bondzie, n.d.).

After receiving critical acclaim for his early self-released recordings, touring worldwide, and eventually supporting acts such as Public Enemy (1982–), Dizzee

Rascal (Dylan Kwabena Mills, 1984–), and others, Sway has seen his albums, as well as his singles, chart. All three albums were produced on Sway's London-based label, Dcypha Productions (2005–), under Island Records (1959–) whose parent company is Universal Music Group (1996–). Sway's latest album, *Preface* (2017) was released on the New Reign Productions label (2014–), based in Nottingham, England.

While still an independent artist, Sway's first hit was "Up Your Speed," which peaked a No. 141 on the U.K. Singles Chart; in 2006, his second hit, "Little Derek," fared better at No. 38. Since 2005, Sway has had nine hit singles on the U.K. Singles Chart with "Still Speedin'" and "Level Up" from *Deliverance*, peaking at Nos. 19 and 8, respectively. Sway is also known for *The Dotted Lines Mixtape* (2007), which features "Black Stars," a remix of English hip hop and grime artist Bashy's (Ashley Thomas, 1985–) song "Black Boys" (2007). Sway dedicated his version to Ghana, which was hosting the 2008 Africa Cup of Nations, the main international association football competition in Africa (1957–), as well as to famous Ghanaians living worldwide as a result of diaspora.

Sway's music has a strong focus on synthesizer, with beats placed further in the background. He strictly raps and is notable for his speed, use of rapid triplets, and storytelling. His lyrical content has addressed how independent artists struggle in a music industry-dominated world, overcoming adversity, his own story as a musician, life on the streets, and religious tolerance, among other topics. Sway has collaborated on his hit recordings with American-born Senegalese rapper, singer-songwriter, and producer Akon (1973–), English-born Nigerian R&B and neo soul singer-songwriter and producer Lemar (Lemar Obika, 1978), and female English rapper and singer Baby Blue (Rachel Estelle Irene Prager, n.d.), among others.

Melissa Ursula Dawn Goldsmith

See also: Ghana; Grime; The United Kingdom

Further Reading

Billen, Andrew. 2006. "No Guns, No Drugs, No Bling." *The Times* (London), January 17, 8.

Mulholland, Garry. 2005. "Bling's Not the Thing: A 22-Year-Old North Londoner Without a Record Deal Beat 50 Cent to Best Hip Hop Award at Last Night's Mobos." *Evening Standard* (London), September 23, 38.

Wood, Andy. 2002. "Hip Hop." In *Companion to Contemporary Black British Culture*, edited by Alison Donnell, pp. 141–42. London: Routledge.

Further Listening

Sway. 2015. *Deliverance.* New Reign Productions/Absolute.

Swaziland

Swaziland is a South African country that attained independence from the United Kingdom in 1968. Since 1986, King Mswati III (HRH Prince Makhosetive, 1968–) has ruled the country, essentially as a dictator who appoints prime ministers and approves parliamentary elections. One of the smallest countries in Africa, Swaziland is a struggling developing country with AIDS/HIV and tuberculosis health crises and has the world's lowest life expectancy. Despite neighboring South Africa, in which hip hop became popular in the early 1980s, Swaziland demonstrated virtually no hip hop activity until the 1990s.

Swaziland Broadcasting and Information Service (SBIS) broadcast traditional and popular music that reflected dominant tastes: gospel, Swazi soul (African jazz and soul using Swati texts), South African *kwaito*, R&B, house, reggae, and country. By the 2000s, Swazi hip hop entered the main stream in Swaziland. Preferred rapping texts are in Swati, English, and Swati street slang. Early 1990s influences came from American and South African hip hop. Small hip hop scenes are centered in the capital city, Mbabane, followed by Manzini. In the 1990s there still was no music industry in Swaziland, so many musicians moved or recorded in neighboring countries; however, in the 2000s, do-it-yourself labels have emerged. Streaming services also help disseminate Swazi music.

Examples of pioneering Swazi hip hop acts from the mid to late 1990s were the rap crew Vamoose (1998*–) and rapper T-Maz (now Maz, Themba Maziya, n.d.) who fused old-school hip hop with R&B, using Swati and English. Active since the early 2000s, rapper and producer Slim Q (Qiniso Dlamini, 1983–), of the Swazi rap crew Stealth Independence (2005–), founded InQgnito (2004–), a label he uses to produce Swazi hip hop artists in Swaziland. Rapper, producer, and label owner Mozaik (Muzi Ngwenya, 1985–) is CEO of Claiming Ground Records (2006–), as well as part of the duo Siyinqaba (2004*–). Other rappers include Psycho Lution (Mzwandile Nxumalo, n.d.), 80 Script (Zolile Motsa, 1991–), Kena (Ayanda Tsela, 1991–), BustaRigo (Mbongeni Ian Manyon, 1981–), and Qibho Intalektual (Qiniso Motsa, 1996*–). Collaborations between these artists often takes place.

Female rapper and singer-songwriter Jazz P (Phephile Hlophe, n.d.) fuses hip hop with reggae and neo soul using English and Swati. Originally from Simunye, Swaziland, Jazz P became frustrated with the slow-moving Swaziland music industry and moved to Maputo, Mozambique, where she founded and fronts the band the Next Generation (2012*–). Her lyrics focus on romance, feminism, and everyday life.

By the 2000s, focus on innovation in Swazi rap has taken place, and rapper, poet, and actor Diba Diba (Banele Mfundo Dlamini, 1992*–) created *Ngwane hop*, which combines R&B and neo soul, using street slang. The intention is to make Ngwane hop a specifically Swazi kind of music, much in the way motswako has become the hip hop of South Africa and Botswana.

Despite its growth, Swazi hip hop faces obstacles. In 2011, South Africa with other countries began boycotting against King Mswati III's dictatorship; this resistance affected Swaziland's recording sales and concerts. That year, American rapper Jadakiss (Jason Phillips, 1975–) withdrew from performing his concert there. As of 2018, the cultural boycott continues.

Melissa Ursula Dawn Goldsmith

See also: Kenya; Kwaito; Political Hip Hop; South Africa

Further Reading

Debly, Teresa. 2014. "Culture and Resistance in Swaziland." *Journal of Contemporary African Studies* 32, no. 3: 284–301.

Mhlambi, Thokozani. 2004. "'Kwaitofabulous': The Study of a South African Urban Genre." *Journal of the Musical Arts in Africa* 1, no. 1: 116–27.

Further Listening
Siyinqaba. 2010. *Siyinqaba: The Album*. InQgnito.

Sweden

Sweden is a progressive democratic socialist country with a high quality of life that includes strong education, healthcare, civil liberties, and equality. This Scandinavian country in Northern Europe that neighbors Norway and Finland has a majority population that is Swedish; the minority populations include Finnish, Sámi, and others. Swedish is the official language, but English is usually learned concurrently, often prior to school age. Other recognized languages include Finnish, Sámi, Meänkieli (a Finnish dialect with Swedish loanwords), Romani, and Yiddish. In the 1980s, after the international distribution of American breakdancing films such as *Wild Style* (1983) and *Beat Street, Breakin', Breakin' 2: Electric Boogaloo*, and *Flashdance* (all 1984), Swedish hip hop culture emerged, first with breakdancing and graffiti in Stockholm, Malmö, and Uppsala. In an effort to attain a broad audience, Swedish hip hop initially favored rap in English.

Swedish folk music includes ballads, *Kulning* (cow-herding calls sung by women), fiddle tunes, and *Gammaldans* (Nordic dance music genres). Traditional instruments include the *Nyckelharpa* (a keyed fiddle), hurdy-gurdy, *Säckpipa* (Swedish bagpipes), harmonicas, clarinets, and accordions. Notable Swedish classical music composers include Johan Helmich Roman (1694–1758), Joseph Martin Kraus (1756–1792), Franz Berwald (1796–1868), and Wilhelm Stenhammer (1871–1927). Many notable singers also hail from Sweden, such as Jenny Lind (Johanna Maria Lind, 1820–1887) and recently, mezzo-soprano Anne Sofie von Otter (1955–). Folk and classical singing in amateur or professional choirs is a popular activity.

Popular music reception has always been strong in Sweden. Played on Sveriges Radio AB (1925–), Sweden's national public radio, American jazz, rock, pop, as well as Swedish pop and folk revival music, were aired by radio DJs throughout most of the 20th century. Sveriges Radio–owned Radio P3 (1964–) initiated Sweden's national record charts, Topplistan (1975–1997) and Hitlistan (1998–2007). After 2007, the chart became the Sverigetopplistan (aka the Swedish Albums and Swedish Singles Charts), which is based on sales data provided by the Grammofonieverantörernas förening (GLF, Swedish Recording Industry Association, 1975–). From 1969 to 1972 and later, since 1987, Sweden holds its equivalent to the American Grammy Awards (1959–), known as the Grammis Awards. Since the 1990s there has been a hip hop and soul music category. Sweden has its own music industry, and popular music by the 1980s and 1990s is diverse with pop, progressive rock, progg (aka progressive musik, meaning alternative music, not progressive rock), punk rock, heavy metal, electronica, soul, and reggae.

EARLY HIP HOP

Drummer and multi-instrumentalist Per Cussion (Per Philip Tjernberg, 1957–) of the reggae and punk band Dag Vag (1978–) visited New York City, where he became inspired by hip hop hits such as Grandmaster Flash and the Furious Five's (1976–1982, 1987–1988) "The Message" (1982). He brought the sound to Stockholm by collaborating with the Brooklyn, New York artist Grandmaster Funk (later GM Funk, Michael White, n.d.). In 1983, they released "Don't Stop," the first hip hop single recorded in Stockholm and the title song of Per Cussion's jazz-funk fusion album.

Subsequent hip hop tracks such as "Payin' the Price" were released as singles from Per Cussion's follow-up album *Beatwave* (1984). Per Cussion's third album, *Everybody's Talking* (1986), focused on fusing hip hop with electronica and neo soul, with songs still inspired by "The Message." Meanwhile, Ice Cold Rockers (IC Rockers, 1984–1991*) was Sweden's first self-contained hip hop collective, consisting of rappers, turntablists, dancers, and graffiti artists. Absent Minded (aka ADL, Adam Baptiste, 1973–), a Muslim rapper of Trinidadian descent born in Sweden, formed one of the country's earliest urban funk and hip hop bands, the Stonefunkers (1987–2001, 2009–), who rapped in English.

Swedish language hip hop emerged about two years later, occurring as numerous acts continued to rhyme in English to gain international appeal. The first rap song in Swedish was MC Tim's (Janus Erik Timothy Wolde, 1975–) "Jag Är Def" ("I'm Def," 1989), but Swedish singer Neneh Cherry's (Neneh Mariann Karlsson, 1964–) album *Raw Like Sushi* (1989) had an international hit hip hop/dance pop single in English with "Buffalo Stance." The trio Just D (meaning Just That, 1990–1995, 2015–), from Stockholm, released the first rap album that was fully in Swedish with its debut album, *1 steg bak å 2 steg fram* (*1 Step Backward, 2 Steps Forward*, 1990). Often compared to Beastie Boys (1981–2012), Just D was an all-white trio. Fusing hip hop and pop, the trio employed humorous skits between tracks that featured rapping and beats, with samples of various Swedish recordings.

Despite racial and/or socioeconomic differences between themselves and subsequent Swedish hip hop groups (Just D's members were from affluent non-immigrant Swedish families), Just D's string of No. 1 hit singles and successful albums, *Svenska Ord* (*Swedish Words*) (1991), *Rock n Roll* (1992), *Tres amigos* (1993), and *Plast* (1995), opened the doors for acts such as Infinite Mass (1991–), Looptroop Rockers (aka Looptroop, 1991–), the Latin Kings (TLK, 1991–2005), Natural Bond (1993–), and Frotté (1996–2006).

TLK, a group from Botkyrka, a southern suburb of Stockholm that is part of the urban public housing project Miljonprogrammet (Million Programm, 1965–1974), included rapper/MC Dogge Doggelito (Douglas Léon, 1975–), who was of Venezuelan descent; he was also a member of the rapping-production duo of Chilean descent known as the Salazar brothers, Salla (Christian Salazar, n.d.) and Chepe (Hugo Salazar, n.d.). The trio is named after the largest Hispanic American street gang, the Chicago-based Latin Kings (Almighty Latin King and Queen Nation, 1954–). TLK raps in its local Rinkeby Swedish, a pidgin language with loanwords from American English slang, as well as in Arabic, Kurdish, Italian, Persian, Spanish, and Turkish. Rinkeby Swedish is a youth vernacular language that is usually spoken in immigrant communities. At times using social realist humor, TLK's themes focus on Latino immigrant life in Stockholm, as well as exposure to crime, racism, and poverty. TLK's sound typically combines East Coast hip hop with salsa, neo soul, and reggae. TLK's debut studio album, *Välkommen till förorten* (*Welcome to the Suburb*, 1994), attained Gold certification and earned two Swedish Grammis. Susbsequent albums are *I skuggan av betongen* (*In the Concrete Shade*, 1997), *Mitt kvarter* (*My Neighborhood*, 2000), and *Omerta* (2003), in addition to a compilation album, *Familia Royal* (2005).

TLK produced Swedish rap acts such as the Stockholm bounce group Fattaru (1998–) and the group Fjärde Världen (Fourth World, 1998–) and paved the way for later Rinkeby artists such as Gambian-born rapper Eboi (aka Erik Lundin, Ibrahima Erik Lundin Banda, 1982–) and Stor (Ulises Infante Azocar, 1987–). Other successful acts who rap in Swedish include Paragon (aka Simon Emanuel, Ivar Simon Emanuel Molin, 1981–), Retarderat Eleverade (Retarded Students, 1999–2000), and Petter (Petter Alexis Askergren, 1974–). The last is a successful rapper-songwriter, who founded the Stockholm record labels BABA Recordings (2012–) and Bananrepubliken (1999–), named after Petter's No. 1, triple-Platinum album (1999) and which signified the start of the Swedish hip hop boom. Since 1998, Petter's albums have charted in Sweden, with his debut album *Mitt sjätte Sinne* peaking at No. 5, with double Platinum certification in Sweden; *Petter* (2001) peaked at No. 16 and *P* peaked at No. 1, both attaining Gold certification in Sweden.

Despite the success of Swedish rap, the language has not replaced English as native or local languages have done in other countries. Absent Minded (1995–2006*) and Sherlock (1995–1997), from Stockholm, and Spotrunnaz (1994–), from Malmö, continued rapping in English. But Sherlock's Thomas Rusiak (Erik Thomas Sihlberg, 1976–), a rapper, singer-songwriter, and producer, later had a solo career and, since 2004, Stockholm duo Snook (slang for Nose, 2000–2009) also shifted to more Swedish rap; however, Kashal-Tee (Samuel Gezelius, 1978–), Headtag (1998–2004*), Loose Cannons (2000*–2002), the Narcissists (aka The Narcs, 2000–2003), and the Casual Brothers (2002–) rap in English. Topics continue to include localized American gangsta themes, drinking or partying rap, romance, and focus on immigrant issues such as feeling out of place or discrimination.

INTO THE 21st CENTURY

Twenty-first-century Swedish acts either opt for English or Swedish only, use dialects of Swedish, or combine languages. They also fuse hip hop with jazz, reggae, dancehall, electronica, neo soul, R&B, and heavy metal. Notable examples include Million Stylez (Kenshin Iryo, 1981–), a Swedish dancehall, reggae, and hip hop artist of Japanese and French descent from Stockholm; and American-born, Lund-raised Timbuktu (Jason Michael Bosak Diakité, 1975–), a hip hop and reggae rapper and television music composer of Malian descent, who works with the funk rock, soul, and Afrobeat band Damn! (1995–). Timbuktu also belongs to Sedlighetsroteln (Vice Squad, 2000–), a collective of Swedish rappers, singers, and producers that includes members from Looptroop and Mobbade Barn Med Automatvapen (MBMA, Bullied Children with Automatic Weapons, 1999*–). Since 2001,

Looptroop's rapper Promoe's (Mårten Edh, b. Nils Mårten Ed, 1976–) solo career has focused on ragga hip hop, with early albums in English, but since 2009, he has recorded in Swedish. Movits! (2007–) is a swing–hip hop fusion band from Luleå, which is located Sweden's northern coast. In 2009, Movits! attained international notoriety when it was interviewed and performed on the American television show *The Colbert Report* (2005–2014). Its album *Ut ur min Skalle!* (*Out of My Head*, 2011) peaked nationally at No. 10. Another band, Maskinen (The Machine, 2007–), fuses hip hop with electronica and *funk carioca* known as *baile funk* (a combination of Miami bass, gangsta rap, and electronica that started in Rio de Janeiro, Brazil and contains samples of accordion and horns, called *stabs*).

More 21st-century Stockholm acts include rappers Nebay Meles (Nebay Alay Shisay Araya, 1997–); Adam Tensta (Adam Momodou Eriksson Taal, 1983–), of Finnish and Gambian descent; Linda Pira (Linda Marie Pira Giraldo, 1985–), of Colombian descent; producer Mack Beats (Marko Saez, 1984–); and the groups Close Creative Comrads (CCC, 2001*–), Highwon (2002*–), Phenomena 3 (PH3, 2010*–), and Kartellen (2008–2016). The most famous hip house group is Swedish House Mafia (2008–2013), who is also from Stockholm.

Numerous acts from Uppsala have also emerged, including MBMA, Afasi & Filthy (2002–2009), and Labyrint (2007–). Emerging from Sundsvall is Supersci (aka Superscientifiku, 1997–), which has a female rapper and singer-songwriter, Remedeeh (Anna Kerttu, n.d.). Lund, the origin of Timbuktu, is also home of his reggae band Helt Off (Completely or Fully Off, 2003–), as well as R&B hip hop rapper Adam Kanyama (1995–). The Malmö scene gave birth to acts such as Advance Patrol (AP, 1998–); hip hop, reggaetón, and Latin music crew, the group Dollar Bill (2002–); rapper-songwriter Lazee (Mawule Kwabla Kulego, 1985–), of Ghanaian descent; and rapper, producer, and entrepreneur Rebstar (Rebin Shah, 1988–), of Persian and Kurdish descent. Rebstar's label Today Is Vintage (2012–) produces, promotes, and distributes Swedish hip hop with the aim to create a "Swedish Invasion."

DIASPORA ACTS

Sweden has become home to a large number of diaspora acts, who still mostly opt to rap in English: Ison & Fille (1994–) has members from Sweden, the United States, and Chile; half of the duo Spotrunnaz is from Zambia; the gay hip hop pioneering group Addis Black Widow (1995–), whose songwriter, rapper Addis Black Widow (aka Pigeon, Armias Pigeon Mamo, n.d.) is from Ethiopia; feminist rapper Feven (Feven Ghebremicael, 1975–), who is from Massawa, Ethiopia (now Eritrea) and has worked with Surinam-born rapper Blues (Raymond Peroti, 1975–); rapper Henok Achido (Henok Meharena, 1982–), of Eritrean descent; Nabila Abdul Fattah (1981–), originally from Lebanon; and Behrang Miri (Seyed Behrang Miri, 1984–) originally from Iran.

Kenya-born, Stockholm-raised Swedish rapper Ken (aka Ken Ring, Kenta Kofot, Ken Kiprono Ring, 1979–) worked with American hip hop and horrorcore band D12's (The Dirty Dozen, 1996–2005, 2007–2017) members on producing Smif-N-Wessun's (aka Cocoa Bravas, 1993–) eponymous album (2007). Ken's output includes *Hip Hop* (2009) and *Akustiken* (2013), which charted nationally. Lazee, who raps in English, has recorded in London. Swedish-born rapper, singer-songwriter, and producer Yarah Bravo (n.d.) is married to London-based, Russian-born, English DJ, recording label owner, writer, radio host, and music promoter DJ Vadim (n.d.) and has collaborated with his project group, One Self (2005–2006). Uppsala rapper Professor P (Petter Tarland, 1985–) and Lund producer DJ Akilles (Viktor Backemar, 1985–) fuse hip hop with jazz (2005–) and have recorded in New York City.

Melissa Ursula Dawn Goldsmith

See also: Finland; Just D; The Latin Kings; The United States

Further Reading

Ackfeldt, Anders. 2012. "'Imma March' toward Ka'ba': Islam in Swedish Hip Hop." *Contemporary Islam* 6, no. 3: 283–96.

Berggren, Kalle. 2014. "Hip Hop Feminism in Sweden: Intersectionality, Feminist Critique, and Female Masculinity." *European Journal of Women's Studies* 21, no. 3: 233–50.

Further Listening

Just D. 1990. *1 steg bak å 2 steg fram* (*1 Step Backward, 2 Steps Forward*). Ricochet/ Telegram.

Ken Ring. 2009. *Hip Hop.* Pope.

Movits! 2011. *Ut ur min Skalle!* (*Out of My Head!*). Universal.

Promoe. 2016. *Fult folk* (*Ugly People*). David Vs. Goliath/Sony Music.

Switzerland

Switzerland is a central Western European country that has had access to American hip hop since the 1980s through the distribution in major cities of American motion pictures such as *Wild Style* (1983) and *Beat Street* (1984), and hip hop subsequently developed in these large cities. Prominent Swiss rappers and breakdancers come from the largest hip hop scenes in Zürich, Basel, Bern, and Lausanne, as well as other metropolitan areas. In the mid-1980s, pioneer rappers wrote texts in American vernacular English rather than in their Swiss-German dialect. But by the late 1980s DJs and groups such as the Geneva band Duty Free (1985–) rapped in their own dialects of Swiss-French, which sparked a national preference for what was called Mundartrap (dialect rap).

Basel hardcore rapping crew P27's (1990–2000)* bilingual hit "Murder by Dialect" (1991), from the album *Overdose Funk*, marked the beginning of rappers' using Swiss mother tongues such as German, French, Italian, and Romansh, with a peppering of American vernacular English. P27 rapper Black Tiger (Urs Baur, n.d.) went on to a solo career that included albums such as the EP *Groovemaischter* (*Groove Masher* or a wordplay on *Groove Mixer* and *Groove Master*, 1998), which featured instrumental hip hop. Other early Swiss hip hop artists included EKR (Thomas Bollinger, 1970–), from Baden bei Zürich; Sens Unik (1987–2010), from Lausanne; and Italian-born Jordanian Luana (aka Chéjah, Stefania Cea, n.d.), from Basel.

Swiss rappers favor at times sound over meaning and like to employ elements such as double entendre, humor, and localization, the latter usually used for consciousness raising. Lyrical content focuses on home city pride, nationalism, progressivism, and discrimination, and some songs take the form of protests. Discrimination remains a constant topic, since many Swiss hip hop artists are immigrant (yet Swiss-born) and have been derogatorily referred to as *Secundo*, which stresses the split between Swiss and immigrant cultures and the latter's Otherness. By 1987, Switzerland not only had a fully formed hip hop music scene but had also begun hosting national breakdancing competitions.

HIP HOP IN THE 2000s

EKR and Luana have had continued success and have worked with artists such as Ultramagnetic MCs (1984–2001, 2006–), Run-D.M.C. (1981–2002), and Grandmaster Flash (1958–). Another pioneering act, Talinn-born Estonian rapper Stress (aka Billy Bear, Andres Andrekson 1977–), from the Lausanne-based rapping crew Double Pact (1994–2006), was the first rapper to top the Swiss Hit Parade. Stress fuses hip hop with pop and soul, rapping in Swiss-French. Ex-members of the short-lived Zürich rapping duo Bligg N Lexx (1999–2000), Bligg (Marco Bliggensdorfer, 1976–) and Lexx (Alex Storrer, 1972–), had successful solo careers and used Swiss-German texts. Bligg has employed a hammered zither in his beats, and his albums *0816* (2008), *Bart aber herzlich* (*Bearded but Friendly* or *Hard but Friendly*, 2010), and *Service Publigg* (2013), reached No. 1 on the Swiss Hit Parade. Post-2000s Swiss acts continue to employ dialects and sometimes different languages.

Examples of rap artists who use local dialects of Swiss-German include Basel's Griot (aka Brewz Bana, Mory Kondé, n.d.), of Guinean descent; Bern's Baze (aka Broccoli George or Dr. Broccoli, Basil Anliker, 1980–) and Dezmond Dez (Cyril Bucher, 1980–); Glarus's Luut and Tüütli (Loud and Clear, 2000–); and Landquart's Sektion Kuchikäschtli (Kitchen Cupboard, 1998–). Rap artists who use other languages include the Italian band Tempo al Tempo (1996–2000*), from Basel, who raps in Italian; Graubünden-based Liricas Analas (1999–), who raps in a Sursilvan dialect of Romansh; and Nyon's Chakal (Rodrigo Figuerdo, 1978–), an immigrant from Caracas, Venezuela, who raps in Spanish, French, and English.

Melissa Ursula Dawn Goldsmith

See also: Germany

Further Reading

Larkey, Edward. 2003. "Just for Fun? Language Choice in German Popular Music." In *Global Pop, Local Language*, pp. 131–52. Jackson: University Press of Mississippi.

Mitchell, Tony. 2003. "Doin' Damage in My Native Language: The Use of 'Resistance Vernaculars' in Hip Hop in France, Italy, and Aotearoa/New Zealand." In *Global Pop, Local Language*, pp. 3–18. Jackson: University Press of Mississippi.

Further Listening

Griot. 2008. *Strossegold* (roughly, *Strobe Gold*). Shotta Music/Universal Music.

Liricas Analas. 2012. *Analium*. Musikvertrieb AG.

Stress. 2003. *Billy Bear*. Universal Music.

Swizz Beatz

(Kasseem Dean, 1978–, Bronx, New York)

Swizz Beatz is a Grammy winning American DJ, rapper, record producer, and songwriter. Though he has released only one album as a soloist, he is known as an R&B and hip hop master producer who plays keyboards, synthesizer, and drums. He has worked with rap mainstays such as Busta Rhymes (1972–), Eve (Eve Jihan Jeffers, 1978–), and Jay-Z (1969–). He is known for eschewing samples in favor of original compositions that feature oddball uses of synthesized instruments, especially percussion sounds such as whistles, bells, and snares; for his use of response calls/vocalizations and yells; for his willingness to work in all musical genres; and for his prodigious output (as of 2018, he has 357 production credits). His songs have made it on 25 occasions into the Billboard R&B or Billboard rap Top 10 charts.

EARLY EXPERIENCE AND SUCCESS

As a boy, Swizz Beatz moved to Atlanta to live with two of his uncles who established Ruff Ryders Entertainment (1988–2010), the hip hop label which produced DMX, the first artist to whom the 16-year-old sold a beat track, "Ruff Ryders' Anthem" (No. 33 on the Hot R&B/Hip-Hop Singles and Tracks). A year later, he produced 10 of the 15 songs on the compilation album *Ryde or Die Vol. 1,* which reached No. 1 on the Billboard 200, and 14 of the 18 tracks on Eve's debut album, *Let There Be Eve . . . Ruff Ryders' First Lady* (1999), which reached the top spot on both the Billboard 200 and the R&B albums chart.

In 2001, Swizz Beatz created Full Surface Records (2001–2009), and after he discovered Philadelphia-based rapper Cassidy, the label became so successful that by 2007 he was able to sign Eve and former Ruthless Records (1987–) mainstay Bone Thugs-N-Harmony (1991–). He has released only two albums of himself on the label, *Swizz Beatz Presents G.H.E.T.T.O. Stories* (2002), on which he appears on half the tracks, and the aforementioned *One Man Band Man,* which reached No. 7 on the Billboard 200. Albums on which he has produced have sold over 80 million copies worldwide. Swizz Beatz is also a fashion designer, painter, and art collector (he owns Warhols, Basquiats, and Dalis). He has married two R&B singers, Mashonda (Mashonda Tifrere, 1979–) and later Alicia Keys (Alicia Augello Cook, 1981–). For the 2010–2011 academic year, he was named the first producer in residence at New York University. As of 2018, Swizz Beatz was serving as vice president of Reebok's sports style marketing, design, and brand music development. He has also been named Global Ambassador for New York City Health and Hospitals Corporation (HHC), has been accepted into the Harvard Business School's Owner/President Management executive program, and has been inducted into the Bronx Walk of Fame, where he received a street named in his honor.

Anthony J. Fonseca

See also: The United States

Further Reading

Chapman, Dale. 2008. "'Tha Ill, Tight Sound': Telepresence and Biopolitics in Post-Timbaland Rap Production." *Journal of the Society for American Music* 2, no. 2: 155–75.

Micallef, Ken. 2007. "Beat Bender." *Remix* 9, no. 1 (January): 26.

Further Listening

Swizz Beatz. 2002. *Swizz Beatz Presents G.H.E.T.T.O. Stories.* DreamWorks Records.

Swizz Beatz. 2007. *One Man Band Man.* Universal Motown.

Syria

Syria has seen hip hop serve as a vehicle for its youth to express concerns as they face rapid social and political change. Early in his presidency, Bashar Al Assad (2000–) instituted domestic reforms, allowing new commercial radio stations. "Good Morning Syria" (Al Madina FM) played both Syrian and Western music, bringing American hip hop artists such as 50 Cent (1975–) to Syrian airwaves. In 2007, the Syrian government reversed its reforms, blocking social media sites, claiming they encouraged militants. In 2011, this was expanded to a complete shutdown of Syria's Internet, which coincided with public protests that heralded the beginning of the Syrian Civil War. With the onset of war, hip hop has become increasingly important as an outlet for youth to cope with revolution, sectarianism, censorship, displacement, and exile.

BEGINNINGS

Syrian rap emerged in the 1990s, culminating in the old-school stylings of rap crew Murder Eyez (1999*) from Aleppo, who were featured on the internationally known "Beit Il Hip Hop" (2011) mixtape by Palestinian American FredWreck (aka FredWreck Nassar, Farid Karam Nassar, 1972–). Rap group Sham MCs (n.d.) released *Crossword* (2009*), the first full-length Syrian rap CD album. Like many Arab rappers, they began by rapping in English and French but later rapped in local dialects, creating an authentically Syrian rap style. Three rappers from Damascus and Homs, Syria formed the group LaTlaTeh (2012*–). The trio layered slow groove style rap with traditional Syrian instruments and beats, sometimes offering a direct auditory portrayal of their subject. For example, the onomatopoeic refrain of "Boom Boom Bam" (2012*) depicts the explosion of a car bomb; this refrain frames detailed accounts of the death experiences of young men killed in that event, symbols of the violent deaths of countless Syrians.

DIASPORA ARTISTS AND INTERNATIONAL ATTENTION

Hip hop artists in the Syrian diaspora have inspired Syrian rappers still inside Syria, while bringing Syrian rap styles to a worldwide audience. *The Mammoth Tusk* (2009), the debut album of Lebanese Syrian Eslam Jawaad (Wissam Khodur, n.d.), was considered an international step forward for local Arabic hip hop because established artists such as Cilvaringz (Tarik Azzougarh, 1979–), who is the rapper, manager, and producer of the Wu-Tang Clan (1992–), supported it. Jawaad was the first to record tracks in the classical "Foos-hha" Arabic language, founding a new style called Foos-hop; however, the best-known Syrian rapper is Omar Offendum (1981–), a Syrian American raised in Washington, DC. Since 2000, his output has focused on Arab youth, human rights, government oppression, and revolution, as demonstrated in his first full-length solo album, *SyrianamaricanA* (2011). He appeared on the song "#Jan25," which expressed solidarity with Egyptian revolutionaries and went viral in 2011. In "#Syria" Offendum pays homage to *dabke* musician Ibrahim Qashoush (1977–2011), who was cruelly martyred, his vocal chords cut out, after public performances of his song "Yalla Erhal Ya Bashar" ("Come on, Leave, Bashar," 2011). Offendum's sampling adds layers of meaning to the song, as he uses audio of Qashoush's chanting his famous words, while the beat features violin and cello, lending a cinematic air. The accompanying video incorporates real footage of the protests and subsequent government retaliation. Omar Offendum produced both "#Jan25" and "#Syria" in collaboration with Iraqi Canadian rapper the Narcicyst (Yassin Alsalman, 1982–), and worked with the nonprofit Islamic Relief U.S.A. in 2015 to draw attention to the continued plight of Syrians.

As life in Syria becomes increasingly perilous, surviving Syrian hip hop artists have fled to Beirut, Paris, and elsewhere. Refugee rappers include Nick Helou (1995*–), Marshall B (Basel Esa, n.d.), and Watar (aka Chord, anonymous, n.d.), formerly of LaTlaTeh. Other hip hop artists, such as brothers Mohamed and Yaser Jamous (n.d.), and Gilgamesh (Raed Ghoneim, n.d.) first performed and recorded in the Yarmouk Refugee Camp in Damascus, and have since left Syria. They continue to rap in support of oppressed Syrians.

Jennifer L. Roth-Burnette

See also: Political Hip Hop

Further Reading

Aidi, Hishaam 2011. "The Grand (Hip Hop) Chessboard Race, Rap, and *Raison d'etat*." *Middle East Report* 260 (Fall): 25–39.

Gana, N. 2012. "Rap and Revolt in the Arab World." *Social Text* 30, no. 4 (113): 25–53.

Gosa, Travis L., and Erik Nielson, eds. 2015. *Hip Hop and Obama Reader*. Oxford, England: Oxford University Press.

Taviano, Stefania. 2013. "Global Hip Hop: A Translation and Multimodal Perspective." *Textus* 26, no. 3: 97–112.

Further Listening

Jawaad, Eslam. 2009. *The Mammoth Tusk*. Eslamophobic Music.

Offendum, Omar. 2010. *SyrianamaricanA*. Self-released.

T

Taiwan

Taiwan's hip hop music is usually rapped in Hokkien or Mandarin, and songs are often less vulgar than with American hip hop; the subject matter includes working conditions, love, friendship, money, and culture. Taiwan's first hip hop artists recorded in the early 1990s, and a few artists have established themselves since. Some of the bigger names include L.A. Boyz (1991–1997); Da Mouth (Dá zuǐbā, 2007–), from Irvine, California; Soft Lipa (Dan bao, 1982–), from Tainan, Taiwan; and Machi (Májí, 2003–), MC HotDog (Yáo Zhōngrén, 1978–), and Dog G (Peh-ōe-jī, aka Dwagie, Tseng Kuan-jung, 1984–), from Taipei. Early Taiwanese hip hop was popularized by L.A. Boyz, whose albums include *Shiam!* (*Shine*, 1992); *Jump* (1992), and *Fantasy* (1994). The title song of *Jump* is reminiscent of "Jump" by Kriss Kross (1991–2001), and *That's the Way* (1994) includes a hip hop rendition of "That's the Way I Like It" by KC and the Sunshine Band (1973–1985, 1993–). L.A. Boyz's initial interest in hip hop came from dances band members learned while in Orange County and Los Angeles, and from fashion encountered in Compton and South Central Los Angeles. Its musical style combines hip hop, new jack swing, and techno dance.

More recent artists include Da Mouth (Big Mouth), Machi, MC HotDog, Dog G, and Soft Lipa. Da Mouth was formed by artists from various nations: Canadian-Taiwanese MC40 (Xue Shi Ling, 1983–), Korean-Taiwanese-American male vocalist Harry (anonymous, n.d.), Japanese-Taiwanese DJ Huang (anonymous, n.d.), and Japanese female vocalist Aisa Senda (1982–), from Ginowan. The group, whose music owes quite a bit to boy and girl band sounds, is known as the Asian version of the Black Eyed Peas (1995). A couple of its albums are *Da Mouth* (2007), *Wáng yuán kǒu lì kǒu* (*Players*, 2008), and *One Two Three* (2010). Machi, a nine-member band, often collaborated with well known foreign hip hop artists such as Missy Elliott (1971–). Most of its hits include rap in Hokkien, and its popular albums include *2nd Opus* (2004) and *Superman* (2005). Hits include "Giving U What U Want," and "Retribution" (both 2005). MC HotDog is known for his two famous hits, "Wǒ de shēng huó" and "Hán Líu lái xí" ("My Life" and "The Korea Invasion," respectively, 2005*). Some of his songs, such as "Hā Gǒu Bāng" ("The HotDog Crew," 2005*) make use of turntables. His album *Wake Up* (2006) contains the hit song "Wǒ ài Tái mèi" ("I Love Taiwanese Girls"), which samples the R&B 1972 hit "I'll Be Around," by the Spinners (1954–). He later had another hit single, "Mr. Almost" (2008). Dog G, who started in the early 2000s and has collaborated with MC HotDog, is best known for his pro-Taiwan nationalist hit single, "Taiwan Song" (2002). Soft Lipa has collaborated with Jabberloop (2004–), a jazz quintet from Kyoto, Japan in his aim to fuse rap with jazz. He is known for rapping over both jazz and hip hop beats, and notably uses a soft voice with a relaxed vocal timbre when he raps over smooth jazz. His albums include *Moonlight* (2010) and *Renovate* (2013), and his single hits include "I Want You" (2010) and "Last Morning (2012)."

Kheng Keow Koay

See also: China; The United States

Further Reading

Liew Kai, Khiun. 2006. "Xi Ha (Hip Hop) Zones within Global Noises: Mapping the Geographies and Politics of Chinese Hip Hop." *Perfect Beat* 7, no. 4: 52–81.

Schweig, Meredith. 2016. "Young Soldiers, One Day We Will Change Taiwan": Masculinity Politics in the Taiwan Rap Scene." *Ethnomusicology* 60, no. 3: 383–410.

Talib Kweli

(Talib Kweli Greene, 1975–, Brooklyn, New York)

Talib Kweli is a hip hop rapper, songwriter, entrepreneur, and social activist who started out with a guest appearance on the Cincinnati, Ohio–based rap group Mood's (aka Three Below Zero, 1993–) album *Doom* (1997). He then joined with fellow Brooklyn rapper Mos Def (1973–) to form the duo Black Star (1997–) and record for Rawkus Records (1995–2007). Kweli went on to have a successful solo career, often collaborating with some of the most recognizable names in rap, including Kanye West (1977–) and Pharrell (1973–). His third album, *Eardrum* (2007), reached No. 2 on both the Billboard 200 and the Top R&B/Hip-Hop Albums chart. His vocal range is tenor or second tenor, and he has a boyish rapping voice, both rare for rap (with notable exceptions in comic rap), and his raps contain references to popular culture and literature, usually in the form of quickly delivered, clever wordplay, and unexpected multisyllabic rhyme and near rhyme. His music varied during his career, as he evolved from hardcore rap beats to neo soul, R&B, and funk influenced beats, often using chill out rhythms, then back to hardcore urban beats.

EARLY YEARS AND INFLUENCES

Kweli grew up in a highly educated environment, being the son of an English professor and a university administrator and having a brother who went on to become a Yale graduate, Supreme Court clerk, and professor of Constitutional Law. Kweli, however, was drawn to the music scene and experimental theatre, and he idolized Afrocentric rap acts such as De La Soul (1987–) and the Native Tongues Collective (1988–1996).

COLLABORATIONS, SOLO PROJECTS, AND AESTHETIC GOALS FOR RAP

As cofounder of Black Star, Kweli got his friend and Cincinnati-based collaborator Hi-Tek (Tony Cottrell, 1976–) to produce the album *Mos Def and Talib Kweli*

Are Black Star (1998). He collaborated with Hi-Tek again on the 2000 album *Train of Thought* and co-organized the anti–police violence project Hip Hop for Respect with Mos Def; he also created his own label, Blacksmith Music (2000–).

In 2001 and 2002, he contributed to the Red Hot Organization's (1990–) musical projects to raise money and awareness for AIDS victims. Kweli's solo debut, *Quality* (2002), was a move toward neo soul and R&B; his *The Beautiful Struggle* (2004) was a return to some of the urban beats and concerns of his early career, intermixed with slow-paced neo soul songs of romance. *Quality* peaked at No. 21 on the Billboard 200, while *The Beautiful Struggle* reached No. 14.

In 2007, he signed Jean Grae (1976–) to Blacksmith Records and released *Eardrum*. In 2010, he collaborated with Hi-Tek for a second album, *Revolutions per Minute*. His next solo studio albums, *Gutter Rainbows* (2011), *Prisoner of Conscious* (2012), *Gravitas* (2014), and *F— the Money* (2015), were all released on his own label, Javotti Media (2011–), and three of the four charted on the Billboard 200.

Kweli's influence on rap culture comes from his crusade to make rap less materialistic and violent, and more eloquent and activist.

Anthony J. Fonseca

See also: Black Nationalism; Mos Def; Native Tongues; Political Hip Hop; The United States

Further Reading
Spady, James G. 2006. "The Fluoroscope of Brooklyn Hip Hop: Talib Kweli in Conversation." Interview with Talib Kweli. *Callaloo* 29, no. 3: 993–1011.

Ware, Tony. 2012. "Idle Warship Rapper Talib Kweli and Singer Res Discuss Defying Musical Definitions, and the Ten-Year Collaboration that Culminated in *Habits of the Heart*." *Electronic Musician* 28, no. 7: 32–40.

Further Listening
Talib Kweli. 2007. *Eardrum*. Blacksmith Music.

Tanzania

Tanzania is an Eastern African presidential constitutional republic of 55.6 million people who descend from several ethnic, linguistic, and religious groups and speak over 100 different languages, although Swahili is considered the national language. Its recent capitals include its current one, Dodoma, and its former one, Dar es Salaam, its largest city and place where most government offices are still located. Tanzanian hip hop, balled *bongo flava*, roughly translated as brain flavor, developed in the 1990s as a fusion of American hip hop, reggae, R&B, Afrobeat, dancehall, and traditional Tanzanian music.

The country's music ranges from traditional African music associated with specific ethnic populations to the vocal- and string-based *taarab*, or sung poetry with Islamic, African (rattles and drums), Middle Eastern (*oud*, zither, and tambourine), and European (guitar) roots, and a distinctive hip hop known as bongo flava, a subset of Swah rap (rap in Swahili). Traditional instruments include tuned goblet drums (similar to the *djembe*), tuned cylindrical drums (similar to the Indian *dhol* or *dholak*), tin rattles, and *ilimba* (a large *kalimba*). Tanzanian music was influenced by dance music (e.g., Cuban *rumba*) in the early 1930s, which introduced brass, Latin percussion, and strings, and later by European elements in the 1960s, which eventually led to a new style called *Swahili jazz*, a fusion of Latin, European, and African music. This evolved into the 1970s laid-back dance sound (called *dansi*) popularized by Orchestre Safari Sound (1970*–1985), which in 1985 became the offshoot bands International Orchestra Safari Sound (1985–1989) and Orchestre Maquis Original (1985–, though technically 1970–). Meanwhile, Vijana Jazz (1971–1990) became the first band to add electronic instruments to dansi. A stripped down dansi music called *mchiriku* emerged later—vocalists sing against three or four different drums accompanied by a keyboard; often outdated speakers are used to produce feedback. Rock music did not become very popular in the country, even though Queen (1970–) lead singer Freddie Mercury (Farouk Bulsara, 1946–1991) was born in Stone Town, Zanzibar (Tanzania).

Reggae became popular in the early 1990s. At present, Ras Nas (Nasibu Mwanukuzi, n.d.), who combines reggae, Afrobeat, and dub poetry, is considered the most popular Tanzanian reggae musician. Early Tanzanian hip hop started as an underground movement in the 1980s, and mainstream rap emerged around 1991 with various rapper competitions. The first rappers rapped in English, imitating American songs, although Saleh Ajabry (n.d.) began rapping in original Swahili lyrics in 1991. Dar es Salaam–based Kwanza Unit (KU, First Unit, 1993–1999) was the first Tanzanian hip hop crew. It was a collective (super crew) inspired by Afrika Bambaataa (1957–) that used rapping texts initially in English, but soon favored Swahili.

Bongo flava's name is credited to a Dar es Salaam radio disc jockey, Mike Mhagama (n.d.), who first used it in 1996. He derived it from the Swahili words *ubongo*, a nickname for Dar Es Salaam that also means brain. Bongo flava's best-known producers include Master J (Joachim Kimario, n.d.), John B (John Blass, n.d.), and dancehall pioneer Dully Sykes (Abdul Sykes, 1980–). The first rap album was recorded by a crew called Mawingu (1992–), which had a minor hit in 1992 with "Oya Msela" ("A Drinker"). Other early Tanzanian hip hop acts included the Hard Blasters (1989–), from Dar Es Salaam, by some accounts the first crew that pioneered the bongo flava sound in Swahili; in 1994, Professor Jay (1975–) became the crew's MC.

Tanzanian hip hop was introduced to the international stage in 2004 when fledgling German record label Out Here Records (2004–) released a 14-track compilation album called *Bongo Flava: Swahili Rap from Tanzania*, which showcased rap crew X Plastaz (1996–), which used trip hop (downtempo) beats against chants and raps in in Maa (Maasai language) and Swahili; the crew became one of the country's most popular rap acts over time. Other popular hip hop acts include rapper Juma Nature (aka Sir Nature, Juma Kassim Ally, 1980–), rap duo Gangwe Mobb (1997–2004), and Mr. II (aka Sugu or 2-proud, Joseph Mbilinyi, 1972–). Juma Nature, founder of the Wanaume rap collective, raps about AIDS, poverty, class and wealth barriers, and self-esteem. Gangwe Mobb, based in the poor Temeke neighborhood in Dar es Salaam, performs music that borders on grime and trap. One of its MCs, Inspector Haroun (Haroun Rashida Kahena, n.d.), went on to form other crews and had a solo career. Songea-based Mr. II, who went on to be elected to the Tanzanian Parliament from 2010 until 2020, rapped about politics and social inequalities and became the most popular Tanzanian rapper in the 1990s. Other hip hop acts include the Makala Brothers (1993–), GWM (aka Gangstas with *Matatisu*, Gangstas with Problems, 1997–2000*), Deplowmatz (aka DPT, Tha De-Plow-Matz, 1992–1999), Bantu Pound (aka Bantu Pound Gangsters, 1993–), Mbeya-based MaNgwair (Albert Kenneth Mangwea, 1982–2013), and Underground Souls (1997–), which performed jazz rap. Female rappers have had difficulty finding success in Tanzania.

Anthony J. Fonseca and Melissa Ursula Dawn Goldsmith

See also: Kenya

Further Reading

Clark, Msia Kibona. 2014. "Gender Representations among Tanzanian Female Emcees." In *Hip Hop and Social Change in Africa: Ni Wakati*, edited by Msia Kibona Clark and Mickie Mwanzia Koster, chap. 9. Lanham, MD: Lexington Books.

Mbuya, Mejah. 2014. "Tanzanian MCs vs. Social Discourse." In *Hip Hop and Social Change in Africa: Ni Wakati*, edited by Msia Kibona Clark and Mickie Mwanzia Koster, chap. 11. Lanham, MD: Lexington Books.

Perullo, Alex. 2012. "Imitation and Innovation in the Music, Dress, and Camps of Tanzanian Youth." In *Hip Hop Africa: New African Music in a Globalizing World*, edited by Eric Charry, chap. 9. Bloomington: Indiana University Press.

Further Listening

Various Artists. 2004. *Bongo Flava: Swahili Rap from Tanzania*. Out Here Records.

Tech N9ne

(Aaron Dontez Yates, 1971–, Kansas City, Missouri)

Tech N9ne is an American rapper-songwriter, record producer, actor, and entrepreneur. His stage is a reference to the TEC-9 semiautomatic pistol, and was given to him because of his quick, staccato rapping style and rhyming, which eventually came to be called the chopper style of rapping (although Tech N9ne claims it stands for his rhyming technique, with the number nine representing the number of completion in Bahá'í and Hinduism). Releasing an album virtually every year since 1999, he has sold over two million copies total, and his music has been used in film, television, and video games.

He is also known for popularizing and spreading the chopper rapping style through his collaboration albums with rappers from the Midwest, South, and both East and West coasts. Tech N9ne's single "Midwest Choppers 2" (2009) from his album *Sickology 101* actually explains his goal of spreading the word on chopper rap through what he called "elite" and "intricate" tongues around the world, including California, New York, Denmark, and Australia. Tech N9ne is revered for his rhyme schemes and chopper style rap abilities; his range of topics, from atmospheric and dark, to uplifting; his creation of rap flow patterns that have a percussive quality (created by his singsong delivery while running words together quickly); his use of varied instrumentation and dramatic gestures; and for his camera presence in music videos.

ALBUMS AND SUCCESS

Born and raised in Kansas City, Missouri, Tech N9ne became a member of a short-lived rap trio named Black Mafia (1990*–1991), which self-released a three-track mixtape in 1991, and he became a member of the group Nnutthowze (1993), which disbanded before recording. He joined Yukmouth's (Jerold Dwight Ellis III, 1974–), Oakland, California–based collective the ReGime (1997–) in 1997. The following year, as a member of the 57th Street Rogue Dog Villians (1998–2002), Tech N9ne released three albums on Hog Style Records (1998–2012) and one 12-inch single.

In 1999, Tech N9ne, along with other guest rappers such as Eminem (1972–), KRS-One (1965–), and Kool G. Rap (Nathaniel Thomas Wilson, 1968–), appeared on the San Francisco rap duo Sway and King Tech's (1990–) song "The Anthem." That year, Tech N9ne cofounded the Strange Music record label and on the Mid-WestSide Records (1996–2006) label released two solo albums, *The Calm Before the Storm Part I* and *The Worst*. He followed those with *Anghellic* (2001) on the JCOR Entertainment label (1998–2004); it sold over 250,000 copies. His fourth studio album, *Absolute Power* (2002), was the first on his Strange Music label, and it topped the sales of *Anghellic* by almost 100,000; however, it did not do as well on the Billboard 200.

Tech N9ne's next six albums on the Strange label, *Project: Deadman* (2004), *Vintage Tech* (2005), *Everready: The Religion* (2006), *Misery Loves Kompany* (2007), *Killer* (2008), and *Sickology 101*, all sold over 100,000 copies. Tech N9ne's 2009 album, *K.O.D.*, marked a turn toward a darker atmosphere, and was his third consecutive album to peak at higher than No. 20 on the Billboard 200. His third *Collabos* album, *The Gates Mixed Plate* (2010), broke his string of albums to sell 100,000 copies, but it became his highest chart performer to date on the Billboard Top R&B/Hip-Hop and Top Rap Albums charts, peaking at Nos. 5 and 4, respectively.

In 2011, Tech N9ne released *All 6's and 7's*, the first to reach the Top 10 on the Billboard 200, peaking at No. 4. It also was his first to reach the top spot on the Top R&B/Hip-Hop and Top Rap Albums charts. He has released six albums since, and two of those *Strangeulation* (2014) and *Special Effects* (2015), have topped the Top R&B/Hip-Hop and Top Rap charts. In 2006, he began his series of collaborative albums called *Tech N9ne Collabos*. As of 2018, Tech N9ne has finished seven *Collabos* albums.

Anthony J. Fonseca

See also: Chopper; The United States

Further Reading

Amter, Charlie. 2007. "Making His Own Flow." Under "Pop Music" in *Los Angeles Times*, July 12, E10.

McCann, Bryan J. 2017. *The Mark of Criminality: Rhetoric, Race, and Gangsta Rap in the War-on-Crime Era*. Tuscaloosa: University of Alabama Press.

Quinn, Eithne. 2005. *Nuthin' But a "G" Thang: The Culture and Commerce of Gangsta Rap*. New York: Columbia University Press.

Further Listening

Tech N9ne. 2003. *Absolute Power*. Strange Music.

Tech N9ne. 2011. *All 6's and 7's*. Strange Music.

Thailand

Thailand is a Southeast Asian constitutional monarchy with a population of 69 million, 14 million of whom live in Bangkok, its capitol and largest city, and its surrounding metropolitan area. Thailand's citizens have existed under a parliamentary democracy and military junta for decades, the latest coup d'état being in 2014. Thai hip hop was first made popular in the 1980s by singer and producer Joey Boy (Apisit Opasaimlikit, 1975–), who collaborated with Canadian reggae singer Snow (Darren Kenneth O'Brien, 1969–) on the song "Fun, Fun, Fun" (1995), a big hit in Thailand. Five years later, he started his own record label, Gancore Club (2000–).

Historically, Thailand went through periods of instability as Indian kingdoms and indigenous states; it also endured 19th-century British and French feuding over colonization (which kept it independent). Thai people lived under a monarchy until 1932, followed by 60 years of military rule prior to 2014. Thai music is influenced by China, India, Laos, and Iran (Persia) in its traditional instrumentation, and more recently its popular music shows a heavy influence of the United States.

Western music has been imported to Thailand since the early 1930s, when Western Classical music, as well as popular music such as show tunes, jazz, and tango reached there. Thai composers such as Montri Tramote (1908–1995) helped popularize Western art and popular music by adopting standard Western musical notation. Jazz is so entrenched in Thai culture that King Prajadhipok (Rama VII, 1883–1941, reigned 1925–1935) and King Bhumibol Adulyadej (1927–2016, reigned 1946–2016) both composed jazz-influenced music. By the 1960s, Thai musicians were emulating American and English rock acts in Bangkok. In the central region of Thailand, however, one kind of popular music originated there, known as *phleng luk thung* or *luk thung* (meaning *child of the field song*) or as Thai country music that focused often on rural topics, pastoral themes, romance, and religious and other traditional cultures. Less explicitly, *Luk Thung* would later serve as political or social commentary and criticism. These popular songs were eventually featured in 1960s and 1970s Thai films.

Joey Boy's influence would be felt by Thai rappers such as Da Jim (aka Dajim, Suwitcha Suphawira, 1977–), who started an underground record label, N.Y.U. Club (2002–) and hosted hip hop radio shows, although his lyrics have led to arrests due to censorship laws. The most popular Thai hip hop acts are Thaitanium (2000–) and Joni Anwar (1981–) of Raptor (n.d.). Thaitanium is a Thai American trio that produced and recorded its first two albums in New York City and released them later in Thailand. Raptor is a duo consisting of Joni Anwar (as Joni Raptor) and Louis Scott (1982–). In the 1990s Raptor began including rap in its songs. Joni Raptor and Scott formed Raptor in their teens, giving them a great appeal to youth, who were influenced by both their music and hip hop fashion, and Raptor's debut album sold over a million copies. Anwar went on to a highly successful solo career.

Anthony J. Fonseca

See also: Anwar, Joni; Laos; Thaitanium

Further Reading

Jirattikorn, Amporn. 2006. "Lukthung: Authenticity and Modernity in Thai Country Music." *Asian Music* 37, no. 1: 24–50.

Poss, Nicholas. 2013. "'Reharmonizing' the Generations: Rap, Poetry, and Hmong Oral Traditional." In *Diversity in Diaspora: Hmong Americans in the Twenty-First Century*, edited by Mark Edward Pfeifer, Monica Chiu, and Kou Yang, chap. 10. Honolulu: University of Hawai'i Press.

Further Listening
Thaitanium. 2002. *P77*. Self-released.

Thaitanium

(2000–, New York City, New York)

Thaitanium is a Thai American rap group that consists of Khan (aka K.H. or King of da Hustle, Khanngoen Nuanual, 1976–), Day (aka Sunny Day, Nay Myo Thant, n.d.), and Way (aka P. Cess, Prinya Intachai, n.d.). The band's members were born in either Bangkok, Thailand, or New York City. Thaitanium raps in both Thai and American urban vernacular languages. As an opening act for 50 Cent (1975–) and the hip hop project Fort Minor (2004–2006, 2015–), a trio that appears on various hip hop tracks, and a live band that tours worldwide, Thaitanium has brought global attention to Thai hip hop. Khan and Day emigrated from Bangkok and started their careers Djing and MCing for house parties in the San Francisco area. In 2000, Thaitanium formed after Khan and Day moved to New York City and met Way. The trio's first two albums, *AA* (2000) and *Thai Riders* (2002), were self-released. Its third album was a hip hop soundtrack for the American film *Province 77* (2002), which was about an expatriate Thai family living in Los Angeles. It tracks their identity struggle between their traditional homeland ties and their new life. The band's other themes include sexual attraction, romance, braggadocio, fame, and ambition.

In 2005, Thaitanium released *RAS* (*Resisting Against Da System*), the same year that Sony BMG Music Entertainment distributed the band's *Thailand's Most Wanted*, which was the first globally distributed Thai hip hop album. That year, Thaitanium began to gain international attention for appearing on tracks of numerous Thai and Japanese hip hop artists, including dance-pop and electropop singer Tata Young (Amita Marie Young, 1980–), from Bangkok; the hip hop group DS455 (1989–), from Yokohama, Japan; and the hip hop group M-Flo (1997–), from Tokyo. In 2006, Thaitanium performed at the MTV Asia Awards. Its album, *Flip Side* (2008), was released on the GMM Grammy label (1983–) and was the band's first global album release. In 2013, Thaitanium was the opening act for 50 Cent and Snoop Dogg (1971–) at the Together Festival in Bangkok.

Thaitanium's subsequent albums and compilations include *Compilation 3: Still Here* (2013), *Thaitanium* (2014), *Still Resisting* (2015), and *16 Years* (2016), all self-released on their Bangkok-based Thaitanium Entertainment label (2010–), which makes it the first Thai hip hop group to publish its own songs. As of 2018, Thaitanium has also focused on other ventures, including its own clothing line, modeling, publishing, and acting.

One interesting aspect of Thaitanium's sound is when it incorporates or implies Thai melodies as loops, as it does in "Too Much" from *P77*. Another interesting technique is using Thai texts to vocalize scratching (turntablism), as in "Doown" ("Cool," 2010). In 2014, rap in English and more closely resemble American gangsta rap than in the past in "Wake Up (Bangkok City)," which featured Snoop Dogg.

Melissa Ursula Dawn Goldsmith

See also: Snoop Dogg; Thailand; Turntablism; The United States

Further Reading

Klangboonkrong, Manta. 2013. "Snoop Dogg Pimps It Up for Bangkok." *The Nation* (Bangkok, Thailand), January 22, 1.

Thamkruphat, Tanya Sangpun. 2005. "As Tough as Thaitanium." *The Bangkok Post*, June 23, 1.

Further Listening

Thaitanium. 2002. *P77.* Self-released.

Thaitanium. 2004. *RAS.* GMM Grammy.

Tijoux, Ana

(Ana María Merino Tijoux, 1977–, Lille, France)

Ana Tijoux is a French Chilean musician born to Chilean parents living in political exile in France during the reign of Augusto Pinochet (1915–2006, in power 1973–1981). Her mother is Chilean sociologist María Emilia Tijoux (1949–). Ana Tijoux moved back to Chile after the return of civil power in 1993, and formed the group Los Gemelos (The Twins, 1995–1997). In 1997, Tijoux was featured on *Mama Funk,* the debut studio album by Los Tetas (The Breasts, 1994–2004, 2011–), a funk band that went on to release five albums and whose *La Medicina* (1997) is considered one of the best Latin American funk albums. That year, she became MC of hip hop group Makiza (1997–2006). By 2001, she and the group's members were pursuing solo careers, and Tijoux moved back to France from 2001 until 2004, when she rejoined Makiza for a tour to promote the rerelease of the group's 1998 debut album, *Vida Salvaje.* Tijoux's big solo break came in 2009 with her second album, *1977,* a collection of Spanish and French autobiographical songs that explored death, friendship, creativity, and fate and which broke completely with Tijoux's pop roots with edgy melodies and harder beats. The lead single, "1977," became an underground hit, placed in the Top 10 in the WorldHipHopMarket.com chart, and was featured in Season Four of *Breaking Bad* (2008–2013). On the strength of *1977,* Tijeaux began a 2010 North American tour. Throughout her oeuvre, Tijoux vocally alternates between a raw, aggressive higher rap register and a laid-back, lower, breathy talk-singing, and her songs vary from sampled rap, to funky brass-infused R&B style hip hop, to experimental rock-infused hip hop. Tijoux has released four solo studio albums, *Kaos* (2007), *1977, La bala* (*The Bullet,* 2011), and *Vengo* (*I Come,* 2014), and one mixtape, *Elefant* (2011).

Anthony J. Fonseca

See also: Chile; France

After living in exile, French-Chilean alternative hip hop rapper and singer-songwriter Ana Tijoux returned to Santiago, where she formed and fronted the Chilean hip hop band Makiza from 1997 until 2006, when she pursued a solo career. By the 2010s Tijoux became one of the best known and most admired female hip hop artists for her breathy talk-singing sound, for addressing topics that range from protesting violence and corruption, to the treatment of women, and for storytelling based on autobiographical content. (Victor Chavez/Getty Images)

Further Reading

Istodor, Luca. 2017. "Ana Tijoux's Radical Crossing of Borders." *Revista: Harvard Review of Latin America* 16, no. 2: 65–66.

Lindholm, Susan. 2017. "Hip Hop Practice as Identity and Memory Work in and in-between Chile and Sweden." *Suomen Antropologi: Journal of the Finnish Anthropological Society* 42, no. 2: 60–74.

Further Listening

Ana Tijoux. 2009. *1977.* Oveja Negra-Potoco Discos.

Timbaland

(Timothy Zachery Mosley, 1972–, Norfolk, Virginia)

Timbaland is an American record producer, turntablist, rapper, and singer-songwriter known primarily for his work with Portsmouth, Virginia rapper and producer Missy

Elliott (1971–), Victoria, British Columbia, R&B and pop singer-songwriter Nelly Furtado (1978–), and Memphis hip hop singer-songwriter Justin Timberlake (1981–). Timbaland has also worked with Washington, DC rapper Ginuwine (Elgin Baylor Lumpkin, 1970–); Brooklyn, New York R&B and pop singer, actress, and model Aaliyah (Dana Haughton, 1979–2001); Brooklyn rapper, producer, and entrepreneur Jay-Z (1969–); Brooklyn rapper-songwriter and producer Nas (1973–); Champaign, Illinois rapper-songwriter Ludacris (1977–); Lagrange, Georgia rapper Bubba Sparxxx (1977–); Bay City, Michigan pop singer-songwriter and producer Madonna (1958–); and Toronto rapper, singer-songwriter, producer and actor Drake (1986–). His 2007 album *Shock Value* was certified Platinum and reached No. 5 on the Billboard 200; it also reached No. 1 in Australia, Austria, and Ireland. He has won four Grammy Awards and has had a total of five songs reach the Billboard Hot 100 Top 10, with two of those, both featuring Furtado, reaching No. 1: "Promiscuous" (2006) and "Give It to Me" (2007); the latter also featured Timberlake.

Timbaland started as a rapper in the duo Timbaland & Magoo (1989–), with schoolmate Melvin Barcliff (n.d.). After joining forces with Missy Elliott, he became part of DeVante Swing's (Donald Earle DeGrate Jr., 1969–) Swing Mob record label (1991–1995), becoming part of a group of musicians known as Da Bassment Cru. Eventually, he got his own imprint label, Mosley Music Group (2005–), associated from 2005 to 2014 with parent label Interscope Records (1989–) and from 2014 on with Epic (1953–), the latter because of Timbaland's success as executive producer of Michael Jackson's (1958–2009) posthumous *Xscape* (2014). Moseley Music Group featured artists such as Furtado, OneRepublic (2002–), and Keri Hilson (1982–). Timbaland's production of Furtado's 2006 album *Loose* (2006) was a commercial success and earned him a BET (Black Entertainment Television) Hip Hop Award for Producer of the Year. As a songwriter he has written or cowritten over 100 hit songs; however, he has been involved in three plagiarism lawsuits. More recent production successes have included V. Bozeman's (Veronika Bozeman, 1988–) R&B hit "What Is Love" (2015) as well as rapper and singer-songwriter Tink's (Trinity Home, 1995–) "Million" (2015), which samples Aaliyah's "One in a Million" (1996, written by Elliott and Timbaland). As of 2018, Timbaland continues producing music.

Timbaland's production sound incorporates self-borrowing and an eclectic use of music ranging from classic soul to psychedelic or Afrofuturist funk, as well as from beatbox effects and turntablism to his trademark stuttering kickdrum, trip hop (downtempo) samples to Bollywood-influenced grooves. By inserting passages or elements from different musical styles (creating unusual juxtapositions or humorous twists), Timbaland's productions often challenge popular music genre expectations.

Anthony J. Fonseca

See also: Elliott, Missy; The United States

Further Reading

Chapman, Dale. 2008. "'That Ill, Tight Sound': Telepresence and Biopolitics in Post-Timbaland Rap Production." *Journal of the Society for American Music* 2, no. 2: 155–75.

Djupvik, Marita B. 2017. "Naturalizing Male Authority and the Power of the Producer."
   Popular Music and Society 40, no. 2: 181–200.

Further Listening
Elliott, Missy. 2001. *Miss E . . . So Addictive.* Elektra.
Elliott, Missy. 2002. *Under Construction.* Elektra.
Timbaland. 1998. *Tim's Bio: Life from da Bassment.* Blackground Records.

T.I.P. Crew

(1996–, Seoul, South Korea)

T.I.P. Crew (Teamwork is Perfect) is the first b-boy crew founded in Korea. In 1996, b-boy Virus (Dae Kyun Hwang, n.d.) founded T.I.P. Crew in Seoul. He wanted to create a crew whose choreography would be known for its large freeze formations, use of contact dance improvisation, and sense of humor. In some street, professional, and competitive shows, the crew has included South Korean flags in its routines, or has preserved South Korean performance traditions. In one showcase-style routine, a member of the crew plays a *piri*—a cylindrical oboe associated with Korean court and folk music—before the accompanying hip hop music begins and the rest of the b-boy crew appears onstage. The members, all similarly attired, dance in pairs, small groups, and as a synchronized crew, often striking multiple-person freezes between moves.

In battles, the crew uses teamwork in its solo entrances, where three or even four members will dance out together, using each other as gymnastic props, finally introducing the soloist through a carefully choreographed flip or slide. T.I.P. Crew's battle routines tend to focus on spins, flips, and gymnastic moves. Since 2001 T.I.P. Crew has hosted and helped organize the international one-on-one b-boy battle in Korea, B-boy Monster Jam. In 2002, the crew was South Korea's first entry into the B-Boy Championship in London.

T.I.P. Crew's international and national accomplishments include winning the U.K. B-Boy Championship in London and Chief Rocker Award (2007), Battle of the Year Korea and Asia (2008), the World B-Boy Classic (2009), and the Red Bull BC One Fingerbreakin' World Championship (2013). It has also finished in second place, as finalists, or as semifinalists in many Battle of the Year Korea competitions. In 2007, they were the first Korean b-boy crew to win the Minister of Culture and Tourism Award. T.I.P. Crew has appeared internationally in television shows and films. Like its more recent rival b-boy crew Gamblerz (2002–), who are also from Seoul, some of T.I.P. Crew's members were arrested for avoiding a mandatory two-year military service. In 2010, b-boy Virus was the first Korean choreographer of an American film, the action-crime comedy *Dancing Ninja*.

Since its inception, T.I.P. Crew has consisted of full-time, professional b-boys, who are known for their supportive attitude toward breakdancing, in addition to their choreographed shows for competition. In 2014, they formed the T.I.P. Dance Academy in Seoul, which emphasizes courses for all ages and dancing levels—in not only hip hop dance, but other kinds of dance styles, from street jazz to bellydancing.

Melissa Ursula Dawn Goldsmith

See also: Battling; Breakdancing; Hip Hop Dance; Korea

Further Reading

File, Curtis. 2013. *Korean Dance: Pure Emotion and Energy.* Korea Essentials No. 15. Seoul: Korea Foundation.

Song, Myoung-Sun. 2014. "The S(e)oul of Hip Hop: Locating Space and Identity in Korean Rap." In *The Korean Wave: Korean Popular Culture in Global Context,* edited by Yasue Kuwahara, chap. 7. New York: Palgrave Macmillan.

Um, Hae-Kyung. 2013. "The Poetics of Resistance and the Politics of Crossing Borders: Korean Hip Hop and 'Cultural Reterritorialisation.'" *Popular Music* 32, no. 1: 51–64.

TLC

(1991–, Atlanta, Georgia)

TLC is a female R&B group originally comprised of T-Boz (Tionne Watkins, 1970–), Left-Eye (Lisa Lopes, 1971–2002), and Crystal Jones (n.d.). Jones, who initiated the band in 1990, was early on replaced by Chilli (Rozonda Thomas, 1971–). Between 1992 and 2002, TLC produced four albums: *Oooooooohhh . . . On the TLC Tip* (1992), *CrazySexyCool* (1994), *FanMail* (1999), and *3D* (2002). It then disbanded after Left-Eye died in a car accident. The group performed in the "new jill swing" style (its version of new jack swing), blending soul-based and R&B-style vocals with the sampling, rapping, and production techniques of hip hop. TLC had four songs top the Billboard chart, "Creep" (1994), "Waterfall" (1995), "No Scrubs" (1999), and "Unpretty" (1999).

FORMATION AND OVERVIEW OF TLC'S SUCCESS

Initially formed in 1991 by Jones, TLC was mentored by Pebbles (Perri Arlette McKissack, 1965–); she managed the group as part of her production company Pebbitone (1989–1996), signing them with producer L. A. Reid (Antonio Marquis Reid, 1956–), who was her husband. His record label, LaFace Records (1989–) produced the band's first three albums. *Oooooooohhh . . . On the TLC Tip* put three songs on the U.S. charts: "Baby-Baby-Baby," "Ain't 2 Proud 2 Beg," and "What About Your Friends." *CrazySexyCool* and *FanMail* both earned the group Grammy awards for Best R&B Album (1995 and 1999), while singles from these albums also garnered Grammys. "Creep" (*CrazySexyCool*) and "No Scrubs" (*FanMail*) both won for Best R&B Performance by a Duo or Group with Vocal. The track "Waterfalls" (1995) from *CrazySexyCool* was nominated for Record of the Year in 1996.

In 2002, Left Eye Lopes died in an automobile accident in Honduras. She had recorded raps for only four tracks of the band's next intended album, *3D*, so the remaining two members completed the album. It, too, achieved success on the charts, making it to No. 6 on the Billboard 200.

FINANCIAL AND LEGAL ISSUES

In the mid-1990s, despite its unprecedented success, the group faced several financial and legal problems. In 1994, Left Eye Lopes was arrested for vandalizing the cars of her boyfriend Andre Rison (1967–), a wide receiver for the Atlanta Falcons (1965–), and burning down his mansion. She was required only to reimburse him and serve time on probation. Soon after, a financial dispute arose between Pebbitone and LaFace Records, and Reid claimed the group's members owed Pebbitone over half a million dollars each. The group filed for bankruptcy in 1995 but rallied for future albums in 1999 and 2002, continuing its association with LaFace Records.

THEMES, PERFORMANCE PRACTICE, AND SOUND

The three women of TLC were remarkable for their frank portrayal of themselves as powerful, sexual, and independent. The 1990s were a decade of liberation for black, female performers, especially on issues of female sexuality and self-reliance. Hip hop groups such as En Vogue (1989–), Salt-N-Pepa (1985–2002, 2007–), and SWV (aka Sisters with Voices, 1990–1999, 2005–) sang openly about sexual pleasure, sexual taboos, and the importance of communication and using protection in sexual relationships. These kinds of songs were part of a complex negotiation of African American womanhood; although they advocated for female independence and self-determined sexuality, they also continued the practice of objectifying women, whether in lyrics, in live performances, or in music videos, where both men and women were treated as sexual objects. TLC was part of this trend, negotiating the power of sex both through its lyrics and in representation. TLC aimed, for instance, to destigmatize condoms by attaching packets to members' clothing, and "Conclusion," the final track on TLC's first album, was an admonition to practice safe sex.

The single "Ain't 2 Proud 2 Beg," for example, places female sexual pleasure front and center, normalizing female desire and objectifying men—essentially flipping the conventional hip hop narrative on its head. The song encourages women to seek sexual satisfaction in their committed relationships, whether or not their partner is in the mood. Musically, it exemplifies new jack swing practices, presenting soul-inspired group harmonies and vocal improvisations in the bridges, layered over propulsive bass and drum grooves, synthesized and looped using a drum machine. The song features a rapped, call-and-response chorus, as well as a rap break by Left Eye Lopes, where she uses her distinctive vocal timbre and lyrical flow to emphasize the importance of mutual satisfaction in sexual relationships, a practice the band would revisit in "Waterfalls." By placing "Ain't 2 Proud 2 Beg" as the first song on their debut album, TLC set the tone for the rest of its catalog, both in terms of style and content.

TLC's albums also included hip hop skits—relatively short introductions and interludes, both scripted and improvised, dramatic and musical, common in mixtapes and albums of the 1990s. Some were comedic, such as "Sexy (Interlude)" from *CrazySexyCool*; some were focused messages, such as "Communicate (Interlude)" from *FanMail*; and some were musical, such as "Intermission I" from *Oooooooohhh . . . On the TLC Tip*. Most, no matter their style, addressed female self-sufficiency.

Those that featured male artists built on hip hop's collaborative culture to give women authority they could not otherwise achieve (female hip hop artists at the time benefited from the sponsorship of established male rappers, through them gaining access to a male-dominated genre). In "Can I Get a Witness (Interlude)" from *CrazySexyCool*, for instance, Busta Rhymes (1972–) performs a soul-based improvisation on his impressions of TLC, his rap indicating that the women of the band knew how to take care of business and were crazy, sexy, and cool women. As the years passed, the number of alternative tracks on TLC's albums diminished, while the tracks themselves became more heavily produced and musically complex. By the time of *3D,* only one of these interlude tracks, "3D Intro," appears, and it acts as a theme song for the album.

Jessica Leah Getman

See also: New Jack Swing; The Sequence; Sisters Underground; The United States

Further Reading

Goodall, Nataki H. 1994. "Depend on Myself: TLC and the Evolution of Black Female Rap." *Journal of Negro History* 79, no. 1 85–93.

Peoples, Whitney A. 2007. "'Under Construction': Identifying Foundations of Hip Hop Feminism and Exploring Bridges between Black Second-Wave and Hip Hop Feminisms." *Meridians: Feminism, Race, Transnationalism* 8, no. 1: 19–52.

Reed, Toya. 1995. "Black Female Music Artists and the New Themes in the Music." *Southern African Feminist Review* 1, no. 1: 60.

Further Listening

TLC. 1992. *Oooooooohhh . . . on the TLC Tip.* LaFace Records/Arista.

TLC. 1995. *CrazySexyCool.* LaFace Records/Arista.

TLC. 1999. *FanMail.* LaFace Records/Arista.

Togo

Togo is a small, mainly tropical rural and agrarian West African country of nearly eight million whose capital and largest city, Lomé, is located on the Gulf of Guinea. It was settled by some 21 ethnic tribes until the 16th century, when it became a slave trade center (part of the Slave Coast region). It was made a German protectorate in 1884, was transferred to France after World War I (1914–1918), and gained its independence in 1960. Since 1967, the Gnassingbé family (via presidential elections) has governed the country. Hip hop dance appeared in Togo around the same time as rapping, turntablism, or beatboxing, making its way into Togo in the 1980s.

Togo's official language is French, but indigenous languages are spoken, and half the country follows indigenous beliefs, with the other half being Christian and

Muslim. Togo's music includes maritime folksongs, as well as percussion-based dance music that uses a diverse set of rhythms and beats, although some of Togo's mountain region tribes base music on stringed instruments and flutes; most traditional music uses the griot praise-singing tradition.

The first popular Togolese musician was ballad singer Bella Bellow (Georgette Adjoavi Bellow, 1945–1973). Western styles of music became more mainstream in Togolese culture in the 1970s with the popularization of Western-style ballads, reggae, ska, and funk, made popular by singer King Mensah (Ayaovi Papavi Mensah, 1971–) and guitarist-singer Peter Solo (1972*–), the latter using call-and-response in many songs.

Political oppression of rap music caused early rap crews such as Djanta Kan (n.d.) to disband as members self-exiled to France. Togolese hip hop music started with Lomé-based rap group Black Syndicate (n.d.), but due to lack of well-funded studios, the production of albums remained scarce. A 1992 concert in Lomé by French Senegalese–Chadian rapper MC Solaar (1969–) led to furthering the local popularity of the Togolese rap crew Force One Posse (1990*–), one of the opening acts—but the band did not achieve broader fame.

Since the 1990s, a few recording studios have surfaced, and more hip hop acts have emerged, such as Bales 2 Rimes (2002–) and ex–Djanta Kan MC Yao Bobby (n.d.), who has toured Africa and Europe with the AURA (Artists United for African Rap) collective.

In 2003, the first Togo hip hop awards ceremony was held, leading to what was supposed to be the annual Togo Hip Hop Awards; however, governmental bans in 2005 stopped most political music from being produced or performed. As of 2018, Togo has made only minor contributions to African hip hop.

Anthony J. Fonseca

See also: France; Political Hip Hop; Reggae

Further Reading

Künzler, Daniel. 2007. "The 'Lost Generation': African Hip Hop Movements and the Protest of the Young (Male) Urban." In *Civil Society: Local and Regional Responses to Global Challenges*, edited by Mark Herkenrath, chap. 3. Zürich, Switzerland: LIT Verlag.

Sautman, Francesca Canadé. 2001. "Hip Hop/Scotch: 'Sounding Francophone' in French and United States Cultures." *Yale French Studies* 100 (Fall): 119–44.

Trap

Trap, an American subgenre of hip hop, is music that refers to urban areas where drug deals occur, whose inhabitants are trapped in a life of desperation. It began in the 1990s in Atlanta, Georgia, an urban metropolis ranked No. 1 in the U.S. income inequality gap by the Brookings Institute in 2014 and 2015. Trap's sound is related to various Southern hip hop subgenres, including crunk and hardcore, as well as West Coast's mobb, and hardcore, and it quickly spread from Atlanta to urban areas such as Houston and Memphis. Its signature sound, which is the product of two Atlanta producers, Shawty Redd (Demetrius Lee Stewart, 1981–) and Lex Luger (Lexus Arnel Lewis, 1991–), is defined by its electronica feel, as it has evolved over decades to sound like a hybrid of hip hop, rave, and EDM (electronic dance music—the term EDM trap is used to differentiate it from rap-based trap).

These two pioneers, and the music's other producers, share a predilection for uneven rhythms, with constant use of double or triple-time hi-hats which have a staccato attack but a lengthy, sometimes reverbed delay, juxtaposed against rhythmic snares and a heavy 808 drum kick sample and sub-bass, usually combined at the tempo at 140 beats per minute. There is also a preference for bleak, throaty, and sometimes threatening vocals; the use of music sequencers and drum samples; and a signature synthesized string, brass, percussions, and woodwind sound that is typically described as cinematic or symphonic.

The resulting music is dark, brooding, and atmospheric, even when it contains a rave or EDM frenetic dance rhythm. Trap songs are usually about drug culture: urban street life, poverty, drug deals, and violence; the songs can best be summed up as a narrative account of the harshness of the inner city and its surrounding neighborhoods.

EARLY TRAP TO 2000

Early producers such as Atlanta's Lil Jon (Jonathan Smith, 1971–), New Orleans's Mannie Fresh (Byron Otto Thomas, 1969–), and Memphis's DJ Paul (Paul Duane Beauregard, 1975–) worked with Atlanta groups such as Dungeon Family (1993–), OutKast (1991–), Goodie Mob (1991–), and Ghetto Mafia (1993–2005). Other acts, such as Port Arthur's UGK (1987–2007) and New Orleans's Master P (1970–), began to rap about the lifestyles of drug dealers. UGK's single "Pocket Full of Stones" (1993) was an early trap song which caught the attention of rap fans, and by the time Master P's "Mr. Ice Cream Man" (1996) became a hit, fans had developed a taste for what they would start to call trap rap.

By the 2000s, trap music had gone mainstream with crossover hits by Atlanta rappers such as T.I. (Clifford Joseph Harris Jr., 1980–) and Young Jeezy (Jay Wayne Jenkins, 1977–). T.I.'s second album, *Trap Muzik* (2003), which was certified Platinum and reached No. 4 on the Billboard 200, solidified the name that had informally been bandied around by fans and critics before. Two years later, Young Jeezy released his second solo album, *Let's Get It: Thug Motivation 101*, which reached No. 2 on the Billboard 200 and was certified Platinum. The music's sound began to develop around this time as well, with the preeminent trap producer of the 2000s, Shawty Redd, whose signature sound could be viewed as a textbook for all subsequent trap artists. Other notable contemporary trap producers included Memphis-based Drumma Boy (Christopher James Gholson, 1983–) and Atlanta-based Zaytoven (Xavier L. Dotson, 1980–).

TRAP IN THE 21ST CENTURY

The 2010s saw prolific producer Lex Luger achieve huge commercial success. Other recent trap producers include Atlanta's Southside (Joshua Howard Luellen, 1989–) and Sonny Digital (Sonny Corey Uwaezuoke, 1991–), and Chicago's Young Chop (Tyree Pittman, 1993–). Since 2010, Chicago's Chief Keef (Keith Cozart,

1995–) has been credited with introducing drill, a new style of trap whose signature producer is Young Chop.

In the last decade drugs and violence have been replaced by more positive messages in trap, making it more palatable to the pop artists such as Beyoncé (1981–), Lady Gaga (1986–), and Katy Perry (1984–). Trap's potential was realized when Philadelphia-based Baauer's (Harry Bauer Rodrigues, 1989–) "Harlem Shake" (2013) hit No. 1 on the Billboard Hot 100, and in 2015 when New Jersey rapper Fetty Wap's (Willie Maxwell II, 1991–) "Trap Queen" went to No. 2. In 2018, Childish Gambino's (Donald McKinley Glover Jr., 1983–) trap-infused protest song, "This Is America," debuted at No. 1 on the Billboard Hot 100, as well as the Hot R&B/Hip-Hop Songs, the Hot Rap Songs, and the Canadian Singles charts. Trap has also influenced dubstep, despite its slower rhythms. As of 2018, trap has gone international, making its way to South Korean K-pop.

Anthony J. Fonseca

See also: Crunkcore; Dirty South; Gangsta Rap; The United States

Further Reading

Balaji, Murali. 2012. "The Construction of 'Street Credibility' in Atlanta's Hip Hop Music Scene: Analyzing the Role of Cultural Gatekeepers." *Critical Studies in Media Communication* 29, no. 4: 313–30.

Grem, Darren E. 2006. "'The South Got Something to Say': Atlanta's Dirty South and the Southernization of Hip Hop America." *Southern Cultures* 12, no. 4: 55–73.

Westhoff, Ben. 2011. *Dirty South: OutKast, Lil Wayne, Soulja Boy, and the Southern Rappers Who Reinvented Hip Hop*. Chicago: Chicago Review Press.

Further Listening

OutKast. 2000. *Stankonia.* LaFace Records.

T.I. 2003. *Trap Musik.* Atlantic.

A Tribe Called Quest

(1985–1998, 2006–2013, 2015–, Queens, New York)

A Tribe Called Quest is an American hip hop group that is generally recognized as the most commercially successful member of Native Tongues (1988–1996). Its members include rapper and producer Q-Tip (Kamaal Ibn John Fareed, 1970–), rapper Phife Dawg (aka Phife, Malik Izaak Taylor, 1970–2016), and DJ and producer Ali Shaheed Muhammad (1970–). Jarobi White (1971–) appeared on the group's first album, *People's Instinctive Travels and the Paths of Rhythm* (1990). The group, its albums, and several of its singles have achieved critical acclaim.

EARLY EFFORTS

Founding members Q-Tip, Phife Dawg, Ali Shaheed Muhammad, and Jarobi White were high school classmates in Queens, New York. In 1989, they produced five demo songs for Geffen Records (1980–) but were not offered a recording contract. Later that year, they signed with Jive Records (1981–), originally a subsidiary of the Zomba label, founded in 1975. With Jive Records, they recorded *People's*

Instinctive Travels (1990). This debut studio album contained singles that the band had recorded for Geffen, including "Can I Kick It?" and "Description of a Fool," as well as new tracks such as "Bonita Applebum." Like other Native Tongues artists such as the Jungle Brothers (1987–2008), Black Sheep (1989–1995, 2000–), and De La Soul (1987–), the band's music promoted Afrocentric ideas, a general sense of positivity, using jazz-based samples against a hip hop beat. The members of the various Native Tongues groups often collaborated and appeared on each other's albums.

THE LOW END THEORY AND MIDNIGHT MARAUDERS

In 1991, ATCQ released its second album, *The Low End Theory*. Unlike *People's Instinctive Travels*, on which Q-Tip had been the solo lyricist on most tracks, *The Low End Theory* featured a good bit of rapping by Phife Dawg. In tracks such as "Check the Rhime," Phife Dawg and Q-Tip engaged in the type of vocal interplay, which was backed by a bass-heavy sound featuring relatively slow tempos and jazz samples, a style that would help to define A Tribe Called Quest's sound. The album was a hands-on project, as the group produced most of the tracks collectively.

The Low End Theory was a commercial and critical success, selling half a million copies within a year of its release and showing up on a number of critics' "best-of" lists. The band's third album, *Midnight Marauders*, was released in 1993, to much commercial and critical success. Fellow Native Tongues Posse member and De La Soul rapper Trugoy the Dove (aka Dave, David Jolicoeur, 1968–) appeared on the single "Award Tour," and Busta Rhymes (1972–), who had also been a guest on *The Low End Theory*, made a memorable appearance in the single "Oh My God."

THE UMMAH

After the release of *Midnight Marauders*, Q-Tip and Muhammed joined forces with producer Jay Dee (aka J Dilla; James Yancey, 1974–2006) to form a production collective called the Ummah, after an Arabic word for both community and brotherhood. Q-Tip and Muhammad, both Muslim, chose the word because it typically refers to the Muslim population in general. In addition to its work with A Tribe Called Quest, the Ummah would later produce music for Q-Tip's 1999 solo album *Amplified* and several singles by Busta Rhymes. The Ummah produced *Beats, Rhymes and Life* (1996) became the band's penultimate album. Jay Dee handled much of the production within the collective, so the album featured fewer samples and possessed a different, darker mood. The group claimed that its use of fewer samples was a response to the overproduced sound that had become all too common in hip hop of the time.

Rapper Consequence (Dexter Raymond Mills Jr., 1977–) appeared on six of the album's tracks, likely at the request of Q-Tip, who was his cousin. Although generally well received by critics, *Beats, Rhymes and Life* was not considered as strong of an album as its predecessors. Prior to the release of their 1998 album *The Love Movement*, band members announced that their fifth album would also be their last.

The album was also produced by the Ummah and featured various solo guests, although Consequence did not appear on *The Love Movement*.

BREAKUP, REUNIONS, AND DEATHS

A Tribe Called Quest officially disbanded following the release of *The Love Movement*. Q-Tip went on to record several solo albums, the first of which was produced by the Ummah. Phife Dawg recorded a single solo album, *Ventilation: Da LP* (2000). Muhammad formed a hip hop supergroup called Lucy Pearl (1999–2002) with Raphael Saadiq (Charles Ray Wiggins, 1966–) of Tony! Toni! Toné! (1988–1997, 2003–) and Dawn Robinson (1965–) of En Vogue (1989–). He also released one solo album, *Shaheedullah and Stereotypes* (2004).

The members of A Tribe Called Quest did reunite at various points in the 2000s for live concert performances. Jay Dee left the Ummah collective in the late 1990s and went on to have an impressive solo production career until he died of a rare blood disorder in 2006. Having kept a low profile due to ill health, Phife Dawg passed away in 2016 of complications related to diabetes. In 2017, remaining members plus Busta Rhymes (1972–) made an appearance on *Saturday Night Live* (1975–) as the musical guests—in a show scheduled just after Donald Trump (1946–) was elected president of the United States. Their performance, as well as the show's tone, expressed both sadness and concern over Trump's political agenda. As of 2018, the remaining members of A Tribe Called Quest do not appear to have any plans for a new album, although they have to date recorded only five albums out of their six-album contract with Jive.

Amanda Sewell

See also: Black Nationalism; Busta Rhymes; De La Soul; Five Percent Nation; Native Tongues; Political Hip Hop; The United States

Further Reading

Sewell, Amanda. 2014. "How Copyright Affected the Musical Style and Critical Reception of Sample-Based Hip Hop," *Journal of Popular Music Studies* 26, no. 2–3: 295–320.

Williams, Justin. 2013. *Rhymin' and Stealin': Musical Borrowing in Hip Hop*. Ann Arbor: University of Michigan Press.

Further Listening

A Tribe Called Quest. 1991. *The Low End Theory*. Jive Records.

A Tribe Called Quest. 1995. *Beats, Rhymes and Life*. Jive Records.

Further Viewing

Rapaport, Michael, dir. 2011. *Beats, Rhymes, and Life: The Travels of A Tribe Called Quest*. Sony.

Trinidad and Tobago

Trinidad and Tobago is a South American twin island parliamentary constitutional republic off the coast of northeastern Venezuela. It was colonized by Spain in the

1500s, but was ceded to the United Kingdom in 1802, finally gaining its independence in 1962 and becoming a republic in 1976, with its capital being Port of Spain. The official language of its one and a half million people is English, and both Trinidadian and Tobagonian English Creole are also spoken. Its ethnic makeup is 77 percent Indian, African, or Dougla (African Indian), and most of its citizens are either Christian or Hindu. Because of petroleum and petrochemicals, Trinidad and Tobago is the third richest country per capita in the Americas, following the United States and Canada. Musically, the islands are known for steel drums (aka steelpan) and tamboo-bamboo percussions, as well as musical styles such as calypso and *soca*, and hybridizations of these with other styles such as *parang, chutney, cariso, extempo, kaiso, pichakaree,* and *rapso*. Calypso became one of the Caribbean's top musical exports with mainstreaming, resulting in stars such as Harry Belafonte (1927–), Lord Kitchener (Aldwyn Roberts, 1922–2000), and Mighty Sparrow (Slinger Francisco, 1935–).

When its popularity waned in the 1970s, calypso was hybridized to form the uptempo African- and Indian-influenced style called soca and combined with hip hop to create rapso. Soca evolved to incorporate elements of funk, soul, *zouk,* and dance. Rapso became influential when Lancelot Layne (n.d.–1990) had a hit with "Blow Away" (1971), and Network Riddum Band (aka Network Rapso Riddum Band, 1979–1986), which featured Brother Resistance (aka Lutalo Masimba, Roy Lewis, n.d.), released its EP *Busting Out* (1981). Like the rock scene, Trinidad and Tobago's hip hop scene is mainly an underground one, represented by new artists such as the duo Omari Thorpe and Vaughn Huggins (n.d.), rappers Denice Millien (1994–) and Lizz (Elizabeth Waldron, 1995–), and rap group Black Royal Dynasty (n.d.).

The island nation's most famous hip hop stars are both Trinidadian-born American rappers, Nicki Minaj (1982–) and Trinidad Jame$ (Nicholas James Williams, 1987–). Nicki Minaj is a New York City–based rapper, singer-songwriter, and model whose three studio albums have all been certified Platinum and have reached either the No. 2 or top spot on the Billboard 200; in 2010, she became the first female solo artist to have seven singles simultaneously chart on the Billboard Hot 100. Trinidad Jame$ is an Atlanta-based rapper and actor who has collaborated with up-and-coming Trindadian acts such as Millien; he has released seven solo albums and mixtapes combined.

Anthony J. Fonseca

See also: Nicki Minaj; The United Kingdom

Further Reading
Gadet, Steve. 2015. "Hip Hop Culture: Bridging Gaps between Young Caribbean Citizens." *Caribbean Quarterly* 61, no. 1: 75–97.
Jackson, Lauren Michele. 2017. "The Rapper Laughs, Herself: Nicki Minaj's Sonic Disturbances." *Feminist Media Studies* 17, no. 1: 126–29.

Further Listening
Nicki Minaj. 2010. *Pink Friday.* Ca$h Money Records/Universal Motown.
Trinidad Jame$. 2015. *No One Is Safe.* Gold Gang Records/Think It's a Game Records.

Trip Hop

(aka Downtempo)

Trip hop, a cultural adaptation of hip hop, came into prominence in the early 1990s in England, particularly in Bristol. The subgenre includes many of the foundations of hip hop, such as looped samples, scratches, and sequencing, but adds more melodic instrumentation and vocal content in the form of singing, with less emphasis on rap. This new subgenre proved advantageous to many of 1990s U.K. hip hop musicians, as their British accents created cognitive dissonance for fans in the American record market (and some international markets), as they were used to a genre sound where vocals were most commonly associated with street slang and the vernacular culture of the Bronx, New York.

THE SOUND

Trip hop has a sound that has been described as to the music version of film noir because of its atmospherics and a lyrical emphasis on drama. Musically, the subgenre is characterized by laid-back tempos and an artful multilayering of instruments, samples, and voices. It emphasizes atmosphere over text, often moving voices back in the mix and moving away from declarative story telling that pervaded hip hop at the time. It shows the strong influence of technology, and while live recording might occur, much of the recorded sound is produced in the studio or on a synthesizer and computer hookup.

Samples from film and preexisting music are pervasive, with special emphasis put on reggae, jazz, hip hop, and soul as source material. The use of samples often involves elaborate changes to the source material, especially in relation to tempo (most often the music is sampled at a rate slower than the original). The resulting texture is often complex, complicated, and murky.

English singer-songwriter Beth Gibbons fronts and writes lyrics for the pioneering Bristol trip hop band Portishead. Gibbons's soft yet unusual coloratura contralto voice and laidback delivery has been influential to trip hop's sound. (Yakub88 /Dreamstime.com)

BRISTOL ORIGINS AND ARTISTS

Many artists labeled as trip hop strongly oppose the subgenre designation, which was first used in the British magazine *Mixmag* to describe a marketing ploy developed solely to white washing the black roots of hip hop to make it more accessible to a white audience. Some artists and scholars also describe the music as the "Bristol Sound." With a Bohemian atmosphere and a diverse population, Bristol did provide an agreeable environment for the blending of the music styles that resulted in trip hop.

Three core Bristol artists popularized trip hop; their influence can be seen on subsequent artists in the subgenre. The bands Massive Attack (1988–) and Portishead (1991–), as well as the singer Tricky (Adrian Nicholas Matthews Thaws, 1968–), all hailed from Bristol, and all had shared contributions to Massive Attack's debut album, *Blue Lines* (1991). Massive Attack had its roots in a DJ collective the Wild Bunch (1983–1989), whose instrumental releases on the Mo' Wax (1992–) label laid the groundwork for the blend of influences that became trip hop.

During the *Blue Lines* period, Massive Attack's core membership included Daddy G (Grantley Evan Marshall, 1959–), Mushroom (Andrew Lee Isaac Vowles, 1967–), rapper 3D (Robert Del Naja, 1965–), and Tricky (as the Tricky Kid), and included programming by Portishead's Geoffrey Barrow (1971–). This downtempo release was intended for headphones, not clubs. Nevertheless, the album included hit singles that were popular on college radio in the United States and showed that fans were, indeed, interested in the laid-back feel.

With two MCs on that first release and a variety on later ones, Massive Attack's sound is more dependent on rap than most other acts associated with trip hop, some of whom include no rap at all in their music. Unlike contemporaneous hip hop songs, the rapping in Massive's output is often relegated to the background, often mumbled, and used as a textural element, rather than a narrative one.

Additional releases extended the Massive Attacks's sound. *Protection* (1994), its last release to include Tricky, as well as *Mezzanine* (1998), which included the addition of roots and reggae singer Horace Andy (Horace Hinds, 1951–), was one of the earliest commercial records released for free on the Internet (before the CD release a month later). *100th Window* (2003), which did not include Daddy G or Mushroom due to creative differences and other personal commitments, included guest vocals by alternative rock singers Sinéad O'Connor (1966–) and Damon Albarn (1968–). *Heligoland* (2010) included several artists who had contributed to previous albums and a smorgasbord of others as well.

In 1994, three years after the release of *Blue Lines*, Portishead, comprising DJ/programmer Barrow, guitarist Adrian Utley (1957–), and cover-song artist Beth Gibbons (1965–), released its debut *Dummy* on the Go! Beat Records label (aka Go! Discs, 1983–), distributed by London Records and later Polydor. Including samples from lounge and soul as well as soundtracks, this album resonated with the public, going Platinum in the United Kingdom and Gold in the United States. Gibbons's voice evoked those of traditional jazz singers, complete with a deep sense of melancholy that infused the album with pathos. Barrow's evocative samples contributed to the darker, filmic aspects of the lyrics. In the same year, Tricky left Massive Attack and then released his first solo effort, *Maxinquaye* (1994). To supplement Tricky's rapping, the disc also featured vocalist Martina (Martina Gillian Topley-Bird, 1975–) whose voice created a melodic, lyrical backdrop to Tricky's declarative style. Tricky speaks of inspiration and prophets and uses his music to channel stories from unknown places, turning his music into performance art, complete with costumes and cross dressing in the media and on stage. The lyrics on *Maxinquaye* speak of romantic longing and confusion, of addiction and frustration, of the pain of life. The sound is layered and dark, with combinations of live instruments, voices, and samples, leaving the listener unsure of the source or meaning of the sounds. The album garnered positive reviews that, reportedly, made him uncomfortable and nearly paralyzed him artistically.

In 1995, Portishead won the prestigious Mercury Music Prize, underscoring their approval by fellow musicians, critics, and the music industry. The group has since released two more studio records, *Portishead* (1997) and *Third* (2008). On both albums, it maintains and develops the sound introduced in *Dummy*. Portishead continued to perform live, often adding extended ensembles of live musicians to provide an unplugged feel.

Coinciding with Portishead's activities, Tricky released his next full-length follow-up to *Maxinquaye*, *Pre Millennium Tension* (1996). It is a sparser album with fewer hooks, though it contains more live instruments. *Angels with Dirty Faces* (1998) covered similar territory, while *Juxtapose* (1999) took him more deliberately in the direction of hardcore hip hop. *Blowback* (2001) and *Vulnerable* (2003) were received with increasing frustration from fans and critics hoping to see a greater sense of development in his work. Tricky's album *Knowle West Boy* (2008) generated a more favorable response to its wide stylistic palette, with influences of lounge, punk, and more. *Mixed Race* (2010), *False Idols* (2013), *Adrian Thaws* (2014), and *Skilled Mechanics* (2016) round out his more recent releases; these continue to include trip hop elements while alternately disappointing and reassuring fans and critics who, inevitably, compare all subsequent Tricky releases to *Maxinquaye*.

NEXT GENERATION, BEYOND BRISTOL

After the initial success of the Bristol trip hop artists, a next generation expanded on the style while adding their own elements. This music can usually be distinguished by a greater clarity of instrumental sound that often includes more acoustic instruments. It is infused with less distortion than that applied by the Bristol artists, while still depending on the technical foundations that create the distinctive sound of trip hop. Morcheeba's (1995–) debut *Who Can You Trust?* (1996) added elements more akin to country and western and folk-rock than to their trip hop foundation. Fronted by vocalist Skye Edwards (Shirley Klaris Yonavieve Edwards, 1974–), Morcheeba achieves the same laid-back cool of earlier trip hop influences, albeit with a less diverse palette than some of its peers. By the release of its second album, *Big Calm* (1998), it was moving toward a more pop-oriented sound, with more straightforward mix and structure; this strategy proved effective as this release led to wider success.

Sneaker Pimps (1994–2005, 2015–) had a much greater dependence on live instruments in its debut album, *Becoming X* (1996), than did the band's peers.

Founded by Chris Corner (1974–) and Liam Howe (1974–), the band grew when it recruited, bassist Joe Wilson (n.d.), percussionist Dave Westlake (1965–), and vocalist Kelli Dayton (aka Kelli Ali, 1974–), who did not stay with the band past the debut album. Its subsequent releases, *Splinter* (1999) and *Bloodsport* (2002), moved progressively away from trip hop and toward electronica and dance music.

The electronic duo Lamb (1996–2004, 2009–) differed from Sneaker Pimps and Morcheeba as it had an almost complete avoidance of acoustic instruments. Lamb achieved a reputation as a successful trip hop act in England, albeit with limited success elsewhere. Producer Andy Barlow (n.d.) and singer-songwriter Lou Rhodes (Louise Rhodes, n.d.) set an atmospheric stage with ethereal vocals, plaintive melodies, and inventive beats. Their eponymous debut (1996) contains their best-known and oft-reused single, "Górecki," which derives inspiration from Polish composer Henryk Górecki's (1933–2010) pathos-ridden *Symfonia pieśni żałosnych* (*Symphony of Sorrowful Songs*), Symphony No. 3, Op. 36 (1976). Overall, many of Lamb's songs are a bit more uptempo, with more structural ebb and flow than that of other trip hop artists. Lamb is sometimes labeled as drum and bass, rather than trip hop.

Aside from some of the major artists who are closely associated with the trip hop subgenre, there are a number who get occasionally swept into the category because their music includes elements of trip hop, though their work might not be as consistently labeled as trip hop. Björk (Björk Guðmundsdóttir, 1965–), Air (1995–), Laika (1993–2003), Goldfrapp (1999), Nightmares on Wax (aka DJ EASE, George Evelyn, 1988–), Thievery Corporation (1995–), and Gorillaz (1998–) all employ sounds and beats that harken back to trip hop. Instrumental trip hop, as exemplified by the works of DJ Shadow (1972–), DJ Krush (Hideaki Ishi, 1962–), and UNKLE (1994–) brings the feel of trip hop but lacks the vocals that are such important elements of some of the more recognized trip hop groups.

The Golden Age of Trip Hop's heyday was in the 1990s. It has passed, but it is music that has as of 2018 worn well with time. Much of the sound has become so commonplace as to become invisible, indistinguishable from other similarly influence material. Because it is defined by sonic elements more than contemporaneous styles, trip hop's artists are able to grow and change, while still maintaining the basic feel of the sound. While some trip hop superstars have moved on, it still provides fertile ground for those who continue to explore its ethos.

Susannah Cleveland

See also: DJ Shadow; Dubstep; Neo Soul; The United Kingdom

Further Reading

DeRogatis, Jim. 2003. *Turn on Your Mind: Four Decades of Great Psychedelic Rock.* Milwaukee, WI: Hal Leonard.

Light, Alan, ed. 1999. *The Vibe History of Hip Hop.* New York: Three Rivers Press.

Reynolds, Simon. 2012. *Energy Flash: A Journey through Rave Music and Dance Culture.* Berkeley: Soft Skull Press.

Wragg, Jeff. 2016. "Just Don't Call It Trip Hop: Reconciling the Bristol Sound Style with the Trip Hop Genre." *Organised Sound* 21, no. 1: 40–50.

Further Listening

Goldfrapp. 2013. *Tales of Us*. Mute.

Lamb. 1996. *Lamb*. Fontana.

Massive Attack. 1991. *Blue Lines*. Wild Bunch Records.

Portishead. 1994. *Dummy*. Go! Beat.

Sneaker Pimps. 2002. *Bloodsport*. Tommy Boy.

Thievery Corporation. 2008. *Radio Retaliation*. Eighteenth Street Lounge Music.

Tuks Senganga

(aka Tuks, Tumelo Kapadisa, 1981–, Mafikeng, South Africa)

Tuks Senganga is a South African hip hop and *motswako* rapper, as well as a record label owner. Motswako, a subgenre of hip hop that emerged in the mid-1990s in Botswana, uses primarily Setswana texts with English raps, combining both with traditional South African rhythms and four-to-the-floor beats; it is popular in South Africa and Botswana. Tuks' vocal range is tenor and his texts are in Setswana, with rare inclusions of English.

EARLY INSPIRATIONS AND INTERESTS IN RAPPING

By age 12, Tuks Senganga was writing poetry inspired by his experiences while growing up in the Bophutatswana, a "homeland" that was specifically formed as part of Apartheid (1948–1991) for black South Africans that spoke Tswana. He witnessed a series of violent coups d'état between 1988 and the 1994, when the homeland enclaves were reincorporated into South Africa, also a difficult transition. By high school, he was rapping and participating in the Mafikeng (now Mahikeng) underground hip hop scene. He also belonged to a couple of rapping crews formed with high school friends.

After graduating from college with a bachelor's degree in multimedia (graphic arts), he was invited to produce a music video, an experience that made him think about producing his own music. He eventually signed a recording contract with Ghetto Ruff (formerly Ku Shu Shu Records, 1991–), a label located in Johannesburg. Before dissolving, Ku Shu Shu Records (1990–1991) produced the legendary Cape Town hip hop crew Prophets of da City (POC, 1988–2001).

His debut album, *Mafoko a me* (*Words Have Me*, 2005), received critical acclaim and won Best Rap Album at the South African Music Awards (SAMAs). *Mafoko a me* was a hip hop and motswako album based on many earlier poems Tuks had written. His popular "525,600" from this album contains Tuks's rapping over a sample of "Seasons of Love" from the 1996 Broadway musical *Rent*.

His second album, *MC Prayer* (2006), began his focus on incorporating praising God and gospel into his rap music. The album was certified Gold in South Africa just four months after its release, but his subsequent albums were not as successful. His third album, *Monopoly* (2008), with songs about how media, music, and religion are used to control people, was released after a two-year hiatus and formation of Tuks's new label, June/July Productions (2008–), originally in partnership with EMI (1931–2012).

Tswanelo's (2010) most popular track was "Let Me Live Now," a song from the album that appealed to gospel music listeners and was followed by *Footprints* (2012) and *Botshe Botshe* (2016). Among many others, Tuks has collaborated with fellow South African hip hop and motswako artists such as Mo'Molemi (Motlapele Morule, 1981–), Hip Hop Pantsula (1980–), Blaklez (Cliff Lesego, n.d.), and hip hip and kwaito rapper Pitch Black Afro (Thulani Ngcobo, 1976*–), as well as Australian R&B and hip hop producer M-Phazes (Mark Landon, 1983–).

Melissa Ursula Dawn Goldsmith

See also: Christian Hip Hop; Motswako; Political Hip Hop; South Africa

Further Reading

Ditsele, Thabo. 2017. "The Promotion of Setswana through Hip Hop and *Motswakolistas*." *Journal of the Musical Arts in Africa* 14, nos. 1–2: 1–14.

Sithole, Siyabonga. 2016. "Rapper Tuks Senganga Back in the Forefront." *The New Age* (Johannesburg, South Africa), December 8, 1.

Further Listening

Tuks Senganga. 2005. *Mafoko a me* (*Words Have Me*). Ghetto Ruff.

Tunisia

Tunisia's hip hop scene emerged in the 1990s, when American rappers such as the Wu-Tang Clan (1992–) gained popularity among young Tunisians. A first wave of Tunisian hip hop groups such as T Men (1997–2013)* and Gangstas Wanted (1997*–) forged a uniquely Tunisian rap style that focused on widespread social problems such as poverty, unemployment, state repression, police brutality, and political strife. The hip hop of Tunisia stands, culturally and stylistically, as part of a broader Maghreb rap phenomenon spanning the North African nations of Algeria, Morocco, Tunisia, and to some extent Libya. Scholars note a parallel between Magrhebian rap and a century-old spoken-word poetry called *rai*. Both arose as urban platforms for the self-expression of disillusioned youth, and both are text-driven, express resistance, and fluidly intermix Arabic, French, and other languages.

POLITICAL ACTIVISM

A second wave of Tunisian hip hop artists, aided by the Internet, released raps that exposed the problems of a growing poor and unemployed youth population. Due to the social policies of former President Ben Ali (1936–), by 2007, Tunisian Internet users totaled around four million, or 40 percent of the population. Over three million Tunisians used social media between 2007 and 2011, though their use was monitored by the Ben Ali regime. In the Internet music climate, Tunisian hip hop groups such as Armada Bizerta (2010*–) greatly enlarged their fan base, while members of the diaspora, such as Delahoja (Férid El Extranjero, n.d.), a Tunisian rapper residing in Spain, added their voices to the Tunisian social cause. Tunisian rapper El Général (Hamada Ben Amor, 1990*–), who claims Tupac Shakur (1971–1996) as a primary influence, made international headlines when he released "Rayes lebled" ("President of the Country"), criticizing Ben Ali. "Rayes lebled" became the anthem of a youth-led protest movement that developed into a revolution in a matter of weeks, leading to the January 2011 fall of the government.

After this Jasmine Revolution (2010–2011), El Général continued to release politically conscious rap, such as "Tounes bledna" ("Tunisia Our Country") and "Rayes lebled 2." El Général is known for adding to hip hop Arabic and French texts, traditional Tunisian instrumental timbres, and an intense focus on the social, political and economic issues that affect young Tunisians. Psycho M (Mouhamed Jandoubi, 1986–) is known for his 2010 release of "Manipulation," a 15–minute rap diatribe against the Tunisian government, Western powers, and their dissimulative and manipulative strategies to impose a status quo. Post-revolution, he performs regularly songs about the role of Islam in the face of a suffering Tunisia. He is joined by a growing community of Tunisian hip hop artists such as Balti (Mohamed Salah Balti, 1980*–), and anonymous rappers DJ Costa (n.d.), and Mastaziano (n.d.), who continue to rap for change in Tunisia.

Jennifer L. Roth-Burnette

See also: Political Hip Hop

Further Reading

Allagui, I. 2014. "Waiting for Spring: Arab Resistance and Change." *International Journal of Communication* 8: 983.

Bouzouita, K. 2013. "Music of Dissent and Revolution." *Middle East Critique* 22, no. 3: 281.

Davies, E. E., and A. Bentahila. 2006. "Code Switching and the Globalization of Popular Music: The Case of North African Rai and Rap." *Multilingua* 25, no. 4: 367.

Gana, N. 2012. "Rap and Revolt in the Arab World." *Social Text* 30, no. 4 113: 25–53.

LeVine, M. 2012. "Music and the Aura of Revolution." *International Journal of Middle East Studies* 44, no. 4: 794–97.

Shannahan, D. S., and Q. Hussain. 2011. "Rap on 'l'Avenue' Islam, Aesthetics, Authenticity, and Masculinities in the Tunisian Rap Scene." *Contemporary Islam* 5, no. 1: 37–58.

Tupac Shakur

(aka Tupac, 2Pac, Lesane Parish Crooks, 1971–1996)

Tupac Shakur was one of the most gifted and influential American hip hop artists of the early 1990s. His delivery exhibited an exceptional control of language, and his lyrics exemplified his strong social consciousness within the gangsta ethos. His legacy is amplified by his violent death in the conflict between East and West Coast hip hop schools. In the two decades since his death, his reputation as one of the greatest hip hop artists has grown, and his music continues to sell at a rate that many living performers can only envy. While the romance of his short life and tragic death may contribute somewhat to the interest of hip hop devotees, it is the exceptional quality of his work, admired by rappers, critics, and fans alike, that makes his albums relevant a generation after they were recorded.

He was born as Lesane Parish Crooks in New York's East Harlem to parents who were members of the Black Panther Party (1966–1982). Around his third birthday, his given name was changed to honor an 18th-century Peruvian revolutionary. His mother raised him, and his early years were spent among family and friends who were involved in social and political activities, including violence as members of the Black Liberation Army (1970–1981).

ARTISTIC TALENTS AND EARLY CAREER

Tupac Shakur's artistic talents were first encouraged when he was 12. The 127th Street Repertory Ensemble in Harlem gave him the opportunity to further develop his talents. After his family moved in 1986 to Baltimore, he enrolled in the Baltimore School for the Arts. Two years later, his family moved to Marin City, California, where he attended Tamalpais High School in Mill Valley, California. Throughout his education, he was a popular student who was active in the arts: He appeared in plays and dances, and he wrote poetry well enough to be accepted into Leila Steinberg's (1961–) Microphone Sessions, a weekly writing workshop for at-risk youths in Oakland. She would be one of his first mentors and helped to launch his career.

His abilities as a rapper were evident as early as his years in Baltimore and became a focus of his schoolwork in California. Steinberg introduced the 19-year-old Tupac Shakur to Atron Gregory (1959–), a local music promoter, who in turn helped the youngster to find work as a dancer and later as a hype man with the hip hop group Digital Underground (1987–2008). His professional debut as a rapper came on the group's "Same Song," which was the lead track on their second release, *This Is an EP Release* (1991); it was also used on the soundtrack for the motion picture *Nothing but Trouble* (1991).

SUCCESSFUL RECORDINGS AND GROWING REPUTATION

Later that same year, he released his first solo album, *2Pacalypse Now* (1991). Although not an exceptionally successful album at that time, achieving only Gold status, its reputation has grown over the years. Its subject matter focused on the inner city's social problems, ranging from racism and poverty, to crime and police brutality, to teenage pregnancy—topics not unexpected for a hip hop album, but delivered with a richer variety of lyrics and beats than could be expected from a 21-year old.

The album *2Pacalypse Now* gained some notoriety in April 1992 after a car thief, who shot and killed a Texas State Trooper, claimed that he had been conditioned to hate police by listening to hip hop. When he was arrested, the thief was listening to "Soulja's Story," a track from *2Pacalypse Now*. Then–U.S. Vice President Dan Quayle (James Danforth Quayle, 1947–, in office 1989–1993) remarked that the album should be withdrawn by its publisher, but nothing came of his comments.

With his name better known, his second album, *Strictly 4 My N.—A.Z.* (1993), debuted at No. 24 on Billboard's Top 200, and achieved wider commercial success, reaching Platinum status, with more of the same content. His third and fourth albums, *Me against the World* (1995) and *All Eyez on Me* (1996), added to his reputation as both a performer and a hip hop personality. *Me against the World* was recorded while Tupac Shakur was involved in a series of legal problems, including a charge of sexual assault, and the album was released just after he entered prison.

Suge Knight (Marion Hugh Knight Jr., 1965–), owner of Death Row Records (1991–2009), then paid a $1.4 million bail bond to get him released while his case was appealed. Tupac Shakur then recorded *All Eyez on Me* for Death Row in payment for that bond. His next project for Death Row, *The Don Killuminati: The 7 Day Theory* (1996), was based on intensive reading and study that he had done while in prison. This album was released shortly after his death.

DEATH AND LEGACY

Tupac Shakur's death came at the hands of an unknown gunman in Las Vegas. In September 1996 he and his entourage attended a boxing match in Las Vegas. Afterward, on the way to a party, his car was stopped at a red light. While he stood up through the sunroof to speak with several women in a nearby vehicle, a third vehicle drew up along the other side, and a gunman fired, striking him four times. He was taken to a hospital, where he died a week later.

Despite extensive investigation by the authorities and others, no one was ever charged with the shooting, although some have speculated that the shooter was a Crips gang member with whom he had had a run-in earlier that evening. The ongoing feud between East Coast and West Coast rappers has also fueled speculation that the Notorious B.I.G. (1972–97) was involved in Tupac Shakur's murder, but the Notorious B.I.G. denied those accusations—and his death by shooting six months later in Los Angeles has kept that theory alive. In 2012, at the Coachella Valley Music & Arts Festival at the Empire Polo Field in Indio, California, a holographic image of Tupac Shakur performed for a crowd of over 80,000.

Scott Warfield

See also: Gangsta Rap; The Notorious B.I.G.; The United States

Further Reading

Dyson, Michael Eric. 2003. *Holler If You Hear Me: Searching for Tupac Shakur.* New York: Basic Civitas Books.

McQuillar, Tayannah, and Fred L. Johnson. 2010. *Tupac Shakur: The Life and Times of an American Icon.* Cambridge, MA: Da Capo Press.

Scott, Cathy. 2014. *The Killing of Tupac Shakur*, 3rd ed. Las Vegas: Huntington Press.

Further Listening

2Pac. 1991. *2Pacalypse Now.* Interscope Records.

2Pac. 1996. *All Eyez on Me.* Interscope/Death Row Records.

Further Viewing

Sean Long, dir. 2001. *Tupac Shakur: Before I Wake.* Sepia Tone Entertainment. Santa Monica, CA: Xenon Pictures.

Turkey

Turkey is a Western Asian country bordered by three seas: the Aegean, the Black, and the Mediterranean. Turkey has a population of 80 million, and about 80 percent of this population identifies as Turks. Kurds are Turkey's largest minority population. Ankara is its capital, while Istanbul, with 14.8 million inhabitants, is its largest city and cultural center. The country has a history of colonization and monarchy until 1922, when the Turkish War of Independence (1919–1923) resulted in Turkish victory against Greece, Armenia, and France (supported in the earlier half of the war by the United Kingdom and Italy), and the establishment of the Republic of Turkey, with a presidential government and western reforms. Many years later, President Recep Tayyip Erdoğan (1954–, in office 2014–) reversed many of the reforms, which threatens freedom of speech and the press.

Turkey's music is heavily influenced by traditional elements that date back to the 11th century, with some elements of Western Asian, Arabic, and Greek music. Westernization, which began in 1926 after the formation of the Republic of Turkey, included the introduction of Western pop music, which lost favor for a short time from 1970 to 1990 when interest Turkey had a resurgence of sociopolitical folk music and Arabesque (aka Arabesk). Despite westernization, between 1924 and 1953, national classification and archiving efforts of Turkish folk music took place. These efforts preserved over 10,000 folksongs. Traditional instrumentation includes the *tanbur* (aka the *saz* or *baglama*, a long-necked plucked lute), the flute, the *kemençe* (a bowed fiddle), the *oud* (a plucked short-necked unfretted lute), the *kanun* (a type of zither), the violin, and in some styles, the drum and the harp. Turkish folk music (*Türkü*) dealt with everyday subjects or was event-oriented. Turkey's popular music shows the influence of the ethnic styles of Greek, Armenian, Albanian, Polish, Azeri, Romani, and Jewish music, along with some western influence. Popular musical instruments in Romani-influenced dance music include clarinet, violin, *kanun*, and *darbuka* (a *djembe*-like drum, or goblet drum). Musical rhyming contests between traveling singers (bards or *aşık*) are also a staple of Turkish folk music, as well as religious music. In such contests, one bard is defeated when he cannot find a rhyme or his story falls apart.

Turkish pop music began in the 1950s when Turkish bands began to cover rock and roll, jazz, and Argentine *tango* with performances by diva singers Ajda Pekkan (Ayşe Ajda Pekkan, 1946–) and Sezen Aksu (Fatma Sezen Yıldırım, 1954–), and continued into the 1960s when popular U.S. and U.K. bands inspired Turkish musicians to produce what came to be called Anatolian rock. Acts such as progressive and psychedelic rocker Cem Karaca (Muhtar Cem Karaca, 1945–2004), singer-songwriter and actor Barış Manço (Tosun Yusuf Mehmet Barış Manço, 1943–1999), and folk and rock band Moğollar (1967–1976, 1993–), led to popular 1970s rock and pop artists such as singer-songwriter and guitarist Bülent Ortaçgil (1950–) and satirical sociopolitical band MFÖ (aka Mazhar-Fuat-Özkan or Mazhar ve Fuat, 1971–), as well as heavy-metal bands such as Bursa-based Mezarkabul (aka Pentagram, 1986–) and Istanbul-based Almora (2001–).

Turkish hip hop began not in Turkey, but with the Turkish migrant worker community in Germany. Most early Turkish hip hop was produced by Turkish Germans, influenced by both German and American hip hop scenes. With music infused by the Arabesque style and samples, they rapped songs about immigration, discrimination, and racism, as well as the plight of the migrant worker. Prior to the emergence of Turkish hip hop, in 1991, Nuremberg-based King Size Terror (1990–1994), a hip hop group of Turkish, Peruvian, and African American origin, produced the first Turkish language rap with the single "Bir Yabancinin Hayati" ("The Life of the Stranger"), which portrayed Turkish youth as strangers in mainstream German culture. King Size Terror led to the creation of Cartel (1995–) as the first successful Turkish hip hop group. Meanwhile, in Bursa, Turkey, trance DJ Mercan Dede (Arkın Ilıcalı, 1966–) was mixing electronic beats with traditional Turkish and religious Sufi songs. Underground Istanbul-based producer Mert Yücel (1977*–) released the album *His* (*Consciousness* or *Feeling*, released as the Mert Yücel Project), the first house music album in Turkey in 1999.

Cartel had problems with violence and incarceration, and at one point was forbidden to perform together, and the band's first album, which contained both German and Turkish rapping, was banned. Another early rap crew, Islamic Force (aka KanAK, 1980s*) wrote songs that challenged racism in English and Turkish, and Berlin-based rapper Kool Savaş (Savaş Yurderi, 1975–) cofounded the rap duo Westberlin Maskulin (1997–2000), as well as the crew Masters of Rap (1996–). Kool Savaş has collaborated with 50 Cent (1975–), among others. Other notable Turkish hip hop acts include Ayben (Ayben Özçalkan, 1982–), a female rapper from Üsküdar, Turkey; Aksit Ugurlu (n.d.), a recording engineer from Germany and Turkey; and rapper and DJ Sagopa Kajmer (aka DJ Mic Check, Silahsiz Kuvvet, Yunus Ozyavuz, 1978–), from Istanbul.

Anthony J. Fonseca and Melissa Ursula Dawn Goldsmith

See also: Cyprus; Germany; Greece

Further Reading

Işik, Nuran Erol, and Muran Can Basaran. 2017. "Unmasking Expressions in Turkish Rap/ Hip Hop Culture: Contestation and Construction of Alternative Identities through Localization in Arabesk Music." In *Hip Hop at Europe's Edge: Music, Agency, and Social Change*, edited by Milosz Miszczynski and Adriana Helbig, chap. 11. Bloomington: Indiana University Press.

Soloman, Thomas. 2005. "'Living Underground Is Tough': Authenticity and Locality in the Hip Hop Community in Instanbul, Turkey." *Popular Music* 24, no. 1: 1–20.

Soloman, Thomas. 2009. "Berlin-Frankfurt-Istanbul." *European Journal of Cultural Studies* 12, no. 3: 305–27.

Soloman, Thomas. 2011. "Hardcore Muslims: Islamic Themes in Turkish Rap between Diaspora and Homeland." In *Muslim Rap, Halal Soaps, and Revolutionary Theater: Artistic Developments in the Muslim World*, edited by Karin van Nieuwkerk, chap. 1. Austin: University of Texas Press.

Further Listening
Islamic Force. 1997. *Mesaj* (*Message* or *Purpose*). De De Records.
King Size Terror. 1991. *The Word Is "Subversion."* Vulkan Verlag.

Turntablism

Turntablism is the art of creating and modifying sounds through the use of two or more turntables (devices that play vinyl albums using an armed needle that can translate the grooves in a vinyl record into sound) and a mixer with a crossfader. Also called scratching, turntablism can involve composing new music, beats, and effects through various techniques that involve moving the armed needle back and forth on the vinyl record, or picking it up and setting it back down to play only certain parts of songs. Turntablism can also involve isolating sampled sounds (usually a musical phrase or two) from preexisting music, creating what is called a loop or hiccup. In early turntablism, the turntablist, commonly called a DJ, would do so by literally picking up the needle and placing it back in its original place, or by shifting it back lightly in a technique called rubbing. Early DJs could also shift quickly between two pieces of music by switching power from one turntable to another through a crossfader device, thereby creating a musical experience that had no breaks between music. Individual turntablists and crews, or teams, have created elaborate techniques and choreographed combinations for both performances and battles. Some of these have made their way onto recordings.

HISTORY, INNOVATORS, AND EARLY EQUIPMENT

The origin of turntablism may be traced back to the 1930s with *musique concrète* experiments that created and distorted previously recorded sounds. These sounds came from nature or were naturally occurring. Sound bites such as sirens, as heard in an urban environment, bomb droppings, or feedback created within a studio could then be incorporated into a musical composition. Just one example of the earliest turntablism is American composer John Cage's (1912–1992) *Imaginary Landscape No. 1* (1939), whose instrumentation includes two variable-speed record players that play previously recorded frequencies on albums (one using original Victor frequency album 84522A and the other using 84522B). These albums are plugged to amplifiers and are played against large Chinese cymbals and a piano whose strings have been muted, all played by a total of four performers.

Other techniques that emerged in the 1950s bear some similar results to turntablism. For example, the practice of using a splicing knife and guided board to splice electroacoustic tape from a reel-to-reel player, and the use special adhesive tape to reattach the electroacoustic tape at a different spot could result in the same effect as crossfading. Using this technique, a music engineer could cut a recorded song on tape into segments and paste it back together in such a way as to create new sounds; how these segments are pasted together creates the new sound. The result can sound chopped up and either recognizable or unrecognizable; in addition, carefully cut and taped segments can result in a seamless auditory continuation from one part of a song to another—much like *cross-fading*, a technique that is used in music editing, both analog and digital. Another technique involves taking tape from a reel-to-reel player and stretching it around a microphone stand, so that playing it will create a *delay* (the tape takes longer to get to the reader). Such delays can be created on turntables by the DJ's either selecting a slower RPM (revolutions per minute, often referred to as record speed) speed or by applying hand pressure to manually slow down the revolutions of a vinyl record. And two or more vinyl record players can add dimension to the delay, as the DJ can be creating two separate RPMs at the same time. And just as tape can be stretched or distressed to create a variety of distorted and scratched sounds, a vinyl record player or turntable can do likewise, even more efficiently, as it offers the DJ/composer more control through scratching.

By the 1950s, sound systems were being created in Kingston, Jamaica, so that music could be played at street parties called *dance halls*. The concept of the sound system included not only equipment, but also the human beings who interacted with the technology, controlling its speed and volume. Such people who were involved in playing the music also engaged audiences to participate. This turntablist came to be known as the *deejay*. Sound systems therefore included record players, speakers, a generator to power large pieces of equipment, and deejays. Music styles such as dancehall, ska, rocksteady, and reggae were played at these parties, and the deejay would announce songs and would perform a *toast*, a kind of monotone talk singing that was a precursor to rap.

Between the 1950s and 1970s, deejays began to use cross-fading and other mixing techniques to fade out one album and fade in another on a two phonograph turntable sound system. They would also briefly play two albums in sync to maintain the continuity of the music and not cause the dancers to have to pause between songs. They began to add turntablist effects, used to further engage dancers through a sound effect. For example, a deejay could bring a song (on an album) to a scratching halt and replace it with a more energetic dance song (on the other album). Because many of the record players used at the time were belt-drive turntables, the deejays could create brief effects, such as a quick scratch (by placing a hand on the album to slow it down enough that the record needle registers a scratch or a backspin—pushing the album backward). However, using too many of these techniques resulted in broken record players, as either the belt would snap or the spin action of the belt would need to be reset. In addition, when stopped manually too often, these belt-drive turntables would start up slowly the next use.

In 1969, the first commercially available direct-drive turntable, the Technics (Panasonic) SP-10, was released. Instead of a belt, the direct-drive turntable used a motor that would rotate the album and was far more durable than a belt-drive turntable. In 1971, another direct-drive turntable, the Technics SL-1100, was made available. It had a more powerful motor than its immediate predecessor.

A young Jamaican living in New York City, Clive Campbell (1955–), noticed the Jamaican sound system setup, which included the use of two SP-10s. His sister threw parties, and to supply the entertainment he began to play records in the apartment, creating a Jamaican-inspired sound system, plugging two turntables plugged into amplifiers: a Shure brand Vocal Master PA system, and two large speaker columns. He also took on the role as album selector. Using the stage name DJ Kool Herc, he spun funk albums such as James Brown's (1933–2006) "Give It Up or Turnit a Loose." By 1973, DJ Kool Herc had begun engaging in turntablism itself when he noticed that people at these parties who liked to dance enjoyed the rhythmic breaks of the songs best, so he created what became known as the break beat by playing an album until the end of the break passage, while cuing a second copy of the same album back to the beginning of the break. Continuing this technique gave the sense of a loop and matched the ideal amount of time that dancers would enjoy—no more than five minutes. He called this technique of album changing the "Merry-Go-Round." Quickly, he realized that not only could he extend the same break, but he could combine two breaks together with two different albums. As the first turntablist, DJ Kool Herc combined turntablism with early DJing. He went beyond toasting and would announce albums using slang words and funny expressions such as "this is the joint!" and "you don't stop" (to accompany the break beat music). He also engaged breakdancers directly in his monologues. Eventually, Kool Herc would drive his sound system (he called it the Herculords, as if it were a band) through the Bronx, playing music at full volume as a way to advertise himself as a DJ. Another way he would advertise was by setting up his sound system in parks. This made DJ Kool Herc a legend in his neighborhood.

One of his observers included Afrika Bambaataa (1957–), who purchased a sound system and invited people, including breakdancers, to join his Universal Zulu Nation (aka Zulu Nation, 1973–). By 1975, DJ Kool Herc had made the break beat popular. He used it in the Incredible Bongo Band's (1972–1974) funk cover of Jerry Lordan's (1934–1995) "Apache" (1960). He also originated the idea of sequences, so that on any given night the DJ became a feature, and his performance could be different as he mixed songs, beats, and rhythm sections with different combinations. Meanwhile, Afrika Bambaataa's Zulu Nation was also contributing by offering outlets for youth—options that could rival gang activity for excitement. Another observer from this time, who went by the name Grandmaster Flash (1958–), took an early interest in collecting and playing albums, as well as DJing. Grandmaster Flash came up with the quick-mix theory, sectioning off parts of albums on his turntables, creating what he called backspin and the double-back.

ENTRY INTO THE MAINSTREAM

A mentee of Grandmaster Flash, Grand Wizzard Theodore (1963–), came up with the idea of scratching, or moving the record back and forth under the stylus. Grandmaster Flash created a showcase for scratching through live shows and on recordings. DJ Grand Mixer DXT (Derek Showard, n.d.) furthered scratching by making it more rhythmic and using two turntables at different velocities to alter the pitch. He made scratching known internationally by using it on Herbie Hancock's (1940–) hit song "Rockit" (1982), a song that made the DJ the star. By the 1980s, scratching become a staple of hip hop, as DJs would provide music for rappers, called MCs, showcasing their skills alongside the verbal skills of the MC. Run-- D.M.C. (1981–2002) made the DJ as band member famous by emphasizing the skills of Jam Master Jay (1965–2002) in their performances and recordings; however, the role of the DJ was quickly downplayed in hip hop, as rappers became the focus of bands, as well as mainstream interest, and the increased use of tapes and other studio techniques and technology made the DJ's skills less relevant as part of the rap crew.

In addition, as a live art, turntablism had challenges with transferring over to recording in its own right: In other words, in sound recordings the visual dimension of the live performance is often felt as missing; despite a DJ's skills or a turntablist's virtuosity, recording solo turntablism or turntablism as instrumental hip hop in the 1980s seemed at best to be geared toward a specialized audience, which was not promising for sales. DJ battles, however, helped in changing this initial attitude.

THE BATTLE AND REINVIGORATING THE SOUND

One of the most important formal battles in turntablism traces back to 1985 when the first DMC World DJ Championships took place in London. The London remix label DMC (Disco Mix Club, 1983–) established this competition, which soon afterward had regional and national competitions that lead into the World Championships. During its first year, this competition was a DJ mixing battle, but by 1986, scratching had been introduced. During a DMC Championship battle, elimination rounds last for two minutes while final sets receive six minutes. In both DJs perform routines that exhibit a team or individual's scratching, mixing, and DJing techniques (including selecting and switching albums), as well as choreographed combinations of these techniques, using any kind of stylus (record needle). Rules for turntablism in less formal competitions more closely resemble those seen in freestyle rap or hip hop dance battles. For example, ciphers (aka cyphers, a circular formation around competitors) form to allow observers and judges to watch closely and allowing for competitors to take turns. Another example is sudden-death rounds, which may be determined by the audience as much as by a battle competitor's or team's accomplishments.

Both locally and globally, the DJ or turntablist battle was responsible for getting youth interested in turntablism as an expressive art, as well as showcasing this art to a broader audience. Pioneering champion crews such as the X-Ecutioners (aka X-Men, 1989–), Invisibl Skratch Piklz, and Beat Junkies (aka World Famous Beat Junkies, 1992–) honed turntablism techniques and brought to turntablism complex techniques such as the crab scratch, created by Invisibl Skratch Piklz's DJ Qbert (1969–), which can involve the use of up to four fingers to coordinate pushing the mixer open and closed while moving the album forward and backward (or backward and forward). The four movements by the four fingers on the crossfader are done quickly and look like a crab. The impression the technique gives is one that sounds like rapid, rhythmic scratching yet faster than what one would be able to do using just the turntable. Other scratching innovations at the time included tearing, orbiting, flaring, chirping, and stabbing, as well as visual turntablism, which is incorporating and manipulating pictures, video, and computer-generated effects into their live performances utilizing a separate video mixer.

Turntablism techniques such as beat juggling, performed by both individuals and crews also developed through battling. Beat juggling involves a variety of scratching skills, as well as beatmatching, matching the beats of at least two playing albums as one fades in and the other fades out, and selecting albums or samples for performance. The combination of these techniques is aimed toward creating a new musical piece or composition. Because many techniques are used and a lot of coordination is involved, crews and individuals have to practice their routines. Though turntablism certainly invites improvisation, special notation—a set of instructions to perform the composition again as well as to remind the turntablists about the composition's structure—has been created by turntablists. This notation often includes consideration of measures, kinds of scratches to be employed, and sections, among other musical aspects, including dynamics and who gets to perform. From battling, other innovations were discovered to make turntablism easier: for example, turning each player 90 degrees—in battle position—places the needle out of the way for the crossfading hand. This technique is now used in noncompetitive scratching. Hamster scratching, often credited to DJ QBert, involves scratching backward first rather than regular scratching, which involves moving the album forward first. By hamster scratching, the scratching hand is a bit closer to the crossfader and increases speed. Many turntablists who still favor regular scratching have come to incorporate some hamster scratching for the ease of hand motion.

Champion crews and their individual members have made albums that have featured turntablism. For example, Rob Swift's studio albums include *Soulful Fruit* (1997), *The Ablist* (1999), *Sound Event* (2002), *Under the Influence* and *Who Sampled This?* (both 2003), *OuMuPo 2* (2004), *War Games* (2005), and *The Architect* (2010), as well as one compilation album, *Airwave Invasion* (2001). In these recordings Rob Swift applied turntablism to jazz, soul, funk, electronica, classical music, and hip hop. Electronica and hip hop have been the most welcoming musical genres to solo turntablism as instrumental music.

TURNTABLISM TODAY

As of 2018, DJing has returned to becoming more of an art form in its own right, more often than not completely divorced from rapping. DJs continue to show off their skills, but not so much in concerts as they do in battles. Many turntablist concerts resemble their electroacoustic forerunners by having the same issues of what should take place visually as prerecorded music is playing onstage and how to coordinate a performance with a large number and variety of sound sources. Not only are there turntablists who select albums and samples and perform live; there are now hybrids of turntablists and music engineers, laptop composers, and live musicians who create loops as they play.

Many turntablists rely on turntablist software such as Serato Scratch Live (2013–), which emulates turntablism, but also simplifies aspects of it. Turntablists who opt to use Serato have the advantage of not having to coordinate large recording collections or other hardware, since Serato works with Digital Audio Workplace software such as Pro Tools (1989–), which includes access to sound filters, virtual instruments, sound effects, music editing tools, beatmaking tools, and mixing tools that can be used to enhance the turntablist's creativity both in live performance and working in the music studio. Across the world, specialized turntablism and DJ schools, as well as several colleges and universities, offer classes and courses on turntablism. Many of these classes give students the option to work with physical turntables and mixers and/or Serato.

Melissa Ursula Dawn Goldsmith and Anthony J. Fonseca

See also: Battling; Cut Chemist; DJ Babu; DJ Bobcat; DJ Jazzy Jeff; DJ QBert; DJ Rap; DJ Shadow; DJ Spinderella; DJ Vadim; Grandmaster Flash; GrandWizard Theodore; Invisibl Skratch Piklz; Jam Master Jay; Kool Herc; Mix Master Mike; Rob Swift; Roc Raida; World Famous Beat Junkies; The X-Ecutioners

Further Reading

Brewster, Bill, and Frank Broughton. 2010. *The Record Players: DJ Revolutionaries.* New York: Black Cat.

Ewoodzie, Joseph C. Jr. 2017. *Break Beats in the Bronx: Rediscovering Hip Hop's Early Years.* Chapel Hill: UNC Press Books.

Falkenberg Hansen, Kjetil. 2015. "DJs and Turntablism." In *The Cambridge Companion to Hip Hop*, edited by Justin Williams, chap. 4. Cambridge, England: Cambridge University Press.

Katz, Mark. 2010. *Capturing Sound: How Technology Has Changed Music.* Berkeley, California: University of California Press.

Katz, Mark. 2012. *Groove Music: The Art and Culture of the Hip Hop DJ.* New York: Oxford University Press.

Miyakawa, Felicia M. 2007. "Turntablature: Notation, Legitization, and the Art of the Hip Hop DJ." *American Music* 25, no. 1: 81–105.

Schloss, Joseph G. 2004. *Making Beats: The Art of Sample-Based Hip Hop.* Middletown, CT: Wesleyan University Press.

Further Listening

Cut Chemist. 2006. *The Audience's Listening.* Warner Bros/A Stable Sound.

Hancock, Herbie. 1983. *Future Shock.* Columbia.

Invisibl Skratch Piklz. 2015. *The 13th Floor.* Self-released.

Kid Koala. 2000. *Carpal Tunnel Syndrome.* Ninja Tune.

Rob Swift. 1999. *The Ablist.* Asphodel.

Rob Swift. 2010. *The Architect.* Ipecac Recordings.

The X-Ecutioners. 1997. *X-Pressions.* Asphodel.

The X-Ecutioners. 2002. *Built from Scratch.* Loud Records/Epic.

1200 Techniques

(1997–2005, Melbourne, Australia)

1200 Techniques was an Australian hardcore hip hop trio that was exceptionally eclectic, fusing hip hop with funk, jazz, electronica, breakbeat, ragga, rock, soul, and drum and bass. Producer, turntablist, and percussionist DJ Peril (Jason Foretti, n.d.) with two brothers, rapper and singer Nfamas (aka N'fa, N'fa Forster-Jones, 1979–) and rapper and singer Kabba (aka Cabba, Kabba Forster-Jones, 1973*–), originally founded the band. In 1998, DJ Peril's own brother, guitarist Kemstar (Simon Foretti, n.d.) joined the band, replacing Kabba after he departed to pursue a career recording electronic dance music and dubstep in London. The band is best known for its debut and second albums, *Choose One* (2002) and *Consistency Theory* (2003), which peaked on Australia's ARIA Albums Chart at Nos. 20 and 38, respectively.

FROM FORMATION TO SUCESS

Since the early 1980s, DJ Peril has been part of Melbourne's emerging hip hop scene as a well known aerosol graffiti artist and member of the Island Boys/Big Pacific (1989–1991)*, one of Melbourne's pioneering rapping crews. N'fa, who was born in London to an Australian mother and a Sierra Leonean father, grew up in Perth, Australia, and, since he was nine years old, wrote songs with his brother Kabba. The band named itself after DJ Peril's turntables, the Technics SL-1200. From the beginning, 1200 Techniques sounded retro and old-school, using funk to back N'fa's gangsta sounding raps in English. Texts focused on the Melbourne street life as a battleground of crime, violence, and poverty. The band's music videos, whether on location or lavishly set (for example, using animation and puppets), showed some entertaining channeling of the Beastie Boys' (1981–2012) approaching and rapping to a camera, as well as creating video moments reminiscent of Public Enemy (1982–), Geto Boys (1986–), Coolio (1963–), and Guerillaz (1998–).

The band's first recording effort, the EP *Infinite Styles*, took place in 2001. Immediately, 1200 Techniques had a popular single with "Hard as Hell," featuring Kemstar's funk-infused opening guitar riff. A year later, it released its successful and critically acclaimed debut album *Choose One*, which was produced on just a $5000 budget in Melbourne by Rubber Records (aka Rubber Chicken, 1989–), a label devoted to Australian underground music; Sony Music (1929–) distributed the album.

The group's biggest hits were "Karma (What Goes Around)" from *Choose One* and "Where Ur At" from *Conspiracy Theory*, both peaking in the Top 40 at Nos. 36 and 35, respectively. It followed its debut album with *Consistency Theory* and three hit songs from that album: "Eye of the Storm," "Where Ur At," and "Fork in the Road" (2004). But in 2005, the band went on a hiatus, which enabled some solo efforts. N'fa released his solo album *Cause an Effect* (2006). Nfa's friend, Australian actor Heath Ledger (1979–2008), directed two music videos for the title track and "Seduction Is Evil (She's Hot)." DJ Peril released *King of Beats* (2006). In 2014, the band released its final EP together, *Time Has Come*.

Melissa Ursula Dawn Goldsmith

See also: Australia; Turntablism

Further Reading

Frilingos, Matt. 2003. "Technical Knockout: 1200 Techniques Throw a Punch for Homegrown Hip Hop: Let's Talk about Techs." Interview with 1200 Techniques. *The Daily Telegraph* (Surry Hills, Australia), July 16, S01.

Moses, Alexa. 2002. "Hip Hop's Indefinables Also Like to Rub a Little Funk in Popular Music." *Sydney Morning Herald*, September 4, 16.

Further Listening

1200 Techniques. 2002. *Choose One.* Rubber Records.
1200 Techniques. 2003. *Consistency Theory.* Rubber Records.

2 Live Crew

(1982–1998, Miami, Florida)

2 Live Crew was an American hip hop group best known for its studio album *As Nasty As They Wanna Be* (1989), which drew criticism both for its explicit sexual content and its problems with alleged copyright infringement. Although the band changed membership in its 16 years of existence, the best-known iteration included DJ Mr. Mixx (anonymous, n.d.) and rappers Fresh Kid Ice (Chris Wong

The American hip hop group 2 Live Crew was at the height of its career in 1989 with its third studio album *As Nasty As They Wanna Be*. At the time, the band's lineup consisted of DJ Mr. Mixx and rappers Fresh Kid Ice, Brother Marquis, and Luke. (Michael Ochs Archives/Getty Images)

Won, 1964–2017), from Port of Spain, Trinidad and Tobago; Brother Marquis (Mark D. Ross, 1967*–), from Rochester, New York; and rapper/promoter Luke (aka Luke Skyywalker, Luther Campbell, 1960–), from Miami. The group's music is characterized by heavy bass, synthesized melodic and drum sounds, samples of comedians such as Richard Pryor (1940–2005) and Cheech and Chong (1971–), and graphic rapped lyrics about women and sex. The band's album *Banned in the U.S.A.* (1990), billed as Luke featuring the 2 Live Crew, was one of the first albums to bear a Parental Advisory sticker from the Recording Industry Association of America (RIAA), a label created to caution parents of explicit lyrics.

The group's first two albums, *The 2 Live Crew Is What We Are* (1986) and *Move Somethin'* (1988), both sold relatively well, but the third album, *As Nasty As They Wanna Be* (1989), propelled 2 Live Crew to national attention. It featured "Me So Horny" and "The F— Shop" and was criticized by the Tupelo, Mississippi–based American Family Association and other culture watchdog groups who claimed that the album should not be sold due to its lyrics. The 2 Live Crew did release a censored version of the album called *As Clean As They Wanna Be*, which sold poorly and did not quiet any of objections to the original version.

In 1990, a United States District Court judge ruled that *As Nasty As They Wanna Be* was obscene and therefore could not be sold legally; three of the group's members were then arrested (the album was the first to be declared obscene in a court of law). In 1992, the Court of Appeals overturned the lower court's ruling, and the United States Supreme Court declined to hear an appeal. The three members of the group were released without incident; however, the group was also sued by Acuff-Rose Music for their unauthorized parody of Roy Orbison's (1936–1988) song "Oh, Pretty Woman" (1964). The case *Campbell vs. Acuff-Rose Music* went all the way to the United States Supreme Court, which held that the group's song was a commercial parody and therefore did not violate copyright.

During the 1990s, the group's personnel changed several times, and although they continued to release albums, none sold as well or achieved as much notoriety as *As Nasty As They Wanna Be*. Further, Luke was forced to change the name of his record label from Luke Skyywalker Records to simply Luke Records after a copyright infringement lawsuit filed by American filmmaker George Lucas (1944–), creator of the *Star Wars* franchise and Luke Skywalker character.

Amanda Sewell

See also: Luke; The United States

Further Reading

Campbell, Luther. 2015. *The Book of Luke: My Fight for Truth, Justice, and Liberty City.* New York: Amistad.

Sanjek, David. 2006. "Ridiculing the 'White Bread Original.'" *Cultural Studies* 20, nos. 2–3: 262–81.

Westoff, Ben. 2011. "Luke Campbell: Bass and Booty." In *Dirty South: OutKast, Lil Wayne, Soulja Boy, and the Southern Rappers Who Reinvented Hip Hop*, chap. 1. Chicago: Chicago Review Press.

Further Listening

2 Live Crew. 1989. *As Nasty As They Wanna Be.* Luke Skyywalker Records.

Uganda

Uganda, like the rest of Africa, has seen a rise in hip hop music popularity since the early 1980s. In 1985, hip hop reached Senegal with groups such as Positive Black Soul (1989–). Tanzania was introduced to MCing before 1989; South Africa saw the rise of groups such as Black Noise (1992–2001), which began as a graffiti and breakdance crew in Cape Town, as well as the rise of *kwaito* in Johannesburg, a variant of house music featuring percussive loop samples, heavy bass, and sung, rapped, and shouted vocals. Uganda's hip hop scene began among university students in the 1990s. Formative groups in the Ugandan hip hop scene, which was popularized at clubs such as Club Pulsations in Kampala, included Bataka Squad (aka Bataka Underground, 1993–). In 2003, members of Bataka Squad helped found the Uganda Hip Hop Foundation, which hosted the first Ugandan Hip Hop Summit and concert in Kampala, and in 2005, members also formed Bavubuka All Starz to bring hip hop music and community together to address social causes.

Breakdancing is popular in Uganda because of the Breakdance Project Uganda (BPU), a youth-empowering organization formed in 2006 that holds b-boy and b-girl events in the country. Uganda's best-known breakdance troupe is Tabu-Flo (2007–), which has competed internationally. Comedians King Kong MC (Alex Lamu, n.d.–2018) and Jaja Bruce (n.d.) have also popularized Ugandan hip hop dance through their comedic dance-off videos posted on YouTube.

LUGAFLOW, LUO-RAP, AND OTHER STYLES

Bataka Squad is the originator of the Lugaflow style, which uses the native Luganda language and is the dominant Ugandan style of hip hop. Luga Flow Army (2011–) is a group of five MCs whose single "Competition" (2013) emphasized local dialect rapping and became a fan favorite, and GNL Zamba (Ernest Nsimbi, 1986–) has made Lugaflow style popular through rapping, filmmaking, and acting.

The second most dominant style of Ugandan hip hop is Luo-rap, whose most famous practitioner was Lumix Da Don (Patrick Lumumba, 1978–2015), an underground Ugandan rapper and record producer who recorded freestyles. Other styles include Kigaflow, Lusoflow, and Lumaflow, all of which are specific to various geographic regions of the country.

CURRENT ARTISTS

Contemporary Ugandan rappers include Keko (1987–), Abramz (Tekya Abraham, 1985*–), Bana Mutibwa (aka Burney MC, Walakira Richard, 1989–), and King

LG (aka King Legend D'Grek, Mpuuga Clifford Magezi Atwooki, n.d.). Keko appeared in the rap collective song "Fallen Heroes" (2010) and followed up with an appearance on the Ugandan hip hop duo Radio and Weasel (2008–) single "How We Do It" remix (2011), an MTV Africa favorite that led to her endorsement deal with Pepsi. Abramz is a socially conscious MC and b-boy and founder of Breakdance Project Uganda, which promotes positive social change and social responsibility. He is also part of the brother-based hip hop duo Abramz and Sylvester (1992–). Bana Mutibwa is a rapper and activist who advocates rapping in local languages, while King LG is a rap and trap artist and producer who promotes underground rap. The future of Ugandan rap rests in the hands of these rappers and others such as Lyrical G (Jeff Kintu, 1978*–) and Navio (Daniel Kigozi, 1983*–), who have both released successful albums with songs that encourage self-improvement, especially in escaping poverty.

Anthony J. Fonseca

See also: Breakdancing; Hip Hop Dance; Keko

Further Reading

Barz, Gregory F., and Gerald C. Liu. 2011. "Positive Disturbance: Tafesh, Twig, HIV/AIDS, and Hip Hop in Uganda." In *The Culture of AIDS in Africa: Hope and Healing in Music and the Arts*, edited by Gregory F. Barz and Judah M. Cohen, chap. 30. New York: Oxford University Press.

Ntarangwi, Mwenda. 2009. "Hip Hop and African Identity in Contemporary Globalization." In *East African Hip Hop: Youth Culture and Globalization*, chap. 2. Urbana: University of Illinois Press.

Slim MC. 2014. "Hip Hop and Social Change in Uganda." In *Hip Hop and Social Change in Africa: Ni Wakati*, edited by Msia Kibona Clark and Mickie Mwanzia Koster, chap. 10. Lanham, MD: Lexington Books.

Ukraine

The Ukraine has a hip hop scene that is closely connected with national identity and politics and is usually found in major cities such as Kiev and Kharkov. During most of the 20th century, the Ukraine was a republic of the Soviet Union, but in 1991, it became an independent republic. Early Ukrainian hip hop was sung in English and Russian, but in the late 1990s, hip hop was written and sung in Ukrainian, as the music became an important marker of social and political identity, although some Ukrainian groups, despite political implications, chose to use Russian in order to reach larger markets in the music industry.

Ukrainian hip hop began to flourish after the Orange Revolution, a series of anti-government protests following an allegedly corrupt election, which took place between November 2004 and January 2005. One song, "Razom Nas Bahato" ("Together We Are Many," 2005), by GreenJolly (1997–2005*), became the unofficial protest anthem in late 2004; a version of the song was Ukraine's official entry for the 2005 Eurovision song contest, where it was awarded twentieth place. GreenJolly disbanded soon afterward.

The best-known Ukrainian hip hop group is TNMK (1989–) from Kharkiv, Ukraine, which did not release its first album, *Zroby Meni Hip Hop* (*Make Me Hip*

Hop), until 1998. In 1997, TNMK won the title of best dance band at Chervona Ruta (1989–), a Ukrainian international music festival usually held in Kiev. Significantly, Chervona Ruta festival rules required the submission of three songs, in Ukrainian. Before this, the band's name had been in Russian, Tanets na Ploshchadi Kongo (Dance in Congo Square). It was changed to the Ukrainian Tanok na Maidani Kongo (TNMK) for the contest.

Ukrainian hip hop includes a lot of rap, and some Ukrainian rap is influenced by reggae; traditional Ukrainian folk music; alternative rock, punk, rap, and funk; and African folk music (due to the influence of African immigrant communities in Ukraine). Popular bands include the acoustic group 5'Nizza (2000–2007, 2015–), from Kharkiv and Tartak (1994–), from Lutsk. Ukrainian hip hop is seen as a vehicle for national, social, political, and ethnic identity, whether through lyrics, language choice, or musical stylistic influences.

Ukrainian language hip hop (Ukrahop) groups include GreenJolly, TNMK, Tartak, Boombox, and Vova ZIL'vova (Volodymyr Parfeniuk, 1983–), the last from Lviv. Russian language groups from Ukraine include 5'Nizza, Tuman (2001–), and Yuzhnyi Tsentral (n.d.) from Moskva.

Terry Klefstad

See also: Russia; Young Paperboyz

Further Reading

Helbig, Adriana. 2014. *Hip Hop Ukraine: Music, Race, and African Migration.* Bloomington: Indiana University Press.

Wanner, Catherine. 1996. "Nationalism on Stage: Music and Change in Soviet Ukraine." In *Retuning Culture: Musical Changes in Central and Eastern Europe*, edited by Mark Slobin, chap. 8. Durham, NC: Duke Univeristy Press.

Further Listening

Tanok na Maidani Kongo (TNMK). 1998. *Zroby meni hip hop* (*Make Me Hip Hop*). Lavina Digital/Nova Records.

Various Artists. 2006. *Ukrainskymy slovamy: Zbirka Ukrainsko-movnoho hip hop* (*With Ukrainian Words: A Collection of Ukrainian-Language Hip Hop*). Age Music Studios.

The United Kingdom

The United Kingdom is a Northern European country that consists of Great Britain, Wales, Scotland, and Northern Ireland, as well as many smaller islands. The vast majority of the nearly 66 million people live in the United Kingdom are white European. There are small pockets of minorities of Asians, blacks, and mixed races, and since the United Kingdom has had a lengthy past of colonizing other countries, it has a strong diaspora rap scene. Hip hop quickly came to England in the early 1980s, just after the Sugarhill Gang's (1979–1985, 1994–) hit "Rapper's Delight" (1979) hit No. 3 on the U.K. Singles Chart. Earlier, the Fatback Band (1970–), an American funk, disco, and R&B band, had U.K. Singles Chart hits with "(Are You Ready) Do the Bus Stop" (1975) and "(Do the) Spanish Hustle" (1976), which reached Nos. 18 and 10, respectively.

The United Kingdom has a lengthy musical heritage. Geographical separation from the European continent led to different music in Great Britain, despite the strength of continental influences. Some musical genres, such as the carol, developed first in Great Britain. Still, England had a tendency to make established continental genres its own. For example, in the late 1500s, Italian *madrigals* were popular in England, but the texts were changed to English, and the subject matter became lighter and humorous. During the late Baroque, one of the country's most famous composers, George Frideric Handel (1685–1759), wrote English language operas based on the Italian Baroque opera; he also made the Italian oratorio English. The United Kingdom is also known for diverse traditional folksongs and folk instruments.

By the 20th and 21st centuries, traditional instruments of the United Kingdom included Celtic *fiddles, harps, bagpipes, penny whistles*, and *bodhráns*. Some surviving traditional music includes dance music such as *jigs, waltzes*, and *reels*. Early popular music included the *broadside ballad* (a narrative song), music hall numbers, and dance music played by bands. By the middle of the 20th century, the United Kingdom had its own popular music charts and had a leading presence in the development of popular music. By the turn of the 21st century, England was the place of origin for numerous musical genres and styles that are related to hip hop. These include dubstep, drum and bass, grime, bhangra-beat, chap hop, trip hop, and trance. England also has a leading presence in the development of experimental hip hop.

Since the early 1970s, punk developed in England, and reggae-influenced punk rock music was already successful and helped pave the way for hip hop there. Early English hip hop was influenced by Jamaican toasting. Some of the earliest examples include brief moments in new wave hits such as Adam and the Ants' (1977–1982) "Ant Rap" from the band's album *Prince Charming* (1981). A year later, Malcolm McLaren's "Buffalo Gals" (1982), from the album *Duck Rock* (1983), became the United Kingdom's first hip hop hit. The song features New York City's World's Famous Supreme Team (1980–1985*). The music, which also became a hit, featured scratching (turntablism) as well as rap. Other tracks from McLaren's album contained scratching and sampling. Meanwhile, as graffiti and breakdancing were becoming commonplace, and club scenes started playing hip hop music in urban London, DJ remixers Simon Harris (1962–) and Froggy (Steve Howlett, 1949–2008) established Music of Life (1986–), the United Kingdom's first independent label that was devoted to hip hop.

MANCHESTER, LEICESTER, BRISTOL, AND BIRMINGHAM

Manchester is home to the Chemical Brothers (1995–) and Ruthless Rap Assassins (1987–1992). Both were a product of the "Madchester," music scene, which included rappers such as MC Tunes (Nicholas William Dennis Hodgson, 1970–), techno and drum-and-bass musician A Guy Called Gerald (Gerald Simpson, 1957–), and techno bands such as 808 State (1987–). Drum and bass duo the Chemical Brothers debuted with *Exit Planet Dust* (1995), which was certified Platinum. Ruthless Rap Assassins rapped using British English and sampled indie rock, reggae, pop, jazz, and classic rock, as well as funk and hip hop. Like the Roots (1987–) in the United States, the band was known for its live performances because it used traditional instrumentation (drum kits, guitars, bass, and keyboards). The band split up in 1992, and three of its members joined with Shaun Ryder (1962–) of Happy Mondays (1980–1993, 2004–) to form Black Grape (1993–1998, 2015–). Leicester hip hop acts include DJ SS (Leroy Small, 1970–), Jehst (William G. Shields, 1979–), Goldie (Clifford Joseph Price, 1965–), and Do'reen (Doreen Waddell, 1965*– 2002). Bristol hip hop acts include Nellee Hooper (Paul Andrew Hooper or Hoop, 1963–), Krust (Kirk Thompson, 1968–), Martina (Martina Gillian Topley-Bird, 1975–), Poetic Pilgrimage (2002*–), Roni Size (Ryan Owen Granville, 1969–), Task Force (1999–), Tinie Tempah (Patrick Chukwuemeka Okogwu, 1988–), Tricky (Adrian Nicholas Matthew Thaws, 1968–), Us3 (1991/1992–), and Frankie Valentine (Franklin Barcey or Fraklyn Barzey, 1962–). Birmingham acts include the Streets (1994–2011*) and Krispy 3 (1987–).

LONDON

London is home to the largest hip hop scene in the United Kingdom, with many of its musicians, including rappers such as Slick Rick (1965–), DJ Rap (1969–), Dizzee Rascal (Dylan Kwabena Mills, 1984*–), and Sway (1982–), as well as rap and hip hop crews such as Coldcut (1986–), the Herbaliser (1995–), Urban Species (1992–2000, 2008–), and the Brand New Heavies (1985–), enjoying international fame. Slick Rick recorded in both England and the United States. Known for his storytelling raps and multiple characters, he saw initial success as MC Ricky D in Barbadian American beatboxer, rapper, and producer Doug E. Fresh's (1966–) Get Fresh Crew (1985–2003). DJ Rap is a Singapore-born English DJ, composer, music engineer, music producer, turntablist, and singer who combines drum and bass (jungle style), house music, EDM (electronic dance music), and later trip hop in her work. Dizzee Rascal was known for his contribution to the grime style of rap. Sway, of Ghanian descent, has had nine hit singles on the U.K. Singles Chart. His music has a strong focus on synthesizer, with beats placed further in the background, and he is known for chopper style rapping, notable for his speed, use of rapid triplets, and biography-based storytelling. Coldcut is an electronic music duo that has fused electronica with hip hop. The Herbaliser is an alternative hip hop group from London that fuses hip hop with jazz. Urban Species fuses hip hop with funk, reggae, dancehall, dubstep, ragga, acid jazz, R&B, soul, blues, and folk music. Urban Species' sound resembles the eclectic alternative groups such as Soul II Soul (1987–1997, 2007–) from England and Arrested Development (1988– 1996, 2000–) from the United States.

Other notable London-based hip hop acts include 4hero (1989–), Akala (Kingslee James Daley, 1983–), Dave Angel (David Anglico Nicholas Gooden, 1966–), Asher D (Ashley Walters, 1982–), Asian Dub Foundation (1993–), Kid Batchelor (Lawrence Batchelor, 1968–), Dreem Teem (1994–), Fabio (Fitzroy Heslop, 1964*–), Fun-Da-Mental (1991–), General Levy (Paul Levy, 1971–), Grooverider (Raymond Bingham, 1967–), Insane Macbeth (Keith Rodgers, 1970*–2016), Jazzy B (Trevor Breseford Romeo, 1963–), Ronny Jordan (Ronald Laurence Albert Simpson,

1962–2014), Kenzie (James MacKenzie, 1986–), Soweto Kinch (1978–), London Posse (1986–1996*), Lowkey (Kareem Dennis, 1986–), M.I.A. (1975–), Ms. Dynamite (Niomi Arleen McLean-Daley, 1981–), N-Dubz (2000–2011), the Nextmen (2000*), Courtney Pine (1964–), Roots Manuva (Rodney Hylton Smith, 1972–), Scratch Perverts (1996–), Adrian Sherwood (Adrian Maxwell Sherwood, 1958–), Shut Up And Dance (1988–), So Solid Crew (1998–), Sonique (Sonia Marina Clarke, 1968–), Stereo MC's (1985–), Young Disciples (1990*–), and ZooNation Dance Company (2002–).

STYLES

The United Kingdom was home to various hip hop movements and new styles, such as dubstep, trip hop, bhangra-beat, and chap hop. In the 1990s, dubstep, an electronic dance music genre, began in South London, introducing fans to experimental remixes that deemphasized vocals and placed the breakbeat, drums, and bass in the foreground. It started as a nightclub phenomenon, but by 2000, dubstep's syncopated rhythm, 138 to 142 beats per minute (bpm), and wobble bass could be heard on radio. London-based producers Benga (Adegbenga Adejumo, 1986–), Skream (Oliver Dene Jones, 1986–), Digital Mystikz (anonymous, n.d.), and Loefah (Peter Livingston, n.d.) started an evolution in dubstep that resulted in a darker, more clipped and minimalist sound, and by 2005, BBC Radio 1 had dubstep-dedicated shows. Baltimore-based English dubstep DJ Joe Nice (2002–) helped with cultivating and promoting dubstep in the United States. Trip hop came into prominence in the early 1990s in Bristol. The genre includes many of the foundations of hip hop, such as looped samples, scratches, and sequencing, but adds more melodic instrumentation and vocal content in the form of singing, with less emphasis on rap. It is characterized by laid-back tempos and an artful multi-layering of instruments, samples, and voices and an emphasis on atmosphere over text, and samples are used to counter the source material, especially in relation to tempo. Massive Attack (1988–), Sneaker Pimps (1994–2005, 2015–), and Portishead (1991–), as well as Tricky, popularized the style while adding their own elements.

Bhangra-beat was popularized by West London–based Panjabi Hit Squad (PHS, 2001–) and Coventry's Panjabi MC (1973–). PHS, a collective of DJ/Producers, combined hip hop rhythms and beats with Indian *bhangra* vocals and instrumentation, BollyHood vocals, and *Desi* beats. In 2002, it collaborated on the single "Stolen (Dil)" with American rapper Jay-Z (1969–), and in 2003, had an international hit with "Hai Hai," which featured rapper Ms Scandalous (Savita Vaid, 1985–). Panjabi MC is known for the bhangra hits "Mundian To Bach Ke" (1998) and "Jogi" (2003). A remix version of the former, "Beware of the Boys," featured Jay-Z. Panjabi MC popularized the combining of Western and traditional instruments such as *tumbi, dhol, dholki,* and *tabla.* He also uses both male and female singers and vocal samples in much of his music. Chap Hop, which vocally can be traced back to Slick Rick, became popular around 2010, paired the language and rhythms of hip hop with the music, values, and aesthetics of the Chappist Movement, which emerged in the late 1990s. Chappism, which both paid homage to and parodied the idea of the proper English gentleman, is epitomized in publications such as *The Chap* magazine, originated in the 2000s in parts of England. Typically, chap hop artists rap using Received Pronunciation English (RP, also known as BBC English), which is the Standard English accent of the United Kingdom, and they employ the grammar and vocabulary of the Queen's English. Most chap hop tracks address English cultural stereotypes, such as cricket playing, pipe smoking, and tea drinking, and many involve the steampunk movement. The artists themselves dress in Victorian- or Edwardian-era style clothing, such as tweed suits and fine hats, and many sport highly cultivated facial-hair styles, such as handlebar mustaches. Important chap hoppers include London's Mr. B the Gentleman Rhymer (1970–), Norwich's Professor Elemental (1975–), and Poplock Holmes (anonymous, 1976–).

NORTHERN IRELAND, WALES, AND SCOTLAND

Northern Ireland's hip hop scene is considerably smaller, with hip hop dance being more popular than music production. Most of its hip hop scenes are in Belfast. If music is produced, its lyrics focus less on politics and more on local life, including partying, as well as on nonlocalized topics such as romance. Belfast rappers use the storytelling style of rap, and usually record in Belfast dialects of English, as for example, local rapper Bee Mark See (Brendan McCarthy, n.d.), and Belfast-born diaspora rapper, such as Jun Tzu (Jonathan Hamilton, 1986*–). Jun Tzu's rap is more political since his father was imprisoned in Ireland for a decade, which is why he moved to Manchester, England. Some diaspora acts from Wales and Scotland moved to England, where they were had successful careers as rappers. These include MC Eric (aka Me One, Eric Martin, 1970–), from Cardiff, Wales and Silibil N' Brains (1998*–), from Dundee, Scotland. Although he was born in Limerick, Ireland, Aphex Twin (Richard David James, 1971–) was raised in England. Others include English-born Nigerian R&B and neo soul singer-songwriter and producer Lemar (Lemar Obika, 1978), and female English rapper and singer Baby Blue (Rachel Estelle Irene Prager, n.d.).

Melissa Ursula Dawn Goldsmith and Anthony J. Fonseca

See also: Chap Hop; Dubstep; Grime; India; Ireland; Trip Hop

Further Reading

Bramwell, Richard. 2015. *U.K. Hip Hop, Grime, and the City: The Aesthetics and Ethics of London's Rap Scenes.* New York: Routledge.

Gerard, Morgan, and Jack Sidnell. 2000. "Reaching Out to the Core: On the Interactional Work of the MC in Drum & Bass Performance." *Popular Music and Society* 24, no. 3: 21–39.

Hall, Joanna. 2013. "Rocking the Rhythm: Dancing Identities in Drum 'n' Bass Club Culture." In *Bodies of Sound: Studies across Popular Music and Dance*, edited by Sherril Dodds and Susan C. Cook, pp. 105–16. Burlington, VT: Ashgate.

Mandaville, Peter. 2009. "Hip Hop, Nasheeds, and 'cool' Sheikhs: Popular Culture and Muslim Youth in the United Kingdom." In *In-Between Spaces: Christian and Muslim Minorities in Transition in Europe and the Middle East*, edited by Christiane Timmerman et al., pp. 149–68. Brussels: P.I.E. Peter Lang.

Sullivan, Paul. 2014. *Remixology: Tracing the Dub Diaspora.* London: Reaktion Books.

Wood, Andy. 2002. "Hip Hop." In *Companion to Contemporary Black British Culture,* edited by Alison Donnell, pp. 141–42. London: Routledge.

Further Listening

Aphex Twin. 2014. *Syro.* Warp Records.

Asian Dub Foundation. 2003. *Enemy of the Enemy.* Virgin Records.

Dizzee Rascal. 2013. *The Fifth.* Dirtee Stank Recordings.

The Herbaliser. 2012. *There Were Seven.* Department H.

Portishead. 2008. *Third.* Island Records.

The United States

The United States is where rap originated, and despite its size, the country's hip hop and rap scene is a local phenomenon. Rap began on the East and West coasts, in several New York City boroughs and in South Central Los Angeles, and moved its way across the United States as major labels emerged in New Orleans and Atlanta, and rap scenes became popular in urban areas such as Oakland, California; Newark, New Jersey; Philadelphia, Pennsylvania; Miami, Florida; and Houston, Texas. The main exception to this rule was Hampton, Virginia (population 138,000), largely because of Jodeci (1988–1996, 2014–) member and producer DeVante Swing (Donald Earle DeGrate Jr., 1969–), whose Hampton-based Swing Mob Collective included locals Missy Elliott (1971–) and Timbaland (1972–), as well as Ginuwine (Elgin Baylor Lumpkin, 1970–). Elliott and Timbaland netted five consecutive Platinum albums, and both have produced for various musicians over three decades; Virginia has also produced the very successful hip hop musician Pharrell (1973–), who has won 10 Grammy Awards and cofounded the production-songwriting duo the Neptunes (1992–).

WEST COAST RAP

Los Angeles

Although Philadelphia's Schoolly D (Jesse Bonds Weaver Jr., 1962–), the Bronx's Boogie Down Productions (1985–1992), and Newark's Ice-T (1958–) drew on gangsta themes, gangsta rap found its voice with the formation of Compton, California–based group N.W.A. (1986–1991). Rapper Eazy-E (1963–1995) cofounded Ruthless Records and N.W.A., and both became the driving force behind gangsta rap. N.W.A. included Eazy-E, Dr. Dre (1965–), Ice Cube (1969–), and Arabian Prince (Kim Nazel, 1965–), and its Platinum albums included *Straight Outta Compton* (1988) and *Efil4za—n* (1991). Five years after the launch of Ruthless, Death Row Records (1991–2008) was cofounded by Dr. Dre, the D.O.C. (Tracy Lynn Curry, 1968–), and Suge Knight (Marion Hugh Knight Jr., 1965–). Dr. Dre, the D.O.C., and Michel'le (Michel'le Toussaint, 1970–) left Ruthless to join Death Row, which then dominated the rap charts with Dr. Dre, Tupac Shakur (1971–1996), and Snoop Dogg (1971–). Gangsta rap became the most popular subgenre of rap music in the 1980s and 1990s. It also became the target of intense criticism by elected officials and law enforcement, leading to labeling and censorship. Nonetheless, gangsta rappers such as Compton's Most Wanted (1987–1993, 2015–) found commercial success and public notoriety. Gangsta rap evolved into various styles, the most popular being G-funk (gangsta funk), which sampled funk albums of the 1970s and used a less aggressive tone, informed by a laid–back vocal delivery. Grammy winning Coolio (1963–) saw his 1996 hit single "Gangsta's Paradise" sell 5 million and rise to No. 1 in 15 countries.

Los Angeles was also home of rap poetry, electronic dance rap, Chicano rap, and experimental turntablism. Aceyalone (1970–) recorded poetry and alternative hip hop. Hip hop and electronica rap stars Black Eyed Peas launched the careers of will.i.am (1975–) and Fergie (Stacey Ferguson, 1975–). Chicano rap combined Latin rhythms, hip hop beats, and gangsta rap, and Kid Frost (aka Frost, Arturo Molina Jr., 1962–) popularized the style in 1990s Los Angeles. Trio Cypress Hill (1988–) became the first certified-Platinum Latino American hip hop act. West L.A.'s Cut Chemist (1972–) became known for his sample–based turntablism. Recent rap has become more socially conscious, as with the work of Compton-based Grammy winner Kendrick Lamar (1987–).

Hip hop dance styles that emerged in the Los Angeles area included clowning, krumping, and crip walking. Clowning and krumping were originated in Compton in 1992 with "Tommy the Clown" (Thomas Johnson, n.d.) as a way to motivate youth living in gang–infested communities. Pioneering krumpers were Compton–based Big Mijo (Jo' Artis Ratti, 1985–) and Tight Eyez (Ceasare Willis, 1985–) and Los Angeles–based Lil'C (Christopher Toler, 1983–). On a more national stage, Don Campbell (1951–), a Midwestern dancer and choreographer, moved to L.A. and created the Campbellock (the prototype of locking). He starred on *Soul Train* (1971–2006) as part of the Lockers (1971–1976). In addition, the Electric Booga-loo was made famous by a West Coast dance crew called the Electric Boogaloos (1977–), which also appeared on *Soul Train*. Boogaloo Sam (Sam Solomon, 1959–) combined the dime stopping moves of locking and the associated stiff, rigid moves of roboting with moves that were so smooth, relaxed, and flowing that they gave the illusion that the dancer had no bones. Asia One (1971–), one of the best-known b-girls in the world, moved to Los Angeles in the 1990s to battle contemporaries Honey Rockwell (Ereina Valencia, n.d.) and Rokafella (1971–). Recently, L.A. became home to jerkin' (aka Doing the Jerk), a dance that gained popularity on both the East and West coasts after New Boyz (2009–2013) and Audio Push (2006–) released associated songs.

Northern California

Northern California's contributions to rap include the Oakland–based Hip Hop Coalition (1997–), which promoted hip hop; it was led by Davey D (David Cook, n.d.), a nationally syndicated radio host and radio show producer. Oakland produced legendary hip hop acts such as MC Hammer (1962–), Michael Franti (1966–), Ant Banks (1966–), and Del the Funky Homosapien (Teren Delvon Jones, 1972–). MC Hammer is today considered the quintessential old-school rapper and dancer, having achieved icon status, winning three Grammys and selling over 50 million albums; Franti became leader of the hip hop, funk, reggae, jazz, folk, and rock band Michael Franti & Spearhead (aka Spearhead, 1994–); Ant Banks's funk–influenced bass lines were influential on West Coast rappers; and Oakland's Del the Funky Homosapien formed hip hop collective Hieroglyphics (1991–) and the Hiero Imperium (1997–) label. In addition, Sacramento's Brotha Lynch Hung's (1969–) debut horrorcore EP, *24 Deep* (1993) helped popularize horrorcore on the West Coast.

Northern California is also known for its contributions to DJing and dance. San Francisco's DJ QBert (1969–) performed regularly with San Francisco–based childhood friend Mix Master Mike (1970–) and cofounded Invisibl Skratch Piklz (1989–2000, 2014–). Mix Master Mike became a Grammy Award winning turntablist and worked as DJ for Beastie Boys (1981–2012). San Jose's DJ Shadow (1972–) used sampling on his innovative album, *Endtroducing. . . .* (1996). On the dance front, Fresno is the home of both Boogaloo Sam and his brother Pop'in Pete (1961–). Pop'in Pete was one of the original poppers, and both were first-generation members of the Electric Boogaloos.

EAST COAST RAP: NEW YORK AND NEW JERSEY

The earliest b-boys included dance crews such as SalSoul (1974–1978) and Rockwell Association (1976–1978), consisting almost entirely of New York–based Puerto Ricans. Ken Swift (1966–) started dancing in 1978; his first crew was the Young City Boys (1978–1980s), but he soon joined the Rock Steady Crew (RSC, 1977–), which also featured Crazy Legs (1966–) and Bronx-based Frosty Freeze (1963–2008). An early example of rapping in music came from the Fatback Band (1970–), with "King Tim III (Personality Jock)" in 1979, considered by many as the first commercially released song with rap. The first song containing rap to reach No. 1 on the Billboard Hot 100 was "Rapture" (1981), by New York punk and new wave band Blondie (1974–1982, 1997–). By this time, rap was becoming more common, and early rap recordings started to emerge: Barbados–born Doug E. Fresh (1966–) became famous for his beatboxing and rapping during the 1980s, and LL Cool J (James Todd Smith, 1968–) released his first studio album, *Radio* (1985), inspired by the rap songs of the Treacherous Three (1978–1984) and the Sugarhill Gang's (1979–1985, 1994–) "Rapper's Delight" (1979), on Sugar Hill Records (1979–1985), led by Sylvia Robinson (1936–2011). His second album, *Bigger and Deffer* (1987), went triple Platinum. Beastie Boys (1980–2012) became one of the great crossover successes in early hip hop, coming into prominence after working with Rick Rubin (Frederick Jay Rubin, 1963–), founder of Def Jam Records (1983–). The band's first studio album went multi-Platinum. Two duos emerged middecade: EPMD (1986–1993) and Eric B. and Rakim (1986–1993, 2016–), both considered integral to the early development of rap music.

Toward the end of the decade, New Rochelle–based Brand Nubian (1989–1995, 1997–) became known for its association with Islam and the Five Percenters, and Yonkers-based DMX (1970–) went from beatboxing to rapping, as his first album, *Flesh of My Flesh, Blood of My Blood* (1988), was released on Def Jam Recordings.

Jungle Brothers (1987–) began fusing old-school hip hop with jazz, funk, electronica, dance, house music, R&B, and Afrobeat and became core members of the New York City hip hop collective Native Tongues (1988–1996), which included A Tribe Called Quest (1985–1998, 2006–2013, 2015–), De La Soul (1987–), and Black Sheep (1989–1995, 2000–2002, 2006–). As turntablism became more complex, DJs such as Roc Raida (Anthony Williams, 1972–2009) and turntablist collaboratives such as the X-Ecutioners (1989–) became popular. The 1980s transitioned into the 1990s with acts such as Brooklyn-born Mos Def (1973–) and Staten Island–based Wu-Tang Clan (1992–). Mos Def later formed the duo Black Star (1997–) with Talib Kweli (1975–). Wu-Tang Clan led to the careers of Ol' Dirty Bastard (Russell Tyrone Jones, 1968–2004), Ghostface Killah (Dennis Coles, 1970–), Method Man (Clifford Smith, 1971–), and Raekwon (Corey Woods, 1970–). Collectively, members of the group have sold over 40 million records. More recent New York City–identified hip hop acts include Atlanta native Kanye West (1977–) and Barbados-born Rihanna (1988–).

The Bronx

Kingston, Jamaica, native Kool Herc (1955–) moved to the Bronx in 1967 and became the first hip hop turntablist. Having moved to the United States from Barbados, Grandmaster Flash (1958–) created Grandmaster Flash and the Furious Five (1976–1982, 1987–1988). He introduced using the beat box drum machine and custom–built instruments, and worked with GrandWizard Theodore (1963–), who is credited with developing turntable scratching. KRS-One (1965–) began recording in 1986 as part of the South Bronx–based trio Boogie Down Productions (1985–1992). Other important early hip hop acts to come out of the Bronx included Afrika Bambaataa (1957–) and Puerto Rican American rapper Big Pun (Christopher Lee Rios, 1971–2000). London-born Slick Rick (1965–) moved to New York, where he teamed up with Doug E. Fresh's Get Fresh Crew (1985–2003). Among more recent hip hop acts one of the most influential is the Welfare Poets (1997–), which introduced the fusion of Afro-Caribbean *bomba y plena* and *rumba*, reggae, blues, bebop, cool and Latin jazz, and 1970s soul. The most famous DJ to come out of the Bronx was Mr. Len (1975–), best known for his role in Brooklyn-based Company Flow (1993–2001). Among breakdancers, the biggest name was Frosty Freeze.

Brooklyn, Queens, and Long Island

One of the boroughs which saw early rap action, Brooklyn was the home of arguably one of the most skilled MCs in hip hop, Big Daddy Kane (1968–), who started as a member of the rap collective the Juice Crew All Stars (1983–1991). Brooklyn also produced Busta Rhymes (1972–) and Jay-Z (1969–). Busta Rhymes was an 11-time Grammy nominee and went on to found the record label Conglomerate/Flipmode Entertainment (1994–), and Jay-Z cofounded the independent label Roc–A–Fella Records (1996–2013). Smif-N-Wessun (1993–) introduced a unique use of smooth jazz rhythm and Jamaican Patois. Nas (1973–) produced seven certified-Platinum albums with an impressive charting record—all have peaked in either the No. 1 or No. 2 position on Billboard's Top R&B/Hip-Hop Albums chart. Shaggy (1968–), who moved to Brooklyn from Kingston, Jamaica, fused reggae with alternative rock, pop, R&B, dancehall, dubstep, and hip hop. Brooklyn also introduced an early successful female rapper, Lil' Kim (1975–), known for her hypersexual performances; she was the only female member of Junior M.A.F.I.A. (1992–1997), which was mentored and promoted by the Notorious B.I.G. (1972–1997). Fab Five Freddy (1959–), a graffiti artist, rapper, and filmmaker, also emerged from the Brooklyn scene.

Long Island may have been the home of diss rap, as Roxanne Shanté (1969–) launched the Roxanne Wars. The Bomb Squad (1986–) became the premiere American hip hop production group, best known for their work with Public Enemy (1982–). Public Enemy's *It Takes a Nation of Millions to Hold Us Back* (1988) and *Fear of a Black Planet* (1990) became rap classics, and cofounders Chuck D (1960–) and Flavor Flav (1959–) joined Def Jam. Long Island's De La Soul (1987–) debuted with *3 Feet High and Rising* (1989), generally regarded one of the greatest hip hop albums of the 1980s. Queens-based A Tribe Called Quest (1985–1993, 2006–2013, 2015–), the most commercially successful member of the Native Tongues Posse, achieved critical acclaim, especially for its 1991 album *The Low End Theory*. Other early Queens hip hop acts included Run-D.M.C. (1981–2002), MC Lyte (1971–), and Salt-N-Pepa (1985–2002, 2007–). Run-D.M.C. achieved rap firsts: the first multi-Platinum record and the first Grammy nomination. MC Lyte was one of the first women rappers to challenge sexism and misogyny. Salt-N-Pepa became one of the first all-female hip hop groups to achieve both commercial and critical success, with a debut album that went Platinum. Recent Queens rappers include 50 Cent (1975–) and Nicki Minaj (1982–), two of the United States' most desired rap acts. 50 Cent became a certified-Platinum musician, and Nicki Minaj, originally from St. James, Trinidad and Tobago, became hip hop's most successful and critically acclaimed female act after she signed with Young Money Entertainment (2005–).

Manhattan (Harlem)

Harlem produced a few highly influential acts. The Last Poets (1968–) became one of hip hop music's earliest influences, introducing rapping, the MC, and beatboxing. Spoonie Gee (1963–) was known for his association with the Treacherous Three, which featured Grammy Award winner Kool Moe Dee (1963–). Kurtis Blow (1959–) was instrumental in mainstreaming hip hop. In 1980, he had the first certified-Gold rap single, "The Breaks," and he became the first rapper to appear on *Soul Train*. Kool Moe Dee started out his solo career in 1987 using an old-school style, but then made the successful transition in 1989 to a more raw delivery, with extended lines and uneven rhythms. At the turn of the decade, two rap icons, Puff Daddy (1969–) and Tupac Shakur emerged, the former becoming a leading producer, performer, entrepreneur, and celebrity, and founder of Bad Boy Records (1993–), and the latter tying social consciousness with the gangsta ethos and becoming the most notable victim of the East and West Coast hip hop wars. Harlem was also the home of an influential rap style, new jack swing, which fused hip hop elements with R&B, sometimes including funk and gospel. The most famous Harlem breakdancer was Popmaster Fabel (1965*–), who became a member of the Rock Steady Crew and introduced West Coast dance styles to the New York scene.

New Jersey

Even though New Jersey native Ice-T moved to Los Angeles and helped establish gangsta rap, New Jersey's rap scene emerged early. South Orange native Lauryn Hill (1975–) eventually earned five Grammy awards for her solo album, *The Miseducation of Lauryn Hill* (1998), a collection of songs that bridge the gap between hip hop, soul, and R&B. She became famous for her collaboration with the South Orange–based Fugees (1992–1997), which included Haitian-born Wyclef Jean (1969–). Queen Latifah (1970–), from Newark, is known as the First Lady of Hip Hop because of her varied career, from being an Afrocentric and feminist rapper to a sitcom actor, film actor, talk show host, and jazz vocalist. In 1995, she cofounded her own label and management company, Flavor Unit Entertainment. Though less commercially successful, Poor Righteous Teachers (1989–1996), from Trenton, was a trio that known for Five Percenter rap. New Jersey is also known as the home of Brick City club, a house music popular from 1995–2000 that consisted of breakbeat music strung together, along with repetitive sound bites to create high-energy dance rhythms.

THE SOUTH

New Orleans

New Orleans' contributions to rap are due largely in part to two record labels, No Limit Records (1990–2003), later revived as No Limit Forever Records (2010–) and Ca$h Money Records (1991–). No Limit was founded in Richmond, California by Master P (1970–), a New Orleans native who, along with his brothers, C-Murder (1971–) and Silkk the Shocker (Vyshonne King Miller, 1975–), created various rap crews and solo acts. In addition, Master P launched the career of his son, Lil Romeo (Percy Romeo Miller, 1989–). Master P went on to found P. Miller Enterprises and Better Black Television (2008–). As a rapper, he has released solo albums, as well as albums with the groups TRU (1995–2002) and 504 Boyz (2000–2005), the latter including Mystikal (Michael Lawrence Tyler, 1970–). In 1995, he moved No Limits to New Orleans and had breakthroughs with the albums *True* (1995), *Ice Cream Man* (1995), and *Ghetto D* (1997). C–Murder is currently incarcerated but has released various albums and has founded the label Bossalinie Records (2000–). Ca$h Money Records was cofounded by Birdman (1969–) and produced Juvenile (Terius Gray, 1975–), Lil Wayne (1982–), Drake (1986–), and Nicki Minaj (Onika Tanya Maraj, 1982–). Lil Wayne went on to found his own imprint, Young Money Entertainment (2005–) and became one of the best–selling artists in any genre. New Orleans is also home to Big Boy Records (1992–2000) and the home of a music style called bounce, which recreates rap as dance party and regional music.

Houston and Miami

Houston's main contribution to rap is the popularization of hardcore rap and horrorcore. About the same time that Detroit–based Esham's (Rashaam Smith, 1973–) debut album *Boomin' Words from Hell 1990* (1989) introduced horrorcore lyrics, Houston–based Ganksta N–I–P's (Lewayne Williams, 1969–) debut album *The South Park Psycho* (1990) was preparing rap fans for Geto Boys (1987–2005), who proved to be influential on both horrorcore and Dirty South. Original members Bushwick Bill (Richard Stephen Shaw, 1966–), Scarface (Brad Terrence Jordan, 1970–), and Willie D (William James Dennis, 1966–) went on to a successful solo careers, and the single "Mind Playing Tricks on Me" (1991) became a genre classic. Miami's contribution to rap music was a style called Miami bass, best represented by the band 2 Live Crew (1982–1998) and its rapper/promoter Luke (1960–), who created a heavy bass, synthesized melodic and drum sound. Cuban American Pitbull (1981–) has released 10 albums since 2004 and has worked with Lil Jon (Jonathan Smith, 1971–).

Atlanta

Atlanta is best known for the subgenres crunkcore and trap, the former a hybrid subgenre of electronica/dance–pop, screamo, and crunk, and the latter being an extreme version of urban rap, concerned with gritty portrayals of urban street life. Atlanta's other contribution, the 1990s Dirty South fad, was a rap style associated with regional slang and speech patterns, danceable beats, and pronounced bass. Snap and trap are two other music styles that came out of Atlanta. Snap is an early to mid-2000s hip hop style derived from crunk. Popular snap artists included D4L (2003–2006). Trap, related to crunk, mobb, and hardcore, took as its topic urban life, including violence, drug deals, and the income gap. It spread from Atlanta to urban areas such as Houston and Memphis, Tennessee. Its signature sound is the product of two Atlanta producers, Shawty Redd (Demetrius Lee Stewart, 1981–) and Lex Luger (Lexus Arnel Lewis, 1991–).

Atlanta is also the home of one of hip hop's best agents, Wendy Day (1962–). Champaign, Illinois' Ludacris (1977–) moved to Atlanta as a teen and worked with Timbaland, guest rapping on the 1998 album *Tim's Bio: From the Motion Picture Life from da Bassment*. He later cofounded Disturbing Tha Peace Records (2000–). His second album for Def Jam, *Word of Mouf* (2001), is a benchmark Dirty South album. Atlanta is the home of three influential hip hop artists, Bronx-born Swizz Beatz (1978–), hip hop trio TLC (1991–2002, 2014–), and Dirty South duo OutKast (1991–2006, 2014–). Swizz Beatz has worked with rap mainstays such as Busta Rhymes, Eve (Eve Jihan Jeffers, 1978–), and Jay-Z. As a boy, he moved to Atlanta to live with two of his uncles who established Ruff Ryders Entertainment (1988–2010), and in 2001, he created Full Surface Records. TLC included rapper Left-Eye Lopes (1971–2002) and produced four Hot 100 No. 1 songs. RIAA-certified-Diamond OutKast (1991–2006, 2014–) fuses hip hop with funk, psychedelic music, drum and bass, electronica, techno/industrial hip hop, R&B, and gospel. It included star rappers André 3000 (André Lauren Benjamin, 1975–) and Big Boi (Antwan André Patton, 1975–).

THE MIDWEST

Although it has produced notable hip hop music and rappers, the Midwest has produced few influential rap movements or record labels. While Chicago is home to jazz and funk composer Herbie Hancock (1940–), spoken-word artist Gil Scott-Heron (1949–2011), female rapper Da Brat (1974–), and more recent popular rappers such as Chance the Rapper (1993–) and Common (1972–), it has lagged behind other urban areas in its rap scene. Hancock's most famous connection to hip hop is his hit song "Rockit" (1983), which featured early turntablism (scratching). Scott-Heron, an influential jazz-poet, is in many respects a rapper prototype, best known for his 1971 single "The Revolution Will Not Be Televised." Da Brat (1974–) became the first solo female rap artist to have a certified-Platinum album and single. Common became known for his verbose and socially conscious lyricism, and Chance the Rapper broke music industry barriers with his multimillion selling self-released mixtape *Coloring Book* (2016).

Other Midwest cities that contributed to hip hop were Indianapolis, St. Louis, Detroit, Cleveland, and Kansas City. Indianapolis-based Babyface (1959–) is an 11-time Grammy winner, known for working with L.A. Reid (Antonio Marquis Reid, 1955–), ultimately cofounding Edmonds Entertainment (aka Babyface Entertainment, 1997–). Senegalese American Akon (1973–) is a St. Louis musician whose 2006 album, *Konvicted*, was certified triple Platinum. Detroit's claim to fame is that it is the adopted home of Eminem (1972–) and his rap crew D12 (1996–). St. Louis native Eminem began with D12, but went on to become one of the world's top-selling solo rappers, with six No. 1 solo studio albums on the Billboard 200. He is also the founder of New York City–based Shady Records (1999–). Detroit can also claim producer J Dilla (1974–2006), known for working with benchmark artists such as A Tribe Called Quest, De La Soul, Busta Rhymes, Common, Erykah Badu (1971–), the Roots (1987–), and the Pharcyde (1989–).

Arguably, however, the biggest contribution to rap from the Midwest was the chopper (rapid) style of delivery. It began in the 1980s in urban areas such as Cleveland, Chicago, and Kansas City. By the early 1990s it had spread to California with the Project Blowed (1994–) movement, led by Aceyalone and his Freestyle Fellowship (1991–2011). Early practitioners included Flint, Michigan's the Dayton Family (1993–) and Chicago's Twista (Carl Terrell Mitchell, 1973–), although Cleveland's Bone Thugs–n–Harmony (1991–) was by far the best–known of the early practitioners of chopper. The style became even more popular when Kansas City underground rapper/songwriter Tech N9ne (1971–), released a number of chopper–heavy collaborative singles.

THE NORTHEAST: PHILADELPHIA AND BOSTON

Some of the earliest rap successes came out of Philadelphia. DJ Jazzy Jeff (1965–), a world DJ champion, cofounded the rap duo DJ Jazzy Jeff & the Fresh Prince. The duo won two Grammy Awards, with the album *He's the DJ, I'm the Rapper* (1988) going triple Platinum. Smith went on to have one of the most successful film careers in modern history. Philadelphia is also the home of the Roots and Jill

Scott (1972–). The Roots have released 11 studio albums and a handful of collaborative albums with musicians such as John Legend (John Roger Stephens, 1978–) and Elvis Costello (Declan Patrick MacManus, 1954–), and has been the house band for Jimmy Fallon's (1974–) *Late Night with Jimmy Fallon* (2009–2014) and *The Tonight Show Starring Jimmy Fallon* (2014–) since 2009. Prolific singer-songwriter Scott became a benchmark alternative hip hop artist, fusing her beats with neo soul, R&B, jazz, and spoken word. North Dakota native but Pittsburgh-based Wiz Khalifa (1987–) has had two albums certified Platinum. Boston has been late to the rap scene, although the city can partly claim Philadelphia's Bahamadia (1976–), who began her career by working with Boston-then-Brooklyn-based Gang Starr (1986–2006). A recent rap phenomenon is Worcester-based (50 miles from Boston) Joyner Lucas (Gary Lucas, 1988–), whose 2017 mixtape *508-507-2209* has spawned two dialogue-based singles, "I'm Sorry" and "I'm Not Racist," which have garnered nearly 120 million YouTube views by mid 2018.

NATIVE AMERICAN AND FIRST NATIONS

Since its earliest years, hip hop artists who identify with being of Native American descent or of First Nations heritage have been involved in hip hop. For example, Melle Mel (aka Grandmaster Melle Mel, Melvin Glover, 1961–) is an African American rapper of Cherokee descent, who may have been the first Native American rapper. Other artists include Wu-Tang Clan's (1991–) founding member Ol' Dirty Bastard (ODB, Russell Tyrone Jones, 1968–2004), who was of Shinnecock (Algonquian) descent. Another example is the Black Eyed Peas's (1995–) Taboo (Jaime Luis Gomez, 1975–), a rapper, singer-songwriter, and actor who is part Shoshone. All of these artists nevertheless lived in urban settings and their contributions do not focus on Natives or related themes.

After urban Native American and First Nations American populations, hip hop reached Native Americans in more rural areas, including most reservations during the early 1980s. John Trudell's (1946–2015) spoken-word poetry and Russell Means's (aka Wanbli Ohitika, Brave Eagle in Lakota, 1939–2012) *rap-ajo* music (rap-ajo is a term Means coined) served as precursors to what became known as Native American hip hop. Trudell was of Mexican and Santee Dakota descent and grew up on the Santee Sioux Reservation in Nebraska. After military service, he moved to San Bernardino, California and began his political activism after relocating to Berkeley, California. In 1969, he became the spokesperson for the United Indians of All Tribes' (1970–) occupation of Alcatraz Island in the San Francisco Bay, an island that is best known as the location of a federal prison from 1934 to 1969. He began broadcasting on a show called *Radio Free Alcatraz* until 1971. Trudell then joined the American Indian Movement (AIM, 1968–), based in Minneapolis. As a multi-instrumentalist and songwriter, Trudell recorded and performed with Jesse Edwin Davis (1944–1988), a guitarist of Kiowa descent, who formed their backing ensemble, the Graffiti Band (1985–1988*). This band accompanied Trudell's songs and spoken-word poetry, which focused on Native American conditions, history, advocacy, anger, and other problems brought on by white man (including addiction, poor health, and poverty). It recorded the mixtape

A.K.A. Grafitti Man on cassette in the 1980s, which was reissued in 1992. Trudell's exemplary recording was *Johnny Damas & Me* (1994).

Means, an Oglala Lakota and libertarian activist, writer, musician, and actor, was also a member of AIM and participated in the Alcatraz occupation. Among other AIM protests, he participated in seizing the Mayflower II, a replica of the original Mayflower, in 1970, in Boston, the Bureau of Indian Affairs (BIA) in Washington, DC, and Wounded Knee in South Dakota. His recordings include the albums *Electric Warrior* (1993) and *The Radical (Album)* (2007). His autobiography, *Where White Men Fear to Tread*, cowritten with Marvin J. Wolf, includes recollections of his father's alcoholism, other family struggles, and his own issues with crime, drugs, and truancy, before finding his political activist calling. General subject matter of his rap-ajo music was similar to Trudell's; however, Means focused much more specifically on his people.

Early Native American hip hop had its roots in 1970s reservation rock (aka rez rock) and punk, which included some rap. Some of these groups include Without Reservation (1970–1980)* and XIT (Crossing of Indian Tribes, 1971*–). Like earlier rez rock, most Native American hip hop prefers American vernacular. Native American languages are generally lightly explored. An early Native American hip hop act was RedCloud (Henry Andrade, 1978–), who ushered in the representation of Native Americans and Hispanic Americans into Christian hip hop in the early 1990s with his combination of gospel and West Coast hip hop. RedCloud took his name after the Lakota Chief who forced out the U.S. Army from the Powder River Basin. He is of Huichol and Mexican descent and was involved in Chicano gang activity and freestyle gangsta rapping in Los Angeles before converting to Christianity. Early Native American hip hop focused on message rap and employed previously composed hip hop beats and samples, but it soon incorporated both real and stereotypical Native American traditional music and instruments. As for the stereotypical, the pan–Native American notion of the powwow and its use of frame drums, chants, and singing vocables pulse through some Native American hip hop. This is sometimes employed in choruses or used for irony.

In 1989, XIT's new leader Tom Bee (n.d.) established Sound of America Records (SOAR, 1989–), the first Native American owned recording label. SOAR records Native American folk, country, rock, new age, electronica, traditional, and hip hop music. Its catalog includes the project group Robby Bee and the Boyz from the Rez's *Reservation of Education* (1993), Julian B's (Julian B. Watson, n.d.) *Once Upon a Genocide* (1994) and *Urban Skins* volumes (1999*–), which fuse Native American hip hop with other kinds of music such as reggae and electronica. In live performances, Julian B has rapped in Muskogee. A contemporary of these acts is the West Coast hip hop crew Funkdoobiest (1989–).

Websites and Internet streaming devoted to Native American and First Nations hip hop have helped spread information about the music. In 1999, the first independent website with a database, REDHIPHOP.COM began. In 2000, NativeHipHop .net superceded it. As a network, it invites new music submissions.

Just a few other Native American hip hop acts include female singer and rapper Solé (Tonya M. Johnston, 1973–), of Choctaw descent; rapper, recording executive, and actor Litefoot (Gary Paul Davis, 1969–), of Cherokee and Chichimeca

(Mexican indigenous) descent; and later Ojibwe rapper Tall Paul (Paul Wenell Jr., 1988*–); Apsáalooke rapper and powwow dancer Supaman (aka Billy Ills, Christian Parrish Takes the Gun, n.d.) and his short-lived group Rezawrecktion (2003–2005); Sicangu Lakota rapper Frank Waln (aka Oyate Teca Obmani, Walks with Young People, 1989–); and LightningCloud (2010*–). The last is a duo of RedCloud and Canadian American rapper, singer-songwriter, electro house DJ, and actress Crystal Lightning (1981–), of Enoch Cree descent. Supaman is notable for his pow-wow dances, using brightly colored headdresses, as well as for his skills as a rapper. As with previous Native American artists, Supaman is also an activist. With Taboo he recorded "Stand Up/Stand N Rock #NoDAPL" (2017) and participated in the Dakota Access Pipeline protests (aka Standing Rock, #NoDAPL, 2016–2017).

Another Native American hip hop artist is hardcore rapper Anybody Killa (aka ABK, Jaymo, Native Funk, Hatchet Warrior, Sawed Off, James Lowery, 1973–), of Lumbee descent and from Detroit. ABK fuses hip hop with funk and electronica. He began rapping in 1995 as Jaymo with his short-lived first duo, Krazy Klan. By 2000, he was pursuing a solo career as Native Funk and released his debut album *Rain from the Sun*. This was followed by *Hatchet Warrior* (2003), which peaked at No. 4 on Billboard's Top Independent Albums chart, No. 42 on Billboard's Top R&B/Hip-Hop Albums chart, and No. 98 on the Billboard 200. Other successful albums followed, all employing Native American hip hop, though he uses hardcore styles such as gangsta rap and horrorcore, ABK thoroughly weaves storytelling based on his Native American experience and his growing up and learning about Lumbee and Cherokee folklore into his lyrics. His rapping delivery stands out because of his lisp. His other albums are *Dirty History* (2004), *Mudface* (2008), and *Medicine Bag* (2010). A new album, *Shape Shifter*, is scheduled for 2018.

Anthony J. Fonseca and Melissa Ursula Dawn Goldsmith

See also: Breakdancing; Chicano Rap; Dirty South; Filmmaking (Feature Films Made in the United States); Gangs (United States); G-Funk; Hip Hop Dance

Further Reading

Cramer, Jennifer, and Jill Hallett. 2010. "From Chi-Town to the Dirty-Dirty: Regional Identity Markers in U.S. Hip Hop." In *The Languages of Global Hip Hop*, edited by Marina Terkourafi, chap. 10. New York: Continuum.

French, Kenneth. 2017. "Geography of American Rap: Rap Diffusion and Rap Centers." *GeoJournal* 82, no. 2: 259–72.

Gosa, Travis L., and Erik Nielson, eds. 2015. *Hip Hop and Obama Reader*. Oxford, England: Oxford University Press.

Mays, Kyle T. 2016. "Promoting Sovereignty, Rapping *Mshkiki* (Medicine): A Critical (Anishinaabeg) Reading of Rapper Tall Paul's 'Prayers in a Song.'" *Social Identities: Journal for the Study of Race, Nation, and Culture* 22, no. 2: 195–209.

Further Listening

ABK. 2003. *Hatchet Warrior*. Psychopathic Records.

Aceyalone. 1998. *A Book of Human Language*. Project Blowed.

ATCQ. 1990. *People's Instinctive Travels and the Paths of Rhythm*. Jive.

Beastie Boys. 1986. *Licensed to Ill*. Def Jam Recordings/Columbia Records.

Beastie Boys. 1989. *Paul's Boutique*. Capitol Records/Beastie Boys.

Blige, Mary J. 1994. *My Life.* Uptown Records/MCA Records.

Chance the Rapper. 2016. *Coloring Book.* Self-released.

Compton's Most Wanted. 2001. *When We Wuz Bangin' 1989–99: The Hitz.* The Right Stuff.

Elliott, Missy. 2001. *Miss E . . . So Addictive.* Elektra.

Eminem. 1999. *The Slim Shady LP.* Aftermath Entertainment/Interscope Records.

Fugees. 1996. *The Score.* Columbia/Ruffhouse Records.

Invisibl Skratch Piklz. 2015. *The 13th Floor.* Self-released.

Jay-Z. 2017. *4:44.* Roc Nation.

Kendrick Lamar. 2017. *DAMN.* Top Dawg Entertainment/Aftermath Entertainment/Interscope Records.

Lil Wayne. 2011. *Tha Carter IV.* Ca$h Money Records.

Nas. 1994. *Illmatic.* Columbia.

Nicky Minaj. 2012. *Pink Friday/Roman Reloaded.* Ca$h Money Records.

The Notorious B.I.G. 1994. *Ready to Die.* Bad Boy Entertainment.

The Notorious B.I.G. 2007. *Greatest Hits.* Bad Boy Entertainment.

N.W.A. 1988. *Straight Outta Compton.* Ruthless Records/Priority Records.

OutKast. 1994. *Southernplayalisticadillacmuzik.* LaFace.

OutKast. 2000. *Stankonia.* LaFace.

Public Enemy. 1990. *Fear of a Black Planet.* Def Jam Recordings.

Public Enemy. 1988. *It Takes a Nation of Millions to Hold Us Back.* Def Jam.

Queen Latifah. 1989. *All Hail the Queen.* Tommy Boy.

Run-D.M.C. 1985. *King of Rock.* Profile Records.

Tupac Shakur (as 2Pac). 1996. *All Eyez on Me.* Death Row Records.

2 Live Crew. 1989. *As Nasty As They Wanna Be.* Luke Skyywalker Records.

West, Kanye. 2013. *Yeezus.* Def Jam Recordings.

Wu-Tang Clan. 1993. *Enter the Wu-Tang (36 Chambers).* Loud Records/RCA.

The Universal Zulu Nation

(formerly Zulu Nation, 1973–, Bronx, New York)

The Universal Zulu Nation was founded in the South Bronx, New York by then-high-schooler Afrika Bambaataa (1957–), a gang (The Black Spades, 1968–) warlord who had just returned from a trip to Africa. He founded it in response to gang violence, the Vietnam War (1955–1975), and the Kent State shootings (1970), in addition to consciousness-raising events such as Woodstock (1969), the black unity movement, and flower power. Afrika Bambaataa and many of the early members came out of local gangs, organizing with the goal of creating a less violent means of community. While its development came at a time when street gangs were arguably already losing hold on the youth of New York, its formation is often credited with curtailing much of the gang activity in the South Bronx of the 1970s through the creation of diversions in the form of hip hop activities and the infusion of a positive message targeted at youth. Since its inception, the Universal Zulu Nation has grown into an international organization aimed at promoting all aspects of hip hop culture and improving communities through hip hop.

FORMATION AND ROLE IN HIP HOP AND COMMUNITY

Originally called the Bronx River Organization, then the Organization, the group eventually adopted the name Zulu Nation, a name derived from the English film *Zulu* (1964) produced by Paramount Pictures that inspired Bambaataa with its images of black people who were fighting for their rights against invading colonizers. The group attracted b-boys, DJs, MCs, and graffiti artists, and early Zulu activities included hosting parties at the Bronx River Neighborhood Community Center. Originally informed by fear of gang culture, the parties largely became gang-free zones where attendees were encouraged to respect one another.

The Zulu Nation became known for raising awareness of black issues in the community and raising the self-esteem of the young members with a focus on education and empowerment. As the group expanded internationally, the word "Universal" was added to its name. It promotes the four main elements of hip hop—DJing, MCing, b-boying, and graffiti writing—but, importantly, also insists on a fifth element, knowledge. This element contributes to the Zulu Nation's support of education and growth in its young members.

In 2016, allegations of child molestation (assaulting underaged boys) against Afrika Bambaataa and a cover up by the Universal Zulu Nation led to turmoil and restructuring, with him and other leaders removed from power. Those leaders expressed hesitation about acting on the allegations, arguing that they had not been thoroughly investigated. In response, the group has since pledged to increase support for victims of molestation and other abuse. As of 2018, its website does not list a new group of leaders.

Susannah Cleveland

See also: Afrika Bambaataa; Gangs (United States); The United States

Further Reading

Fricke, Jim, and Charlie Ahearn. 2002. *The Experience Music Project Oral History of Hip Hop's First Decade: Yes Yes Y'All.* Cambridge, MA: Da Capo Press.

Forman, Murray, and Mark Anthony Neal, eds. 2012. *That's the Joint: The Hip Hop Studies Reader.* 2nd ed. New York: Routledge.

Upper Hutt Posse

(UHP, 1985–, Wellington, New Zealand/Aotearoa)

Upper Hutt Posse (UHP) was originally a reggae band named after the Wellington, New Zealand suburb where the band formed. It became the first band in New Zealand to fuse reggae and rap in both Māori and English. In 1985, the Hapeta brothers—singer, rapper, lyricist, guitarist, and keyboardist Te Kupu (aka D Word, Dean Hapeta, 1966–) and bassist, singer, and rapper MC Wiya (Matthew Hapeta, n.d.)—formed the band. Inspired by the plight of the Māori, particularly the challenges they faced with discrimination and with the preservation of their culture and language, UHP fused the sociopolitical messages of reggae and rap within a New Zealand cultural context.

EARLY INSPIRATION AND STUDIO RECORDINGS

UHP has several major influences: legendary Jamaican reggae singer, songwriter, and guitarist Bob Marley (Robert Nesta Marley, 1945–1981); American jazz poet and jazz, soul, and funk musician Gil Scott-Heron (1949–2011); and the American hip hop group Public Enemy (1981–). Te Kupu's rapping style is inspired by the *haka*, a traditional Māori war chant and posture dance used to overawe any opposition. In 1988, singer Teremoana Rapley (1973–), also from Upper Hutt, joined the group before becoming part of the hip hop trio Moana and the Moahunters (1991–1998) in 1993. UHP and Moana and the Moahunters have collaborated on many recordings and at concerts worldwide.

In 1988, UHP released the first rap record in New Zealand, the 12-inch hip hop single "E tū" (aka "Stand Proud"). The song has a sociopolitical message that borrows from Jamaican reggae musicians and black American musicians and writers; it also pays homage to Māori warrior chiefs during Aotearoa's colonial period. "E tū" appeared on their first studio album *Against the Flow* (1989) and peaked at No. 44 on the New Zealand pop chart.

The band continued to tour and perform in Wellington, including supporting Public Enemy's 1990 concert there, but it took six years before their second album release, *Movement in Demand* (1995). In the meantime, Te Kupu codirected *Solidarity* (1992), a documentary on UHP's visit to the United States. That same year, UHP released the non-album single "Ragga Girl," which was released with the film drama *Once Were Warriors* (1994) and peaked at No. 48 on the New Zealand pop chart.

UHP IN THE 21ST CENTURY

Well into the 21st century, UHP continued its sociopolitical messages about the plight of the Māori in New Zealand, concerned with issues such as poverty and unemployment, as well as threats of losing language and culture. The 2000 album *Mā Te Wā* was a digital reggae release completely in the Māori language. It was followed by the *Te reo Māori Remixes* (*The Language Māori Remixes*, 2002), which featured UHP's previous hits—some tracks redone as dubstep and drum and bass—also completely in the Māori language. In 2003, *Te reo Māori Remixes* won for Best Mana Māori Album at the New Zealand Music Awards.

As new members have come, gone, and returned, UHP remains a band with five to seven core members still led by Te Kupu. Their subsequent studio albums include *Legacy* (2005), the electronica-influenced *Tohe* (*Endurance* or *Insist*, 2010), and the live album *Declaration of Resistance* (2011). In 2016, UHP was awarded the Taite Music Prize.

Melissa Ursula Dawn Goldsmith

See also: New Zealand; Political Hip Hop; Reggae

Further Reading

Allen, Chadwick. 2007. "Rere Ke/Moving Differently: Indigenizing Methodologies for Comparative Indigenous Literary Studies." *Studies in American Indian Literatures* 19, no. 4: 1–26, 217.

Hapeta, Dean. 2000. "Hip Hop in Aotearoa/New Zealand." In *Changing Sounds: New Directions and Configurations in Popular Music*, edited by Tony Mitchell and Peter Doyle, pp. 202–07. Sydney, Australia: University of Technology, Faculty of Humanities and Social Sciences.

Johnson, Henry. 2010. *Many Voices: Music and National Identity in Aotearoa/New Zealand.* New Castle upon Tyne, England: Cambridge Scholars.

Shute, Gareth. 2004. *Hip Hop Music in Aotearoa.* Auckland, New Zealand: Reed.

Further Listening
Upper Hutt Posse. 1989. *Against the Flow.* Southside Records.

Uprock

Uprock, a derivative of rocking, is a type of music and dance that has deep-seeded roots in soul, rock, and funk. Its primary art is steeped in competitive hip hop dance, called battling, which began in the boroughs of New York City in the 1970s. The gist of uprock is to serve as a preparatory dance move, which can then lead into a breakdown, or break; it utilizes what are called "burn moves," aimed at the other performer. Either two dancers or two dance teams face off inside of a circle, where they perform various dance moves which can grow in intensity and skill, after which an audience declares a winner via cheering. Uprock is the rhythmic set up for each member or team to perform the dance. It involves a series of back and forth motions, using steps which place one foot forward on a down beat and then pull back behind the dancer on the subsequent down beat, alternating between each foot. The arms also play an important role in that they are crossed in front of the body during the upright and back position, and then spread out and down when the foot takes its forward downbeat step. The opening up of the arms and forward step of the foot is used to challenge, or "front" the other team or dancer, with the invitation to outperform. This repetitive motion also allows a dancer or team to prepare a more intricate series of steps, which is then performed. Dances then end in a pop or a pose, usually held for a moment, before the dancer returns to the uprock dance move and retreats so that the opposing dancer or team can use its uprock dance move to lead into its competitive dance, in what is called "taking the floor."

Most of the time the uprock dance is performed to an iconic hip hop beat, with a 4/4 (quadruple) meter; in fact, the uprock dance is specifically designed for this beat. Samples from the music of James Brown (1933–2006), Beastie Boys (1981–2012), Jimmy Castor (James Walter Castor, 1940–2012), and other 1960s and 1970s R&B and funk artists serve as underscoring for this classic dance. Dancers utilize hard downbeats and soft upbeats, with loose solo riffs of guitar, saxophone, or lyrics. Much of the singing contains staccato sounds effects and engineered hiccups, which inherently serve as jerks and burns for the dancer. Brown's *Sex Machine* (1970) is one of the most used samples for uprocking, as the dancer can pop arms or kicks to accentuate the verbalizations (the repeated "ha" and "uh" heard throughout the song). In addition, early video of uprocking and rocking show the influence of swing dancing, soft shoe, and tap. All of these influences make uprocking one of the fan favorites in competitive hip hop dancing, where the ultimate goal is to "rock" the opposing dancer or team into an accentuated back and forth motion.

Matthew Schlief

See also: Battling; Breakdancing; Hip Hop Dance

Further Reading

Dodds, Sherril. 2016. "Hip Hop Battles and Facial Intertexts." *Dance Research* 34, no. 1: 63–83.

Sato, Nahoko, Hiroyuki Nunome, and Yasuo Ikegami. 2016. "Key Motion Characteristics of Side-Step Movements in Hip Hop Dance and Their Effect on the Evaluation by Judges." *Sports Biomechanics* 15, no. 2: 116–27.

Urban Species

(1992–2000, 2008–, London, England)

Urban Species is an English band that fuses hip hop with funk, reggae, dancehall, dubstep, ragga, acid jazz, R&B, soul, blues, and folk music. It is best known for its hits from 1993 to 1999 that peaked between Nos. 35 and 56 on the U.K. Singles Chart (now the Official Singles Chart), "Spiritual Love," "Brother," "Listen," and "Blanket." All but the last appeared on their debut studio album, *Listen* (1994), which peaked at No. 43 on the U.K. Albums Chart. Urban Species' second and last studio album was *Blanket* (1998). Urban Species' sound resembles the eclectic alternative groups such as Soul II Soul (1987–1997, 2007–) from England and Arrested Development (1988–1996, 2000–) from the United States. Though its sound was always a combination of hip hop, live rapping, reggae, and other kinds of music, *Blanket* marked a shift to more collaborative songwriting and a greater incorporation of trip hop, acid jazz, soul, funk, and electronic music. Lyrics were concerned with social injustice, romance, and music as escape.

FORMATION, PERSONNEL, COLLABORATIONS

Urban Species was originally an unnamed duo founded in 1988 in Tottenham, North London. It consisted of rapper Mintos (aka MC Mint, Peter Akinrinlola, n.d.) and DJ Renegade (Winston Small, n.d.), school friends who enjoyed listening to rap, electro, reggae, dancehall, blues, and rave music. Renegade's first sampling materials came from his older brother's funk and jazz record collection, and demos were home-produced.

In 1989, Urban Species released its first white label promo, "It's My Thing." The single developed a strong cult following with both underground and mainstream airplay in the United Kingdom and New York City. The duo's repeated success with "Got to Have It" led to a recording contract in 1991 on the Talkin' Loud label (1990–) in London. In 1992, the duo officially became Urban Species. By this time, the band added another school friend, rapper Dr. Slim (aka Doc Slim, Rodney Green, n.d.). The three wanted to perform live, adding local musician friends to play with DAT-recorded samples and beats.

Releasing its studio albums *Listen* and *Blanket*, in addition to its EP *Religion and Politics* (1997), on the Talkin' Loud label, led to Urban Species' collaborating with artists such as French Senegalese–Chadian hip hop and jazz rapper MC Solaar (1969–), English singer-songwriter, multi-instrumentalist, and music engineer Imogen Heap (1977–), the English hip hop and electronic dance group Stereo MCs (1985–), and English rapper and vocalist Blak Twang (aka Taipanic, Tony Rotten, Tony Olabode, n.d.). Touring worldwide, engaging in hip hop education (particularly in Africa), and recording took their toll on the group, and by 1995, DJ Renegade had departed. By the recording of *Blanket*, Dr. Slim had also been replaced, by Tukka Yoot (n.d.).

Between 2000 and 2008, Urban Species went on hiatus; however, its members reunited in 2008 and returned to touring and recording, working with producer Raw Deal (Jim Robins, n.d.). As of 2018, Urban Species is working on a third album.

Melissa Ursula Dawn Goldsmith

See also: Dubstep; Reggae; The United Kingdom

Further Reading

Bradley, Lloyd. 2013. "'If You're Not Dancing, F— Off.'" In *Sounds Like London*, chap. 8. London: Profile Books.

Wood, Andy. 2002. "Hip Hop." In *Companion to Contemporary Black British Culture*, edited by Alison Donnell, pp. 141–42. London: Routledge.

Further Listening

Urban Species. 1994. *Listen*. Talkin' Loud.

Urban Species. 1998. *Blanket*. Talkin' Loud.

V

Venezuela

Venezuela's hip hop scene, which began in the mid-1990s, is tied to the country's polarized politics since Hugo Chavez (1954–2013), a well known hip hop fan, took office in 1999, and is controlled by government censorship of radio. For some, the rap lifestyle has become dangerous because of the music's criticisms of the government. Rappers often depict urban violence in their lyrics, and hint at military crackdowns on free speech, both of which the government does not officially acknowledge.

Several Venezuelan hip hop artists have been the victims of violence. Rapper Onechot (Juan David Chacón, 1977*–) released the music video for "Rotten Town" in 2010, a song that depicted Venezuela's capital city Caracas as "embassy of hell." In 2012, Onechot was shot twice in the head (he survived). Rather than investigating his shooting, authorities investigated his depiction of Caracas. Arguably the best known of all Venezuelan rappers, Maracay, Venezuela–based Canserbero (aka El Can, Tyrone José González Orama, 1988–2015), whose album *Muerte* (*Dead*, 2012) is considered a classic, was killed in what was called a murder-suicide, although the hip hop community suspects otherwise. Despite threats, the country's hip hop scene found outlets—free downloads on the Internet and Venezuelan hip hop artists regularly tour Latin America; their live performances, rather than record sales, are their primary source of income.

Other important hip hop acts include male artists El Prieto (aka Prieto Gang, Colombia, Arvei Angulo Rivas, 1982–), McKlopedia (Ramsés Meneses, 1986*–), and Master (Jorney Madriz, n.d.), and female rappers include Gabylonia (María Gabriela Vivas Sojo, 1987*–). The Hip Hop Revolucion (HHR, 2003–), a coalition of hip hop groups, unites the community through several festivals and dozens of hip hop schools through the associated EPATU (2010–) arts and urban traditions program, where breakdancing, MCing, graffiti art, turntablism, and politics are taught five days a week.

Anthony J. Fonseca

See also: Political Hip Hop

Further Reading

Carruyo, Light. 2005. "*La gaita Zuliana* [*The Zuliana Bagpipe*]: Music and the Politics of Protest in Venezuela." *Latin American Perspectives* 32, no. 3: 98–111.

Marsh, Hazel. 2016. *Hugo Chávez, Alí Primera, and Venezuela: The Politics of Music in Latin America*. London: Palgrave McMillan.

Further Listening

Canserbero. 2012. *Muerte* (*Dead*). VinilHRecords.

Vietnam

Hip hop culture in Vietnam faces numerous government obstacles such as censorship, threat of imprisonment, and retaliation against rappers whose music protests the current socialist government. Due to former colonial influence, American and French hip hop made it to Vietnam in the late 1980s. Early non-English-speaking Vietnamese artists favored and phonetically imitated American rappers before creating their own Viet Rap, which uses Vietnamese texts. Without access to beat-making technology, early Viet Rap rappers would rap over American hip hop beats and samples. Though it is illegal to post videos that criticize the government, contain violent or sexual texts, or protest negative aspects of Vietnamese life such as poverty and hunger, Viet Rap artists began circumventing government censorship by using streaming services by the late 1990s.

Following the overthrow of French colonial administration and the Vietnam War (1955–1975) that unified North and South Vietnam, the communist regime imposed censorship on music and artists critical of the government. Threats and reprisals against rappers are still a major concern under the current government. For example, in 2012, rapper and singer-songwriter Viet Khang (aka, Minh Tri, Vô Minh Tri, 1978–) was sentenced to four years imprisonment for criticizing the government and posting onto YouTube his songs, "Anh Là Ai" and Viet Nam Toi Dau" ("Who Are You" and "Vietnam Where I Am," both 2011).

The first Viet Rap recording took place in the United States. Vietnamese American Thai Viet G's (Thai Minh Ngo, 1983*–) song "Vietnamese Gang" (1997, later released on *Portland Love*, 2001) contained both English and Vietnamese texts. Other artists produced Viet Rap videos soon after. These included Saigon-based Nah's (aka Son Nah, Son Nguyen, 1991"DMCS" (aka "Dịt Mẹ Cong San," "F—Communism," 2015), which was released while he studying at Oklahoma State University.

In the 2000s, two Vietnamese rappers found international success and are now considered the King and Queen of Vietnamese hip hop. Wowy (Nguyen Ngoc Minh Huy, 1989*–) avoids rapping about the government or social issues, opting for non-localized gangsta rap themes or focusing on Buddhist spiritualism and compassion. Suboi (aka Quiet Bunny, Hang Lam Trang Anh, 1990–), who raps in English and Vietnamese, released a 2016 video of herself freestyle rapping and interacting with then–U.S. President Barack Obama (1961–). It went viral. Suboi learned English while rapping to recordings by Eminem (1972–) and Snoop Dogg (1971–). Her lyrics emphasize romance, social pressure, family, and daily life in Vietnam. On her studio albums, *Walk* (2010) and *Run* (2014), she circumvents censorship by employing words and phrases with double meanings.

Melissa Ursula Dawn Goldsmith

See also: France; Political Hip Hop

Further Reading

Harfenist, Ethan. 2015. "Censorship Doesn't Keep Vietnam's Rappers from Speaking Their Piece." *Los Angeles Times*, July 13.

Olson, Dale A. 2008. *Popular Music of Vietnam: The Politics of Remembering, the Economics of Forgetting.* New York: Routledge.

The Virgin Islands

The Virgin Islands are located between the Caribbean Sea and the Atlantic Ocean, divided as the United States (mainly Saint Croix, Saint John, and Saint Thomas), British (mainly Anegada, Jost Van Dyke, Tortola, and Virgin Gorda), and Spanish (mainly Culebra and Vieques) Virgin Islands. The last, a territory of Puerto Rico, are also known as the Puerto Rican Virgin Islands. Overall, more current research is needed on the music of the Virgin Islands. The major centers for early Virgin Islands hip hop were Tortola and Saint Thomas, and by the mid-1980s, tourists and traveling citizens had brought hip hop music and films to the Virgin Islands and nightclubs had begun playing it. Because Jamaican reggae, pan-Caribbean calypso, and American rock and jazz were the dominant musical tastes, 1990s hip hop was perceived as alternative music. Raps that do exist are in English, often localizing gangsta rap themes, protesting against local socioeconomic issues, or emphasizing romance. Because there is virtually no music industry there, most Virgin Islands hip hop artists approach rap and breakdancing as hobbies—creating mixtapes with rap over previously composed beats and samples and sharing among friends.

The Virgin Islands are nevertheless the origin of several successful hip hop artists, many who also record reggae and R&B or infuse hip hop with these music genres. Singer-songwriter, rapper, and dancer Iyaz (Keidran Jones, 1987–) records hip hop, reggae, and R&B. The title track and "Solo" from Iyaz's debut studio album *Replay* (2009) peaked at Nos. 2 and 32, respectively, on the Billboard Hot 100. Songwriting and producing duo Rock City (aka R. City, Planet VI, 2003–) fuses hip hop with reggae, calypso, R&B, and pop. In 2006, Rock City began writing songs for pop and hip hop artists such as Iyaz, Sean Kingston (Kisean Anderson, 1990–), and Rihanna (1988–). Rock City released several mixtapes and a debut studio album, *What Dreams Are Made of* (2015).

Virgin Islands' singer-songwriter, rapper, and dancer Iyaz's musical style includes hip hop, reggae, and R&B. Iyaz's "Replay" and "Solo" from his studio album *Replay* (2009) became international hits and peaked at No. 2 and No. 32, respectively, on the Billboard Hot 100. (Jun Sato/Getty Images)

Singer-songwriter and producer Verse Simmonds (Maurice Simmonds, n.d.) moved to Los Angeles. He later formed the production duo the Jugganauts (1996*–) and has written for Jay-Z (1969–), R. Kelly (1967–), and Kanye West (1977–), among others. In 2009, Verse Simmonds began his own solo career in Atlanta, Georgia with "Buy You a Round (Up and Down)," which peaked at No. 55 on the Billboard's Hot R&B/Hip-Hop Songs. Rappers Dem Rude Boyz (2013–) fuse gangsta rap and alternative hip hop with reggae and dancehall. Dem Rude Boyz moved to Atlanta and released *Grindin' the Mixtape* (2014) on its own label, Dem Rude Boyz Entertainment (2013–).

Melissa Ursula Dawn Goldsmith

See also: Jamaica; Reggae; The United Kingdom; The United States

Further Reading

Francis, Dale. 2014. *The Quelbe Commentary: Anthropology in Virgin Islands Music.* Bloomington: Iuniverse.

Pinckney, Warren P. 1992. "Jazz in the U.S. Virgin Islands. *American Music* 10, no. 4: 441–67.

Further Listening

Iyaz. 2010. *Replay.* Beluga Heights/Reprise Records.

W

The Welfare Poets

(WP, 1997–, Bronx, New York)

The Welfare Poets (WP) is an American hip hop group-turned-collective that fuses Afro-Caribbean *bomba y plena* (bomba and plena are kinds of Puerto Rican dance music that use percussion—plena focuses on contemporary events, including politics and satire), as well as rumba, reggae, blues, bebop, cool and Latin jazz, and 1970s soul, which it incorporates into its rap and slam poetry recordings. The band's musical roots are American, Puerto Rican, Cuban, and Jamaican. Its influences include the pioneering hip hop collective the Last Poets (aka the Original Last Poets, 1968–) and poet/singer-songwriter Gil Scott-Heron (1949–2011). The group's lyrics offer social and political commentary on issues such as race, police brutality, the economy, gentrification, and the environment, as well as criticism and protest of the U.S. government's relations with Puerto Rico and its treatment of Puerto Ricans—all in support of the Puerto Rican Independence Movement and the Black Liberation efforts.

WP's symbol is a two-headed axe of Changó, a weapon of justice, with the red, black, and green Lares flag, suggesting the unification of oppressed people from the African Diaspora and Indigenous Americas. Its members are often engaged in community education and local-to-global cultural activism.

BEGINNINGS AND RECORDINGS

In 1990, Rayzer Sharp (Raymond Ramirez, 1970–) and Hector Rivera (1971–) met at Cornell University and began writing poetry to be accompanied by congas and percussion instruments. But the Welfare Poets was not fully established until Rayzer and Rivera returned to their home, the Puerto Rican section of the Bronx, New York, where activist, trumpeter, and vocalist Poppa (Dahu Ala, n.d.) of Harlem and vocalist Angel Rodriguez (1954–) of the Bronx joined them. Rodriguez became the group's arranger and contributed lyrics, while Ramirez, the group's lead MC (emcee), wrote lyrics, published songs, and managed the group.

WP's albums took several years to come to fruition, as the tracks were honed through performances at workshops and during tours worldwide. Its first studio album, the self-released *Project Blues* (2000), began in 1997 as a project for the band after an early expansion, adding bassist and Cornell friend Djibril Toure (n.d.) and guitarist Mike Angel (n.d.). *Project Blues* contained Scott-Heron–inspired lyrics about the group's inner city New York community, accompanied by blues, Latin Jazz, and Caribbean-influenced rhythms.

The second album, *Rhymes for Treason* (2005), showcased WP's transition into a collective. This album was its largest ensemble recording, and it included songs such as "Sak Pase," "The Media," and "Freedom," all of which further explored Afro-Caribbean music and jazz. During the album's release, the group toured Latin America for the first time. Rodriguez and Ala left shortly afterward.

WP's two fundraising compilations, *Cruel and Unusual Punishment* (2006) and *The Puerto Rican Freedom Project* (2009), supported anti–death penalty campaigns and raised awareness of Puerto Rican political prisoners and their families. The first compilation marked the addition of MC/emcee and hip hop producer the Legendary MIC (M. Pacheco, n.d.) from Harlem, and a former student of the collective's hip hop workshops in the Bronx. The album featured over 20 musicians from around the world, and it was also the final project for founding members Rivera and Toure. In 2007, WP completed its first tour to Europe.

Warn Them (2009) features a smaller ensemble and is the group's first album that is hip hop only, combining both old- and new-school styles. The backgrounds of the 16 tracks are a combination of beats, samples, and drumming, with Rayzer's (and at times Legendary's) rap and vocals in the foreground. The title track is representative of the themes addressed on the album, which include the problem of fake MCs in general, multinational corporations, and right-wing governments, as well as negative commentary on social contradictions, polluting the environment, capitalism, and exploitation of oppressed peoples. "Warn Them" also marks the group's first major music video release. Other tracks such as "Feel Something," "So Alive," and "Last of the Po' Ricans" represent the group's uplifting hip hop themes, such as surviving and even succeeding despite struggles against the system; "Feeling" narrates a dream of encountering revolutionary figures.

Between 2012 and 2013, its members toured and taught workshops in Iceland to assist refugees (mainly from Africa and the Middle East) with the organizations No Borders Iceland and Saving Iceland. Its members shot a documentary, *No Human Being Is Illegal: The Story and Struggle of the Other Hidden People of Iceland* (2013), as well as the video for "So Alive," a track on its album *Warn Them* (2009). As of 2018, WP is still active and continues to attract a cult following, but have released only three albums.

Melissa Ursula Dawn Goldsmith

See also: Iceland; The Last Poets; Political Hip Hop; Puerto Rico; Reggae; The United States

Further Reading

Cramer, Lauren M. 2017. "Pulse of the People: Political Rap Music and Black Politics." *Journal of African American History* 102, no. 2: 285–87.

Minister of Information JR. 2011. "Twentieth Anniversary of the Welfare Poets: An Interview wit' Founding Member Rayzer." *The San Francisco Bay View National Black Newspaper*, March 26.

Saleh-Hanna, Viviane. 2010. "Crime, Resistance, and Song: Black Musicianship's Black Criminology." In *Popular Culture, Crime, and Social Control*, edited by Mathieu Deflem, pp. 145–72. Sociology of Crime, Law, and Deviance, vol. 14. Bingley, England: Emerald.

Further Listening

WP. 2000. *Project Blues.* Self-released.

WP. 2005. *Rhymes for Treason.* Self-released.

WP. 2009. *Warn Them.* Poor Rican Productions.

West, Kanye

(Kanye Omari West, 1977–, Atlanta, Georgia)

Kanye West is an American rapper, singer, songwriter, and music producer known for his brash personality and thoughtful lyrics. His sound and style are experimental and flamboyant and have influenced other artists. Raised in a middle-class lifestyle, he was not exposed to poverty, gang violence, or drugs. In fact, his father was a photographer for *The Atlanta Journal-Constitution* before becoming a church counselor and his mother was an English professor. When he was three, his parents divorced, and he moved to Chicago with his mother, eventually studying at Chicago's American Academy of Art and then transferring to Chicago State University to study English. He dropped out of school at the age of 20 to focus on a music career.

FROM ENGLISH MAJOR TO MUSIC CAREER

West, who by 1996 was producing for local rap artists in Chicago, moved to New York City in 2001 to work with Roc-A-Fella Records (1996–2013). He wrote five songs for rapper Jay-Z's (1969–) album *The Blueprint* (2001), which included sped-up samples of classic rock and soul songs. Over 420,000 copies of the album were sold in its first week, and it became certified double Platinum. Its success led to West's involvement in work by other hip hop artists, including Foxy Brown (Inga DeCarlo Fung Marchand, 1978–), Ludacris (1977–), and DMX (1970–).

West lacked the gangsta image and background of other rappers, so multiple record companies, including Capitol, rejected him. Roc-A-Fella eventually signed him. Despite a serious 2002 car accident, he recorded the single "Through the Wire," setting the framework for his debut album, *The College Dropout* (2004), which juxtaposed gospel choirs and string arrangements against programmed drums; it produced two critically acclaimed singles, "Jesus Walks" and "Slow Jamz." His debut album peaked at the No. 2 position on the Billboard 200, became certified triple Platinum, and won the Grammy for Best Rap Album.

West's second album, *Late Registration* (2005), enjoyed similar success and accolades: It won Best Rap Album, Best Rap Solo Performance for the single "Gold Digger," and Best Rap Song for "Diamonds from Sierra Leone." He collaborated with film composer Jon Brion (1963–) for his sophomore album and incorporated complex samples and a live string orchestra, drawing inspiration from English trip hop group Portishead (1991–). The album showcased West's storytelling abilities and featured lyrics about poverty, blood diamond trades, self-reflection, and the U.S. healthcare system.

Eager to continue exploring various storytelling methods and to appeal to arena anthems, West drew inspiration from electronic music, house music, 1980s rock, the synth-pop, and folk music for the sound and lyrics of *Graduation* (2007). Most of the lyrics convey West's ambivalence toward his newfound fame and success, oscillating between extreme self-confidence and intense self-doubt. *Graduation* ended the reign of "gangsta" rap in mainstream media.

TRAGEDY AND MORE RECENT ALBUMS

Within months, in 2007, West lost his mother unexpectedly and had his engagement called off. The events influenced the content of his fourth album, *808s and Heartbreak* (2008), for which he used an autotune vocal processor for lead vocals and the Roland TR–808 Rhythm Composer (a drum machine) to create a radical change in his style. He also experimented with a minimalistic, electronic R&B sound. West's style continued to break away from the boasting and materialistic themes prominent in mainstream hip hop and rap, and his introspective lyrics for this album influenced artists such as Drake (1986–) and Frank Ocean (Christopher Edwin Breaux, 1987–).

West implemented a maximalist style for his fifth album, *My Beautiful Dark Twisted Fantasy* (2010), which touched on themes of consumerism and race. He adopted a more aggressive sound for *Yeezus* (2013), adding components of acid house, punk rock, industrial music, and Chicago drill; its themes included modern race relations. *The Life of Pablo* (2016) features the vocal talents of a variety of artists, including Rihanna (1988–), Kid Cudi (Scott Ramon Seguro Mescudi, 1984–), Chris Brown (1989–), and Kendrick Lamar (1987–), as well as elements of gospel and soul. In 2018, West created a hip hop industry controversy when he expressed his support for President Donald Trump (1946– ; in office 2016–), despite what the industry saw as racist policies.

Celeste Roberts

See also: Estelle; The United States

Further Reading

Cullen, Shaun. 2016. "The 'Innocent' and the 'Runaway:' Kanye West, Taylor Swift, and the Cultural Politics of Racial Melodrama." *Journal of Popular Music Studies* 28, no. 1: 33–50.

Lynne, Douglas. 2013. *Kanye West: Grammy-Winning Hip Hop Artist and Producer.* North Mankato, MN: ADBO.

Further Listening

West, Kanye. 2004. *The College Dropout.* Roc-A-Fella Records.
West, Kanye. 2008. *808s and Heartbreak.* Roc-A-Fella Records.
West, Kanye. 2013. *Yeezus.* Def Jam Recordings.

will.i.am

(William James Adams, 1975–, Los Angeles, California)

will.i.am is a rapper, hip hop and R&B singer, songwriter, keyboardist, record producer, technology entrepreneur, and sometime actor. He is best known as one of the two original founding members of the Grammy Award winning group from Los Angeles, the Black Eyed Peas (1995), and has remained with the band its entire recording career. He has also released four moderately successful solo albums while also producing songs for other notable artists.

Born William Adams in East Los Angeles, he was raised in housing projects in one of the few African American families in a predominantly Hispanic community. He studied fashion merchandising. His first band was the socially conscious rap group Atban Klann (aka A Tribe Beyond a Nation or Tribal Nation, 1991–1995), which was signed to Eazy-E's Ruthless Records (1987–2010*) in 1992, but a first album, tentatively titled *Grass Roots*, never came to fruition.

Along with other Black Eyed Peas members—apl.de.ap (Allan Pineda Lindo, 1974–), Fergie (Stacy Ann Ferguson, 1975–), and Taboo (Jaime Luis Gomez, 1975–), will.i.am has been the

Of all the founding members of the American hip hop group the Black Eyed Peas, will.i.am (pictured in 2006) has enjoyed the most successful concurrent solo and production career. Among others, he has produced hip hop acts like Nicki Minaj, Rihanna, and Usher. (KMazur/WireImage/Getty Images)

the recipient of seven Grammies, eight American Music Awards, and three World Music Awards. He was one of the group's songwriters and was its main rapper and keyboardist. The band's hit albums included *Elephunk* (2003), which peaked at No. 14 on the Billboard 200 and sold 8.5 million copies; *Monkey Business* (2005), which reached No. 2 and sold 10 million copies; and *The E.N.D.* (2009), which reached No. 1 and sold 11 million copies. Its hit songs included "Where Is the Love," "Hey Mama," "Let's Get It Started," "Don't Phunk with My Heart," and "My Humps," as well as three No. 1 songs, "Boom, Boom, Pow," "I Gotta Feeling," and "Imma Be."

His solo albums, many released while with the Black Eyed Peas, are *Lost Change* (2001), *Must B 21* (2003), *Songs about Girls* (2007), and *#willpower* (2013). He has worked with Cartoon Network series creator Genndy Tartakovsky (1970–) on various series soundtracks as well, and in 2008, he produced a political album, *Change is Now: Renewing America's Promise*, in support of Barack Obama's presidential campaign. His "Reach for the Stars" is the first song broadcast from Mars, by the Curiosity rover.

His solo music and collaborations as a producer can best be described as high energy rave music, heavily influenced by electronica and synth-pop, with lots of vocal modulation, autotuning, sound-bite usage, and sampling. He has produced songs with Ke$ha (Kesha Rose Sebert, 1987–), Eazy-E (1964–1995), Britney Spears (1981–), Miley Cyrus (Destiny Hope Cyrus, 1992–), Lady Gaga (1986–), Nicki Minaj (1982–), and Michael Jackson (1958–2009), among many others. He often stars in videos featuring music that he produces, sometimes as a singer/performer and sometimes as the video's main character.

Anthony J. Fonseca

See also: Black Eyed Peas; The United States

Further Reading

Boucher, Geoff. 2006. "Minding the Peas: Will.i.am and His Mates Have Captured the Interest of Hip Hop Fans and Corporate America." *Los Angeles Times*, March 29, E1.

Devitt, Rachel. 2008. "Lost in Translation: Filipino Diaspora(s), Postcolonial Hip Hop, and the Problems of Keeping It Real for the 'Contentless' Black Eyed Peas." *Asian Music* 39, no. 1: 108–34.

du Lac, J. Freedom. 2006. "The Prince of the Peas: His Group Took a Rap for Being More Pop Than Hip Hop, but Will.i.am Adams Is Hot." *The Washington Post*, April 22, C01.

Wiz Khalifa

(Cameron Jibril Thomaz, 1987–, Minot, North Dakota)

Wiz Khalifa is an American rapper, singer-songwriter, actor, and record sub-label owner based in Pittsburgh, Pennsylvania. He has had four Top 10 hits on the Billboard Hot 100, with two reaching No. 1, "Black and Yellow (2010) and "See You Again" (2015), and one chart-topping album on the Billboard 200, *Blacc Hollywood* (2014). In addition, his albums *Rolling Papers* (2011) and *O.N.I.F.C.* (2012) both were certified Platinum and reached No. 2 on the Billboard 200, with all three albums topping both the Rap and Top R&B/Hip-Hop Albums charts, spawning three No. 1 on Billboard's Hot Rap Songs. No overnight success story, Khalifa released his digital (.mp3) mixtape debut *Prince of the City: Welcome to Pistolvania* and debut album *Show and Prove* in 2006, both in conjunction with Pittsburgh-based independent label Rostrum Records (2003–), founded by Benjy Grinberg (n.d.), a former Arista Records (1974–2011) developer who wanted to create a label that would develop artists over time; Wiz Khalifa would form his sub-label, Taylor Gang, in 2008.

After a short-lived contract with Warner (1958–) in 2008, he returned to Rostrum and ihiphop Distribution (2009–) for the album *Deal or No Deal* (2009), which was bolstered by his opening for Wu-Tang Clan (1992–) member U-God (Lamont Jody Hawkins, 1970–) in a 2009 Music Marathon in New York City and his appearance at the 2010 South by Southwest Music Festival, at Soundset 2010, at Rock the Bells, and on the 50-city sold-out Waken Baken Tour.

He achieved success in 2011, when he and Rostrum signed a distribution deal with Atlantic Records (1947–). This came from lots of hard work: while he was developing, Rostrum and Taylor Gang released several mixtapes, including *Flight School* (2009) and *Kush and OJ* (2010) for free download to create a fanbase for his laid back, trip hop (downtempo) melodies and slow-paced rapping. Also in 2011, he won Best New Artist at the BET Awards. He then went on to collaborate with Curren$y (Shante Scott Franklin, 1981–), Miley Cyrus (Destiny Hope Cyrus, 1992–), and Juicy J (Jordan Michael Houston, 1975–) for his next studio projects.

In 2015, Wiz Khalifa toured with Fall Out Boy (2001–2009, 2013–). In 2016, he released the album *Khalifa* on his Taylor Gang label, in conjunction with Rostrum and Atlantic, but his relationship with Grinberg reached an impasse when he sued Rostrum for $1 million in compensation. The album was not commercially successful, failing to achieve Gold certification.

As of 2018, an album tentatively titled *Rolling Papers 2* is scheduled for release on the same labels. Wiz Khalifa has been an activist for legalization of cannabis—many of his songs are about marijuana.

Anthony J. Fonseca

See also: The United States

Further Reading

Gibbs, Adrienne Samuels. 2011. "Baking Brownies with Wiz Khalifa." *Ebony* 66, no. 6: 34.

Inkster, Becky, and Akeem Sule. 2015. "Drug Term Trends in American Hip Hop Lyrics." *Journal of Public Mental Health* 14, no. 3: 169–73.

Pawson, Mark, and Brian C. Kelly. 2014. "Consumption and Community: The Subcultural Contexts of Disparate Marijuana Practices in Jam Band and Hip Hop Scenes." *Deviant Behavior* 35, no. 5: 347–63.

Further Listening

Wiz Khalifa. 2011. *Rolling Papers.* Atlantic/Rostrum Records.

World Famous Beat Junkies

(aka Beat Junkies, 1992–, Long Beach and Los Angeles, California)

World Famous Beat Junkies is a DJ crew currently located in Glendale, California, the location of its own DJ School, the Beat Junkie Institute of Sound (2017–). Originally called Beat Junkies, the crew was founded in 1992 by DJ and producer J-Rocc (aka Chief Rocca, the Funky President, Jason Jackson, n.d.). Original core members included DJ Rhettmatic (Nazareth Nizra, n.d.) and Melo-D (David Mendoza, n.d.). The most famous core member, Filipino American turntablist and producer DJ Babu (aka Babu, The Turntablist, Melvin Babu, Chris Oroc, 1974–), joined later, as well as Shortkut (Jon Cruz, 1975–) and D-Styles (Dave Cuasito, 1972–), both ex-members of San Francisco–based rival DJ crew Invisibl Skratch Piklz (1989–2000, 2014–). By the early 1990s, the Beat Junkies competed at DJ battles in Southern California. It is a multiracially diverse crew known for stimulating a resurgence of interest in turntablism by developing advanced skills, its smooth beat juggling style—creating an original composition by manipulating two or more samples, using two or more turntables and one or more mixers, its choreographed combinations that included intelligent and entertaining pauses, its practice of group lip-syncing while scratching, and its creation of hiccoughing grooves. During late 1990s battles, the Beat Junkies mostly used regular scratching as the foundation of its sound, but with far less stress on uniformity (in-sync scratching) than its East Coast predecessors such as the X-Ecutioners (aka X-Men, 1989–), which makes the Beat Junkies look relaxed in competition.

Among many other battles and championships, individual members of the Beat Junkies won the Disco Mix Club (DMC) title as West Coast Champions with Shortkut (1994 and 1998), Babu (1995), and Rhettmatic (1996). In 1997 and 1998, the Beat Junkies won the International Turntable Federation (ITF) World Team Championships. Meanwhile, starting in 1997, the crew established its own recording label, Beat Junkie Sound, which produced individual members' mixtapes and remixes before releasing D-Styles's instrumental hip hop and turntablist solo debut studio album, *Phatazmagorea* (2002). The crew retired from battles in 1998; however, as the World Famous Beat Junkies, it has judged many DMC Chamionships and DJ battles and it has been committed to in-person instruction of turntablist skills at all levels.

Members continue recording solo projects and collaborating with other hip hop artists. For example, DJ Babu has produced over a hundred albums and has performed as a member of the duo the Likwit Junkies (2003–2005) and the alternative hip hop trio Dilated Peoples (1992–). D-Styles has appeared on albums by X-Ecutioners' member Rob Swift (1972–) and Japanese DJ Kentaro (Kentaro Okamoto, 1982*–), among others, in addition to producing X-Ecutioners' member Roc Raida's (1972–2009) songs "Razorblade Alcohol Slide" on *Crossfaderz* (2000) and "The Murder Faktory" on *Champion Sounds* (2003). The World Famous Beat Junkies also continues to run its own record pool (to provide to members exclusive cuts and edits), clothing line, and radio station, Beat Junkie Radio (2015–). New members have joined the crew, though its core members remain. In early 2017, American actor, comedian, director, and podcast host Michael Rapaport (1970–), who won critical acclaim directing the documentary *Beats, Rhymes & Life: The Travels of a Tribe Called Quest* (2011), in a popular video posted on YouTube interviewed and performed with the crew at the the Beat Junkie Institute of Sound.

Melissa Ursula Dawn Goldsmith

See also: Battling; Dilated Peoples; DJ Babu; Turntablism; The United States; The X-Ecutioners

Further Reading

Katz, Mark. 2012. "Turntablism: 1989–96." In *Groove Music: The Art and Culture of the Hip Hop DJ*, chap. 5. New York: Oxford University Press.

Smith, Sophy. 2013. *Hip Hop Turntablism, Creativity, and Collaboration*. Burlington, VT: Ashgate.

Werde, William. 1999. "The Real Spin Doctors: Turntables in Hand, Mixmasters Live a Sample Life." *The Washington Post*, February 7, G01.

Further Listening

D-Styles. 2002. *Phantazmagorea*. Beat Junkie Sound.

World Famous Beat Junkies. 2013. *Beat Junkie Sound Presents the Beat Junkie Picture Disc Collection*. Beat Junkie Sound.

Wu-Tang Clan

(1992–, Staten Island, New York)

The Wu-Tang Clan is a New York–based hip hop collective of MCs who represent one of the most respected groups in hip hop. With an aesthetic drawn from Kung-Fu films, the name derives from the Hong Kong film *Shaolin and Wu Tang* (1983), a drama about two battling martial arts schools. In fact, Kung-Fu forms important aspects of the band's identity, underscoring common hip hop themes of self-defense, identity, and battle. The collective also uses elements of mafia culture, usually found in its samples and sound.

FORMATION AND FIRST ALBUMS

The Wu-Tang Clan grew out of another group, the short-lived All In Together Now Crew (1992), which included cousins RZA (Robert Fitzgerald Diggs, 1969–), GZA (aka The Genius, Gary Grice, 1966–), and Ol' Dirty Bastard (ODB, Russell Tyrone Jones, 1968–2004). The addition of Ghostface Killah (Dennis Coles, 1970–), Method Man (Clifford Smith, 1971–), Raekwon (Corey Woods, 1970–), U-God (aka Universal-God, Lamont Hawkins, 1970–), Inspectah Deck (Jason Hunter, 1970–), and Masta Killa (Jamal Irief Elgin Turner, b. Elgin Turner, 1969–) led to the formation of the Wu-Tang Clan.

Dissatisfied with prospective record deals, the members agreed to chip in $100 each to record their first single, the self-released "Protect Ya Neck" (1993). After touring successfully and seeing the single played on college radio stations, they signed to Loud Records (1991–2012), a then-small independent rap label in New York City. The selection of Loud, despite other offers, came about because of the label's willingness to offer a small advance in exchange for the group's maintaining creative control, as well as the freedom for individual members to sign deals with other labels; this arrangement supported Wu-Tang Clan's ambition of subverting the usual conventions of the music industry, ensuring the greatest likelihood for all of the members' subsequent commercial success. Collectively, members of the group have earned six Platinum albums and sold over 40 million records.

The collective's first release on Loud (the label that distributed the first four full Wu-Tang Clan studio albums), *Enter the Wu-Tang (36 Chambers)* (1993) introduced the martial arts themes and metaphors that would pervade all of its music. Intended, in part, as a launching pad for the solo careers of all of the MCs, it was followed by just such success; individual members have recorded for a variety of labels, with the RZA producing or coproducing most releases. The first solo project, Method Man's *Tical* (1994), produced by Def Jam Recordings (1984–), which was certified Platinum the next year, proved the success of the freedom strategy and has been followed by multiple releases and side projects by the other members that have seen both commercial and critical success.

In 1997, the larger group reconvened for their second album, *Wu-Tang Forever*, which sold heavily immediately. Additional side projects filled the time between that release and the next, *The W* (2000). The next full album, *Iron Flag* (2001) was recorded without ODB, who was in prison on numerous charges, including escaping for a month. In 2004, a final, live album and DVD that included previously released material, *Disciples of the 36 Chambers: Chapter 1,* came out shortly before ODB's death. It represented the 36th Wu-Tang family release and the last group album until their 2007 release on SRC, *8 Diagrams*, which received a lukewarm response. Further releases *Legendary Weapons* (2011), produced by Entertainment One Music (2009–), a compilation album with some new material, and *A Better Tomorrow* (2014), on Warner Bros. Records (1958–) round out the widely available releases.

LYRIC CONTENT, SOUND, MYTHOLOGY, AND CLOTHING BRAND

Lyrically, the Wu-Tang Clan is known for gritty, urban rhymes that do not gloss over the reality of daily life in the ghetto. Each MC maintains his own vocal and poetic style that gives the band's collective output a widely diverse sound. Each MC brings in other collaborators, supplementing his style with the efforts of other creators. Band members have brought Brooklyn and Staten Island, New York–based other acts, such as Sunz of Men (1994–), Cappadonna (Darryl Hill, 1969–), and Killarmy (1995–), under their wing, granting them the brand of the Wu-Tang and supporting their work. Much of what makes the Wu-Tang Clan different from its contemporaries are the mythology and storytelling that surrounds the collective.

The band's culture has become so robust that the RZA penned a guidebook, *The Wu-Tang Manual: Enter the 36 Chambers, Vol. One* (2004), as a method to explain its mysteries. Acting as a master or a guide in the *Manual*, RZA takes the reader through the foundations of the first Wu-Tang album, with illumination on the themes of spirituality, kung fu, and chess that pervade the record and resultant Wu-Tang culture. In this work, he explains much of the symbolism that transmits meaning to the group's oeuvre, from numerology to spiritual interpretation.

In addition to the careful planning around recording, the Wu-Tang Clan have managed its brand in more tangible ways, too. The launch of Wu-Wear Clothing in 1995 allowed its members some control over distribution of clothing with the band's logo in a brick-and-mortar store on Staten Island. Members also developed a comic book line, *The Nine Rings of Wu-Tang* (Image Comics, 2001–) and a Kung-Fu video game, *Wu-Tang: Shaolin Style* (Activision Success, 1999), both of which sold successfully.

A CONTROVERSIAL ALBUM SALE

A "secret" album, *Once Upon a Time in Shaolin*, of which only one copy, a CD, was pressed, was auctioned off and purchased in 2015 by controversial pharmaceutical CEO and entrepreneur Martin Shkreli (1983–) for two million dollars; upon learning who the buyer was, the Clan donated a significant amount of the proceeds to charity. The group members' public feuding about the marketing strategy around this release reflects growing public discord that has pervaded much of the press surrounding Wu-Tang Clan since the early 2000s.

Susannah Cleveland

See also: Black Nationalism; Fashion; Political Hip Hop; The United States

Further Reading

Blanco, Alvin. 2011. *The Wu-Tang Clan and RZA: A Trip through Hip Hop's 36 Chambers.* Santa Barbara, CA: Praeger.

Bradley, Adam, and Andrew Dubois, eds. 2010. "The Wu-Tang Clan." Under "Part 3: 1993–99: Rap Goes Mainstream" in *The Anthology of Rap*, pp. 532–69. New Haven, CT: Yale University Press.

RZA. 2004. *The Wu-Tang Manual: Enter the 36 Chambers, Vol. One.* New York: Riverhead.

RZA and Chris Norris. 2009. *The Tao of Wu.* New York: Riverhead.

Further Listening

Wu-Tang Clan. 1993. *Enter the Wu-Tang (36 Chambers).* Loud Records.

Wu-Tang Clan. 2001. *Iron Flag.* Loud Records/Epic.

Further Viewing

Salzy (Christoffer Salzgeber), dir. 2004. *Wu-Tang Clan: Disciples of the 36 Chambers: Chapter 2.* New York: Wu Tang Productions/Sanctuary Records.

X

The X-Ecutioners

(aka X-Men, 1989–, New York City, New York)

The X-Ecutioners is an American turntablist and DJ crew that was originally known as the X-Men and led by DJ Roc Raida (Anthony Williams, 1972–2009). The X-Ecutioners are best known for their award-winning turntablist skills, seminal turntablist innovations, and ability to revitalize turntablism during the Golden Age of Hip Hop (1986–1994)—a time when MCs and rappers dominated hip hop's foreground.

As with beatboxing, turntablism was a live performance art that faced challenges when studio recording and engineering threatened to replace it. The X-Ecutioners' debut studio album *X-Pressions* (1997) was the first full-length album that featured turntablism as its focus. The X-Ecutioners were the first turntablist crew to have mainstream success, with albums that charted on the Billboard 200. The crew's second and third studio albums, *Built from Scratch* (2002) and *Revolutions* (2004), peaked at Nos. 15 and 118, respectively. Both albums also peaked at Nos. 13 and 50, respectively, on Billboard's Top R&B/Hip-Hop Albums chart, which was dominated by rappers. In workshops and in films, the X-Ecutioners were active in educating the public about turntablism history and its techniques, as well as discussing its beat juggling combinations and patterns. Not only did members interview for the American documentary *Scratch* (2001), but the X-Ecutioners made its own DVD, *Built to Scratch* (2004), which serves as a turntablist and DJ tutorial.

The X-Men originally formed with the intention to win the Superman Battle for World Supremacy, a turntablist battle that featured DJ and producer Clark Kent (Rodolfo Franklin, 1967–) as MC. The X-Men began performing in Harlem, New York, as an 11-member crew. The crew took its name after writer Stan Lee (Stanley Martin Lieber, 1922–) and artist Jack Kirby's (Jacob Kurtzberg, 1917–1994) Marvel Comics (1939–) fictional 1960s comic book superheroes—mutants born with superhuman capabilities (1963–). Some original members were Roc Raida; Johnny Cash (anonymous, n.d.); Sean C (aka Sean Cane, Deleno Matthews, n.d.); EPMD's (1986–1993, 1997–1999, 2006–) first DJ, Diamond J (anonymous, n.d.); Dr. Butcher (Andrew Venable, n.d.); and Steve D (aka Steve Dee, Steve Thomas, n.d.).

Around 1986, Steve D created beat juggling, which at the time he called "the funk." The X-Men adapted and developed beat juggling—where two or more musical excerpts or samples (for example, a break, a drumbeat groove, or vocal or instrumental phrases) are used to create a new composition by manipulating them through looping, mixing and cross-fading, pauses (cutting), scratching, or adding sound effects—incorporating it into its battle and showcasing performances. The crew's beat juggling performances, sometimes improvised, required both musical and choreographed physical timing as well as a sense of musical direction and focus while mixing and composing.

Steve D and other founding members left the X-Men, but by 1991, Rob Swift (Rob Aguilar, 1972–) had joined, followed in 1993 by Mista Sinista (Joel Wright, 1970–), both mentored by Dr. Butcher. In 1996, DJ Total Eclipse (Keith Bailey, 1977–) joined after winning the first ITF (International Turntablist Federation, 1996–) World Championship.

In the meantime, members of the X-Men established themselves by winning major turntablist battles such as DMC U.S.A. (aka Disco Mix Club), affiliated with the New York City Regional DJ Battle and the DMC World DJ Championships (1985–). Early recognition came to Rob Swift, who won the DMC East Coast DJ Championship the same year he joined the X-Men; Mista Sinista would earn the same title in 1996. Other early recognition came to Roc Raida, who became the DMC U.S. DJ Champion (1994/1995) and World DJ Champion (1995). The X-Men also participated, though they were defeated, in an ITF Team Battle, a showcase exhibit against the San Francisco turntablist crew, Invisibl Skratch Piklz (aka Shadow of the Prophet, 1989–). This showcase was captured on film, demonstrating that all X-Men members scratched regular style and used their left hands mostly for scratching, and their right hands mostly for mixing.

In 1997, the X-Men signed a recording deal with Asphodel (1992–), an San Francisco experimental indie label that specialized in hip hop, electronica, and spoken word. Concerned with the possibility of facing a lawsuit with Marvel Comics over their name, the X-Men became the X-Ecutioners. By the time their debut album *X-Pressions* was released (1997), the X-Ecutioners consisted of four remaining members: Roc Raida; Rob Swift; Mista Sinista; and Total Eclipse. Though the album did not chart, its critical acclaim led to signing with the more prominent hip hop label Loud Records (1991–) and two later hit albums, *Built from Scratch* and *Revolutions*.

Both albums included collaborations with other turntablists and turntablist crews such as the alternative hip hop duo Gang Starr's (1986–2003) DJ Premier (aka Preem, Premo, or Primo, Christopher Edward Martin, 1966–); Beat Junkies (aka World Famous Beat Junkies, 1992–) rappers such as Kool G Rap (Nathaniel Thomas Wilson, 1968–); and Wu-Tang Clan's (1992–) Ghostface Killah (Dennis Coles, 1970–) and Inspectah Deck (Jason Hunter, 1970–); as well as hip hop groups such as Cypress Hill (1988–) and alternative or indie post-punk groups such as Tom Tom Club (1981–).

Mista Sinista left in 2003 and Rob Swift left in 2004; both, as well as Roc Raida, focused on solo careers that included releasing more albums. Meanwhile, the X-Ecutioners continued on by recruiting top turntablists. In 2004, DJ Precision (Perrin Wright, n.d.) and DJ Boogie Blind (Dameon Tompkins, n.d.) joined. Other new members into the 2010s included Exotic E (anonymous, n.d.) and Boogie Boy (formerly Booji Boy, anonymous, n.d.).

Subsequent albums include the collaboration album *General Patton vs. The X-Ecutioners* (2005) and *Ground Xero* (2008). The last is credited to Ill Insanity (2008–), a turntablist collective consisting of Rob Swift, with the X-Ecutioners members Total Eclipse and DJ Precision. New members have also won major turntablist battles. Released just a year before his unexpected and untimely death, Roc Raida also produced, along with DJ Qbert (1969–), a founding member of Invisible Skratch Piklz. Since 2014, Rob Swift teaches DJ Skills and Styles is a Professor at the New School for Liberal Arts in New York City.

Melissa Ursula Dawn Goldsmith

See also: Battling; Invisibl Skratch Piklz; Rob Swift; Roc Raida; Turntablism; The United States

Further Reading

Katz, Mark. 2012. "Turntablism: 1989–96" and "Legitimacy: 1996–2002." In *Groove Music: The Art and Culture of the Hip Hop DJ.* New York: Oxford University Press.

Webber, Stephen. 2008. *DJ Skills: The Essential Guide to Mixing and Scratching.* Burlington, MA: Focal Press.

Further Listening

The X-Ecutioners. 2002. *Built from Scratch.* Loud Records.

Further Viewing

Davis, Jake, dir. 2004. *Built to Scratch.* New York: Koch Records.

Yemen

Yemen's hip hop scene was first cultivated by American Yemeni AJ (Hagage Abul-Gowee Masaed, 1963*–), who released his first rap song, "Yemen," in 1997, followed by an album, *Nights in Arabia* (1999*). His beats and hooks incorporate distinctly Yemeni melodies and pop-style orchestral riffs, with traditional instruments such as the *oud* and the *mizmar*, paired with hard-driving rap verses. AJ collaborates with classical Yemeni singers Hussein Muhib (n.d.), Fouad Al-Kibsi (n.d.), Fuad Al-Sharjabi (n.d., founder of the 2007 Yemen Music House), Ibrahim Al-Taefi (n.d.), and Abdurahman Al-Akfash (n.d.). AJ's "No Terrorists Please" (2010)*, featuring Hussein Muhib on the refrain, reaches across generations with its blending of rap and classical Yemeni music as it calls on government leaders to eliminate terrorism. In 2008, the French and German Cultural Centers and the Sana'a Governorate arranged the first Yemeni rap and hip hop dance workshop and competition in Yemen's capital city Sana'a, for which winners received training from international artist-judges in their fields. In 2009, the first public Yemeni Rap Festival occurred. Yemeni hip hop is often political, with songs before and after the Yemeni Revolution of 2011 that protested unemployment, economic conditions and government corruption. Rapper Kawi (anonymous, n.d.) and the band Wohoush al Yemen (Yemen's Monsters, n.d.) were active in the protests that led to the ousting of President Ali Abdullah Saleh (1942–) in 2012.

DANCE AND ART ELEMENTS

Yemeni hip hop culture includes rap, breakdancing (highlighted in the 2014 American documentary *Shake the Dust*), street art, and graffiti. Mohamed Al-Ansi (n.d.) encourages political mobilization through his street art at Change Square, a revolutionary encampment near Sana'a University, which is also a common site for the performance of protest music. Rock City breakdancing, founded by Farj Al-Badani (n.d.) and Hussein Al-Habashi (n.d.), blends Western hip hop moves with *taekwondo*, gymnastics, and traditional Yemeni dance. When the Rock City crew won the Sea of Talents competition (2012), they used prize money to expand training for local youth. Java Jamz (n.d.), a rap crew comprised of over 30 artists, was founded by Mohammed Hijazi (n.d.) and Suhail Al-Doa'eis (n.d.), who pooled their funds to purchase recording and editing equipment. They used their studio space to make recordings and to train others in song writing, singing, dancing, and skateboarding, while spreading awareness for freedom and peace.

FEMALE ARTISTS

Amani Yahya, (1993*–) first performed at a coffee shop near her home in Sana'a, sparking outrage in conservative Yemeni society. Newspaper coverage of her performances with friend and guitarist Alaa' Haider (n.d.), describing two women performing without hijab or abaya, led to anonymous threats to the women. Amani, who learned from recordings of Lil Wayne (1982–), raps in English, hoping to make the world aware of women's rights, child marriage, and sexual harassment in Yemen. Monika (anonymous, n.d.), another aspiring female rapper, also feels pressure not to perform rap as a Yemeni woman.

LYRICS AND MUSICAL INFLUENCE

Many Yemeni rappers combine English and Arabic lyrics. This is true both for Yemen-based bands such as Military Mind (n.d.), Sari Killer (n.d.), and Mad Marino (n.d.), and for diaspora artists such as California-based Smokie Almo (1989–), Nadir Mohammed Haidar (n.d.), and Moscow-based Nadeem Al-Eryani (aka Yung Sheikh, n.d.). Traditional Yemeni Jewish music has influenced the rap of Diwon (Erez Safar, 1979–), a Yemeni American DJ whose music blends hip hop, Afrobeat, and Arab sounds. The Element Music Band (n.d.) releases YouTube grunge-rap music with traditional Yemeni instruments and vocal melodies. Aspiring rapper Faris Othrub (1997–) participates with other Yemeni rappers in web forums where new Arab rappers learn from professionals.

Jennifer L. Roth-Burnette

See also: Israel; Political Hip Hop; The United States

Further Reading

Seigneurie, Ken. 2012. "Discourses of the 2011 Arab Revolutions." *Journal of Arabic Literature* 43, nos. 2–3: 484–509.

Schuyler, Philip D. 1997. "*Qat*, Conversation, and Song: A Musical View of Yemeni Social Life." *Yearbook for Traditional Music* 29: 57–73.

Further Viewing

Adam Sjöberg, dir. 2014. *Shake the Dust.* Toluca Lake, CA: Dave Stewart Entertainment. Bond/360.

Young Paperboyz

(2007–, Nigeria; Ukraine)

Young Paperboyz is a Nigerian- and Ukrainian-based hip hop, R&B, electronic dance, and dance pop duo. While studying in the Ukraine for graduate school, Nigerian students Mayor Boss (1986–) and Della Ratta (1987–) recorded a demo tape in 2007. The single got the duo, which took its stage name from a childhood nickname, noticed by local radio DJs, and the two continued to grow their fanbase through Facebook and other social media.

Young Paperboyz released its first official single in 2008. "You Know" became a local hit, propelled mainly through radio airplay. Its success inspired the duo to follow up with a 13-track debut album, *Moving* (2009), which spawned two other singles, "Rozkachai" and "Moving." The album was well received not only in the Ukraine, but also in Nigeria and Germany. In 2010, Young Paperboyz released a second single, "Livin' on the Edge," leading to the band's first Ukrainian tour.

In 2010, the duo released a new, freely downloadable mixtape with 21 tracks, *Young Paperboyz Lavish Life*, as well as the single "Live it Up." The next mixtape, *Naija Boss*, was released in 2012, after Mayor Boss's graduation with a master's of science degree in pharmacy, and was freely downloadable on SoundCloud, iTunes, Amazon, iHeartRadio, Google Play, and Spotify. This mixtape produced three singles, "Pop It Up," "5 Million Girls," and "Shake Am." The duo's long-awaited second album, *Naija Boss Techno Reloaded*, was released in 2013. The music videos for the singles "Make Love, Hit It" and "Party People" were released. The duo's third studio album, *Life of the Boys*, was released in 2015. It featured the single "Scrabble."

The Young Paperboyz's sound can best be compared to that of the Black Eyed Peas (1995–) in that it emphasizes dance rhythms over song structure or lyrics, is highly autotuned (both singing and rapping are autotuned), and takes as its major concerns love, romance, sex, and partying. Rarely are there any songs about social or political concerns featured on the band's studio albums. The duo's videos generally emphasize lavishness—stylish clothing, limousines, and adoring, scantily clad women.

Anthony J. Fonseca

See also: Nigeria; Ukraine

Further Reading

Inyabri, Idom T. 2016. "Youth and Linguistic Stylization in Naija Afro-Hip Hop." *Sociolinguistic Studies* 10, nos. 1–2: 89–108.

Shipley, Jesse Weaver. 2017. "Parody after Identity: Digital Music and the Politics of Uncertainty in West Africa." *American Ethnologist* 44, no. 2: 249–62.

Shonekan, Stephanie. 2012. "Nigerian Hip Hop: Exploring a Black World Hybrid." In *Hip Hop Africa: New African Music in a Globalizing World*, edited by Eric Charry, chap. 7. Bloomington: Indiana University Press.

Further Listening

Young Paperboyz. 2012. *Naija Boss.* Mayor Boss Promotion.

Z

Zambia

Zambia is a landlocked South African country that neighbors the Democratic Republic of Congo, Angola, Tanzania, Malawi, Mozambique, Botswana, Namibia, and Zimbabwe. Though Zambia has experienced rapid economic growth since the 2010s, freedom of speech is threatened and its Christian majority possesses extreme conservative views toward women and homosexuals. By the late 1980s, hip hop nevertheless arrived in Zambia, with activity taking place mainly in its capital, Lusaka. Zambian hip hop, which emerged by the early 1990s, favors English, the country's official language, but it also uses Lusaka's main local language, Nyanja (Chewa). Song themes include politics, street violence, romance, and HIV/AIDS. Some rap is religious (Christian themes).

Pioneering hip hop acts included Chennai-born and Zambian-raised rapper-turned-playback-singer Blaaze (Lakshmi Narasimha Vijaya Rajagopala Sheshadri Sharma Rajesh Raman, 1975–), Chilu Lemba (1975–), Holstar (aka The Host, The Holstar, Duncan Sodala, 1982–), Daddy Zemus (Anthony Kafunya, 1968–2001), and the Perth, Australia–based Zambian rapper C.R.I.$.I.$. (aka Mr. Swagger, Chisenga Katongo, n.d.). The rap duo Black Muntu (1999–2005) increased the national popularity of hip hop with its debut album *Wisakamana* (1999) and second album *Kokoliko* (2002).

As of 2010, the most popular Zambian rap group is Lusaka-based Zone Fam (2009–). In early 2011, its hit single "Shaka Zulu on 'em," released on the album *The Business (Foreign Exchange)*, led to international airplay. Zone Fam's hardcore rapping style is mostly in English, but includes Nyanja, Bemba, Tonga, and Zulu languages. The group fuses hardcore and alternative hip hop with R&B. Zone Fam, which includes its manager Holstar, has collaborated with Zambian rappers Slapdee (Mwila Musonda, n.d.) and Macky 2 (aka MK, DJ Bugar, Flava Boy, Mulaza Kaira, 1984–). Macky 2's younger brother, Chef 187 (Kondwani Kaira, n.d.) is also a successful artist who fuses hip hop with R&B and *kalindula*—an energetic musical style that uses the kalindula, a Zambian crafted electric bass guitar that is also called a banjo. PilAto (Fumba Chama, 1984–), who has been arrested and received death threats for his harsh political rap against Zambia's former President Michael Sata (1937–2014, in office 2011–2014), also fuses these styles.

Other acts since the 2000s include Cleo (aka Cleo Ice Queen, Clementina Mulenga, 1989–) and Kan 2 (Kantu Habanji Siachingili, 1990–) two female rappers and singers who record hip hop, Afropop, and dancehall music, as well as Just Slim (Paul Chilupe Banda, 1989–), B'Flow (Brian Mumba Kasoka Bwembya (1986–), Petersen Zagaze (Mukubesa Mundia, 1982–), and the Harare-based

Zimbabwean-Zambian-Ghanaian rapping crew 25toLyf (2014–). Another Zimbabwean-Zambian act is the Innovators (2000–), a rapping duo that formed in Grahamstown, Eastern Cape, South Africa.

Melissa Ursula Dawn Goldsmith

See also: Political Hip Hop

Further Reading

Mensah, Atta Annan. 1970. "The Music of Zumaile Village, Zambia." *African Music* 4, no. 4: 96–102.

Ntarangwi, Mwenda. 2007. "Hip Hop, Westernization, and Gender in East Africa." In *Songs and Politics in Eastern Africa*, edited by Kimani Njogu and Hervé Maupeu, chap. 12. Dar es Salaam, Tanzania: Nyota.

Further Listening

Zone Fam. 2011. *The Business (Foreign Exchange).* Slam Dunk Records.

Zeus

(Game Goabaone Bantsi, 1986–, Serowe, Botswana)

Zeus is a Motswana motswako rapper, singer-songwriter, creative writer, recording label owner, and philanthropist. In the early 2000s, while still in his teens, Zeus created his stage name based on his interest in Greek gods and the powerful all-father of Greek gods, as well as his desire to be a serious and respected MC. Typical of motswako artists, Zeus primarily interweaves rapping texts in Setswana—a Tswana language that is Botswana's lingua franca, which is also spoken by a large population in South Africa—with American vernacular. He sometimes fuses *motswako* with reggae.

Zeus has released three critically acclaimed studio albums: *Freshly Baked* (2009); *The Flipside* (2009), and *African Time* (2013). His debut and second album were released on his own label, D.I.Y. Entertainment (2007–) whereas his third album was released on the Universal Music Group (1996–) label. The label change signifies Zeus's shift from recording in Gaborone, Botswana to Johannesburg, a move that is common among many Motswana musicians simply because the music industry is much larger in South Africa. His mixtape, *Honey, I'm Home* (2012), also features Zeus in the role of MC. His lyrical content focuses on unity, national pride, sociopolitical and economic commentary about South Africa, rapper braggadocio, and hate, among other topics.

African Time has more serious content than the first two albums, with songs criticizing South Africa's economic disparity (as one of richest nations for its resources) as well as offering uplifting messages about changing for the better. Zeus is a tenor, though he rarely sings but rather chants rapping texts with featured collaborators. Zeus' music videos for national hits such as "Gijima" (2008), "Imagination" (2008), and "Champagne Music" (2010), and South African hit "#Datswasup" (2012) have also attained critical acclaim. His videos at times show parties, sexualized dancing, women being objectified, as well as scenes that address his lyrical content.

Zeus has collaborated with many notable South African musicians: motswako artist Hip Hop Pantsula (1980–), Tanzanian-born rapper Tumi Molekane (1981–), and R&B, neo soul, and acid jazz singer-songwriter and producer RJ Benjamin (Roy J. Benjamin, n.d.). South African motswako rapper Nomadic (formerly Mr T, Tebogo Mapine, n.d.), of Motswana descent, also a graphic artist, designed the album cover of Zeus's *African Time.*

Melissa Ursula Dawn Goldsmith

See also: Botswana; Motswako; South Africa

Further Reading

Ditsele, Thabo. 2017. "The Promotion of Setswana through Hip Hop and *Motswakolistas.*" *Journal of the Musical Arts in Africa* 14, nos. 1–2: 1–14.

Rapoo, Connie. 2013. "Urbanized Soundtracks: Youth Popular Culture in the African City." *Social Dynamics: A Journal of African Studies* 39, no. 2: 368–83.

Rapoo, Connie. 2014. "Reconfiguring the City: Contemporary Youth Performance and Media Entertainment in Gaborone." *Botswana Notes and Records* 45: 66–76.

Further Listening

Zeus. 2008. *Freshly Baked.* D.I.Y. Entertainment.

Zeus. 2010. *The Flipside.* D.I.Y. Entertainment.

Zeus. 2015. *African Time.* Universal Music Group.

Zimbabwe

Zimbabwe is a South African country of 16 million who speak 16 official languages, including English. Its capital and largest city is Harare. With a history of states and kingdoms, and brief colonization, it became a self-governing annexed British colony in 1923 known as Southern Rhodesia (1923–1953). Briefly the United Kingdom consolidated Southern and Northern Rhodesia as the Central African Federation (aka Federation of Rhodesia and Nyasaland (1953–1963), which was ultimately split Northern Rhodesia into Zambia and Nyasland into Malawi. In 1965, Southern Rhodesia gained independence from the United Kingdom and became Rhodesia, followed by 15 years of a racially based civil war from 1964 to 1979 known as the Zimbabwe War of Liberation (aka Rhodesian Bush War, Second Chimurenga), which resulted in the end of white minority rule (Zimbabwe's vast majority is Shona, followed by Ndebele, and tiny minority populations of white Africans of European descent and Africans of Indian descent). In 1980, a peace agreement established universal enfranchisement and the country's official name—Zimbabwe, which was recognized by the UN.

Under Prime Minister Robert Mugabe (1924–, in office 1987–2017), Zimbabwe has become authoritarian, rife with human rights violations—this has made it difficult for rappers to become mainstream, despite the fact that folk and popular music dominate the Zimbabwean music scene. Traditional or folk music is essential to the country's culture, used in ceremonies, work songs, and songs of protest. The main instrument is the *mbira*, which is a *kalimba* (thumb piano) set inside of a gourd or other material that acts as a resonator. Having made a comeback as an instrument, the mbira has been recently incorporated into pop music in Zimbabwe and around the world, as in the music of Seattle-based hip hop duo Shabazz Palaces (2009–).

Other important kinds of music include guitar styles such as *jit* (aka *tuku music*), *sungura*, and *bulawayo*, as well as flute-based African jazz, *chimurenga* (modernized, sociopolitical mbira music), and gospel. Congolese rumba (*souk*) is also popular in Zimbabwe. A new style of music called *urban grooves* emerged in the late 1990s, fusing hip hop with American R&B and neo soul, and world music, including Zimbabwean popular music. Early urban grooves acts include Maskiri (Alishias Musimbe, 1980–), Stunner (Desmond Chideme, 1980–), and Neville Sigauke (n.d.). Hip hop never became as popular as Zimbabwean *museve*, Jamaican reggae, or South African *kwaito*. Some of the more popular rap artists in Zimbabwe include pioneers Herbert Schwamborn (Herbert Qwela Schwamborn, 1973–) and Laygwan Sharkie (n.d.), who were both members of Harare-based rap crew A Peace of Ebony (n.d.).

Current popular rappers include Harare-based 25toLyf (2000–), which has members from Zimbabwe, Ghana, and Zambia and rap in English; Comrade Fatso (Samm Farai Monro, n.d.); and duo Divided Kingdom Republic (2005–), who now record in Shona and English from their home in London. Among breakdancers, the crew Crazy BOYZ Dance (2001–) became popular in Harare. Among diaspora rappers, American Mizchif (Hechichamunorwa Mount Zion Kwenda, 1976–2014) became internationally famous. With Mugabe being deposed in a coup d'état by the Zimbabwe National Army in 2017, the fate of hip hop as of early 2018 is uncertain, as no one knows if the new regime under Emmerson Dambudzo Mnangagwa (1942–, in office 2017–) will be more lenient or possibly more authoritarian.

Anthony J. Fonseca

See also: Breakdancing

Further Reading

Chari, Tendai. 2009. "Continuity and Change: Impact of Global Popular Culture on Urban Grooves Music in Zimbabwe." *Muziki: Journal of Music Research in Africa* 6, no. 2: 170–91.

Veit-Wild, Flora. 2009. "'Zimbolicious': The Creative Potential of Linguistic Innovation: The Case of Shona-English in Zimbabwe." *Journal of Southern African Studies* 35, no. 3: 683–97.

Appendix 1: Frequently Mentioned Hip Hop Artists

Arranged in alphabetical order by stage name, this list contains internationally known hip hop artists and includes alternative stage names or nicknames as well as year and place of birth. These artists are mentioned frequently in this book. An asterisk by a date, place, or name indicates that the information was unverifiable.

Aceyalone (Edwin Maximilian Hayes Jr., 1970–, Los Angeles, California)

Afrika Bambaataa (aka Afrika Bambaataa Aasim, Kevin Donovan, 1957–, Bronx, New York)

Akon (Aliaume Badara Thiam, 1973–, St. Louis, Missouri)

Allen, Harry (1964–, Brooklyn, New York)

Ant Banks (Anthony Banks, 1966–, Oakland, California)

Anwar, Joni (aka Joni Raptor, 1981–, Bangkok, Thailand)

Ashanthi (Ashanthi De Alwis, 1981*–, Colombo, Sri Lanka)

Ashanti (Ashanti Shequoiya Douglas, 1980–, Glen Cove, New York)

Asia One (Anonymous, 1971–, Denver, Colorado)

Awadi, Didier (aka DJ Awadi, Didier Sourou Awadi, 1969–, Dakar, Senegal)

Babyface (Kenneth Brian Edmonds, 1959–, Indianapolis, Indiana)

Bahamadia (Antonia Reed, 1976–, Philadelphia, Pennsylvania)

Banks, Azealia (1991–, New York City, New York)

Ben Sharpa (Kgotso Semela, 1979–, Johannesburg, South Africa)

Beyoncé (Beyoncé Giselle Knowles, 1981–, Houston, Texas)

Big Daddy Kane (Antonio Hardy, 1968–, Brooklyn, New York)

Big Pun (Christopher Lee Rios, 1971–2000, Bronx, New York)

Birdman (aka Baby, Bryan Williams, 1969–, New Orleans, Louisiana)

Blige, Mary J. (Mary Jane Blige, 1971–, Bronx, New York)

Briggs (Adam Briggs, 1986–, Shepparton, Victoria, Australia)

Brotha Lynch Hung (Kevin Danell Mann, 1969–, Sacramento, California)

Brothablack (Shannon Narrun Williams, 1978–, Sydney, Australia)

Bubba Sparxxx (Warren Anderson Mathis, 1977–, LaGrange, Georgia)

Bubbles (aka Hanifa, Hanifa McQueen-Hudson, 1969–, Wolverhampton, England)

Busta Rhymes (aka Busta Rhymez, Trevor Smith Jr., 1972–, Brooklyn, New York)

Campbell, Don (aka Campbellock, 1951–, St. Louis, Missouri)

Chance the Rapper (Chancelor Jonathan Bennett, 1993–, Chicago, Illinois)

Christie Z-Pabon (1969*–, Pennsylvania*)

Chuck D (Carlton Douglas Ridenhour, 1960–, Queens, New York)

C-Murder (Corey Miller, 1971–, New Orleans, Louisiana)

Common (aka Common Sense, Lonnie Rashid Lynn Jr., 1972–, Chicago, Illinois)

Coolio (Artis Leon Ivey Jr., 1963–, Compton, California)

Crazy Legs (Richard Colón, 1966–, Bronx, New York)

C-Real (Cyril-Alex Gockel, 1984–, Hohoe, Ghana)

Cut Chemist (Lucas MacFadden, 1972–, Los Angeles, California)

Da Brat (Shawntae Harris, 1974–, Chicago, Illinois)

Danger Mouse (Brian Joseph Burton, 1977–, White Plains, New York)

Davenport, N'Dea (1966–, Atlanta, Georgia)

Davey D (David Cook, n.d., n.p.)

Davy D (aka Davy DMX, David Reeves, 1960–, Beckley, West Virginia)

Day, Wendy (anonymous, 1962–)

DJ Babu (aka Babu, The Turntablist, Melvin Babu, Chris Oroc, 1974–, Washington, DC)

DJ Bobcat (aka Bobcat, Bobby Ervin, 1967–, Los Angeles, California)

DJ Jazzy Jeff (Jeffrey Allen Townes, 1965–, Philadelphia, Pennsylvania)

DJ QBert (Richard Quitevis, 1969–, San Francisco, California)

DJ Rap (formerly Ambience, Charissa Saverio, 1969–, Singapore)

DJ Shadow (Joshua Paul Davis, 1972–, San Jose, California)

DJ Spinderella (Deidra Muriel Roper, 1971–, Brooklyn, New York)

DJ Vadim (aka Daddy Vad, Andre Gurov, One Self, Vadim Alexsandrovich Peare, Leningrad, U.S.S.R., now Saint Petersburg, Russia, n.d.)

DMX (Earl Simmons, 1970–, Mount Vernon, New York)

Doug E. Fresh (Douglas E. Davis, 1966–, Christ Church, Barbados)

Dr. Dre (Andre Romelle Young, 1965–, Compton, California)

Drake (Aubrey Drake Graham, 1986–, Toronto, Canada* [possibly Memphis, Tennessee])

Eazy-E (Eric Lynn Wright, 1963–1995, Compton, California)

Eedris Abdulkareem (Eedris Turayo Abdulkareem Ajenifuja, 1974–, Kano, Nigeria)

EL (aka E.L., LOMI, Elom Adablah, 1986–, Accra, Ghana)

ELDee (aka eLDee the Don, Lanre Dabiri, 1977–, Kaduna, Nigeria)

Elliott, Missy (aka Misdemeanor, Melissa Arnette Elliott, 1971–, Portsmouth, Virginia)

Eminem (Marshall Bruce Mathers III, 1972–, St. Joseph, Missouri)

Enow, Stanley (aka Bayangi Boy, 1986–, Bamenda, Cameroon)

Erykah Badu (Erica Abi Wright, 1971–, Dallas, Texas)

Estelle (Estelle Fanta Swaray, 1980–, London, England)

Fab Five Freddy (aka Fab 5 Freddy, Fred Brathwaite, 1959–, Brooklyn, New York)

50 Cent (Curtis James Jackson III, 1975–, Queens, New York)

Flavor Flav (aka Flav, William Jonathan Drayton Jr., 1959–, Long Island, New York)

Franti, Michael (1966–, Oakland, California)

Frosty Freeze (aka The Freeze to Please, Mr. Freeze, Wayne Frost, 1963–2008, Bronx, New York)

Grandmaster Flash (Joseph Saddler, 1958–, Bridgetown, Barbados)

GrandWizard Theodore (aka Grand Wizzard Theodore, Theodore Livingston, 1963–, Bronx, New York)

Hancock, Herbie (Herbert Jeffrey Hancock, 1940–, Chicago, Illinois)

Heap, Imogen (Imogen Jennifer Heap, 1977–, London, England)

Hill, Lauryn (Lauryn Noelle Hill, 1975–, South Orange, New Jersey)

Hip Hop Pantsula (aka HHP, Jabba, Jabulani Tsambo, 1980–, Mafikeng, now Mahikeng, South Africa)

Ice Cube (O'Shea Jackson, 1969–, Los Angeles, California)

Ice Prince (Panshak Henry Zamani, 1986–, Minna, Nigeria)

Ice-T (Tracy Lauren Marrow, 1958–, Newark, New Jersey)

Iggy Azalea (Amethyst Amelia Kelly, 1990–, Sydney Australia)

Ivy Queen (Martha Ivelisse Pesante Rodríguez, 1972–, Añasco, Puerto Rico)

J Dilla (aka Jay Dee, James Dewitt Yancey, 1974–2006, Detroit, Michigan)

Jam Master Jay (Jason Mizell, 1965–2002, Brooklyn, New York)

Jay-P (Paul Omiria Epeju, 1987–, Kampala, Uganda)

Jay-Z (Shawn Corey Carter, 1969–, Brooklyn, New York)

Jean Grae (Tsidi Ibrahim, 1976–, Cape Town, South Africa)

Jesse Jagz (aka Jago, Jesse Garba Abaga, 1984–, Jos, Nigeria)

Jones, Quincy (aka Q, Quincy Delight Jones Jr., 1933–, Chicago, Illinois)

Keko (Jocelyne Tracey Keko, 1987–, Tororo, Uganda)

Ken Swift (Kenneth Gabbert, 1966–, New York City, New York)

Kendrick Lamar (Kendrick Lamar Duckworth, 1987–, Compton, California)

K'Naan (Keinan Abdi Warsame, Keynaan Cabdi Warsame, 1978–, Mogadishu, Somalia)

Kool Herc (aka Kool DJ Herc, DJ Kool Herc, Clive Campbell, 1955–, Kingston, Jamaica)

Kool Moe Dee (Mohandes Dewese, 1963–, Harlem, New York)

KRS-One (aka KRS, Blastmaster KRS-One, Teacha, Lawrence Parker, 1965–, Bronx, New York)

Kurtis Blow (Kurt Walker, 1959–, Harlem, New York)

Lil' Kim (Kimberly Denise Jones, 1975–, Brooklyn, New York)

Lil Wayne (Dwayne Michael Carter Jr., 1982–, New Orleans, Louisiana)

LL Cool J (James Todd Smith, 1968–, Bay Shore, New York)

Ludacris (Christopher Brian Bridges, 1977–, Champaign, Illinois)

Luke (aka Luke Skyywalker, Luther Roderick Campbell, 1960–, Miami, Florida)

Marley Marl (Marlon Lu'ree Williams, 1962–, Queens, New York)

Master P (Percy Robert Miller, 1970–, New Orleans, Louisiana)

mc chris (Christopher Brendan Ward IV, 1975–, Libertyville, Illinois)

MC Frontalot (Damian Hess, 1973–, San Francisco, California)

MC Hammer (Stanley Kirk Burrell, 1962–, Oakland, California)

MC Lars (Andrew Robert Nielsen, 1982–, Berkeley, California)

MC Lyte (Lana Michele Moorer, 1971–, Queens, New York)

MC Opi (Janette Oparebea Nelson, 1971–, London, England)

MC Solaar (Claude M'Barali, 1969–, Dakar, Senegal)

Melle Mel (aka Mele Mel, Grandmaster Melle Mel, Melvin Glover, 1961–, Bronx, New York)

M.I. (Jude Abaga, 1981–, Jos, Nigeria)

M.I.A. (aka Maya, Mathangi Arulpragasam, 1975–, London, England)

Mix Master Mike (Michael Schwartz, 1970–, San Francisco, California)

Molekame, Tumi (aka MC Fatboy, Tumi, Stogie T, Boitumelo Molekane, 1981–, Tanzania)

Mos Def (aka Yasiin Bey, Dante Terrell Smith, 1973–, Brooklyn, New York)

Mr. B The Gentleman Rhymer (James Burke, 1970–, London, England)

Mr. Len (Leonard Smythe, 1975–, Bronx, New York)

Naeto C (Naetochukwu Chikwe, 1982–, Houston, Texas)

Nas (aka Nasty Nas, Nasir Ben Olu Dara Jones, 1973–, Brooklyn, New York)

Nicki Minaj (Onika Tanya Maraj, 1982–, Port of Spain, Trinidad and Tobago)

9th Wonder (aka 9thmatic, Patrick Denard Douthit, 1975–, Winston Salem, North Carolina)

The Notorious B.I.G. (aka Biggie Smalls, Christopher George Latore Wallace, 1972–1997)

Panjabi MC (Rajinder Singh Rai, 1973–, Coventry, England)

Pharrell (Pharrell Lanscilo Williams, 1973–, Virginia Beach, Virginia)

Pitbull (Armando Christian Pérez, 1981–, Miami, Florida)

Pop'in Pete (Timothy Earl Solomon, 1961–, Fresno, California)

Popmaster Fabel (Jorge Pabon, 1965*–, Harlem, New York)

Professor Elemental (Paul Alborough, 1975–, Norwich, England)

Professor Jay (formerly N—a J, Joseph Haule, 1975–, Songea, Tanzania)

PSY (Park Jae-sang, 1977–, Seoul, Korea)

Puff Daddy (aka P. Diddy, Love, Brother Love, Sean John Combs, 1969–, New York City, New York)

Queen Latifah (Dana Elaine Owens, 1970–, Newark, New Jersey)

Queen Pen (Lynise Walters, 1972–, Brooklyn, New York)

Rihanna (Robyn Rihanna Fenty, 1988–, Saint Michael, Barbados)

Rob Swift (Robert Aguilar, 1972–, Queens, New York)

Robinson, Sylvia (Sylvia Vanderpool, 1936–2011, New York City, New York)

Roc Raida (aka Grandmaster Roc Raida, Anthony Williams, 1972–2009, New York City, New York)

Rokafella (Ana García, 1971–, New York City, New York)

Roxanne Shanté (Lolita Shanté Gooden, 1969–, Long Island, New York)

Sarkodie (Michael Owusu Addo, 1985–, Tema, Ghana)

Scott, Jill (1972–, Philadelphia, Pennsylvania)

Scott-Heron, Gil (Gilbert Scott-Heron, 1949–2011, Chicago, Illinois)

Shaggy (Orville Richard Burrell, 1968–, Kingston, Jamaica)

Slick Rick (aka Rick the Ruler, MC Ricky D, Richard Martin Lloyd Walters, 1965–, London, England)

Smith, Will (Willard Carroll Smith Jr., 1968–, Philadelphia, Pennsylvania)

Snoop Dogg (aka Snoop Lion, Snoop Doggy Dogg, Calvin Cordozar Broadus Jr., 1971–, Long Beach, California)

Spoonie Gee (aka The Love Rapper, Gabriel Jackson, 1963–, Harlem, New York)

Suge Knight (Marion Hugh Knight Jr., 1965–, Compton, California)

Sway (Derek Andrew Safo, 1982–, London, England)

Swizz Beatz (Kasseem Dean, 1978–, Bronx, New York)

Talib Kweli (Talib Kweli Greene, 1975–, Brooklyn, New York)

Tech N9ne (Aaron Dontez Yates, 1971–, Kansas City, Missouri)

Tijoux, Ana (Ana María Merino Tijoux, 1977–, Lille, France)

Timbaland (Timothy Zachery Mosley, 1972–, Norfolk, Virginia)

Tuks Senganga (aka Tuks, Tumelo Kapadisa, 1981–, Mafikeng, South Africa)

Tupac Shakur (aka Tupac, 2Pac, Lesane Parish Crooks, 1971–1996)

West, Kanye (Kanye Omari West, 1977–, Atlanta, Georgia)

will.i.am (William James Adams, 1975–, Los Angeles, California)

Wiz Khalifa (Cameron Jibril Thomaz, 1987–, Minot, North Dakota)

Zeus (Game Goabaone Bantsi, 1986–, Serowe, Botswana)

Appendix 2: The 100 Most Influential Global Hip Hop Record Labels

This is a selective list of recording labels that specialize in hip hop, produce a large number of hip hop albums, and/or lead the initiative for producing hip hop in a country (giving the label a historical significance). This list includes year(s) of operation and location(s).

Aftermath Entertainment (1996–, Santa Monica, California)

Akwaaba Music (2008–, Accra, Ghana)

Alerce (1976–, Santiago, Chile)

American Recordings (1988–, Los Angeles, California)

Asere Records (2002–, Havana, Cuba)

Asphodel (1992–, San Francisco, California)

Asylum Down (2012–, Accra, Ghana)

Babygrande Records (2001–, New York City, New York)

Bad Boy Entertainment (1993–, New York City, New York)

Bassivity Music (2005–, Belgrade, Serbia)

B-Boy Records (1986–, Bronx, New York)

Blacksmith Records (2005–2012, New York City, New York)

Boogie Down Productions (BDP, 1985–1992, South Bronx, New York)

Bossalinie Records (2000–, New Orleans, Louisiana)

Calif Records (2000–, Nairobi, Kenya)

Capitol Records (1942–, Los Angeles, California; see Redline Records)

Ca$h Money Records (1991–, New Orleans, Louisiana, and Miami, Florida)

CashTime Life (2010–, Johannesburg, South Africa)

The Chap-Hop Business Concern (2012–, London*, England)

Chocolate City (2005–, Lagos and Abuja, Nigeria)

Chrysalis Records (1969–, London, England)

Cobiana Records (2001–, Washington, DC)

Cold Chillin' Records (aka Prism Records, 1986–1998, New York City, New York)

The Conglomerate (aka Flipmode Entertainment, 1994–2011, 2011–, Brooklyn, New York)

Death Row Records (1991–2008, Los Angeles, California)

Def Jam Recordings (1983–, Queens, New York)

Def Jam South (1999–, New York City, New York)

Definitive Jux Music (1997–, New York City, New York)

Delicious Vinyl (1987–, Los Angeles, California)

Disturbing tha Peace (DTP, 2000–, Atlanta, Georgia)

Duck Down Music (1995–, New York City, New York)

Elefant Traks (1998–, Sydney, Australia)

Face II Face Records (1993*–, Houston, Texas)

Ghetto Ruff (aka Ku Shu Records, 1991–, Johannesburg, South Africa)

Golden Era Records (2008*–, Stirling, Australia)

The Goldmind, Inc. (1997–, New York City, New York)

Grand Hustle Records (aka Grand Hustle Entertainment, 2002–, Atlanta, Georgia)

G-Unit Records (2003–, Santa Monica, California; see Interscope Records)

Huh! Records (1995–, Auckland, New Zealand)

The Inc. Records (aka Murder Inc. Records, 1999–2012, New York City, New York)

Interscope Records (aka Interscope Geffen, 1989–, Santa Monica, California; see G-Unit Records)

Island Records (1959–, Kingston, Jamaica; now headquartered in London, England)

Jive Records (1981–, New York City, New York)

Jugoton (1947–, Zagreb, Croatia)

Karaļūdens (2013–, Riga, Latvia)

Kennis Music (1998–, Lagos, Nigeria)

Knirckefritt (2011*–, Oslo, Norway)

Koch Records (aka Entertainment One Music, 1987–2009, Port Washington, New York)

Komuna (1985–, Belgrade, Serbia)

LaFace Records (1989–2001, Atlanta, Georgia)

Loud Records (1991–2012, New York City, New York)

Luke Records (1990–, Miami, Florida)

Machete Music (2005–, San Juan, Puerto Rico; see Universal Music Group)

Mapane Records (1998–2006, Yaoundé, Cameroon)

Matador (1989–, New York City, New York)

Menart Records (1994–, Ljubljana, Slovenia)

Mo' Wax (1992–, London, England)

Motherland Empire (2013*–, Douala, Cameroon)

New No Limit (2001–, Los Angeles, California; see No Limit Forever and No Limit Records)

Nika (1990–, Ljubljana, Slovenia)

Ninja Tune (1990–, London, England)

No Limit Forever (2010–, Los Angeles, California; see New No Limit and No Limit Records)

No Limit Records (1990–2003, New Orleans, Louisiana; was headquartered in Richmond, California; see New No Limit and No Limit Forever)

Obese Records (1995–2007, Melbourne, Australia)

Pandisc Music Corporation (1981–, Miami, Florida)

Paradise Records (2000–, Freetown, Sierra Leone)

Priority Records (1985–, Los Angeles, California)

Profile Records (1980–, New York City, New York)

Rähinä Records (2003–, Helsinki, Finland)

Rap-A-Lot Records (1986–, Houston, Texas)

Rawkus Records (1995–2001, New York City, New York)

Redline Records (2000–, Stockholm, Sweden; see Capitol Records and Virgin EMI Records)

Renegades of Bump (2010–, Vilnius, Lithuania)

Roc-A-Fella Records (1996–2013, New York City, New York)

Ruff Ryders Entertainment (1988–2010, Yonkers, New York; see Ruff Ryders Indy)

Ruff Ryders Indy (2010– New York City, New York; see Ruff Ryders Entertainment)

Ruthless Records (1987–2010*, Compton, California)

Selfmade Records (2005–, Düsseldorf, Germany)

Shady Records (1999–, New York City, New York)

Shanachie (1976–, Newton, New Jersey)

Skillions Records (2008–, Accra, Ghana)

So Def Recordings (1993–, Atlanta, Georgia)

Spring Records (1967–1990*, New York City, New York)

Sugarhill Records (1979–1985, Englewood, New Jersey)

Talkin' Loud (1990–, London, England)

Tee Productions (1995–, Oslo, Norway)

Telegram Records Stockholm (1987–2006, Stockholm, Sweden; see Warner Bros. Records)

Today Is Vintage (2012–, Malmö, Sweden)

Tommy Boy Entertainment (aka Tommy Boy Records, 1981–, New York City, New York)

Universal Music Group (aka UMG, 1996–, London, England; now headquartered in Santa Monica, California; see Machete Music, Universal Music Records, and Virgin EMI Records)

Universal Music Records (1934–1996, Santa Monica, California; see Universal Music Group)

Univision Records (2001–2008, Woodland Hills, California)

Uptown Records (1986–1999, Harlem, New York)

Urban Pacifika Records (1993–, Auckland, New Zealand)

Virgin EMI Records (aka EMI, 1931–, London, England; see Universal Music Group)

Volition (1984–2000s*, Sydney, Australia)

Warner Bros. Records (aka WEA and Warner Music Group, 1958–, New York City; was also headquartered in Hollywood, California; now headquartered in Burbank, California; see Telegram Records Stockholm)

Wrasse Records (1998–2005, London, England)

XL Recordings (1989–, London, England)

Young Money Entertainment (2005–, New Orleans, Louisiana)

Zomloa Records (aka Zomba Music Group, 1975–, Yaoundé, Cameroon)

Appendix 3: Editor-Recommended Top Hip Hop Music Videos Worldwide

Arranged by country of production and sometimes by artist's origin, this list uses a global focus on hip hop videos produced. Also included are the names of the artists, the songs, and the albums on which the songs were released and each album's release year.

Algeria: Intik, "Soldat" ("Soldier"), released as a single (2009)

Australia: Hilltop Hoods, featuring Montaigne and Tom Thum, "1955," *Drinking from the Sun, Walking under Stars Restrung* (2016); 1200 Techniques, "Karma," *Choose One* (2002)

Australia and United States: Bliss n' Eso, featuring Nas, "I Am Somebody," *Circus in the Sky* (2013)

Austria: Texta, "Die dramaturgie der ereigniße" ("The Dramaturgy of the Events"), *Grotesk* (2011)

Belgium: Benny B, "Vous êtes fous!" ("You're All Crazy"), *L'Album* (1990)

Botswana and South Africa: Cashless Society, "Hottentot Hop (Bantu 1, 2)," *African Raw Material, Vol. 1* (2003)

Brazil: Racionais MC's, "Diário de um detento" ("Diary of a Detainee"), *Sobrevivendo no inferno* (*Surviving in Hell*, 1997)

Burkina Faso: Smockey, "Insoumission" ("Disobedience"), *Pre'volution: Le président, ma moto et moi* (*Pre'volution: The President, My Motorcycle, and Me*, 2015); Tim Winsey, "Zèssa," *Zèssa* (2004)

Cameroon: Stanley Enow, "Hein pére" ("Hey/All right, Father"), *Soldier Like Ma Papa* (2015)

Canada: Drake, "Marvin's Room," *Take Care* (2011); K'Naan, "Take a Minute," *Troubadour* (2009)

Canada and Cambodia: Honey Cocaine, "Hella Illy," *Like a Drug* (2014)

Canada and United Kingdom: DJ A.P.S., "Tabba," *Bobby Friction & Nihal Present . . .* (2004)

China and United States: MC Jin, "Learn Chinese," *The Rest Is History* (2003)

Czech Republic: Gipsy.cz, "Žigulik," *Upgrade* (2013)

Denmark: Malk de Koijn, "Braget" ("Crash"), *Toback to the Fromtime* (2011); Outlandish, "Warrior // Worrier," *Warrior // Worrier* (2012)

Dominican Republic: La Materialista, "La chapa que vibran" (loosely, "The A—That Shakes"), *Trayectoria* (*Trajectory*, 2015)

Ecuador: Mateo Kingman, "Sendero del monte" ("Mountain Trial") and "Lluvia" ("Rain"), *Respira* (*Breathe*, 2016)

France: Ana Tijoux, "1977," *1977* (2009), and, featuring Shadia Mansour, "Somos Sur" ("We Are the South"), *Vengo* (*I Come*, 2014)

France and South Africa: Chinese Man, featuring Tumi Molekane, "Once upon a Time," *The Groove Sessions, Vol. 3* (2014)

Germany: Peter Fox, featuring the Cold Steel Drumline, "Alles neu" ("Everything Is New"), *Stadtaffe* (*City Monkey*, 2008); XAVAS, "Schau nicht mehr zurück" ("I Don't Look Back Anymore"), *Gespaltene persönlichkeit* (*Split Personality*, 2012)

Greece: Imiskoúmbria (aka Imiz or The Semi Sardines), "To Voukolikó" ("The Duchess"), *Ta imiskoúmbria* (*The Hemisphere*, 1996)

Guatemala: Kool Savas, "Aura," *Aura* (2011); Rebeca Lane, "Reina del caos" ("Queen of Chaos"), released as a single (2017)

Iceland: Quarashi, "Bassline," *Jinx* (2001), and "Chicago," released as a single (2016); Reykjavíkurdætur (Daughters of Reykjavik), "Ógeðsleg" ("Disgusting"), *RVK DTR* (2016); Úlfur Úlfur, featuring Kött Grá Pje (Gray Cat), "Brennum allt" ("Burn Everything"), *Tvær plánetur* (*Two Planets*, 2015)

India: Sofia Ashraf, "Kodaikanal Won't," released as a single (2015)

Indonesia: Batik Tribe, "Indo Yo . . . Ey," *Melangkah* (*Stepping*, 2008)

Iran: Salome MC, "Drunk Shah, Drunk Elder," *I Officially Exist* (2013)

Ireland: The Rubberbandits, "I Want to Fight Your Father," released as a single (2011), and as "Ba mhaith liom bruîon le d'athair" ("I Want to Fight Your Father"), released as a single (2015); Rusangano Family, "Soul Food," *Let the Dead Bury the Dead* (2016)

Italy: Emis Killa, "Cult," *Terza stagione* (*Third Season*, 2016)

Latvia: Reinis Kapone, featuring ansis, "Gotham," *Katafalks* (*Hearse*, 2017)

Lithuania: G&G Sindikatas, "Tiems, kas raso" ("For Those Who Are Deaf"), *Išvien* (*United*, 2008)

Mali: Mokobé Traore, "Mali Forever," *Mon Afrique* (2007)

Mexico: Control Machete, "Si Señor," *Artilleria pesada, presenta . . .* (*Heavy Artillery, Presents . . .* , 1999); Mare Advertencia Lirika, "Bienvenidx," *Siempre viva* (*Immortal*, 2016)

New Zealand: Moana and the Tribe, "Whole World's Watching," *Rima* (2014); Otara Millionaires Club, "How Bizarre," *How Bizarre* (1995); Sisters Underground, "In the Neighbourhood," *Proud: An Urban-Pacific Streetsoul Compilation* (1994)

Nigeria: Ice Prince, "Aboki" ("Friend"), *Fire of Zamani* (*Fire of the Past*, 2013); Iyanya, "Kukere" ("Don't Worry"), *Desire* (2013); Jesse Jagz, "Redemption," *Jagz Nation, Vol. 1: Thy Nation Come* (2013), and "Murder Dem," released as a single (2013)

Poland: Donatan and Cleo, "Brać" ("Take" or "Assume," among other possible translations), *Hiper Chimera* (2014)

Puerto Rico: Ivy Queen, "Vendetta," *Vendetta: The Project* (2015)

Senegal: Didier Awadi, "Ma révolution," *Ma révolution* (*My Revolution*, 2011); Daara J Family, "Tomorrow," *School of Life* (2010)

South Africa: Die Antwoord, "Fatty Boom Boom" and "I Fink U Freeky," *Ten$ion* (2012); Hip Hop Pantsula, "Mpitse" ("Miss Me"), *Dumela* (*Believe*, 2009); Tuks Senganga, featuring Thembisile, "Ticket to Jozi," *MC Prayer* (2006)

South Korea: PSY, "Gangnam Style," *Psy 6 (Six Rules)* (2012); Tymee, "Cinderella," released as a single (2016)

Tanzania: Professor Jay, "Ndio mzee" ("Yes, Sir"), *Machozi jasho na damu* (*Tears of Sweat and Blood*, 2001)

Turkey and Germany: Eko Fresh, "Köln Kalk ehrenmord" ("Cologne Kalk Honor Killing"), *Ekrem* (2011)

Uganda: Keko, featuring Madtraxx, "Make You Dance," released as a single (2012)

Ukraine: Tanok na Maidani Kongo (TNMK, "Dance in Congo Square"), "Fidel," *Dzerkalo* (*The Mirror*, 2014)

United Kingdom: Dizzee Rascal, "I Don't Need a Reason," *The Fifth* (2013), and "Space," *Raskit* (2017); M.I.A., "Paper Planes," *Kala* (2007); Mr. B The Gentleman Rhymer, "Chap Hop History," *Flattery Not Included* (2008); Panjabi Hit Squad, featuring Ms Scandalous, "Hai Hai," *The Streets* (2002); Professor Elemental, "Fighting Trousers," *The Indifference Engine* (2010)

United Kingdom and United States: Panjabi MC, featuring Jay-Z, "Mundian to bach ke" ("Beware of the Boy," Jay-Z remix), *Beware* (2003)

United States: Azealia Banks, "212," *1991* (2012) and *Broke with Expensive Taste* (2014); Beastie Boys, "Sabotage," *Ill Communication* (1994); Chance the Rapper, "Same Drugs," *Coloring Book* (2016); Childish Gambino, "This Is America," released as a single (2018); C-Murder, "Down 4 My Ns," *Trapped in Crime* (2000); Cypress Hill, "Insane in the Brain," *Black Sunday* (1993); D12, "My Band," *D12 World* (2004), and "Purple Hills" ("Purple Pills"), *Devil's Night* (2001); Missy Elliott, "Work It," *Under Construction* (2002), and, featuring Pharrell, "WTF (Where They From)," released as a single (2015); Geto Boys, "My Mind Playing Tricks on Me," *We Can't Be Stopped* (1991); Herbie Hancock, "Rockit," *Future Shock* (1983); Talib Kweli, "Violations," *Gravitas* (2014), and "Listen!!!," *Eardrum* (2007); Joyner Lucas, "I'm Sorry," *508–507–2209* (2017), and "I'm Not Racist," released as a single (2017); N.W.A., "F— tha Police," *Straight Outta Compton* (1988); OutKast, "B.O.B." ("Bombs over Baghdad"), *Stankonia* (2000); Poor Righteous Teachers, "Easy Star," *Pure Poverty* (1991); Public Enemy, "Fight the Power," *Fear of a Black Planet*

(1990); Gil Scott-Heron, "The Revolution Will Not Be Televised," *The Revolution Will Not Be Televised* (1974); Tupac Shakur (as 2Pac), "So Many Tears," *Me against the World* (1995); The Welfare Poets, "Warn Them," *Warn Them* (2009); Kanye West, featuring Chosan, "Diamonds from Sierra Leone," *Late Registration* (2005)

United States and Barbados: Nicki Minaj, "Pound the Alarm," *Roman Reloaded* (2012)

Zambia: Zone Fam, "Contola" ("Take Control" in Nyanja), released as a single (2012)

Appendix 4: Hip Hop Films and Documentaries

This appendix lists feature and documentary films that focus on hip hop as main subject matter or as backdrop as well as films that were important to the development or perception of hip hop. Feature films are narrative films such as dramas, comedies, thrillers, biopics, and musicals that are over 45 minutes in length. Excluded are film shorts and precursors such as *Foxy Brown* (1974, United States) and *Scarface* (1983, United States). Because they contain fictional narratives, mockumentaries are listed under "Feature Films." Documentaries have a nonfictional narrative. Though intended to list film titles beyond the scope of the entries, this appendix is by no means exhaustive; many made-for-television and DVD films, including sequels, have been excluded.

FEATURE FILMS

Above the Rim (1994, United States)

Ali G Indahouse (2002, United Kingdom)

All Eyez on Me (2017, United States)

Anuvahood (2011, United Kingdom)

Baller Blockin' (2000, United States)

Bamboozled (2000, United States)

Banlieue 13 (*District B13*, aka *B-13*, 2004, France)

Beat Street (1984, United States)

Bodied (2017, United States)

Body Language (2011, Netherlands)

Bomb the System (2002, United States)

Born to Dance (2015, New Zealand)

Boyz n the Hood (1991, United States)

Breakin' and *Breakin' 2: Electric Boogaloo* (1984, United States)

Brooklyn Babylon (2001, United States and France)

The Bros. (2007, United States)

Brown Sugar (2002, United States)

Carmen: A Hip Hopera (2001, United States)

CB4 (1993, United States)

Ching fung dik sau (*Mismatched Couples*, 1985, Hong Kong)

Colors (1988, United States)

Cool as Ice (1991, United States)

Coz ov Moni: The First Pidgin Musical Film in the World and *Coz ov Moni 2 (FOKN Revenge)* (2010 and 2013, Ghana)

Da Hip Hop Witch (2000, United States)

Dance Flick (2009, United States)

Dead Presidents (1995, United States)

Death of a Dynasty (2003, United States)

Do the Right Thing (1989, United States)

Don't Be a Menace to South Central While Drinking Your Juice in the Hood (1996, United States)

8 Mile (2002, United States)

Fear of a Black Hat (1993, United States and United Kingdom)

Feel the Noise (2007, United States)

Flashdance (1983, United States)

Fly by Night (1992, United States)

G (2002, United States)

Gang Related (1997, United States)

Get Rich or Die Tryin' (2005, United States)

Girls Town (1996, United States)

Honey (2003, United States)

'Hood (1998, Japan)

The Horrible Dr. Bones (2000, United States)

House Party (1990, United States)

Hustle and Flow (2005, United States)

Identity Crisis (1989, United States)

Idlewild (2006, United States)

Ill Manors (2012, United Kingdom)

Juice (1992, United States)

Junction 48 (2016, Israel)

Kadhalan (1994, India)

Kidulthood, *Adulthood*, and *Brotherhood* (2006, 2008, and 2016, United Kingdom)

Knights of the City (originally *Cry of the City*, 1986, United States)

Krush Groove (1985, United States)

Lean on Me (1989, United States)

Malibu's Most Wanted (2003, United States)

Marci X (2003, United States)

Meesaya murukku (*Twirl Your Moustache*, 2017, India)

Menace II Society (1993, United States)

Morris from America (2016, United States and Germany)

New Jack City (1991, United States)

Notorious (2009, United States)

1 More Hit (2007, United States)

Out Kold (2001, United States)

Paper Soldiers (2002, United States)

Patti Cake$ (2017, United States)

Phat Beach (1996, United States)

π (aka *Pi*, 1998, United States)

Province 77 (2002, United States and Thailand)

Qu'Allah bénisse la France! (*May Allah Bless France!*, 2014, France)

Rappin' (1985, United States)

Rome and Jewel (2006, United States)

Sài gòn yo! (*Saigon Electric!*, 2011, Vietnam)

Save the Last Dance (2005, United States)

Shockumentary (1997, United States)

Slam (1998, United States)

Snipes (2002, United States)

Step Off (originally *Battle*, 2011, United States)

Stockholmsnatt (*Stockholm Night*, aka *The King of Kungsan*, 1987, Sweden)

Stomp the Yard (2007, United States)

Straight out of Brooklyn (1991, United States)

Straight Outta Compton (2015, United States)

Tales from the Hood (1995, United States)

Thicker Than Water (1999, United States)

Tokyo Tribe (2014, Japan)

Tougher Than Leather (1988, United States)

Tyttö sinä olet tähti (*Beauty and the Bastard*, 2005, Finland)

The Warriors (1979, United States)

Wave Twisters (2001, United States)

Whiteboyz (1999, France and United States)

Wild Style (1983, United States)

You Got Served and *You Got Served: Beat the World* (2004 and 2011, United States)

Zebrahead (1992, United States)

Zeiten ändern dich (*Times Change You*, 2010, Germany)

DOCUMENTARIES

African Underground: Democracy in Dakar (2007, United States and Senegal)

Alternative Freedom (2006, United States)

And You Don't Stop: 30 Years of Hip Hop (2004, United States)

Arotzim shel za'am (*Channels of Rage*, 2003, Israel)

Asia One: Expect the Unexpected (2013, United States)

Backstage (2000, United States)

Bad Rap (2016, United States)

Basic Equipment (1998, Australia)

Beat This: A Hip Hop History (1984, United States)

Beatboxing: The Fifth Element of Hip Hop (2011, United States)

Beats, Rhymes, and Life: The Travels of A Tribe Called Quest (2011, United States)

Beef, Beef II, Beef III, and *Beef IV* (2003, 2004, 2005, and 2007, United States)

Big Fun in the Big Town (1986, Netherlands)

Big Pun: Still Not a Player (2002, United States)

Biggie and Tupac (2002, United Kingdom)

Biggie Smalls: Rap Phenomenon (2009, United Kingdom)

Black Tape (2015, Germany)

Bomb It and *Bomb It 2* (2007 and 2010, United States)

Bouncing Cats (2010, United States)

Breath Control: The History of the Human Beat Box (2002, United States)

Buenos Aires Rap (2014, Argentina)

Built to Scratch (2004, United States)

The Carter (2009, United States)

Copyright Criminals (2009, United States)

Counting Headz: South Afrika Sistaz in Hip Hop (2007, South Africa)

Dave Chappelle's Block Party (2006, United States)

Diamonds in the Rough: A Ugandan Hip Hop Revolution (2007, Uganda)

Downtown 81 (formerly *New York Beat*, filmed in 1980, released in 2000, United States)

Electro Rock (1985, United Kingdom)

Exit through the Gift Shop (2010, United Kingdom)

A Family Underground (2009, United States)

Freestyle: The Art of Rhyme (2000, United States)

Fresh Dressed (2015, United States)

The Freshest Kids: A History of the B-Boy (2002, United States)

Girl Power (2016, Czech Republic)

Good Copy, Bad Copy (2007, Denmark)

The Great Hip Hop Hoax (2013, United Kingdom)

Hali halisi (*The Real Situation*, 1999, Netherlands and Tanzania)

Hamilius: Hip Hop Culture in Luxembourg (2010, Luxembourg)

Hang the DJ (1998, Canada)

The Heart of Krump (2005, United States)

Hip Hop Colony (2006, Kenya)

Hip Hop: Beyond Beats and Rhymes (2006, United States)

Hip Hop Evolution (2016, Canada)

The Hip Hop Fellow (2012, United States)

Hip Hop Kabul (2013, Afghanistan)

The Hip Hop Project (2006, United States)

Hip Hop Revolution (2007, South Africa)

Hip Hop-eration (2014, New Zealand)

History and Concept of Hip Hop Dance (2010, United States)

Hustler's Convention (2015, United States)

I Am Hip Hop: The Chicago Hip Hop Documentary (2008, United States)

I Love Hip Hop in Morocco (2007, United States and Morocco)

Infamy (2005, United States)

Jails, Hospitals, and Hip Hop (2000, United States)

Jay-Z: Fade to Black (2004, United States)

Just for Kicks (2005, United States)

Kroonjuwelen: Hard Times, Good Times, Better Times (*Crown Jewels*, 2006, Netherlands)

Letter to the President (2005, United States)

Living the Hiplife (2007, Ghana)

Moi c'est moi—Ich bin ich (*I Am I*, 2011, Switzerland)

Money, Power, Respect: Hip Hop Billion Dollar Industry (2012, United States)

Mongolian Bling (2012, Mongolia and Australia)

Mr. Devious: My Life (2007, South Africa)

Nas: Time Is "Illmatic" (2014, United States)

Nerdcore for Life (2008, United States)

Nerdcore Rising (2008, United States)

Ni Wakati! (*It's Time!*, 2010, Tanzania and Kenya)

Notorious B.I.G.: Bigger Than Life (2007, United States)

Our Vinyl Weighs a Ton: This Is Stones Throw Records (2013, United States and France)

Overspray 1.0 (2006, United States)

Planet B-Boy (2007, United States)

Public Enemy: It Takes a Nation: The First London Invasion Tour 1987 (2005, United States)

Rap Sheet: Hip Hop and the Cops (2006, United States)

Redder Than Red (2005, England, Germany, and United States)

Rhyme and Punishment (2011, United States)

Rhyme and Reason (1997, United States)

Right On! Poetry on Film (1971, United States)

Rize (2005, United States)

Rock the Bells (2006, United States)

Ruthless Memories: Preserving the Life and Legend of Eric (Eazy-E) Wright (2012, United States)

Sample This (2012, United States)

Sarabah (2012, Senegal)

Scratch (2001, United States)

Shake the Dust (2014, United States)

The Show (1995, United States)

Slingshot Hip Hop (2008, United States and Palestine)

Solidarity (1992, New Zealand)

Something from Nothing: The Art of Rap (2012, United Kingdom)

Sonita (2015, Switzerland)

Stations of the Elevated (1981, released in 2000, United States)

Style Wars and *Style Wars 2* (1983 and 2013, United States)

This Is the Life (2008, United States)

Tupac: Resurrection (2003, United States)

Tupac Shakur: Before I Wake (2001, United States)

Tupac Shakur: Thug Angel (2002, United States)

Turn It Loose! (2009, United Kingdom)

2 Turntables and a Microphone: The Life and Death of Jam Master Jay (2008, United States)

Underground Hip Hop in China (2011, China and United States)

United States of Africa: Beyond Hip Hop (2011, Burkina Faso, Senegal, South Africa, and United States)

Uprising: Hip Hop and the L.A. Riots (2012, United States)

Welcome to Death Row (2001, United States)

What Ever Happened to Hip Hop? (2009, United States)

Will einmal bis zur sonne (*I Want to Go to the Sun*, 2002, Germany)

The Wonder Year (2011, United States)

Wreckin' Shop from Brooklyn (1992, United States)

Wu: The Story of the Wu-Tang Clan (2007, United States)

Wu-Tang Clan: Disciples of the 36 Chambers, Chapter 2 (2004, United States)

Zim Hip Hop Documentary (2013, Zimbabwe)

Appendix 5: Countries with Severely Restricted Underground Activity

This list includes countries that as of 2018 have governments that severely restrict hip hop activity to the extent that underground performance is forbidden, censored, and/or punished. Hostility from the government leads to banning or censorship and may be accompanied by rappers' being threatened with lawsuits, detention, imprisonment, torture, exile or banishment, and/or death. Nearly all of these countries rank worst in the world for freedom of expression in addition to other human rights violations, according to the 2017 Human Rights Watch (1978–) World Report, the Committee to Protect Journalists (1981–), and the 2017 World Press Freedom Index. Some countries had earlier hip hop activity until new governments came into power. Boldfaced countries are not covered as entries in this book, mainly because they have too little verifiable hip hop activity.

Afghanistan

Albania

Algeria

Angola

Argentina

Armenia

Azerbaijan

Bahrain

Bangladesh

Belarus

Brunei

Burundi

Cambodia

Central African Republic

Chad

Chile

China

Comoros

Croatia

Cuba

Democratic Republic of the Congo (see entry for Congo)

Djibouti

East Timor

Ecuador

Egypt

Equatorial Guinea

Eritrea

Ethiopia

The Gambia

Georgia

Guatemala

Guinea

Guinea-Bissau

Honduras

Indonesia

Iran

Iraq

Ivory Coast

Jordan

Kazakhstan

Kenya

Kyrgyzstan

Laos

Lebanon

Liberia

Libya

Malaysia

The Maldives

Mali

Morocco

Mozambique

Myanmar

North Korea (see entry for Korea)

Oman

Pakistan

Palestine

Papua New Guinea

Paraguay

Peru

Qatar

Republic of Congo (see entry for Congo)

Russia

Rwanda

Saudi Arabia

Singapore

Somalia

South Sudan (see entry for Sudan)

Sudan

Swaziland

Syria

Tajikistan

Thailand

Tibet

Togo

Tunisia

Turkey

Turkmenistan

Uganda

Ukraine

United Arab Emirates

Uzbekistan

Venezuela

Vietnam

Yemen

Zimbabwe

Glossary

This glossary provides brief definitions for terms and concepts that are frequently mentioned throughout the book, including terminology associated with hip hop, ethnomusicology/anthropology, musical rudiments, musical production and recording, and dance. When a term is also an entry in the book, this is indicated. This glossary also draws connections between related terms and concepts.

Aborigines
A word most often used to describe indigenous Australians. In a larger sense, *aborigine* describes populations that are native to a particular land.

Accent
An emphasis or stress on certain beats in music or on certain words or syllables. It is sometimes called a *stress*.

Acoustic Instruments
Nonelectric musical instruments that do not require electronic amplification. Acoustic instruments often need to be recorded by using microphones rather than by plugging cables directly into a recording device.

Aerophones
Musical instruments that need air to create sound. Examples are woodwinds (flutes, oboes, and clarinets), brass instruments (trumpets, trombones, tubas, and horns), and bellow-blown instruments (accordions) as well as didgeridoos, bagpipes, and whistles.

Album
Originally pressed on vinyl, a collection of recorded tracks (usually songs) that may be, but are not necessarily, unified by a concept or narrative. An album contains more tracks than an EP, or single. For the purposes of this book, the word *album* is synonymous with CD or digital album, terms that differ based simply on format, including physical versus virtual. *See also:* LP; EP

Album or Singles Certification
See Music Recording Sales Certification.

Alliteration
The repetition of the same consonant sound in poems, raps, or songs, usually at the beginnings of words.

Alto (Contralto)
Usually the lowest vocal range assigned to a female singer.

Amplifier
1. An electronic device similar to a speaker or monitor into which electric instruments can be plugged to be heard. Most amplifiers allow for the regulation of high- and low-end frequencies as well as volume control. 2. Any device attached to an acoustic instrument to make it louder—for example, a gourd placed around a kalimba or mbira so that the instrument can be better heard.

Analog Synthesizer
A synthesizer, with origins in the 1900s, that creates or modifies sounds by using analog circuits and signals. Though analog synthesizers appeared in the earliest hip hop music with the Roland TB-303 bass synthesizer, Roland TR-808 programmable drum machine, Oberheim polyphonic synthesizers, and a variety of vocoders, by the mid-1980s they had been replaced by more affordable digital synthesizers and samplers. *See also:* Digital Synthesizer

And Beat (Off Beat)
A weak beat in between strong beats in music. For example, in quadruple meter (four beats per measure), the *and beat* falls between the numbered beats: | 1-and-2-and-3-and-4-and | 1-and-2-and-3-and-4-and |.

Assonance
Repetition of the same vowel sound in poems, raps, or songs.

Autotune
Automated vocal processing used to correct pitch. The process usually corrects off-pitch notes by a semitone, using either an audio processor (originally called Auto-Tune, after a device manufactured by Antares Audio Technologies), or auto-tuning software, as found in a vocal performer box.

Baritone
Usually the middle vocal range assigned to a male singer. The baritone is the most common male vocal range.

Bass
1. Usually the lowest vocal range assigned to a male singer. 2. The lowest musical part in music (as with the double bass or electric bass). It establishes a song's harmonic rhythm as well as its groove (the part of a song that indicates how it should be danced to) and generally complements the drum rhythm. A melody composed for the bass is sometimes called a *bassline*.

Battle
In hip hop, a competitive tradition between two or more individuals or groups to determine who is best at their art. Hip hop battles are also used to showcase talent. They take place in hip hop dance (e.g., breakdancing), MCing (rapping), and DJing (turntablism or scratching). ***See also the entry for Battling.***

B-Boy
Derived from *beat-boy*, an urban nickname from the early 1980s to describe a male hip hop dancer who expresses himself through breakdancing moves that accompany a breakbeat.

Beat
The regular pulse of a musical piece that divides it into equal segments of time.

Beatboxing
The practice of making drum and synthesizer sounds using mostly the mouth and nose. Beatboxing is a way to create a beat when no instrumentation is available, as found in rap street battling. Skilled beatboxers can create both a beat and a melodic line simultaneously. *See also the entry for Beatboxing.*

Beatmaking
The process of creating or composing a beat for a song using either an acoustic or analog instrument (such as a drum kit) or a digital instrument (such as a synthesizer).

Beatmapping
A music engineer's technique for taking a song's rhythmic information and remixing it, creating a mash-up with another song, or composing a new song. Professional Digital Audio Workstation software such as Pro Tools or Digital Performer can be used, but less expensive software like Sony's Acid Pro can also perform beatmapping through automation. *See also:* Digital Audio Workstation

Beatmatching
During a DJ or turntablist's performance, the practice of synchronizing an album's upcoming track with a currently playing track. This synchronization involves *shifting the pitch* (changing the pitch—higher or lower—without playing the new track faster or slower) or *timestretching* (changing the duration of the track without altering the new track's pitch). These techniques may be used in music engineering, especially mixing.

Beats per Minute (bpm)
The measurement of a tempo based on the number of beats played in one minute. The term bpm allows for a description of the music to both musically trained and musically untrained people—the higher the bpm, the faster the music.

B-Girl
Derived from *b-boy*, an urban nickname from the mid-1980s for a female hip hop dancer who expresses herself through breakdancing moves that accompany a breakbeat. Many female hip hop dancers do not use this term to describe themselves, opting instead for *breakdancer* or *hip hop dancer*.

Bling
Wealth, in the form of jewelry, cars, lavish homes, and wads of cash, that is pursued for ostentatious display. In hip hop culture, the display of bling may be proportionate to musical skill.

Breakbeat

The part of a hip hop song where all music except the beat stops. Breakbeats tend to be repetitive (which involves looping a musical phrase) and predictable, for the benefit of the b-boy and b-girl crews that dance to them. The most popular break-beats are samples, often from funk.

Breakdancing

An acrobatic form of dance performed to hip hop music by b-boy and b-girl crews. Breakdancing, originally called breaking, involves both floor work (footwork) and gymnastics-style acrobatics, such as flips and headstands (which usually go into a head spin). It also involves controlled freezes and can be a team or individual event. *See also the entry for Breakdancing.*

Bridge

A brief instrumental or vocal passage that leads to the main sections of a musical piece. Bridges often offer contrast to these sections as well. They often take place just before the final refrain (chorus) toward the end of a song. *See also:* Form

Cadence

Melodic, harmonic, and/or rhythmic musical gestures that give a sense of strong or weak resolution, internal pause, or final pause. In simple terms, cadences are pauses that occur at the end of a piece or within a piece. Cadences differ from *rests* in that they are full pauses.

Call-and-Response

A follow-the-leader song pattern in which a lead voice or instrument performs a phrase (the call) with the expectation that another voice (or voices) or instrument will answer the phrase (the response). The most common hip hop call-and-response follows the pattern "Everybody say . . . ," which is followed by the word(s) the audience is prompted to say. This is done to engage dancers and concertgoers.

Censorship

The censoring (silencing) of a song (or more specifically, its lyrics) either by making it illegal or by labeling it so that only certain people can legally buy it. In the United States, censorship usually occurs because of sexual or violent imagery; in other countries, it can also occur because of political messages (usually against the regime in power).

Chopping

Selecting an excerpt or aspect of a song (for example, the bassline, drum break, hook, or sound bite) that is sampled, thus "chopping" out part(s) of the song. This is not to be confused with *chopper,* which is a style of rapping. *See also the entry for Chopper.*

Chord

Three or more simultaneously played pitches or notes. Musicians can do what is called a "cheat" and play two or more simultaneous pitches to outline or suggest a chord, which may have a harmonic, nonharmonic, or passing function.

Chordophones

Musical instruments played by manipulating one or more strings. These include harps, lutes, lyres, and zithers. Examples include violins and cellos (classified as strings in a symphonic orchestra), acoustic and electric guitars, and acoustic and electric bass guitars, as well as koras and cimbaloms. Though pianos have strings, they are classified as keyboard or percussion instruments as well as chordophones because they are played by striking keys, which in turn causes the striking of strings, not by fingers or picks but by hammers.

Chorus

See: Refrain

Copyright

See: Musical Copyright

Countermelody

A melody that is played as either accompaniment or counterpoint to the main melody. The countermelody may be placed in the foreground or background. The most famous pop music example is Simon and Garfunkel's 1966 hit "Scarborough Fair/Canticle," in which Art Garfunkel sings the main melody, based on a traditional song, and Paul Simon sings a countermelody about soldiers in war. A countermelody usually harmonizes with the main melody. *See also:* Harmony

Cover

A performance of a previously performed song. A cover is often called a rendition or version and can be interpreted the same way as a previous performance or in a new way by changing one or more aspects of a song, such as its tempo or meter. Hip hop renditions of non–hip hop songs often apply hip hop beats and different instruments. A cover employs most of a song, if not all, unlike sampling, which uses just an excerpt. *See also:* Meter; Sampling; Tempo

Crew

A team or group of members that focus on one or more aspects of hip hop (for example, a beatboxing crew, a dancing crew, a graffiti crew, a rap crew, or a DJ crew). All crewmembers may be from the same geographic place, though many crews consist of members from different locations. In battles in which a crew competes, the crew represents its home or community as much as itself.

Crossfader

The part of a DJ mixer—often controlled by a horizontal lever between two turntables—that enables the DJ to fade out one album's track while fading in another album's track. Set in the middle, the crossfader allows for two playing albums to be heard at the same audio level; the crossfader can therefore also be used for balancing. The crossfader is important to beatmatching in turntablism. *See also:* Beatmatching; Mixer; Turntablism

Cross-fading

In music engineering, cross-fading is a technique used to create a single track out of the best results from multiple takes so that the recording sounds like a single performance. Cross-fading may also be used for sound editing, mostly to eliminate or fade out unwanted sound, as well as for mixing, such as fading an instrument in or out. All can be done using digital audio workplace software. *See also:* Digital Audio Workstation

Cypher
A circle that is typically formed in breakdancing and rapping battles as well as in poetry slam challenges. The cypher usually includes the participants, but it may at times also include audience members who judge events. The main competitors step inside the cypher to showcase their moves or rapping talents.

Dancehall
See Dub.

Deejay
Not to be confused with a DJ (who can be a turntablist or a radio disc jockey), a deejay selects *riddims* (Jamaican patois for rhythm), instrumental accompaniments to a song found in reggae, dancehall, soca, calypso, or reggaetón music. The deejay adds a vocal part to the riddim through toasting (talk-singing with a monotone melody) to engage audiences during a live performance. Deejaying usually takes place at parties or informal musical events that involve dancing.

Delivery
A rapper or singer's style. Delivery can involve speed, emphasis, tone, loudness, flow, and attitude, ranging from laid-back and relaxed to angry and in-your-face confrontational.

Digital–Audio Interface
A box-shaped hardware device that connects an instrument or a controller to a computer serving as a digital audio workstation so that it can provide the best audio input. This leads to accurate outputs through headsets or monitors (as opposed to what is delivered by a computer's sound card, which is distorted to various degrees). Input devices range from electric musical instruments to controllers and synthesizers. *See also:* Monitor or Stereo

Digital Audio Workstation (DAW)
A device and software combination that is used for producing and recording music, spoken word, podcasts, and radio. It is also used for sound designing and scoring live concerts and performances, motion pictures, videos, television shows, and multimedia events. State-of-the-art DAWs are self-contained and integrated, often including mixing consoles (or software that creates an on-screen console), manual or automated equalizing/balancing options, surface controllers, keyboard and guitar synthesis ability, multitrack and sequencing functionality, audio conversion (software plug-ins that produce effects), and data storage. As of 2018, examples of professional-grade software DAWs include Pro Tools, Digital Performer, REAPER, and Ableton Live—all can be purchased for home use. DAWs have made it possible to create one's own beats at home, sometimes even on a laptop, instead of relying on a commercial recording studio.

Digital Synthesizer

A synthesizer with origins in late 1979 with the Casio VL-1, the first commercial digital synthesizer. Digital synthesizers produce digital signal processing (DSP), used to create or modify sounds. The digital synthesizer can be thought of as a computer with a keyboard interface (such as the Kurzweil). By the mid-1980s, digital synthesizers had replaced more expensive and limited analog synthesizers, though virtual analog synthesizers have been made since the 1990s for musicians who prefer analog modeling or a sound closer to an analog synthesizer. Synthesis techniques and faster ways to program digital synthesizers in comparison to analog synthesizers have also led to the disuse of analog synthesizers. An earlier popular digital synthesizer in hip hop was the Yamaha DX7.

Diss (Diss Track)

A disrespectful song or recording of a song intended to embarrass and ridicule other artists, celebrities, or types of people in general (e.g., doubters, haters, exes) for personal gratification and to create commercially marketable feuds.

DJ

Either a turntablist (also called a beatmaker or producer) or a radio disc jockey. Several radio DJs have gone on to become beatmakers and producers.

Downbeat

The first beat of any measure of music. It is expected to get the heaviest stress in that measure.

Drum Kit

A traditional analog instrument that is actually a series of drum types (such as bass kick, tom, and snare), cymbals (such as hi-hats and risers), and percussion instruments (such as bells, wood blocks, and toothed vibrating instruments such as the vibraslap). The term *drum kit* can also refer to a type of limited synthesizer played by striking fixed areas with drumsticks. The synthetic drum kit is meant to replace the analog drum kit, but preference for the analog continues in live music. The synthetic kit is preferred for its portability, as its sounds can be set to any number of drum types or percussion instruments.

Drum Machine

An electronic musical instrument that imitates the sound of drums, other kinds of percussion instruments, and basslines. Having origins in the 1930s, drum machines in hip hop began as analog instruments that used sound synthesis but were replaced by more affordable digital drum machines that used sampling. The most popular drum machine in early hip hop was the Roland TR-808, followed later by Oberheim's DMX. Digital synthesizers also have drum machine sounds and virtual instruments that can be controlled by keyboard and manipulated by using digital audio workplace (DAW) software. In hip hop, drum machines are often used instead of live drummers with drum kits because of a low budget, concerns for time in the studio, and other reasons. *See also:* Digital Audio Workstation; Digital Synthesizer

Dub or Dancehall
Music stressing a previously recorded bass and rhythm that is used by a deejay or DJ, who can talk, toast, rap, or sing over the music with a microphone.

Dynamics
The loudness or softness of music.

Electrophones
Musical instruments that require electricity. Examples are synthesizers, drum machines, electric guitars and basses, vibraphones, and turntables.

End Rhyme
A rhyme that occurs at the end of a line of poetry, rap, or sung lyrics. End rhymes can be couplets (two consecutive lines that rhyme) or a variation (for example, even numbered lines rhyming). Lyrics that contain a too-fixed rhythm and nothing but end rhymes are called singsong, as they are reminiscent of children's songs and taunts.

EP
Known as an extended-play record, an EP is a collection of songs and/or vignettes (originally pressed on vinyl), but with fewer tracks than are found on an album or LP. Most EPs range from four to seven songs.

Flow
The rhythmic quality of the vocal delivery of a rapper. Words that describe a rapper's flow would be *gentle, smooth, disjointed,* and like terms.

Form
The underlying structure of a musical piece, text, and/or performance. For example, a hip hop song can have the same music to accompany each verse of rap text. This form is known as *strophic.* It can also have a refrain (also called a chorus) inserted between verses. Different music used throughout a rap song is known as *through-composed.* The form of a musical piece, whether it is a rap or dance song (vocal or instrumental), therefore depends on repetition. Hip hop songs may have, for example, a *rounded binary form,* giving a sense of an A section (with or without a chorus), a B section, and then the A section again. But most of the time, a hip hop song is thought of as containing this general form, which can be modified: *intro, hook, verse,* hook, *bridge,* second verse, hook, and *outro. See also:* Bridge; Hook; Intro or Introduction; Outro; Verse

Four-to-the-Floor
See Meter.

Freestyle
A type of rapping that is supposed to be either prewritten as a template that can be improvised on or a rap that is made up on the spot. In rap music, an argument persists over which of these two methods of composing is the proper way to freestyle.

Graffiti Art
Detailed urban art done with spray paint and signed by the artist using an iconic image that represents his or her work. Originally, graffiti was guerrilla art,

meaning that it was done in secret and was technically illegal (it was sometimes called *bombing*, as in the phrase *bombing the suburbs*). Some early graffiti was gang-related, used to demarcate a gang's territory. Since the early 2000s, graffiti has become more mainstream and has been commissioned by city councils and private companies, which now view it as a kind of mural painting. Illegal graffiti can still be seen on bridges, public edifices, and trains. *See also the entry for Graffiti Art.*

Griot
A French term that applies to a wandering minstrel who praises a person or a historical event in song or sings about heritage. Griots either are accompanied by or accompany themselves with musical instruments. One type of griot is the West African *jali*. *See also the entry for Griot.*

Groove
The rhythmic feel of a piece of music, created often as an accompanying repeated pattern and melody played by the bass, drums, keyboards, and/or guitars (known as the rhythm section). It is usually associated with jazz, funk, rock, and soul, but it is also found in hip hop. The groove is usually established at the beginning of a song, typically in an *introduction*. Its basis can be a *vamp* or a *riff*. *See also:* Intro or Introduction; Riff; Vamp

Harmony
The progression of chords composed to accompany a main vocal or instrumental melody. A countermelody or accompanying melody may be part of a musical piece's harmony. In rap, most rappers are not accompanied by harmonizing backup singers; however, harmonies may be created and suggested between the rapping or singing voice and the accompanying musical instruments. *See also:* Chord

Hook
A memorable short musical idea, melody, excerpt, phrase, or riff in a musical piece. The hook of a song is usually the catchiest part and becomes most famous.

Hype Man
A type of MC or toaster whose job involves engaging the audience or crowd through wild fashion and side commentary on a song's main lyrics. The hype man may also serve as a vocal harmonizer. The most famous use of a hype man in rap was Public Enemy's Flavor Fav, who serves as a comic sidekick to MC Chuck D. *See also the entry for hype man.*

Idiophones
Musical instruments that are struck to vibrate to create sound. Examples are bells, rattles, and rhythm sticks. Many idiophones are percussion instruments.

Improvisation
The act of composing while performing. Improvisation is normally associated with jazz bands and rock jam bands but can be used in rap when the MC is skilled at freestyle.

Internal Rhyme
Rhyme that occurs not at the ends of lines but within a line itself. In rap, the ability to create interior rhyme as well as exterior rhyme is considered a sign of superior skill.

Intro or Introduction
The beginning section of a musical piece that precedes the main melody, first verse, or hook. Not all musical pieces have introductions, and sometimes introductions may return later in a song. Introductions may also contain *vamps* and can establish a song's *groove*. *See also:* Form, Groove, Vamp

Key
An arrangement of pitches and chords that give a sense of musical coherence because of their fixed relationship to a home pitch or home chord. Key is normally associated with Western music. *See also:* Chord; Harmony

Lamellophones
Idiophones that create sound through vibrating tongues (sometimes called *lamellas*) or strips, which are usually metal. Examples of lamellophones are the kalimba, mbira, jaw harp, and comb. *See also:* Idiophones

Loop
A repeated musical phrase, usually created by using music software or a turntable-mixer setup. A loop can be an original composition or a sample. *See also:* Looping; Sample

Looping
The process of creating a loop. *See also:* Loop

LP
A shortened version of long-playing record. LPs were originally pressed on vinyl. LPs were used by DJs (turntablists) to manually create scratches, loops, and breakbeats. The term *LP* can be used synonymously with *album*, as both are based on the idea of a group of songs released together as a collection. *See also:* Album

MC
A shortened version of *emcee*. MC is synonymous with *rapper*, and rap bands can have many MCs. MCs and DJs are the most common rap band members. DJs typically do not rap; rather, they play turntables, serve as hype men (or women), and/or produce via a soundboard. ***See also the entry for MC.*** *See also:* DJ; Hype Man

Measure
A grouping of beats, indicated in visual musical notation by bar lines. Related to meter and time signature, a measure is a segment of music containing a set number of beats of a specific length.

Melody
A succession of pitches, notes, or chords that are organized into a recognizable and predictable pattern to create a tune or musical phrase.

Membranophones
Musical instruments that have a stretched membrane that vibrates when struck, scratched, strummed, or blown to create sounds. Examples of membranophones are kick drums, snare drums, bass drums, bodhrans, cuicas, and tambourines as well as kazoos, mirlitons, and *swazzles*. Because they are struck, many membranophones are also *idiophones*. *See also:* Idiophones

Message Rap
Rap music that is lyrically about politics, society, and/or community and can be either critical or positive in tone. Message rap stands in contrast to party rap, which is about sex, drugs, dancing, and bling, or braggadocio, which involves bragging on one's musical skills or songwriting. Five percenter rap and some gangsta rap are kinds of message rap.

Metaphor
A comparison that differs from a simile in that it does not use the word *like* or *as*. A simile equates two items with *like* or *as*, as in the M.I.A. example "I fly like paper, get high like planes" ("Paper Planes"), while metaphor simply equates two items, as in the Nas example "I never sleep, cause sleep is the cousin of death" ("N.Y. State of Mind"). *See also:* Simile

Meter
A regular grouping of beats in music. The most common meter in hip hop is quadruple or 4/4 meter (pronounced "four-four"), which groups four quarter beats (not to be confused with notes) per measure, creating a | 1-2-3-4 | 1-2-3-4 | count, also known as *four to the floor*. *See also:* Beat

Mixtape
A usually free (via social media or download) collection of songs intended to either introduce a new musician to the public or create hype for a new album release. Mixtapes were originally burned onto audiocassettes but are now released virtually as downloaded files.

Monitor or Stereo
A speakerlike device used in music studios, sometimes called a studio monitor. A set of right and left monitors is used to gauge or monitor the precise sounds of a recording (as opposed to what is delivered by a computer's sound card, which is distorted to various degrees). *See also:* Digital–Audio Interface; Speakers

Motive
A brief musical (instrumental or vocal) idea that is repeated throughout a song.

Music Recording Sales Certification
A system of certifying that a music recording has shipped or sold a previously defined number of copies. Although the number of copies is universal, the term used to certify the recording varies per country. In addition, the threshold quantity needed to achieve a status varies by type of recording (album, single). Almost all countries follow some variation of the Recording Industry Association of America (RIAA) certification categories, which are named after precious materials: Silver,

Gold, Platinum, and Diamond. The number required for these certifications depends on the population of the territory where the recording is released, although original Gold and Silver record awards were presented to artists by their own record companies to publicize their sales achievements. In 1958, the RIAA introduced its Gold record award program for records of any kind, albums or singles, that achieved one million dollars in retail sales. The Platinum certification was introduced in 1976 for the sale of one million units (measurable by albums, audiocassettes, or compact discs), album or single, with the Gold certification redefined to mean sales of 500,000 units, album or single. The International Federation of the Phonographic Industry (IFPI) was founded in 1996 and currently grants the award for album sales over one million within Europe and the Middle East. The Independent Music Companies Association (IMPALA) was founded in 2000 and launched in 2005 to recognize sales on a pan-European basis. The IFPI operates in 66 countries and services affiliated industry associations in 45 countries.

Musical Copyright
The specific set of copyright licenses for music. The most important musical copyright license is known as mechanical rights, which are the record of instructions for recreating a musical piece. For songwriters, mechanical rights are responsible for most of the royalties, the revenue they earn from a musical piece. Many people who do not understand music copyright confuse mechanical rights with royalties. Musicians wishing to cover or sample songs, no matter the size of the sample or manipulation, need to pay a mechanical rights fee to the original copyright owner to legally use the music (including the words). If copyrightable material is added (for example, new lyrics or an inserted original melody), then a notification of intent should be sent to the copyright owner. Other important musical copyright licenses are recording and performance rights; however, there are intricacies (for example, there is a separate copyright license for streaming music). The recording copyright license covers the recorded performance and its use by others, whereas performance rights cover performing the piece in public and other aspects of performance. Hip hop has posed many challenges with musical copyright. For example, artists have argued that sampling falls under fair use, an exception loophole that allows use of material without permission, because the music samples or excerpts are brief and considered an insignificant portion of an entire musical piece. The same has been argued about beatmapping. Worldwide, however, despite the need to get permission from the copyright owner, samples, musical excerpts, grooves, basslines, melodies, and other parts of musical pieces continue to be used without permission. This frequent practice has led to another challenge for copyright owners: many people violate copyright laws. Even though the copyright owner may win a lawsuit easily, most do not have the effort, time, or money to challenge every musician who uses music without permission. *See also:* Beatmapping; Sampling

Off Beat
See And Beat.

Ostinato
A melodic or rhythmic pattern that repeats throughout a musical piece.

Outro

Music composed and engineered to serve as a memorable end melody of a song. In hip hop, the outro could be music heard for the first time or reused music from an earlier part of a song. An example of an outro is Coolio's "Gangsta's Paradise," which allows its vamp to enter the foreground at the end, adds a group of choir singers, and reaches a climax before the song begins its final fade-out. *See also:* Form

Phrase

In music, a brief passage in the melody that is made meaningful by a brief or lengthy pause (cadence) and/or harmonic progression. In vocal music, the lyrics are often sung in the melody and the phrases correspond to language; commas, ends of lines, or periods can be helpful in identifying phrases. One musical phrase is "Twinkle, twinkle, little star." Another is "Now, this is a story all about how" (from Will Smith's theme song to the American television show *The Fresh Prince of Bel-Air*). Both phrases are meaningful units that begin songs; the end of the first is indicated by a brief pause as well as a comma and a line break, whereas the end of the second is indicated only by a line break. The next line, which in each case completes both the thought and the sentence, is another musical phrase. In music, as in poetry, complete ideas are often created by two back-to-back phrases, where the second phrase provides meaningful and (in a song) musical completion. *See also:* Cadence; Harmony; Melody

Producer

A preproduction individual who finances a music project, such as a single, an EP, or an album, by paying for recording time, postproduction editing, and possibly touring expenses. Some producers are also postproduction producers, that is, music engineers who may or may not be musicians. These engineers edit the raw recorded tracks that make up a song (usually each instrument, including a vocalist, is recorded on a different track) with the intention of making the song sound more professional. A postproduction producer will edit (via a process called cutting, copying, and cross-fading), add effects to, mix (i.e., determine which sounds are placed in the foreground or background and where they are heard), and master (i.e., make sure sound levels are correct) a song.

Promoter

The person who promotes a band (not to be confused with a *hype man*). A promoter may also manage a band's tour or a performance venue.

Rapping

A type of music vocal, usually performed by an MC, that is similar to talk-singing except that it is more oriented toward rock and funk conventions, whereas talk-singing is oriented more toward the conventions of theatrical musicals. Both rap and talk-singing differ from spoken word because they require a musical beat; they differ from singing because the performer does not break into song. *See also:* MC; Spoken Word; Talk-Singing

Refrain

Repeated lyrics that occur in a song. A refrain is usually set to the same, repeated melody, making up the catchiest part of the song. It is commonly called a chorus, and it usually occurs at the end of each verse or stanza. *See also:* Verse

Register

The total pitch range (the highest and lowest musical sound or note) of any musical instrument. An instrument's register is often divided between its upper and lower pitches.

Rest

A pause or silence of distinct length in music. Some rests are used for emphasis or to introduce a dramatic shift.

Rhythm

1. The duration or length of musical sounds. 2. The organization of stressed and unstressed beats into a distinct and predictable pattern that can be followed by singers, rappers, and dancers.

Riff

A short and repeated melodic and rhythmic musical phrase that is often memorable. It is usually played with rhythm-section instruments such as basses or guitars (usually with drums). A riff can serve as accompaniment in the background but can also occur in the foreground (for example, when it becomes part of a refrain or chorus). A *groove* may be based on a riff. *See also:* Groove; Refrain

Sample

A recording or an excerpt from a previously recorded musical piece that is incorporated and mixed into a new recording. In hip hop music, some kinds of samples are spoken or sung musical excerpts, whereas others include melodic hooks, basslines, brass parts, and/or percussive effects. Sampling is the use and manipulation of samples. *See also:* Sampler; Sampling

Sampler

1. A hardware device, which may be a musical instrument such as a synthesizer, that provides and/or manipulates music samples (e.g., by pitch, by duration, or through applying effects). 2. A sound recording of tracks recorded by various artists that serves as a collection that is representative of a music studio's work. *See also:* Sample; Sampling

Sampling

Taking a sample or musical excerpt from a previously recorded piece and adding it to a newly composed song. Sampling can be the use of samples as they are, but more likely the samples will be manipulated in a variety of ways and will add meaning to the new song. Manipulations include altering the duration or pitch (samples can be assigned to different pitches or notes on a digital synthesizer, or pitch can be altered using digital audio workstation or music editing software), looping, and reversing. An example of sampling in hip hop is M.I.A.'s "Paper Planes," which samples the Clash's song "Straight to Hell." In the original recording of "Straight to Hell," the song is sung from the point of view of a xenophobic, anti-immigration individual. "Paper Planes," however, is an ironicized song sung from the point of view of an immigrant who is criminal and greedy, preying on every xenophobic fear. *See also:* Sample; Sampler

Scat Singing
Singing by vocal improvisation that usually uses not recognizable words but rather vocables, nonsense syllables, vocal sound effects, and/or nonsense words and phrases (jazz icon Jon Hendricks was able to use scat techniques to sing pre-written lyrics). Often associated with vocal jazz, scat singing requires treating the voice as if it were an instrument in the band, and most scat singing is improvised. *See also:* Improvisation; Vocable

Scratching
1. Another word for *turntablism*. 2. A turntablism technique that involves the DJ's creating a scratching sound with a vinyl record album by manually moving the album forward, backward, or both under the record player's needle. *See also:* DJ; Turntables; Turntablism

Simile
A comparison using *like* or *as. See* Metaphor *for examples.*

Single
A song that is released independently of its parent album. Originally recorded on one side of a 45-RPM vinyl record, singles were usually accompanied by either a different version of the same song or another single on the record's other side (called its B side). *See also:* Album; EP

Slam Poetry
Spoken poetry that is usually improvised or based on a template, similar to free-style rap or jazz improvisation. Slam poetry tends to have an aggressive tone. It owes its origins to the West Coast beat poetry performance happenings of the 1960s, where a poet would improvise or freestyle to the accompaniment of music, usually created by bongos, piano, and a bass instrument (such as a stand-up bass). Slam poetry also differs from beat poetry and rap in that it does not always adhere to a musical beat. The overall sound of words is less prioritized in slam poetry than in beat poetry and some rap. *See also:* Freestyle; Improvisation; Spoken Word

Slang
See Vernacular.

Soprano
Usually the highest vocal range assigned to a female singer.

Sound Bite
A sampled spoken-word phrase or sentence from a speech, monologue, or dialogue (as from a film, news clip, or television show), used either to help create a mood for a song or to ironicize its lyrics. Rap music also uses domestic sound bites, such as a father talking to his son as in TRU's 1997 album *Tru 2 da Game. See also:* Sample; Sampling

Speakers
See Monitor or Stereo.

Spoken Word

A kind of sound recording that features either unaccompanied spoken-word arts (such as poetry, prose reading, or closet drama) or such spoken-word arts set against background music, as in Gil Scott-Heron's 2010 album *I'm New Here*. Spoken word differs from rap in that it is not usually spoken to the musical beat.

Stanza

See Verse.

Stress

See Accent.

Syncopation

Accenting or stressing an unexpected beat, such as a weak beat. For example, in quadruple or 4/4 meter (four beats per measure), the expected stresses are on beats 1 (the downbeat) and 3. In syncopation, the stress gets shifted to unexpected beats 2 and 4: | 1-**2**-3-**4** |. In a more complex example, syncopation can also take place on a weak beat such as an "and beat" (off beat), happening between beats: | 1-and-2-**and**-3-and-4-**and** |. *See also:* Beat; Meter

Synthesizer

See Analog Synthesizer *and* Digital Synthesizer.

Talk-Singing

A type of music vocal where the vocalist talks rhythmically, approaching song but never breaking into it. The most famous talk-singing occurs in stage musicals, the most recognized being Meredith Willson's *The Music Man* with songs such as "Rock Island" and "(Ya Got) Trouble." Talk-singing differs from rapping because it uses stage musical conventions rather than rock or funk conventions. Talk-singing also has its roots in cabaret singing and is related to *Sprechstimme* (speech-song employed and notated by composers such as Arnold Schoenberg in Western art music). *See also:* Rapping

Tempo

The speed of music. Words that are used describe or indicate tempo include *fast* and *slow* in rock and rap and *allegro* (meaning fast) and *adagio* (meaning slow) in classical music.

Tenor

Usually the highest vocal range assigned to a male singer.

Text

Another word for song lyrics or spoken word.

Toasting

The art of engaging with the audience via rhymed spoken word. Toasting differs from rapping because it is more monotonous in its delivery and addresses the audience directly. A toaster differs from a hype man because he or she does not have to be part of the rap crew and because he or she does not serve as comic relief. In some respects, the toaster plays the role of the *deejay* as it was strictly conceived, as akin to a master of ceremonies. *See also:* Deejay

Track
1. A distinct section or musical piece, often numbered, on a sound recording. 2. In hip hop and its literature, a track is synonymous with the word *song*. 3. In music production, a file created when recording a single voice or instrument; songs are created by recording various tracks and playing them simultaneously using music production software.

Turntables
The instrument used by a turntablist or DJ. Most turntables include two direct-drive record players, on which vinyl albums can be spun, and a control panel between the two that allows for switching back and forth between turntables via use of a crossfader, a mixer, and controls for speed. *See also:* Turntablism

Turntablism
The art of creating and modifying sounds through the use of two or more turntables and a mixer with a crossfader. Also called scratching, turntablism can involve composing new music, beats, and effects by scratching, rubbing, speeding up, or slowing down previously recorded albums. The turntablist is commonly called a DJ. Individuals and DJ crews have created elaborate techniques and combinations in performances and battles as well as on recordings. The origins of turntablism may be traced back to the 1930s, with musique concrète experiments that created and distorted previously recorded sounds. ***See also the entry for turntablism.*** *See also:* Turntables

Upbeat
1. The last beat in a musical measure that anticipates the downbeat. To the ear, the upbeat is less stressed than the downbeat. The upbeat is sometimes called the *pickup* or *anacrusis*, which means "pushing up." 2. A word to describe a fast or energetic musical piece. *See also:* Downbeat; Measure

Vamp
A repeated musical passage or section that is harmonically sparse. The vamp has roots in blues, jazz, soul, gospel music, and other kinds of popular music (e.g., funk, reggae, R&B, and hip hop) and is used as either an accompaniment or introduction. As an introduction, vamps are often played as a performer gets ready to start a song. Vamps can also be used this way for dancers getting ready to begin their routine. An example of a vamp in hip hop is played by the synthesizer in Missy Elliott's "Work It" from her studio album *Under Construction* (2002). Another example is found in Booker T. & the M.G.'s funky instrumental song "Green Onions" (1962), where the Hammond M3 organ vamp is introduced. It is later exchanged with the bass guitar. *See also:* Intro or Introduction

Vernacular
Another word for slang. Vernacular is the style of language used in a localized area. It is related to a dialect in that it contains words and expressions from that dialect; however, vernacular can also contain expressions that represent a community, such as a neighborhood or municipality. It plays a large role in rapping because rappers use the language of the urban streets, in a localized fashion, since street language differs per community and geographic location.

Verse
The sections of a song that change and are not usually repeated, as opposed to the refrain (chorus), which contains the song's hook and is repeated, usually between each verse. While refrains articulate the overall theme of a song and are therefore standard, verses can be narrative and chronological in nature, telling a story from beginning to end, or can serve as different examples of the same overall idea. *See also:* Hook; Refrain

Vixen
Also called a video vixen, a young woman who stars in a male soloist's or male group's rap video, generally scantily clad and performing sexually suggestive dances or moves. Some vixens have gone on to become rappers in their own right.

Vocable
A vocal sound that is not a recognized word. Popular songs often include vocables, which are usually used as part of the refrain or hook. Generally, rap music uses fewer vocables than other pop genres, as vocables lend themselves to singing rather than rapping. *See also:* Hook; Refrain

Vocal Processing
The act of inserting a voice processor or autotuning device, during production, between the microphone used by a singer, rapper, or spoken-word artist and either a recording device (in the studio) or output device (when live). Vocal processing can also occur postproduction using various kinds of mixing and mastering software (vocal effects can be layered and combined). Virtually all vocals are processed, to some degree, in popular music, usually to adjust pitch, reverb, balance, and wetness/dryness. Vocals that are overprocessed sound robotic and/or distorted and are generally described as autotuned. *See also:* Autotune

Selected Bibliography

The study of hip hop around the world is interdisciplinary, which is reflected in the following selected list of English-language resources on hip hop. The first section lists books whose subject matter is solely hip hop. For biographies, autobiographies, memoirs, polemics, and books with chapters or sections on hip hop, see the "Further Reading" sections in the entries. The last two sections of this bibliography list peer-reviewed journals and periodicals that offer numerous articles on hip hop. Excluded are periodicals that rarely cover hip hop or contain mostly reviews.

BOOKS

Bailey, Julius, ed. *Jay-Z: Essays on Hip Hop's Philosopher King.* Jefferson City, NC: MacFarland, 2011.

Basu, Dipannita, and Sidney J. Lemelle, eds. *The Vinyl Ain't Final: Hip Hop and the Global of Black Popular Culture.* Ann Arbor, MI: Pluto Press, 2006.

Bradley, Adam, and Andrew Dubois, eds. *The Anthology of Rap.* New Haven, CT: Yale University Press, 2010.

Brewster, Bill, and Frank Broughton. *The Record Players: DJ Revolutionaries.* New York: Black Cat, 2010.

Chang, Jeff. *Can't Stop Won't Stop: A History of the Hip Hop Generation.* New York: Picador, 2005.

Charnas, Dan. *The Big Payback: The History of the Business of Hip Hop.* New York: New American Library, 2010.

Charry, Eric, ed. *Hip Hop Africa: New African Music in a Globalizing World.* Bloomington: Indiana University Press, 2012.

Clark, Msia Kibona, and Mickie Mwanzia Koster, eds. *Hip Hop and Social Change in Africa: Ni Wakati.* Lanham, MD: Lexington Books, 2014.

Coleman, Brian. *Check the Technique: Liner Notes for Hip Hop Junkies.* New York: Villard, 2007.

Condry, Ian. *Hip Hop Japan: Rap and the Paths of Cultural Globalization.* Durham, NC: Duke University Press, 2006.

Dennis, Christopher. *Afro-Colombian Hip Hop: Globalization, Transcultural Music, and Ethnic Identities.* Lanham, MD: Lexington Books, 2012.

Durand, Alain-Philippe, ed. *Black, Blan, Beur: Rap Music and Hip Hop Culture in the Francophone World.* Lanham, MD: Scarecrow, 2002.

Dyson, Michael Eric. *Holler If You Hear Me: Searching for Tupac Shakur.* New York: Basic Civitas Books, 2003.

Dyson, Michael Eric, and Sohail Daulatzai, eds. *Born to Use Mics: Reading Nas's "Illmatic."* New York: Basic Civitas Books, 2010.

Edwards, Paul. *How to Rap: The Art and Science of the Hip Hop MC.* Chicago: Chicago Review Press, 2009.

Edwards, Paul. *How to Rap 2: Advanced Flow and Delivery Techniques.* Chicago: Chicago Review Press, 2013.

Fernandes, Sujatha. *The Edge: In Search of the Global Hip Hop Generation.* New York: Verso, 2011.

Forman, Murray. *The 'Hood Comes First: Race, Space, and Place in Rap and Hip Hop.* Middletown, CT: Wesleyan University Press, 2002.

Forman, Murray, and Mark Anthony Neal, eds. *That's the Joint: The Hip Hop Studies Reader.* 2nd ed. New York: Routledge, 2004.

Fricke, Jim, and Charlie Ahearn. *The Experience Music Project Oral History of Hip Hop's First Decade: Yes Yes Y'all.* Cambridge, MA: Da Capo Press, 2002.

Garcia, Ana "Rokafella." Introduction to *We B*Girlz* by Nika Kramer and Martha Cooper. New York: powerHouse Books, 2005.

George, Nelson. *Hip Hop America.* New York: Viking Press, 1998.

Gosa, Travis L., and Erik Nielson, eds. *Hip Hop and Obama Reader.* Oxford, UK: Oxford University Press, 2015.

Helbig, Adriana. *Hip Hop Ukraine: Music, Race, and African Migration.* Bloomington: Indiana University Press, 2014.

Hess, Mickey, ed. *Hip Hop in America: A Regional Guide.* 2 vols. Santa Barbara, CA: Greenwood, 2010.

Hess, Mickey, ed. *Icons of Hip Hop: An Encyclopedia of the Movement, Music, and Culture.* 2 vols. Westport, CT: Greenwood Press, 2007.

Kajikawa, Loren. *Sounding Race in Rap Songs.* Oakland: University of California Press, 2015.

Katz, Mark. *Groove Music: The Art and Culture of the Hip Hop DJ.* New York: Oxford University Press, 2012.

Krims, Adam. *Rap Music and the Poetics of Identity.* Cambridge, England: Cambridge University Press, 2000.

Light, Alan, ed. *The Vibe History of Hip Hop.* New York: Three Rivers Press, 1999.

Martinez, George, and Christopher Malone. *The Organic Globalizer: Hip Hop, Political Development, and Movement Culture.* New York: Bloomsbury Academic, 2014.

Miller, Matt. *Bounce: Rap Music and Local Identity in New Orleans.* Amherst: University of Massachusetts Press, 2012.

Miller, Paul (DJ Spooky), ed. *Sound Unbound: Sampling Digital Music and Culture.* Cambridge, MA: MIT Press, 2008.

Miszczynski, Milosz, and Adriana Helbig, eds. *Hip Hop at Europe's Edge: Music, Agency, and Social Change.* Bloomington: Indiana University Press, 2017.

Mitchell, Tony, ed. *Global Noise: Rap and Hip Hop outside the U.S.A.* Middletown, CT: Wesleyan University Press, 2001.

Miyakawa, Felicia. *Five Percenter Rap: God Hop's Music, Message, and Black Muslim Mission.* Bloomington: Indiana University Press, 2005.

Monteyne, Kimberley. *Hip Hop on Film: Performance, Culture, Urban Space, and Genre Transformation in the 1980s.* Jackson: University Press of Mississippi, 2013.

Nitzsche, Sina A., and Walter Grünzweig, eds. *Hip Hop in Europe: Cultural Identities and Transnational Flows.* Zürich, Switzerland: LIT Verlag, 2013.

Ntarangwi, Mwenda. *East African Hip Hop: Youth Culture and Globalization.* Urbana: University of Illinois Press, 2009.

Oliver, Richard, and Tim Leffel. *Hip Hop, Inc.: Success Strategies of the Rap Moguls.* New York: Thunder's Mouth Press, 2006.

Pardue, Derek. *Brazilian Hip Hoppers Speak from the Margins: We's on Tape.* New York: Palgrave Macmillan, 2011.

Pardue, Derek. *Cape Verde, Let's Go: Creole Rappers and Citizenship in Portugal.* Urbana-Champaign: University of Illinois Press, 2015.

Pinn, Anthony B., ed. *Noise and Spirit: The Religious and Spiritual Sensibilities of Rap Music.* New York: New York University Press, 2003.

Price, Emmett G. III. *Hip Hop Culture.* Santa Barbara, CA: ABC-CLIO, 2006.

Quinn, Eithne. *Nuthin' but a "G" Thang: The Culture and Commerce of Gangsta Rap.* New York: Columbia University Press, 2005.

Rajakumar, Mohanalakshmi. *Hip Hop Dance.* Santa Barbara, CA: Greenwood, 2012.

Rausch, Andrew J. *I Am Hip Hop: Conversations on the Music and Culture.* Lanham, MD: Scarecrow, 2011.

Reeves, Marcus. *Somebody Scream! Rap Music's Rise to Prominence in the Aftershock of Black Power.* New York: Faber and Faber, 2008.

Richardson, Elaine. *Hip Hop Literacies.* New York: Routledge, 2006.

Rivera, Raquel Z. *New York Ricans from the Hip Hop Zone.* New York: Palgrave Macmillan, 2002.

Romero, Elena. *Free Stylin': How Hip Hop Changed the Fashion Industry.* Santa Barbara, CA: Praeger, 2012.

Rose, Tricia. *Black Noise: Rap Music and Black Culture in Contemporary America.* Middletown, CT: Wesleyan University Press, 1994.

Sarig, Roni. *Third Coast: OutKast, Timbaland, and How Hip Hop Became a Southern Thing.* Cambridge, MA: Da Capo Press, 2007.

Saucier, P. Khalil. *Necessarily Black: Cape Verdean Youth, Hip Hop Culture, and a Critique of Identity.* Michigan State University Press, 2015.

Schloss, Joseph G. *Foundation: B-Boys, B-Girls, and Hip Hop Culture in New York.* Oxford: Oxford University Press, 2009.

Shute, Gareth. *Hip Hop Music in Aotearoa.* Auckland, New Zealand: Reed, 2004.

Spady, James G., H. Samy Alim, and Samir Meghelli. *Tha Global Cipha: Hip Hop Culture and Consciousness.* Philadelphia: Black History Museum Publishers, 2006.

Tanz, Jason. *Other People's Property: A Shadow History of Hip Hop in White America.* New York: Bloomsbury, 2007.

Terkourafi, Marina, ed. *The Languages of Global Hip Hop.* New York: Continuum, 2010.

Tucker, Boima. *Musical Violence: Gangsta Rap and Politics in Sierra Leone.* Uppsala, Sweden: Nordiska Afrikainstitutet, 2013.

Walter, Carla Stalling. *Hip Hop Dance: Meanings and Messages.* Jefferson, NC: McFarland, 2007.

Wang, Oliver, ed. *Classical Material: The Hip Hop Album Guide.* Toronto: ECW Press, 2003.

Wang, Oliver. *Legions of Boom: Filipino American Mobile DJ Crews in the San Francisco Bay Area.* Durham, NC: Duke University Press, 2015.

Webber, Stephen. *DJ Skills: The Essential Guide to Mixing and Scratching.* Burlington, MA: Focal Press, 2008.

Weis, Ellen R. *Egyptian Hip Hop: Expressions from the Underground.* Cairo Papers in Social Science, vol. 34, no. 1. Cairo: American University in Cairo Press, 2016.

Westoff, Ben. *Dirty South: OutKast, Lil Wayne, Soulja Boy, and the Southern Rappers Who Reinvented Hip Hop.* Chicago: Chicago Review Press, 2011.

Williams, Justin, ed. *The Cambridge Companion to Hip Hop.* Cambridge, England: Cambridge University Press, 2015.

Williams, Justin. *Rhymin' and Stealin': Musical Borrowing in Hip Hop Music.* Ann Arbor: University of Michigan Press, 2013.

Woodstra, Chris, John Bush, and Stephen Thomas Erlewine. *Old School Rap and Hip Hop.* New York: Backbeat Books, 2008.

JOURNALS

Journals with the most articles on hip hop are boldfaced.

African American Review (1967–)
African Conflict and Peacebuilding (2011–)
Alter/Nativas: Latin American Cultural Studies Journal (2013–)
American Ethnologist (1972–)
American Quarterly (1949–)
Anthropological Quarterly (2001–)
Asian Music (1969–)
Callaloo (1976–)
Centro Journal (1987–)
CLCWeb: Comparative Literature and Culture (1999–)
Contemporary Islam (2001–)
Contemporary Music Review (1984–)
CR: The New Centennial Review (2001–, formerly *The Centennial Review*, 1961–1999)
Critical Sociology (1969–)
Critical Studies in Media Communication (2000–, formerly *Critical Studies in Mass Communication*, 1984–1999)
Cultural Studies (1987–)

Dance Research (1982–)
Diaspora (1991–)
Ethnic and Racial Studies (1978–)
Ethnomusicology (1953–)
Ethnomusicology Forum (2004–)
Feminist Media Studies (2001–)
Geojournal (1977–)
International Journal of Bilingual Education and Bilingualism (1998–)
International Journal of Communication (2007–)
International Journal of Critical Pedagogy (2008–)
International Journal of Heritage Studies (1994–)
International Journal of Qualitative Studies in Education (1988–)
International Journal of Urban and Regional Research (1977–)
Journal of African Cultural Studies (1998–, formerly *African Languages and Cultures*, 1988–1997)
Journal of Black Studies (1970–)
Journal of Hip Hop Studies (2012–)
Journal of Music and Dance (2011–)
Journal of Negro History (1916–)
Journal of Pan African Studies (1987–)
Journal of Poetry Therapy (1987–)
Journal of Popular Culture (1967–)
Journal of Popular Music Studies (1988–)
Journal of Sociolinguistics (1997–)
Journal of Southern African Studies (1975–)
Journal of the Society for American Music (2007–)
Journal of World Popular Music (2014–)
Journal of Youth Studies (1998–)
Language and Communication (1981–)
Linguistics and Education (1989–)
Meridians: Feminism, Race, Transnationalism (2001–)
Middle East Critique (1992–)
Multilingua: Journal of Cross-Cultural and Interlanguage Communication (1982–)
Muziki: Journal of Music Research in Africa (1969–)
Organised Sound (1996–)
Perfect Beat (1992–)
Poetics (1971–)
Popular Communication (2003–)
Popular Music (1981–)
Popular Music and Society (1995–)
Postmodern Culture (1990–)
Social Dynamics: A Journal of African Studies (1975–)
Social Identities: Journal for the Study of Race, Nation, and Culture (1995–)
Southern Cultures (1994–)
TDR: The Drama Review (1955–)

Transition (1961–)
Women and Performance: A Journal of Feminist Theory (1983–)

MAGAZINES, NEWSLETTERS, AND NEWSPAPERS

American Music Review (1971–)
Ebony (1945–)
Eureka Street (1991–)
The Guardian (1821–)
JazzTimes (1970–)
Los Angeles Times (1881–)
Middle East Report (1973–)
The New York Times (1851–)
Newsletter-Institute for Studies in American Music (1971–)
Newsweek (1933–)
Remix (1999–2009)
Rolling Stone (1967–)
The San Francisco Bay View National Black Newspaper (1976–)
Spin (1985–)
Time (1923–)
The Washington Post (1877–)

About the Editors and Contributors

EDITORS

MELISSA URSULA DAWN GOLDSMITH is a musicologist who studies popular music, film music, and 20th-century music aesthetics. Her projects focus on jazz poetry sound recordings, William S. Burrough's musicality, and music criticism of the Doors. She is currently a Visiting Lecturer in the Department of Music and Visiting Associate Professor in the Department of Graduate and Continuing Education at Westfield State University in Massachusetts. Her PhD in musicology is from Louisiana State University in Baton Rouge. Among other publications, she has coauthored *The Encyclopedia of Musicians and Bands on Film* (Rowman & Littlefield, 2016) with Paige A. Willson and Anthony J. Fonseca. She is also composer, sound engineer, and co-owner of Dapper Kitty Music—MLMC Media—in Northampton, Massachusetts. Melissa first heard hip hop while growing up in Santa Monica, California, when a friend challenged her to a pillow fight to Frankie Smith's funky rap song "Double Dutch Bus" (1981). She first encountered global hip hop at the Santa Barbara Film Festival, in which Māori dancers and rappers from Napier, New Zealand, performed onstage.

ANTHONY J. FONSECA is the Library Director/Associate Professor of Alumnae Library at Elms College in Chicopee, Massachusetts. His PhD in literature is from the University of Louisiana, Lafayette. Among other publications, Tony has coauthored four books with Libraries Unlimited's Genreflecting series (*Hooked on Horror*) and three books on horror topics (*Encyclopedia of the Zombie: The Walking Dead in Popular Culture and Myth*, *Richard Matheson's Monsters: Gender in the Stories, Scripts, Novels, and* Twilight Zone *Episodes*, and *Ghosts in Popular Culture and Legend*). He has written many articles and book chapters on various topics, including international music cultures, high school–to–college transitions, vampire themed music, Ramsey Campbell, and Robert Aickman. He is also a songwriter, multi-instrumentalist, sound engineer, and co-owner of Dapper Kitty Music and an independent publisher and owner of Gothic and Main Publishing in Northampton, Massachusetts. He prefers intelligent lyrics and complex rap vocals, beats, and instrumentation to lazy canned beats and nonsense vocalizations or senseless scatting (he is a fan of Jon Hendricks, who proves lyrics can be scatted).

CONTRIBUTORS

ANTONETTE ADIOVA is an independent scholar specializing in Filipino and Filipino American music. Her PhD in musicology is from the University of Michigan, Ann Arbor. Antonette's academic interests include music and dance in Filipino festivals, folklorization, applied ethnomusicology, and popular music. She first became interested in hip hop after watching music videos on MTV every day after school. Tupac Shakur's "California Love" (1996), featuring Dr. Dre, is one of her favorite hip hop songs.

J. RYAN BODIFORD recently earned his PhD in ethnomusicology from the University of Michigan, Ann Arbor, School of Music, Theatre, and Dance. His dissertation is titled "Sharing Sounds: Musical Innovation, Collaboration, and Ideological Expression in the Chilean Netlabel Movement." Ryan's research focused on electropop, electronica, and electroacoustic composers and musicians in Chile and their use of technology to create and share music both individually and in collectives.

SUSANNAH CLEVELAND is currently the Head Librarian of the Music Library and Bill Schurk Sound Archives at Bowling Green State University in Ohio. Her previous publications include works focusing on music librarianship, use of research music materials, and collection and use of popular music in academia. Her first exposure to hip hop was incredibly square: as a fourth-grader, she encountered K-Tel's 1983 release *Get Dancin': Hot Hits to Get You Movin'*, which included Grandmaster Flash and the Furious Five's "The Message."

JACQUELINE M. DeMAIO was born in South Florida and raised with hip hop pulsing through her veins. By age six, she was enrolled in hip hop dance classes, which deepened her fondness for the entire genre. Jaqui earned a bachelor of arts in English from Nicholls State University in Thibodaux, Louisiana. Her southern roots form the basis of her appreciation for the passionate and rapidly growing hip hop scenes in the southern United States. Miami bass and bounce music remain her favorite musical styles.

CHRISTINE LEE GENGARO is an educator, writer, and musician. A tenured Associate Professor in the Music Department at Los Angeles City College, Christine teaches music theory, voice, and music history. Her PhD in musicology is from the University of Southern California. Her articles on film music and classical music in media appear in numerous journals and books, and she has been program annotator for the Los Angeles Chamber orchestra since 2007. She is the author of *Listening to Stanley Kubrick: The Music in His Films* and *Experiencing Chopin* (Rowman & Littlefield, 2013 and 2017, respectively). The first hip hop song she remembers hearing is Melle Mel's classic "White Lines (Don't Don't Do It)" (1983).

JESSICA LEAH GETMAN earned her PhD in musicology from the University of Michigan, Ann Arbor, School of Music, Theatre, and Dance, where she serves as the inaugural Managing Editor of the George and Ira Gershwin Critical Edition. In addition to critical editing, Jessica specializes in film and television music, popular music in science fiction media, and amateur music making that is produced by fandom. Jessica is also conducting research on glitch hop music. Her article on the music used in the original *Star Trek* series (1966–1969) appeared in the *Journal of the Society for American Music*.

LINDSEY E. HARTMAN is a doctoral student in Experimental Music & Digital Media at the Louisiana State University (LSU), College of Music and Dramatic Arts in Baton Rouge, Louisiana. At LSU, Lindsey has been a member of Laptop Orchestra of Louisiana, has created music installment pieces for presentations, and has worked as a graduate assistant at Music Resources at LSU Libraries. Her interests include music technology, composition, and musicology.

LAURON JOCKWIG KEHRER is an Assistant Professor of Music in the Music Department at the College of William & Mary in Williamsburg, Virginia, where she teaches courses on American popular music, hip hop, and Western art music. Her PhD in musicology is from the Eastman School of Music, University of Rochester, where she also completed a master of arts in ethnomusicology and a graduate certificate from the Susan B. Anthony Institute for Gender, Sexuality, and Women's Studies. Lauron's research focuses on the intersections of race, gender, and sexuality in American popular music, especially hip hop.

TERRY KLEFSTAD is an Associate Professor of Music at the School of Music at Belmont University in Nashville, Tennessee. Her PhD in musicology is from the University of Texas at Austin. Terry's first encounter with hip hop was as a teenager when her little brother began listening to Run-D.M.C. and Beastie Boys. She is drawn to rap music with a strong social justice message, and her articles on Slavic hip hop build on her work in music and politics (including composer Dmitri Shostakovich). Terry's most recent publication is a biography of Nashville musician William Pursell (University Press of Mississippi, 2018).

KHENG KEOW KOAY is an Associate Professor at the Department of Music at National Sun Yat-Sen University in Taiwan. A native of Penang, Malaysia, and a pianist, Kheng Keow earned her PhD in musicology at the University of Melbourne, Australia. Her areas of specialization include 20th- and 21st-century Western art music and aesthetics as well as music analysis and theory. In addition, she has strong secondary interests in popular music, such as hip hop, and film music. Kheng Keow has authored *The Kaleidoscope of Women's Sounds in Music of the Late Twentieth and Early Twenty-First Centuries* (Cambridge Scholars, 2015), and her articles have appeared in *Theoria* and *Tempo*, among other music journals.

KATY E. LEONARD teaches in the Music Department at Harvard University, where she is also the Resident Dean of Eliot House and Assistant Dean of Harvard College. Her PhD in ethnomusicology is from Brown University. Katy has studied and performed Irish/classical flute, Ghanaian drumming and dance, and Javanese gamelan. Her research and teaching interests include roots music, hip hop culture, rock history, virtual and physical community, music and political movements, and the arts in civic community engagement.

BABACAR M'BAYE is an Associate Professor in the Department of English and Pan-African studies at Kent State University in Ohio. His PhD in American Culture Studies is from Bowling Green State University. Babacar's research interests are diverse: postcolonial studies; black Atlantic theories and methods; the relationships between intellectuals of Africa and the black diaspora; African influences in African American, African Caribbean, African British, and African Canadian literatures; black travel writings; and the representations of immigration, race, class, gender, sexuality, and hybrid identities in black literatures, music, films, and cultures. Among many article publications, Babacar is the author of *Black Cosmopolitanism and Anti-colonialism: Pivotal Moments* (Routledge, 2017) and *The Trickster Comes West: Pan-African Influence in Early Black Diasporan Narratives* (University Press of Mississippi, 2009). He is also the co-editor of *Crossing Traditions: American Popular Music in Local and Global Contexts* (Scarecrow, 2013).

BRYAN J. McCANN is an Assistant Professor of Rhetorical Studies in the Department of Communication Studies at Louisiana State University in Baton Rouge, Louisiana. He earned his PhD from the Communication Studies Department (Rhetoric and Language) at the University of Texas at Austin. Bryan's interest in hip hop grew from his experiences as a scholar, teacher, and activist interested in mass incarceration. His recent book *The Mark of Criminality: Rhetoric, Race, and Gangsta Rap in the War-on-Crime Era* (University of Alabama Press, 2017) describes the intersection of gangsta rap and tough-on-crime politics during the 1980s and 1990s.

SABIA McCOY-TORRES is an Assistant Professor at the Roger Thayer Stone Center for Latin American Studies at Tulane University in New Orleans, Louisiana. Her PhD in anthropology is from Cornell University. Sabia's research and teaching specializations include Afro-diasporic circum-Caribbean studies as well as race and gender/sexuality studies and popular performance (especially in reggae). Since 2016, Sabia has been a contributing editor to *Transforming Anthropology*.

JAMES McNALLY is an ethnomusicologist whose research investigates popular music in Brazil and the United States, with theoretical focuses on questions of race and ethnicity, media studies, experimental music, and the African diaspora. His dissertation, "São Paulo Underground: Musical Innovation and Independent Cultural Production in Brazilian Experimental Music Practice" (University of Michigan, Ann Arbor) examines these issues in the context of a multistylistic independent experimental music scene in Brazil. As a musician, he performs with the University of Michigan Vencedores Samba Bateria and Javanese Gamelan Ensemble. James enjoys making hardware-hacked instruments in his spare time.

CELESTE ROBERTS was born and raised in South Louisiana, where storytelling assumes several forms: Cajun folklore; oil and gas rhetoric; blended languages; and food versus music. All have rooted within her a love for communication and its ability to unite people of various cultures and lifestyles. Celeste earned her bachelor of arts in English from Nicholls State University, located across the street from the bayou in Thibodaux, Louisiana. Growing up in the 1990s, she first heard hip hop dance music on Top 40 radio stations and loved the catchy beats. As she grew up, she discovered earlier hip hop music and began to appreciate the messages, talent, and fusion that the genre exemplifies.

JENNIFER L. ROTH-BURNETTE holds a PhD in music from New York University and heads the Innovation Team at the University of Alabama in Tuscaloosa, where she works with faculty from across the university to incorporate emerging technologies for teaching. Jennifer teaches courses in music and political movements, music history, and world music, while working on metadata applications for research on medieval melodic design, global hip hop, and perception of learning.

MATTHEW SCHLIEF is an Assistant Professor of Scenic Design and Production Coordinator at Texas Tech University in Lubbock, Texas. He is also a Resident Designer for Outpost Theatre Company in Lubbock, Classical Theatre Co. in Houston, and Creede Repertory Theatre in Colorado. Matt's awards include the Houston Press Theatre for Best Design for *Bloody Bloody Andrew Jackson* (2012), the Broadway World Best of Houston Award for lighting design for *Sweeney Todd* (2013), and several Kennedy Center American College Theater Festival Awards for Meritorious Achievement in Design (2014–2017).

AMANDA SEWELL is a freelance academic editor and independent scholar in Traverse City, Michigan. Her PhD in musicology is from Indiana University Jacobs School of Music in Bloomington. She specializes in hip hop, including nerdcore, music copyright, and the art of music sampling. Amanda's articles have appeared in the *Journal of Popular Music Studies* and the *Journal of the Society for American Music*, and she has also written a book chapter for *The Cambridge Companion to Hip Hop* (2015).

SCOTT WARFIELD is an Associate Professor of Music History at the School of Music at the University of Central Florida in Orlando, where he teaches in all areas of music history and literature through the graduate level. Scott's most recent publications include a dozen entries on musical theatre topics in the second edition of *The Grove Dictionary of American Music* (Oxford University Press, 2013), essays on Richard Strauss and the business of music in *The Cambridge Companion to Richard Strauss* (Cambridge University Press, 2010) and the Strauss-Hugo von Hofmannsthal collaboration in the journal *Ars Lyrica* (2014–2015), and a revised chapter on the rock musical in the third edition of *The Cambridge Companion to the Musical* (2017).

PAIGE A. WILLSON is an Instructional Associate Professor of Costume Design and Technology in the School of Theatre and Dance at the University of Houston in Texas as well as a costume and mask designer for theatre, dance, and performance art. Paige's master of fine arts in costume, lighting, and scenic design is from the

University of Houston Theatre School. From 2004 to 2009, she was crafts master/milliner at the Tony Award–winning Alley Theatre. Paige's dye and millinery work have been shown nationwide. Her masks have been in curated exhibitions at Art on Broad Street in Augusta, Georgia, as well as at Rice University and the Catalina Coffee in Houston. She was also the costume designer for many Houston productions, including the Houston Shakespeare Festival, Generations: A Theatre Company, and Mildred's Umbrella. She is co-author of *The Encyclopedia of Musicians and Bands on Film* (Rowman & Littlefield, 2016) and has written on the use of music and costuming in two female vampire films, *Dracula's Daughter* (1936) and *Nadja* (1994).

Index

Page numbers in **bold** indicate the location of main entries.